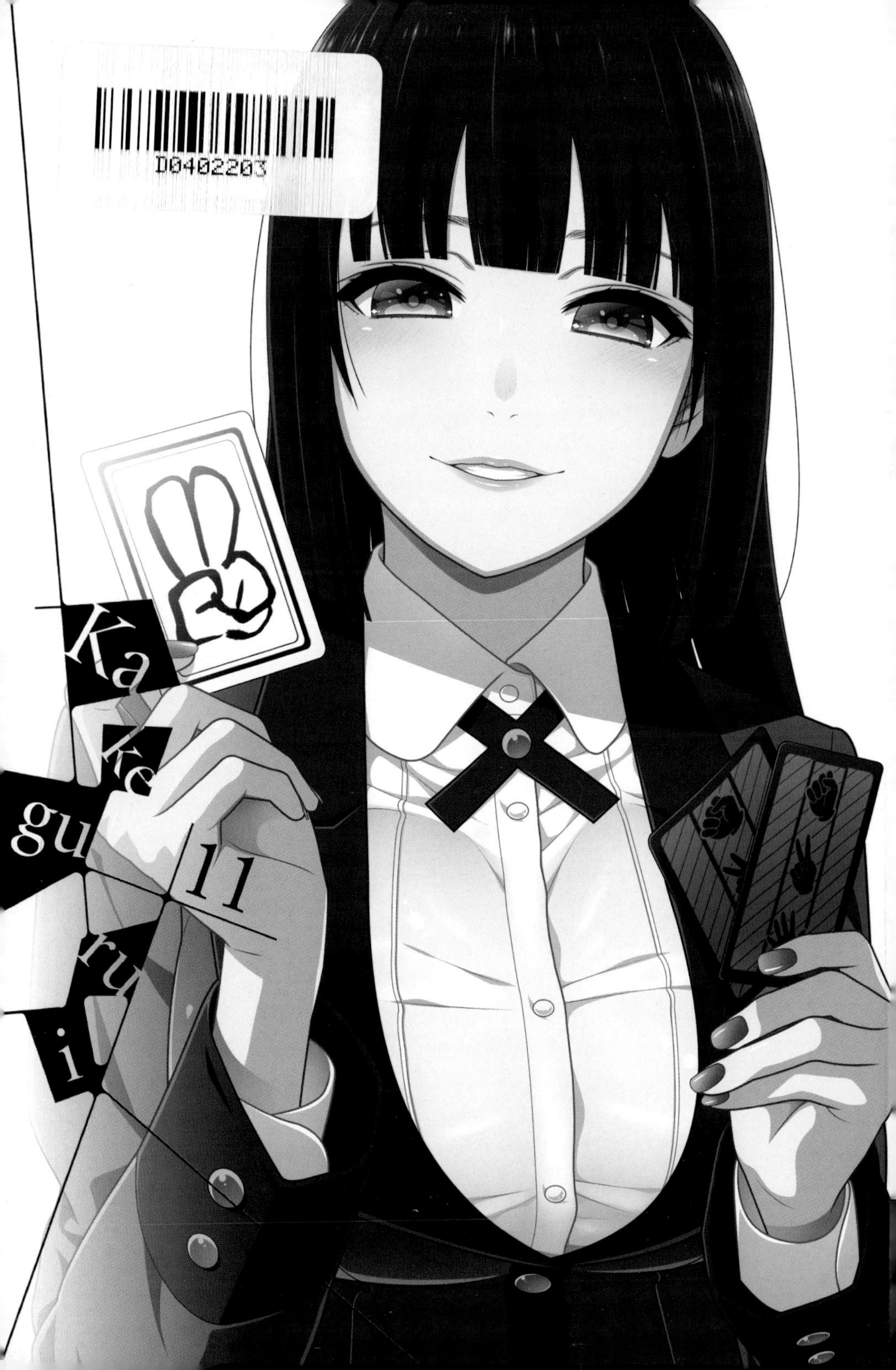
Kakegurui
11

⑪

K
A
K
E
G
U
R
U
I

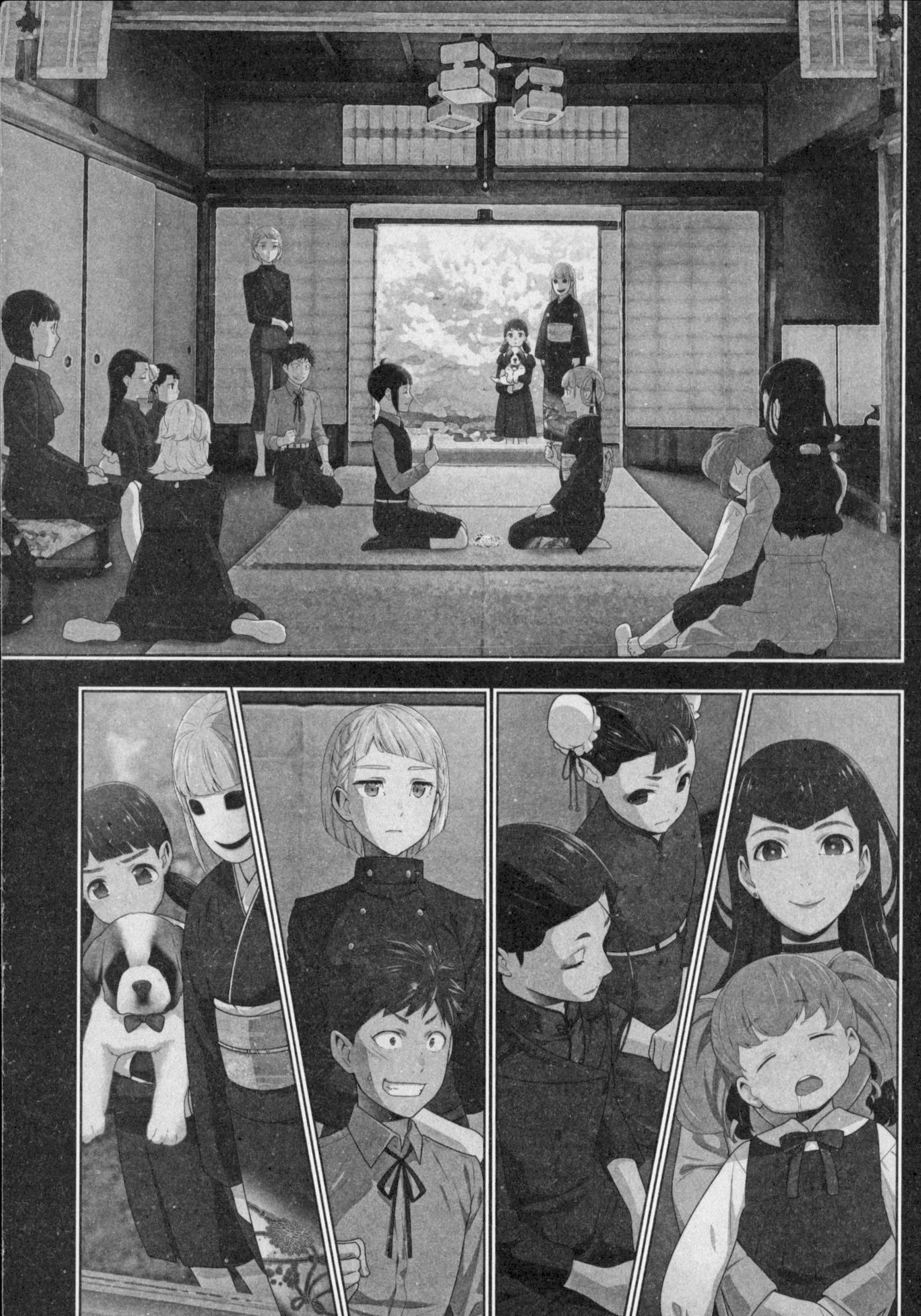

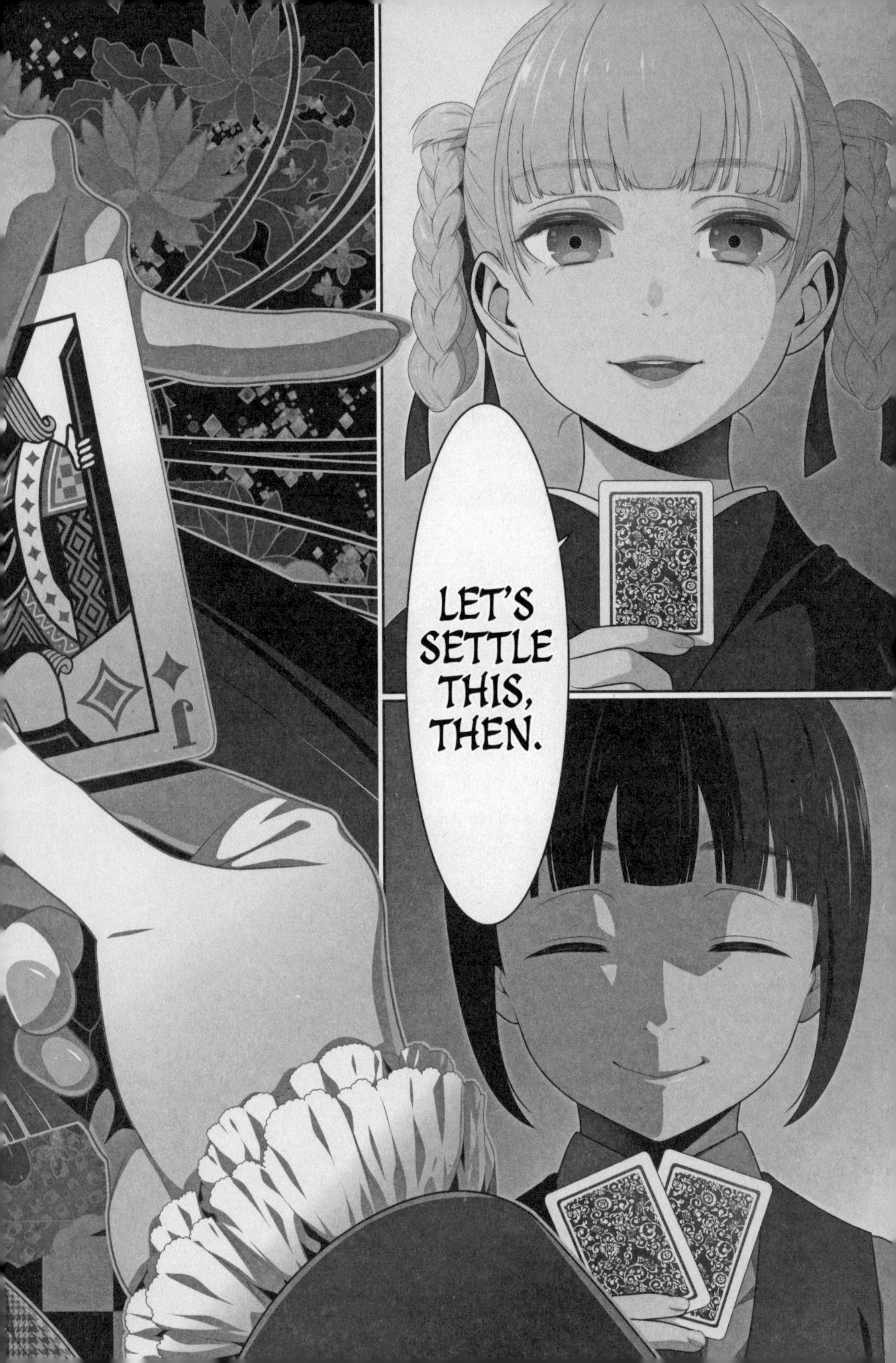
LET'S SETTLE THIS, THEN.

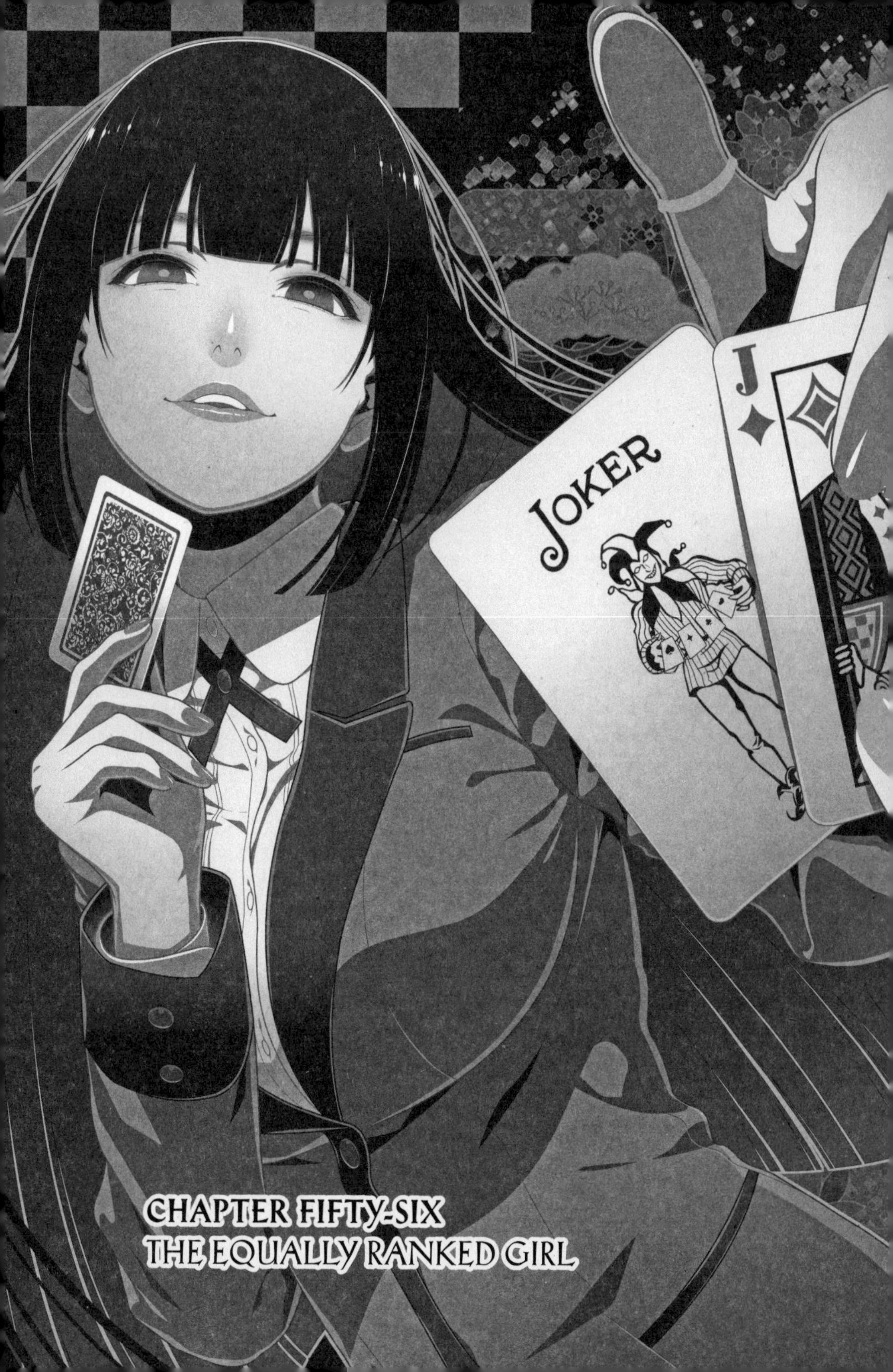
JOKER
J

CHAPTER FIFTY-SIX
THE EQUALLY RANKED GIRL

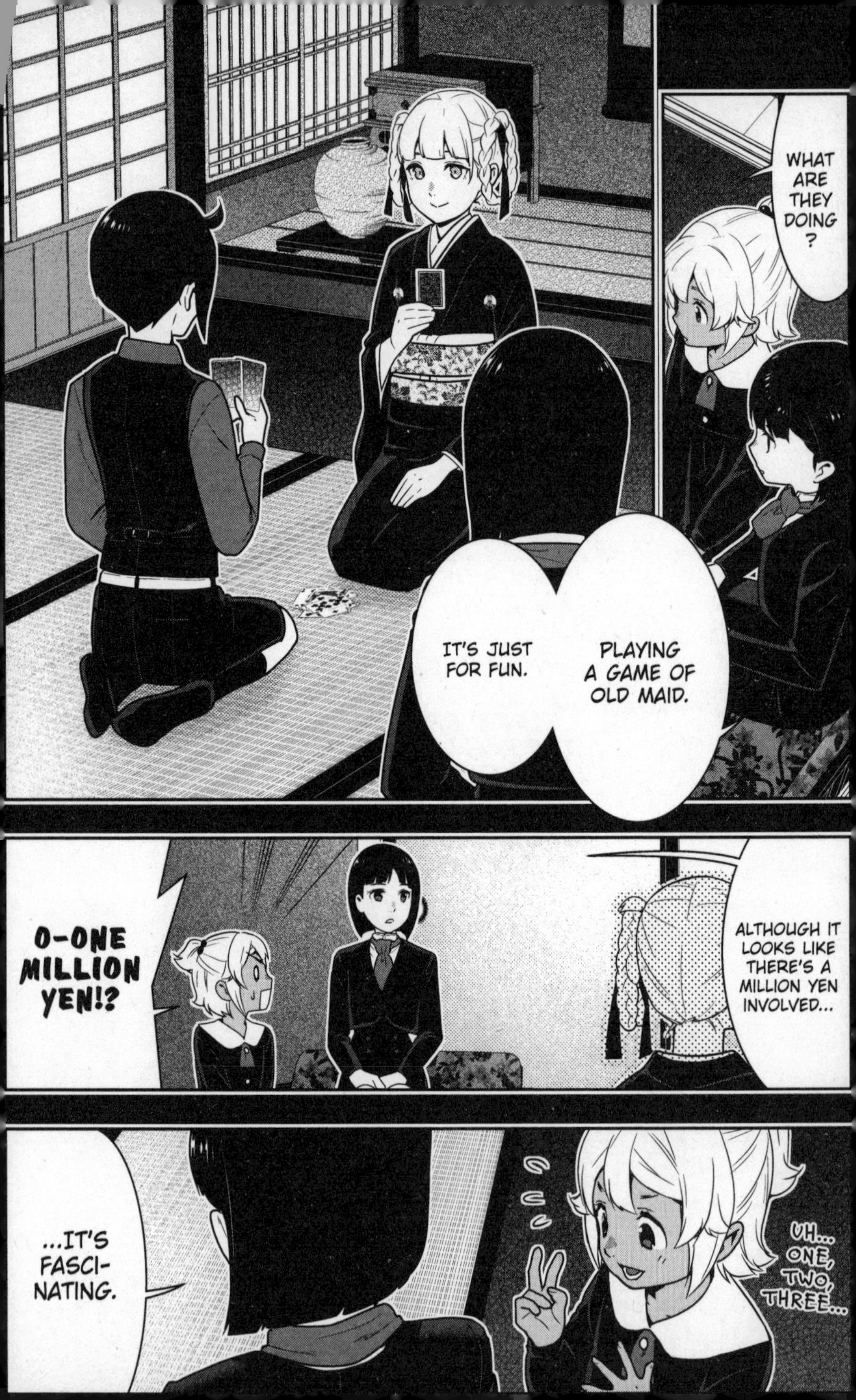
WHAT ARE THEY DOING?
PLAYING A GAME OF OLD MAID.
IT'S JUST FOR FUN.
ALTHOUGH IT LOOKS LIKE THERE'S A MILLION YEN INVOLVED...
O-ONE MILLION YEN!?
UH... ONE, TWO, THREE...
...IT'S FASCI-NATING.

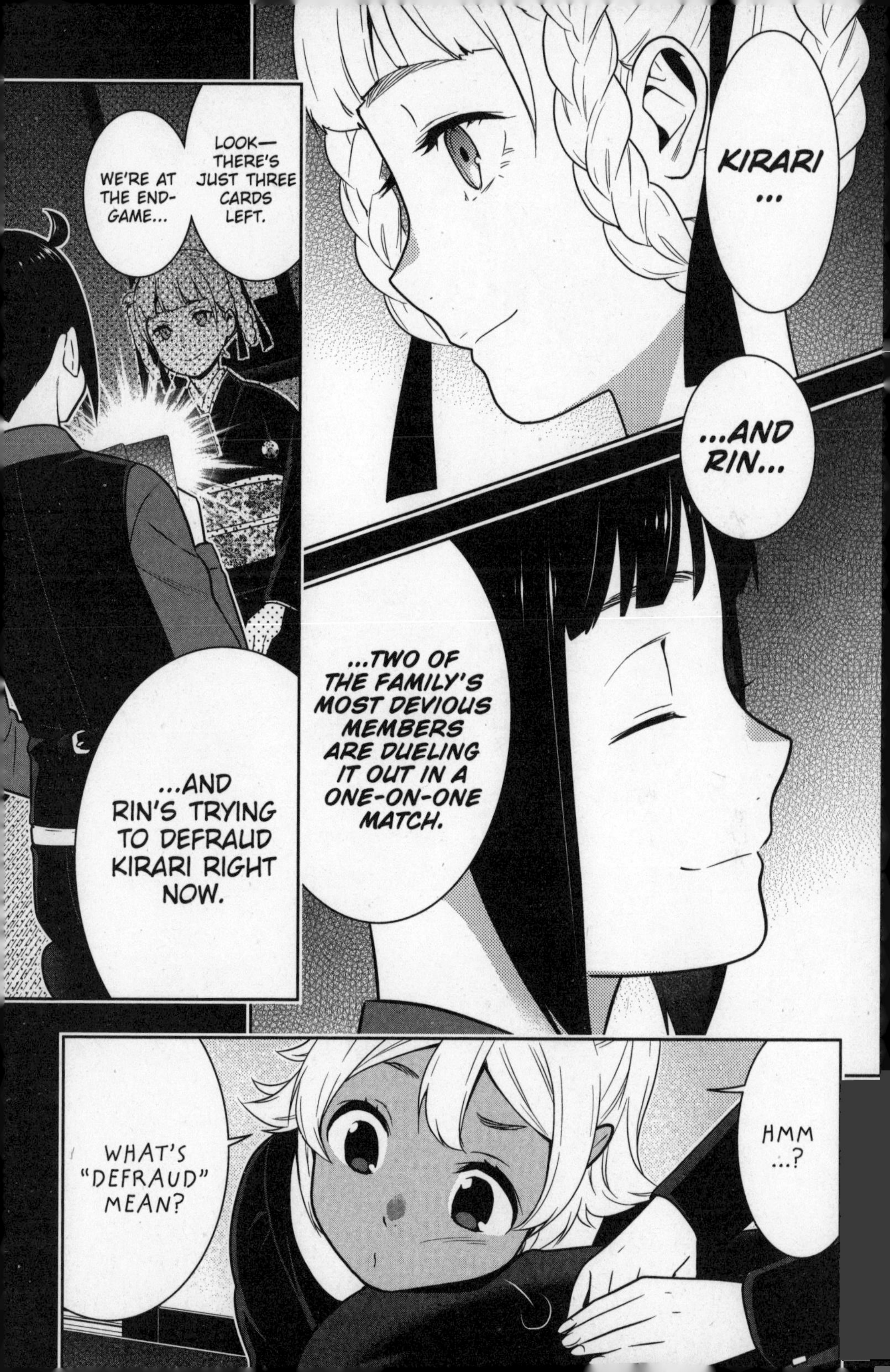
KIRARI ...
...AND RIN...
...TWO OF THE FAMILY'S MOST DEVIOUS MEMBERS ARE DUELING IT OUT IN A ONE-ON-ONE MATCH.
LOOK—THERE'S JUST THREE CARDS LEFT.
WE'RE AT THE END-GAME...
...AND RIN'S TRYING TO DEFRAUD KIRARI RIGHT NOW.
HMM ...?
WHAT'S "DEFRAUD" MEAN?

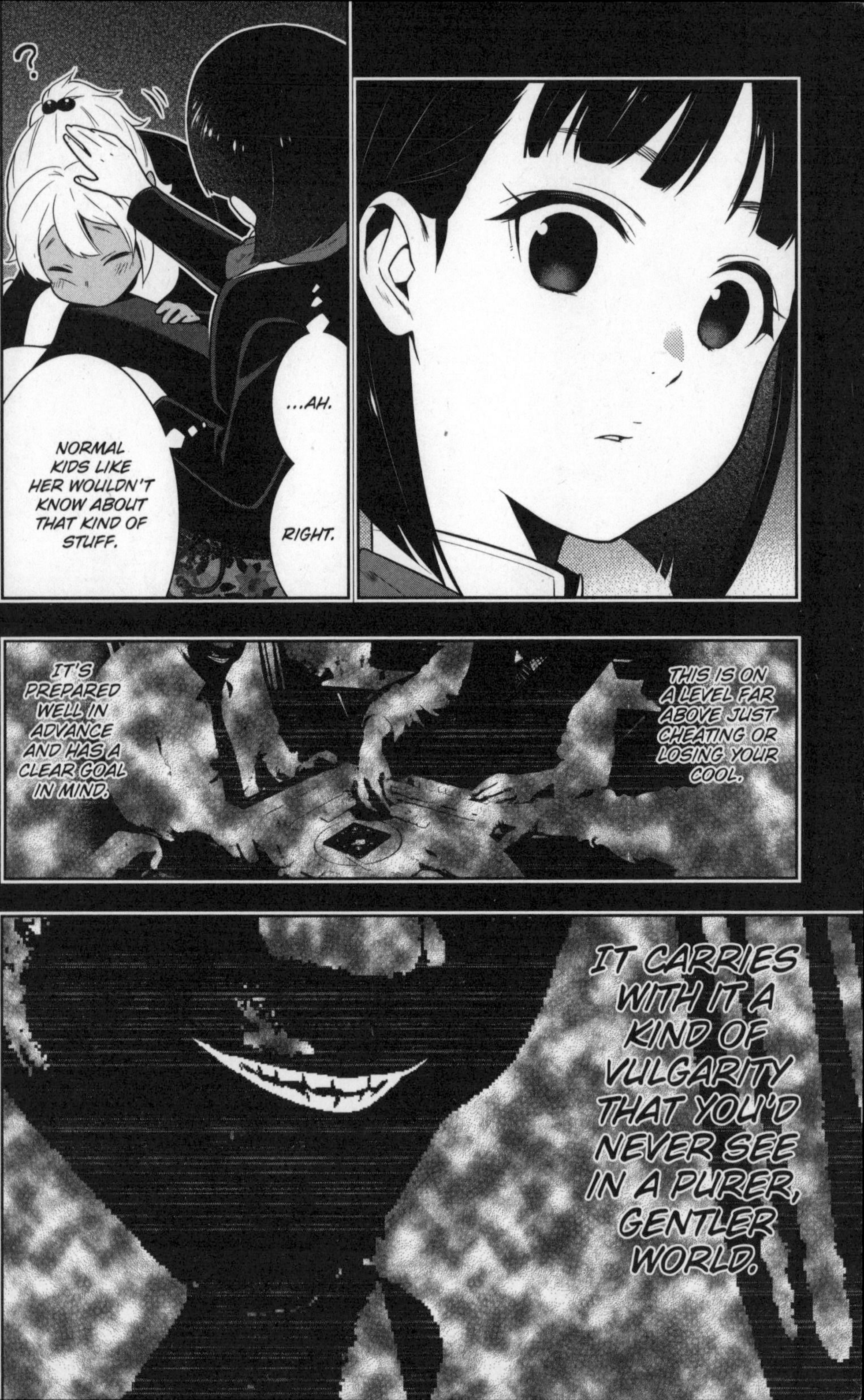
?
...AH.
RIGHT.
NORMAL KIDS LIKE HER WOULDN'T KNOW ABOUT THAT KIND OF STUFF.
THIS IS ON A LEVEL FAR ABOVE JUST CHEATING OR LOSING YOUR COOL.
IT'S PREPARED WELL IN ADVANCE AND HAS A CLEAR GOAL IN MIND.
IT CARRIES WITH IT A KIND OF VULGARITY THAT YOU'D NEVER SEE IN A PURER, GENTLER WORLD.

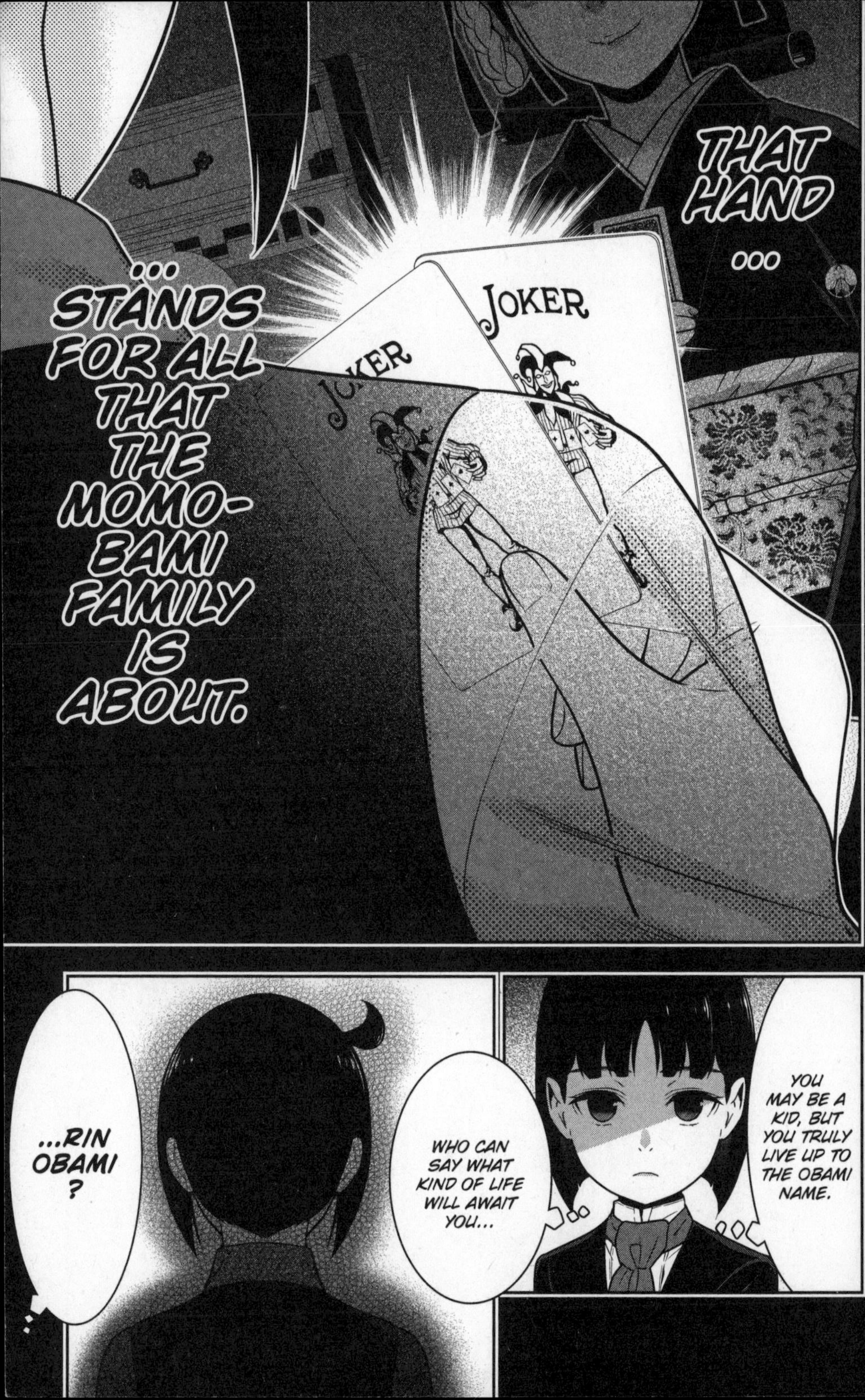
THAT HAND...
...STANDS FOR ALL THAT THE MOMOBAMI FAMILY IS ABOUT.
YOU MAY BE A KID, BUT YOU TRULY LIVE UP TO THE OBAMI NAME.
WHO CAN SAY WHAT KIND OF LIFE WILL AWAIT YOU...
...RIN OBAMI?

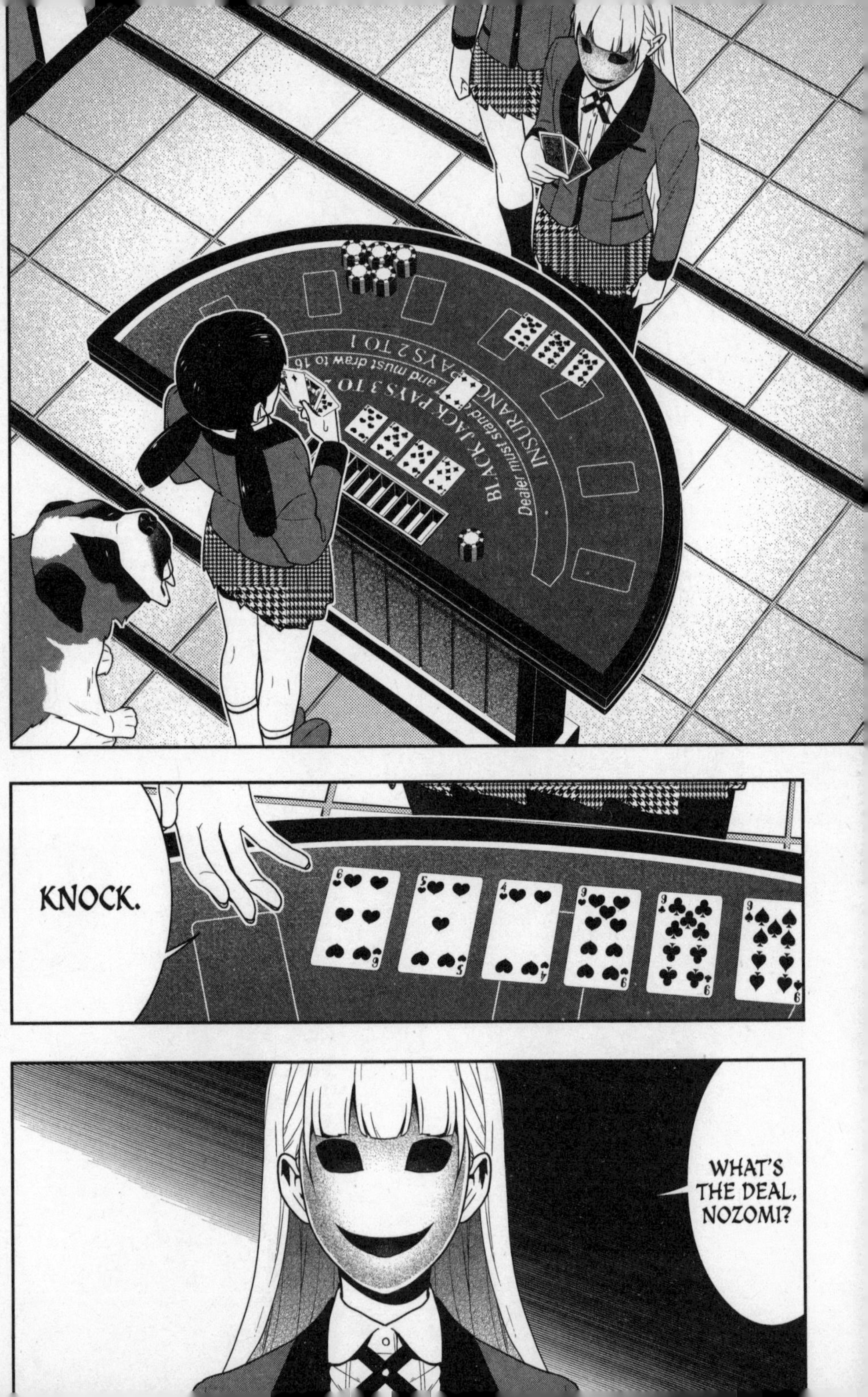
KNOCK.
WHAT'S THE DEAL, NOZOMI?

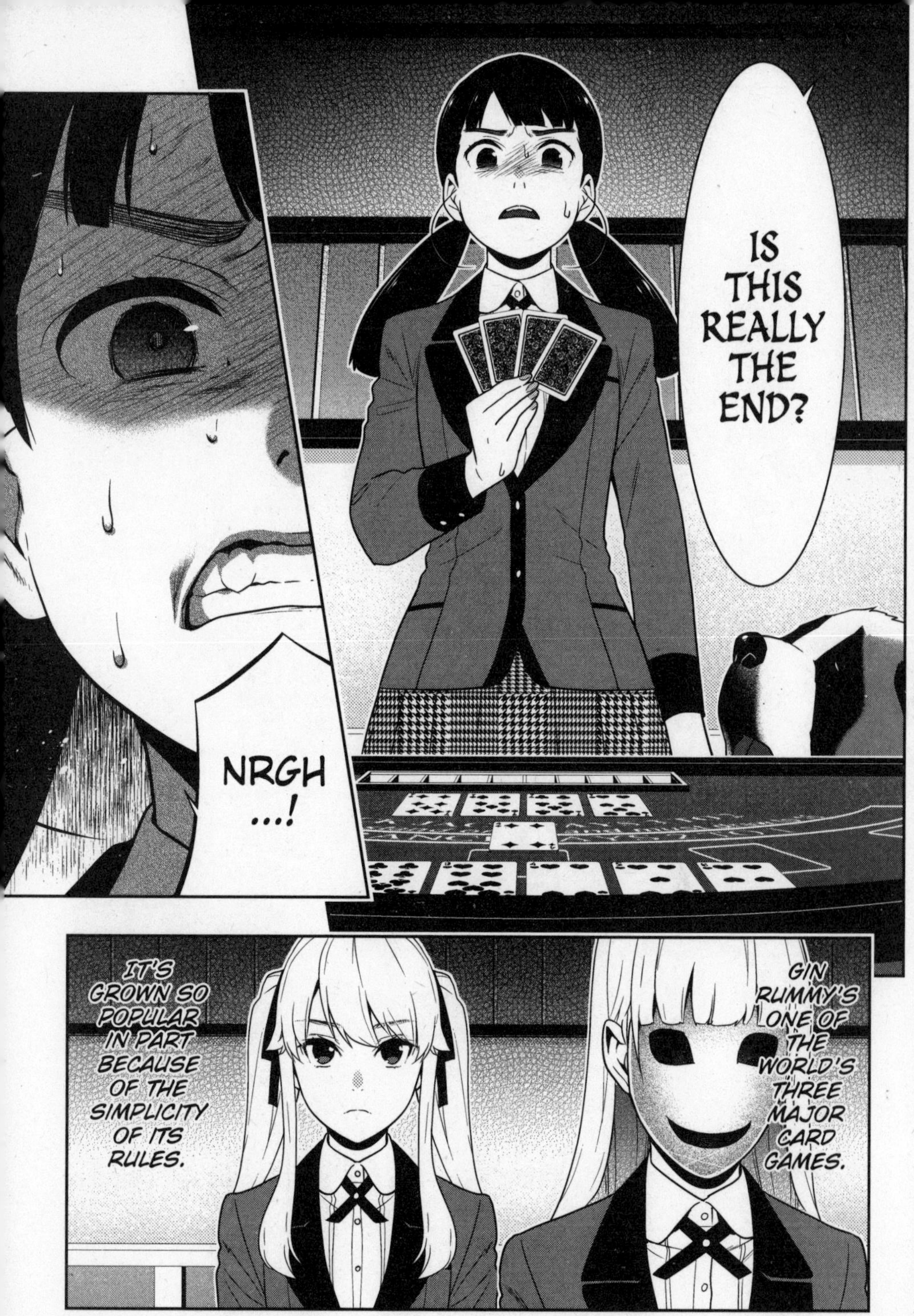
IS THIS REALLY THE END?
NRGH ...!
GIN RUMMY'S ONE OF THE WORLD'S THREE MAJOR CARD GAMES.
IT'S GROWN SO POPULAR IN PART BECAUSE OF THE SIMPLICITY OF ITS RULES.

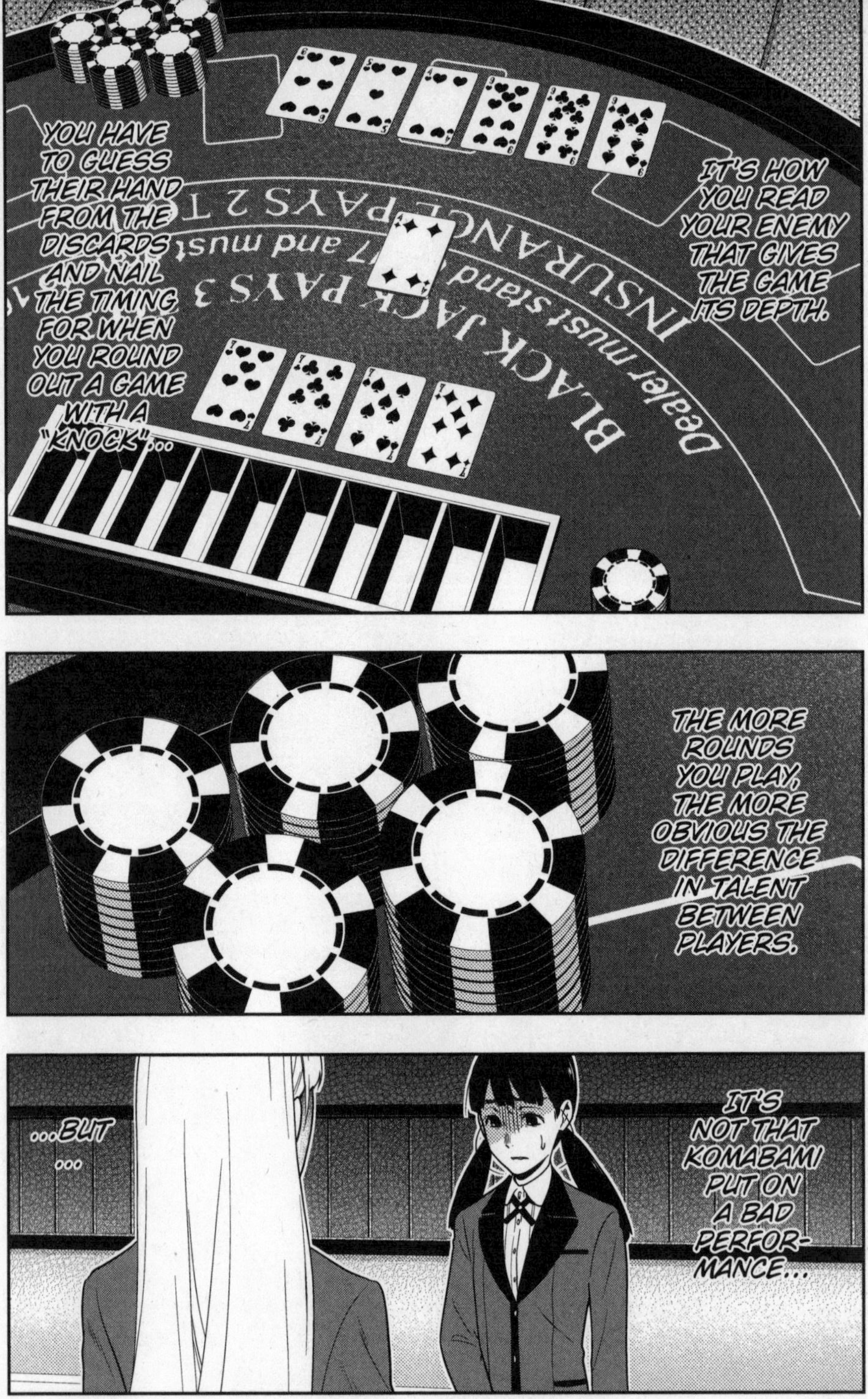
YOU HAVE TO GUESS THEIR HAND FROM THE DISCARDS AND NAIL THE TIMING FOR WHEN YOU ROUND OUT A GAME WITH A "KNOCK"...
IT'S HOW YOU READ YOUR ENEMY THAT GIVES THE GAME ITS DEPTH.
THE MORE ROUNDS YOU PLAY, THE MORE OBVIOUS THE DIFFERENCE IN TALENT BETWEEN PLAYERS.
IT'S NOT THAT KOMABAMI PUT ON A BAD PERFORMANCE...
...BUT ...

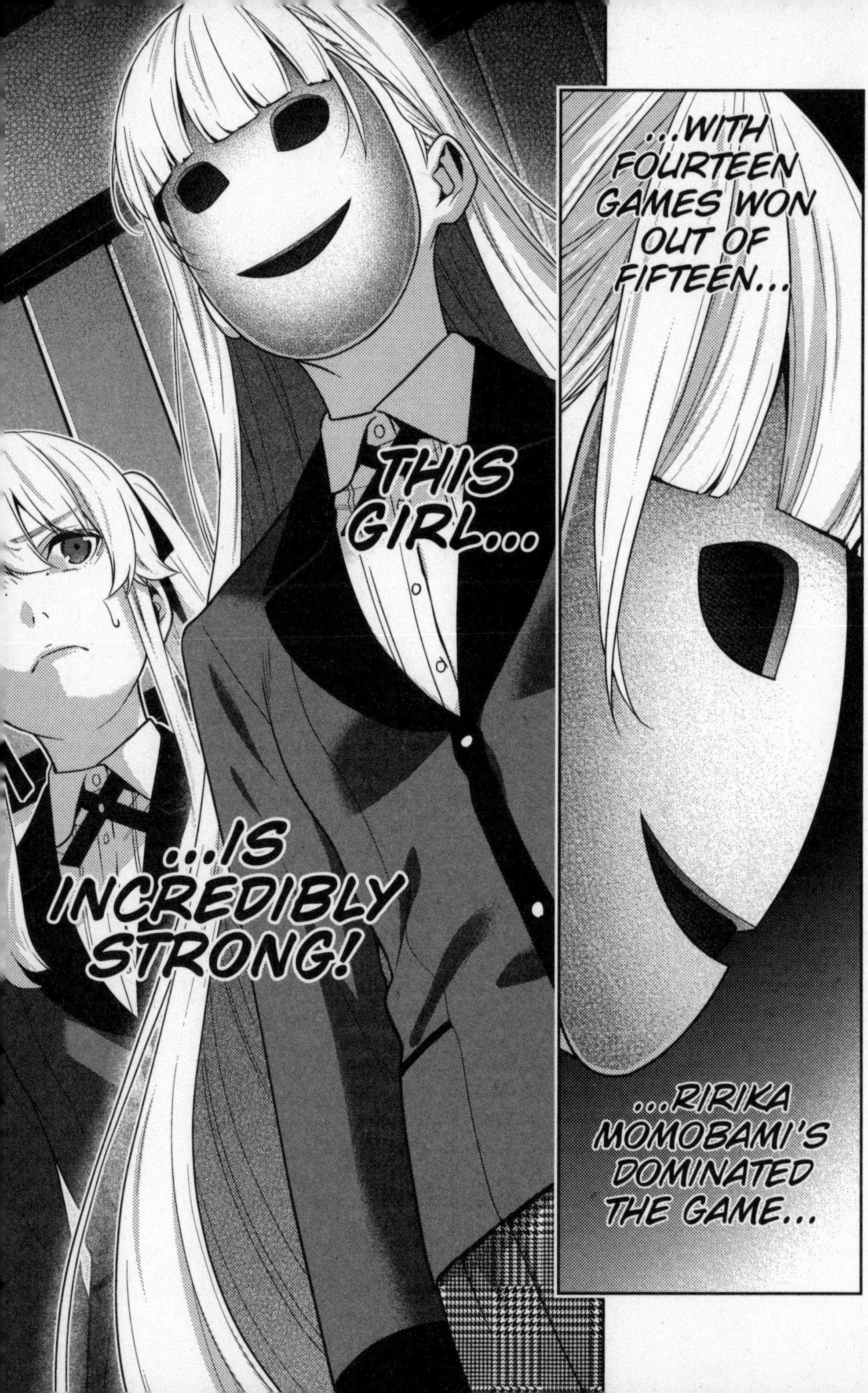
...WITH FOURTEEN GAMES WON OUT OF FIFTEEN...
...RIRIKA MOMOBAMI'S DOMINATED THE GAME...
THIS GIRL...
...IS INCREDIBLY STRONG!

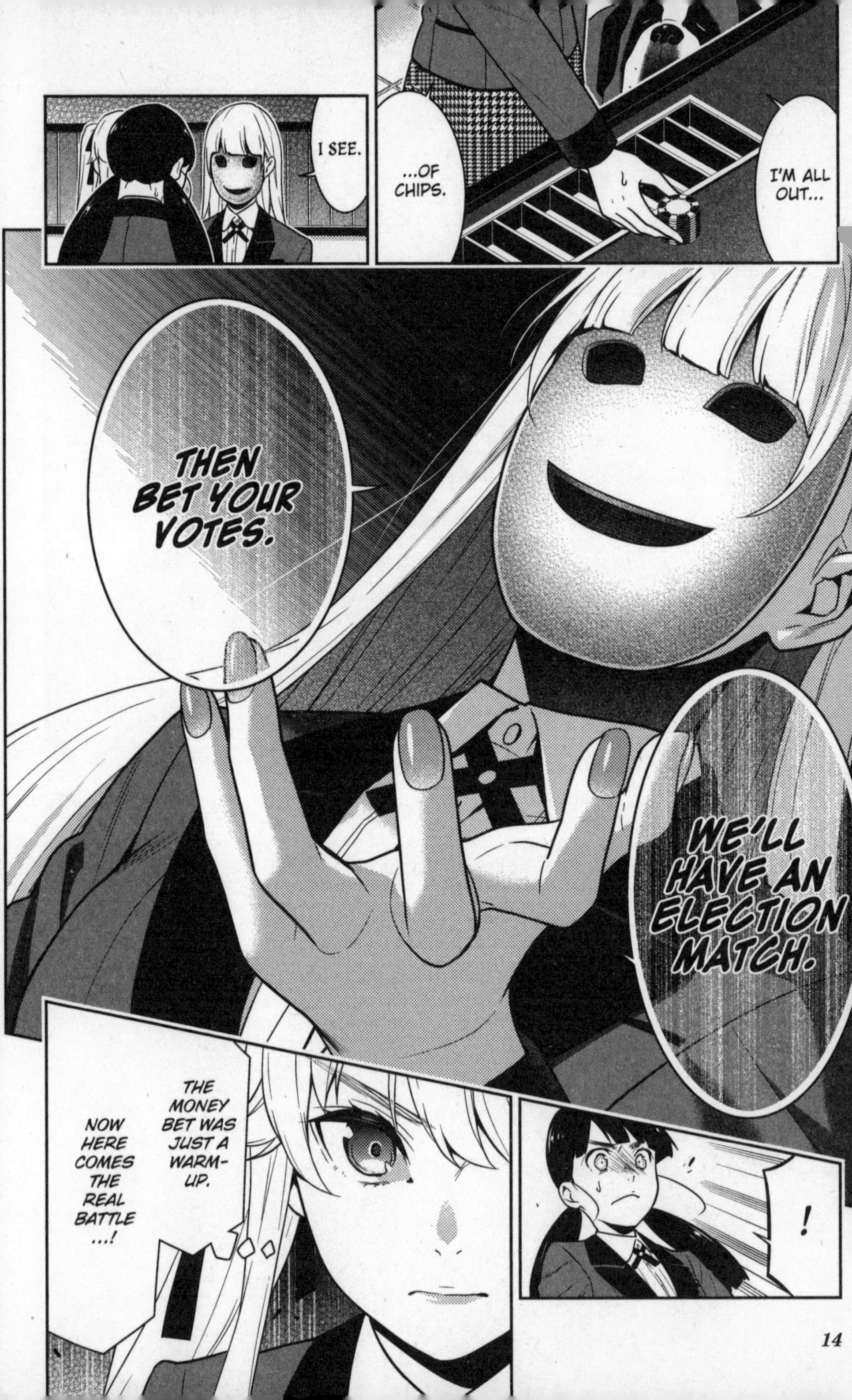

I'M ALL OUT...
...OF CHIPS.
I SEE.
THEN BET YOUR VOTES.
WE'LL HAVE AN ELECTION MATCH.
!
!
THE MONEY BET WAS JUST A WARM-UP.
NOW HERE COMES THE REAL BATTLE...!

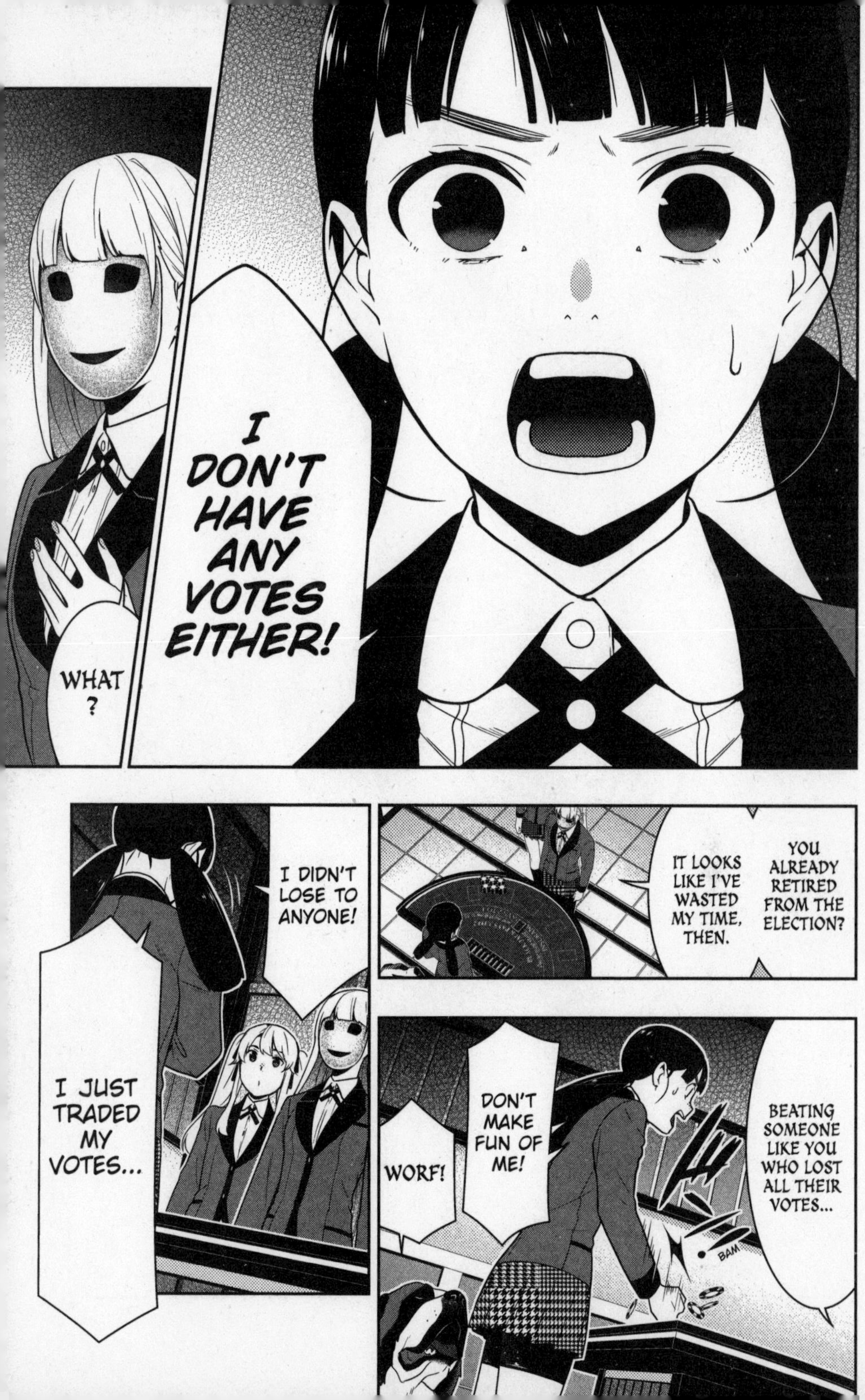
I DON'T HAVE ANY VOTES EITHER!
WHAT?
YOU ALREADY RETIRED FROM THE ELECTION?
IT LOOKS LIKE I'VE WASTED MY TIME, THEN.
BEATING SOMEONE LIKE YOU WHO LOST ALL THEIR VOTES...
BAM
DON'T MAKE FUN OF ME!
WORF!
I DIDN'T LOSE TO ANYONE!
I JUST TRADED MY VOTES...

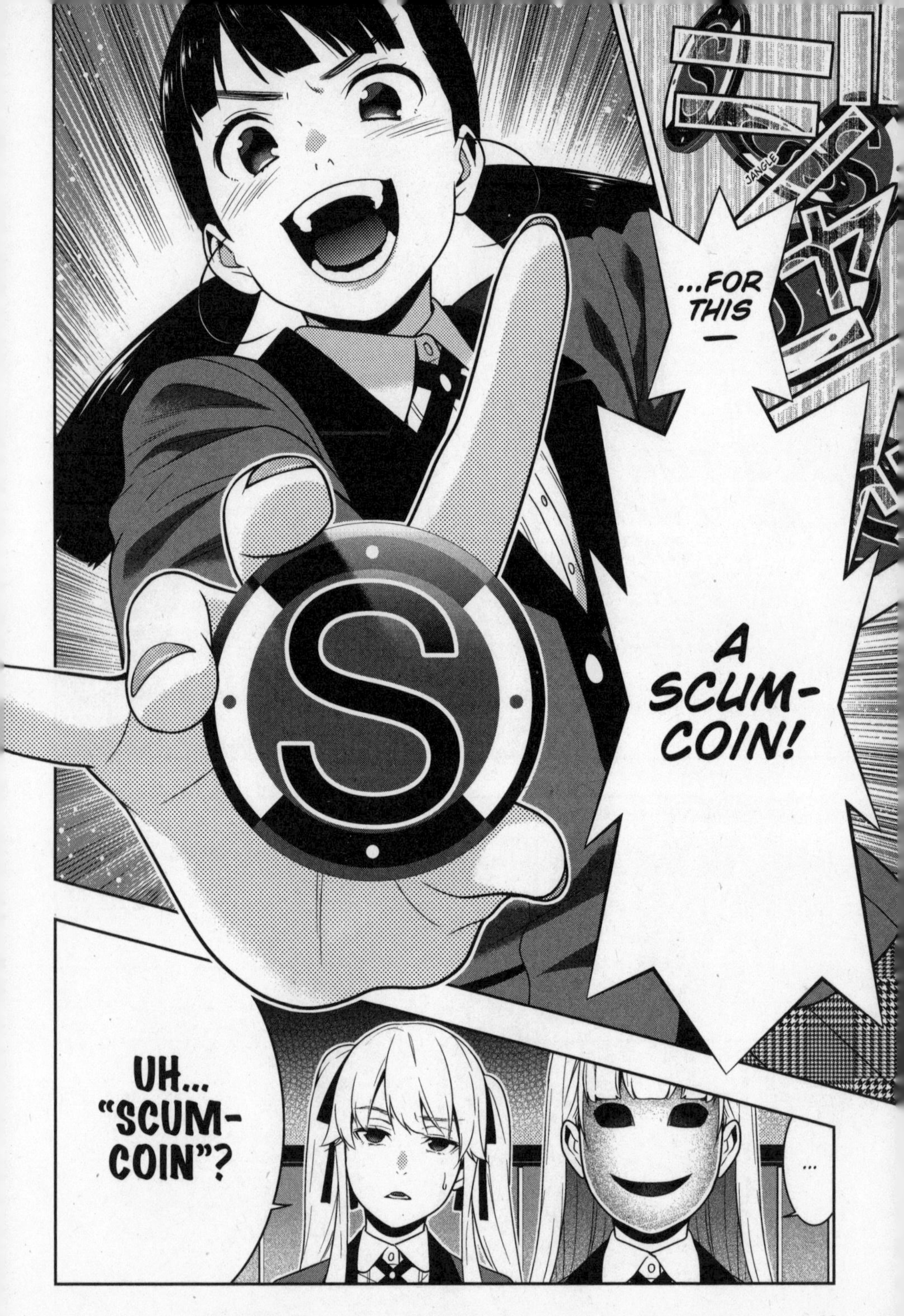
JANGLE
...FOR THIS—
A SCUM-COIN!
...
UH... "SCUM-COIN"?

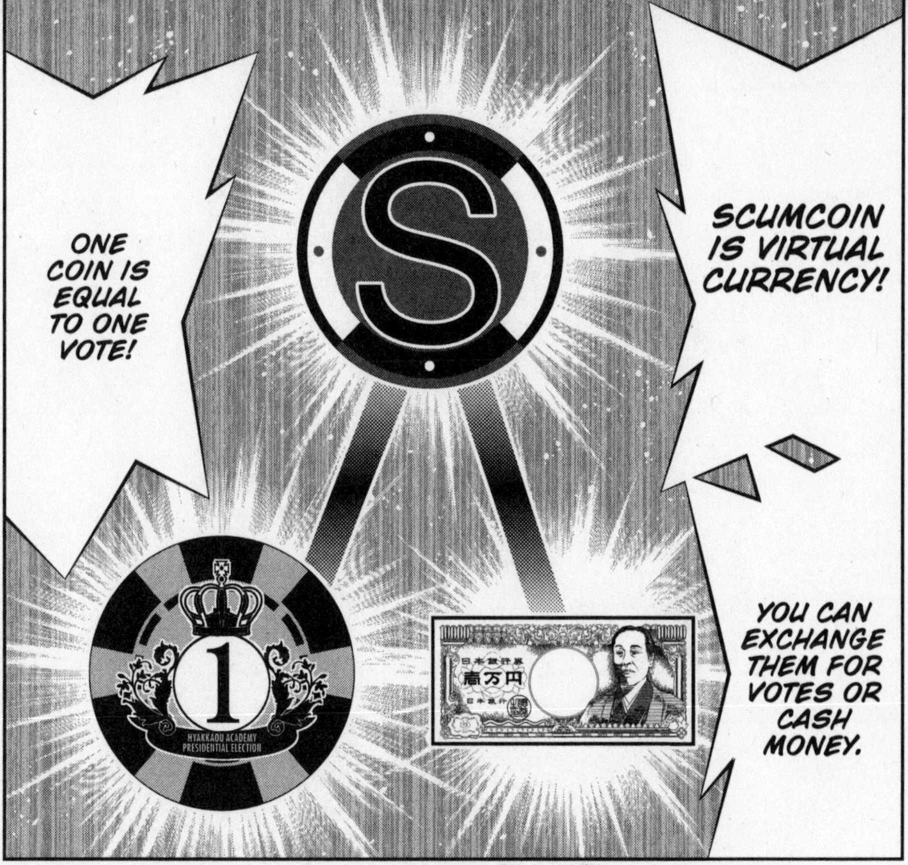
SCUMCOIN IS VIRTUAL CURRENCY!
ONE COIN IS EQUAL TO ONE VOTE!
HYAKKAOU ACADEMY PRESIDENTIAL ELECTION
YOU CAN EXCHANGE THEM FOR VOTES OR CASH MONEY.

BILL: 10,000 YEN

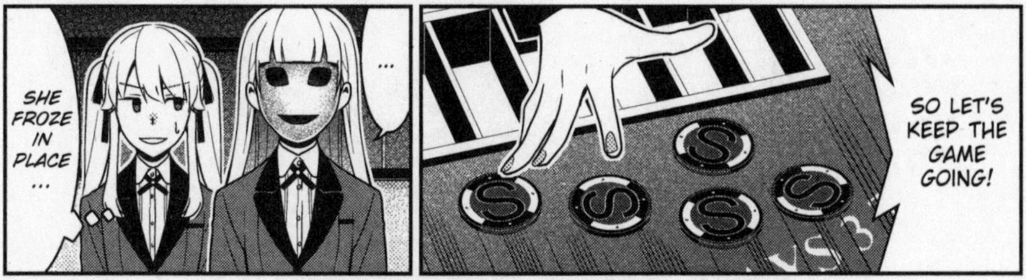
SO LET'S KEEP THE GAME GOING!
...
SHE FROZE IN PLACE...

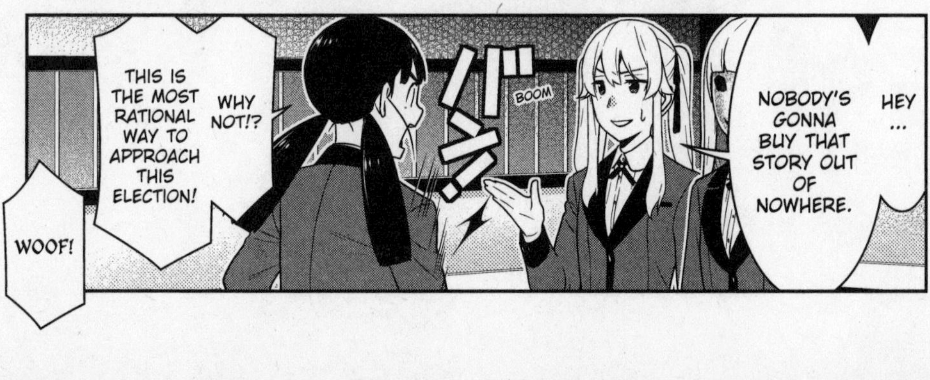
HEY...
NOBODY'S GONNA BUY THAT STORY OUT OF NOWHERE.
BOOM
WHY NOT!?
THIS IS THE MOST RATIONAL WAY TO APPROACH THIS ELECTION!
WOOF!

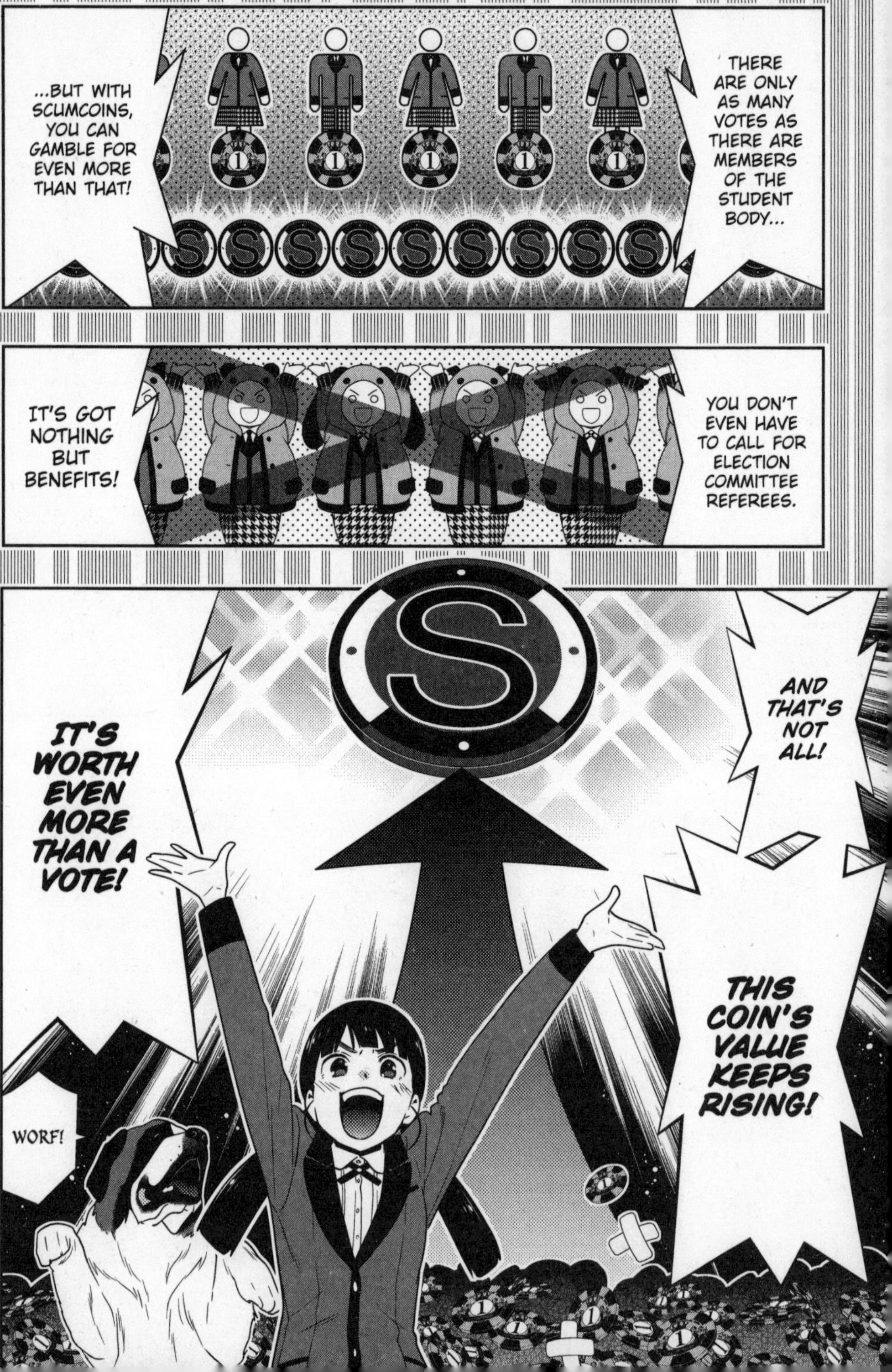

THERE ARE ONLY AS MANY VOTES AS THERE ARE MEMBERS OF THE STUDENT BODY...
...BUT WITH SCUMCOINS, YOU CAN GAMBLE FOR EVEN MORE THAN THAT!
YOU DON'T EVEN HAVE TO CALL FOR ELECTION COMMITTEE REFEREES.
IT'S GOT NOTHING BUT BENEFITS!
AND THAT'S NOT ALL!
IT'S WORTH EVEN MORE THAN A VOTE!
THIS COIN'S VALUE KEEPS RISING!
WORF!

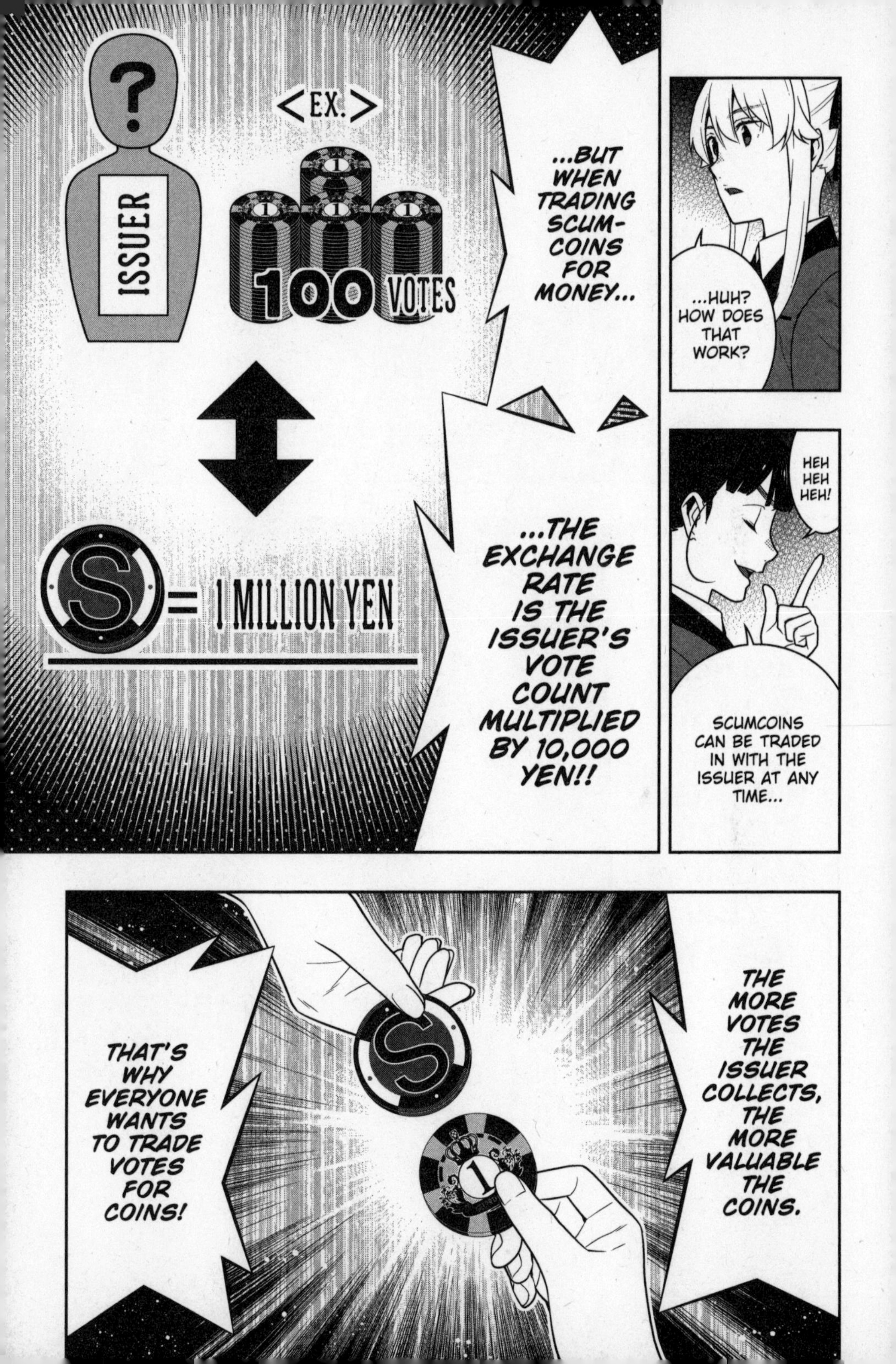
...HUH? HOW DOES THAT WORK?
HEH HEH HEH!
SCUMCOINS CAN BE TRADED IN WITH THE ISSUER AT ANY TIME...
...BUT WHEN TRADING SCUM-COINS FOR MONEY...
?
ISSUER
<EX.>
100 VOTES
...THE EXCHANGE RATE IS THE ISSUER'S VOTE COUNT MULTIPLIED BY 10,000 YEN!!
S = 1 MILLION YEN
THE MORE VOTES THE ISSUER COLLECTS, THE MORE VALUABLE THE COINS.
THAT'S WHY EVERYONE WANTS TO TRADE VOTES FOR COINS!

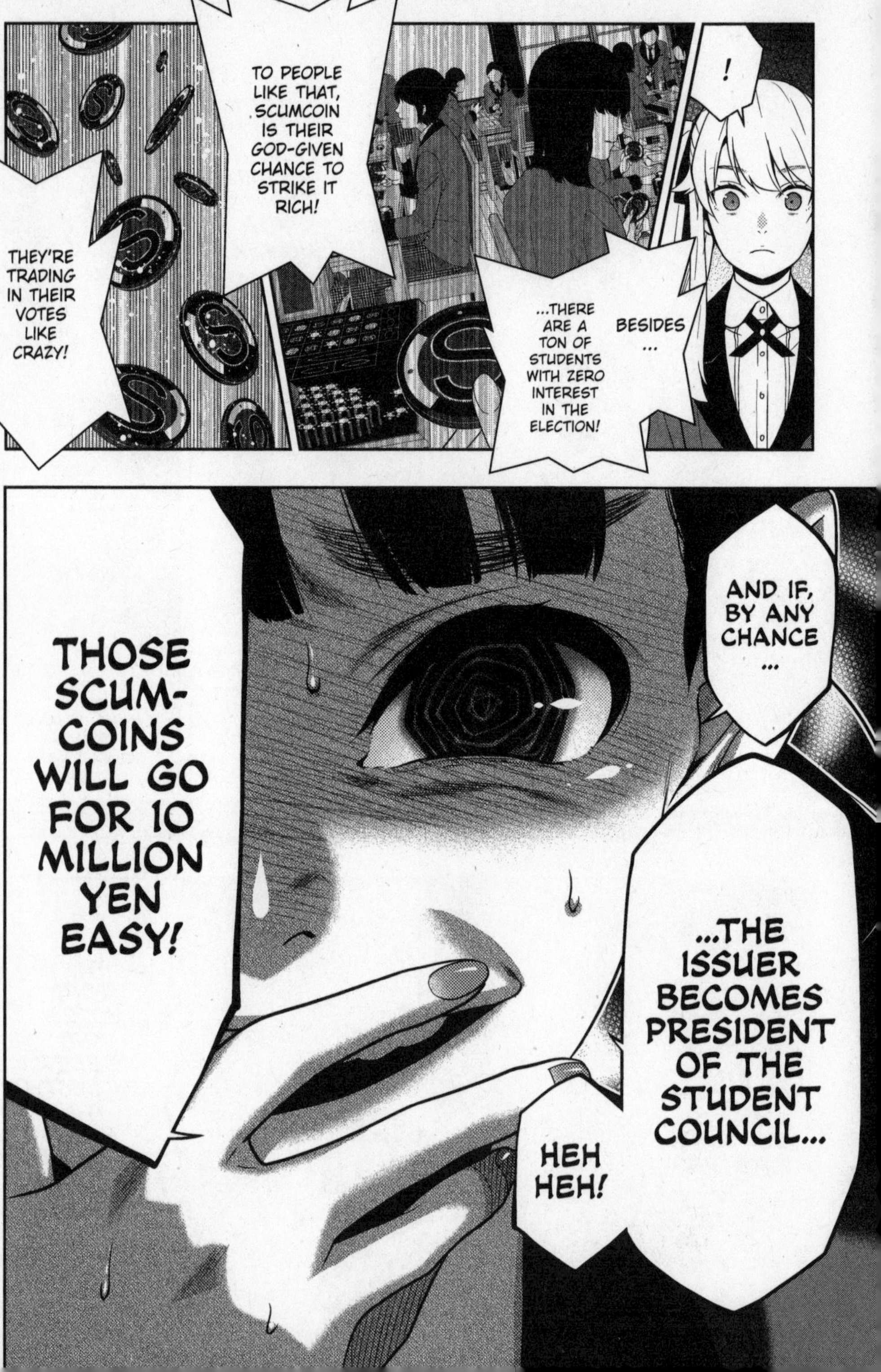
!
BESIDES ...
...THERE ARE A TON OF STUDENTS WITH ZERO INTEREST IN THE ELECTION!
TO PEOPLE LIKE THAT, SCUMCOIN IS THEIR GOD-GIVEN CHANCE TO STRIKE IT RICH!
THEY'RE TRADING IN THEIR VOTES LIKE CRAZY!
AND IF, BY ANY CHANCE ...
...THE ISSUER BECOMES PRESIDENT OF THE STUDENT COUNCIL...
HEH HEH!
THOSE SCUM-COINS WILL GO FOR 10 MILLION YEN EASY!

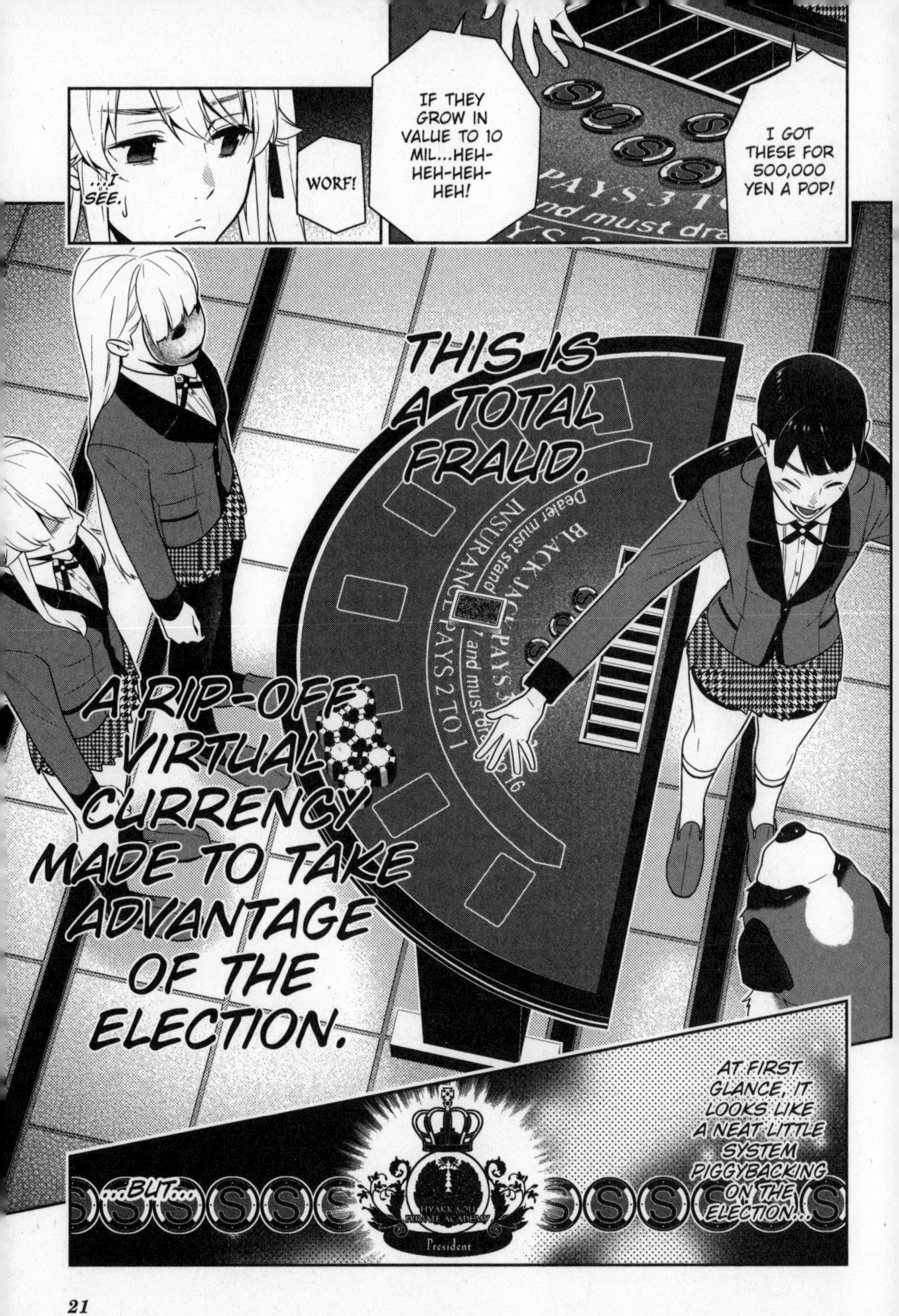

I GOT THESE FOR 500,000 YEN A POP!
IF THEY GROW IN VALUE TO 10 MIL...HEH-HEH-HEH-HEH!
WORF!
...I SEE.
THIS IS A TOTAL FRAUD.
A RIP-OFF VIRTUAL CURRENCY MADE TO TAKE ADVANTAGE OF THE ELECTION.
AT FIRST GLANCE, IT LOOKS LIKE A NEAT LITTLE SYSTEM PIGGYBACKING ON THE ELECTION...
HYAKKAOU PRIVATE ACADEMY
President
...BUT...

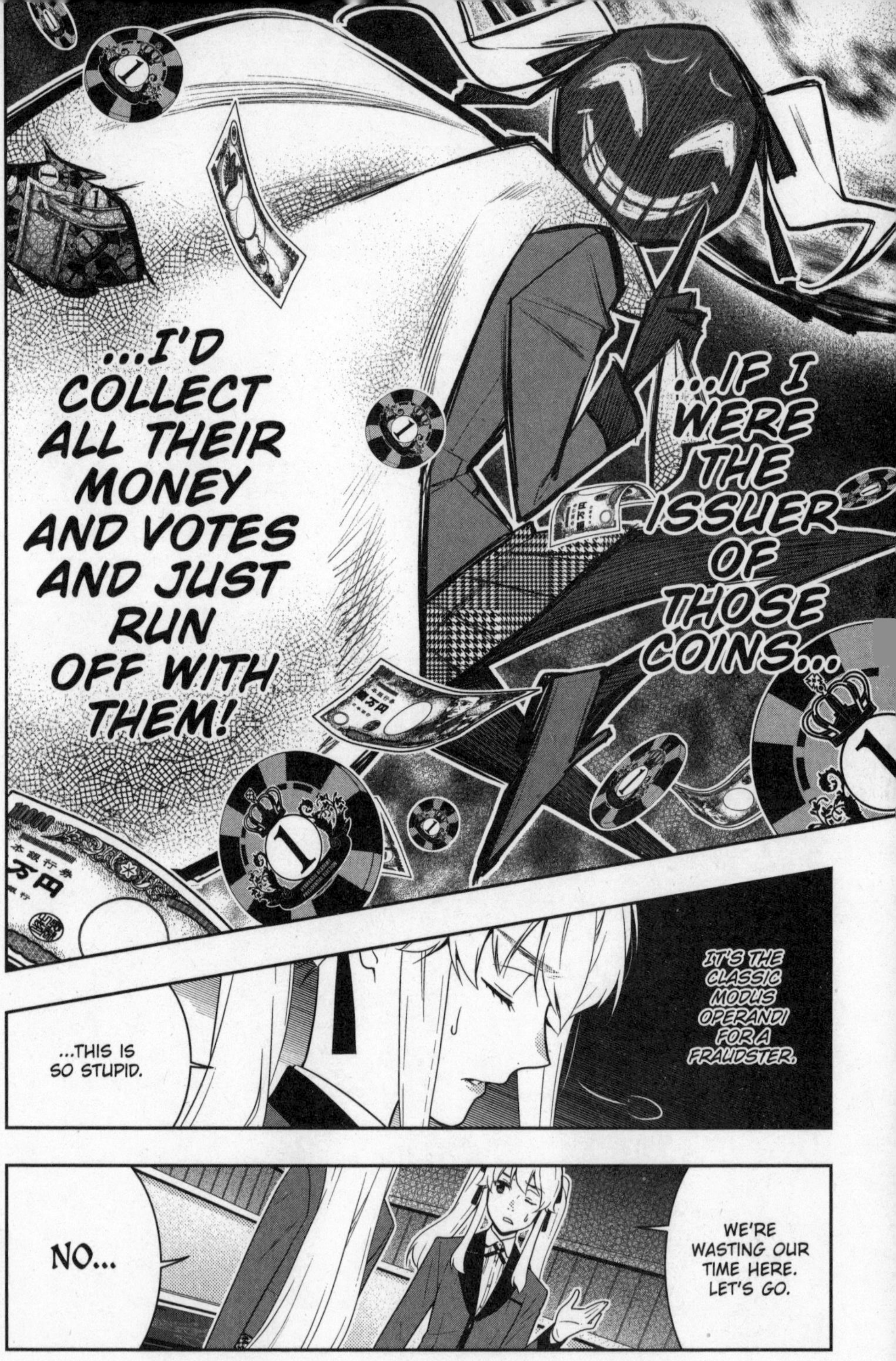
...IF I WERE THE ISSUER OF THOSE COINS...
...I'D COLLECT ALL THEIR MONEY AND VOTES AND JUST RUN OFF WITH THEM!
IT'S THE CLASSIC MODUS OPERANDI FOR A FRAUDSTER.
...THIS IS SO STUPID.
WE'RE WASTING OUR TIME HERE. LET'S GO.
NO...

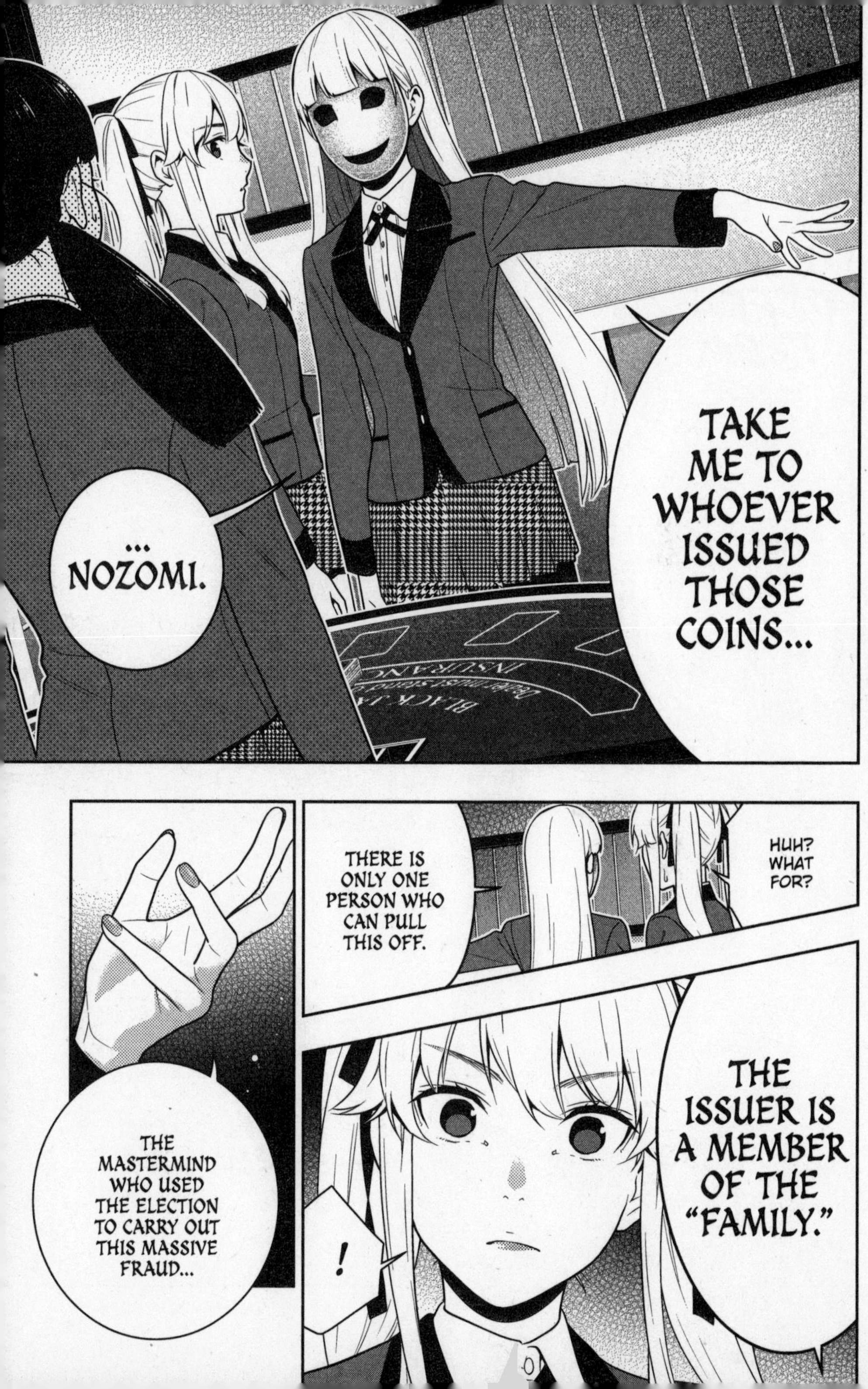
TAKE ME TO WHOEVER ISSUED THOSE COINS...
...NOZOMI.
HUH? WHAT FOR?
THERE IS ONLY ONE PERSON WHO CAN PULL THIS OFF.
THE ISSUER IS A MEMBER OF THE "FAMILY."
!
THE MASTERMIND WHO USED THE ELECTION TO CARRY OUT THIS MASSIVE FRAUD...

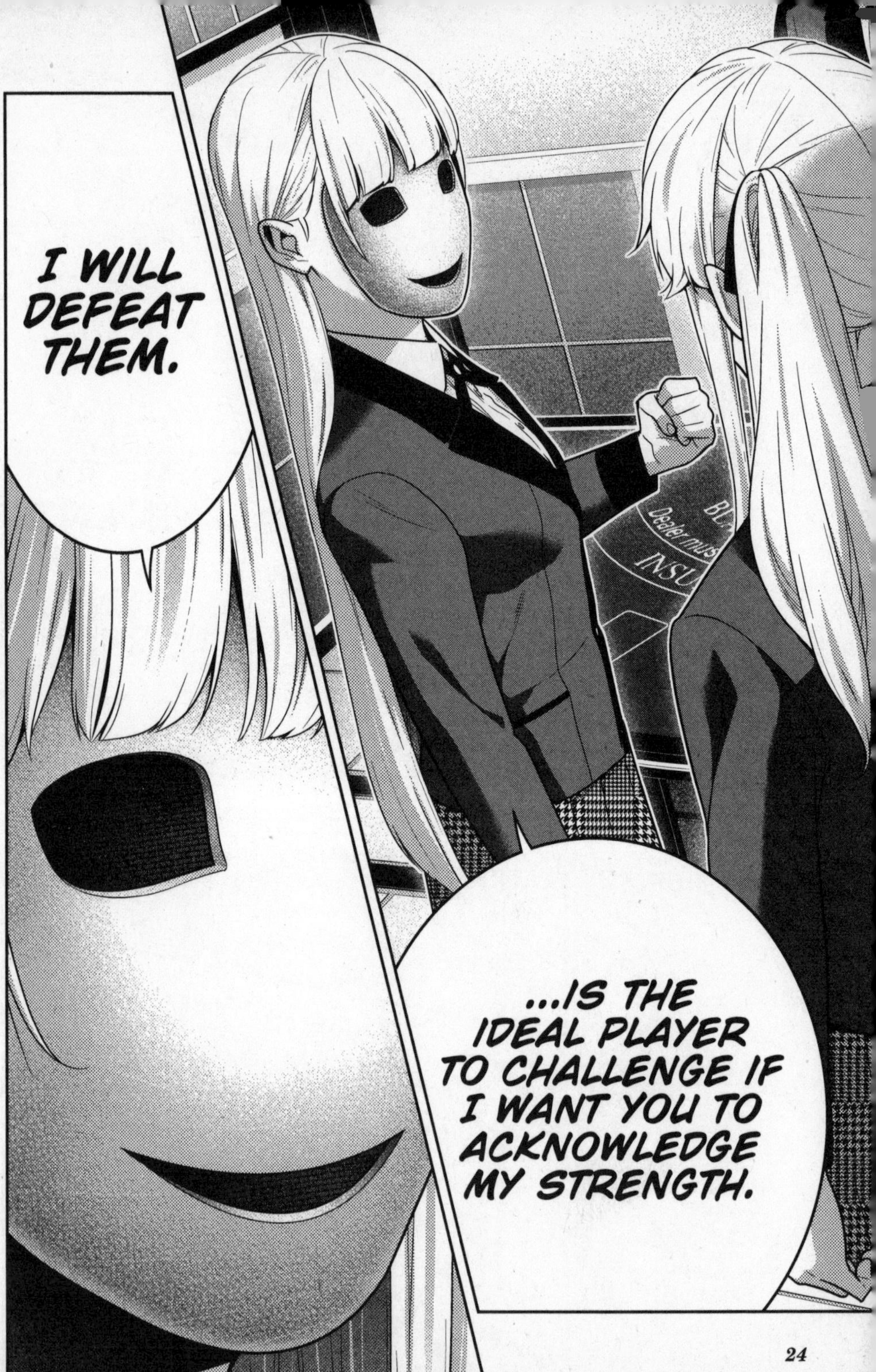
...IS THE IDEAL PLAYER TO CHALLENGE IF I WANT YOU TO ACKNOWLEDGE MY STRENGTH.
I WILL DEFEAT THEM.

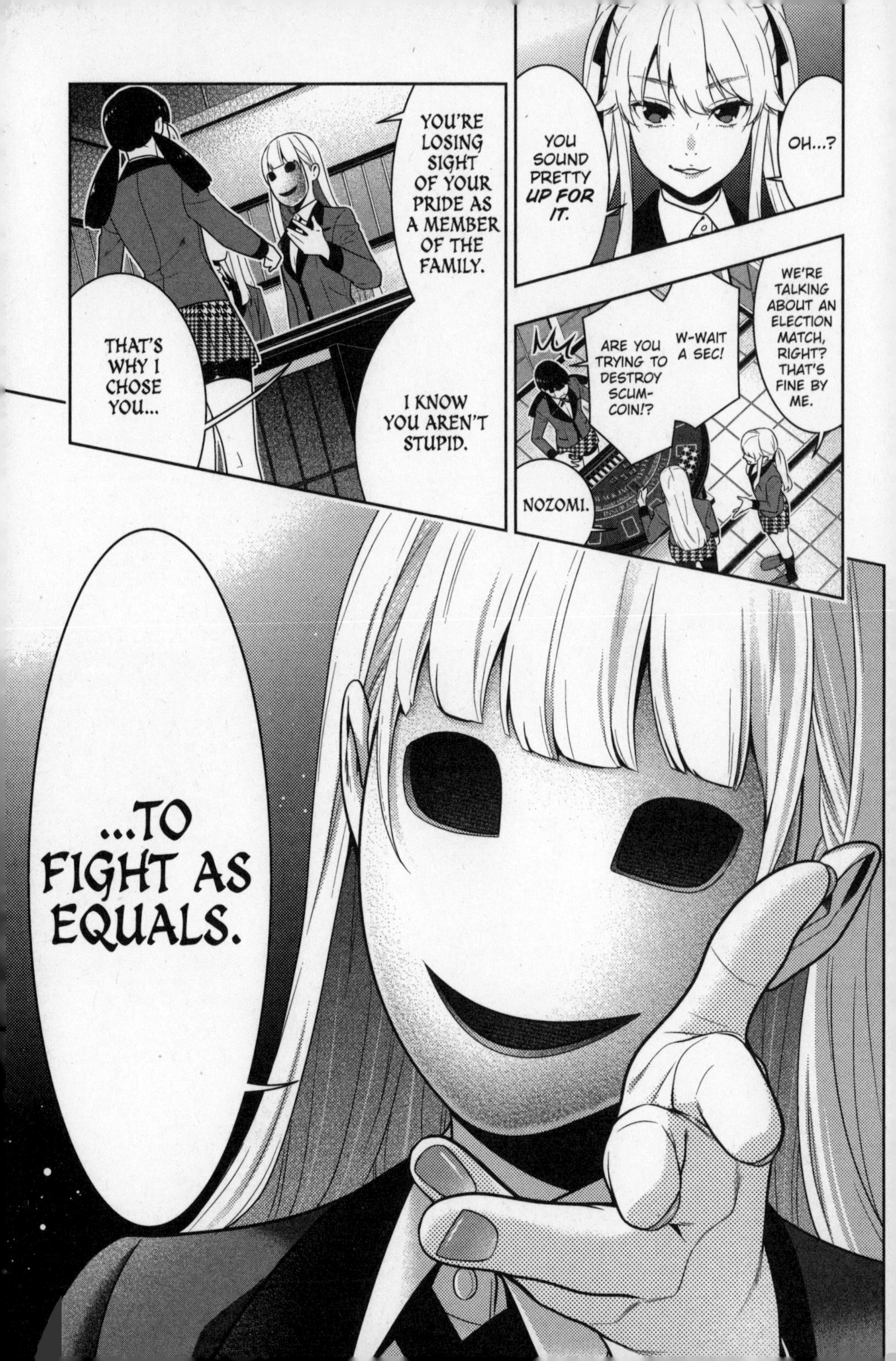
OH...?
YOU SOUND PRETTY *UP FOR IT.*
WE'RE TALKING ABOUT AN ELECTION MATCH, RIGHT? THAT'S FINE BY ME.
W-WAIT A SEC!
ARE YOU TRYING TO DESTROY SCUM-COIN!?
NOZOMI.
YOU'RE LOSING SIGHT OF YOUR PRIDE AS A MEMBER OF THE FAMILY.
I KNOW YOU AREN'T STUPID.
THAT'S WHY I CHOSE YOU...
...TO FIGHT AS EQUALS.

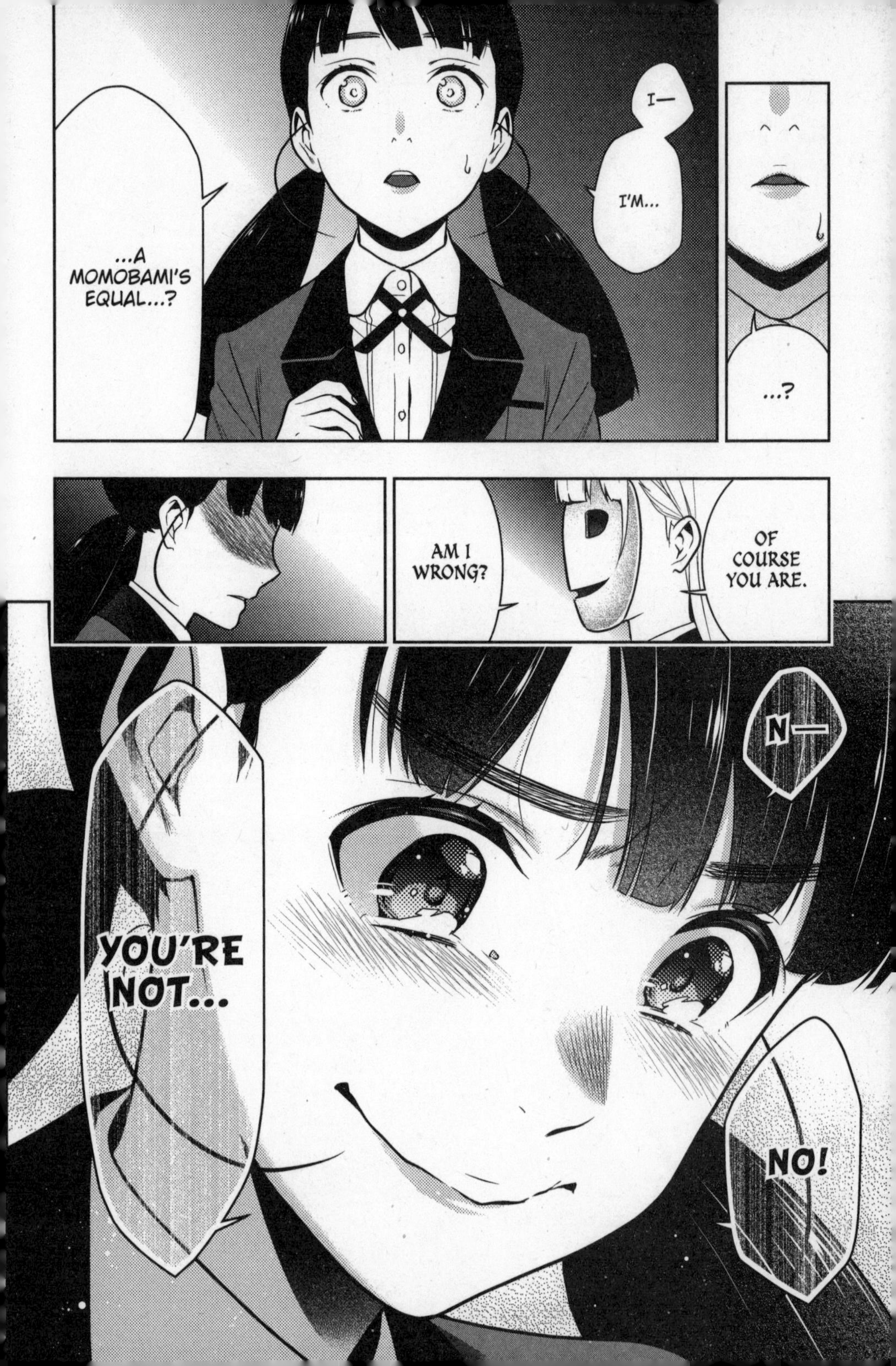
...?
I—
I'M...
...A MOMOBAMI'S EQUAL...?
OF COURSE YOU ARE.
AM I WRONG?
N—
YOU'RE NOT...
NO!

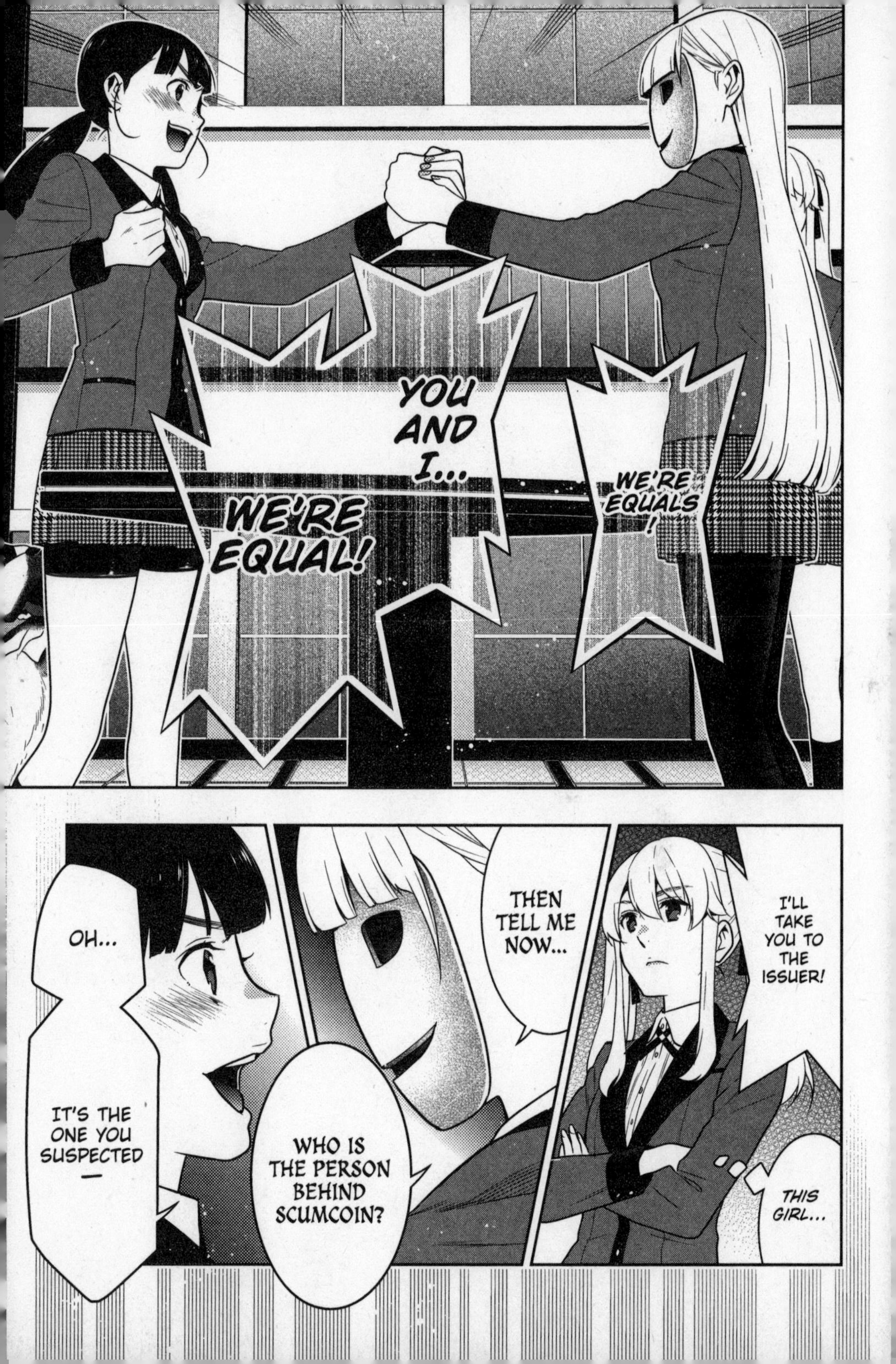
YOU AND I...
WE'RE EQUAL!
WE'RE EQUALS!
I'LL TAKE YOU TO THE ISSUER!
THIS GIRL...
THEN TELL ME NOW...
WHO IS THE PERSON BEHIND SCUMCOIN?
OH...
IT'S THE ONE YOU SUSPECTED —

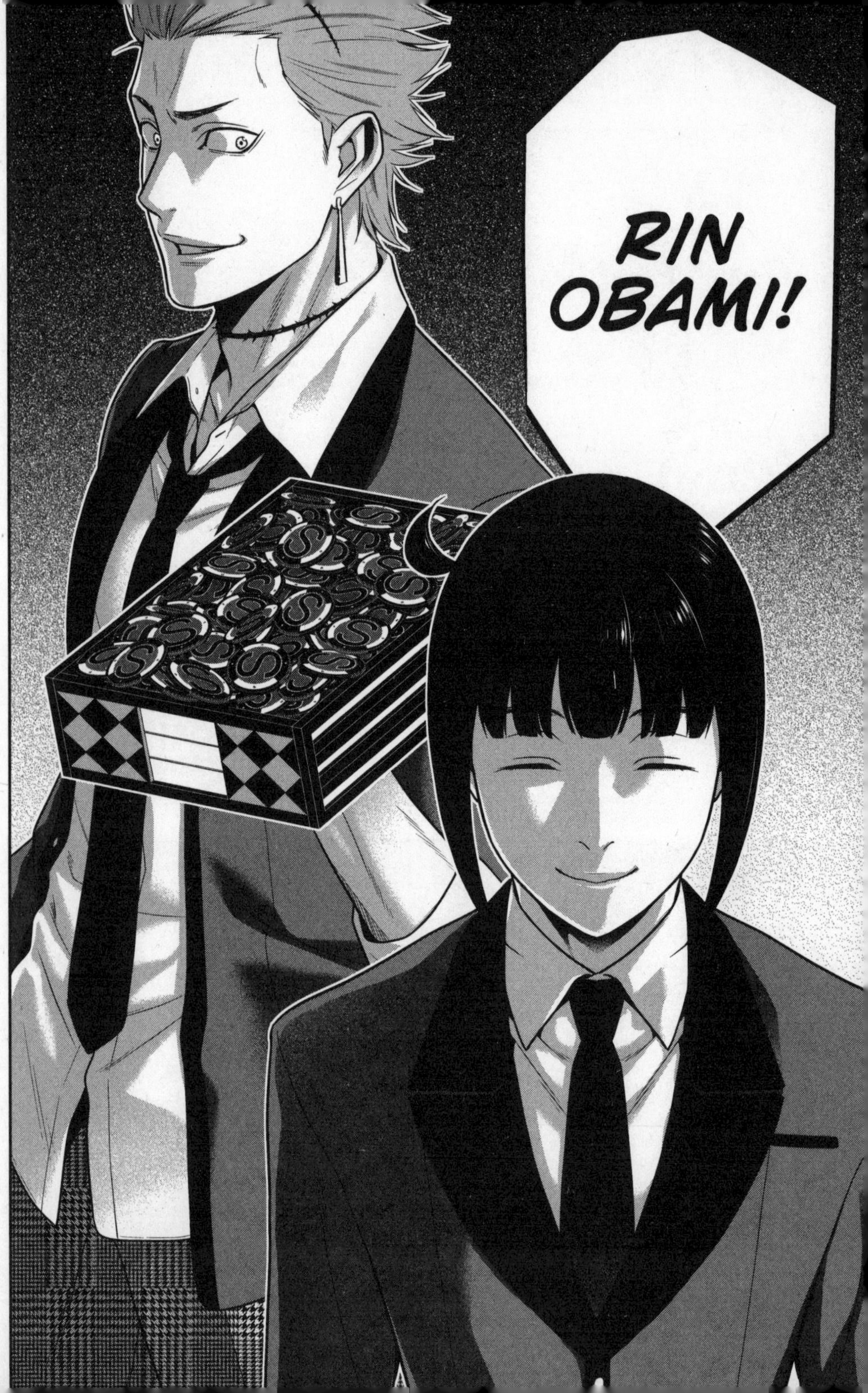
RIN OBAMI!

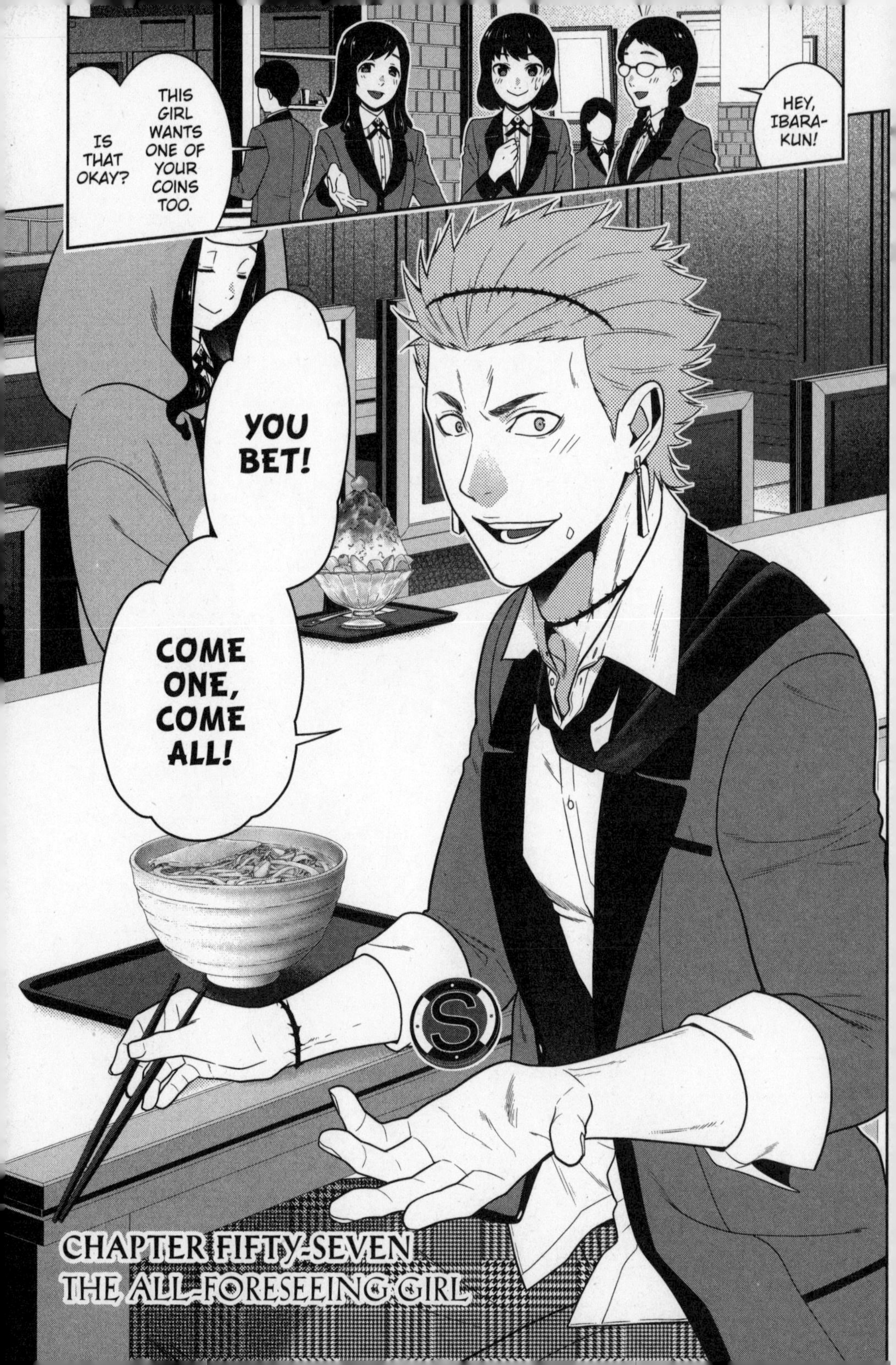
HEY, IBARA-KUN!
THIS GIRL WANTS ONE OF YOUR COINS TOO.
IS THAT OKAY?
YOU BET!
COME ONE, COME ALL!

CHAPTER FIFTY-SEVEN
THE ALL-FORESEEING GIRL

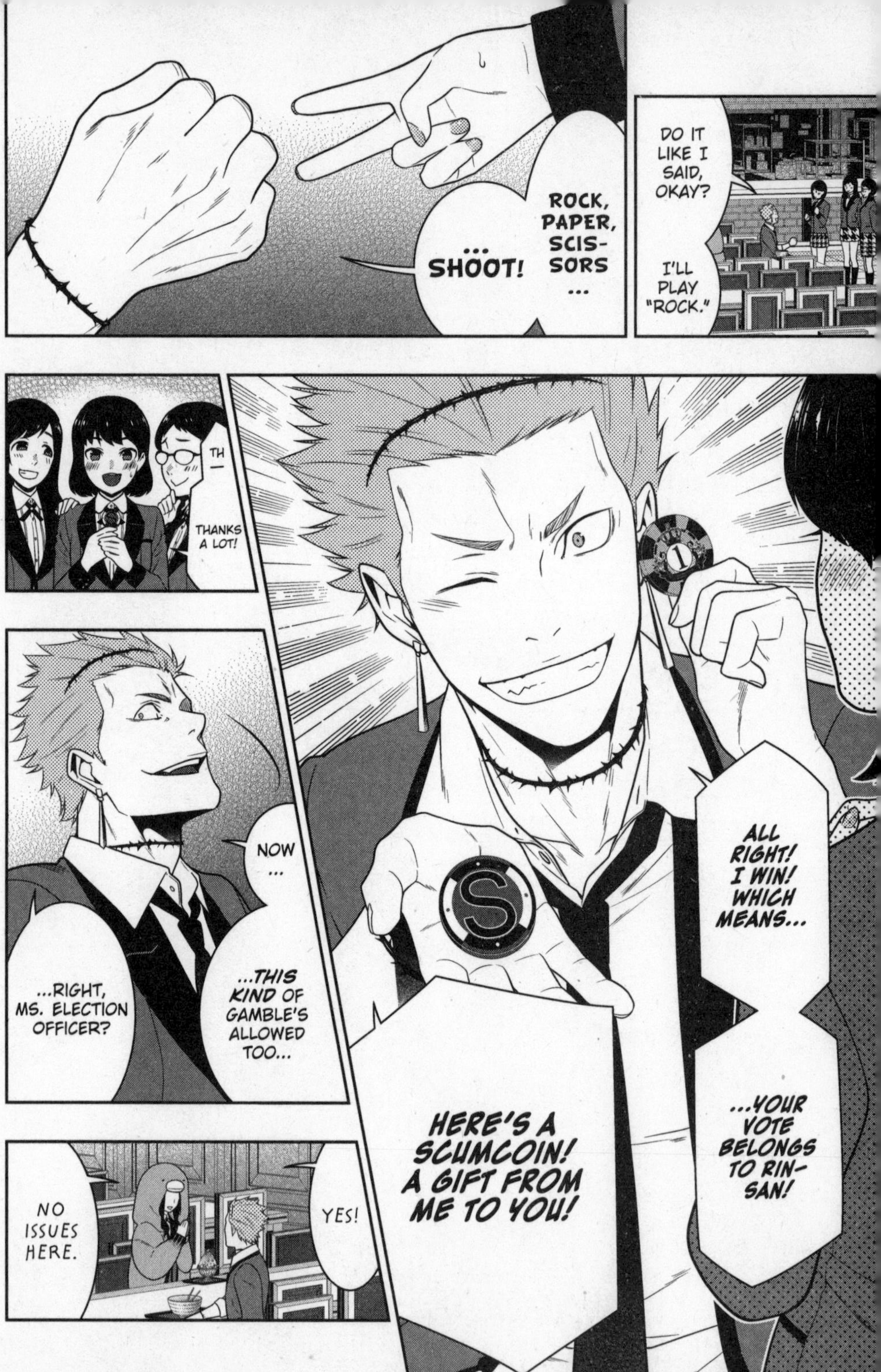
DO IT LIKE I SAID, OKAY?
I'LL PLAY "ROCK."
ROCK, PAPER, SCIS-SORS ...
... SHOOT!
ALL RIGHT! I WIN! WHICH MEANS...
...YOUR VOTE BELONGS TO RIN-SAN!
HERE'S A SCUMCOIN! A GIFT FROM ME TO YOU!
TH—
THANKS A LOT!
NOW ...
...THIS KIND OF GAMBLE'S ALLOWED TOO...
...RIGHT, MS. ELECTION OFFICER?
YES!
NO ISSUES HERE.

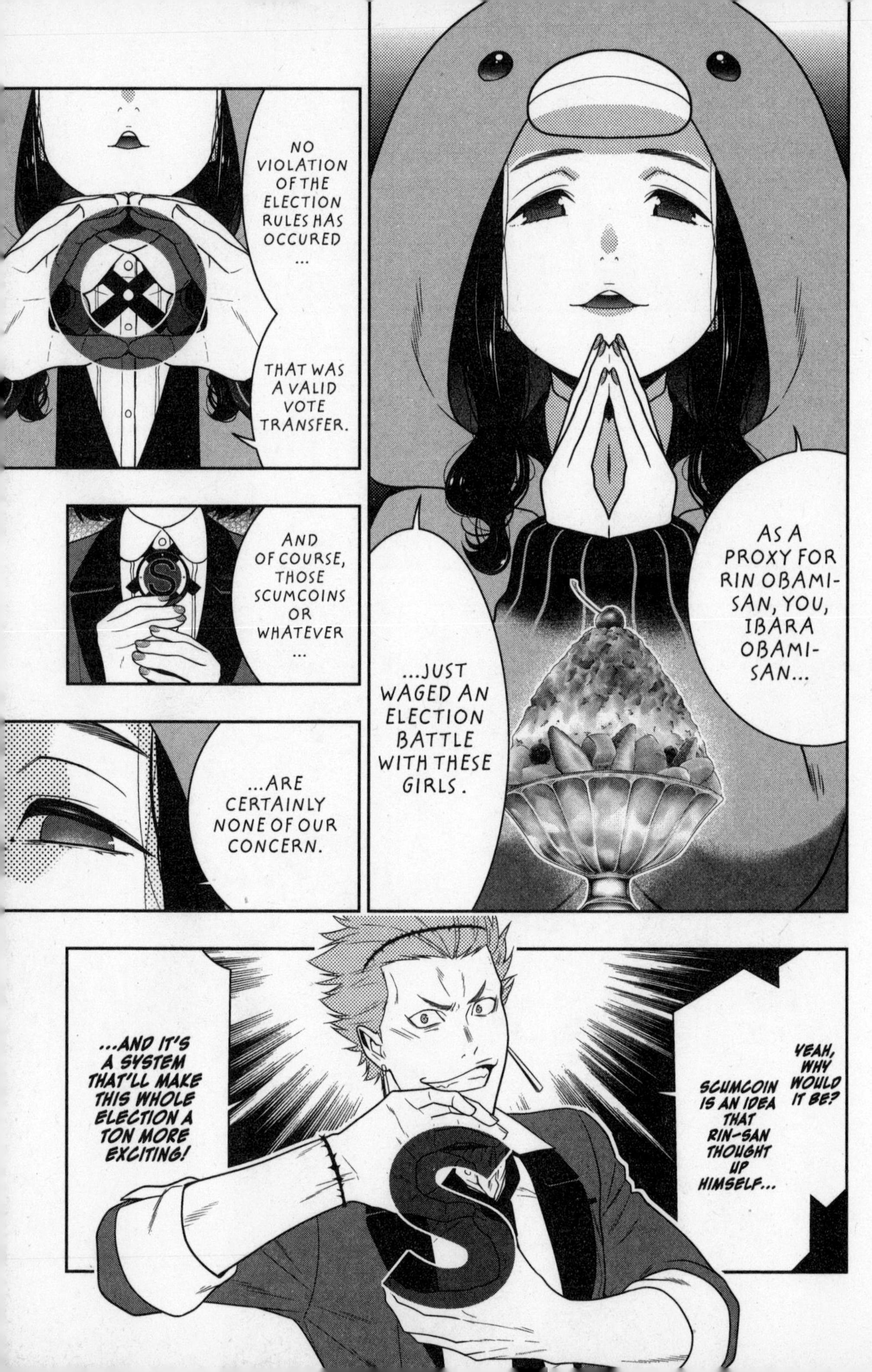
AS A PROXY FOR RIN OBAMI-SAN, YOU, IBARA OBAMI-SAN...
...JUST WAGED AN ELECTION BATTLE WITH THESE GIRLS.
NO VIOLATION OF THE ELECTION RULES HAS OCCURED ...
THAT WAS A VALID VOTE TRANSFER.
AND OF COURSE, THOSE SCUMCOINS OR WHATEVER ...
...ARE CERTAINLY NONE OF OUR CONCERN.
YEAH, WHY WOULD IT BE?
SCUMCOIN IS AN IDEA THAT RIN-SAN THOUGHT UP HIMSELF...
...AND IT'S A SYSTEM THAT'LL MAKE THIS WHOLE ELECTION A TON MORE EXCITING!

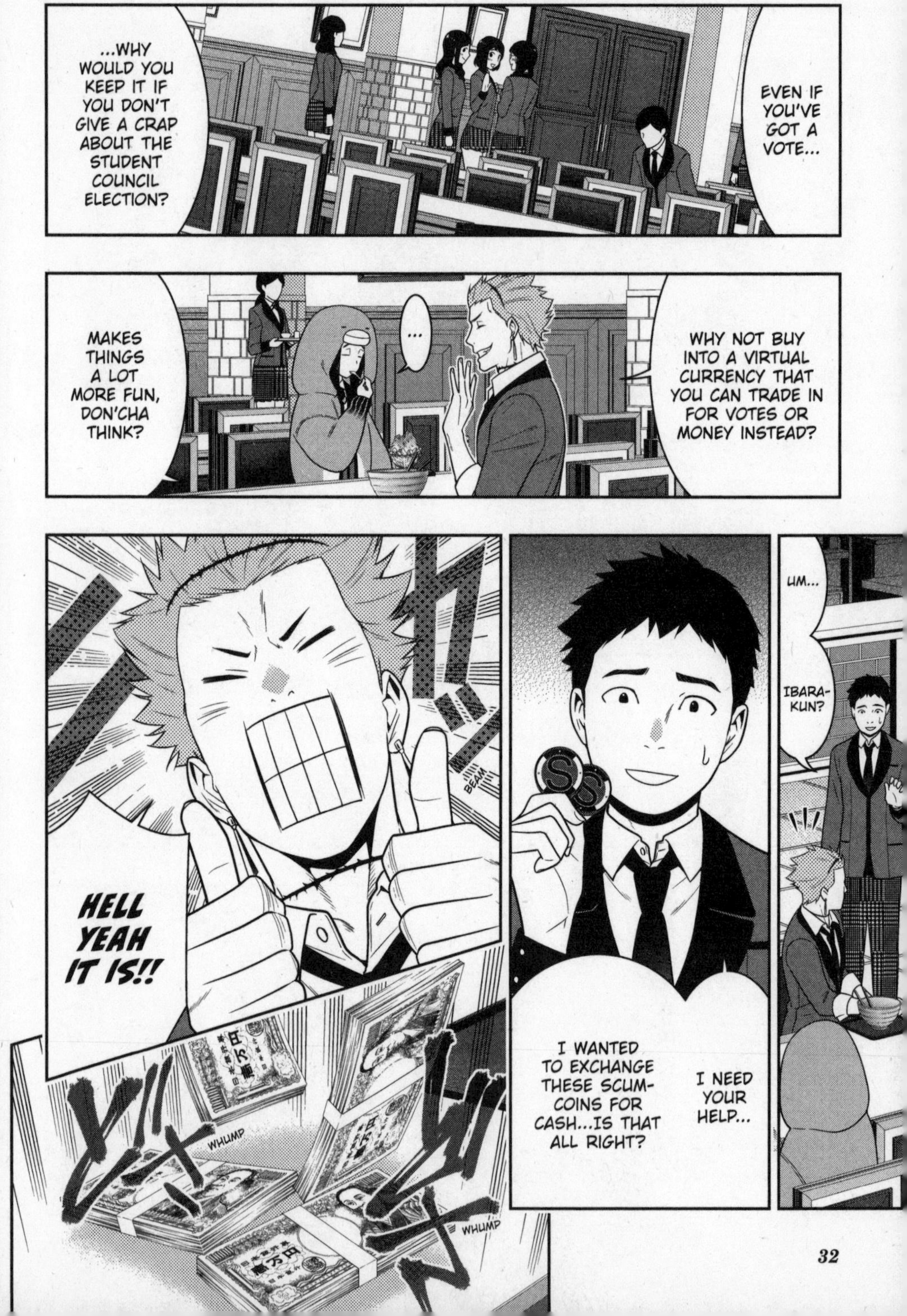
EVEN IF YOU'VE GOT A VOTE...
...WHY WOULD YOU KEEP IT IF YOU DON'T GIVE A CRAP ABOUT THE STUDENT COUNCIL ELECTION?
WHY NOT BUY INTO A VIRTUAL CURRENCY THAT YOU CAN TRADE IN FOR VOTES OR MONEY INSTEAD?
...
MAKES THINGS A LOT MORE FUN, DON'CHA THINK?
UM...
IBARA-KUN?
I NEED YOUR HELP...
I WANTED TO EXCHANGE THESE SCUM-COINS FOR CASH...IS THAT ALL RIGHT?
BEAM
HELL YEAH IT IS!!
WHUMP
WHUMP

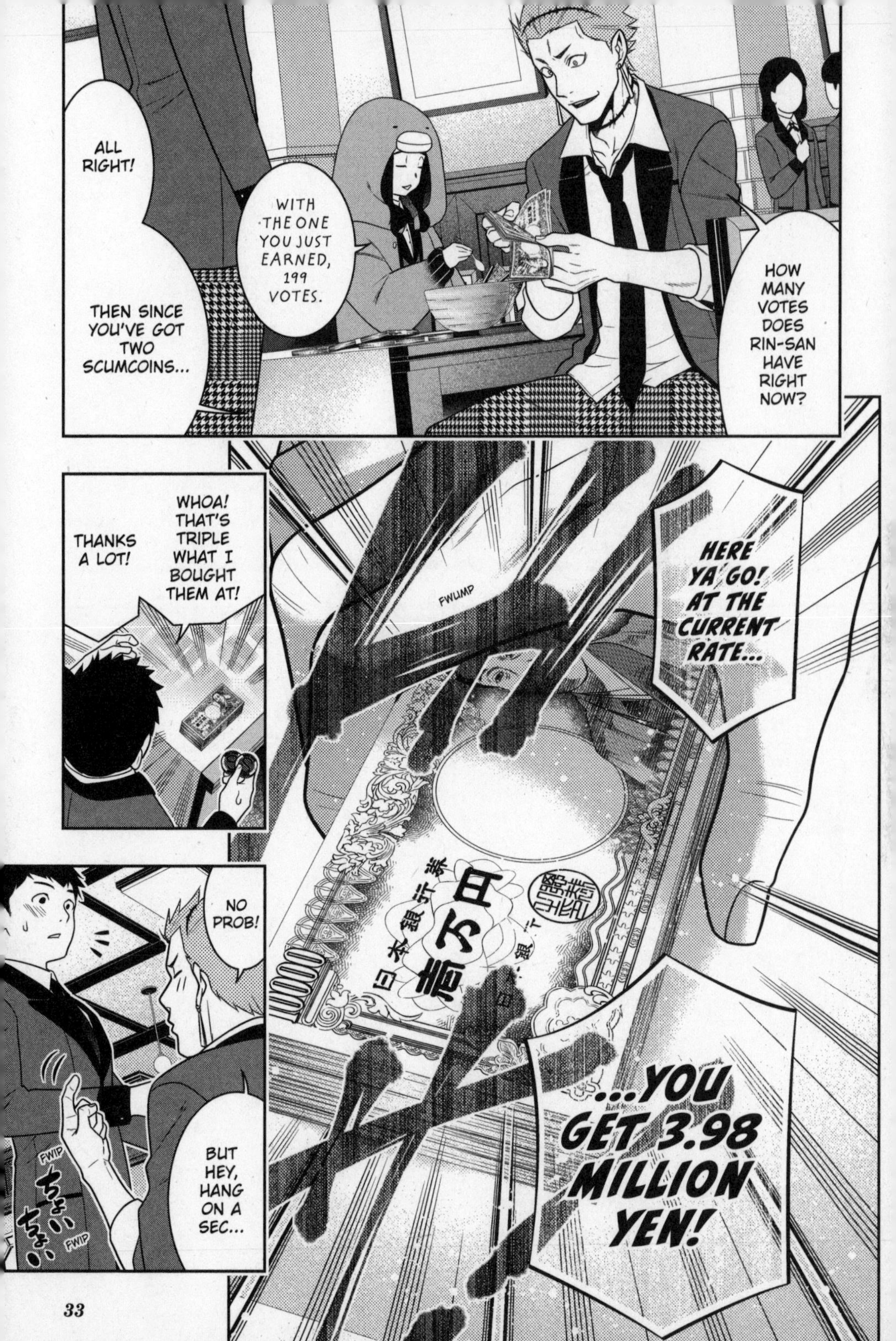
HOW MANY VOTES DOES RIN-SAN HAVE RIGHT NOW?
WITH THE ONE YOU JUST EARNED, 199 VOTES.
ALL RIGHT!
THEN SINCE YOU'VE GOT TWO SCUMCOINS...
HERE YA GO! AT THE CURRENT RATE...
FWUMP
...YOU GET 3.98 MILLION YEN!
WHOA! THAT'S TRIPLE WHAT I BOUGHT THEM AT!
THANKS A LOT!
NO PROB!
BUT HEY, HANG ON A SEC...
FWIP
ちょい
ちょい
FWIP

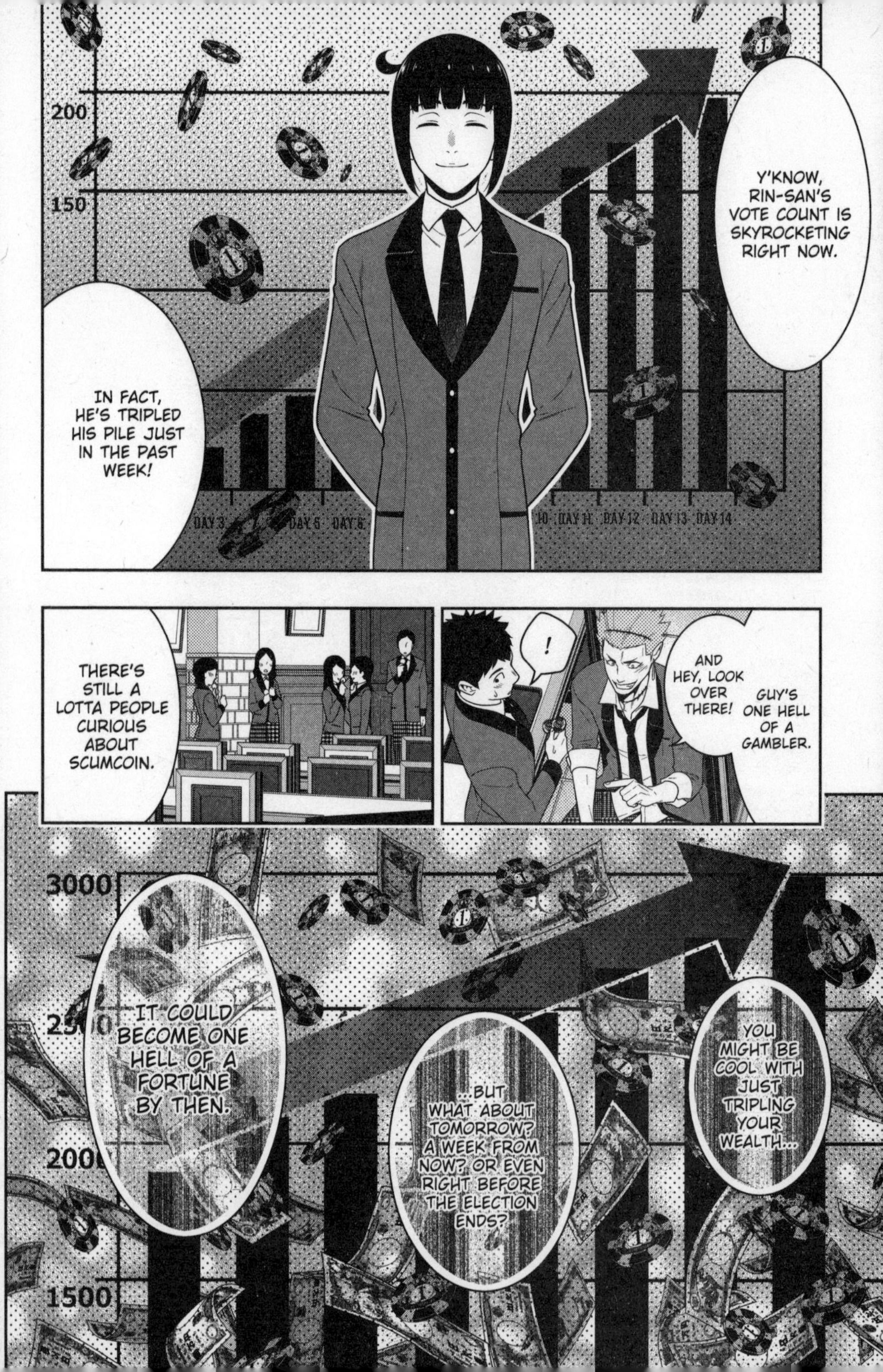
200
150
DAY 3
DAY 5
DAY 6
DAY 11
DAY 12
DAY 13
DAY 14
Y'KNOW, RIN-SAN'S VOTE COUNT IS SKYROCKETING RIGHT NOW.
IN FACT, HE'S TRIPLED HIS PILE JUST IN THE PAST WEEK!
AND HEY, LOOK OVER THERE!
GUY'S ONE HELL OF A GAMBLER.
!
THERE'S STILL A LOTTA PEOPLE CURIOUS ABOUT SCUMCOIN.
3000
1500
YOU MIGHT BE COOL WITH JUST TRIPLING YOUR WEALTH...
...BUT WHAT ABOUT TOMORROW? A WEEK FROM NOW? OR EVEN RIGHT BEFORE THE ELECTION ENDS?
IT COULD BECOME ONE HELL OF A FORTUNE BY THEN.

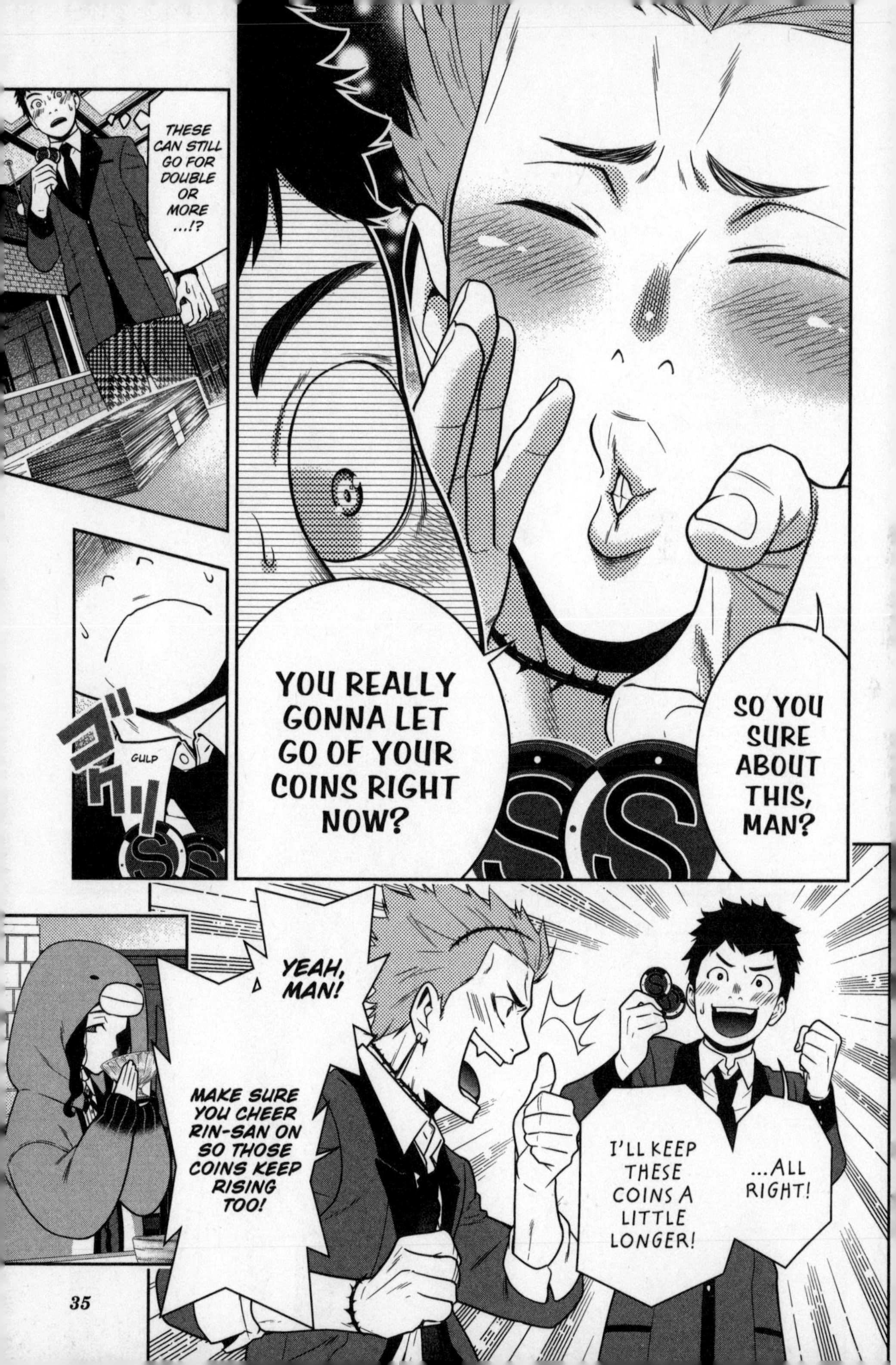
SO YOU SURE ABOUT THIS, MAN?
YOU REALLY GONNA LET GO OF YOUR COINS RIGHT NOW?
THESE CAN STILL GO FOR DOUBLE OR MORE ...!?
GULP
...ALL RIGHT!
I'LL KEEP THESE COINS A LITTLE LONGER!
YEAH, MAN!
MAKE SURE YOU CHEER RIN-SAN ON SO THOSE COINS KEEP RISING TOO!

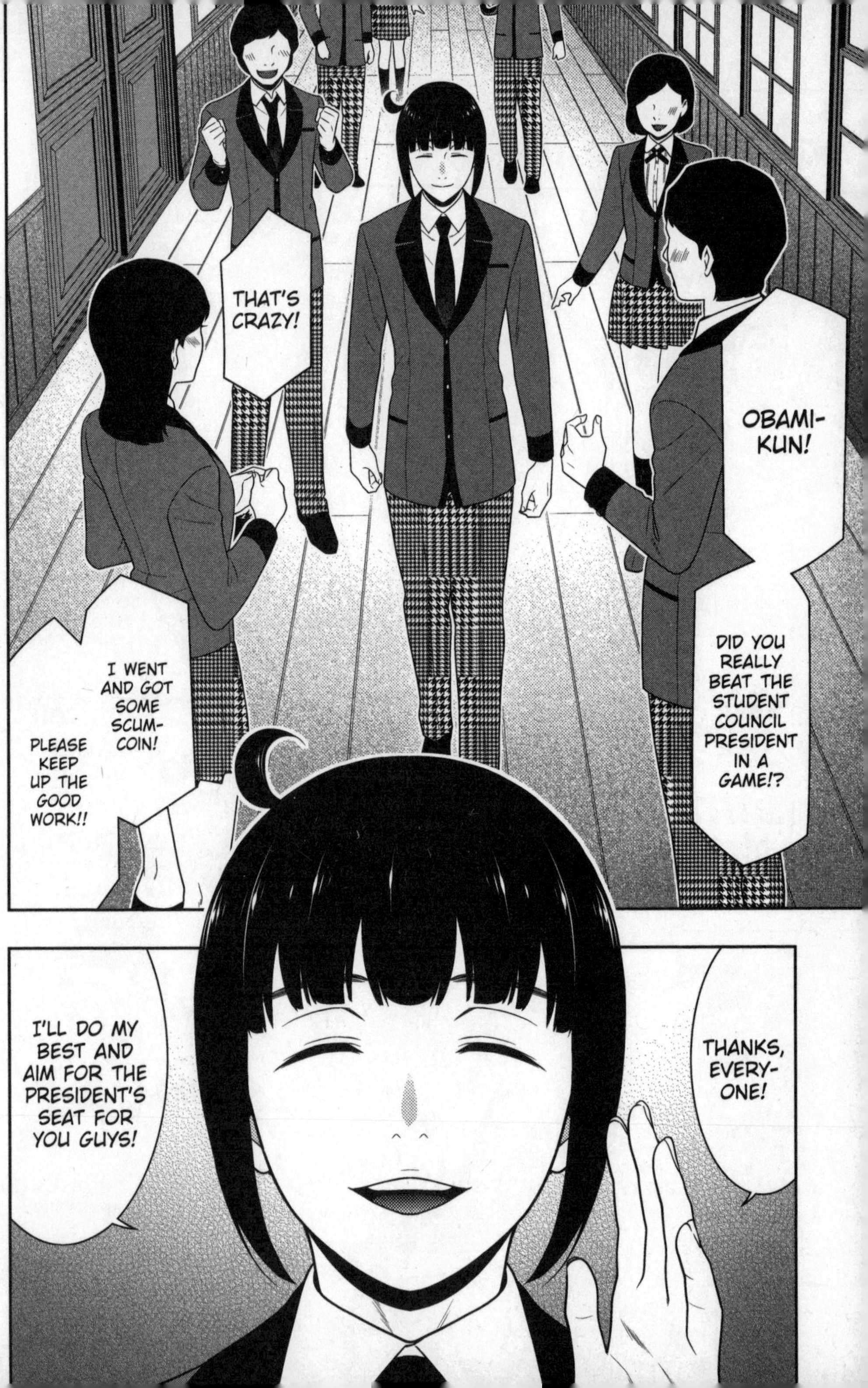
OBAMI-KUN!
DID YOU REALLY BEAT THE STUDENT COUNCIL PRESIDENT IN A GAME!?
THAT'S CRAZY!
I WENT AND GOT SOME SCUM-COIN!
PLEASE KEEP UP THE GOOD WORK!!
THANKS, EVERYONE!
I'LL DO MY BEST AND AIM FOR THE PRESIDENT'S SEAT FOR YOU GUYS!

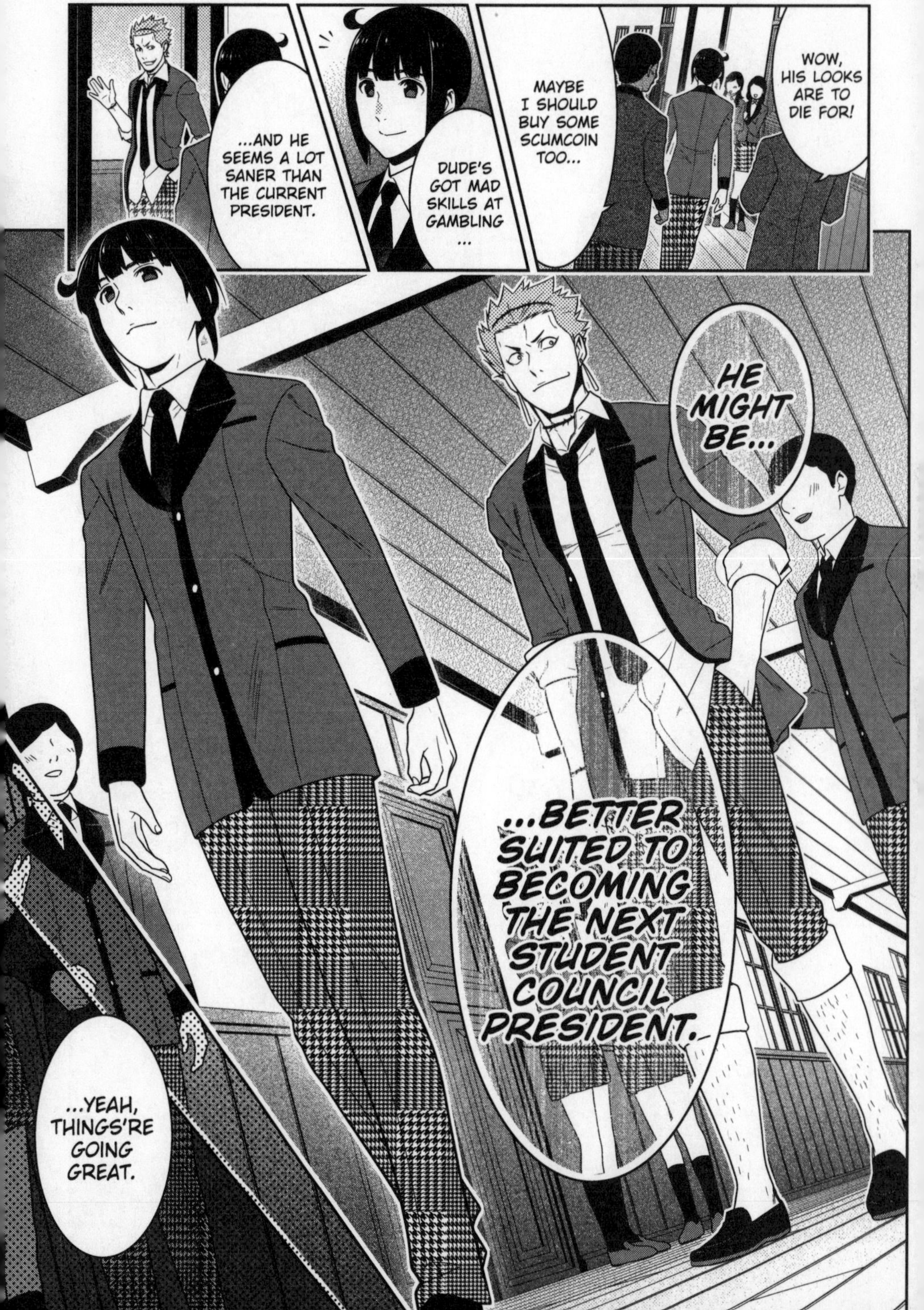
WOW, HIS LOOKS ARE TO DIE FOR!
MAYBE I SHOULD BUY SOME SCUMCOIN TOO...
DUDE'S GOT MAD SKILLS AT GAMBLING...
...AND HE SEEMS A LOT SANER THAN THE CURRENT PRESIDENT.
HE MIGHT BE...
...BETTER SUITED TO BECOMING THE NEXT STUDENT COUNCIL PRESIDENT.
...YEAH, THINGS'RE GOING GREAT.

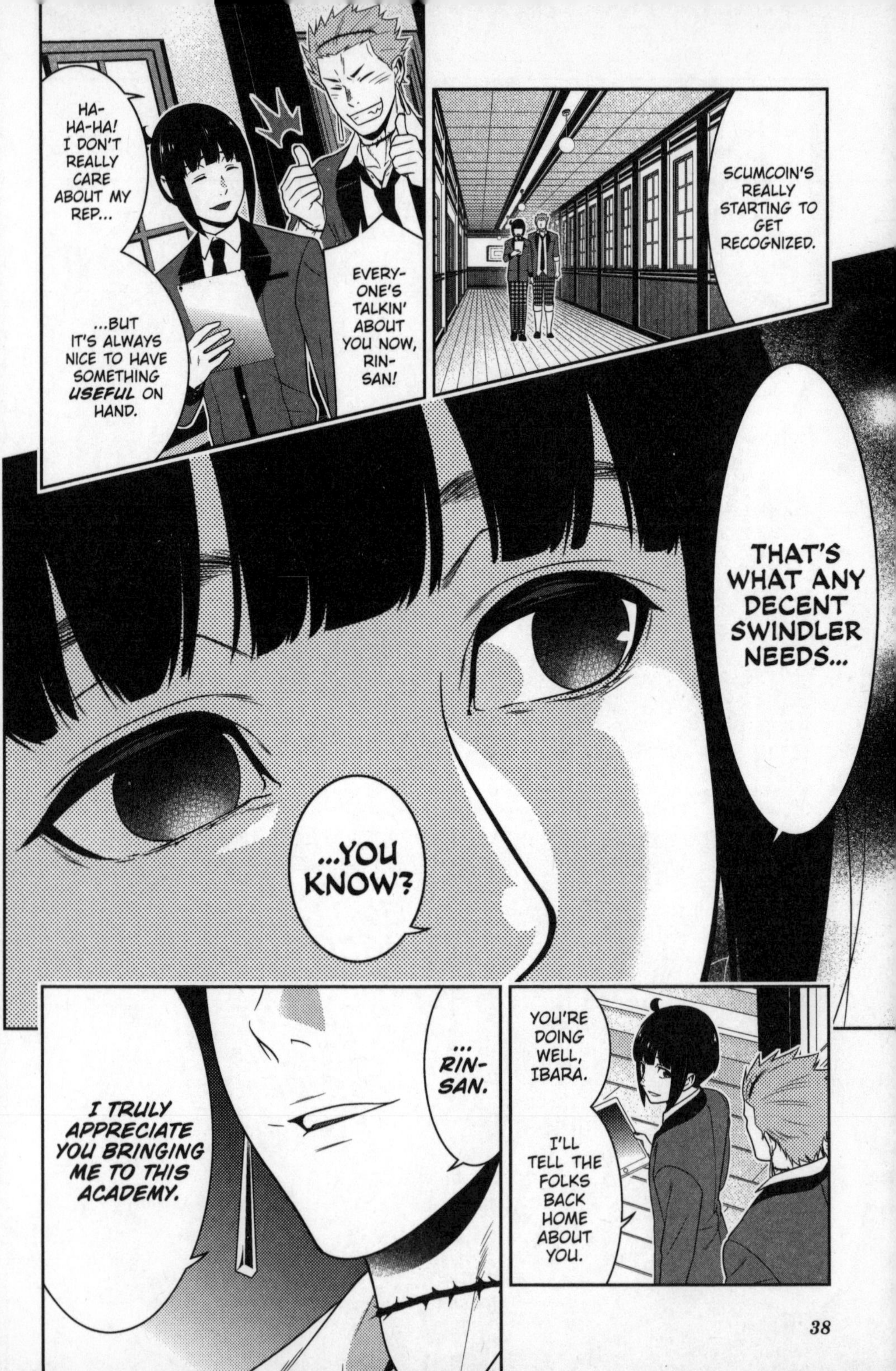
SCUMCOIN'S REALLY STARTING TO GET RECOGNIZED.
EVERY-ONE'S TALKIN' ABOUT YOU NOW, RIN-SAN!
HA-HA-HA! I DON'T REALLY CARE ABOUT MY REP...
...BUT IT'S ALWAYS NICE TO HAVE SOMETHING *USEFUL* ON HAND.
THAT'S WHAT ANY DECENT SWINDLER NEEDS...
...YOU KNOW?
YOU'RE DOING WELL, IBARA.
I'LL TELL THE FOLKS BACK HOME ABOUT YOU.
...RIN-SAN.
I TRULY APPRECIATE YOU BRINGING ME TO THIS ACADEMY.

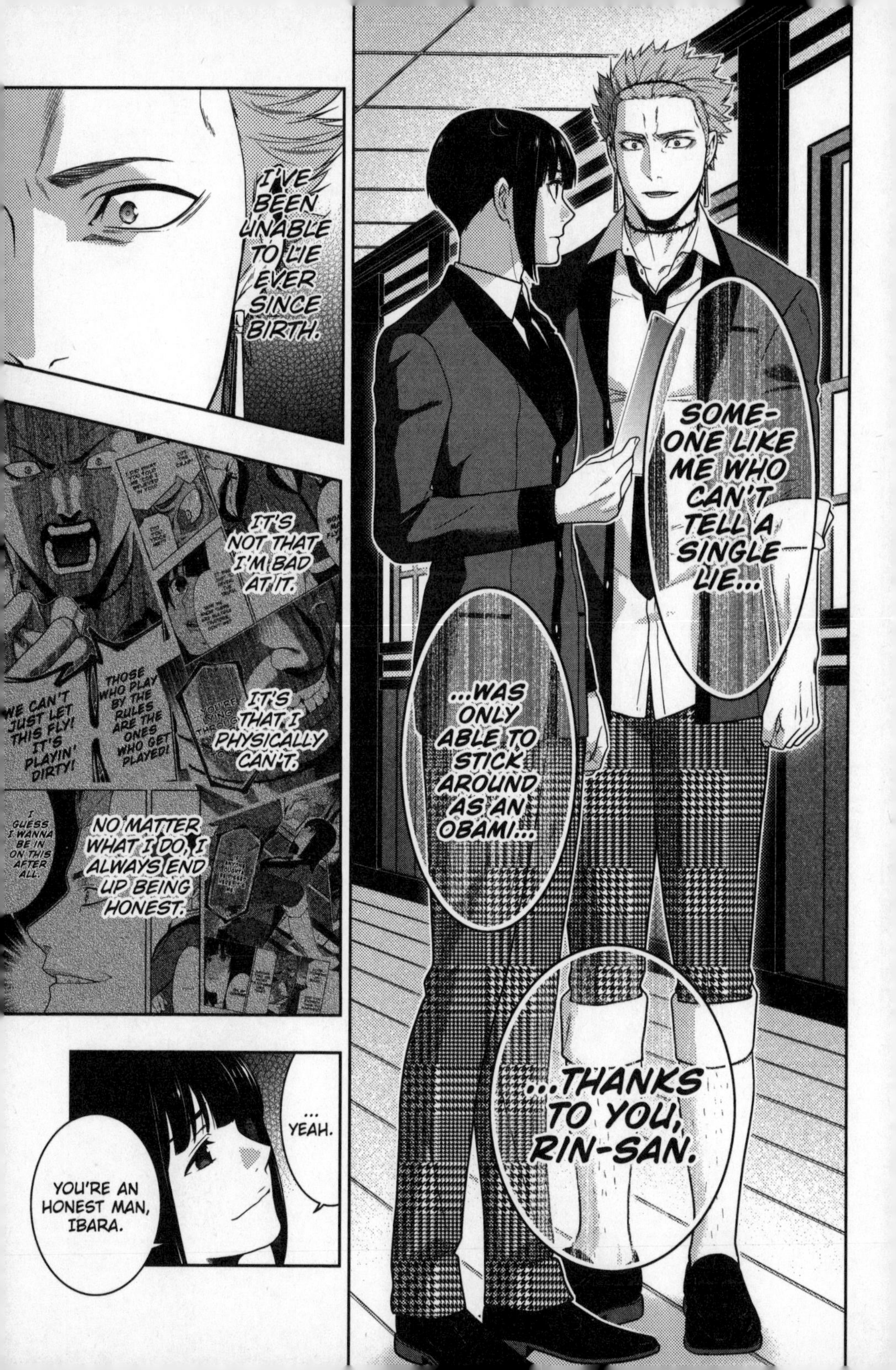

SOME-ONE LIKE ME WHO CAN'T TELL A SINGLE LIE...
...WAS ONLY ABLE TO STICK AROUND AS AN OBAMI...
...THANKS TO YOU, RIN-SAN.
I'VE BEEN UNABLE TO LIE EVER SINCE BIRTH.
IT'S NOT THAT I'M BAD AT IT.
IT'S THAT I PHYSICALLY CAN'T.
THOSE WHO PLAY BY THE RULES ARE THE ONES WHO GET PLAYED!
WE CAN'T JUST LET THIS FLY! IT'S PLAYIN' DIRTY!
NO MATTER WHAT I DO, I ALWAYS END UP BEING HONEST.
I GUESS I WANNA BE IN ON THIS AFTER ALL.
...YEAH.
YOU'RE AN HONEST MAN, IBARA.

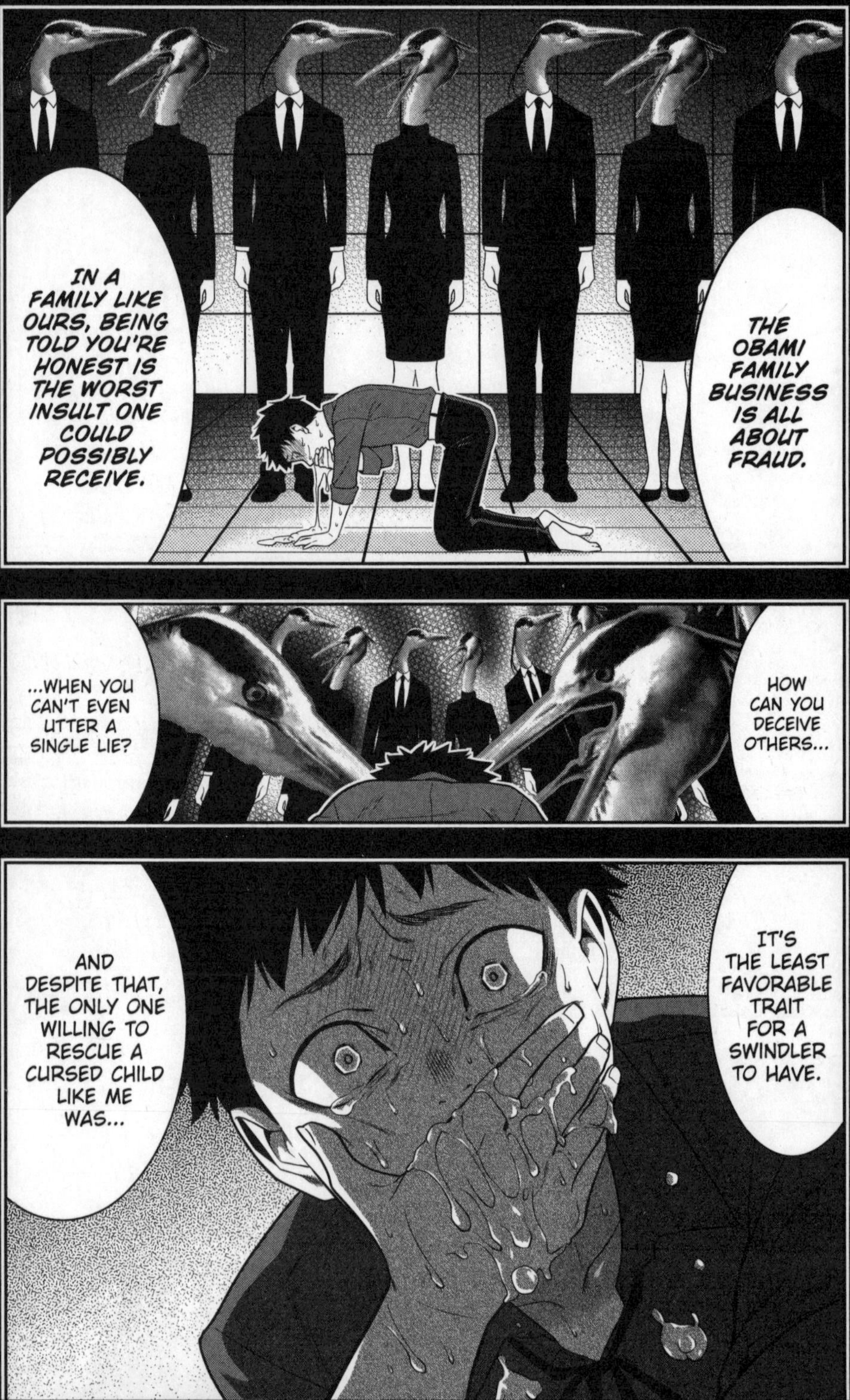
THE OBAMI FAMILY BUSINESS IS ALL ABOUT FRAUD.
IN A FAMILY LIKE OURS, BEING TOLD YOU'RE HONEST IS THE WORST INSULT ONE COULD POSSIBLY RECEIVE.
HOW CAN YOU DECEIVE OTHERS...
...WHEN YOU CAN'T EVEN UTTER A SINGLE LIE?
IT'S THE LEAST FAVORABLE TRAIT FOR A SWINDLER TO HAVE.
AND DESPITE THAT, THE ONLY ONE WILLING TO RESCUE A CURSED CHILD LIKE ME WAS...

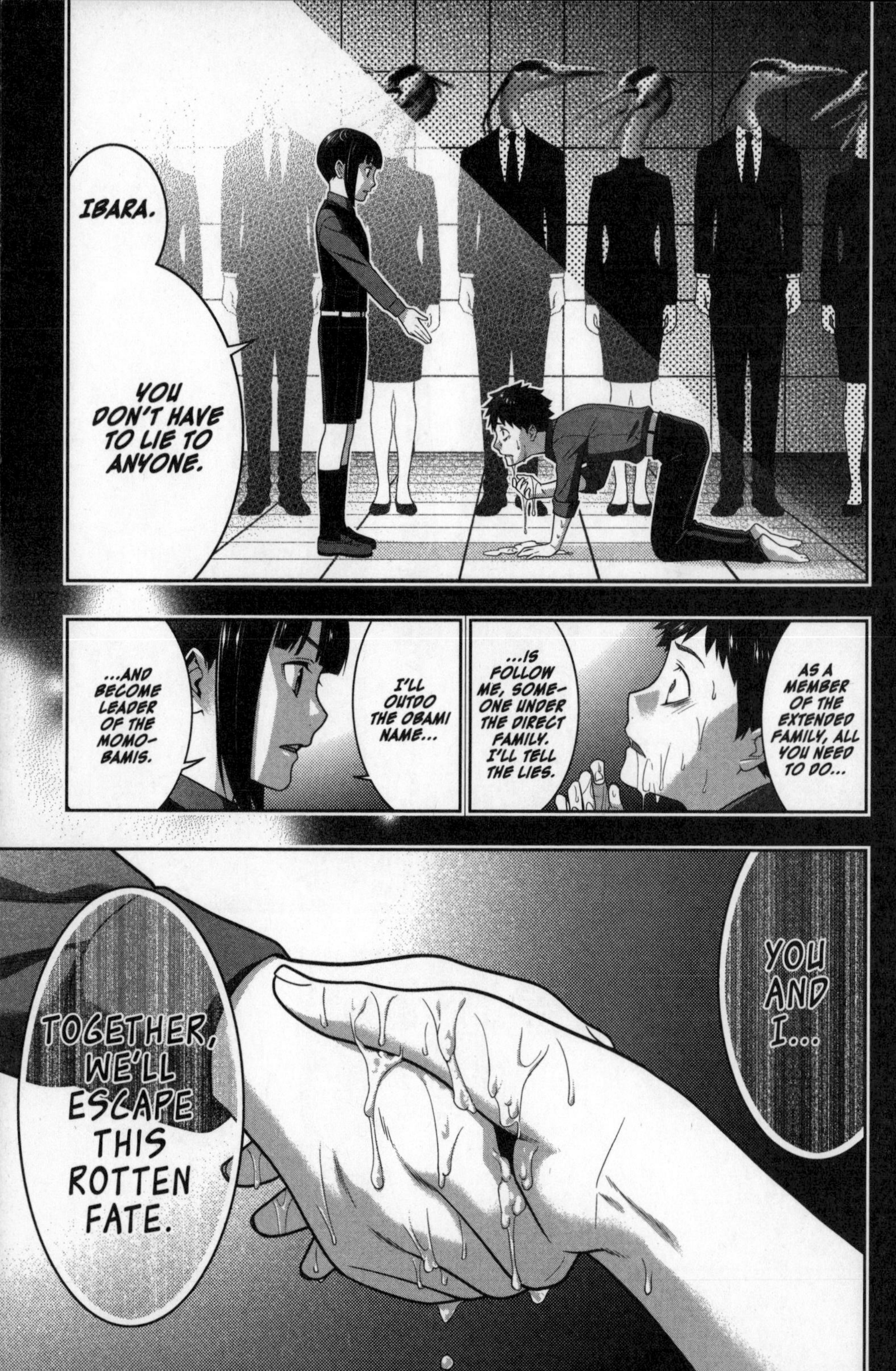
IBARA.
YOU DON'T HAVE TO LIE TO ANYONE.
AS A MEMBER OF THE EXTENDED FAMILY, ALL YOU NEED TO DO...
...IS FOLLOW ME, SOMEONE UNDER THE DIRECT FAMILY. I'LL TELL THE LIES.
I'LL OUTDO THE OBAMI NAME...
...AND BECOME LEADER OF THE MOMOBAMIS.
YOU AND I...
TOGETHER, WE'LL ESCAPE THIS ROTTEN FATE.

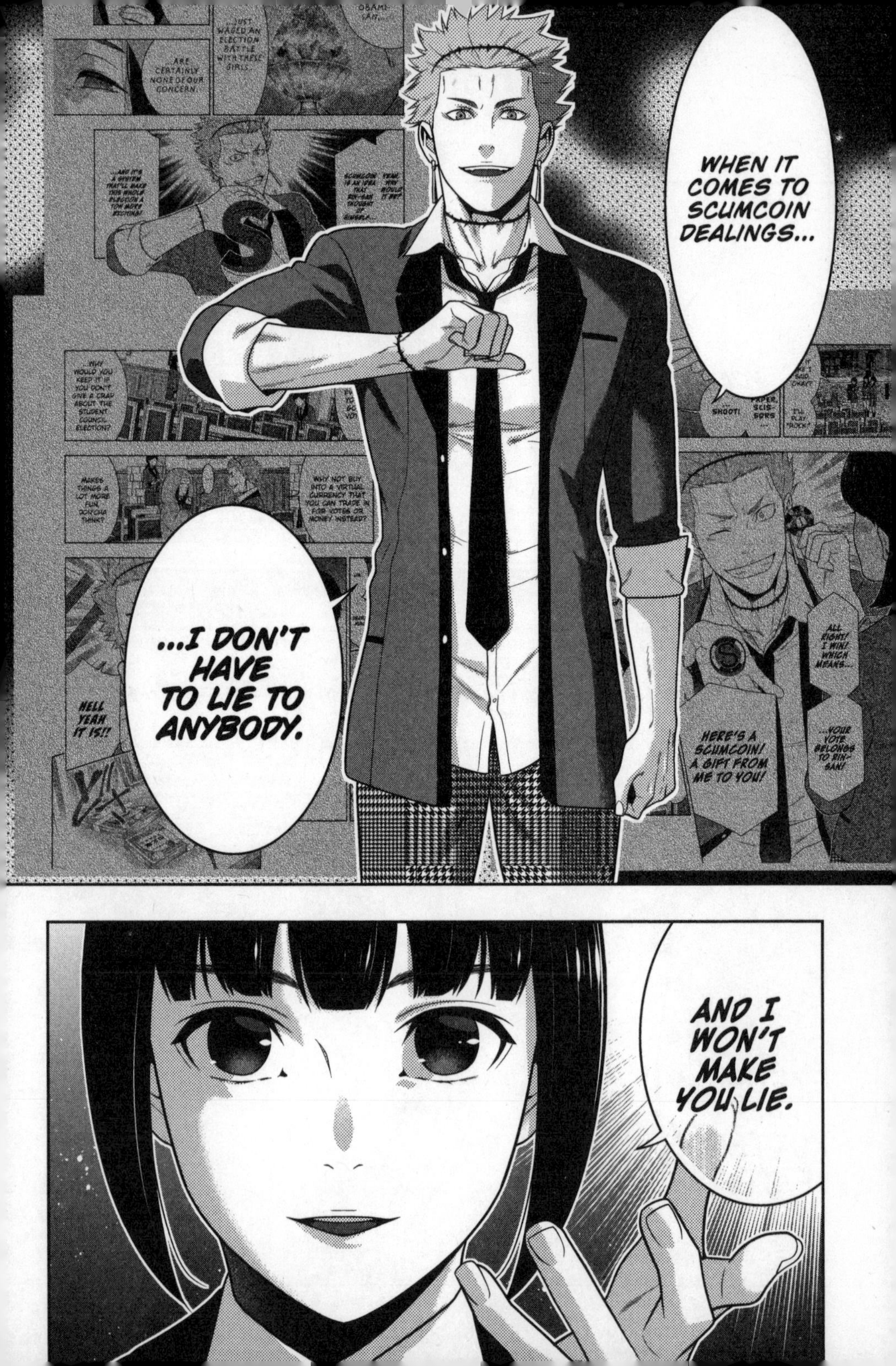
WHEN IT COMES TO SCUMCOIN DEALINGS...
...I DON'T HAVE TO LIE TO ANYBODY.
...JUST WAGED AN ELECTION BATTLE WITH THESE GIRLS...
...ARE CERTAINLY NONE OF OUR CONCERN.
...WHY WOULD YOU KEEP IT IF YOU DON'T GIVE A CRAP ABOUT THE STUDENT COUNCIL ELECTION?
SHOOT!
WHY NOT BUY INTO A VIRTUAL CURRENCY THAT YOU CAN TRADE IN FOR VOTES OR MONEY INSTEAD?
MAKES THINGS A LOT MORE FUN, DONCHA THINK?
ALL RIGHT! I WIN! WHICH MEANS...
...YOUR VOTE BELONGS TO RIN-SAN!
HERE'S A SCUMCOIN! A GIFT FROM ME TO YOU!
HELL YEAH IT IS!!
AND I WON'T MAKE YOU LIE.

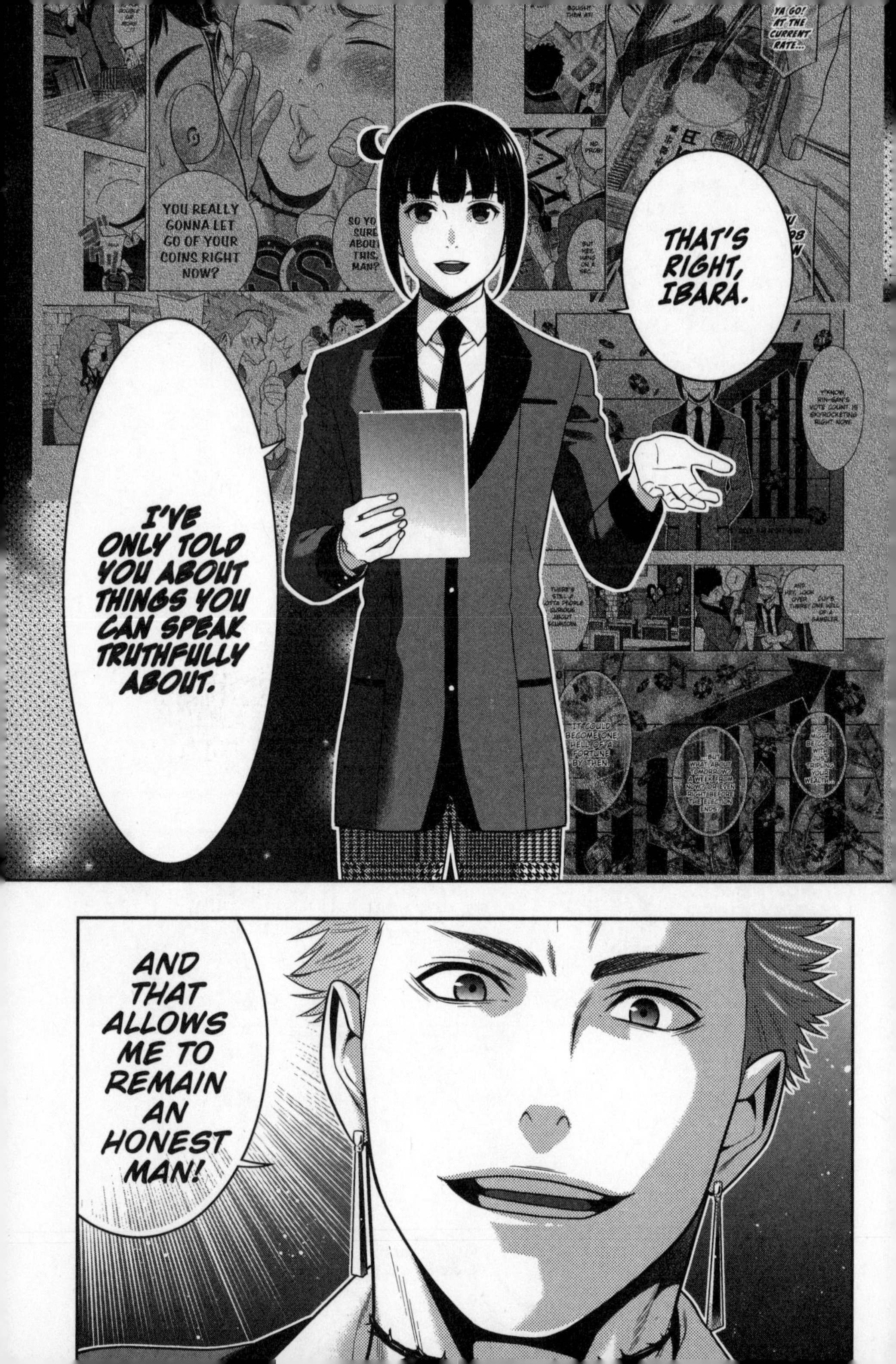
YA GO! AT THE CURRENT RATE...
Y'KNOW, RIN-GAN'S VOTE COUNT IS SKYROCKETING RIGHT NOW.
YOU REALLY GONNA LET GO OF YOUR COINS RIGHT NOW?
THAT'S RIGHT, IBARA.
I'VE ONLY TOLD YOU ABOUT THINGS YOU CAN SPEAK TRUTHFULLY ABOUT.
AND THAT ALLOWS ME TO REMAIN AN HONEST MAN!

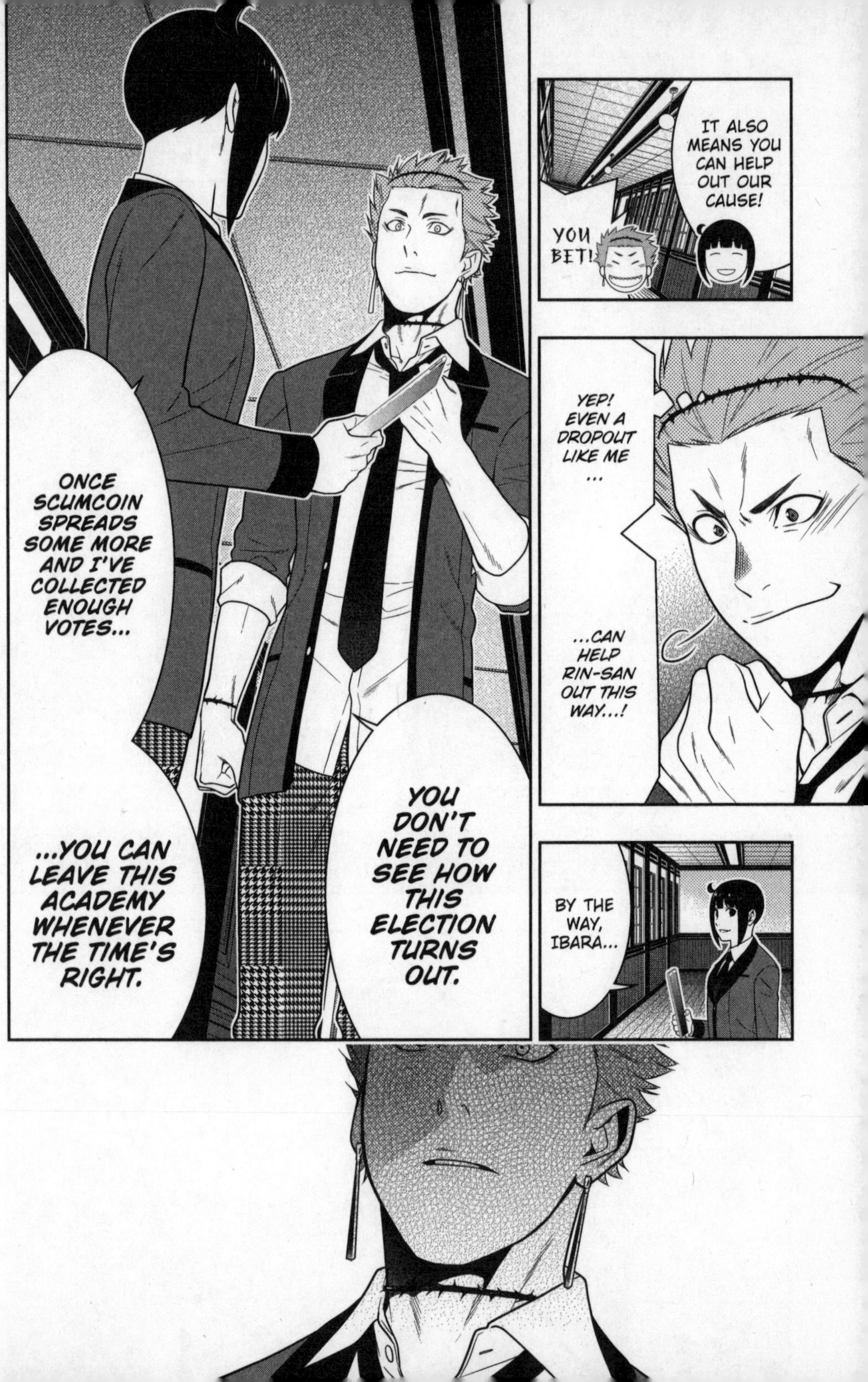
IT ALSO MEANS YOU CAN HELP OUT OUR CAUSE!
YOU BET!
YEP! EVEN A DROPOUT LIKE ME ...
...CAN HELP RIN-SAN OUT THIS WAY...!
BY THE WAY, IBARA...
ONCE SCUMCOIN SPREADS SOME MORE AND I'VE COLLECTED ENOUGH VOTES...
...YOU CAN LEAVE THIS ACADEMY WHENEVER THE TIME'S RIGHT.
YOU DON'T NEED TO SEE HOW THIS ELECTION TURNS OUT.

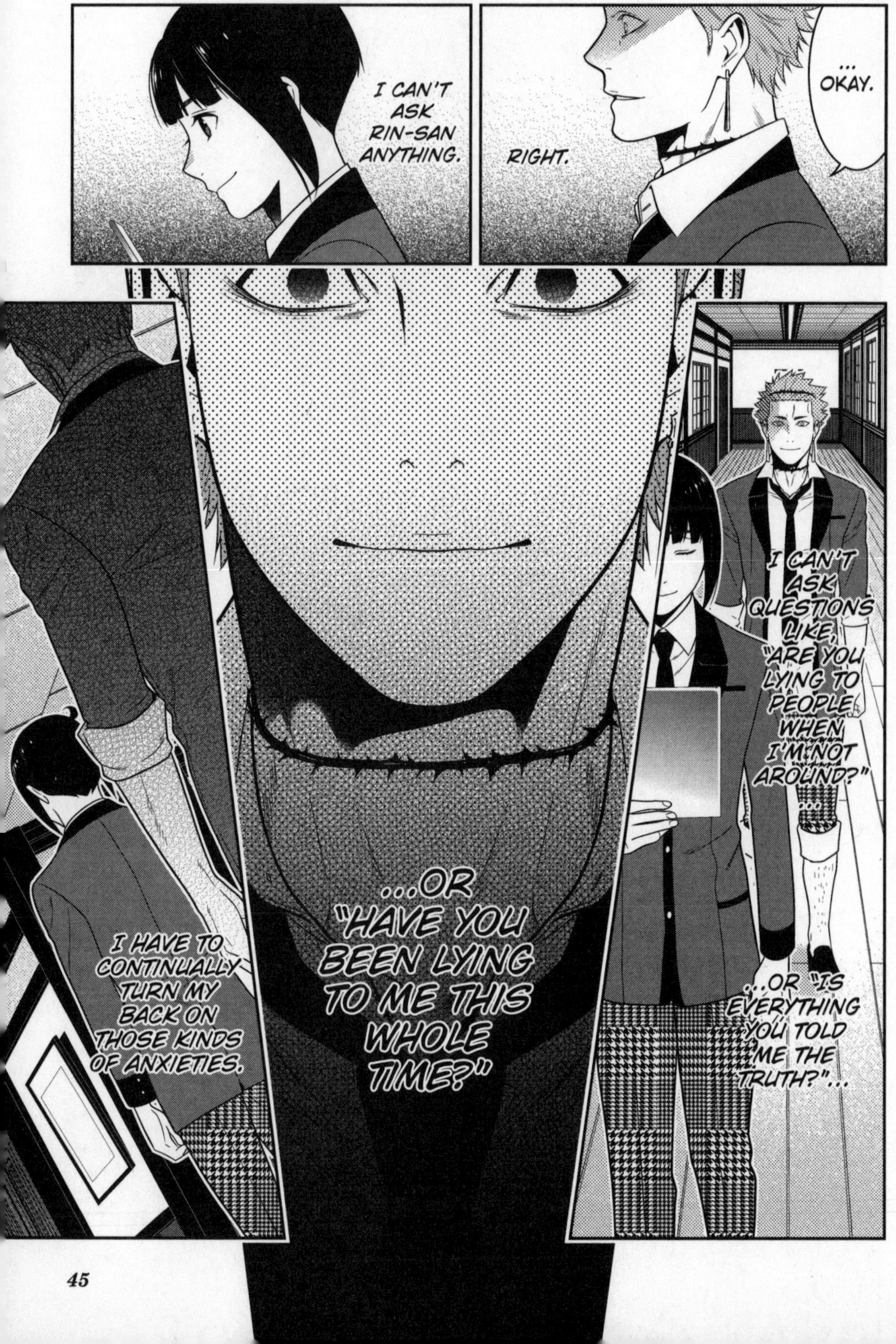
...OKAY.
RIGHT.
I CAN'T ASK RIN-SAN ANYTHING.
I CAN'T ASK QUESTIONS LIKE, "ARE YOU LYING TO PEOPLE WHEN I'M NOT AROUND?"...
...OR "IS EVERYTHING YOU TOLD ME THE TRUTH?"...
...OR "HAVE YOU BEEN LYING TO ME THIS WHOLE TIME?"
I HAVE TO CONTINUALLY TURN MY BACK ON THOSE KINDS OF ANXIETIES.

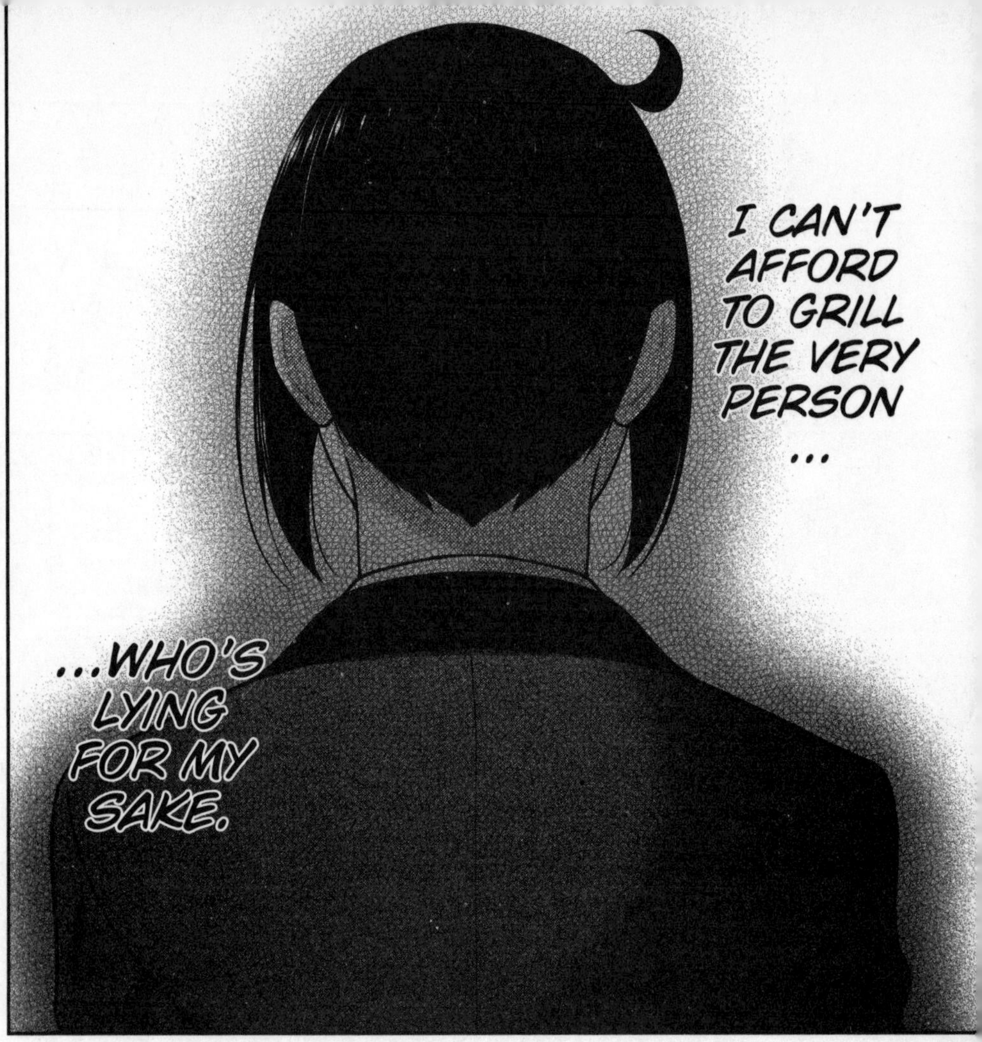
I CAN'T AFFORD TO GRILL THE VERY PERSON ...
...WHO'S LYING FOR MY SAKE.

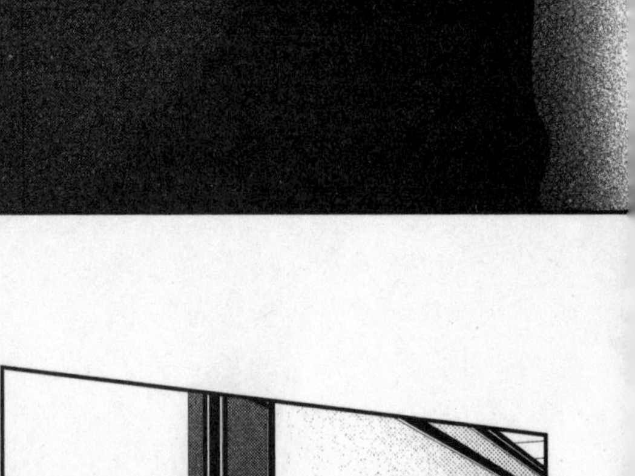
D.C. SISTERS
NNN

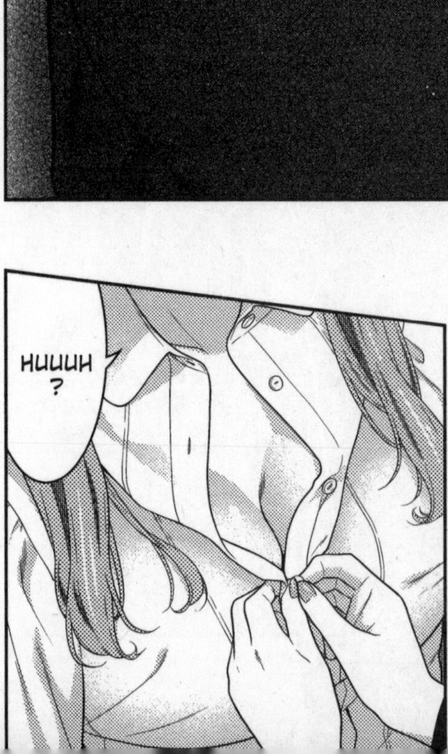
HUUUH ?

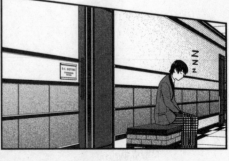

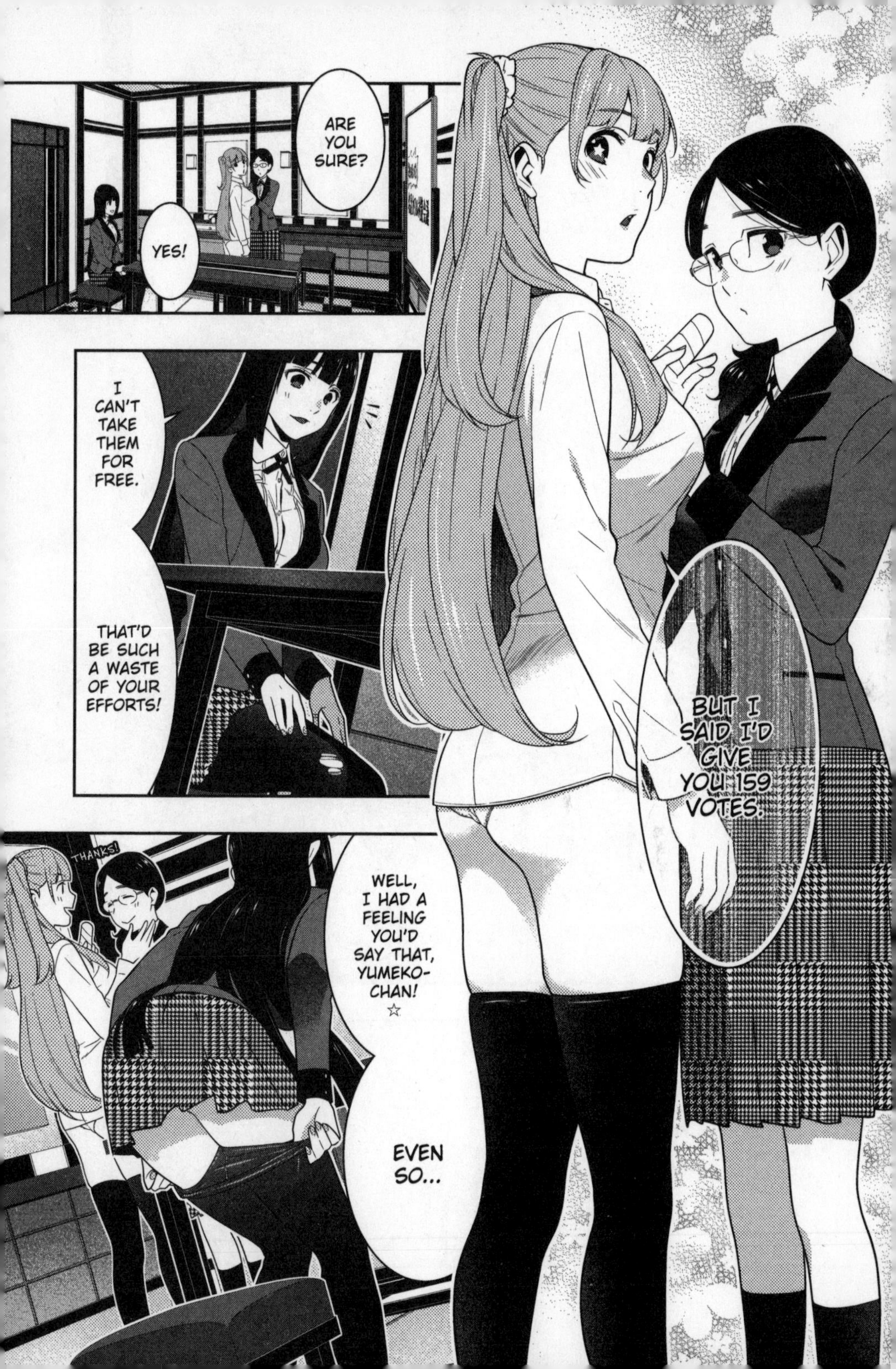
BUT I SAID I'D GIVE YOU 159 VOTES.
ARE YOU SURE?
YES!
I CAN'T TAKE THEM FOR FREE.
THAT'D BE SUCH A WASTE OF YOUR EFFORTS!
WELL, I HAD A FEELING YOU'D SAY THAT, YUMEKO-CHAN! ☆
THANKS!
EVEN SO...

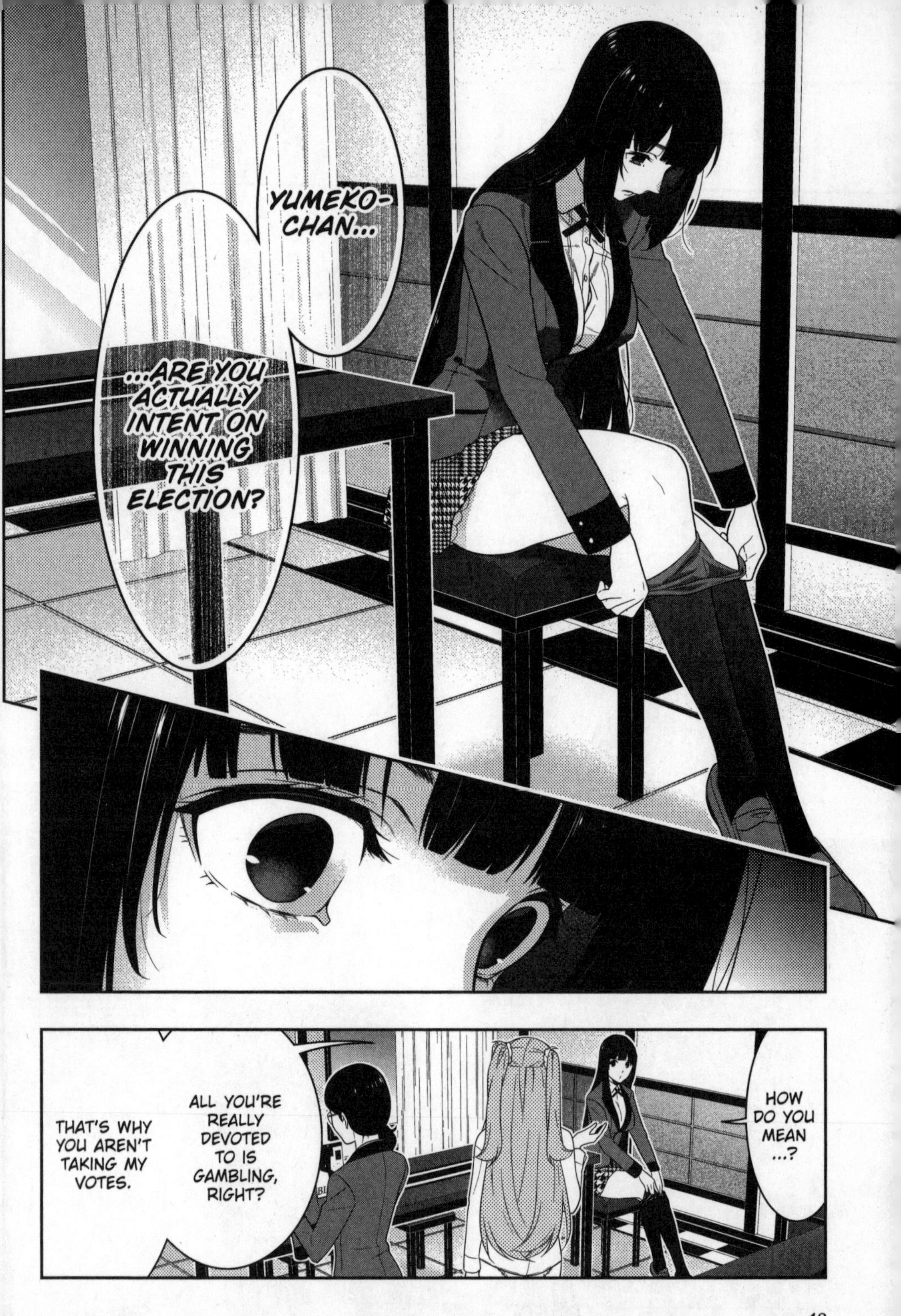
YUMEKO-CHAN...
...ARE YOU ACTUALLY INTENT ON WINNING THIS ELECTION?
HOW DO YOU MEAN ...?
ALL YOU'RE REALLY DEVOTED TO IS GAMBLING, RIGHT?
THAT'S WHY YOU AREN'T TAKING MY VOTES.

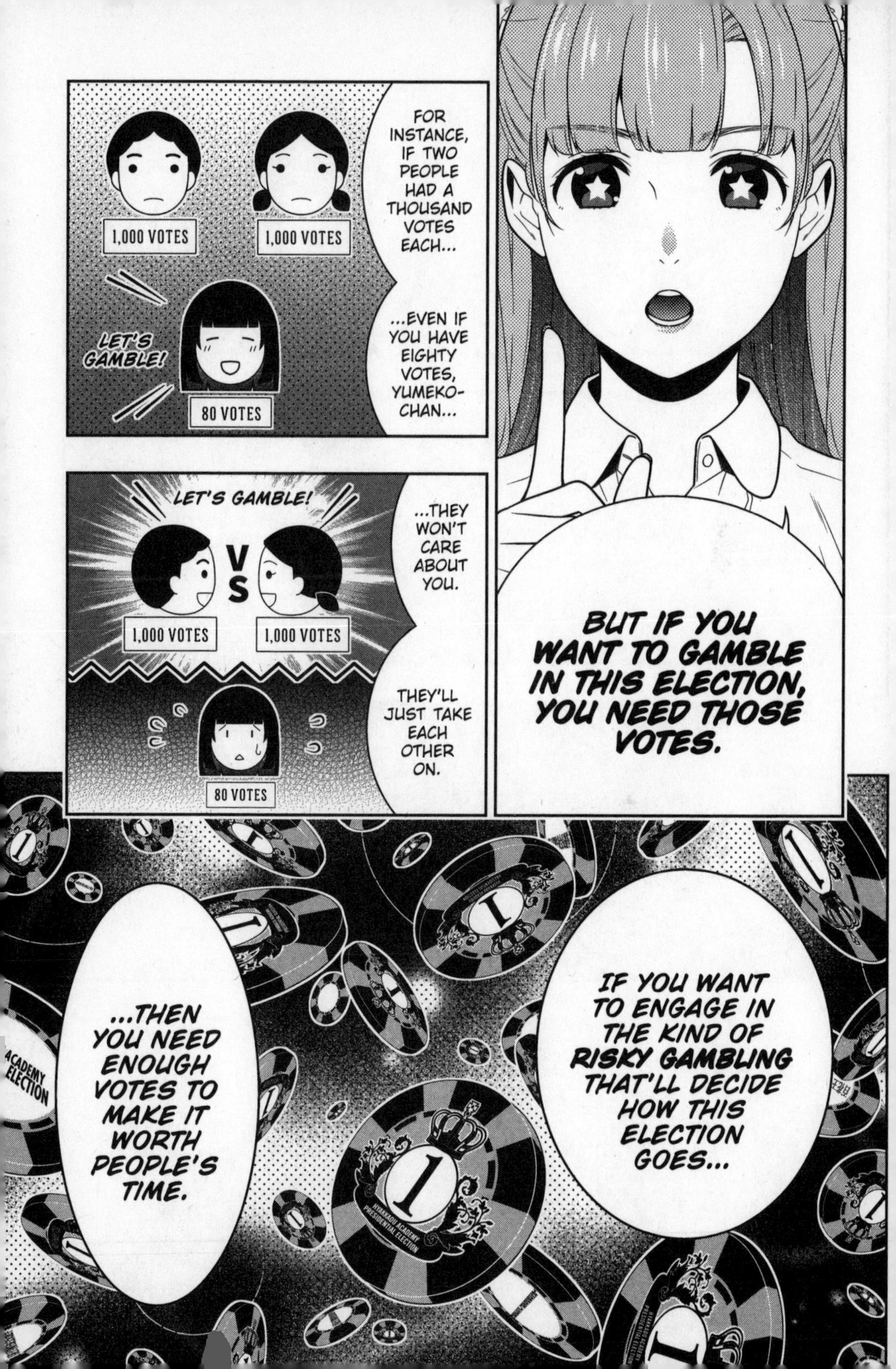
BUT IF YOU WANT TO GAMBLE IN THIS ELECTION, YOU NEED THOSE VOTES.
FOR INSTANCE, IF TWO PEOPLE HAD A THOUSAND VOTES EACH...
1,000 VOTES
1,000 VOTES
...EVEN IF YOU HAVE EIGHTY VOTES, YUMEKO-CHAN...
LET'S GAMBLE!
80 VOTES
...THEY WON'T CARE ABOUT YOU.
LET'S GAMBLE!
VS
1,000 VOTES
1,000 VOTES
THEY'LL JUST TAKE EACH OTHER ON.
80 VOTES
IF YOU WANT TO ENGAGE IN THE KIND OF RISKY GAMBLING THAT'LL DECIDE HOW THIS ELECTION GOES...
...THEN YOU NEED ENOUGH VOTES TO MAKE IT WORTH PEOPLE'S TIME.
ACADEMY ELECTION
HYAKKAOU ACADEMY PRESIDENTIAL ELECTION

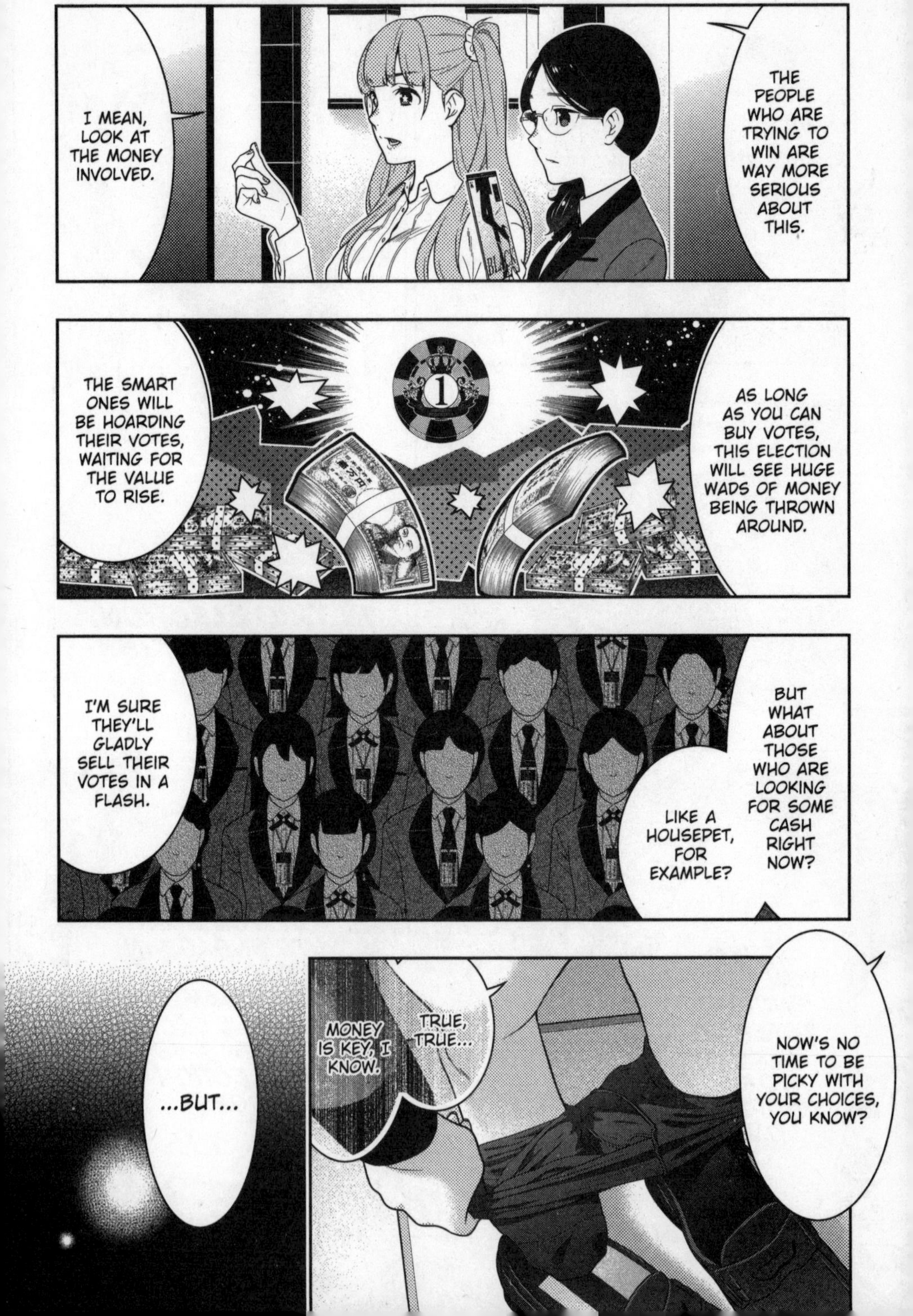
THE PEOPLE WHO ARE TRYING TO WIN ARE WAY MORE SERIOUS ABOUT THIS.
I MEAN, LOOK AT THE MONEY INVOLVED.
AS LONG AS YOU CAN BUY VOTES, THIS ELECTION WILL SEE HUGE WADS OF MONEY BEING THROWN AROUND.
THE SMART ONES WILL BE HOARDING THEIR VOTES, WAITING FOR THE VALUE TO RISE.
BUT WHAT ABOUT THOSE WHO ARE LOOKING FOR SOME CASH RIGHT NOW?
LIKE A HOUSEPET, FOR EXAMPLE?
I'M SURE THEY'LL GLADLY SELL THEIR VOTES IN A FLASH.
NOW'S NO TIME TO BE PICKY WITH YOUR CHOICES, YOU KNOW?
TRUE, TRUE...
MONEY IS KEY, I KNOW.
...BUT...

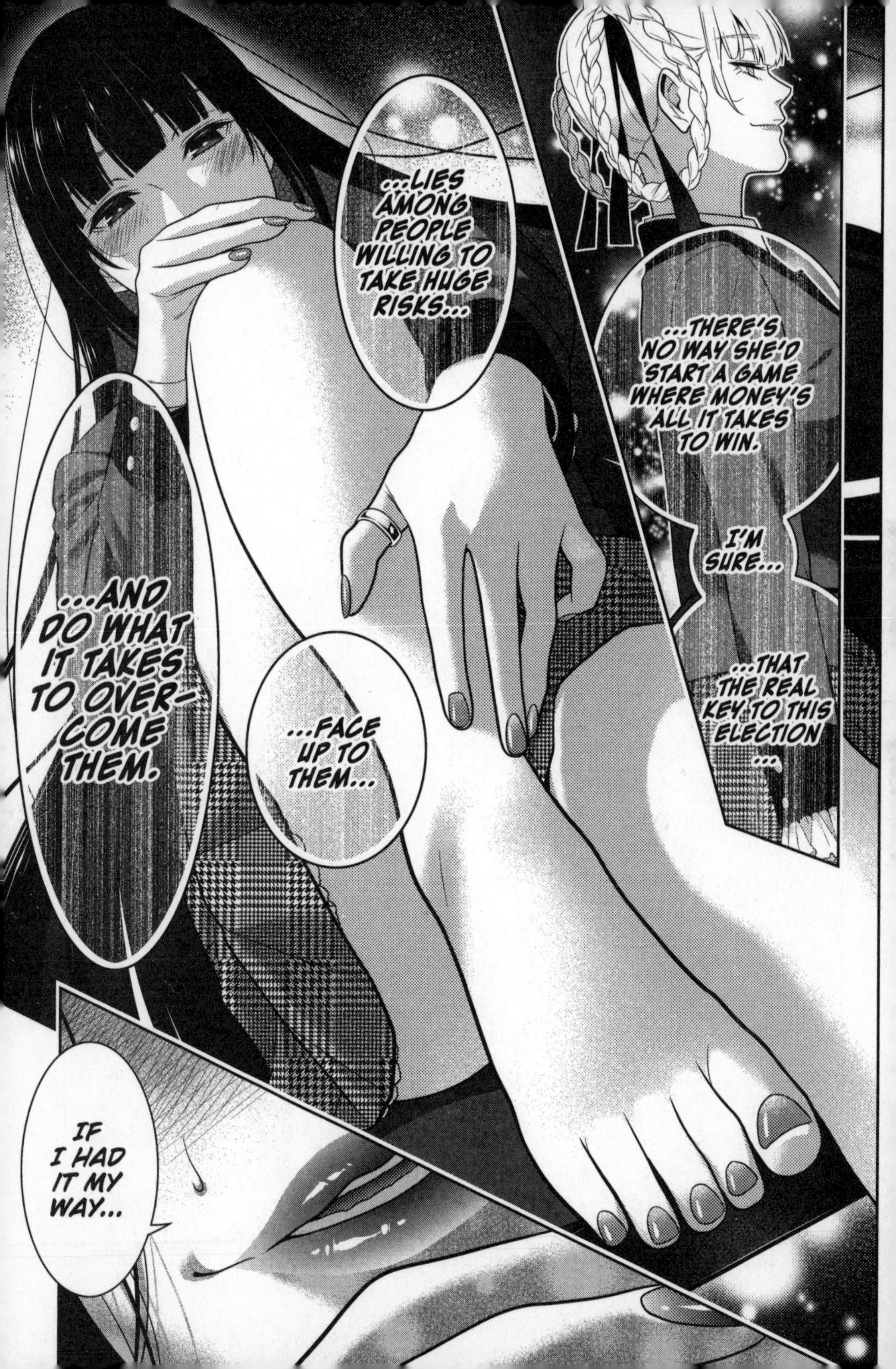
...THERE'S NO WAY SHE'D START A GAME WHERE MONEY'S ALL IT TAKES TO WIN.
I'M SURE...
...THAT THE REAL KEY TO THIS ELECTION...
...LIES AMONG PEOPLE WILLING TO TAKE HUGE RISKS...
...FACE UP TO THEM...
...AND DO WHAT IT TAKES TO OVER-COME THEM.
IF I HAD IT MY WAY...

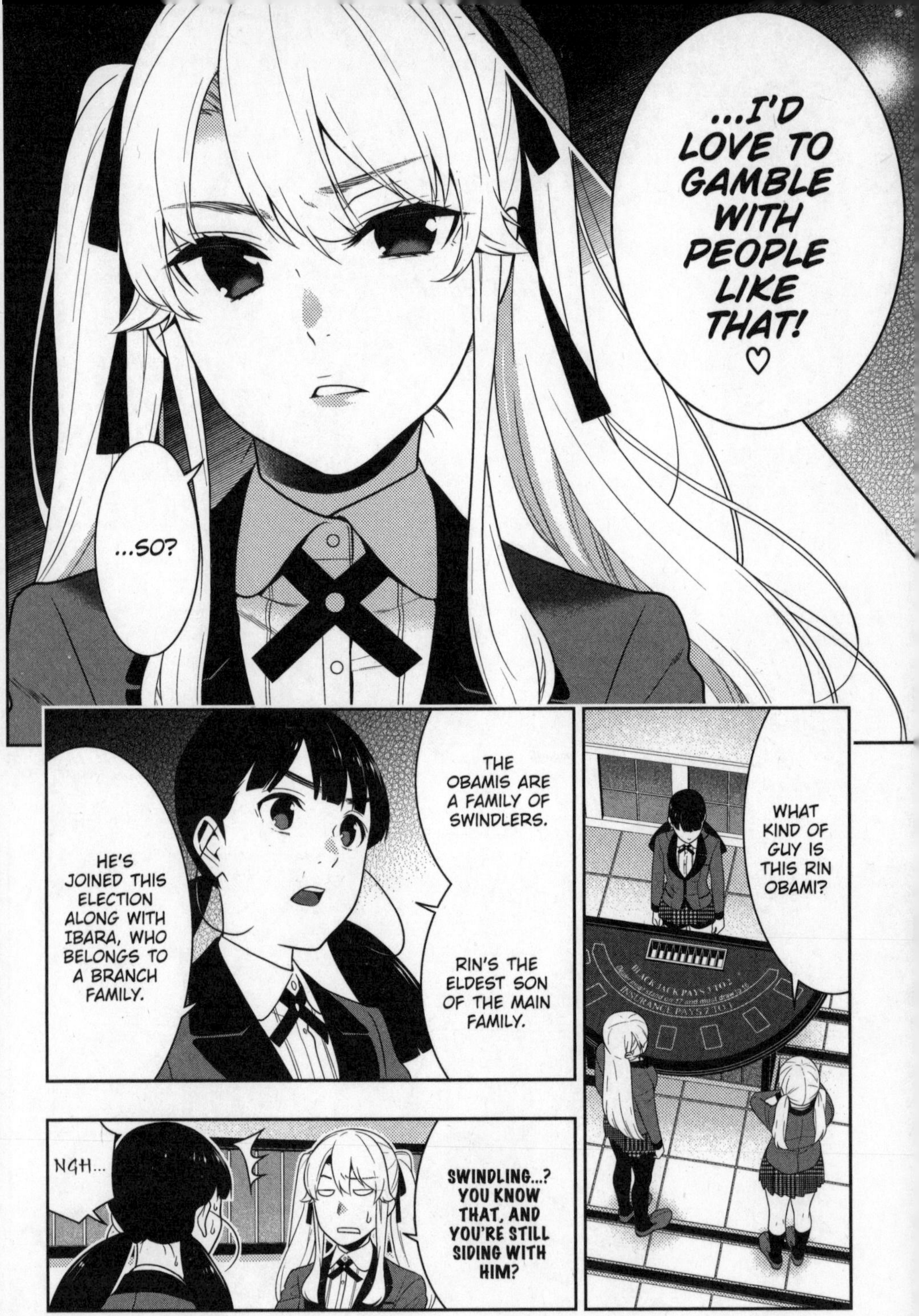
...I'D LOVE TO GAMBLE WITH PEOPLE LIKE THAT! ♡
...SO?
WHAT KIND OF GUY IS THIS RIN OBAMI?
THE OBAMIS ARE A FAMILY OF SWINDLERS.
RIN'S THE ELDEST SON OF THE MAIN FAMILY.
HE'S JOINED THIS ELECTION ALONG WITH IBARA, WHO BELONGS TO A BRANCH FAMILY.
SWINDLING...? YOU KNOW THAT, AND YOU'RE STILL SIDING WITH HIM?
NGH...

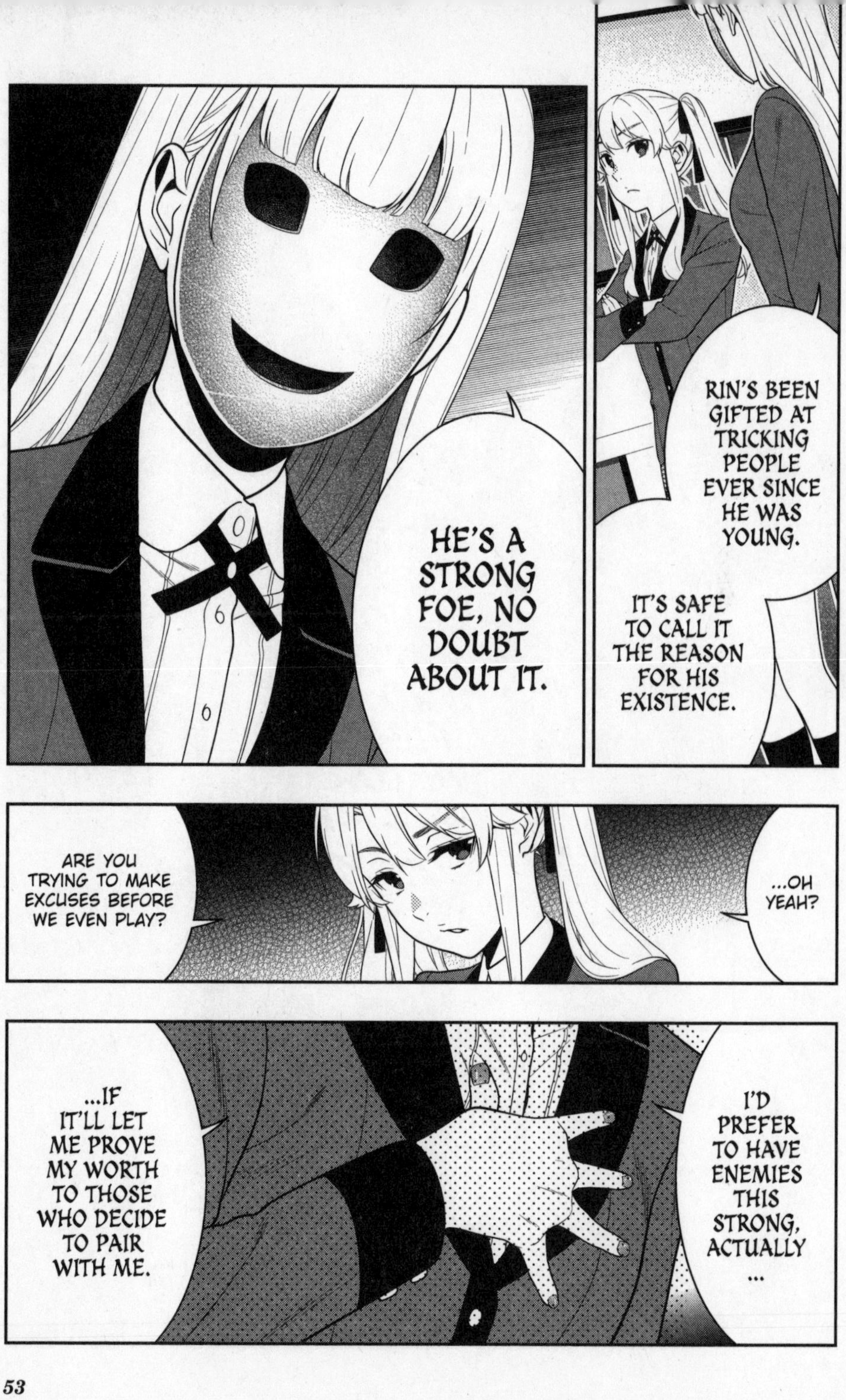
RIN'S BEEN GIFTED AT TRICKING PEOPLE EVER SINCE HE WAS YOUNG.
IT'S SAFE TO CALL IT THE REASON FOR HIS EXISTENCE.
HE'S A STRONG FOE, NO DOUBT ABOUT IT.
...OH YEAH?
ARE YOU TRYING TO MAKE EXCUSES BEFORE WE EVEN PLAY?
I'D PREFER TO HAVE ENEMIES THIS STRONG, ACTUALLY ...
...IF IT'LL LET ME PROVE MY WORTH TO THOSE WHO DECIDE TO PAIR WITH ME.

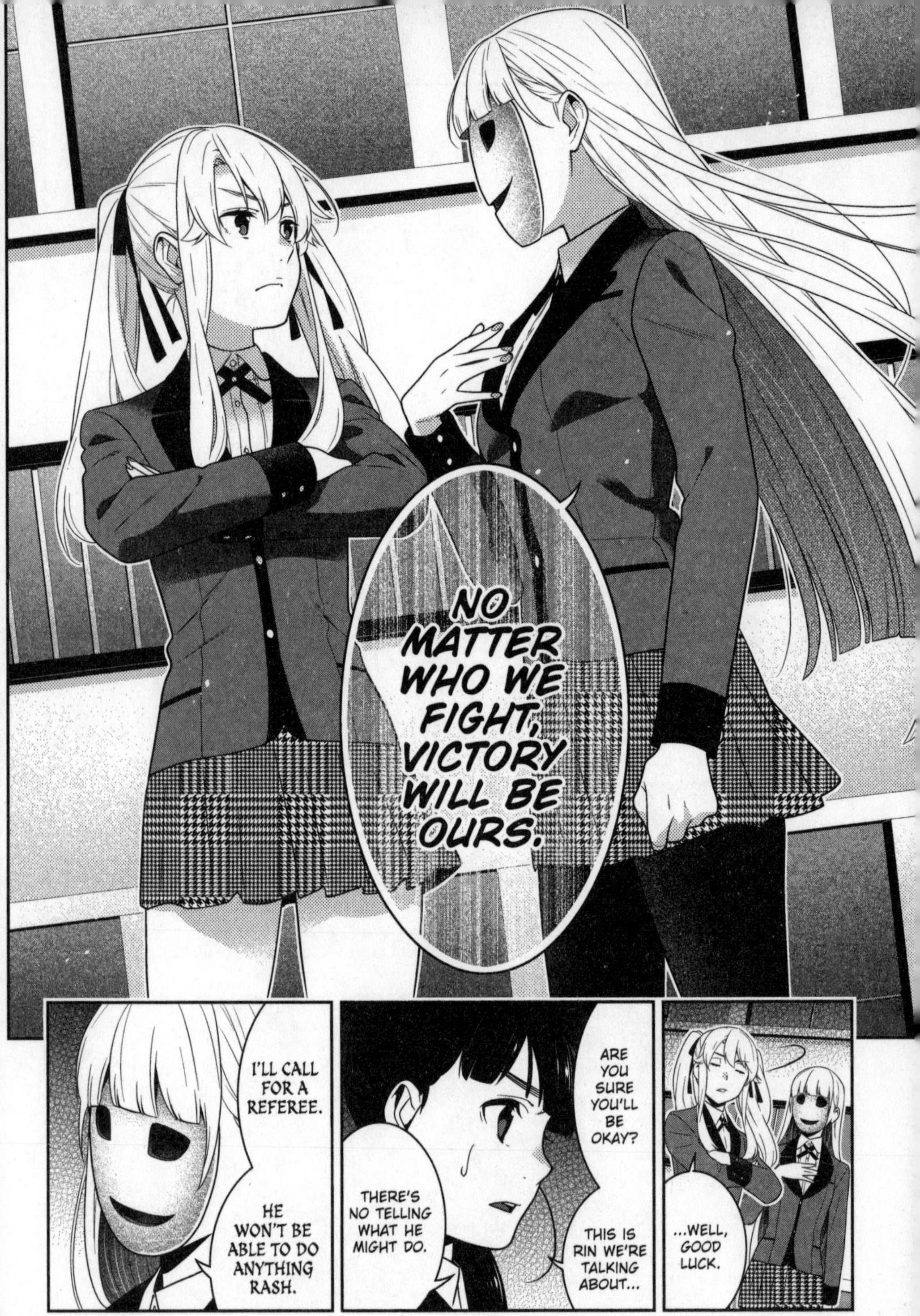
NO MATTER WHO WE FIGHT, VICTORY WILL BE OURS.
ARE YOU SURE YOU'LL BE OKAY?
THIS IS RIN WE'RE TALKING ABOUT...
THERE'S NO TELLING WHAT HE MIGHT DO.
I'LL CALL FOR A REFEREE.
HE WON'T BE ABLE TO DO ANYTHING RASH.
...WELL, GOOD LUCK.

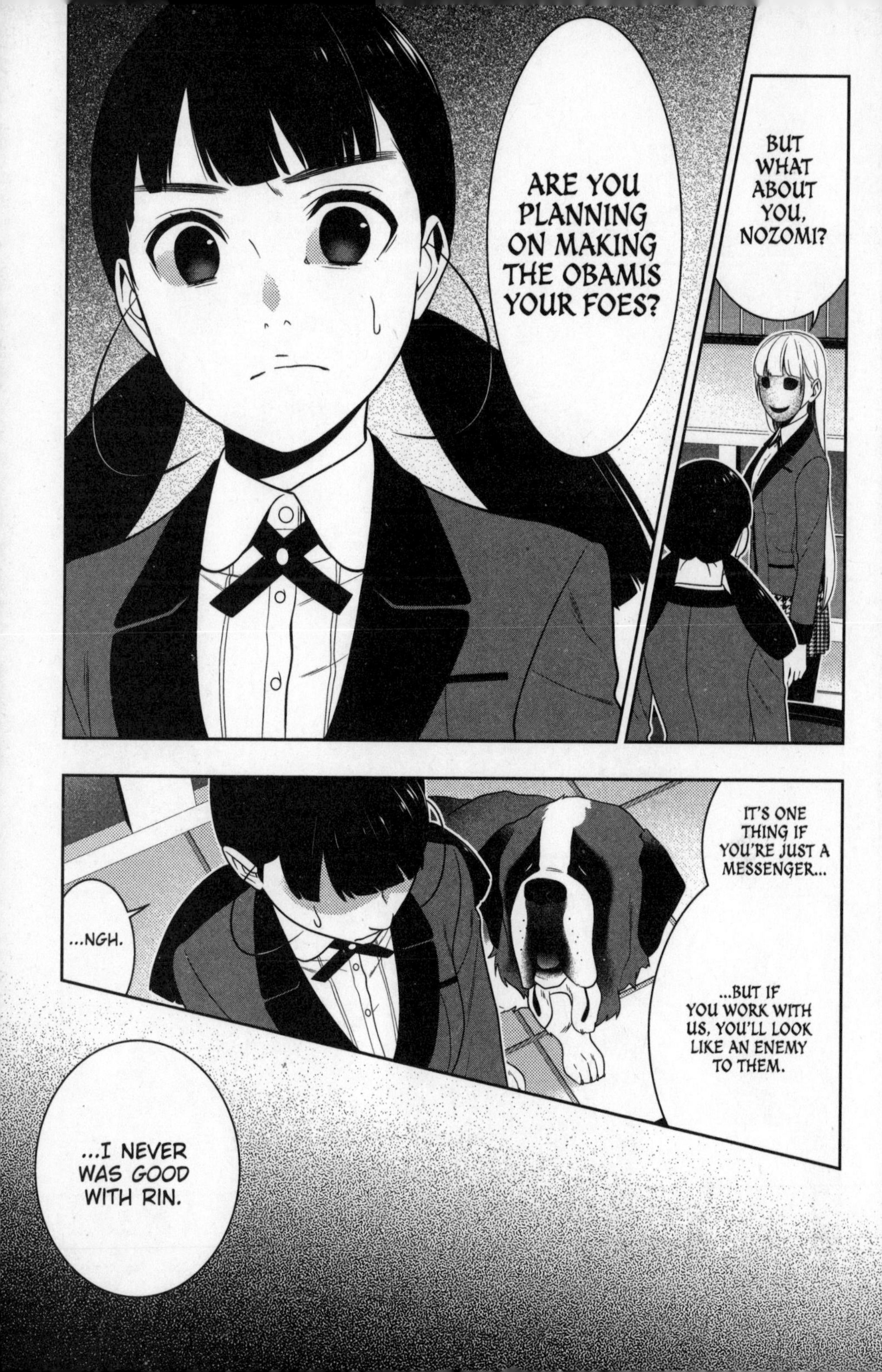
BUT WHAT ABOUT YOU, NOZOMI?
ARE YOU PLANNING ON MAKING THE OBAMIS YOUR FOES?
IT'S ONE THING IF YOU'RE JUST A MESSENGER...
...BUT IF YOU WORK WITH US, YOU'LL LOOK LIKE AN ENEMY TO THEM.
...NGH.
...I NEVER WAS GOOD WITH RIN.

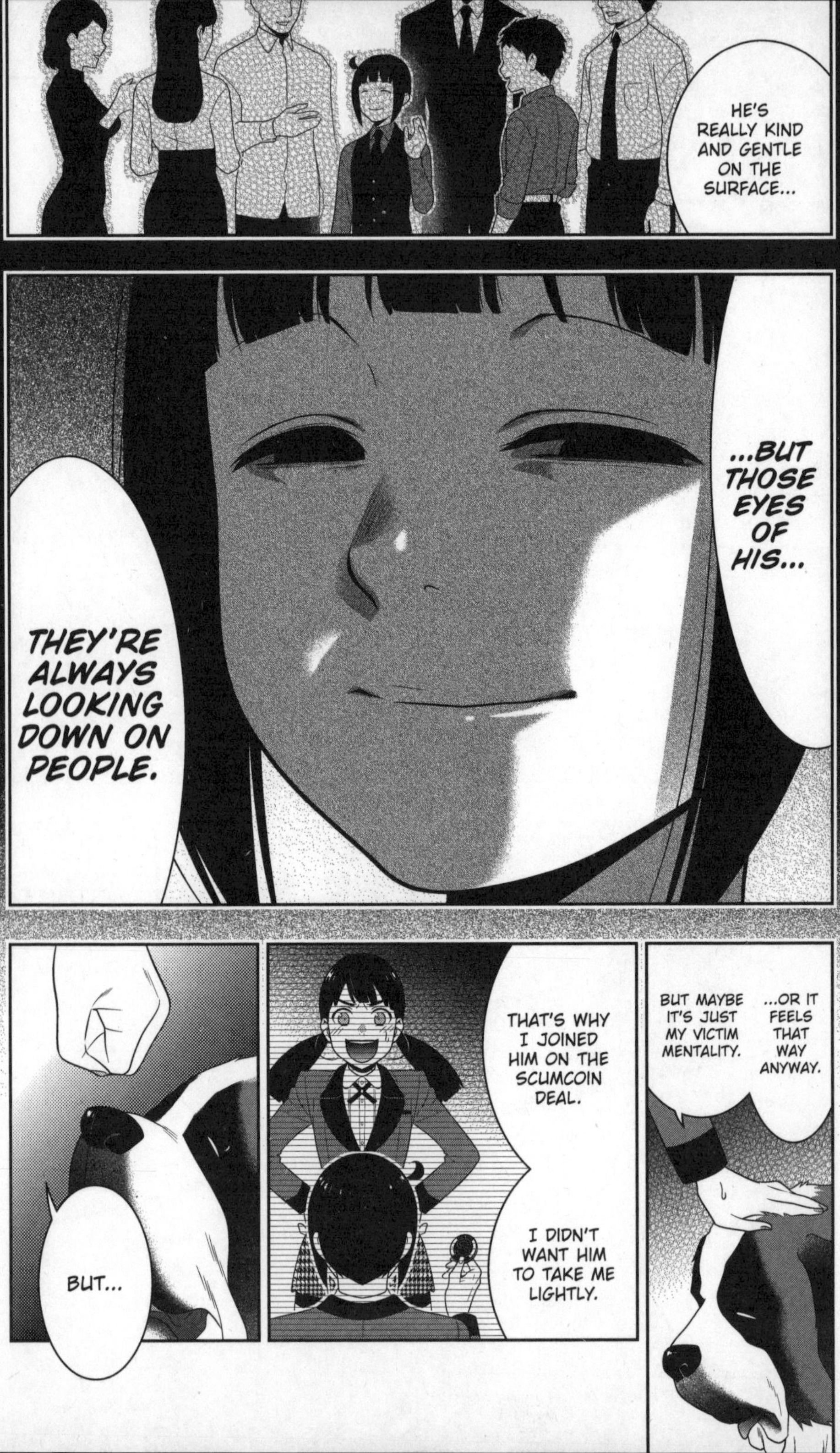
HE'S REALLY KIND AND GENTLE ON THE SURFACE...
...BUT THOSE EYES OF HIS...
THEY'RE ALWAYS LOOKING DOWN ON PEOPLE.
...OR IT FEELS THAT WAY ANYWAY.
BUT MAYBE IT'S JUST MY VICTIM MENTALITY.
THAT'S WHY I JOINED HIM ON THE SCUMCOIN DEAL.
I DIDN'T WANT HIM TO TAKE ME LIGHTLY.
BUT...

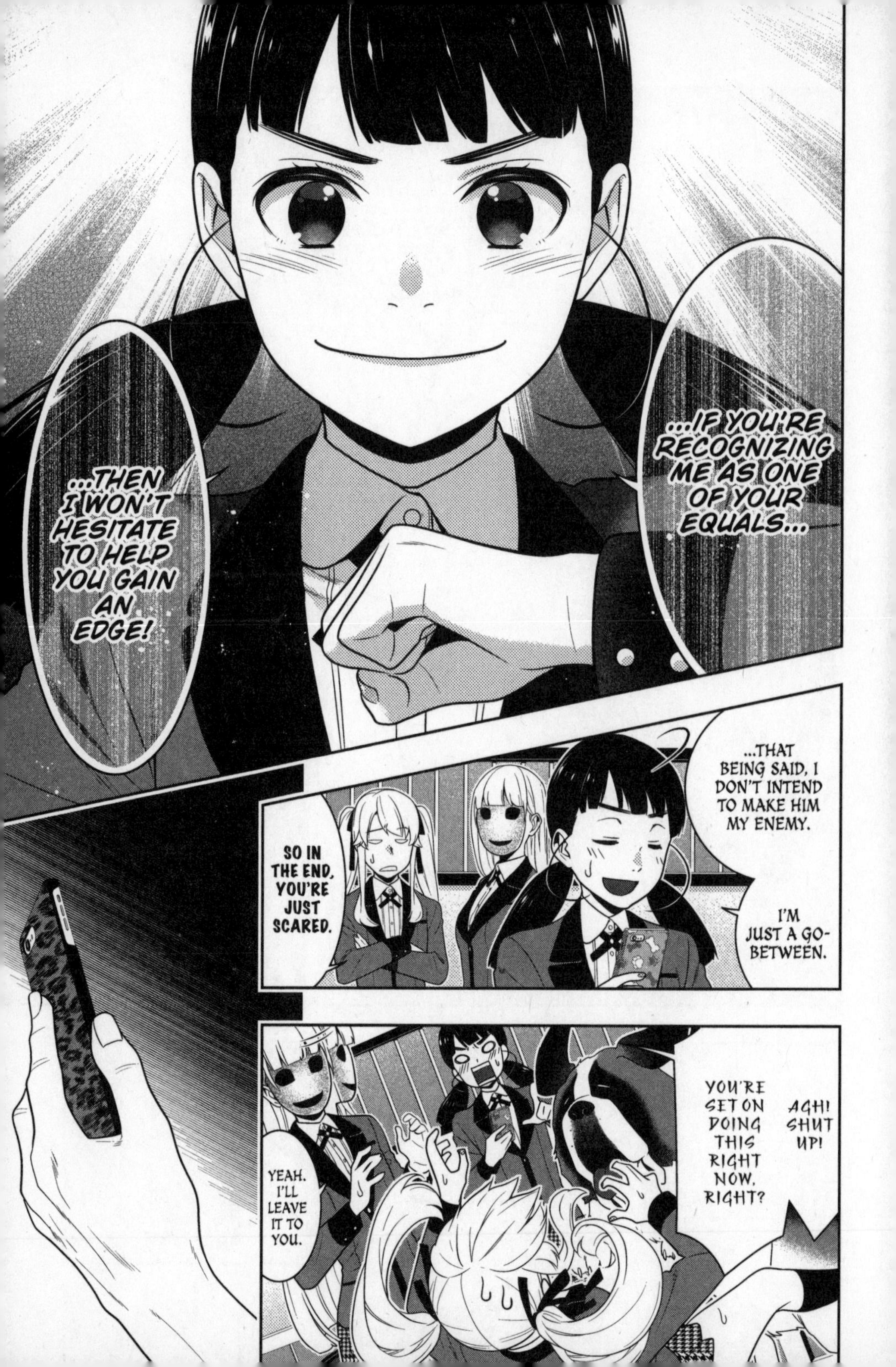
...IF YOU'RE RECOGNIZING ME AS ONE OF YOUR EQUALS...
...THEN I WON'T HESITATE TO HELP YOU GAIN AN EDGE!
...THAT BEING SAID, I DON'T INTEND TO MAKE HIM MY ENEMY.
I'M JUST A GO-BETWEEN.
SO IN THE END, YOU'RE JUST SCARED.
AGH! SHUT UP!
YOU'RE SET ON DOING THIS RIGHT NOW, RIGHT?
YEAH. I'LL LEAVE IT TO YOU.

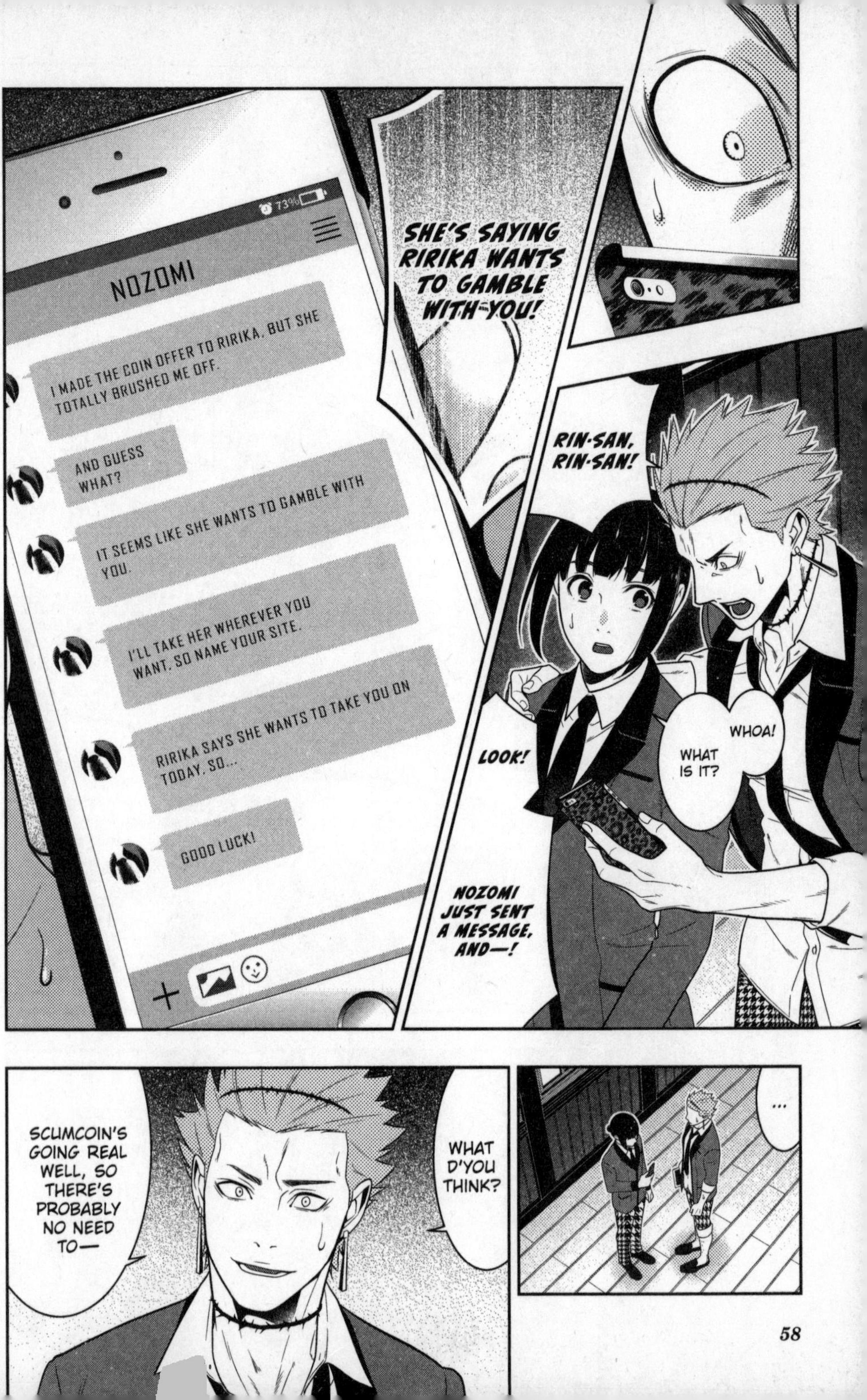
RIN-SAN, RIN-SAN!
NOZOMI JUST SENT A MESSAGE, AND—!
LOOK!
WHOA!
WHAT IS IT?
SHE'S SAYING RIRIKA WANTS TO GAMBLE WITH YOU!
73%
NOZOMI
I MADE THE COIN OFFER TO RIRIKA, BUT SHE TOTALLY BRUSHED ME OFF.
AND GUESS WHAT?
IT SEEMS LIKE SHE WANTS TO GAMBLE WITH YOU.
I'LL TAKE HER WHEREVER YOU WANT, SO NAME YOUR SITE.
RIRIKA SAYS SHE WANTS TO TAKE YOU ON TODAY, SO...
GOOD LUCK!
...
WHAT D'YOU THINK?
SCUMCOIN'S GOING REAL WELL, SO THERE'S PROBABLY NO NEED TO—

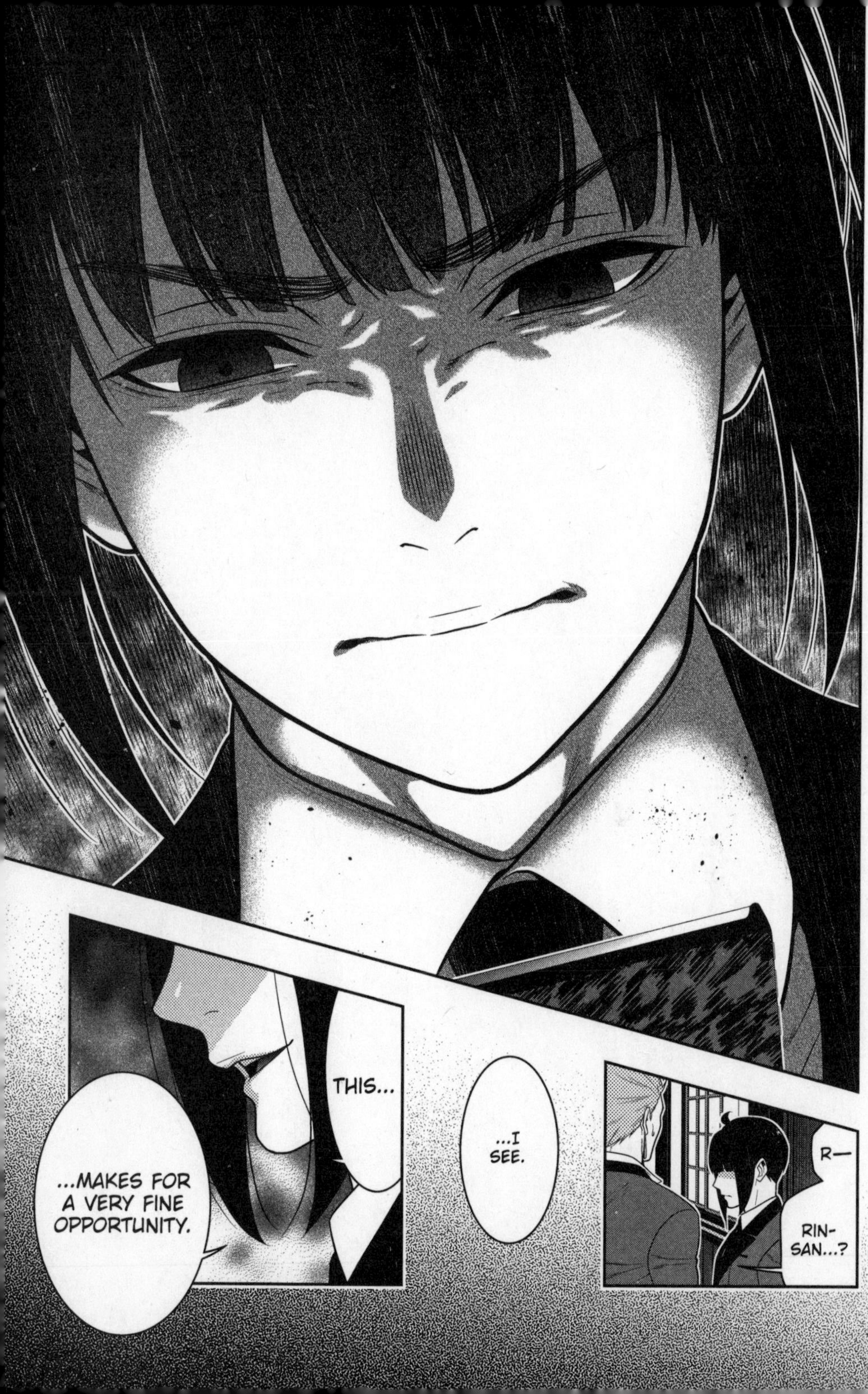
R—
RIN-SAN...?
...I SEE.
THIS...
...MAKES FOR A VERY FINE OPPORTUNITY.

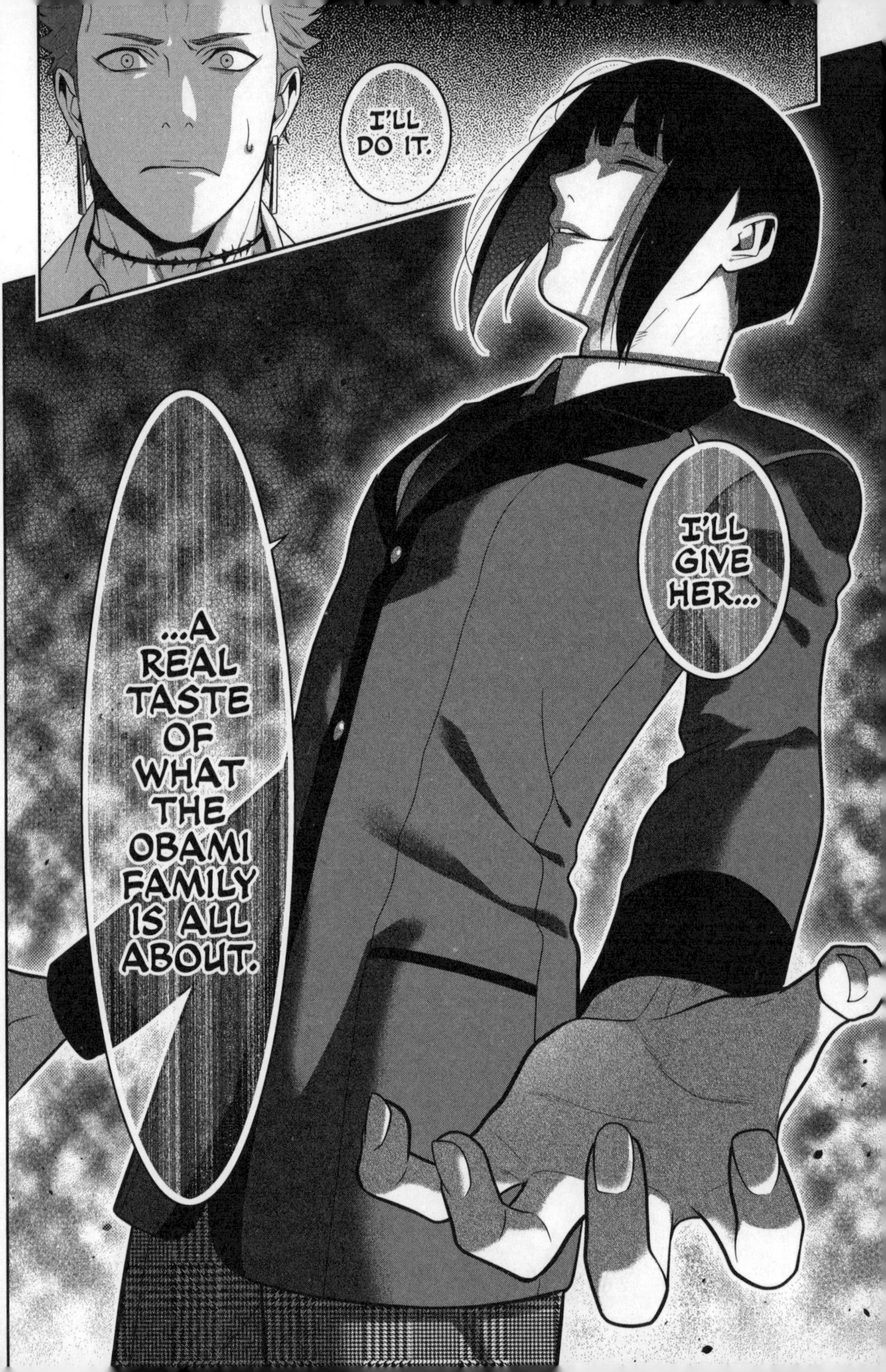
I'LL DO IT.
I'LL GIVE HER...
...A REAL TASTE OF WHAT THE OBAMI FAMILY IS ALL ABOUT.

CHAPTER FIFTY-EIGHT
THE IMMORAL GIRL

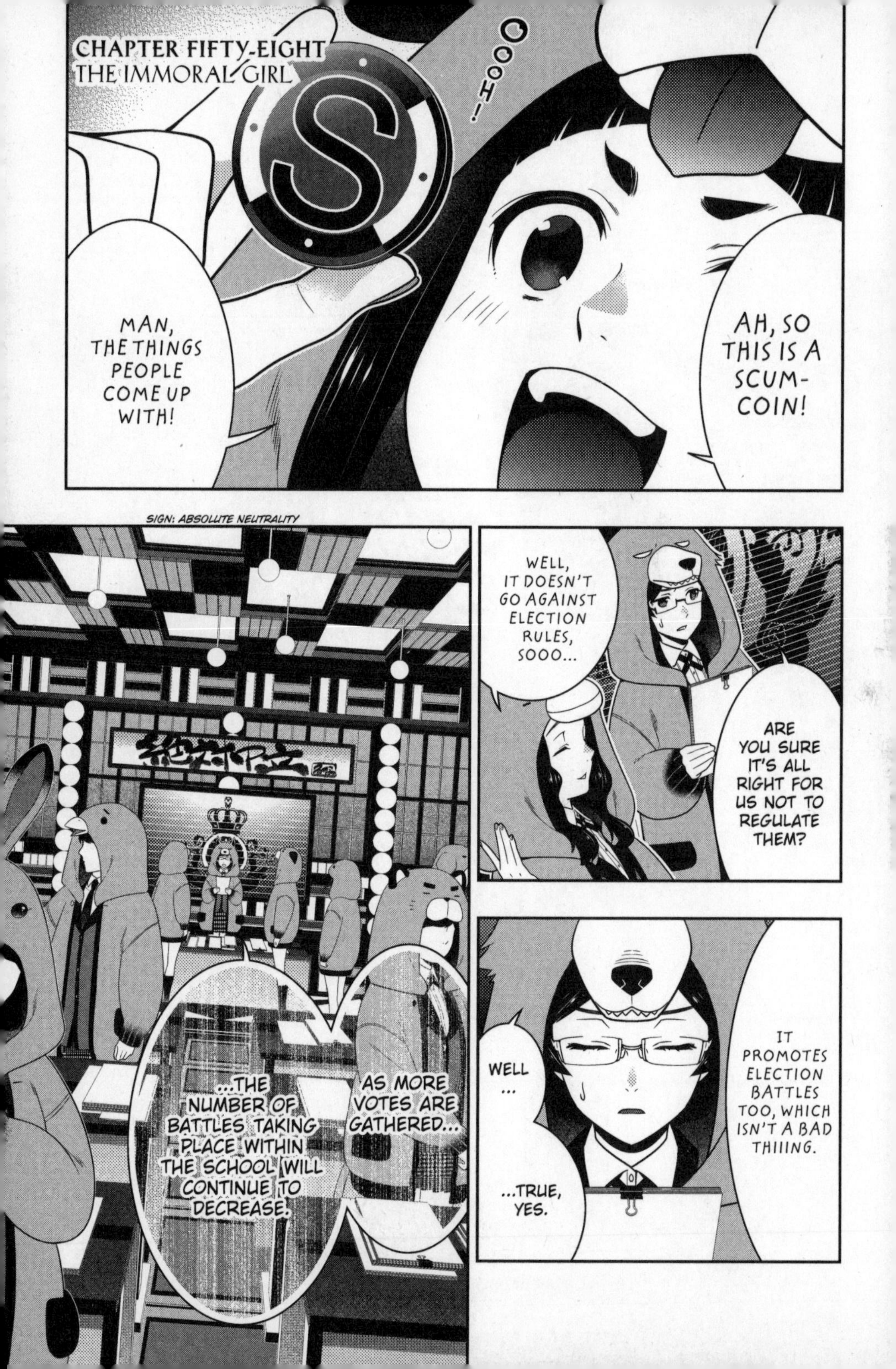
OOOH...!
AH, SO THIS IS A SCUM-COIN!
MAN, THE THINGS PEOPLE COME UP WITH!
SIGN: ABSOLUTE NEUTRALITY
ARE YOU SURE IT'S ALL RIGHT FOR US NOT TO REGULATE THEM?
WELL, IT DOESN'T GO AGAINST ELECTION RULES, SOOO...
IT PROMOTES ELECTION BATTLES TOO, WHICH ISN'T A BAD THIIING.
WELL...
...TRUE, YES.
AS MORE VOTES ARE GATHERED...
...THE NUMBER OF BATTLES TAKING PLACE WITHIN THE SCHOOL WILL CONTINUE TO DECREASE.

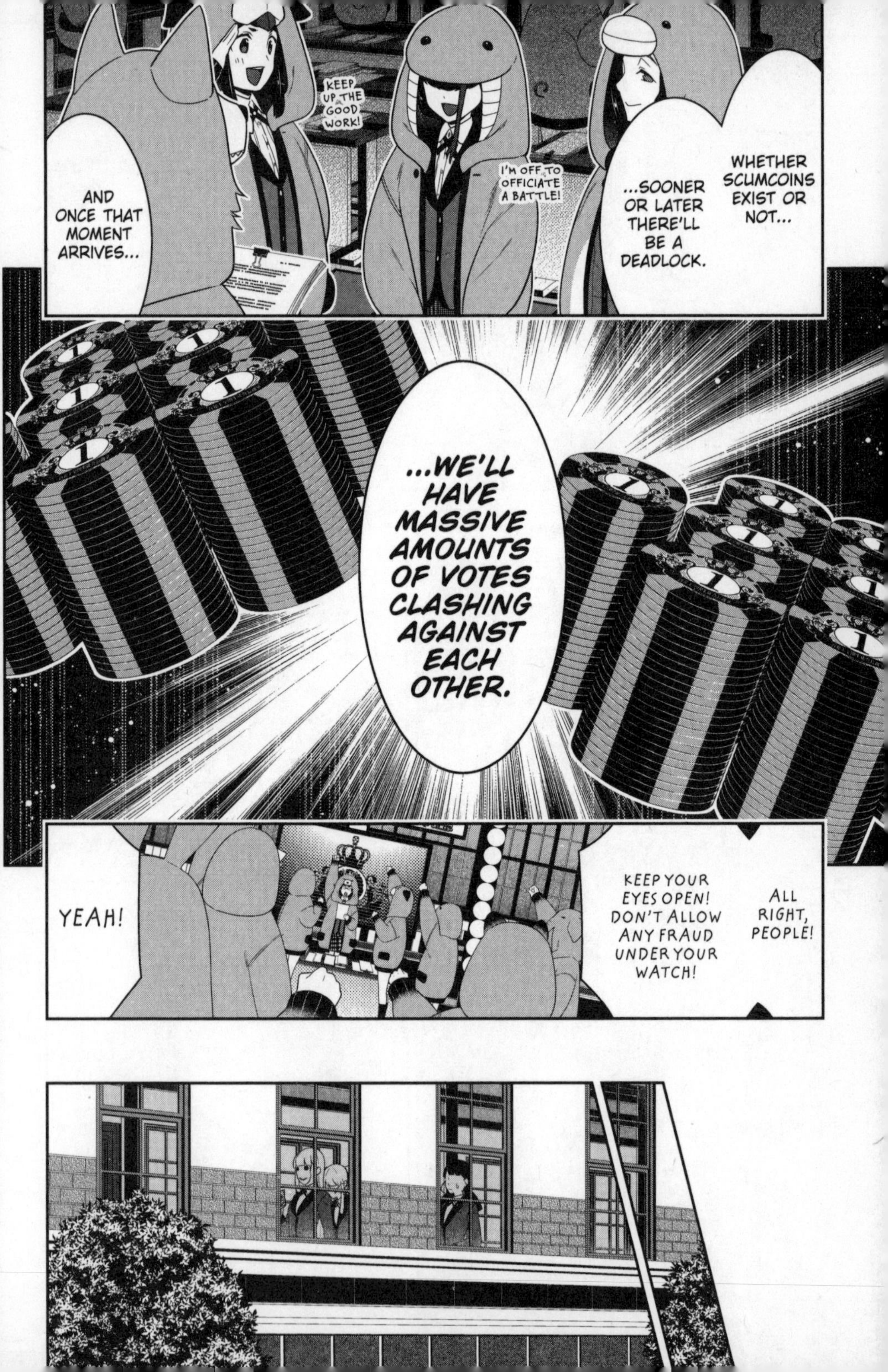
WHETHER SCUMCOINS EXIST OR NOT...
...SOONER OR LATER THERE'LL BE A DEADLOCK.
I'M OFF TO OFFICIATE A BATTLE!
KEEP UP THE GOOD WORK!
AND ONCE THAT MOMENT ARRIVES...
...WE'LL HAVE MASSIVE AMOUNTS OF VOTES CLASHING AGAINST EACH OTHER.
ALL RIGHT, PEOPLE!
KEEP YOUR EYES OPEN! DON'T ALLOW ANY FRAUD UNDER YOUR WATCH!
YEAH!

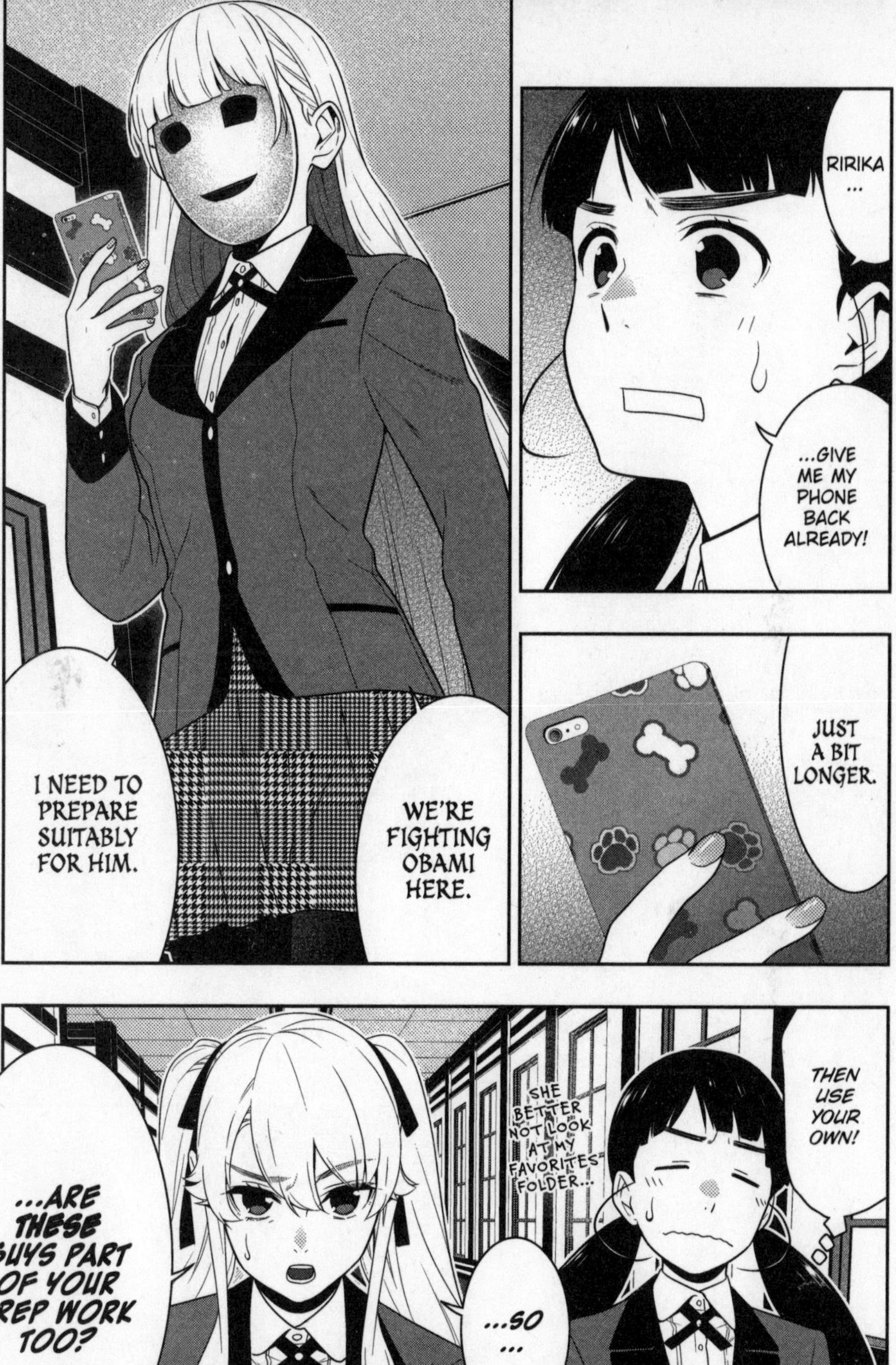
RIRIKA ...
...GIVE ME MY PHONE BACK ALREADY!
JUST A BIT LONGER.
WE'RE FIGHTING OBAMI HERE.
I NEED TO PREPARE SUITABLY FOR HIM.
THEN USE YOUR OWN!
SHE BETTER NOT LOOK AT MY FAVORITES FOLDER...
...SO ...
...ARE THESE GUYS PART OF YOUR PREP WORK TOO?

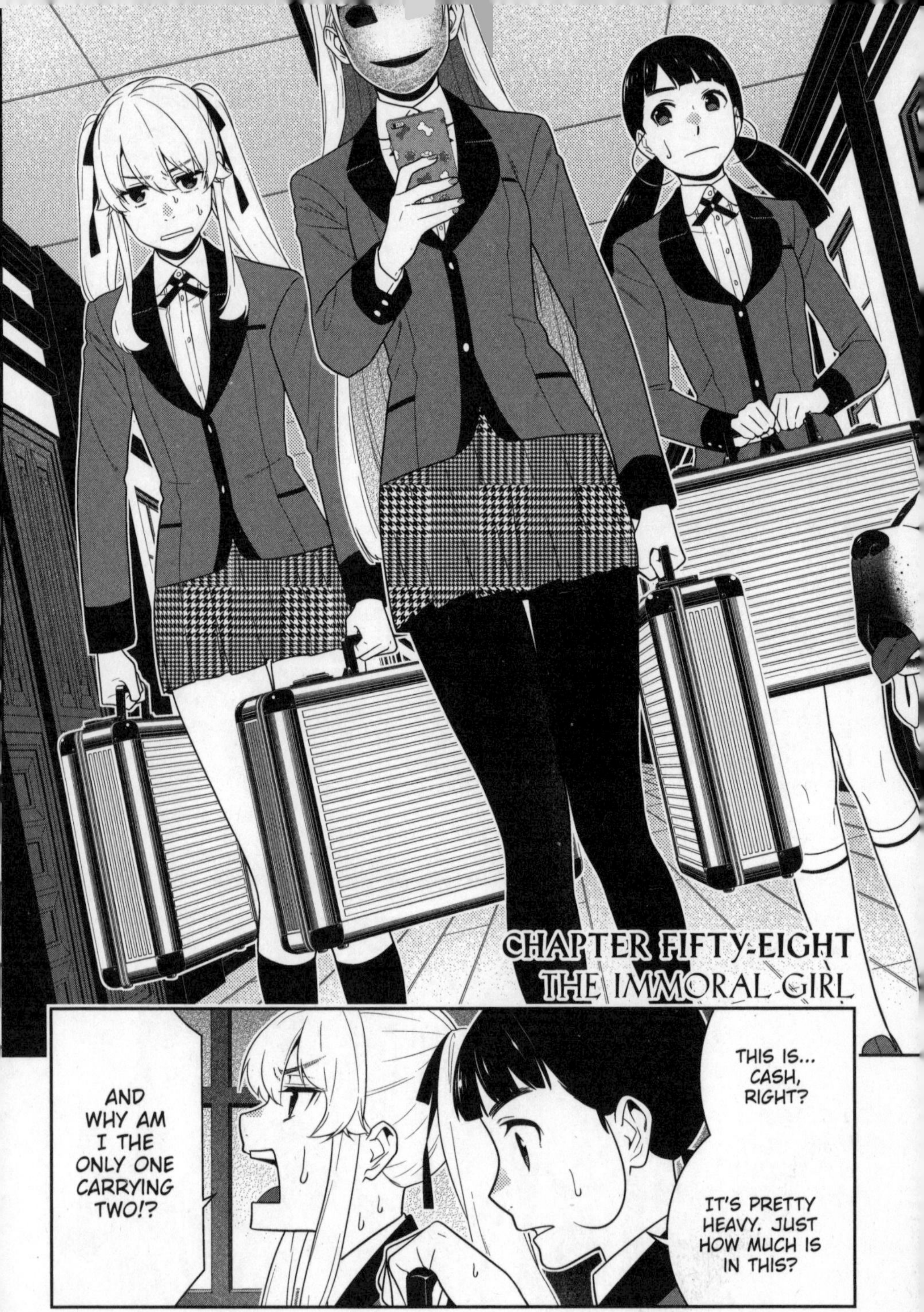
CHAPTER FIFTY-EIGHT
THE IMMORAL GIRL
THIS IS... CASH, RIGHT?
IT'S PRETTY HEAVY. JUST HOW MUCH IS IN THIS?
AND WHY AM I THE ONLY ONE CARRYING TWO!?

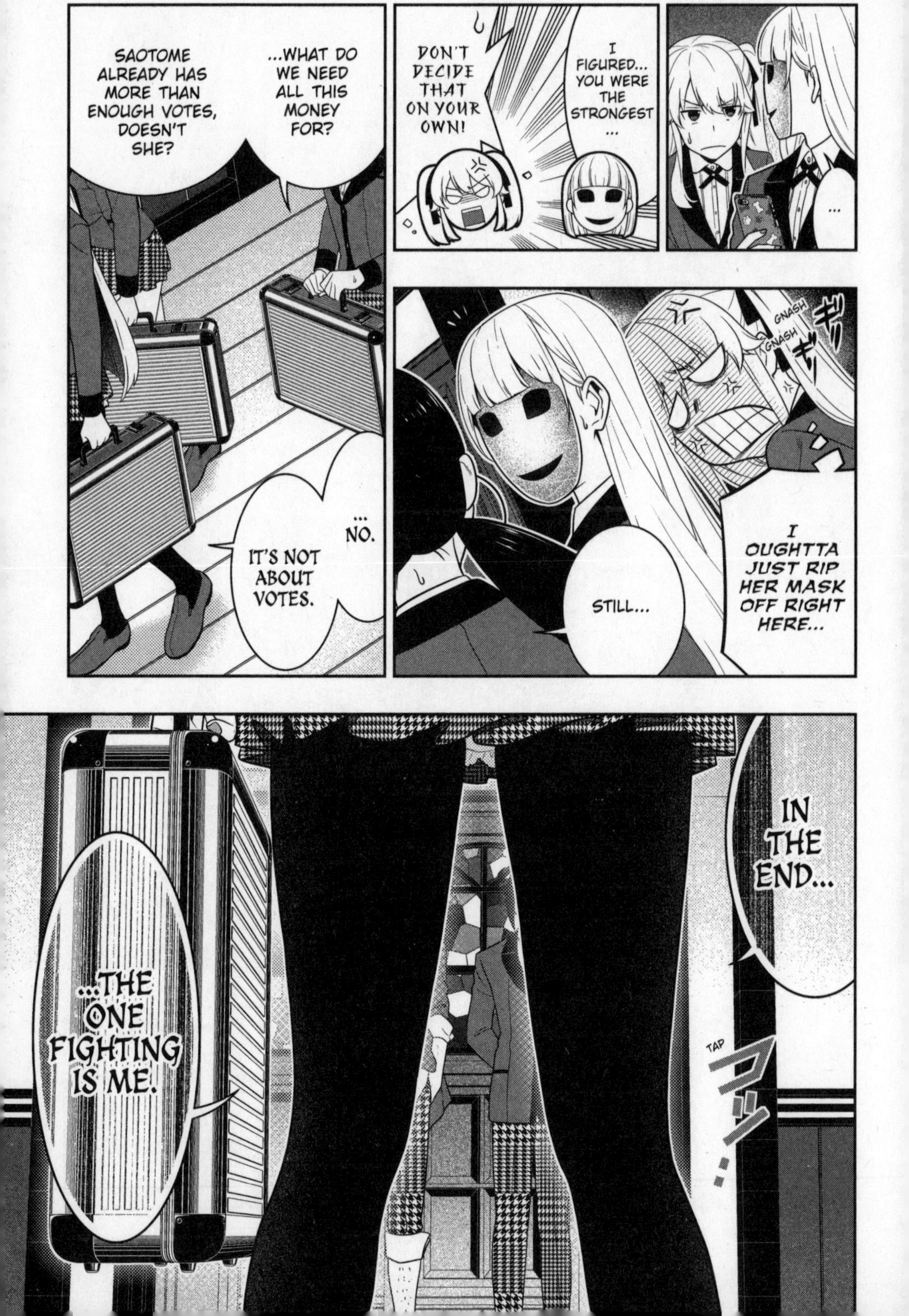
...
I FIGURED... YOU WERE THE STRONGEST ...
DON'T DECIDE THAT ON YOUR OWN!
GNASH GNASH
I OUGHTTA JUST RIP HER MASK OFF RIGHT HERE...
STILL...
...WHAT DO WE NEED ALL THIS MONEY FOR?
SAOTOME ALREADY HAS MORE THAN ENOUGH VOTES, DOESN'T SHE?
... NO.
IT'S NOT ABOUT VOTES.
IN THE END...
TAP
...THE ONE FIGHTING IS ME.

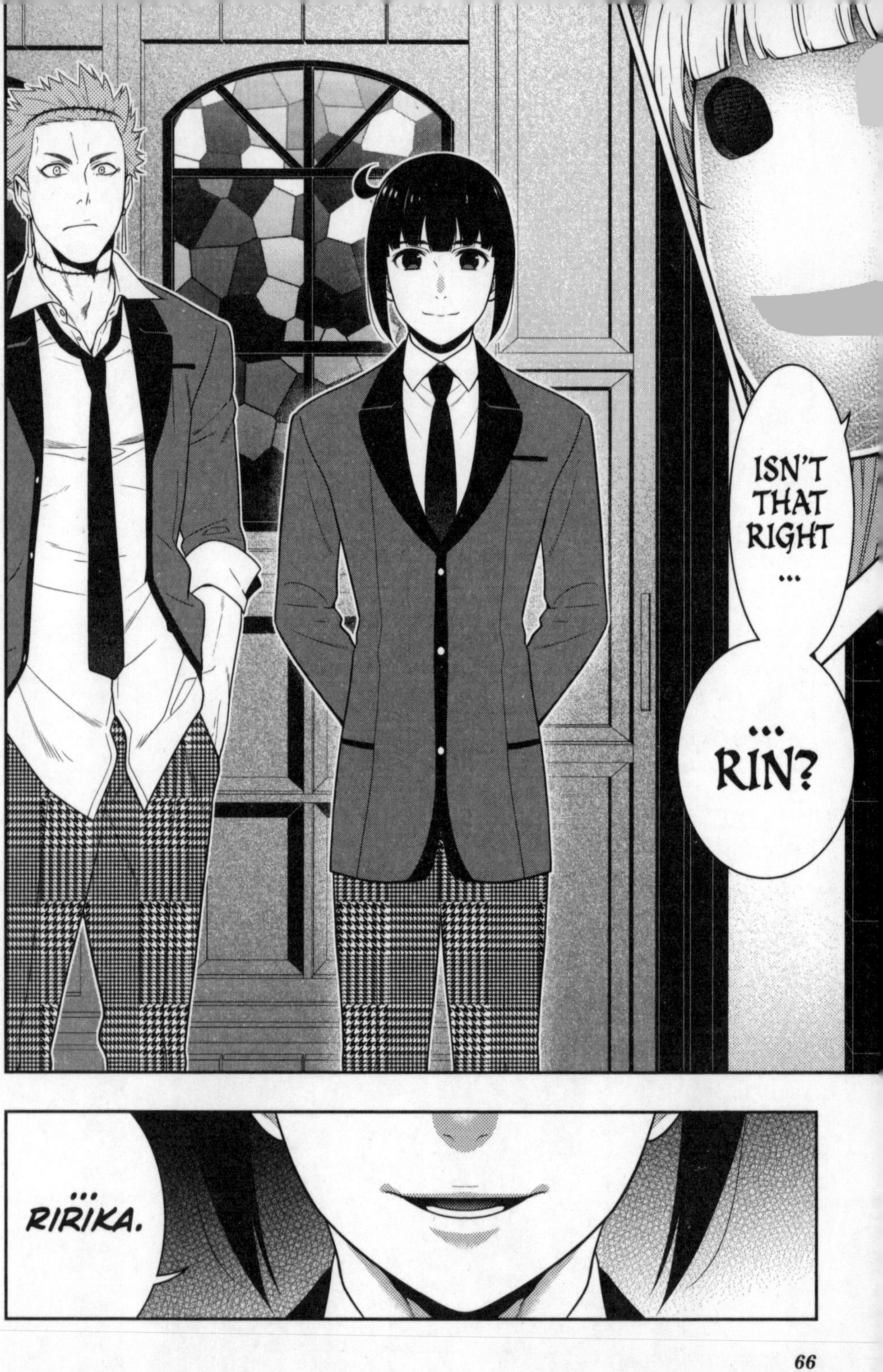
ISN'T THAT RIGHT ...
... RIN?
... RIRIKA.

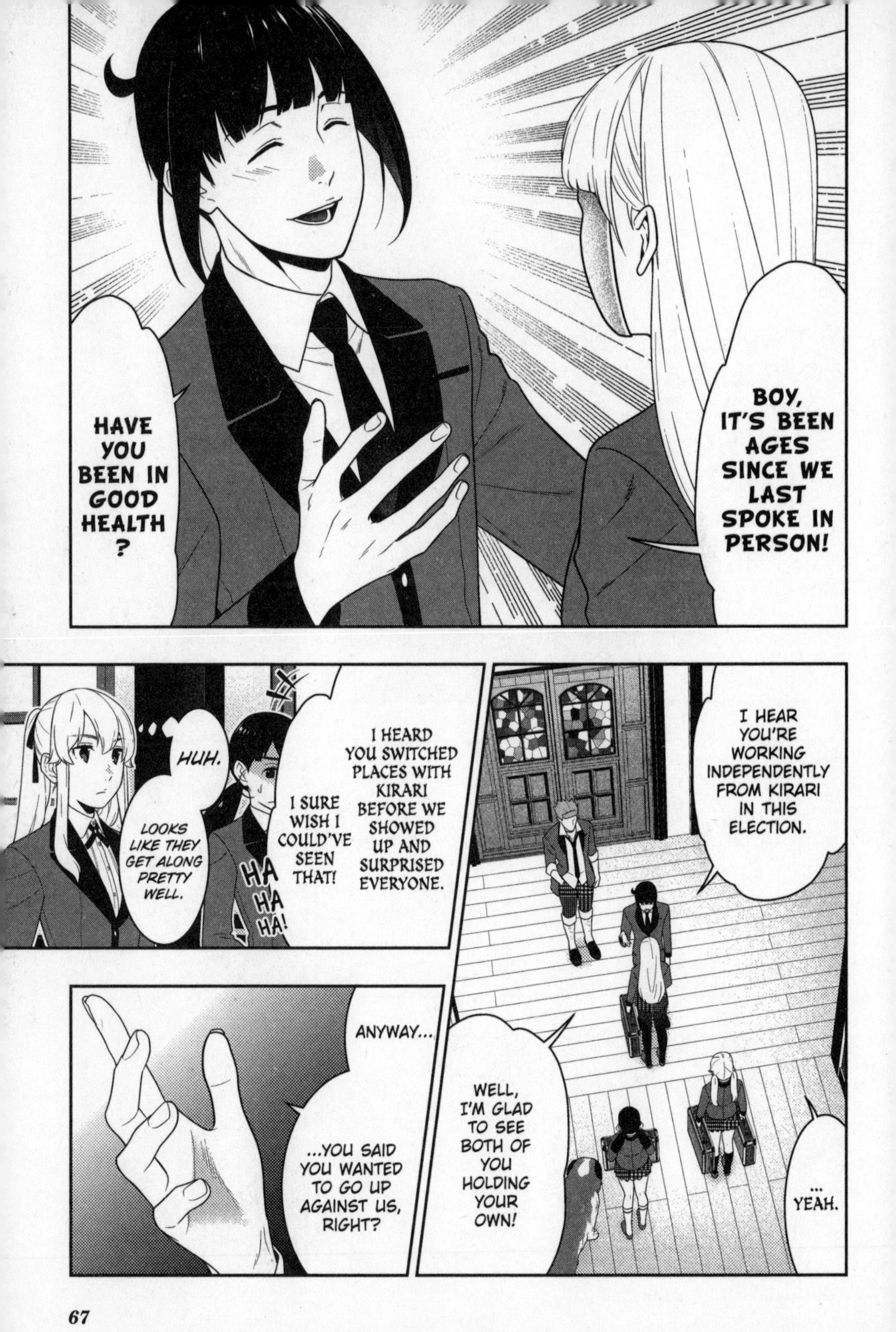
BOY, IT'S BEEN AGES SINCE WE LAST SPOKE IN PERSON!
HAVE YOU BEEN IN GOOD HEALTH?
I HEAR YOU'RE WORKING INDEPENDENTLY FROM KIRARI IN THIS ELECTION.
...YEAH.
WELL, I'M GLAD TO SEE BOTH OF YOU HOLDING YOUR OWN!
I HEARD YOU SWITCHED PLACES WITH KIRARI BEFORE WE SHOWED UP AND SURPRISED EVERYONE.
I SURE WISH I COULD'VE SEEN THAT!
HA HA HA!
HUH.
LOOKS LIKE THEY GET ALONG PRETTY WELL.
ANYWAY...
...YOU SAID YOU WANTED TO GO UP AGAINST US, RIGHT?

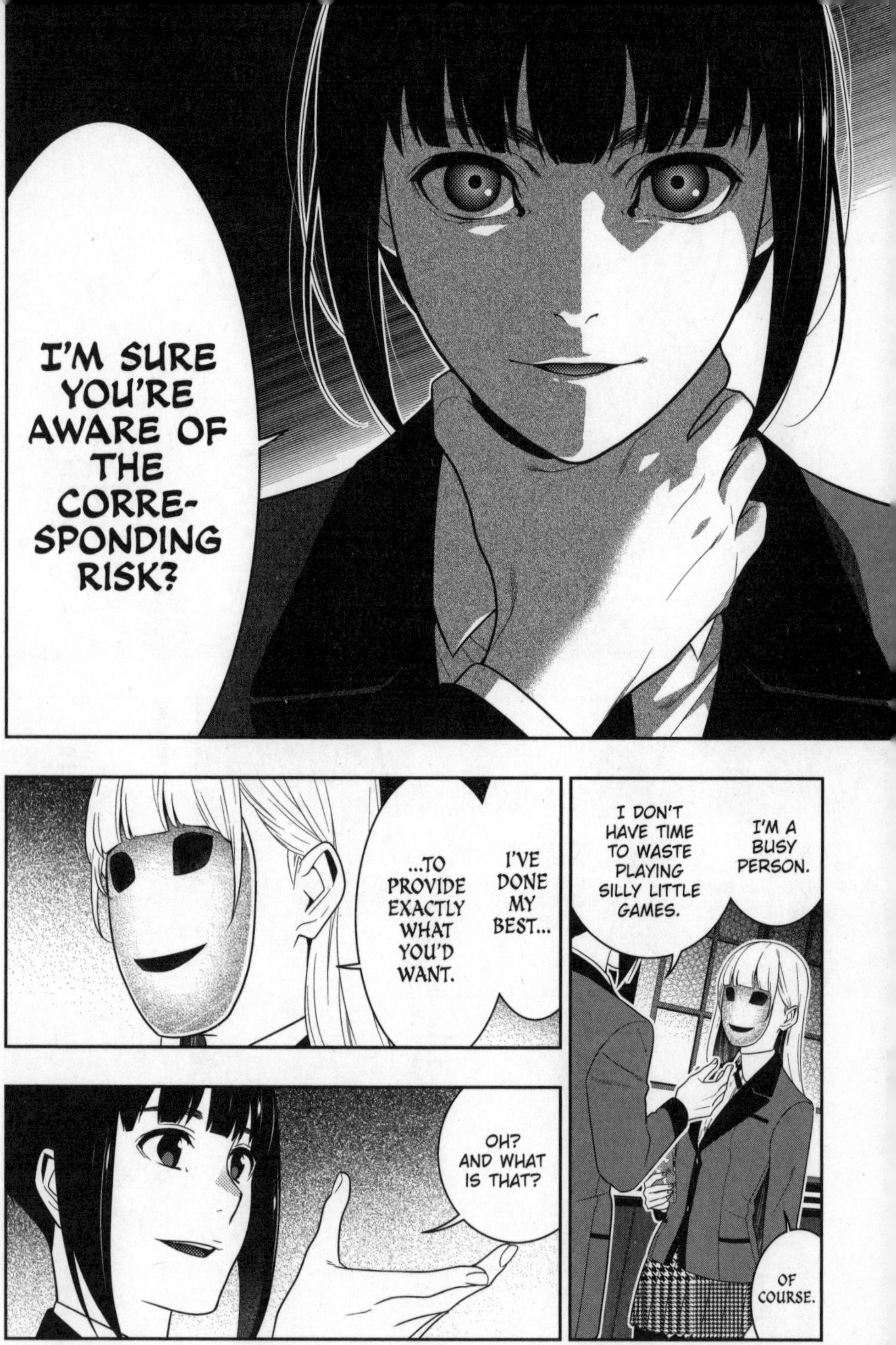
I'M SURE YOU'RE AWARE OF THE CORRE-SPONDING RISK?
I'M A BUSY PERSON.
I DON'T HAVE TIME TO WASTE PLAYING SILLY LITTLE GAMES.
OF COURSE.
I'VE DONE MY BEST...
...TO PROVIDE EXACTLY WHAT YOU'D WANT.
OH? AND WHAT IS THAT?

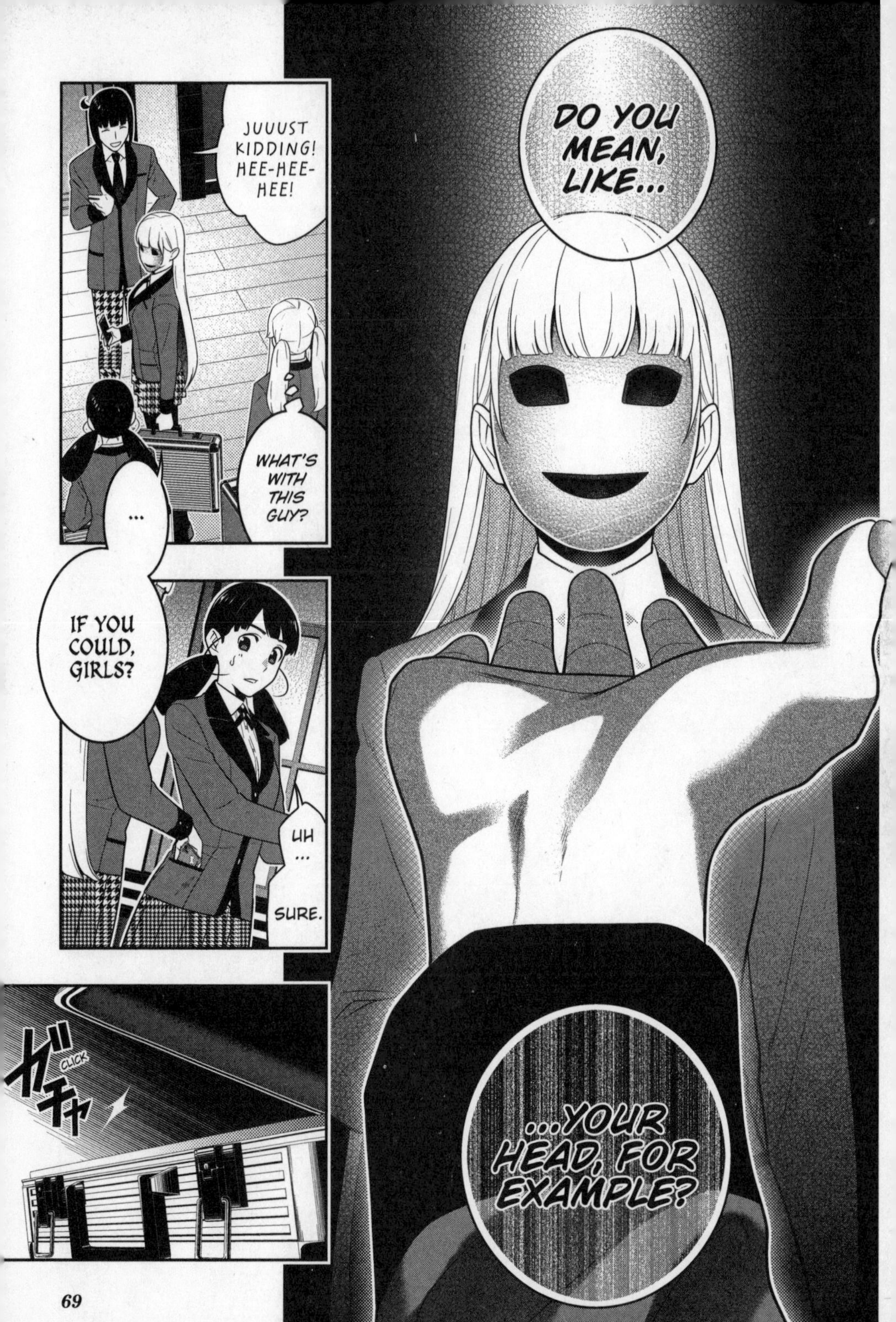
DO YOU MEAN, LIKE...
...YOUR HEAD, FOR EXAMPLE?
JUUUST KIDDING! HEE-HEE-HEE!
WHAT'S WITH THIS GUY?
...
IF YOU COULD, GIRLS?
UH ...
SURE.
ガチャ
CLICK

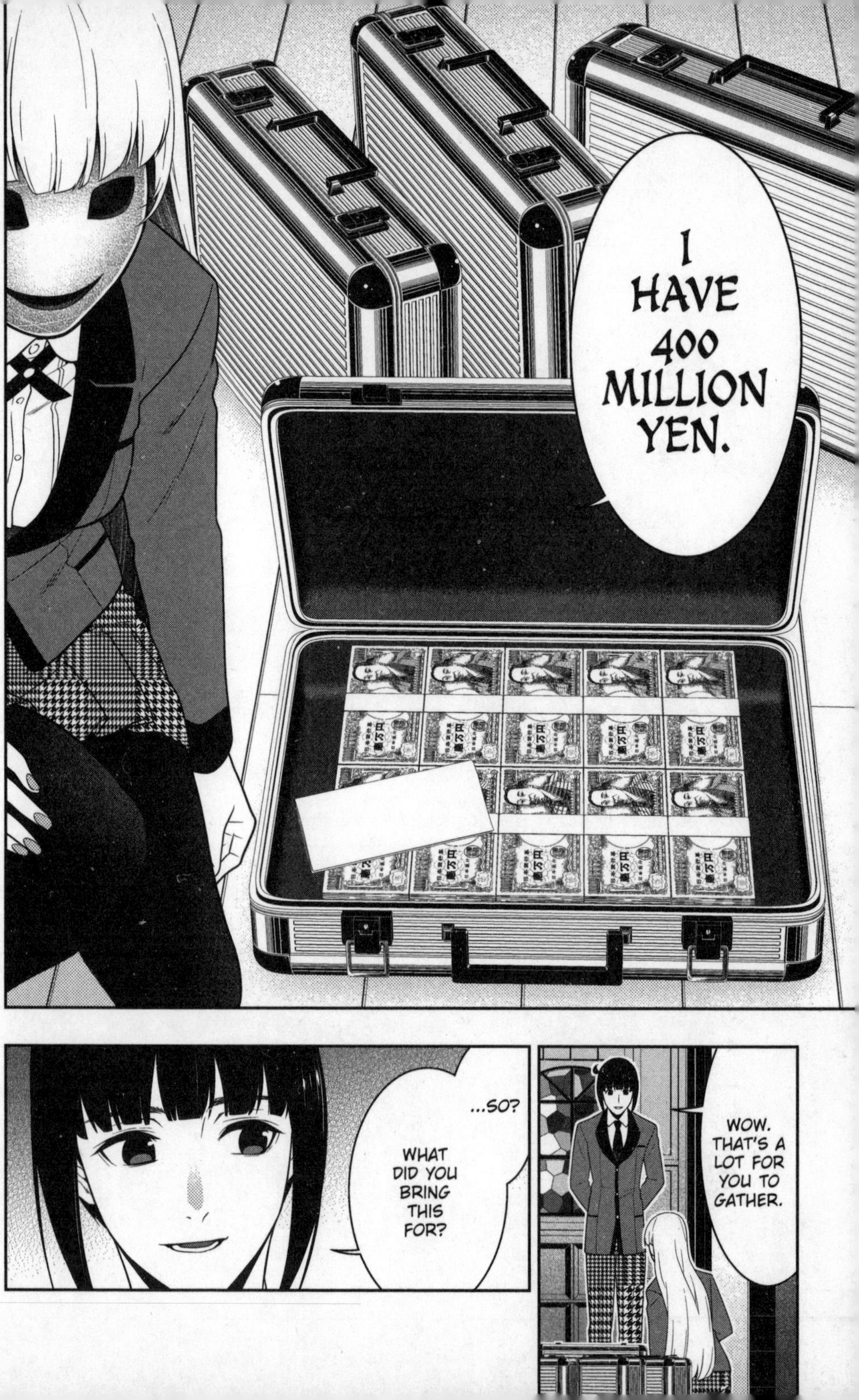
I HAVE 400 MILLION YEN.
WOW. THAT'S A LOT FOR YOU TO GATHER.
...SO?
WHAT DID YOU BRING THIS FOR?

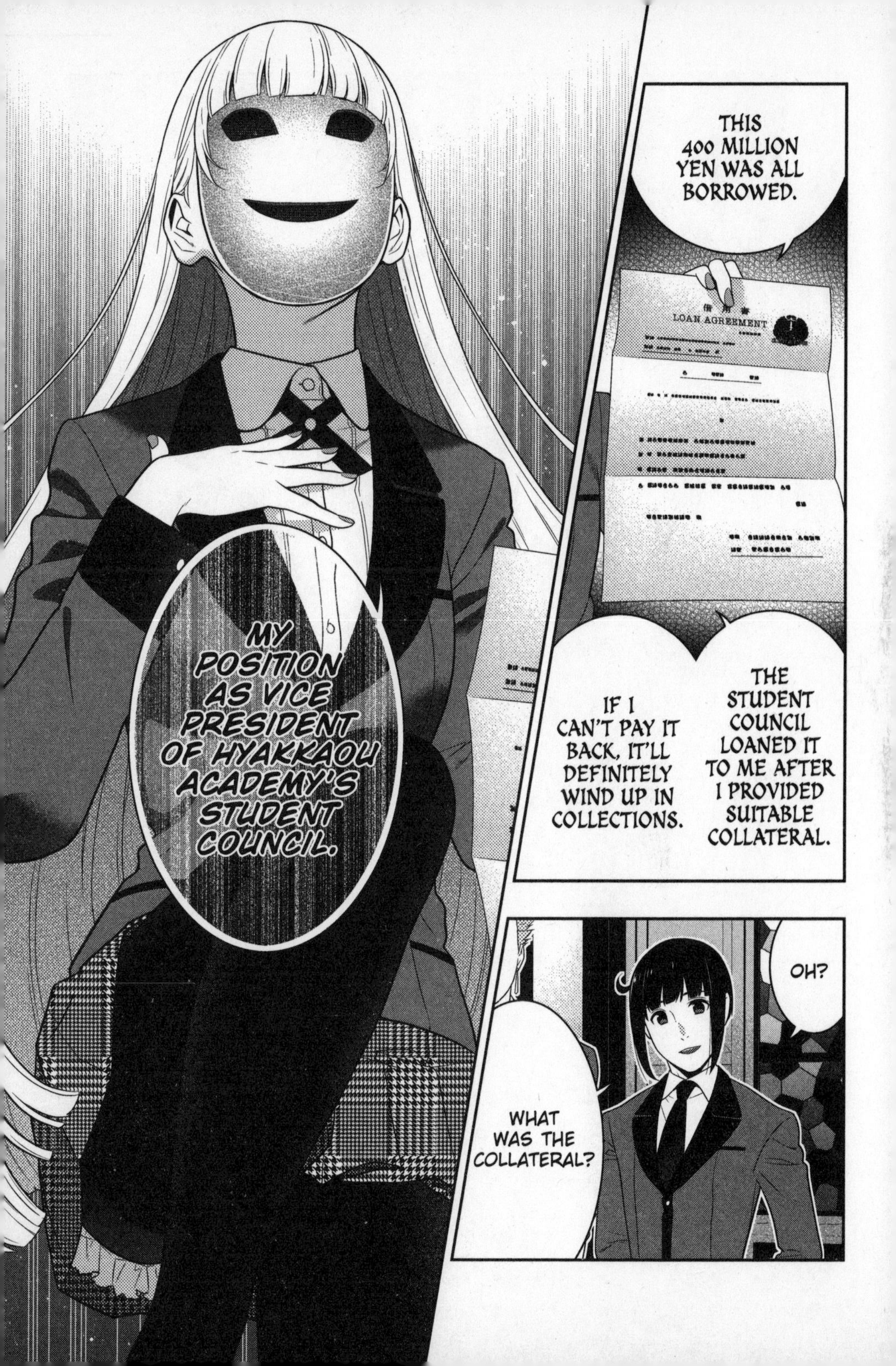
THIS 400 MILLION YEN WAS ALL BORROWED.
LOAN AGREEMENT
THE STUDENT COUNCIL LOANED IT TO ME AFTER I PROVIDED SUITABLE COLLATERAL.
IF I CAN'T PAY IT BACK, IT'LL DEFINITELY WIND UP IN COLLECTIONS.
OH?
WHAT WAS THE COLLATERAL?
MY POSITION AS VICE PRESIDENT OF HYAKKAOU ACADEMY'S STUDENT COUNCIL.

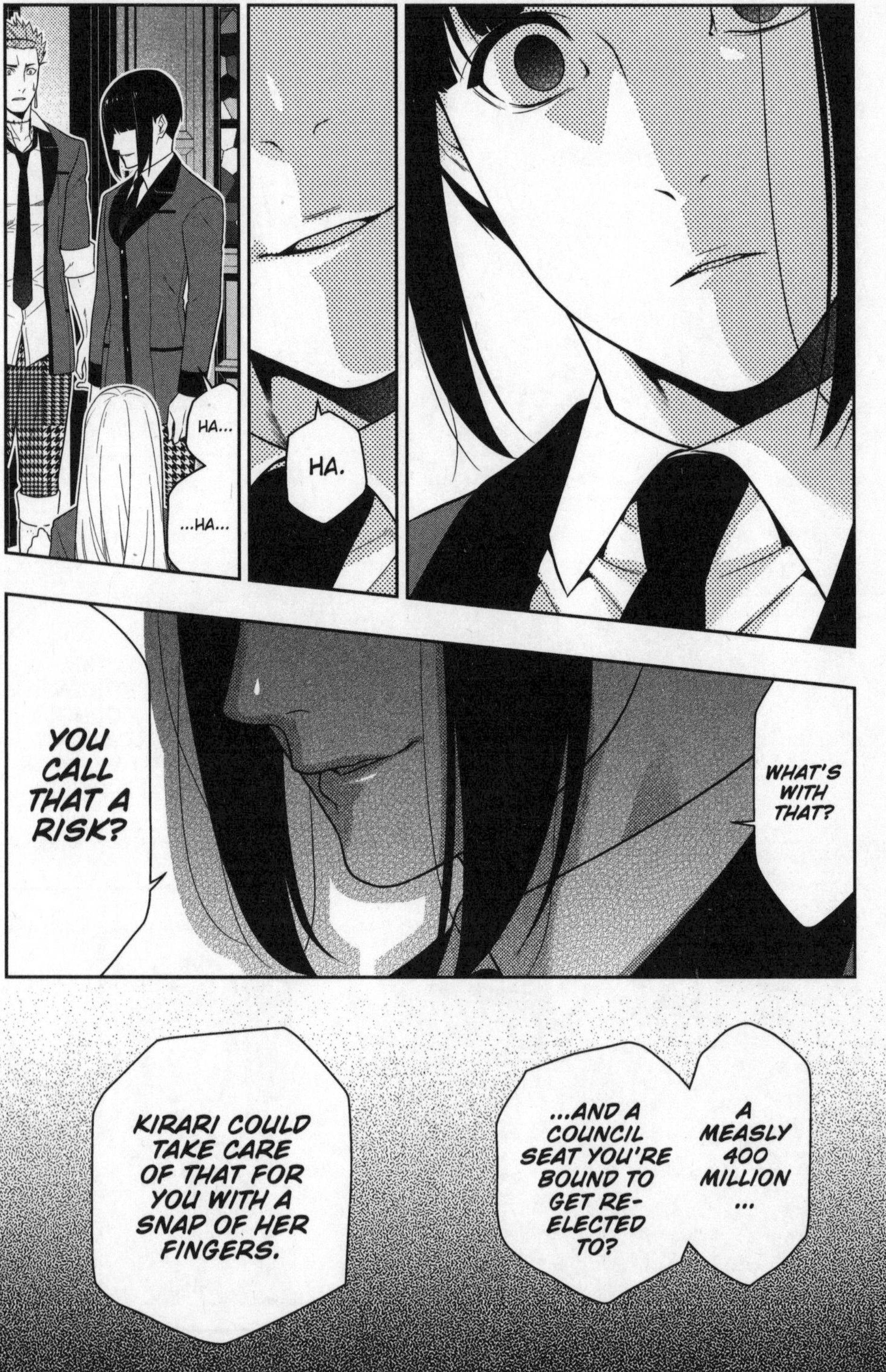
HA.
HA...
...HA...
WHAT'S WITH THAT?
YOU CALL THAT A RISK?
A MEASLY 400 MILLION ...
...AND A COUNCIL SEAT YOU'RE BOUND TO GET RE-ELECTED TO?
KIRARI COULD TAKE CARE OF THAT FOR YOU WITH A SNAP OF HER FINGERS.

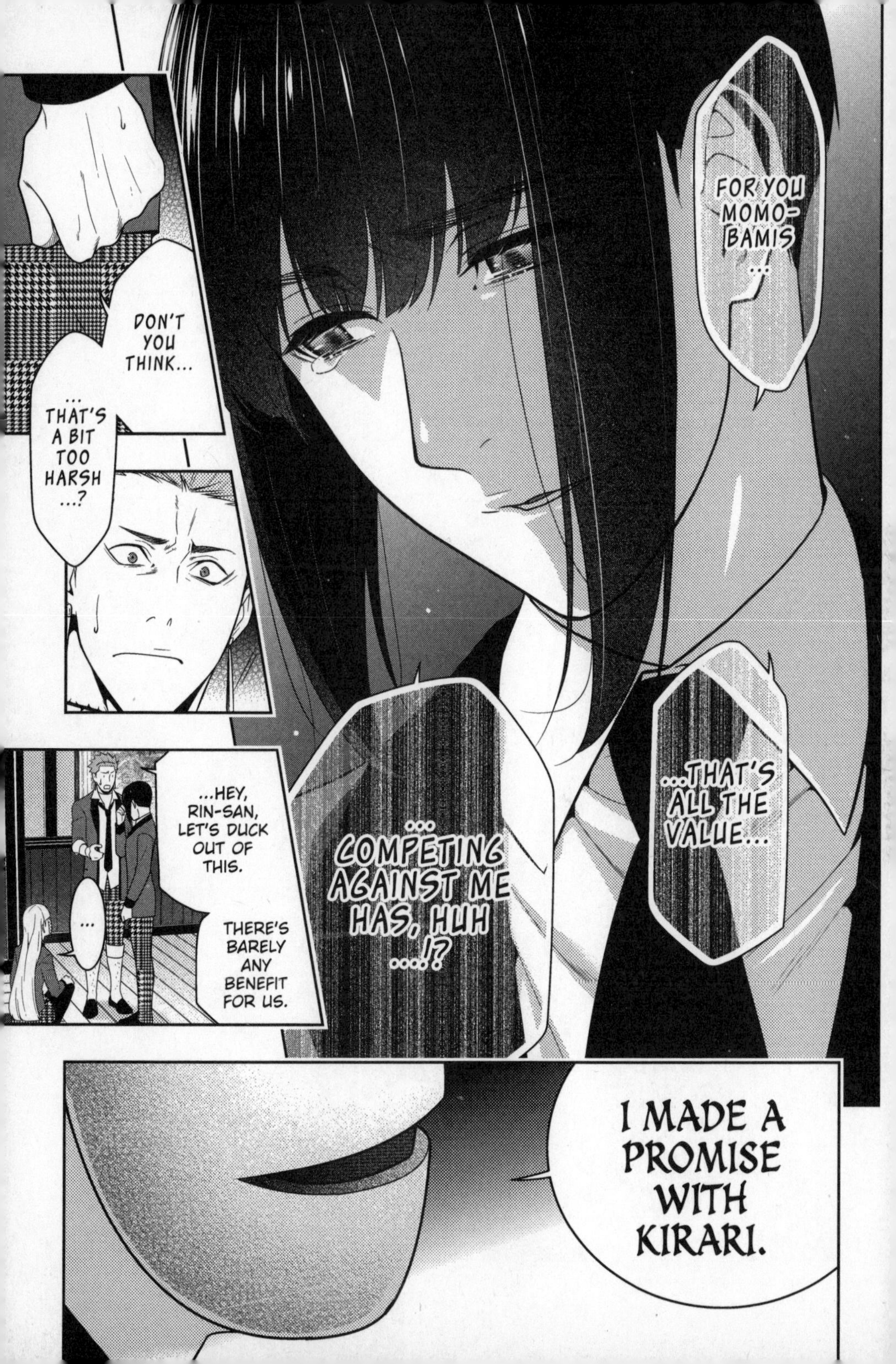
FOR YOU MOMO-BAMIS ...
...THAT'S ALL THE VALUE...
...COMPETING AGAINST ME HAS, HUH ...!?
DON'T YOU THINK...
...THAT'S A BIT TOO HARSH ...?
...HEY, RIN-SAN, LET'S DUCK OUT OF THIS.
THERE'S BARELY ANY BENEFIT FOR US.
...
I MADE A PROMISE WITH KIRARI.

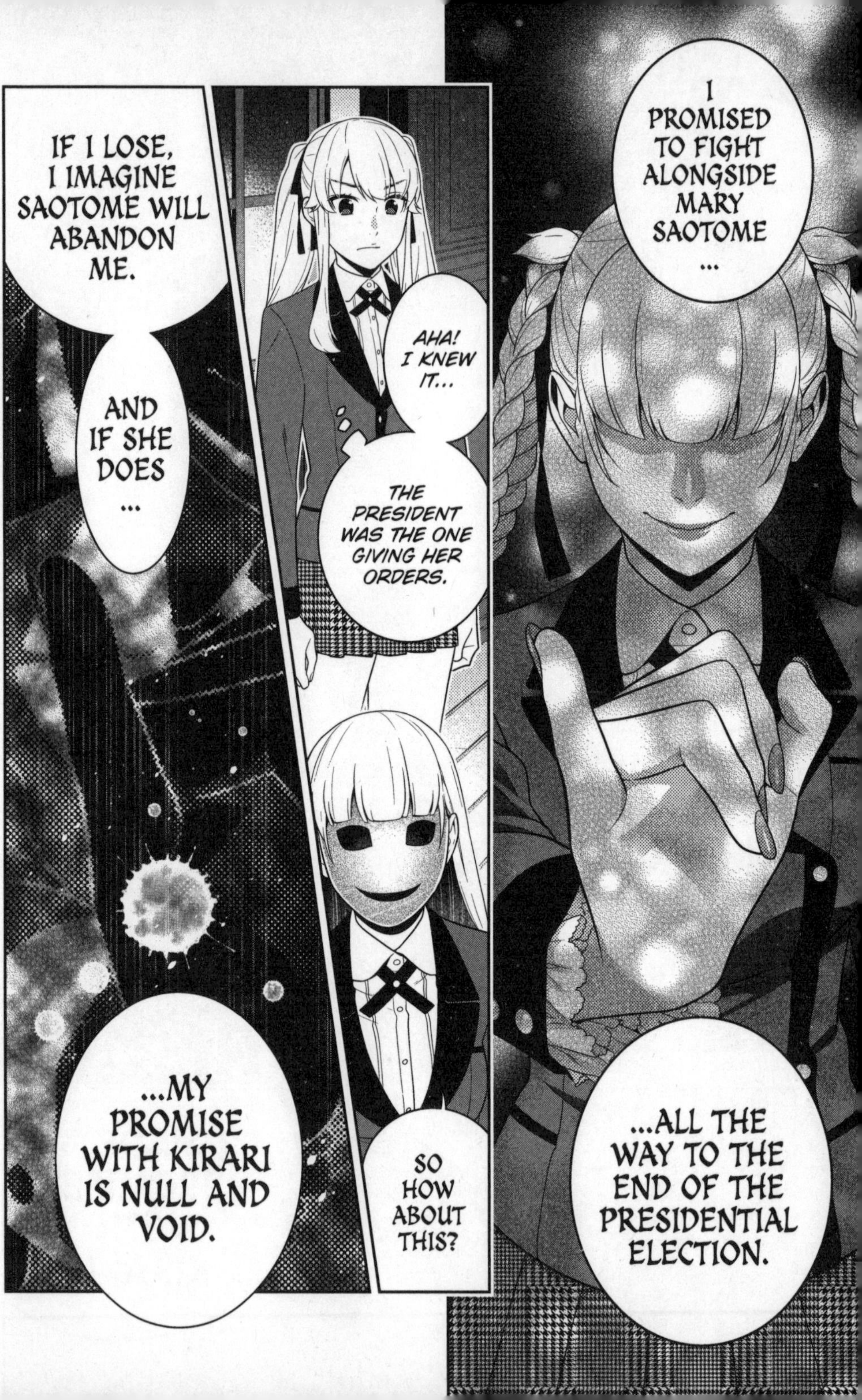
I PROMISED TO FIGHT ALONGSIDE MARY SAOTOME...
...ALL THE WAY TO THE END OF THE PRESIDENTIAL ELECTION.
AHA! I KNEW IT...
THE PRESIDENT WAS THE ONE GIVING HER ORDERS.
SO HOW ABOUT THIS?
IF I LOSE, I IMAGINE SAOTOME WILL ABANDON ME.
AND IF SHE DOES...
...MY PROMISE WITH KIRARI IS NULL AND VOID.

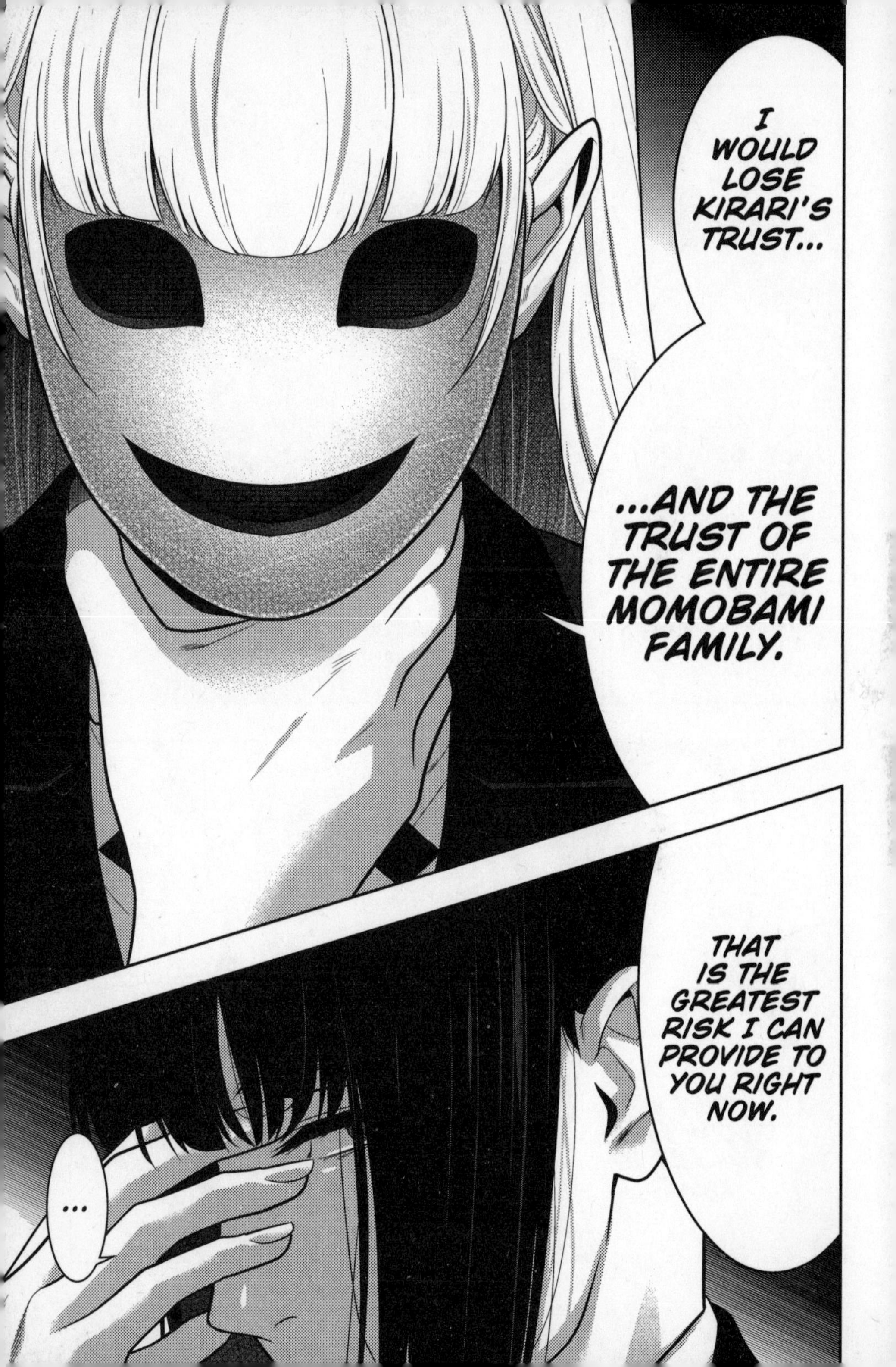
I WOULD LOSE KIRARI'S TRUST...
...AND THE TRUST OF THE ENTIRE MOMOBAMI FAMILY.
THAT IS THE GREATEST RISK I CAN PROVIDE TO YOU RIGHT NOW.
...

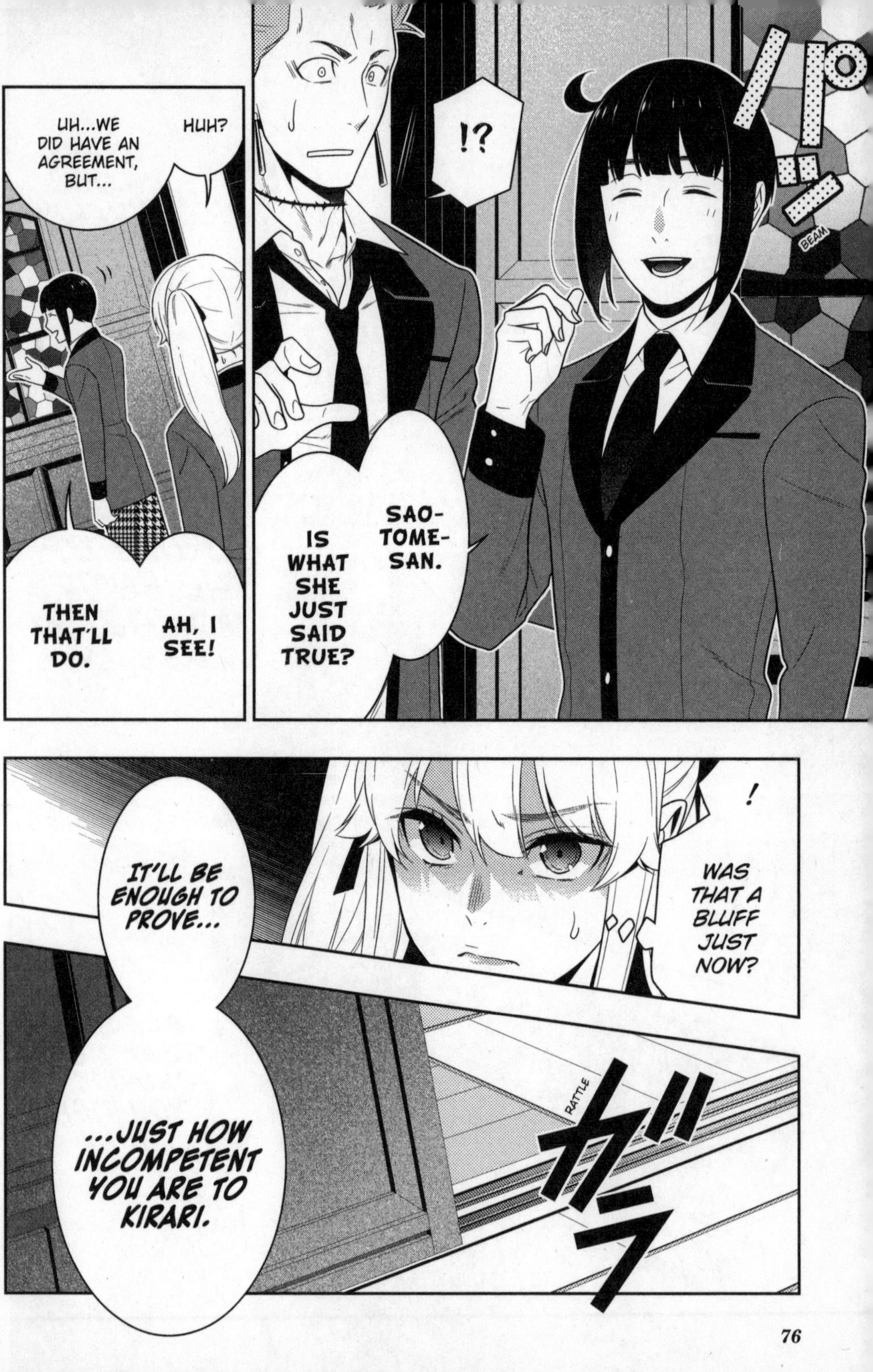
BEAM
!?
SAO-TOME-SAN.
IS WHAT SHE JUST SAID TRUE?
HUH?
UH...WE DID HAVE AN AGREEMENT, BUT...
AH, I SEE!
THEN THAT'LL DO.
!
WAS THAT A BLUFF JUST NOW?
IT'LL BE ENOUGH TO PROVE...
...JUST HOW INCOMPETENT YOU ARE TO KIRARI.
RATTLE

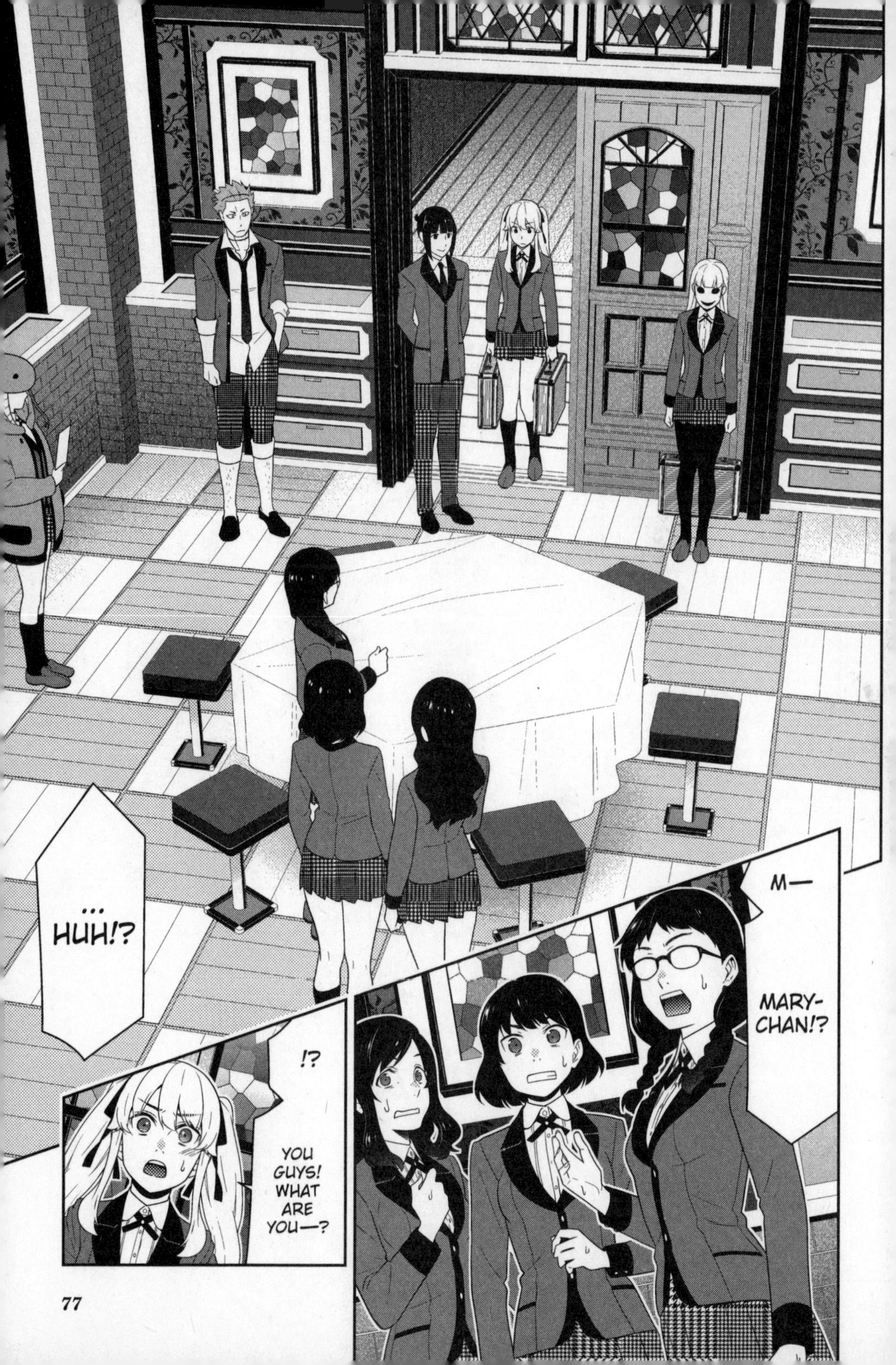

... HUH!?
M—
MARY-CHAN!?
!?
YOU GUYS! WHAT ARE YOU—?

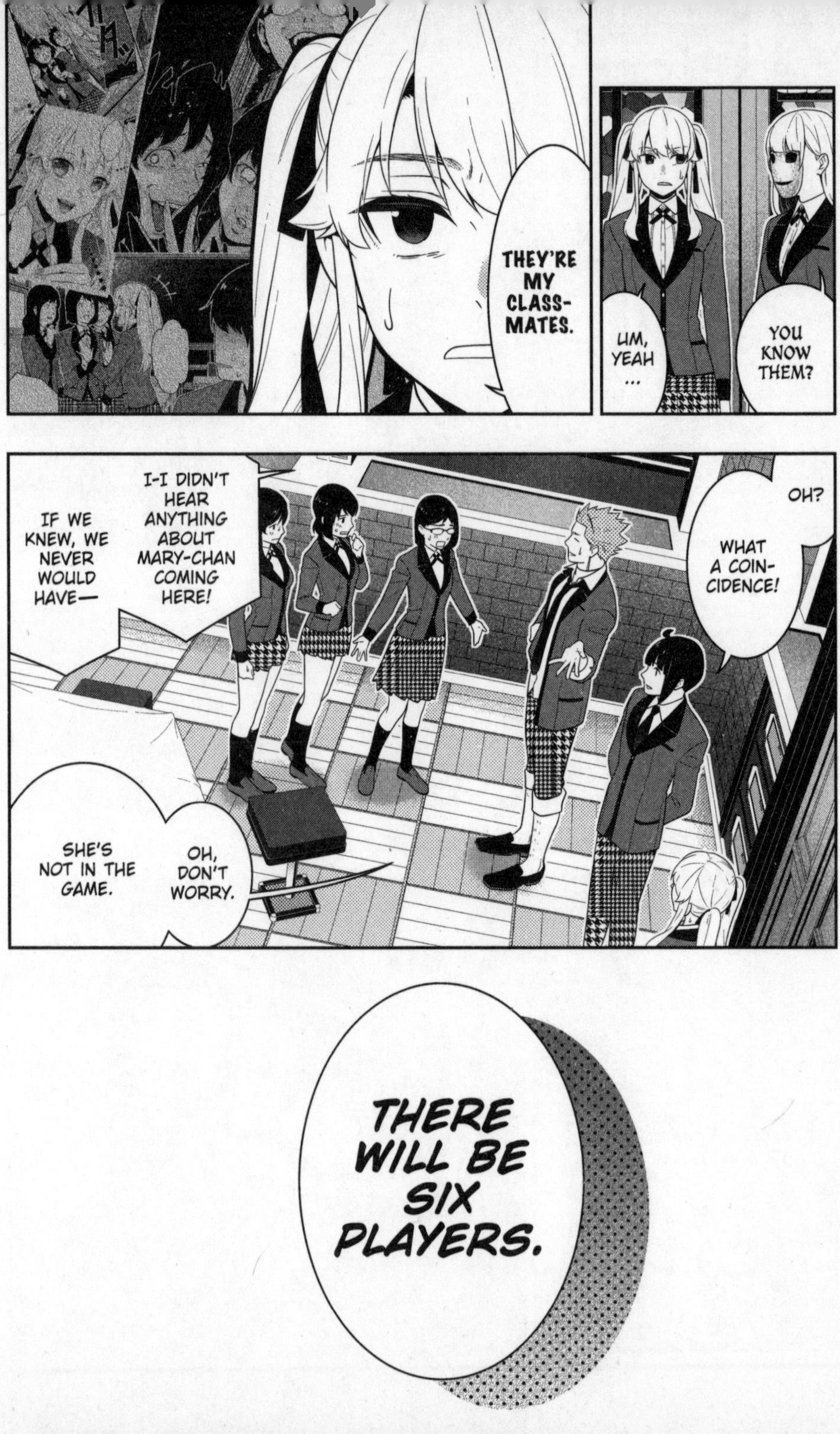
YOU KNOW THEM?
UM, YEAH ...
THEY'RE MY CLASSMATES.
OH?
WHAT A COINCIDENCE!
I-I DIDN'T HEAR ANYTHING ABOUT MARY-CHAN COMING HERE!
IF WE KNEW, WE NEVER WOULD HAVE—
OH, DON'T WORRY.
SHE'S NOT IN THE GAME.
THERE WILL BE SIX PLAYERS.

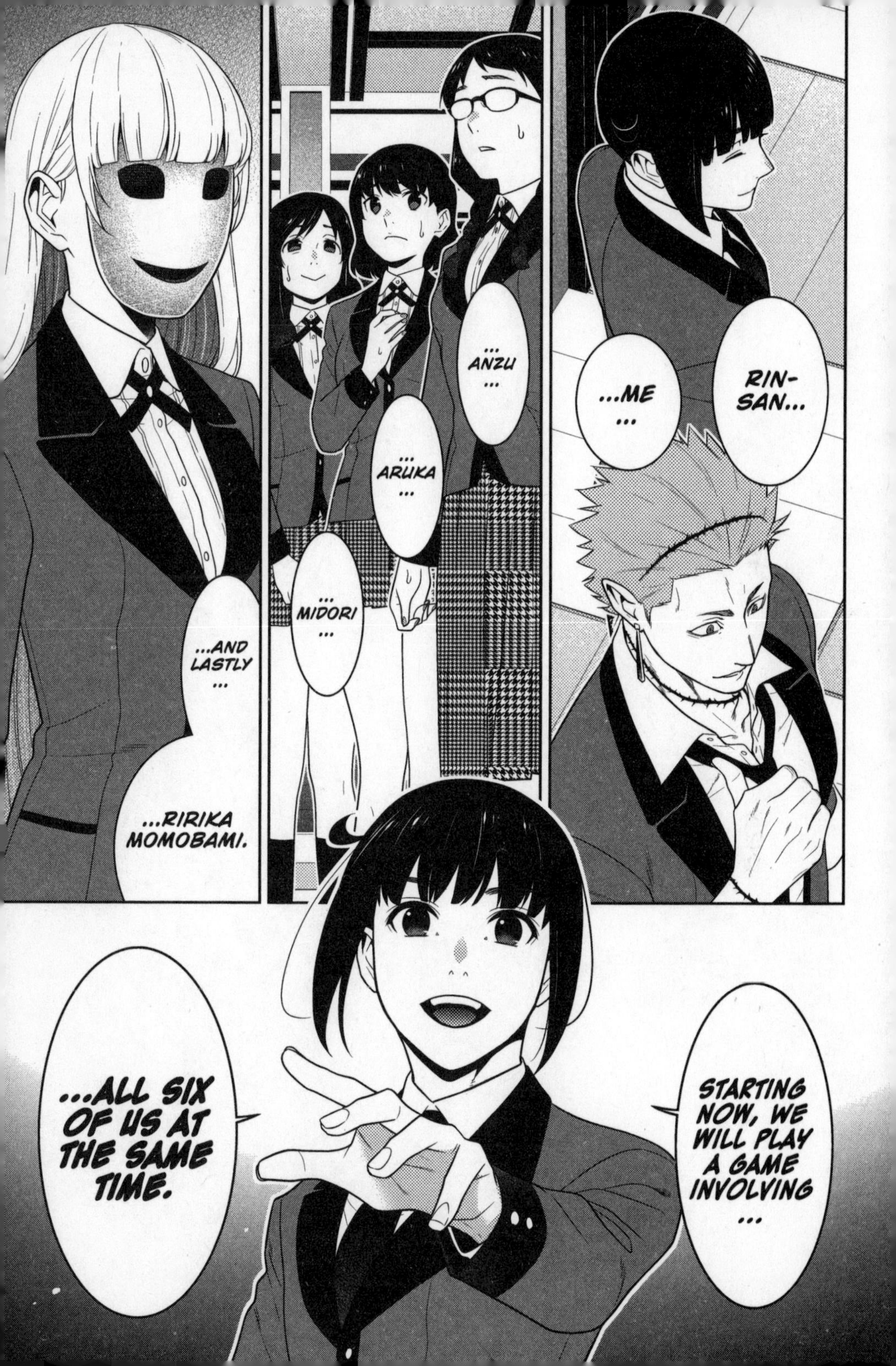
RIN-SAN...
...ME...
...ANZU...
...ARUKA...
...MIDORI...
...AND LASTLY...
...RIRIKA MOMOBAMI.
STARTING NOW, WE WILL PLAY A GAME INVOLVING...
...ALL SIX OF US AT THE SAME TIME.

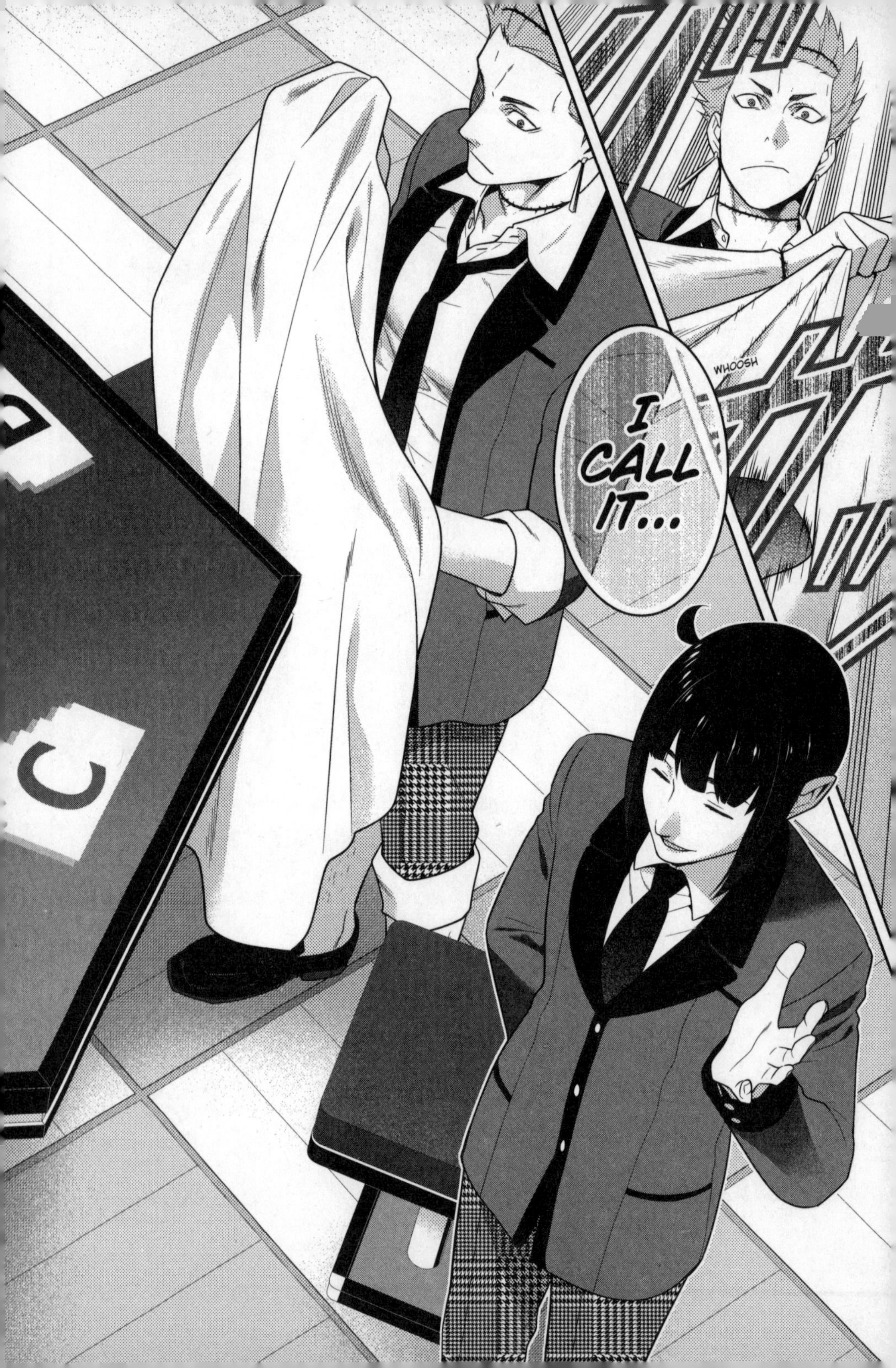
WHOOSH
I CALL IT...

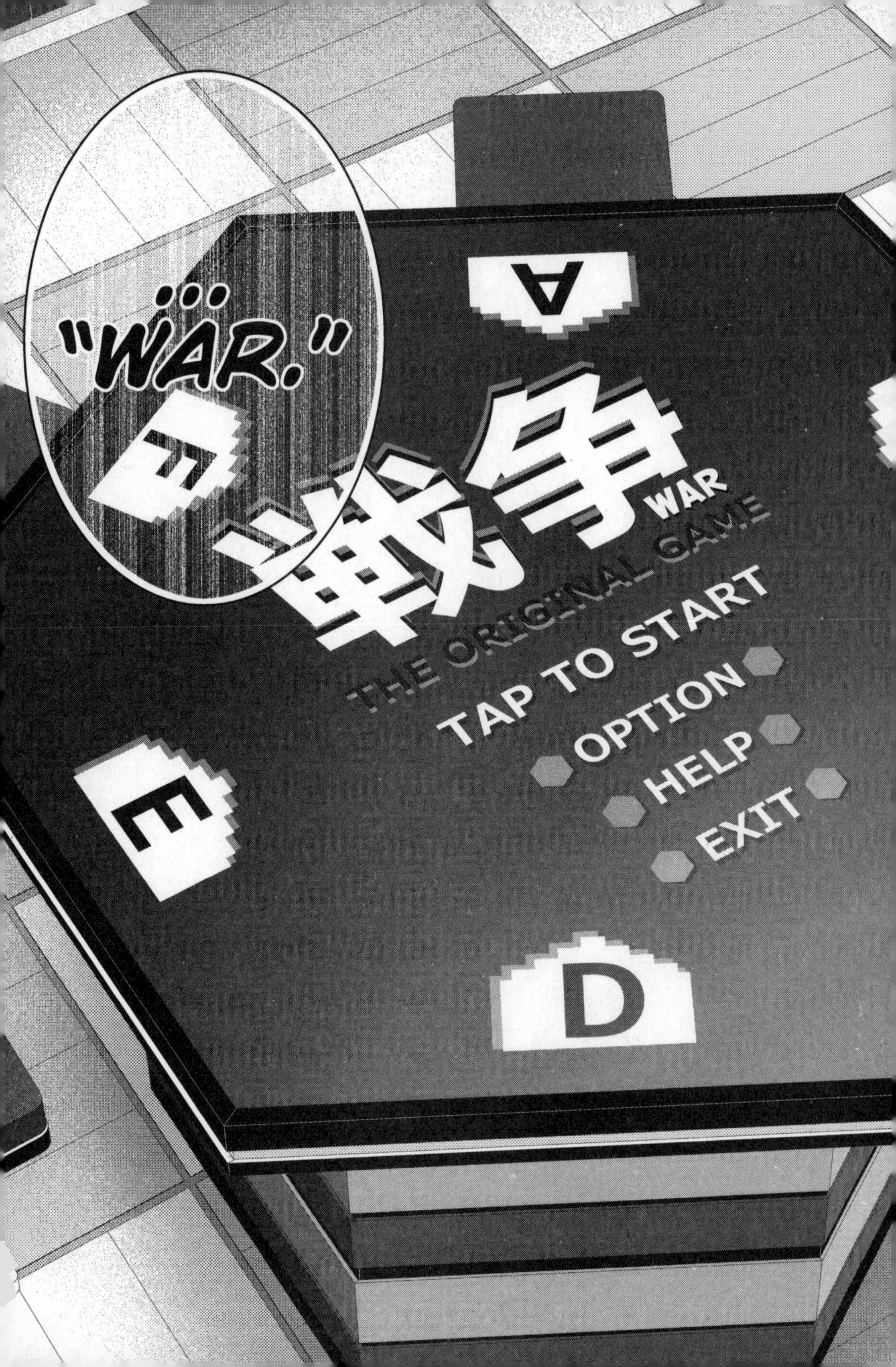
..."WAR."
A
戦争
WAR
THE ORIGINAL GAME
TAP TO START
OPTION
HELP
EXIT
E
D

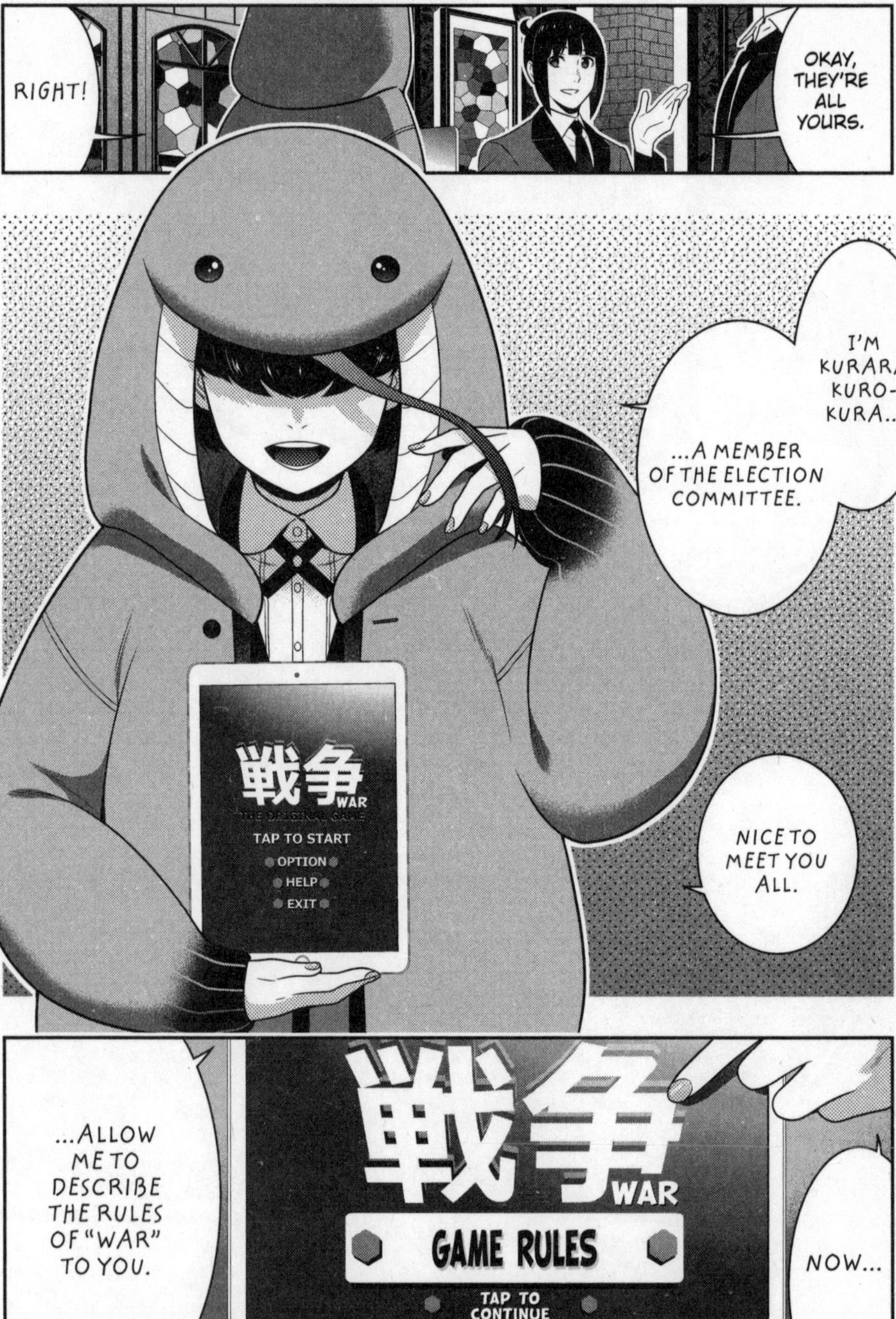
OKAY, THEY'RE ALL YOURS.
RIGHT!
I'M KURARA KURO-KURA...
...A MEMBER OF THE ELECTION COMMITTEE.
NICE TO MEET YOU ALL.
戦争 WAR
TAP TO START
OPTION
HELP
EXIT
NOW...
戦争 WAR
GAME RULES
TAP TO CONTINUE
...ALLOW ME TO DESCRIBE THE RULES OF "WAR" TO YOU.

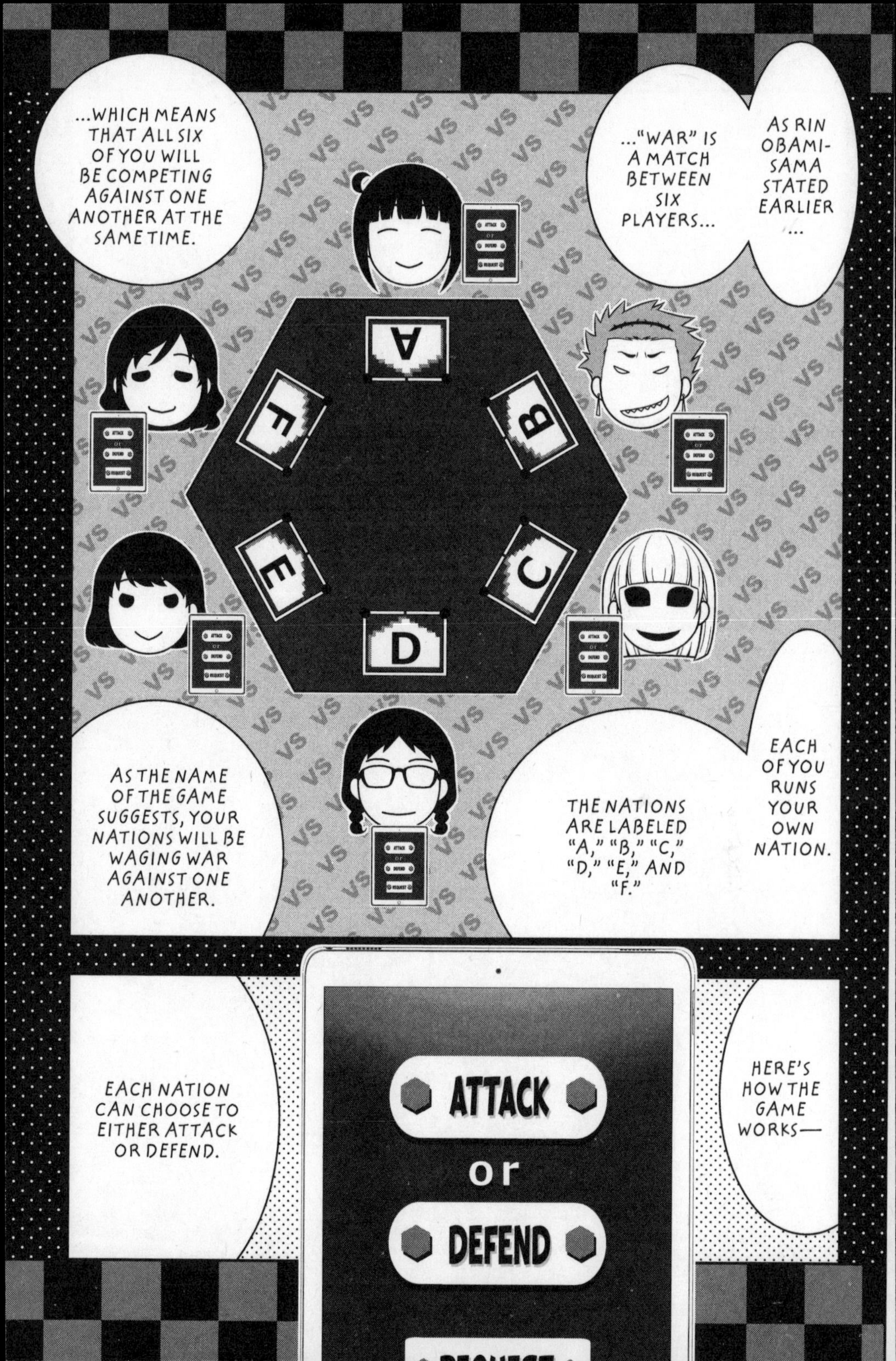
AS RIN OBAMI-SAMA STATED EARLIER...
..."WAR" IS A MATCH BETWEEN SIX PLAYERS...
...WHICH MEANS THAT ALL SIX OF YOU WILL BE COMPETING AGAINST ONE ANOTHER AT THE SAME TIME.
A
B
C
D
E
F
EACH OF YOU RUNS YOUR OWN NATION.
THE NATIONS ARE LABELED "A," "B," "C," "D," "E," AND "F."
AS THE NAME OF THE GAME SUGGESTS, YOUR NATIONS WILL BE WAGING WAR AGAINST ONE ANOTHER.
HERE'S HOW THE GAME WORKS—
ATTACK
or
DEFEND
EACH NATION CAN CHOOSE TO EITHER ATTACK OR DEFEND.

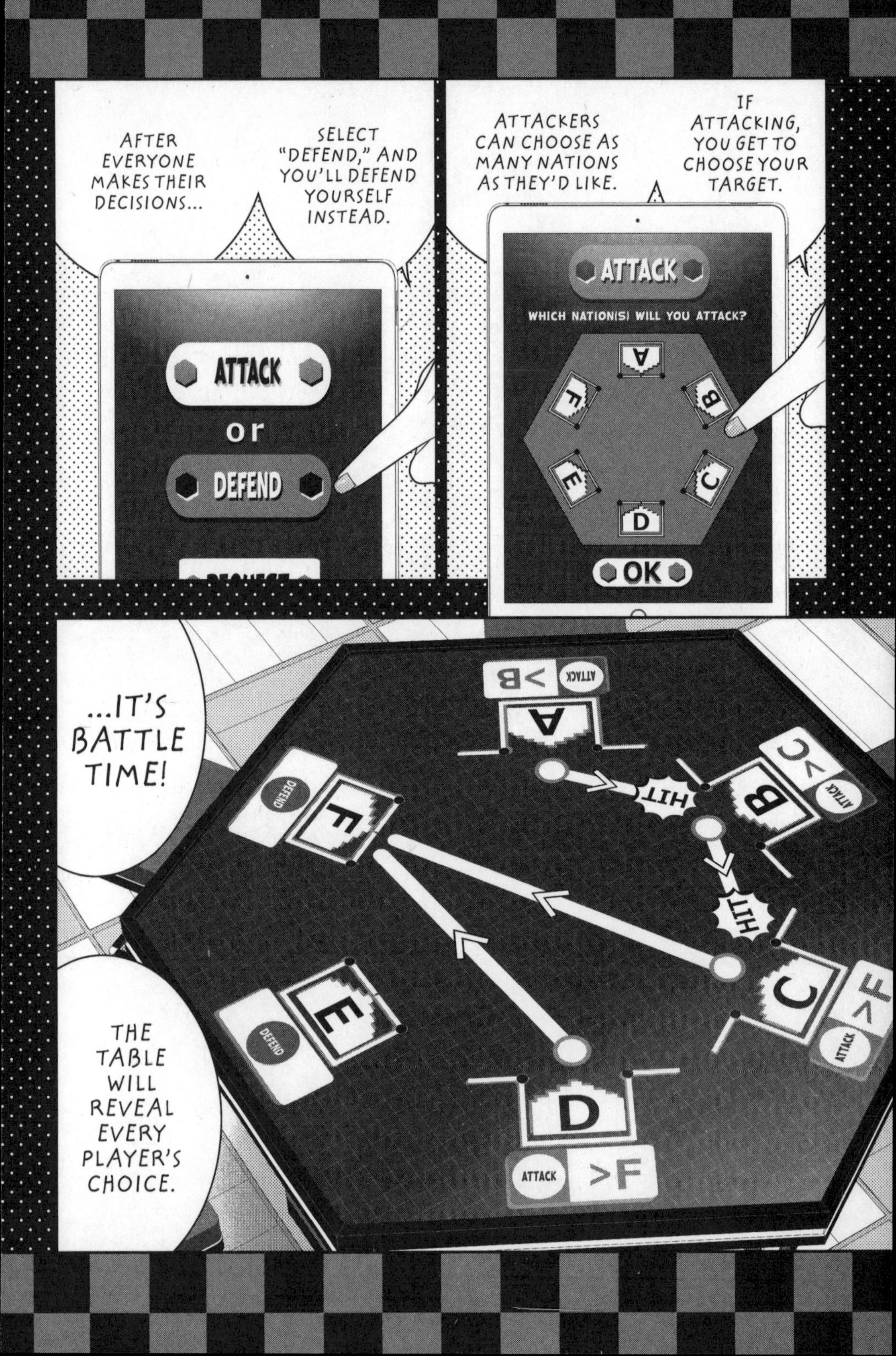
IF ATTACKING, YOU GET TO CHOOSE YOUR TARGET.
ATTACKERS CAN CHOOSE AS MANY NATIONS AS THEY'D LIKE.
ATTACK
WHICH NATION(S) WILL YOU ATTACK?
OK
SELECT "DEFEND," AND YOU'LL DEFEND YOURSELF INSTEAD.
AFTER EVERYONE MAKES THEIR DECISIONS...
ATTACK
or
DEFEND
...IT'S BATTLE TIME!
THE TABLE WILL REVEAL EVERY PLAYER'S CHOICE.
ATTACK >B
ATTACK >C
HIT
HIT
DEFEND
ATTACK >F
DEFEND
ATTACK >F

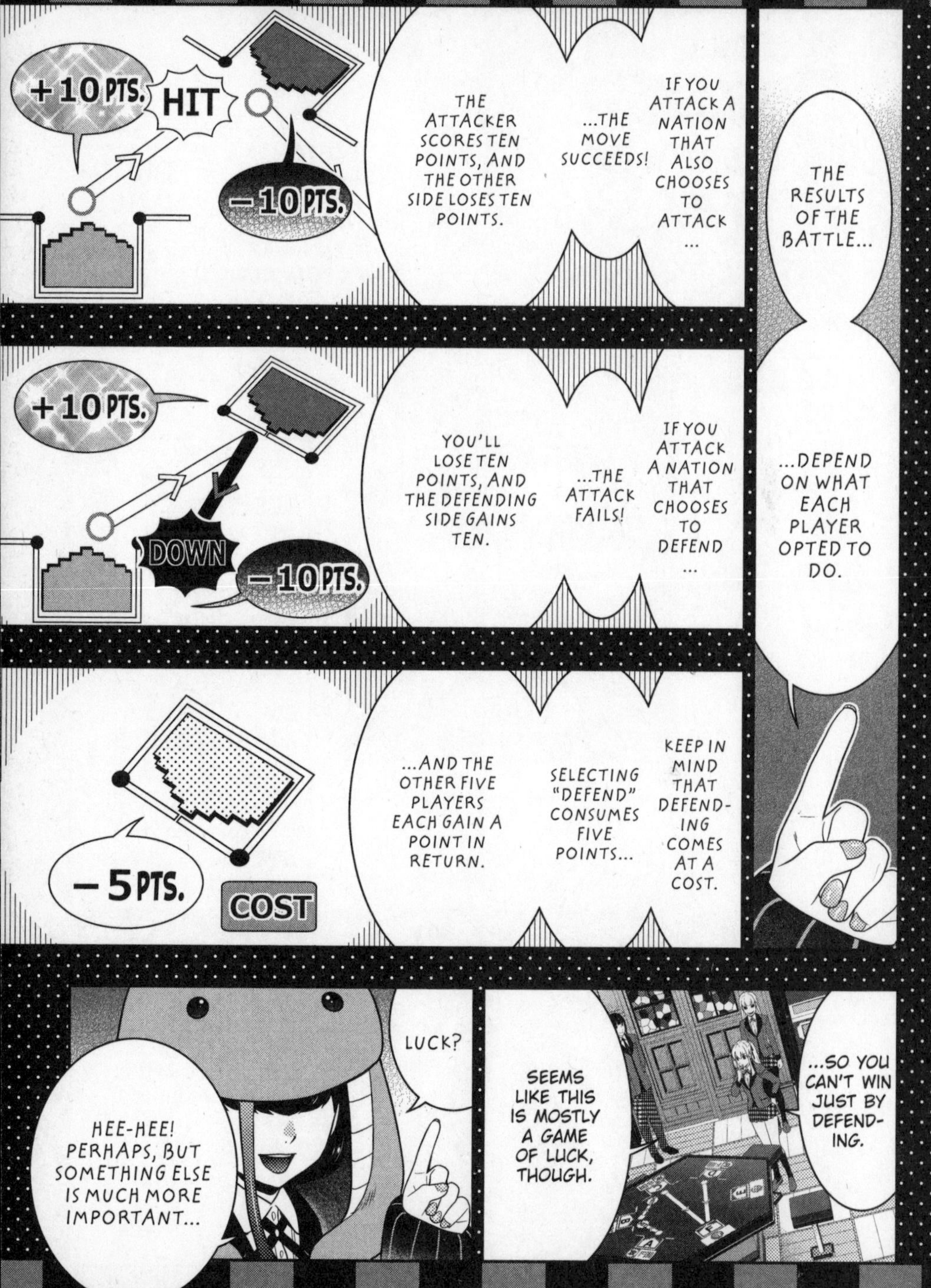
THE RESULTS OF THE BATTLE...
...DEPEND ON WHAT EACH PLAYER OPTED TO DO.
IF YOU ATTACK A NATION THAT ALSO CHOOSES TO ATTACK...
...THE MOVE SUCCEEDS!
THE ATTACKER SCORES TEN POINTS, AND THE OTHER SIDE LOSES TEN POINTS.
HIT
+10 PTS.
−10 PTS.
IF YOU ATTACK A NATION THAT CHOOSES TO DEFEND...
...THE ATTACK FAILS!
YOU'LL LOSE TEN POINTS, AND THE DEFENDING SIDE GAINS TEN.
+10 PTS.
DOWN
−10 PTS.
KEEP IN MIND THAT DEFENDING COMES AT A COST.
SELECTING "DEFEND" CONSUMES FIVE POINTS...
...AND THE OTHER FIVE PLAYERS EACH GAIN A POINT IN RETURN.
−5 PTS.
COST
...SO YOU CAN'T WIN JUST BY DEFENDING.
SEEMS LIKE THIS IS MOSTLY A GAME OF LUCK, THOUGH.
LUCK?
HEE-HEE! PERHAPS, BUT SOMETHING ELSE IS MUCH MORE IMPORTANT...

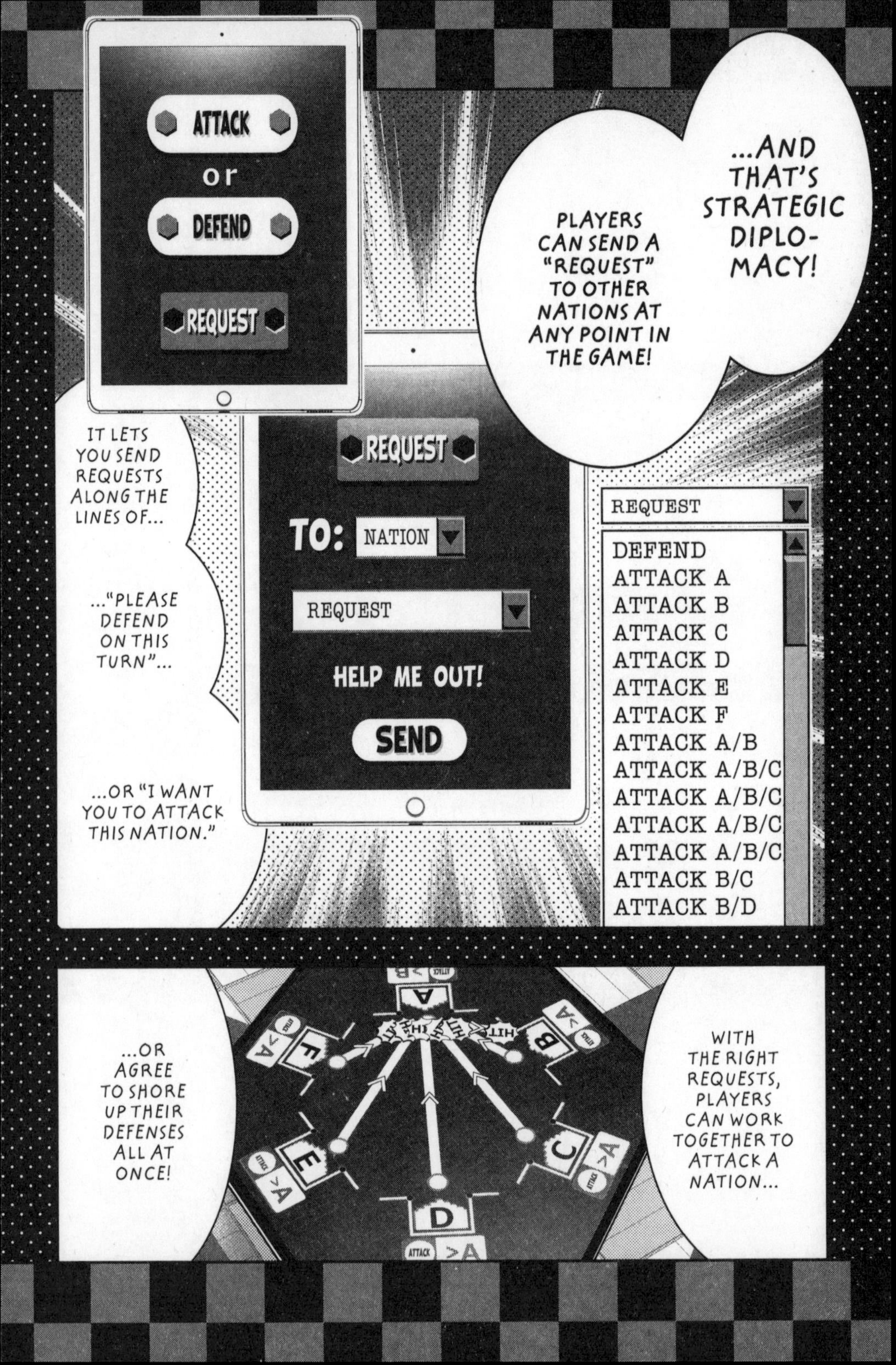

...AND THAT'S STRATEGIC DIPLOMACY!
PLAYERS CAN SEND A "REQUEST" TO OTHER NATIONS AT ANY POINT IN THE GAME!
ATTACK
or
DEFEND
REQUEST
REQUEST
DEFEND
ATTACK A
ATTACK B
ATTACK C
ATTACK D
ATTACK E
ATTACK F
ATTACK A/B
ATTACK A/B/C
ATTACK A/B/C
ATTACK A/B/C
ATTACK A/B/C
ATTACK B/C
ATTACK B/D
REQUEST
TO: NATION
REQUEST
HELP ME OUT!
SEND
IT LETS YOU SEND REQUESTS ALONG THE LINES OF...
..."PLEASE DEFEND ON THIS TURN"...
...OR "I WANT YOU TO ATTACK THIS NATION."
WITH THE RIGHT REQUESTS, PLAYERS CAN WORK TOGETHER TO ATTACK A NATION...
A
B
C
D
E
F
HIT
...OR AGREE TO SHORE UP THEIR DEFENSES ALL AT ONCE!

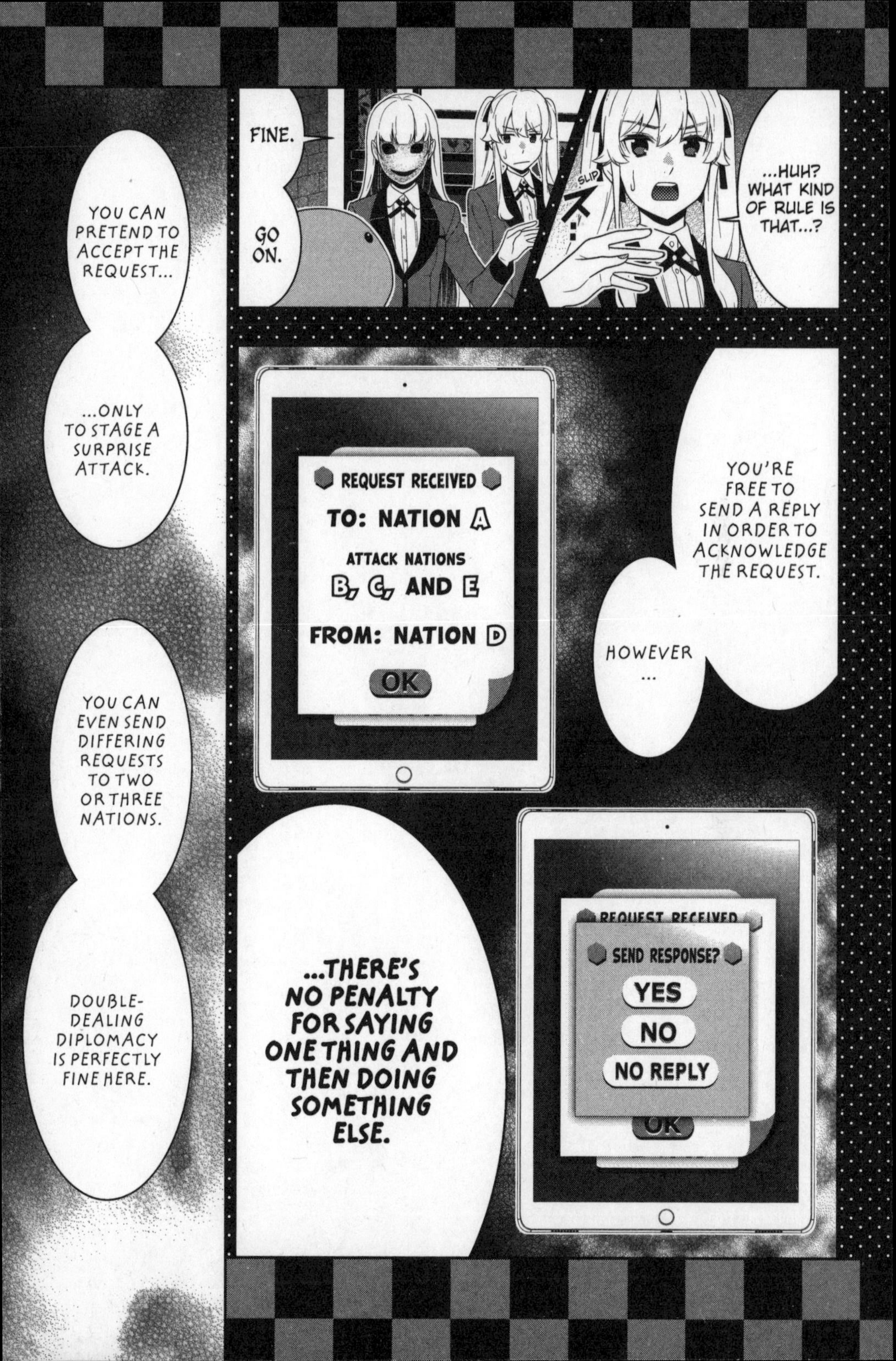

...HUH? WHAT KIND OF RULE IS THAT...?
SLIP
FINE.
GO ON.
REQUEST RECEIVED
TO: NATION A
ATTACK NATIONS B, C, AND E
FROM: NATION D
OK
YOU'RE FREE TO SEND A REPLY IN ORDER TO ACKNOWLEDGE THE REQUEST.
HOWEVER...
SEND RESPONSE?
YES
NO
NO REPLY
OK
...THERE'S NO PENALTY FOR SAYING ONE THING AND THEN DOING SOMETHING ELSE.
YOU CAN PRETEND TO ACCEPT THE REQUEST...
...ONLY TO STAGE A SURPRISE ATTACK.
YOU CAN EVEN SEND DIFFERING REQUESTS TO TWO OR THREE NATIONS.
DOUBLE-DEALING DIPLOMACY IS PERFECTLY FINE HERE.

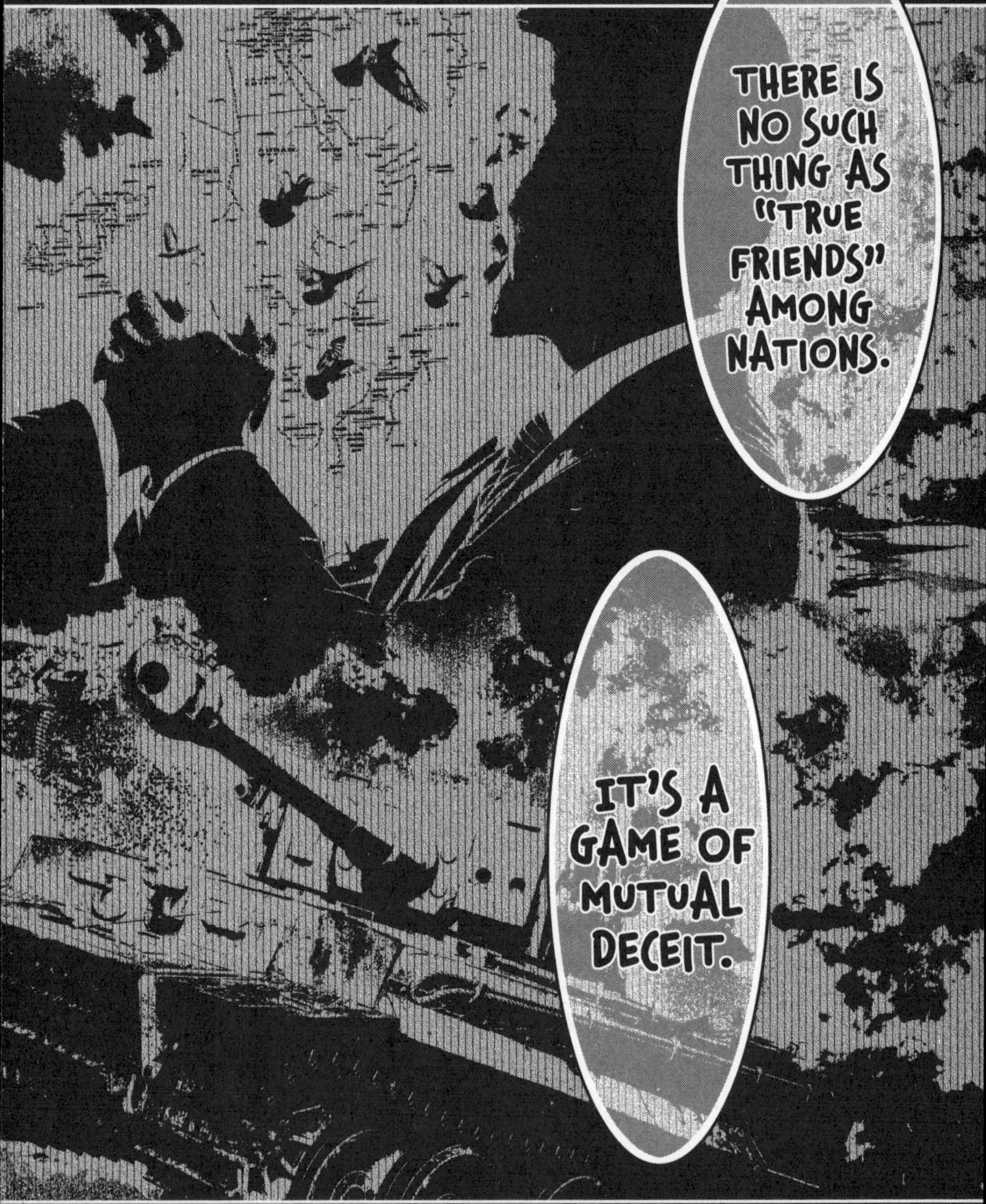
THERE IS NO SUCH THING AS "TRUE FRIENDS" AMONG NATIONS.
IT'S A GAME OF MUTUAL DECEIT.

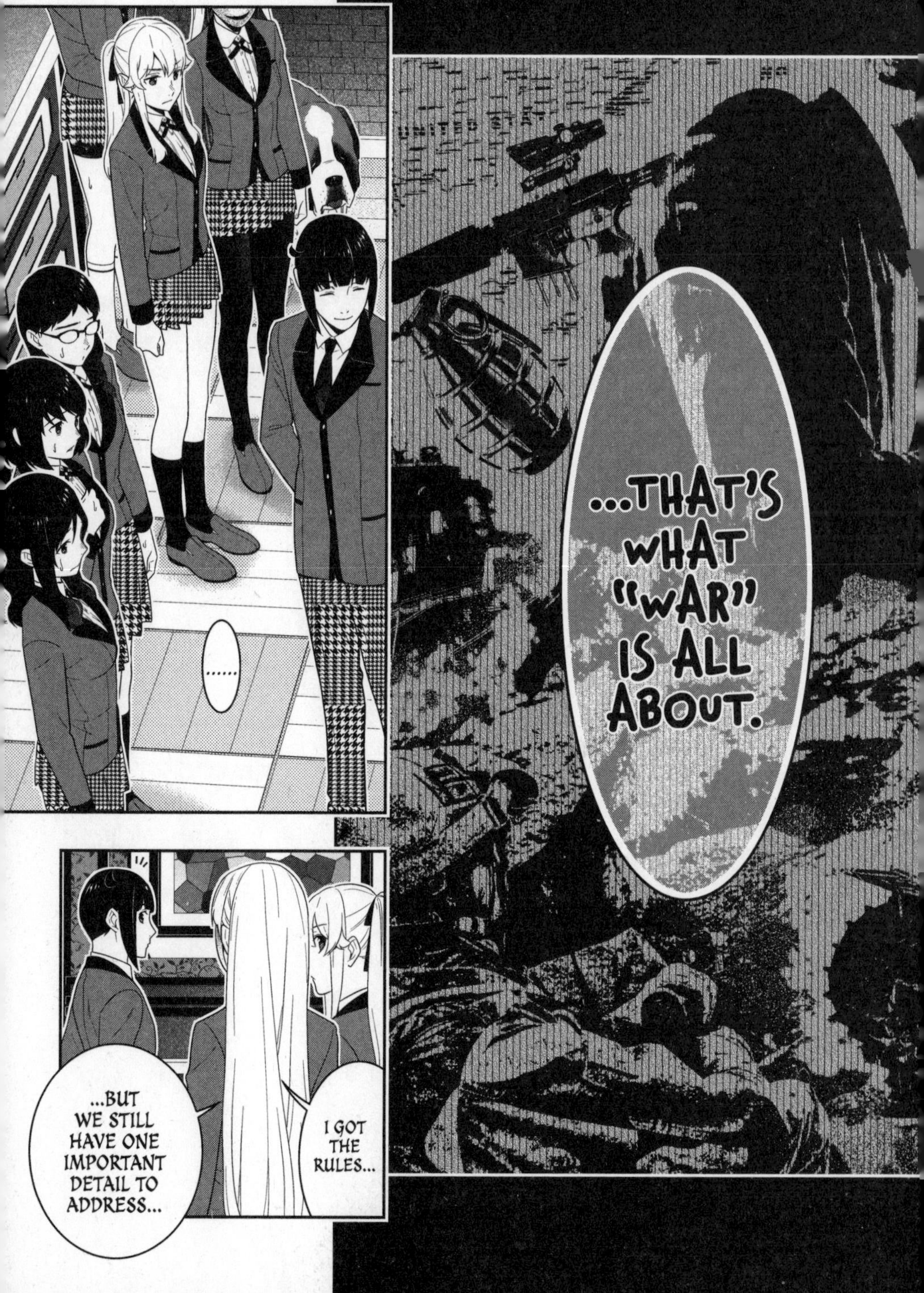
UNITED STAT
...THAT'S WHAT "WAR" IS ALL ABOUT.
......
I GOT THE RULES...
...BUT WE STILL HAVE ONE IMPORTANT DETAIL TO ADDRESS...

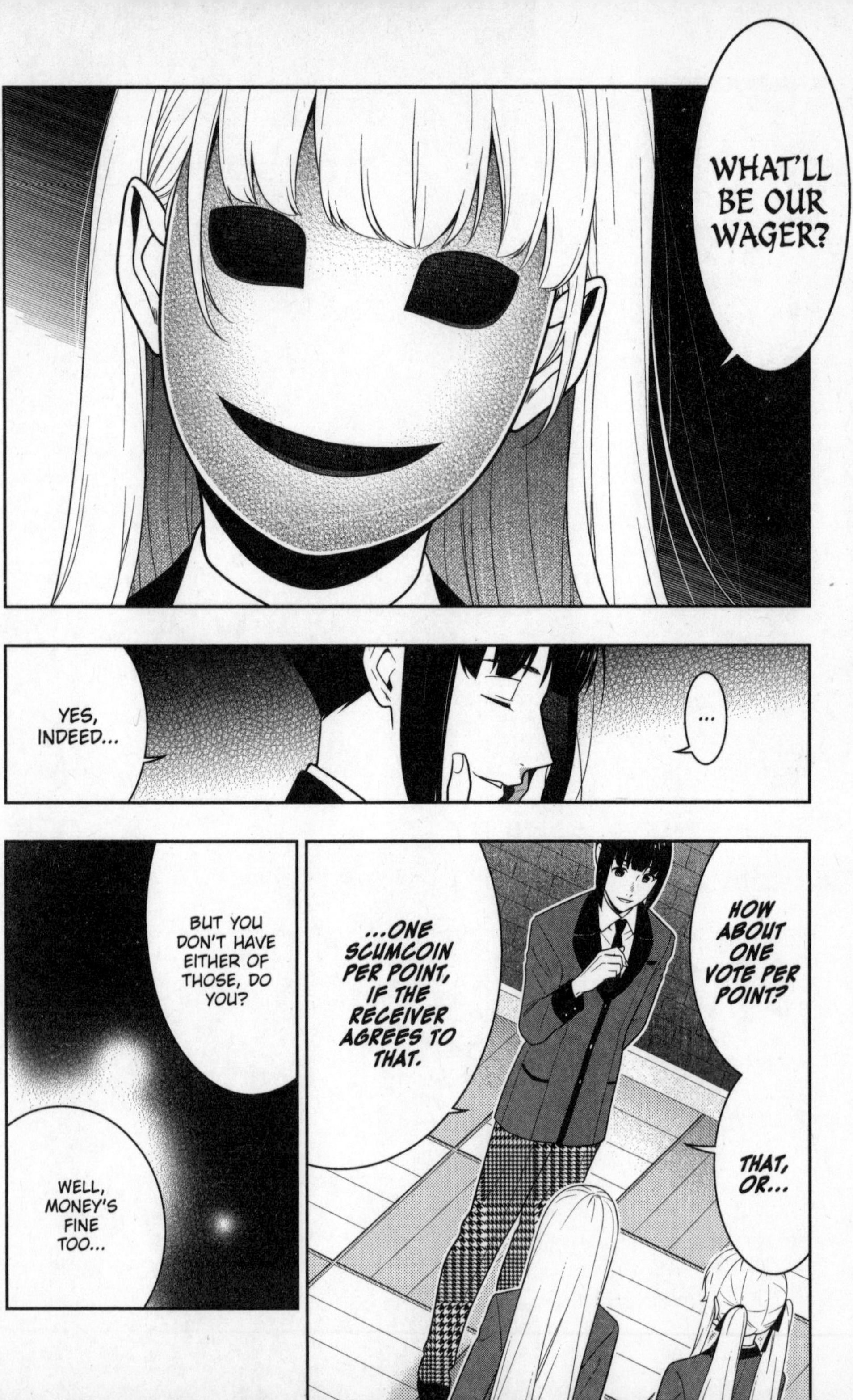
WHAT'LL BE OUR WAGER?
...
YES, INDEED...
HOW ABOUT ONE VOTE PER POINT?
THAT, OR...
...ONE SCUMCOIN PER POINT, IF THE RECEIVER AGREES TO THAT.
BUT YOU DON'T HAVE EITHER OF THOSE, DO YOU?
WELL, MONEY'S FINE TOO...

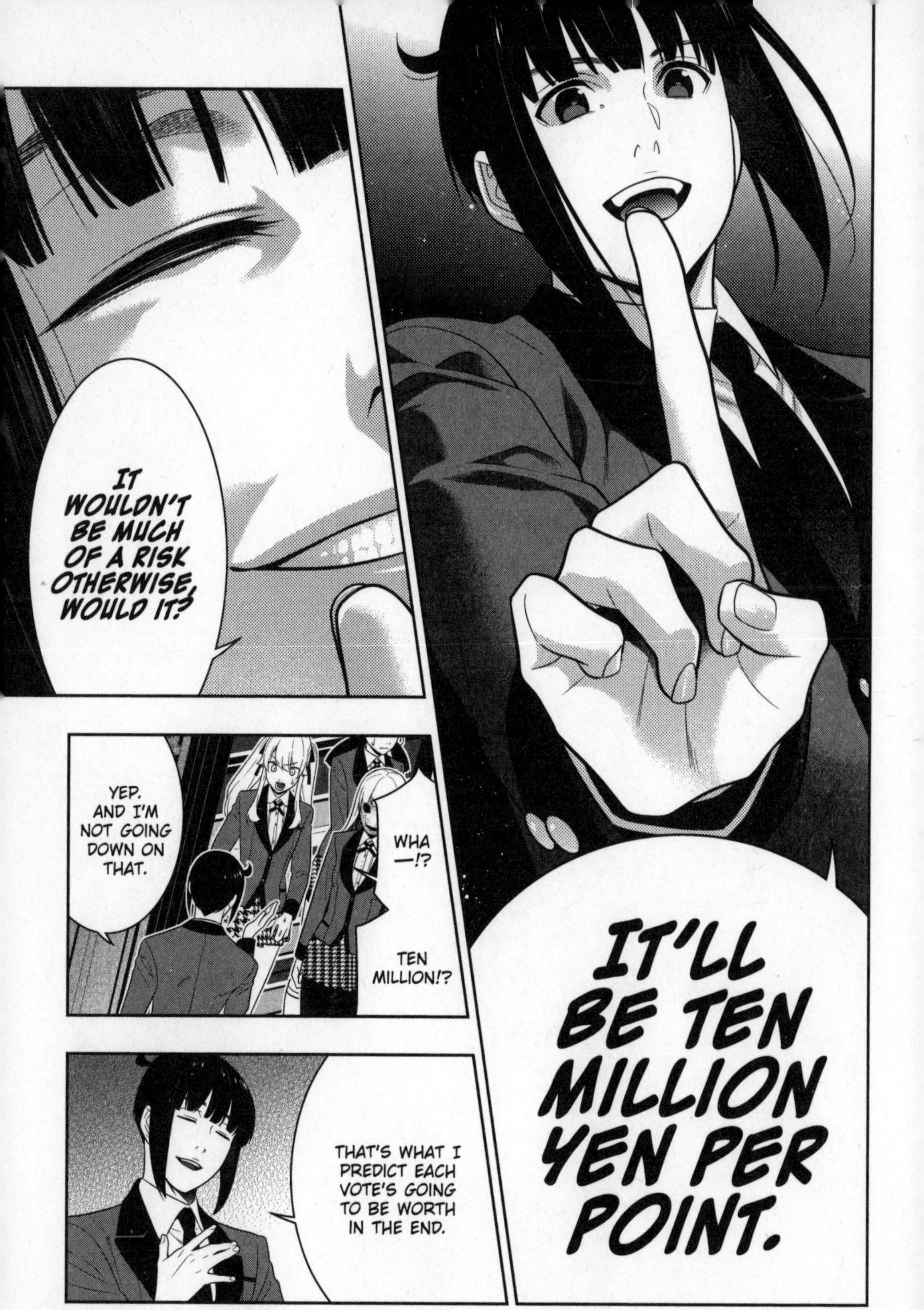
IT'LL BE TEN MILLION YEN PER POINT.
IT WOULDN'T BE MUCH OF A RISK OTHERWISE, WOULD IT?
WHA—!?
TEN MILLION!?
YEP. AND I'M NOT GOING DOWN ON THAT.
THAT'S WHAT I PREDICT EACH VOTE'S GOING TO BE WORTH IN THE END.

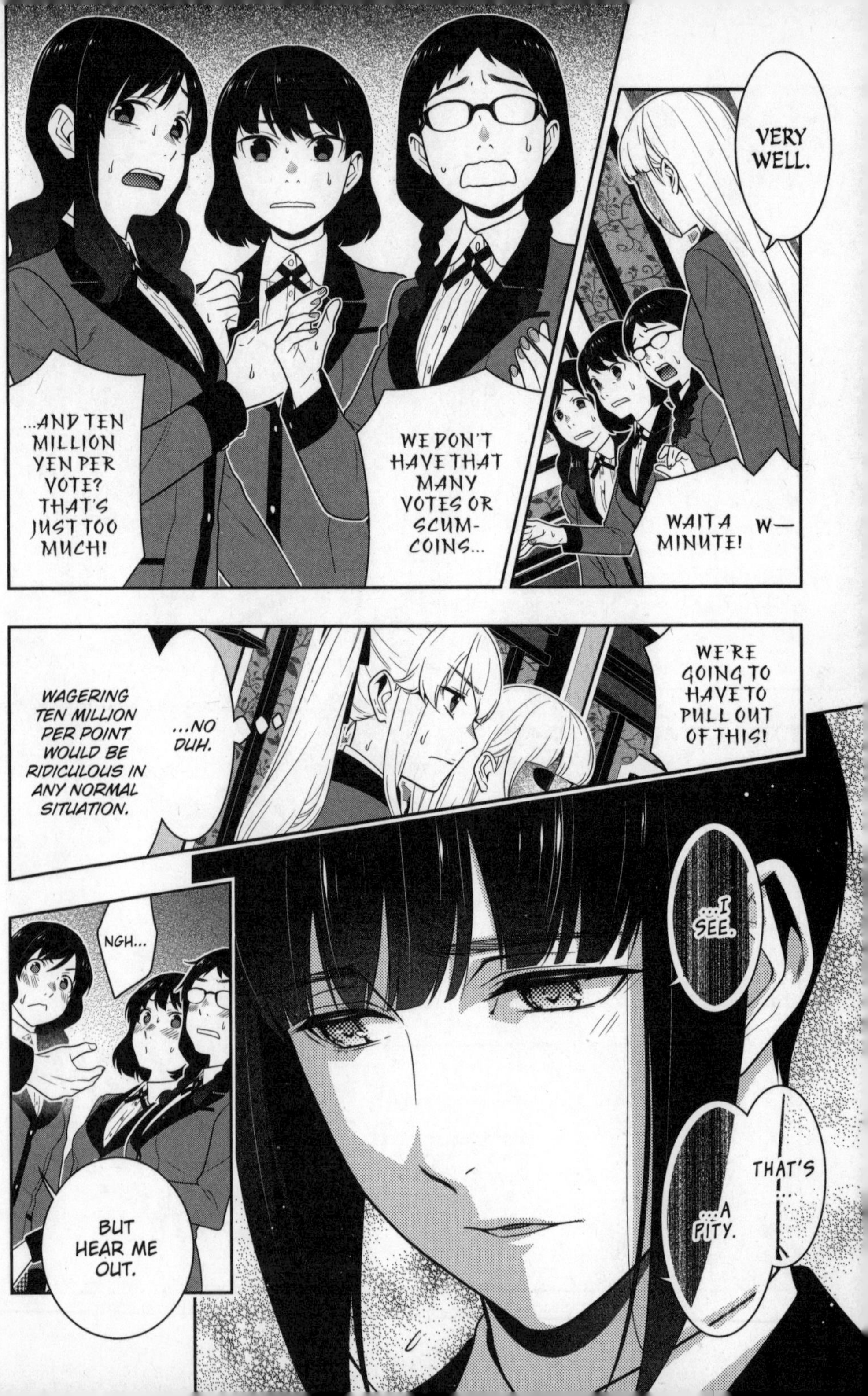
VERY WELL.
W—
WAIT A MINUTE!
WE DON'T HAVE THAT MANY VOTES OR SCUM-COINS...
...AND TEN MILLION YEN PER VOTE? THAT'S JUST TOO MUCH!
WE'RE GOING TO HAVE TO PULL OUT OF THIS!
...NO DUH.
WAGERING TEN MILLION PER POINT WOULD BE RIDICULOUS IN ANY NORMAL SITUATION.
...I SEE.
THAT'S...
...A PITY.
NGH...
BUT HEAR ME OUT.

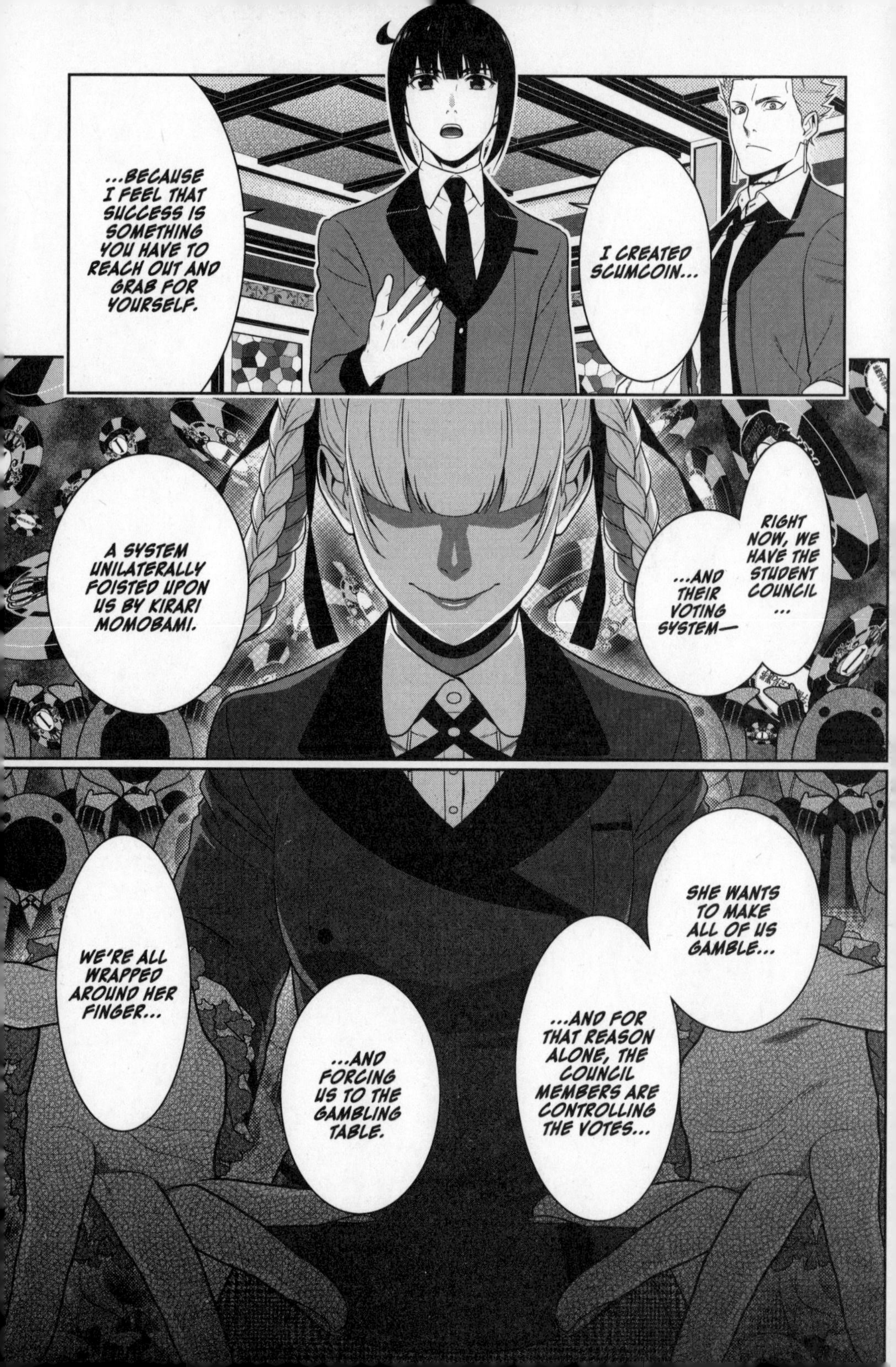
I CREATED SCUMCOIN...
...BECAUSE I FEEL THAT SUCCESS IS SOMETHING YOU HAVE TO REACH OUT AND GRAB FOR YOURSELF.
RIGHT NOW, WE HAVE THE STUDENT COUNCIL ...
...AND THEIR VOTING SYSTEM—
A SYSTEM UNILATERALLY FOISTED UPON US BY KIRARI MOMOBAMI.
SHE WANTS TO MAKE ALL OF US GAMBLE...
...AND FOR THAT REASON ALONE, THE COUNCIL MEMBERS ARE CONTROLLING THE VOTES...
WE'RE ALL WRAPPED AROUND HER FINGER...
...AND FORCING US TO THE GAMBLING TABLE.

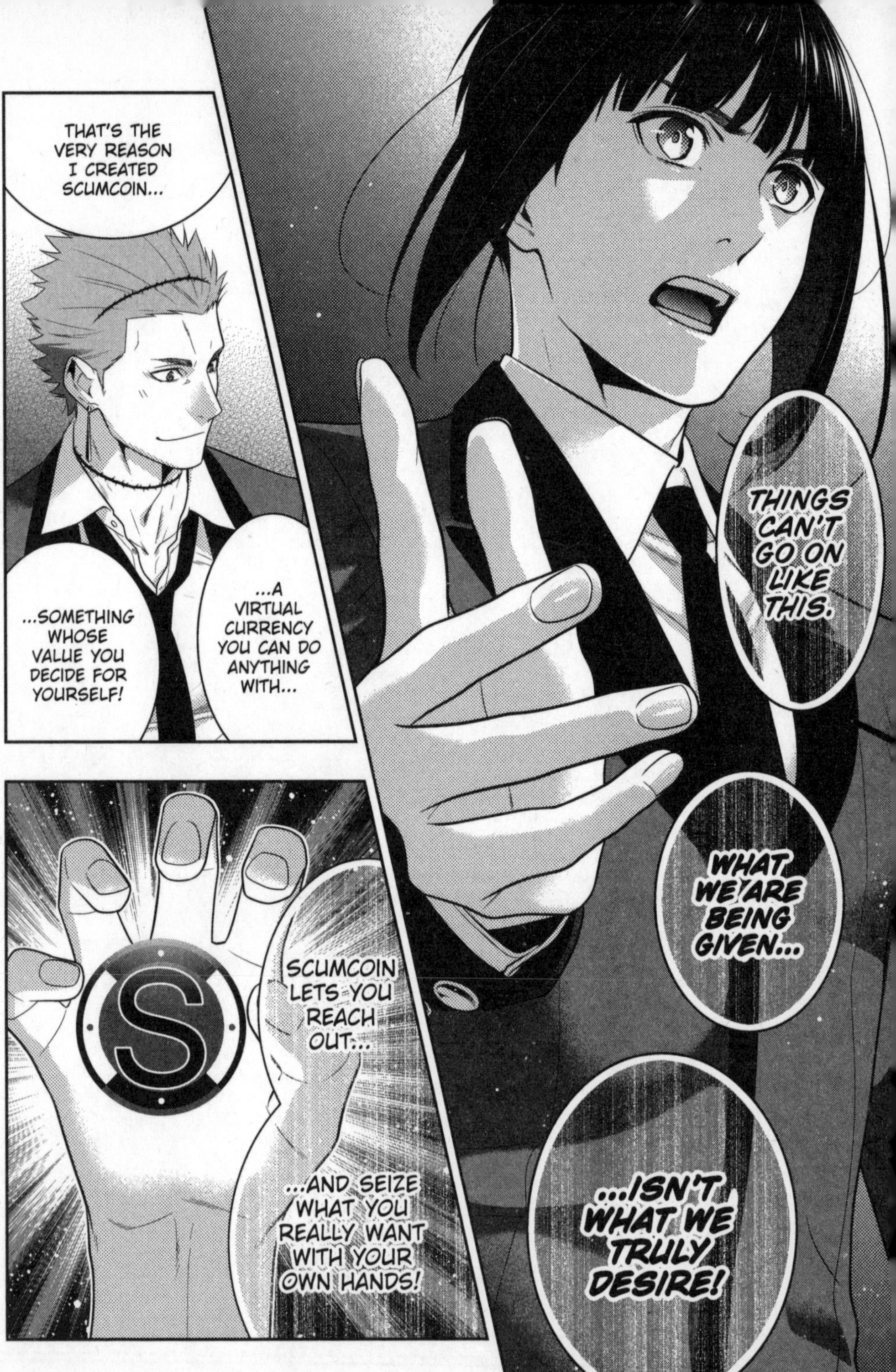
THINGS CAN'T GO ON LIKE THIS.
WHAT WE ARE BEING GIVEN...
...ISN'T WHAT WE TRULY DESIRE!
THAT'S THE VERY REASON I CREATED SCUMCOIN...
...A VIRTUAL CURRENCY YOU CAN DO ANYTHING WITH...
...SOMETHING WHOSE VALUE YOU DECIDE FOR YOURSELF!
SCUMCOIN LETS YOU REACH OUT...
...AND SEIZE WHAT YOU REALLY WANT WITH YOUR OWN HANDS!

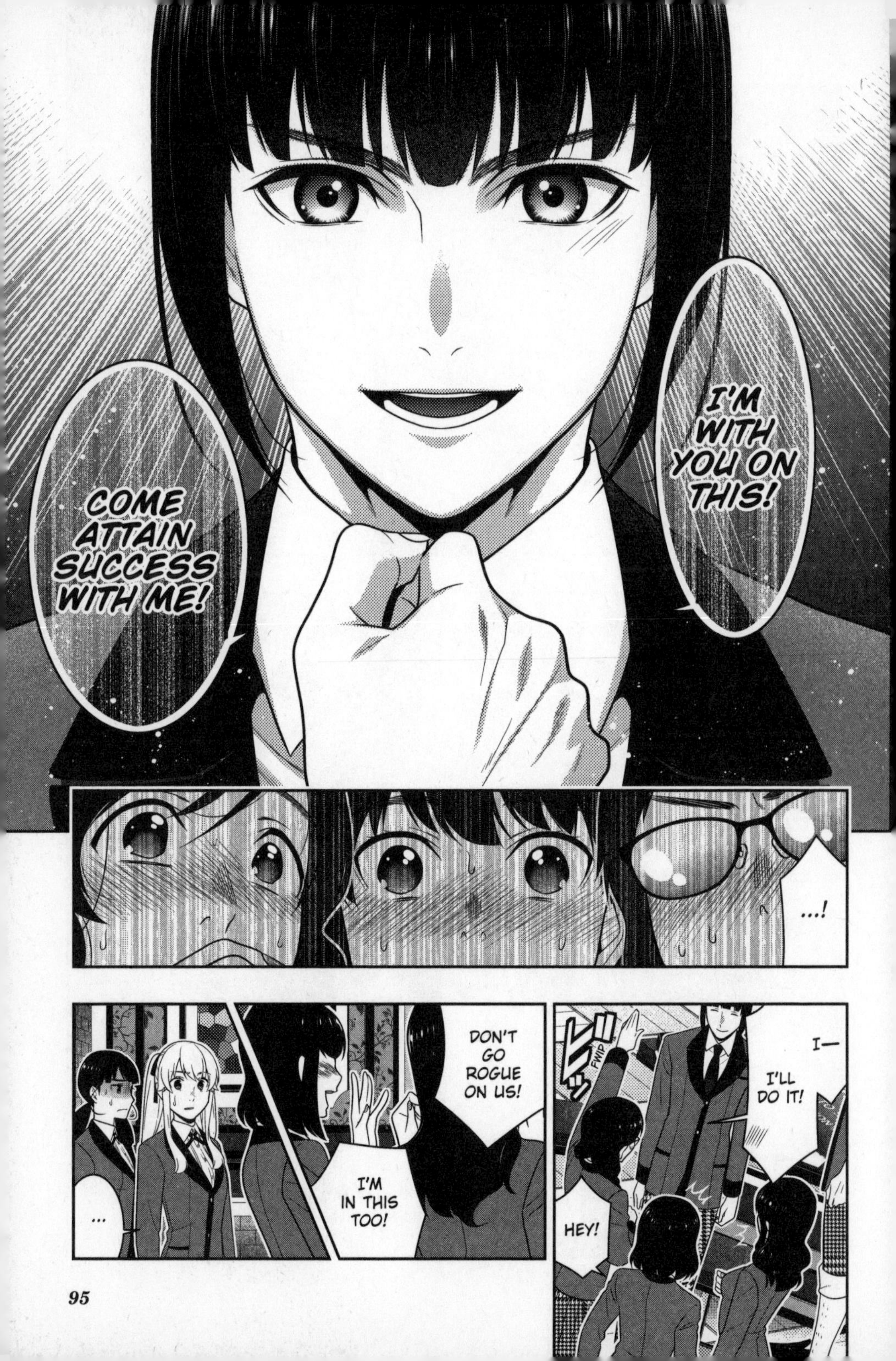
I'M WITH YOU ON THIS!
COME ATTAIN SUCCESS WITH ME!
...!
I—
I'LL DO IT!
FWIP
HEY!
DON'T GO ROGUE ON US!
I'M IN THIS TOO!
...

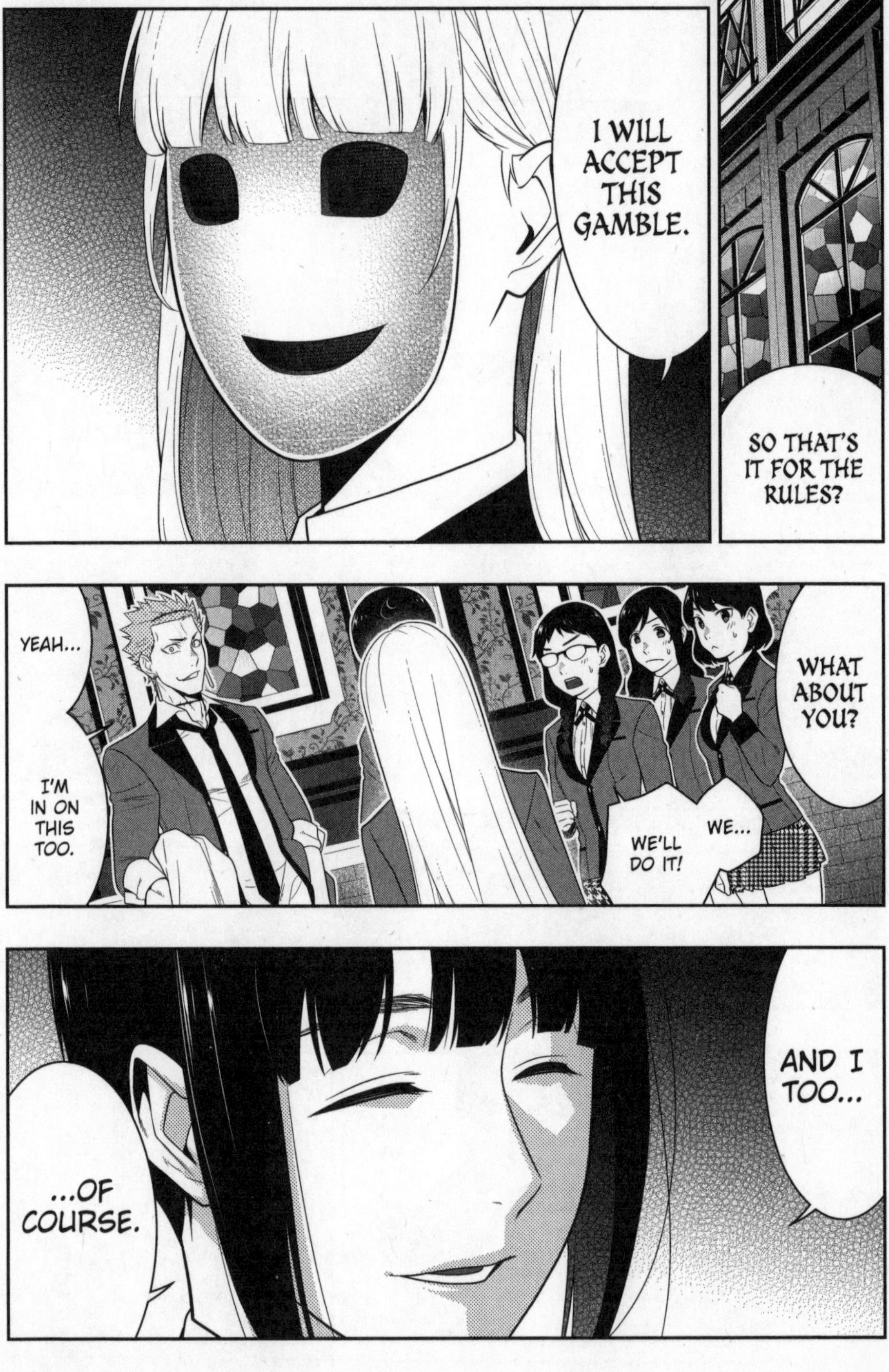
SO THAT'S IT FOR THE RULES?
I WILL ACCEPT THIS GAMBLE.
WHAT ABOUT YOU?
WE...
WE'LL DO IT!
YEAH...
I'M IN ON THIS TOO.
AND I TOO...
...OF COURSE.

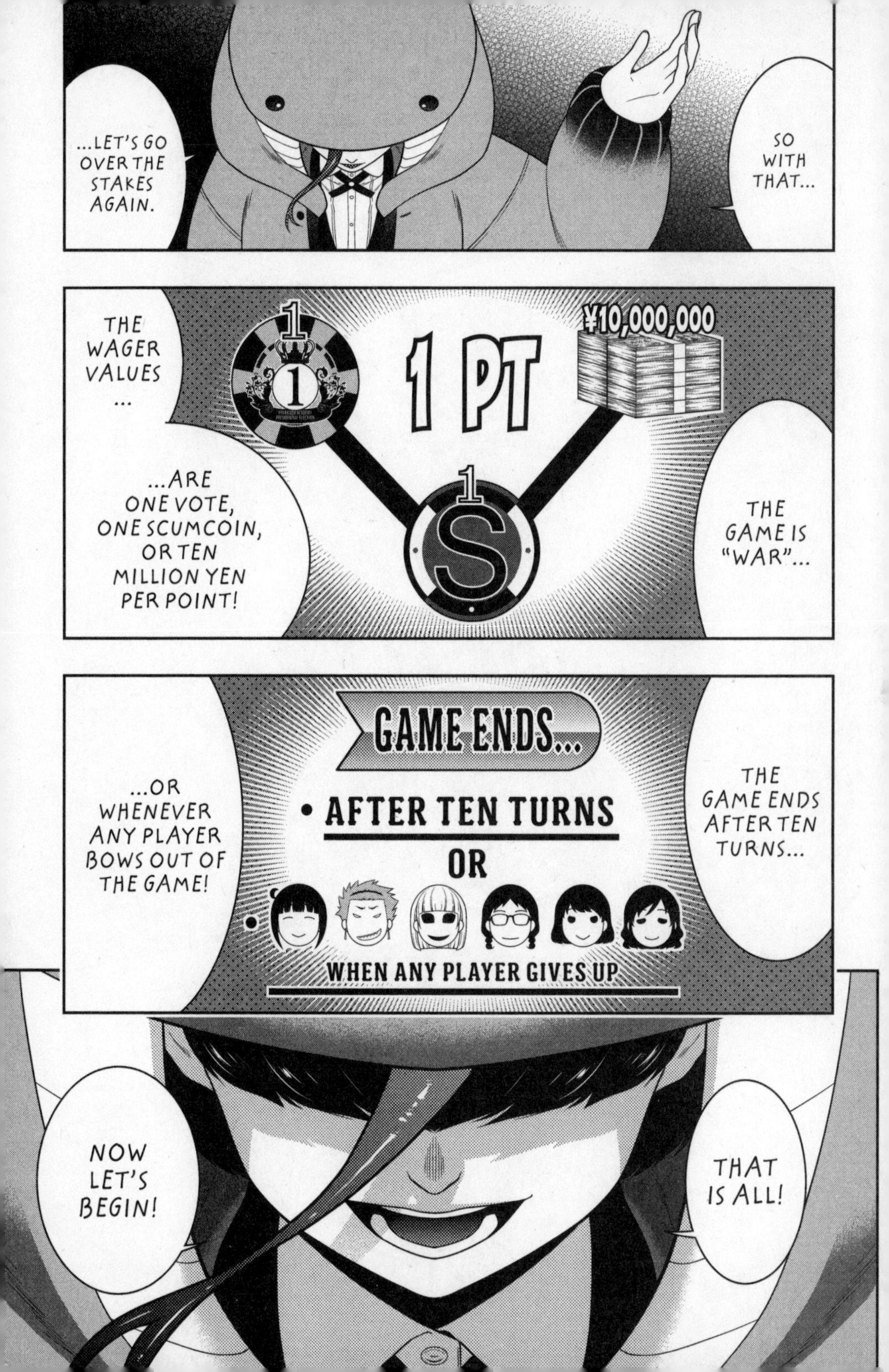
SO WITH THAT...
...LET'S GO OVER THE STAKES AGAIN.
THE GAME IS "WAR"...
THE WAGER VALUES ...
1 PT
¥10,000,000
...ARE ONE VOTE, ONE SCUMCOIN, OR TEN MILLION YEN PER POINT!
THE GAME ENDS AFTER TEN TURNS...
GAME ENDS...
• AFTER TEN TURNS
OR
• WHEN ANY PLAYER GIVES UP
...OR WHENEVER ANY PLAYER BOWS OUT OF THE GAME!
THAT IS ALL!
NOW LET'S BEGIN!

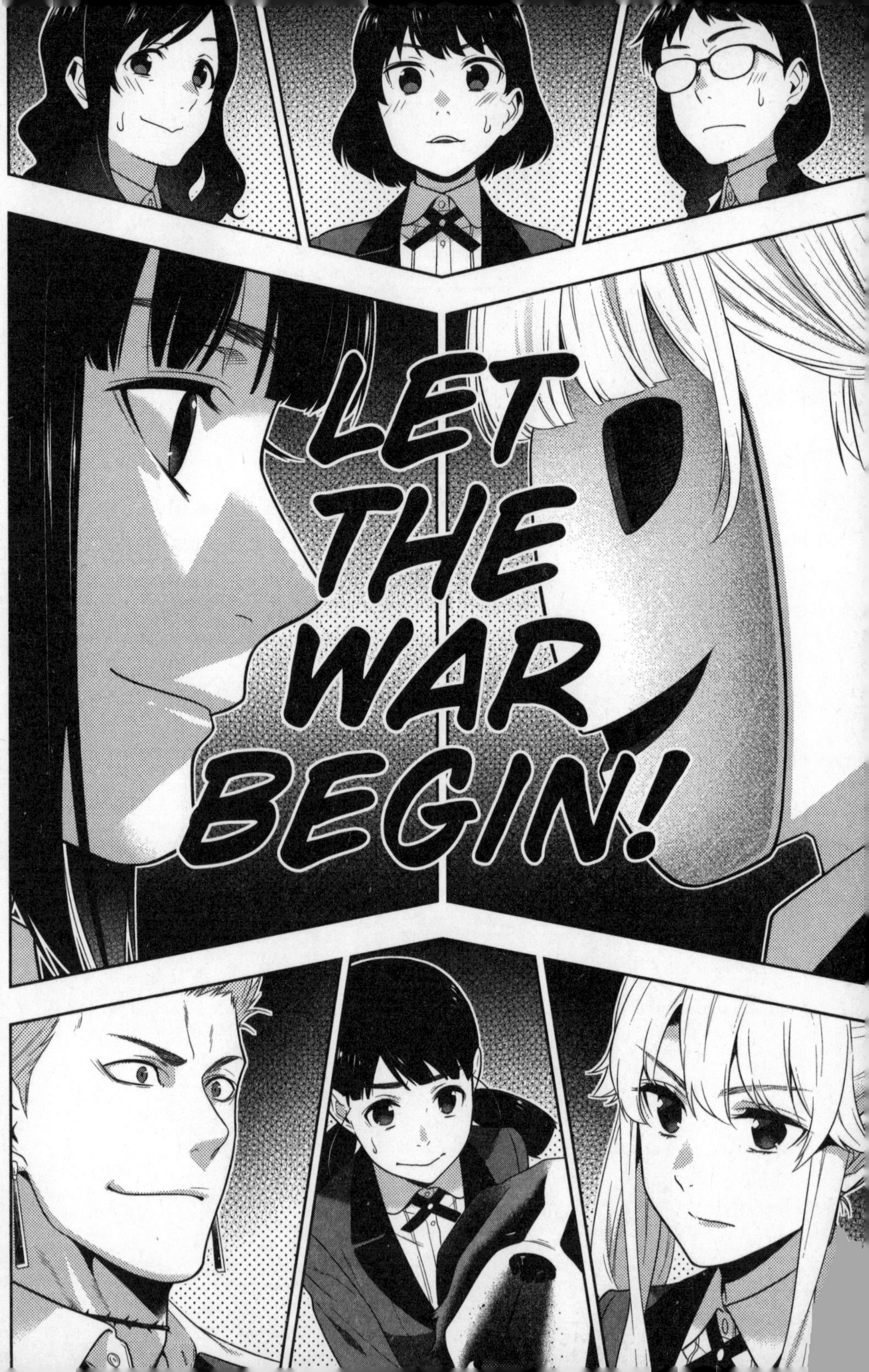
LET THE WAR BEGIN!

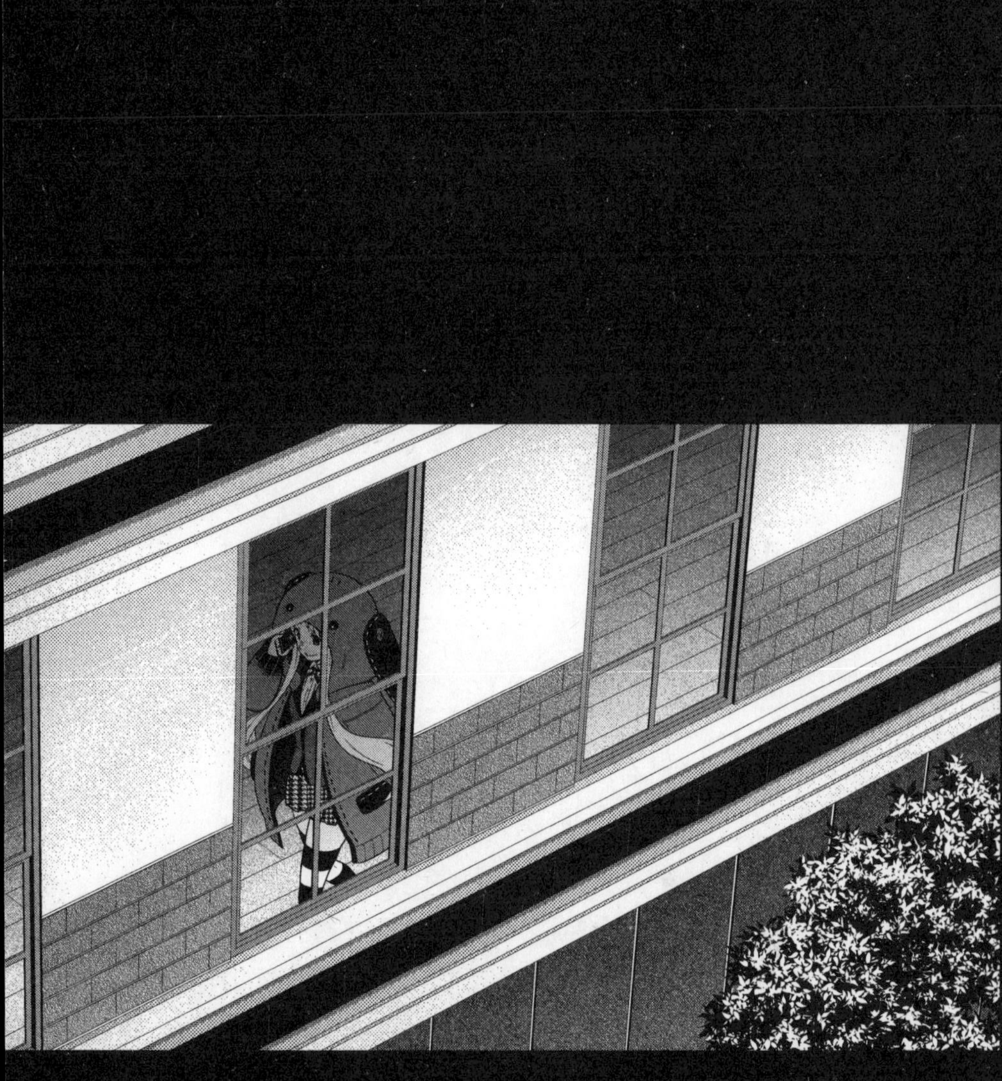

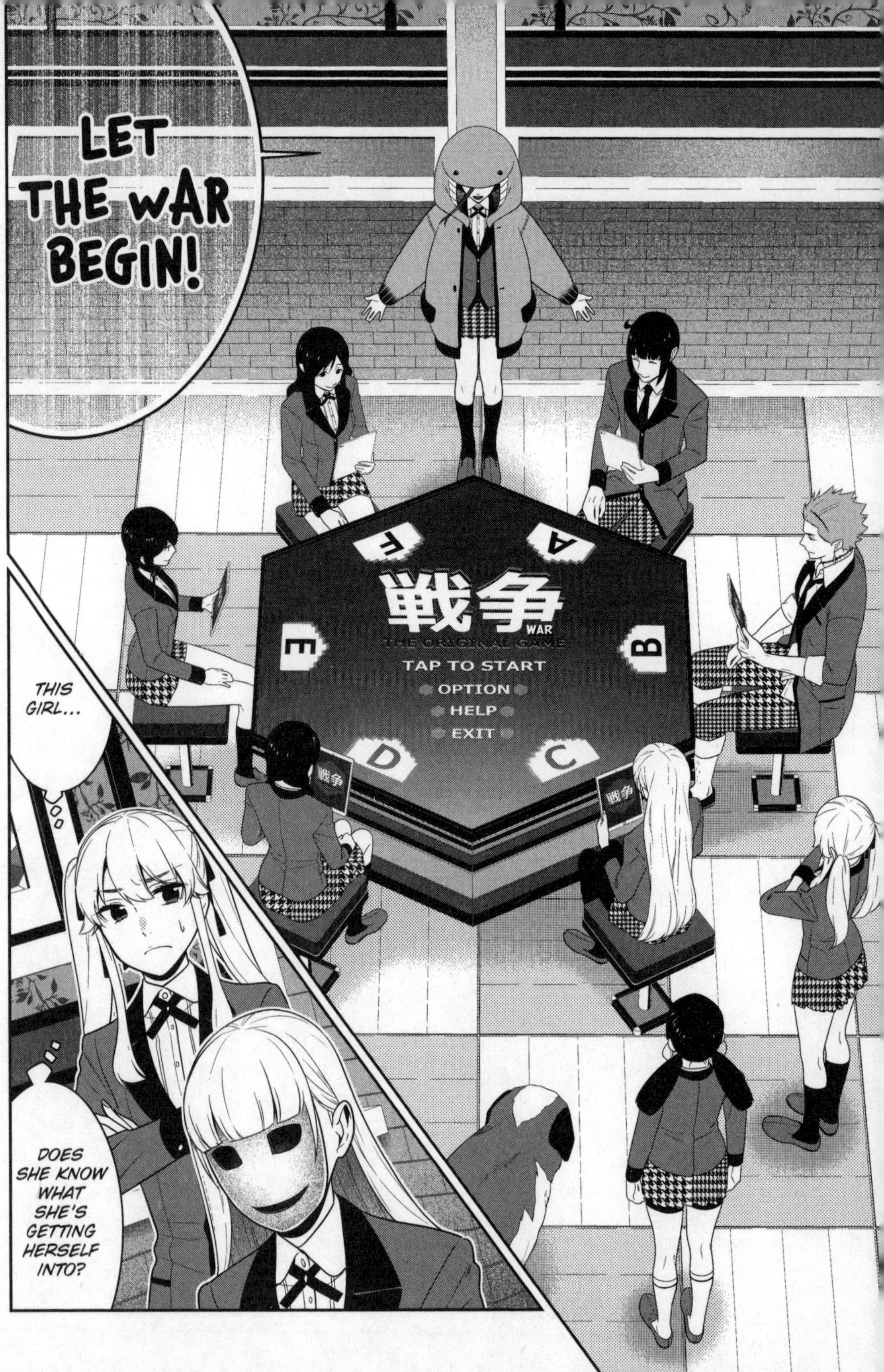
LET THE wAR BEGIN!
戦争
WAR
THE ORIGINAL GAME
TAP TO START
OPTION
HELP
EXIT
A
B
C
D
E
F
戦争
戦争
THIS GIRL...
DOES SHE KNOW WHAT SHE'S GETTING HERSELF INTO?

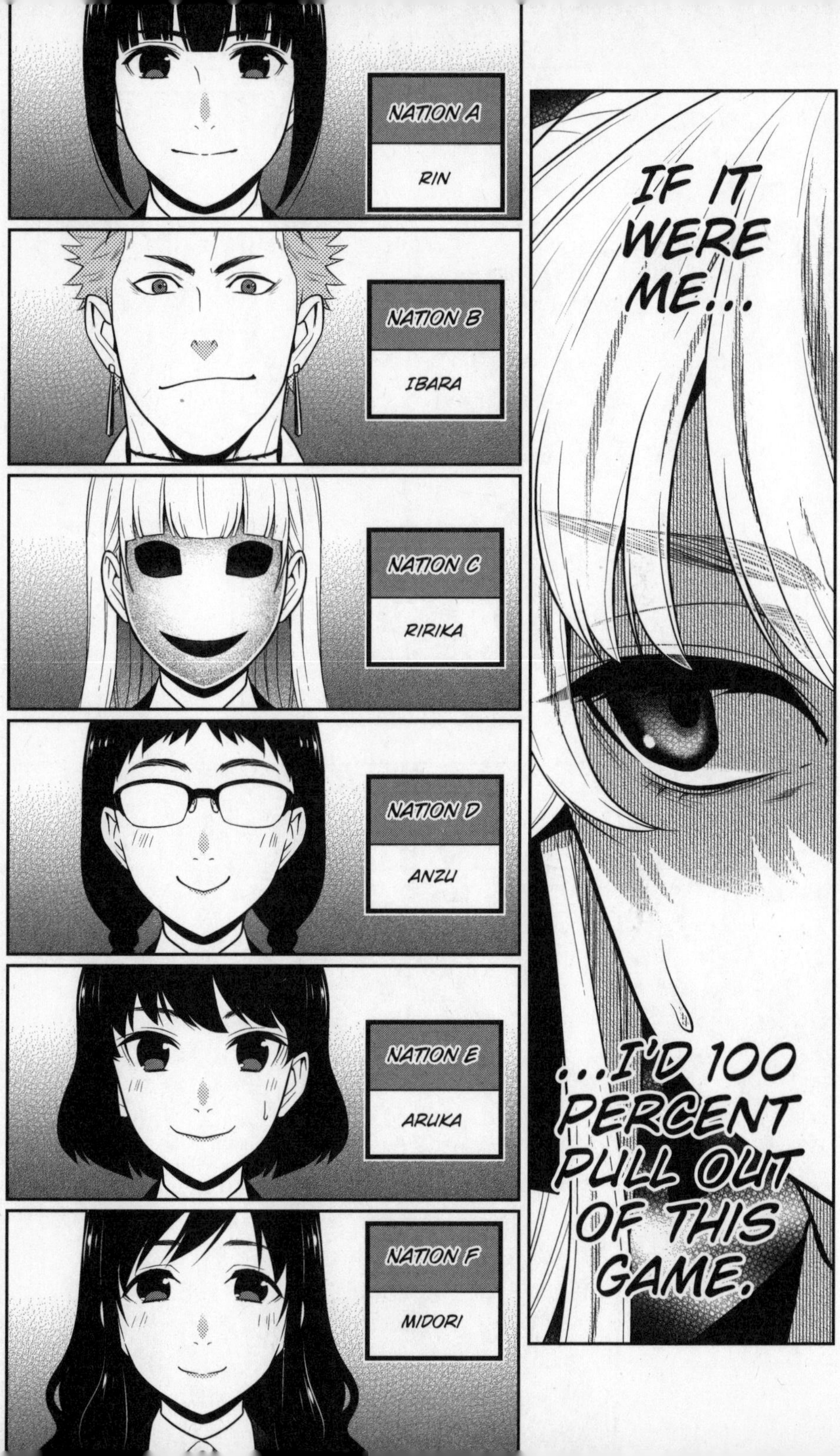

IF IT WERE ME...
...I'D 100 PERCENT PULL OUT OF THIS GAME.
NATION A
RIN
NATION B
IBARA
NATION C
RIRIKA
NATION D
ANZU
NATION E
ARUKA
NATION F
MIDORI

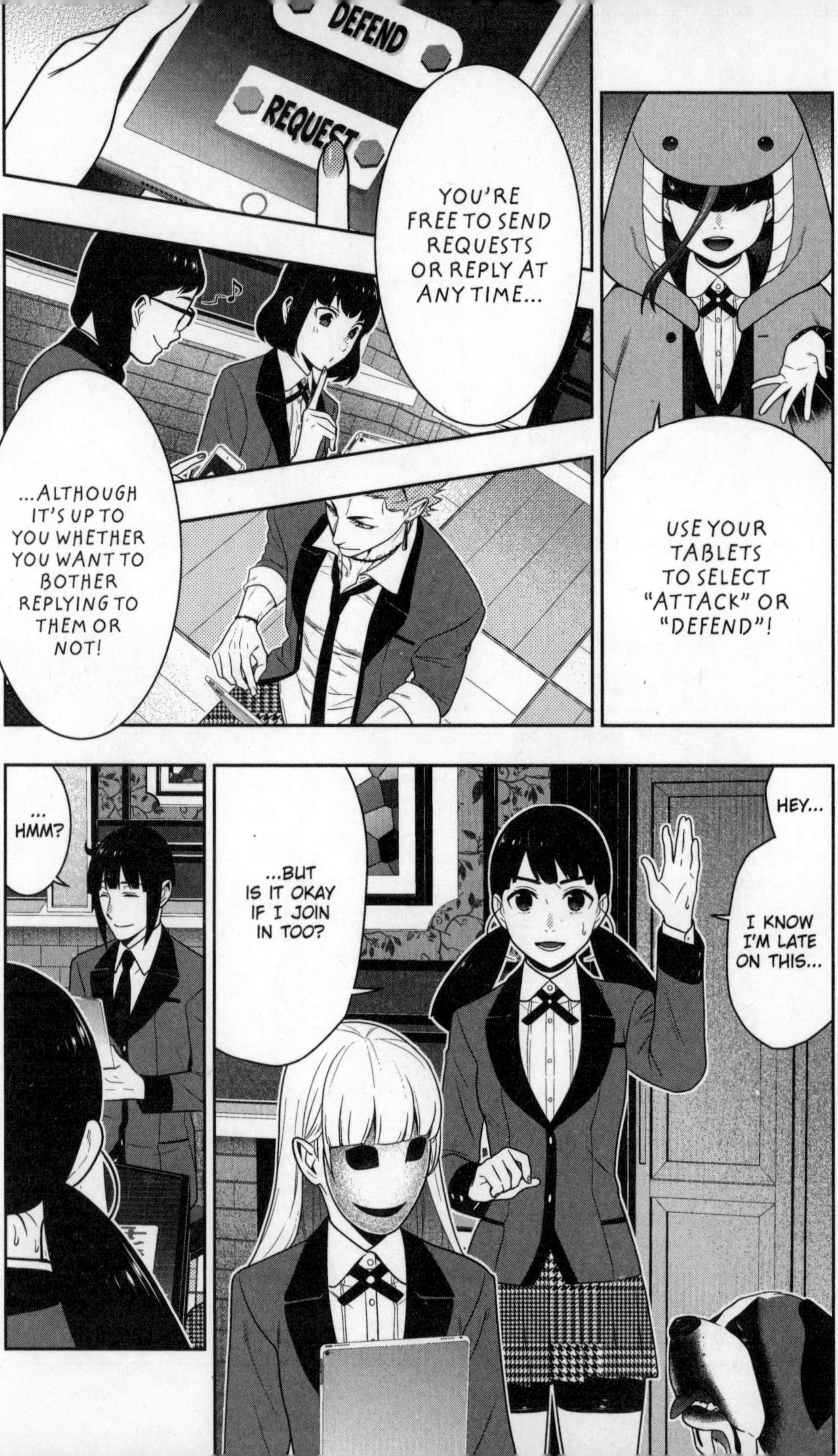

USE YOUR TABLETS TO SELECT "ATTACK" OR "DEFEND"!
DEFEND
REQUEST
YOU'RE FREE TO SEND REQUESTS OR REPLY AT ANY TIME...
...ALTHOUGH IT'S UP TO YOU WHETHER YOU WANT TO BOTHER REPLYING TO THEM OR NOT!
HEY...
I KNOW I'M LATE ON THIS...
...BUT IS IT OKAY IF I JOIN IN TOO?
... HMM?

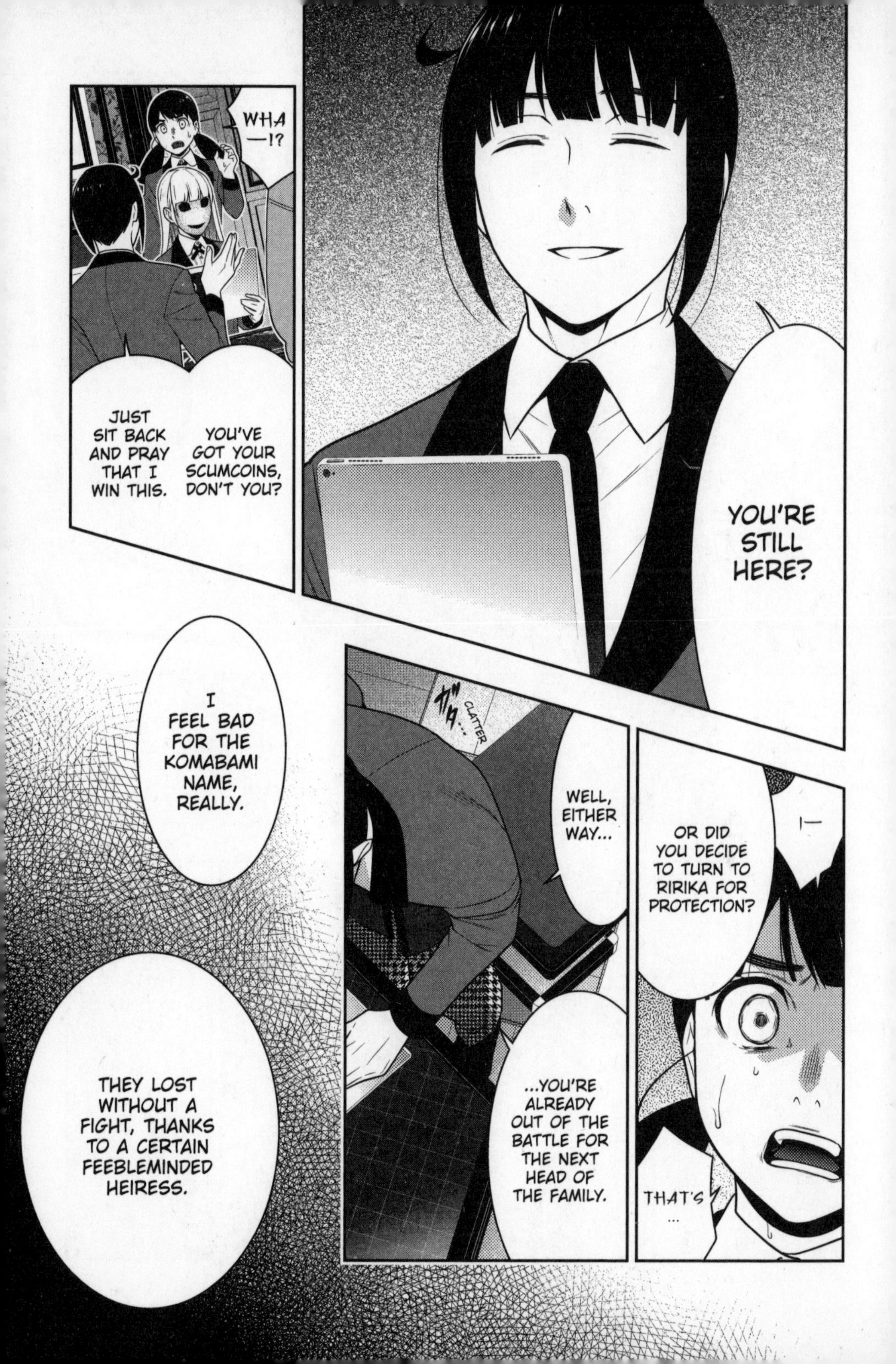
YOU'RE STILL HERE?
WHA—!?
YOU'VE GOT YOUR SCUMCOINS, DON'T YOU?
JUST SIT BACK AND PRAY THAT I WIN THIS.
OR DID YOU DECIDE TO TURN TO RIRIKA FOR PROTECTION?
!—
THAT'S ...
CLATTER
WELL, EITHER WAY...
...YOU'RE ALREADY OUT OF THE BATTLE FOR THE NEXT HEAD OF THE FAMILY.
I FEEL BAD FOR THE KOMABAMI NAME, REALLY.
THEY LOST WITHOUT A FIGHT, THANKS TO A CERTAIN FEEBLEMINDED HEIRESS.

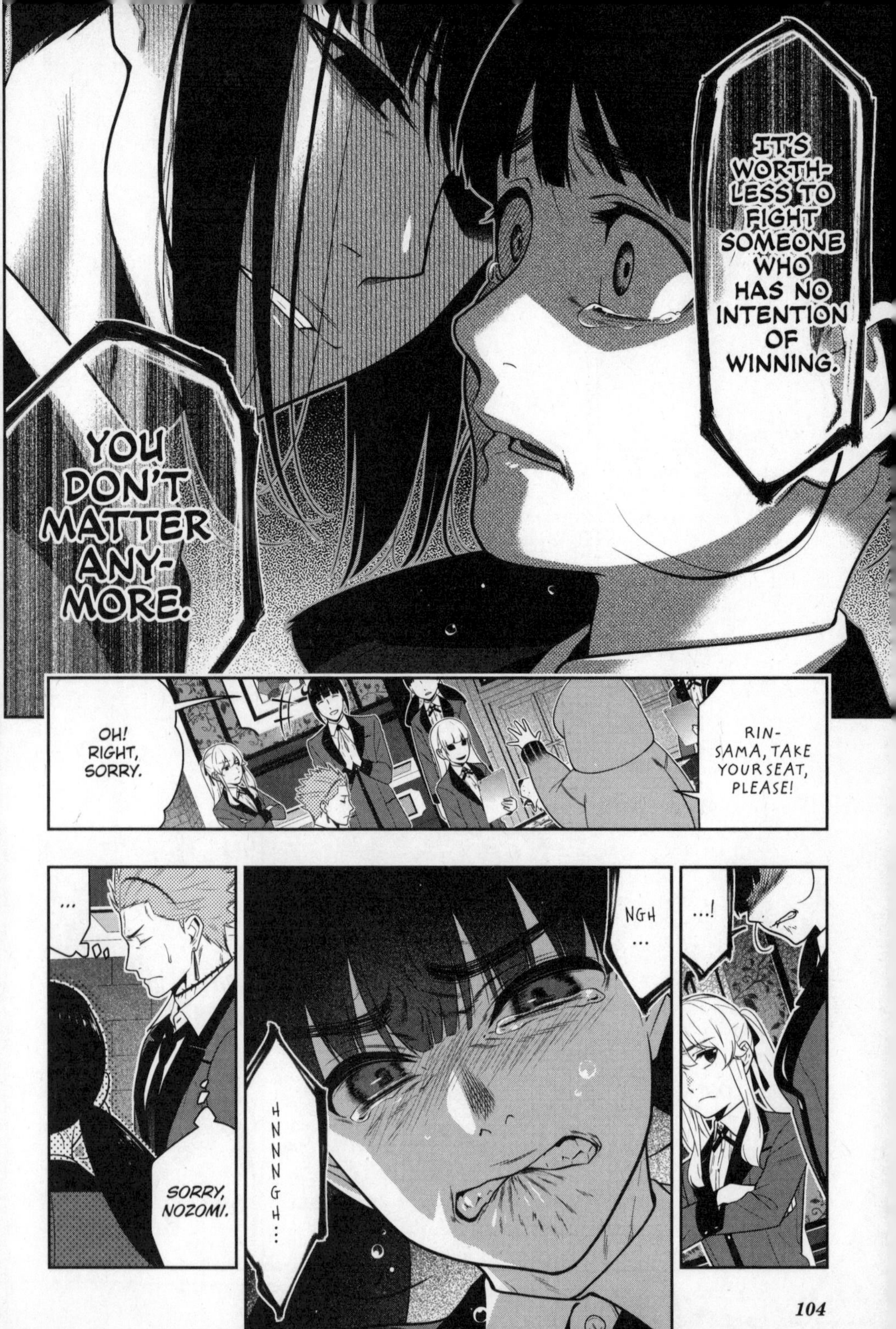
IT'S WORTHLESS TO FIGHT SOMEONE WHO HAS NO INTENTION OF WINNING.
YOU DON'T MATTER ANYMORE.
RIN-SAMA, TAKE YOUR SEAT, PLEASE!
OH! RIGHT, SORRY.
...!
NGH ...
HNNNGH...
...
SORRY, NOZOMI.

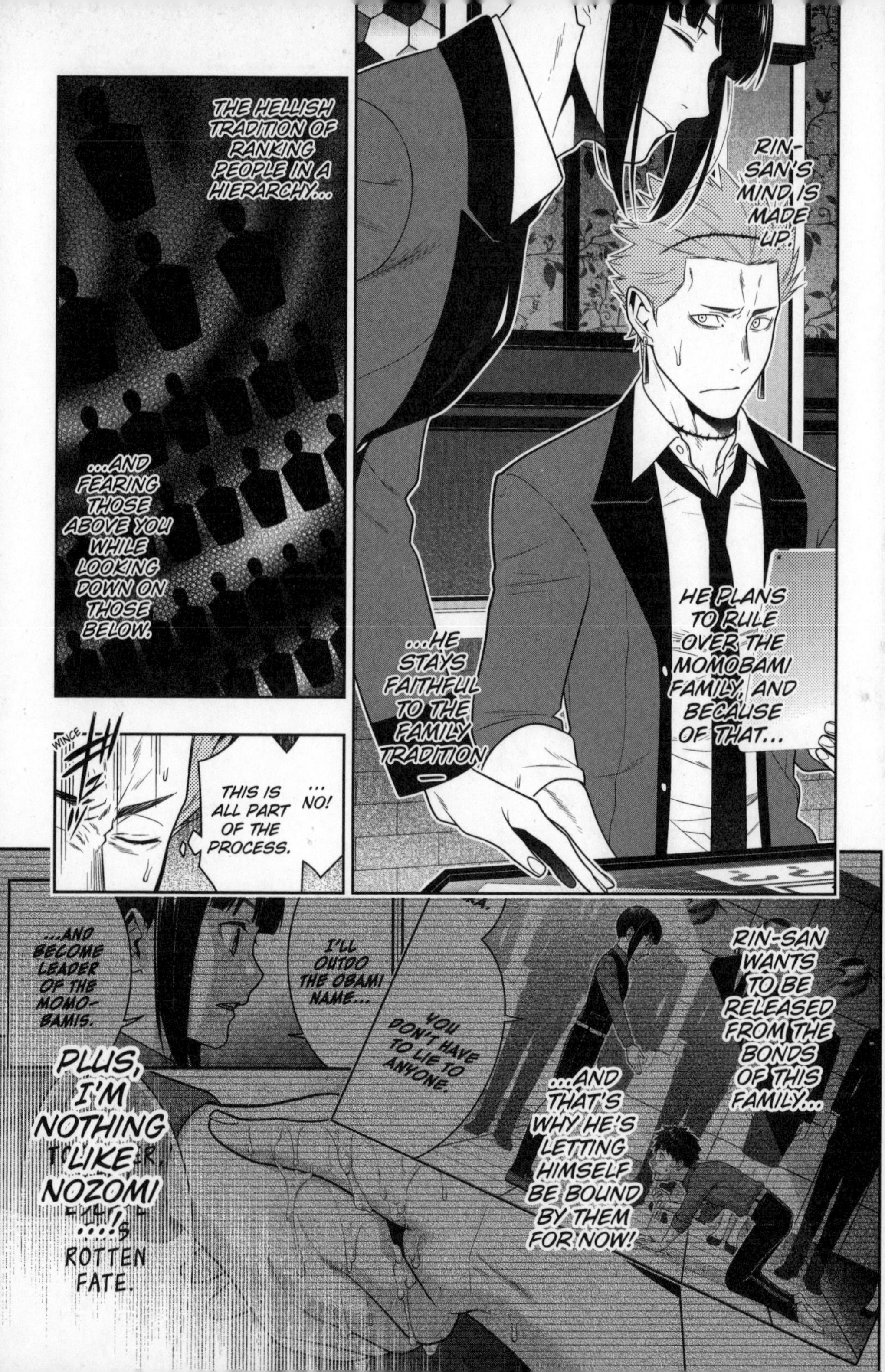
RIN-SAN'S MIND IS MADE UP.
HE PLANS TO RULE OVER THE MOMOBAMI FAMILY, AND BECAUSE OF THAT...
...HE STAYS FAITHFUL TO THE FAMILY TRADITION—
THE HELLISH TRADITION OF RANKING PEOPLE IN A HIERARCHY...
...AND FEARING THOSE ABOVE YOU WHILE LOOKING DOWN ON THOSE BELOW.
WINCE
...NO!
THIS IS ALL PART OF THE PROCESS.
RIN-SAN WANTS TO BE RELEASED FROM THE BONDS OF THIS FAMILY...
...AND THAT'S WHY HE'S LETTING HIMSELF BE BOUND BY THEM FOR NOW!
YOU DON'T HAVE TO LIE TO ANYONE.
I'LL OUTDO THE OBAMI NAME...
...AND BECOME LEADER OF THE MOMO-BAMIS.
PLUS, I'M NOTHING LIKE NOZOMI
ROTTEN FATE.

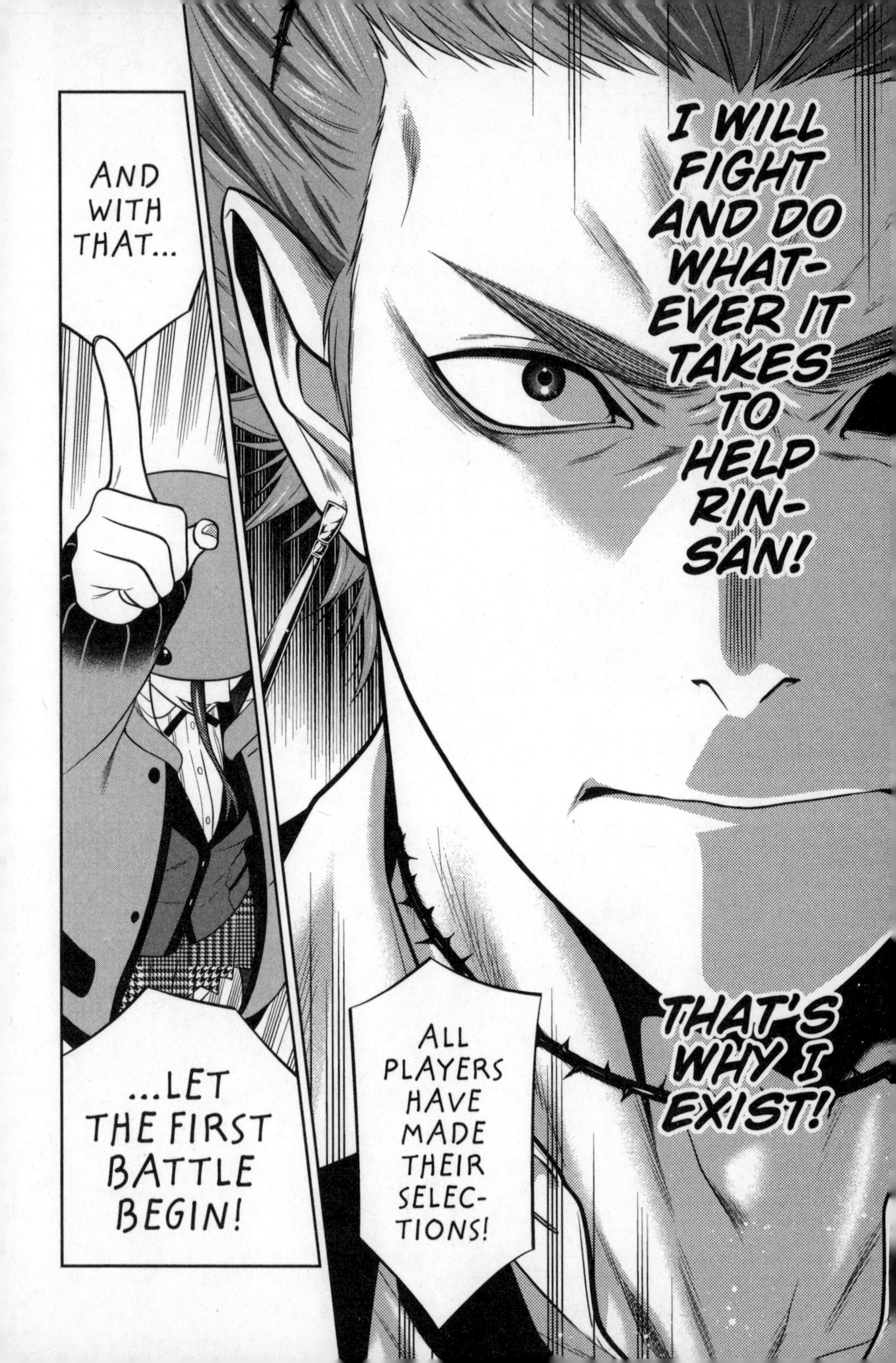
I WILL FIGHT AND DO WHAT-EVER IT TAKES TO HELP RIN-SAN!
THAT'S WHY I EXIST!
ALL PLAYERS HAVE MADE THEIR SELEC-TIONS!
AND WITH THAT...
...LET THE FIRST BATTLE BEGIN!

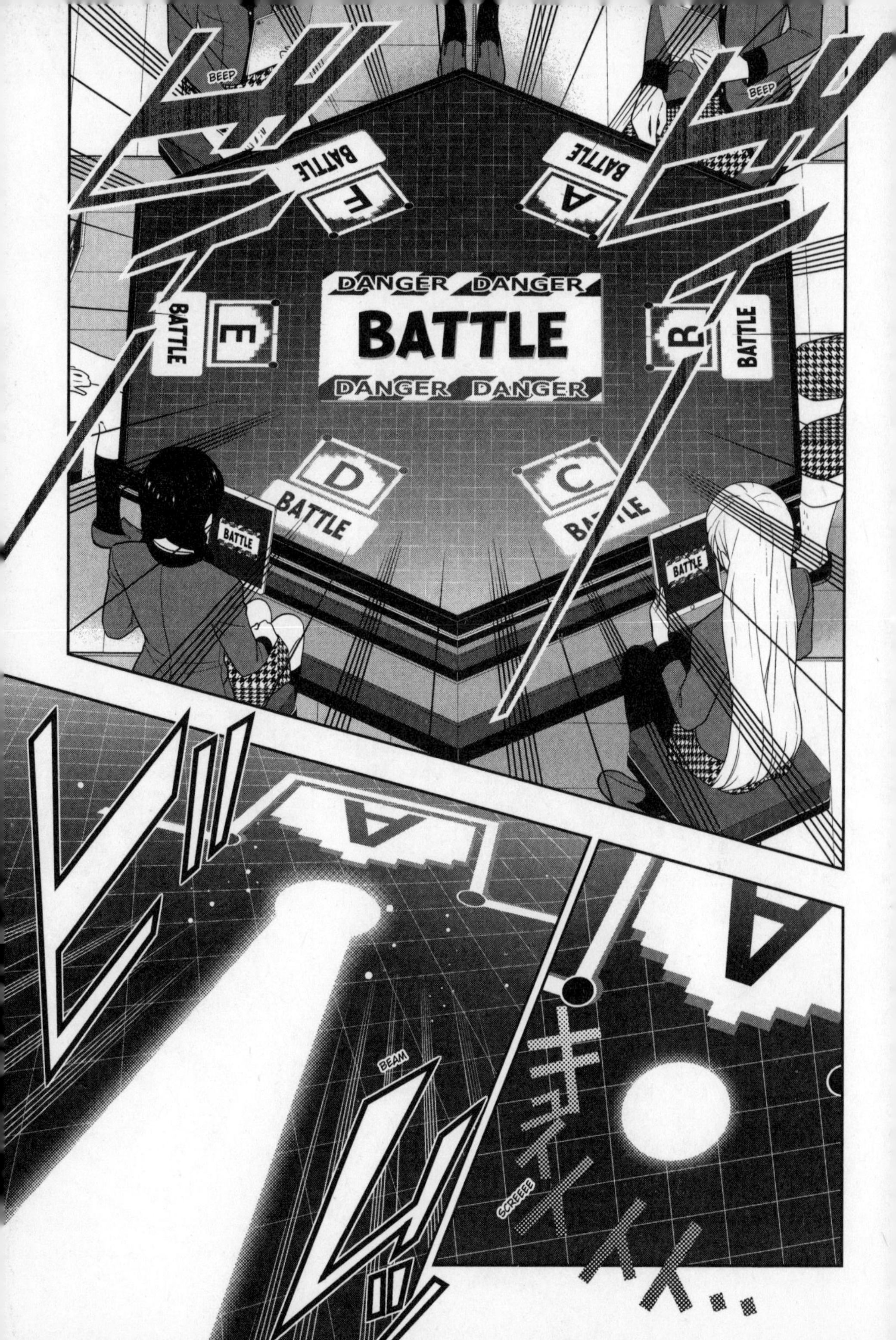
BEEP
BEEP
BATTLE
BATTLE
DANGER DANGER
BATTLE
DANGER DANGER
BATTLE
BATTLE
BATTLE
BATTLE
BATTLE
BATTLE
SCREEEE
BEAM

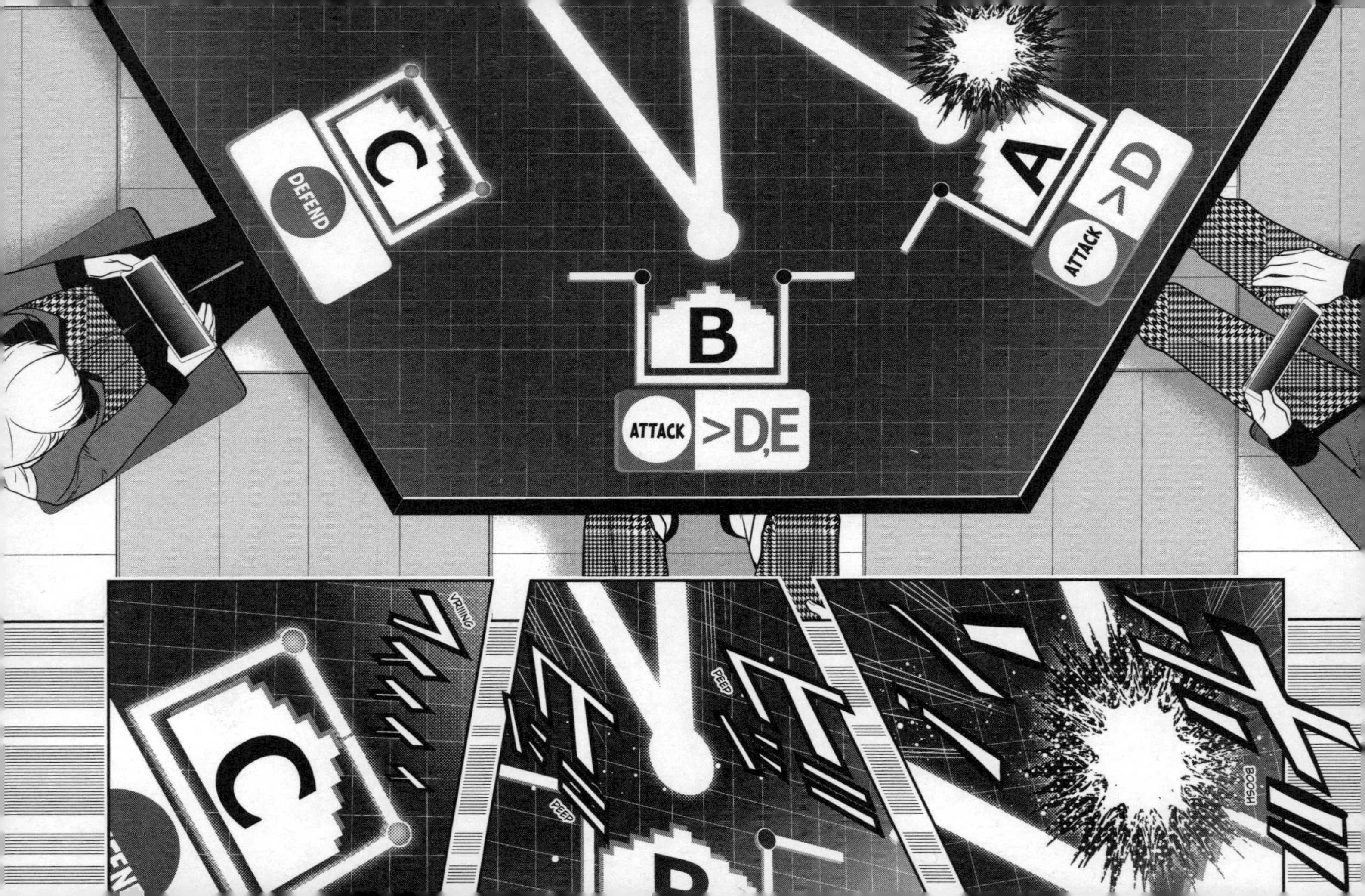

ATTACK
>D
A
B
ATTACK
>D,E
C
DEFEND
BOOSH
PEEP
PEEP
VRIING
C

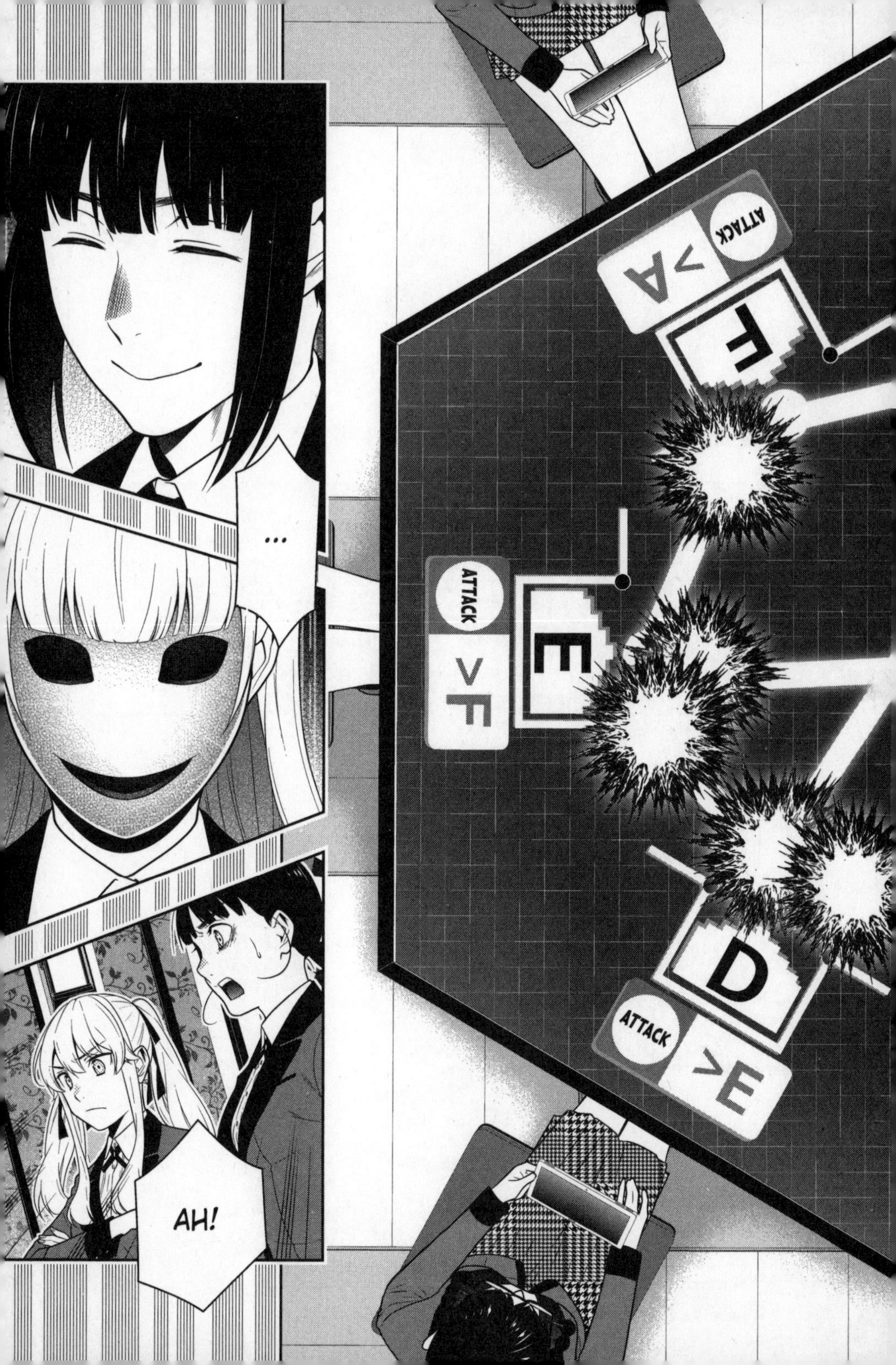
ATTACK
>A
F
E
ATTACK
>F
D
ATTACK
>E
...
AH!

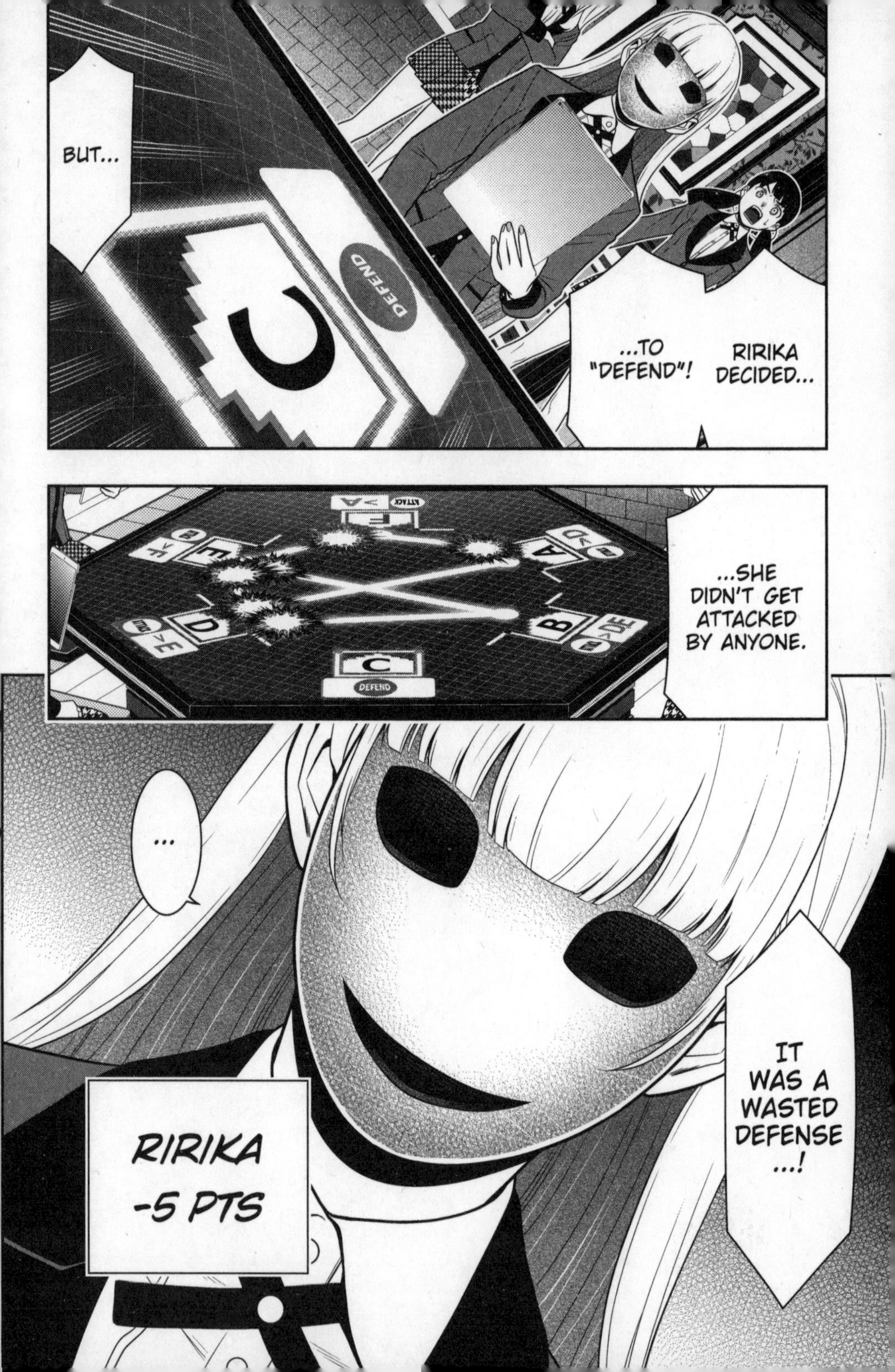
RIRIKA DECIDED...
...TO "DEFEND"!
BUT...
DEFEND
...SHE DIDN'T GET ATTACKED BY ANYONE.
IT WAS A WASTED DEFENSE ...!
...
RIRIKA -5 PTS

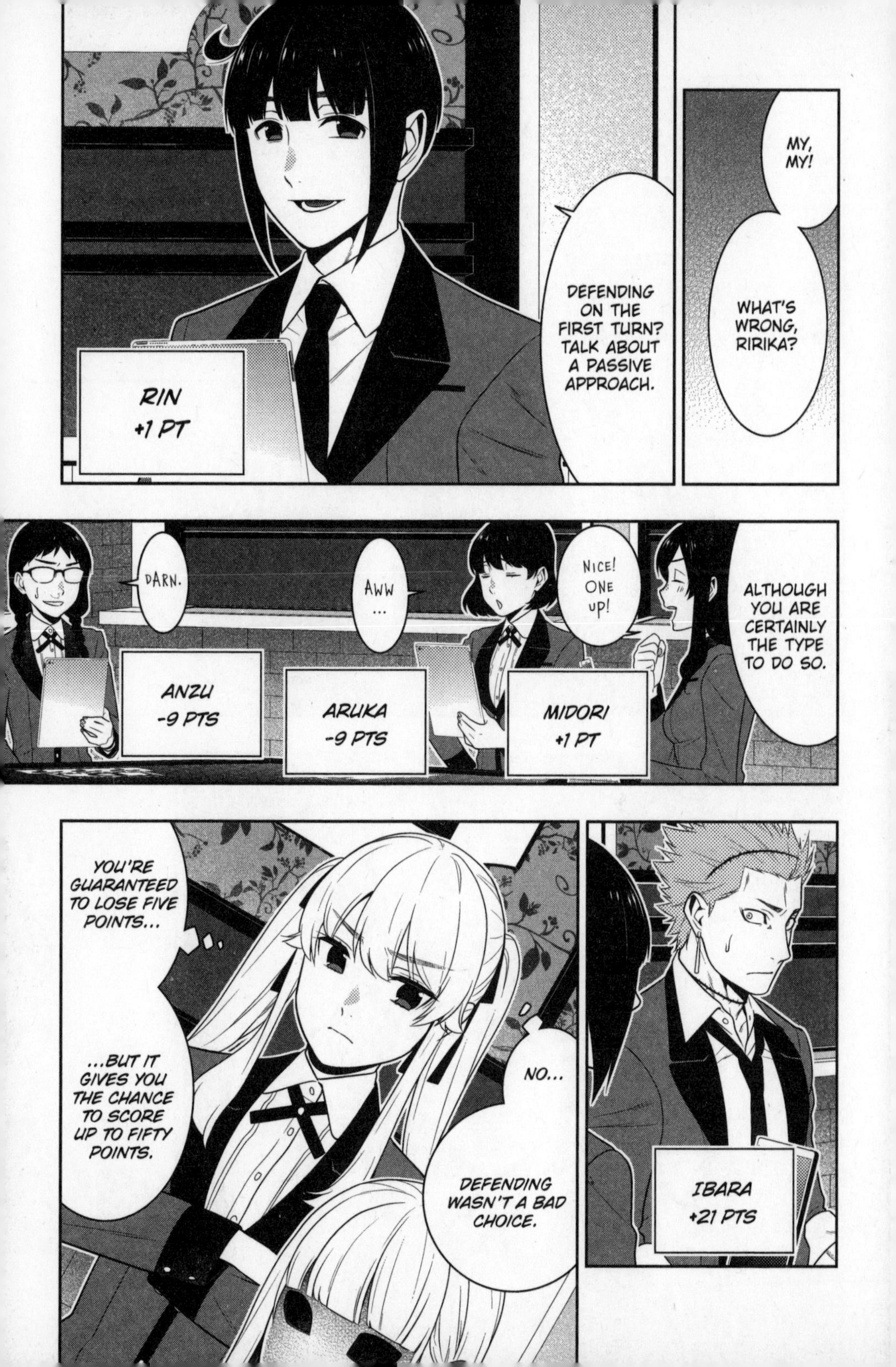
MY, MY!
WHAT'S WRONG, RIRIKA?
DEFENDING ON THE FIRST TURN? TALK ABOUT A PASSIVE APPROACH.
RIN +1 PT
ALTHOUGH YOU ARE CERTAINLY THE TYPE TO DO SO.
NICE! ONE UP!
MIDORI +1 PT
AWW...
ARUKA -9 PTS
DARN.
ANZU -9 PTS
IBARA +21 PTS
NO...
DEFENDING WASN'T A BAD CHOICE.
YOU'RE GUARANTEED TO LOSE FIVE POINTS...
...BUT IT GIVES YOU THE CHANCE TO SCORE UP TO FIFTY POINTS.

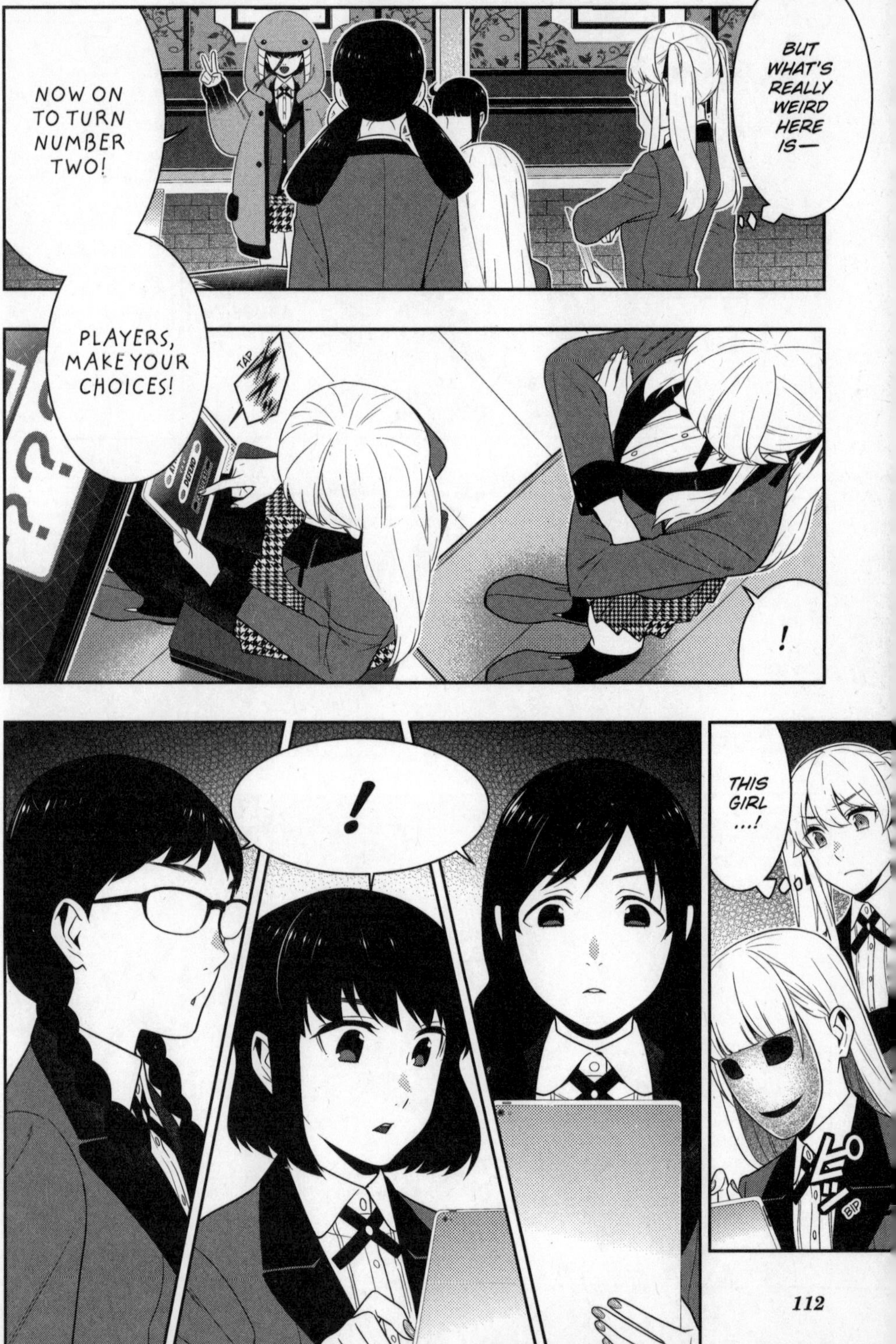
BUT WHAT'S REALLY WEIRD HERE IS—
NOW ON TO TURN NUMBER TWO!
PLAYERS, MAKE YOUR CHOICES!
TAP
!
THIS GIRL ...!
BIP
!

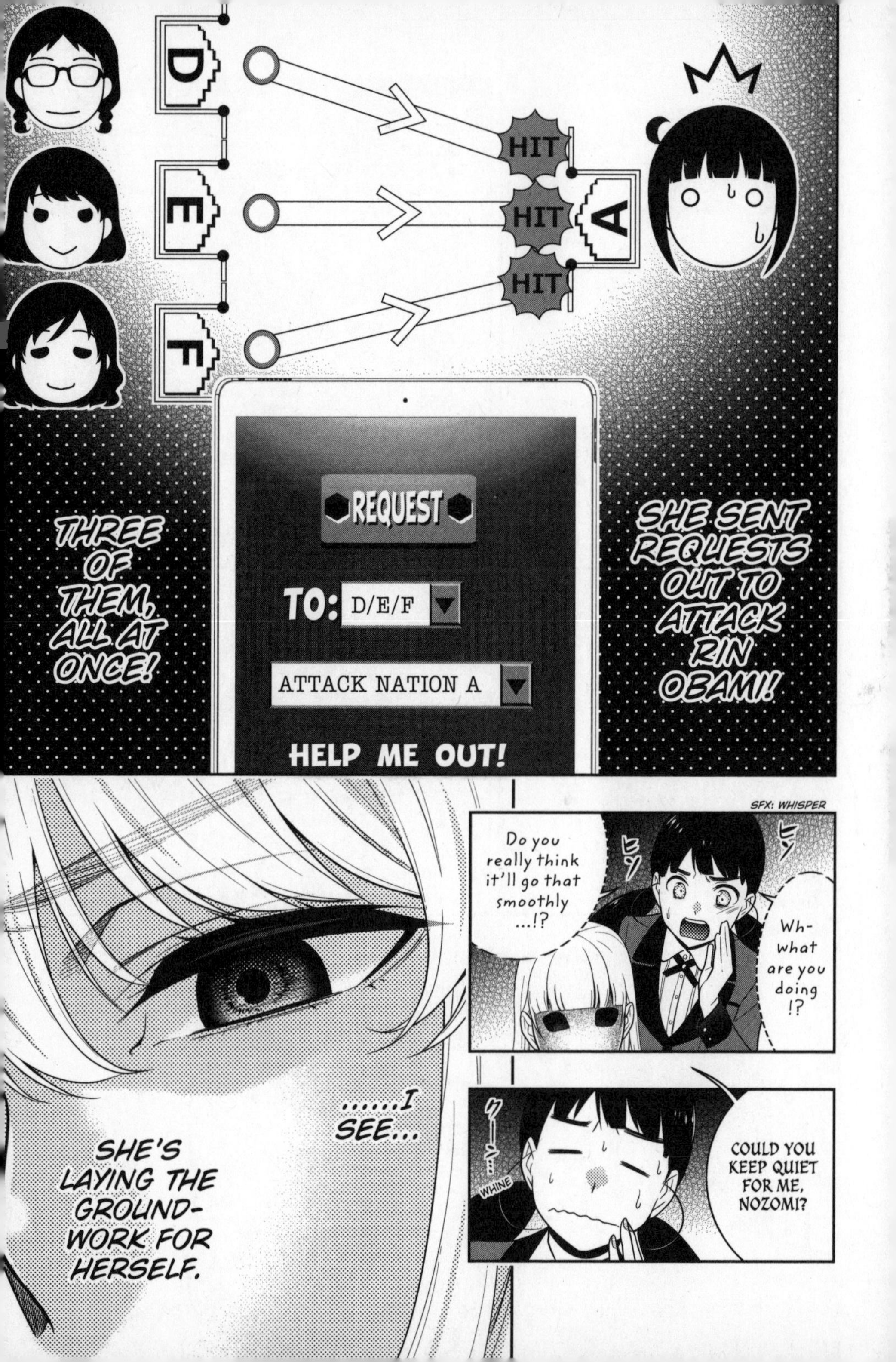

SHE SENT REQUESTS OUT TO ATTACK RIN OBAMI!
A
HIT
HIT
HIT
D
E
F
REQUEST
TO: D/E/F
ATTACK NATION A
HELP ME OUT!
THREE OF THEM, ALL AT ONCE!
SFX: WHISPER
Do you really think it'll go that smoothly ...!?
Wh-what are you doing!?
COULD YOU KEEP QUIET FOR ME, NOZOMI?
WHINE
......I SEE...
SHE'S LAYING THE GROUND-WORK FOR HERSELF.

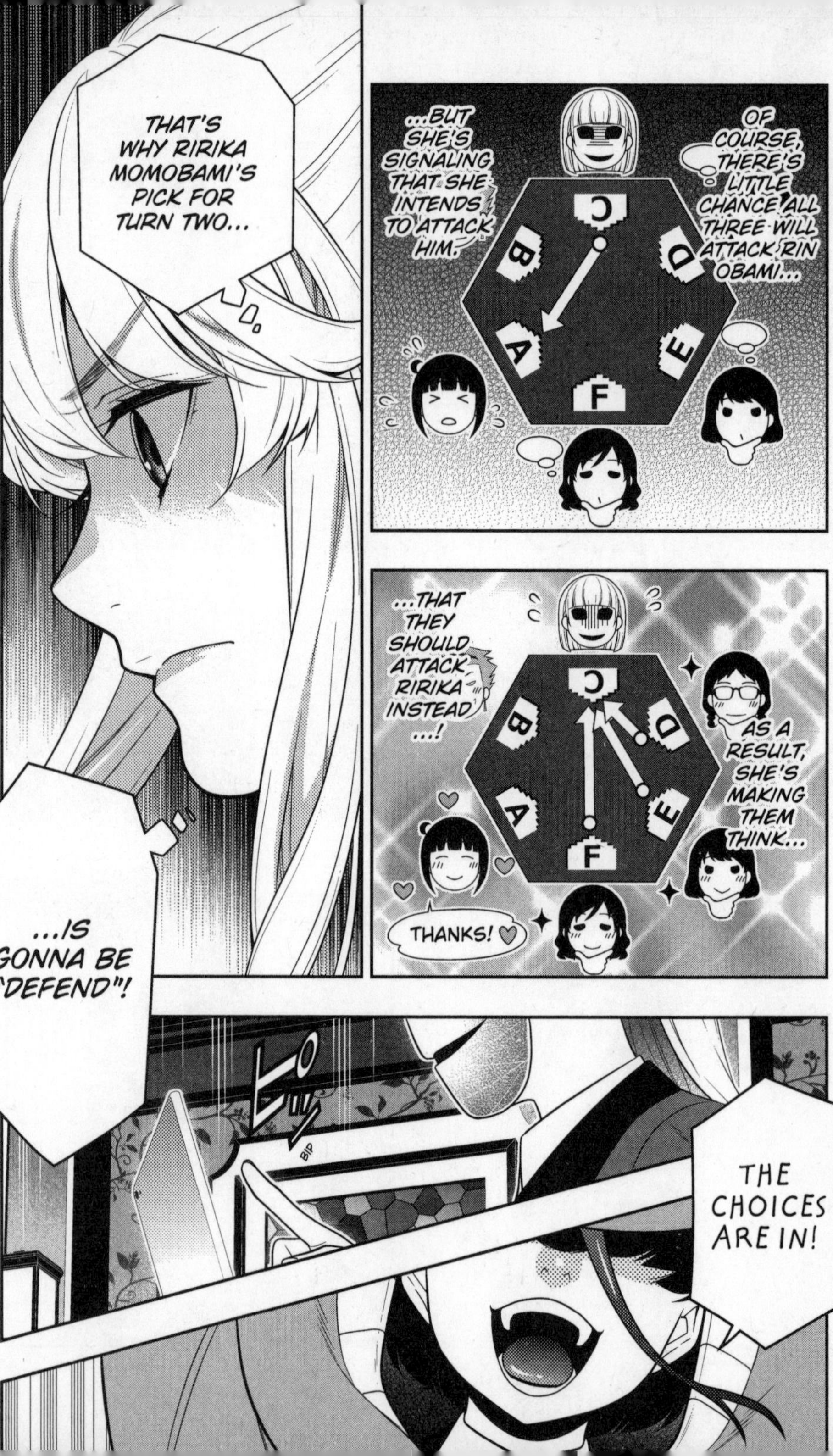
OF COURSE, THERE'S LITTLE CHANCE ALL THREE WILL ATTACK RIN OBAMI...
...BUT SHE'S SIGNALING THAT SHE INTENDS TO ATTACK HIM.
AS A RESULT, SHE'S MAKING THEM THINK...
...THAT THEY SHOULD ATTACK RIRIKA INSTEAD...!
THANKS!
THAT'S WHY RIRIKA MOMOBAMI'S PICK FOR TURN TWO...
...IS GONNA BE "DEFEND"!
BIP
THE CHOICES ARE IN!

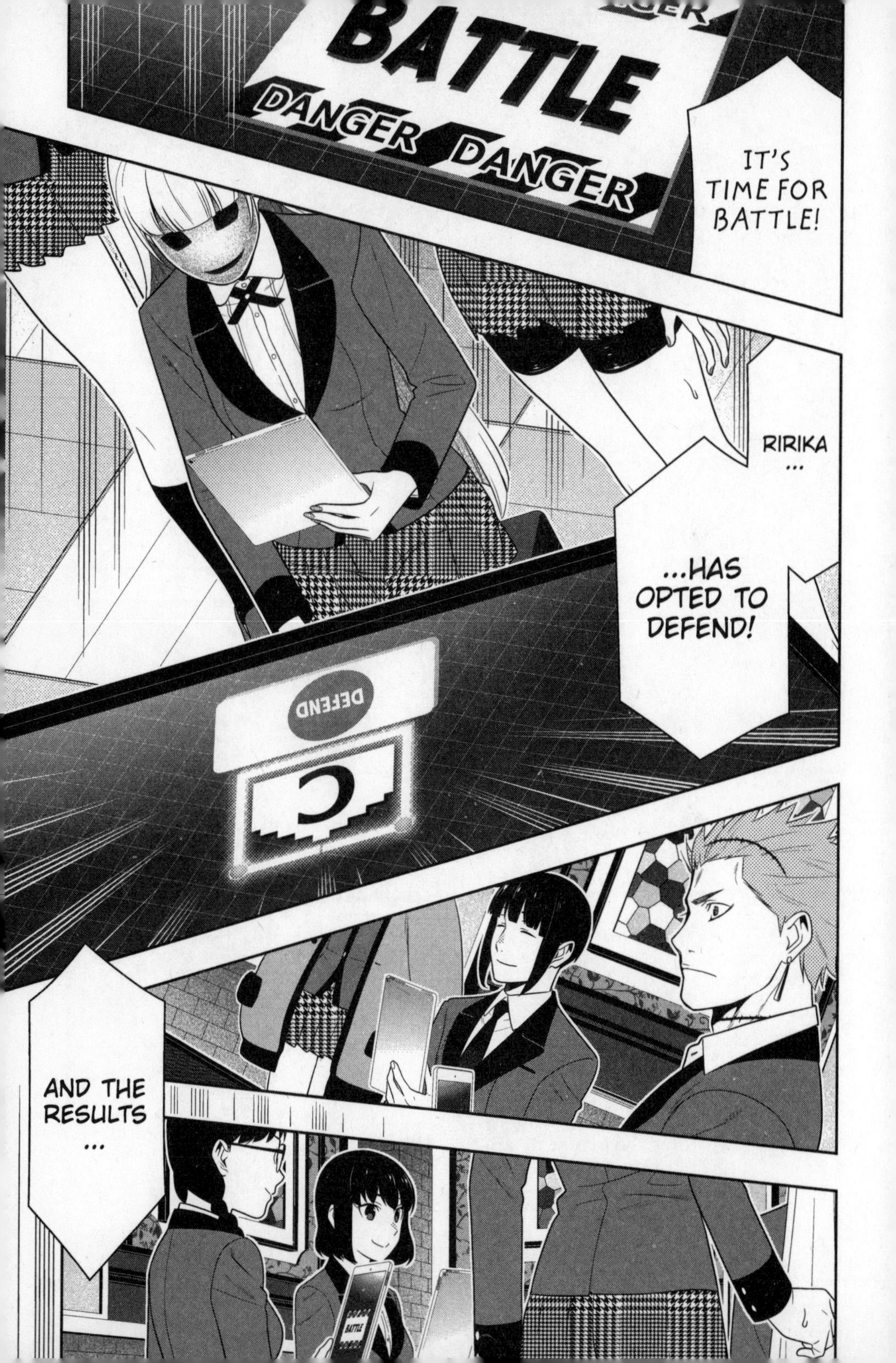
BATTLE
DANGER DANGER
DANGER
IT'S TIME FOR BATTLE!
RIRIKA ...
...HAS OPTED TO DEFEND!
DEFEND
C
AND THE RESULTS ...
BATTLE

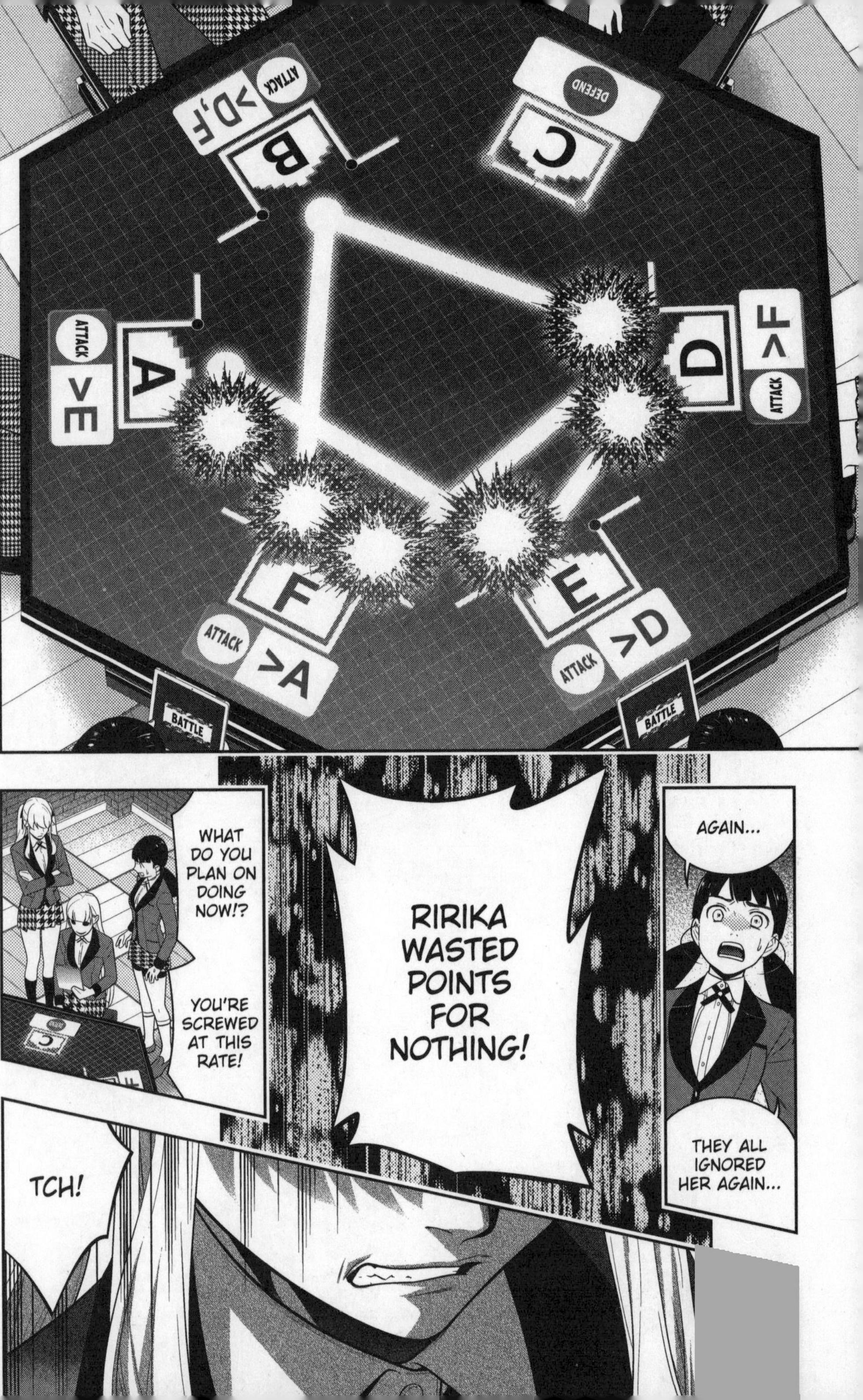
ATTACK
B
>D,F
DEFEND
C
D
ATTACK
>F
A
ATTACK
>E
E
ATTACK
>D
F
ATTACK
>A
BATTLE
BATTLE
AGAIN...
THEY ALL IGNORED HER AGAIN...
RIRIKA WASTED POINTS FOR NOTHING!
WHAT DO YOU PLAN ON DOING NOW!?
YOU'RE SCREWED AT THIS RATE!
TCH!

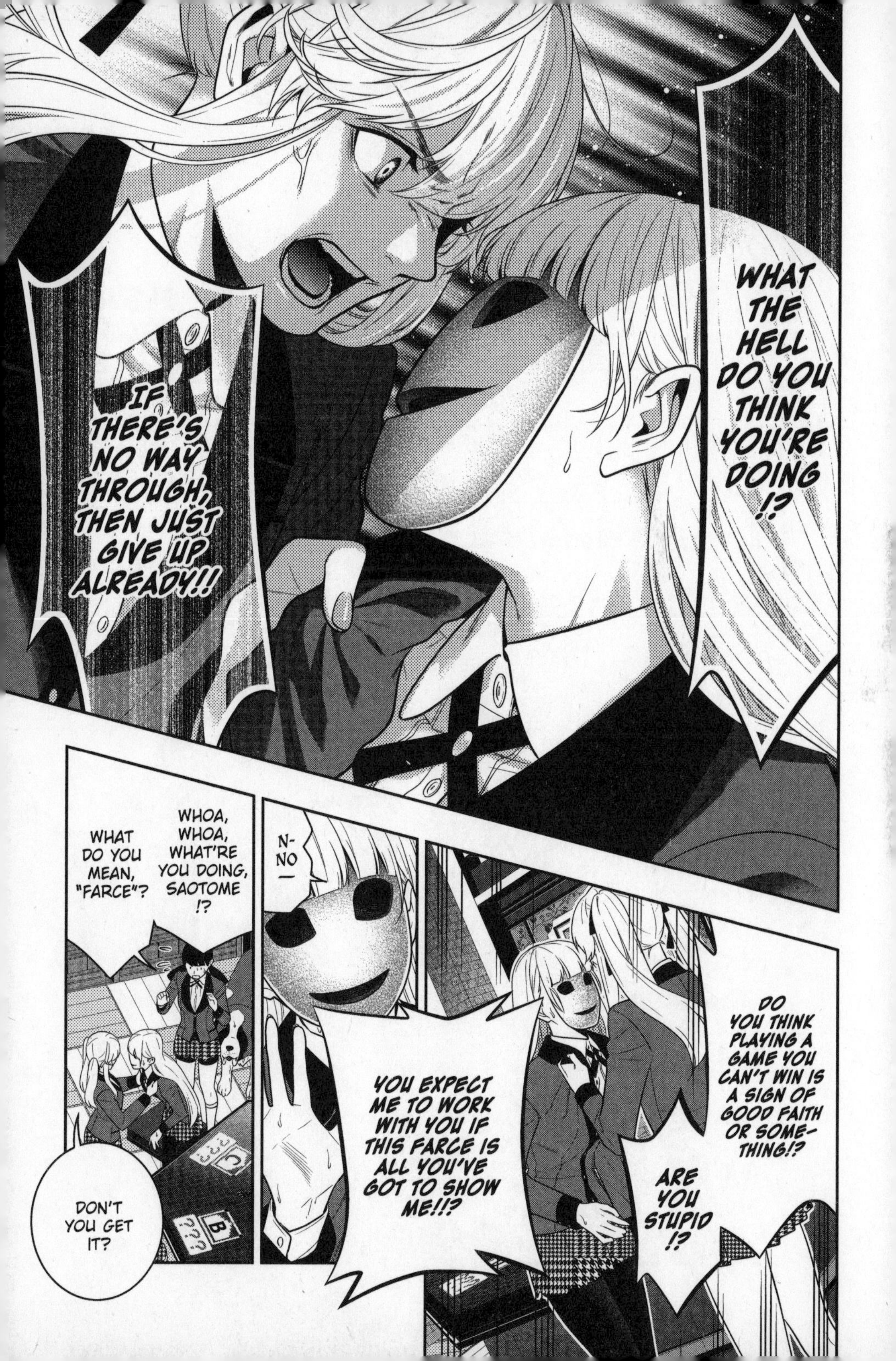
WHAT THE HELL DO YOU THINK YOU'RE DOING!?
IF THERE'S NO WAY THROUGH, THEN JUST GIVE UP ALREADY!!
DO YOU THINK PLAYING A GAME YOU CAN'T WIN IS A SIGN OF GOOD FAITH OR SOME-THING!?
ARE YOU STUPID!?
YOU EXPECT ME TO WORK WITH YOU IF THIS FARCE IS ALL YOU'VE GOT TO SHOW ME!!?
N-NO—
WHOA, WHOA, WHAT'RE YOU DOING, SAOTOME!?
WHAT DO YOU MEAN, "FARCE"?
DON'T YOU GET IT?

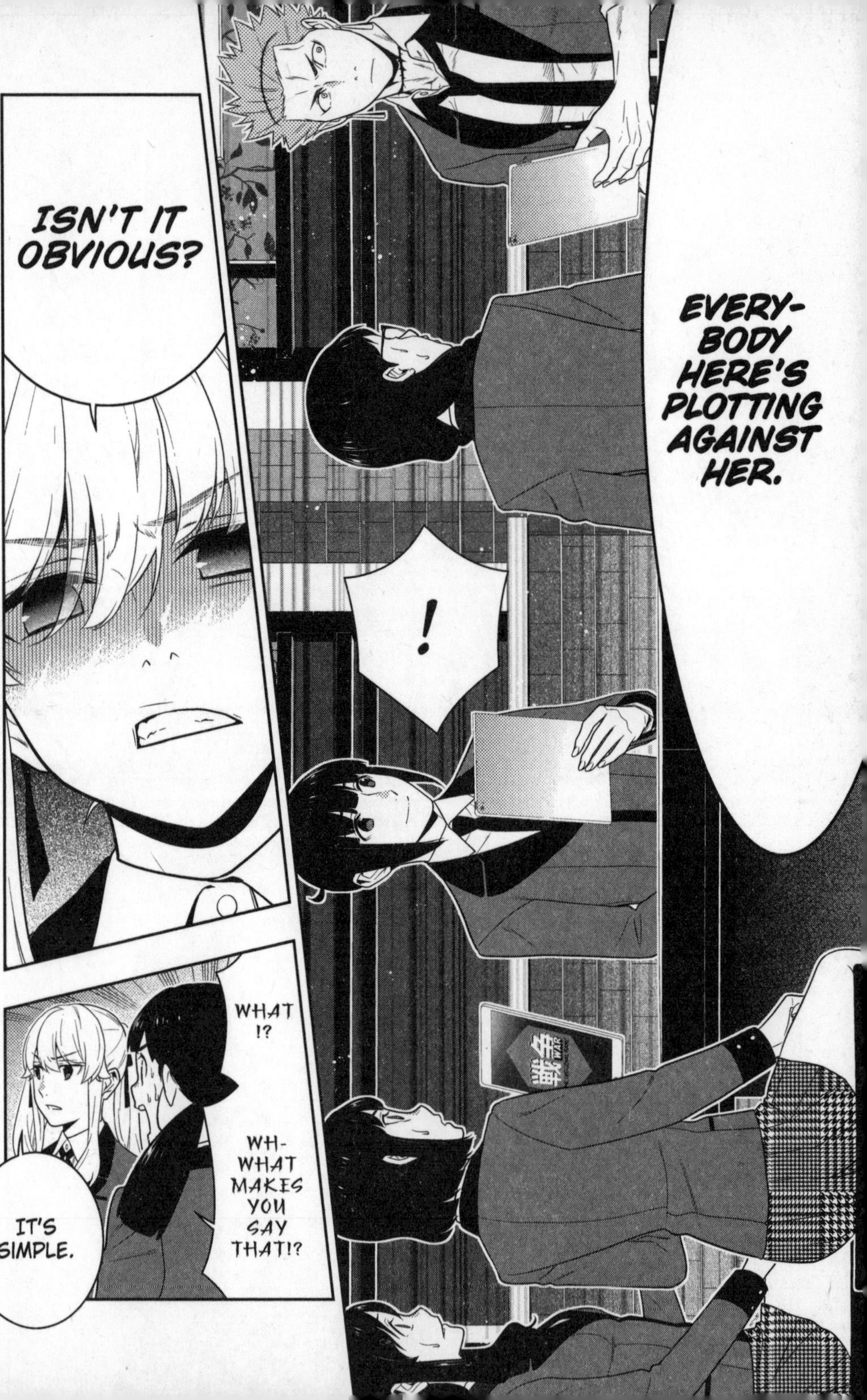
EVERY-
BODY
HERE'S
PLOTTING
AGAINST
HER.
!
ISN'T IT
OBVIOUS?
WHAT
!?
WH-
WHAT
MAKES
YOU
SAY
THAT!?
IT'S
SIMPLE.

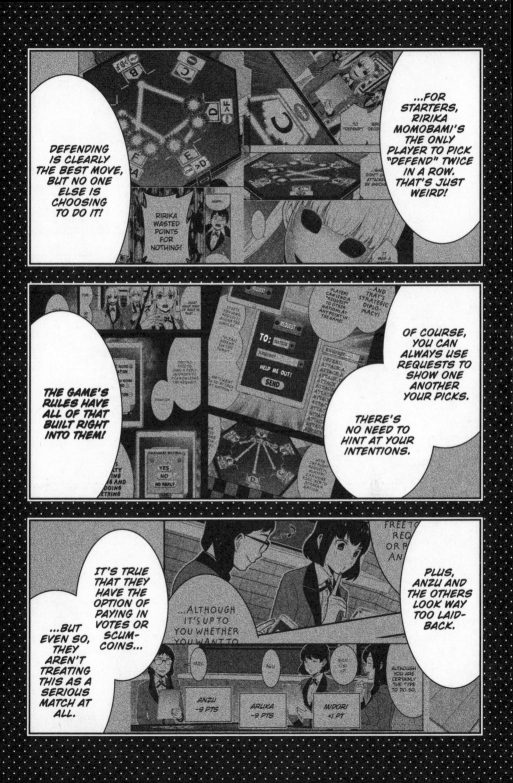

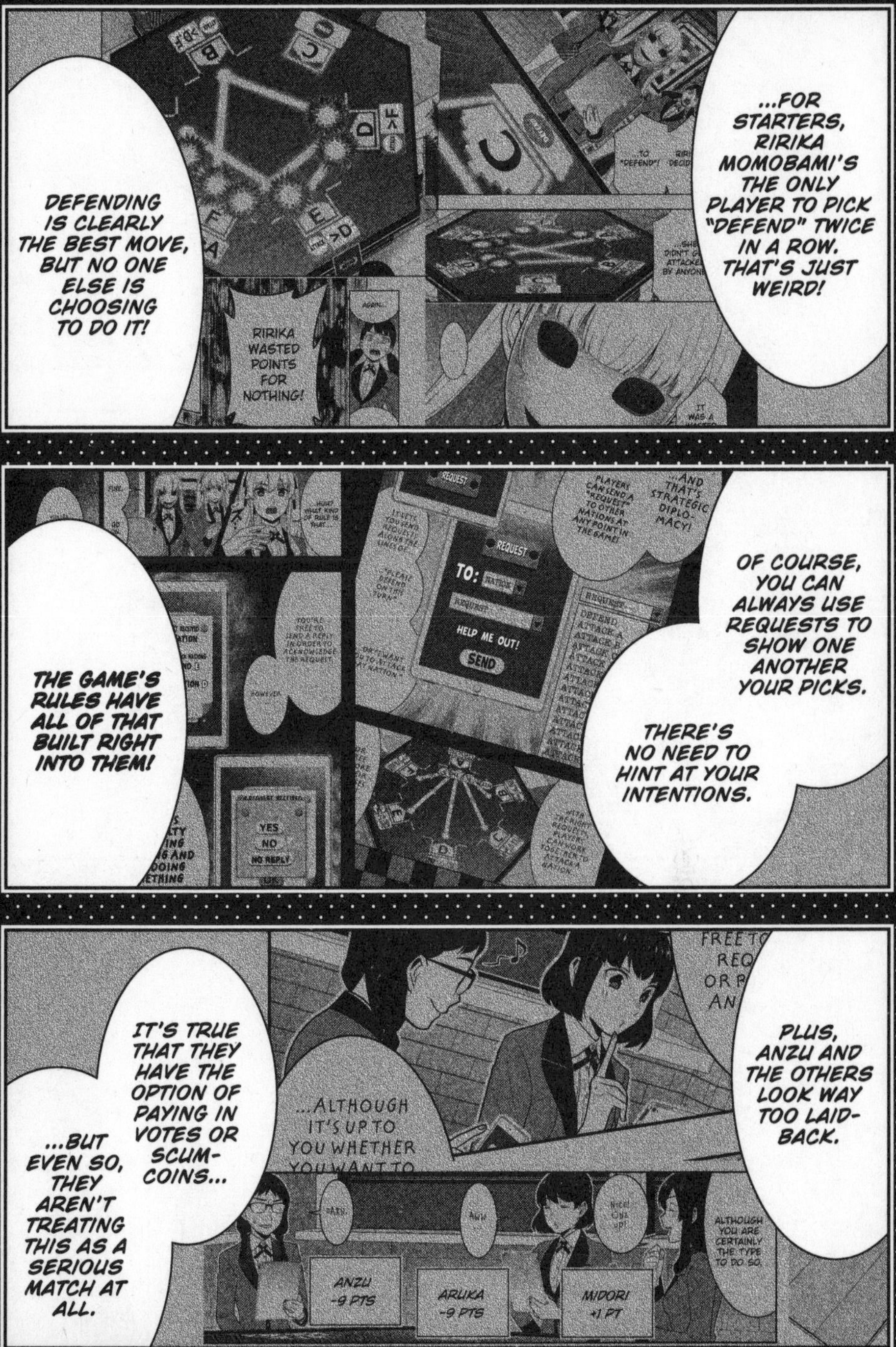
...FOR STARTERS, RIRIKA MOMOBAMI'S THE ONLY PLAYER TO PICK "DEFEND" TWICE IN A ROW. THAT'S JUST WEIRD!
RIRIKA WASTED POINTS FOR NOTHING!
DEFENDING IS CLEARLY THE BEST MOVE, BUT NO ONE ELSE IS CHOOSING TO DO IT!
...AND THAT'S STRATEGIC DIPLO-MACY!
REQUEST
TO:
HELP ME OUT!
SEND
OF COURSE, YOU CAN ALWAYS USE REQUESTS TO SHOW ONE ANOTHER YOUR PICKS.
THERE'S NO NEED TO HINT AT YOUR INTENTIONS.
YES
NO
NO REPLY
THE GAME'S RULES HAVE ALL OF THAT BUILT RIGHT INTO THEM!
PLUS, ANZU AND THE OTHERS LOOK WAY TOO LAID-BACK.
...ALTHOUGH IT'S UP TO YOU WHETHER YOU WANT TO
IT'S TRUE THAT THEY HAVE THE OPTION OF PAYING IN VOTES OR SCUM-COINS...
...BUT EVEN SO, THEY AREN'T TREATING THIS AS A SERIOUS MATCH AT ALL.
ALTHOUGH YOU ARE CERTAINLY THE TYPE TO DO SO.
MIDORI +1 PT
ARUKA -9 PTS
ANZU -9 PTS

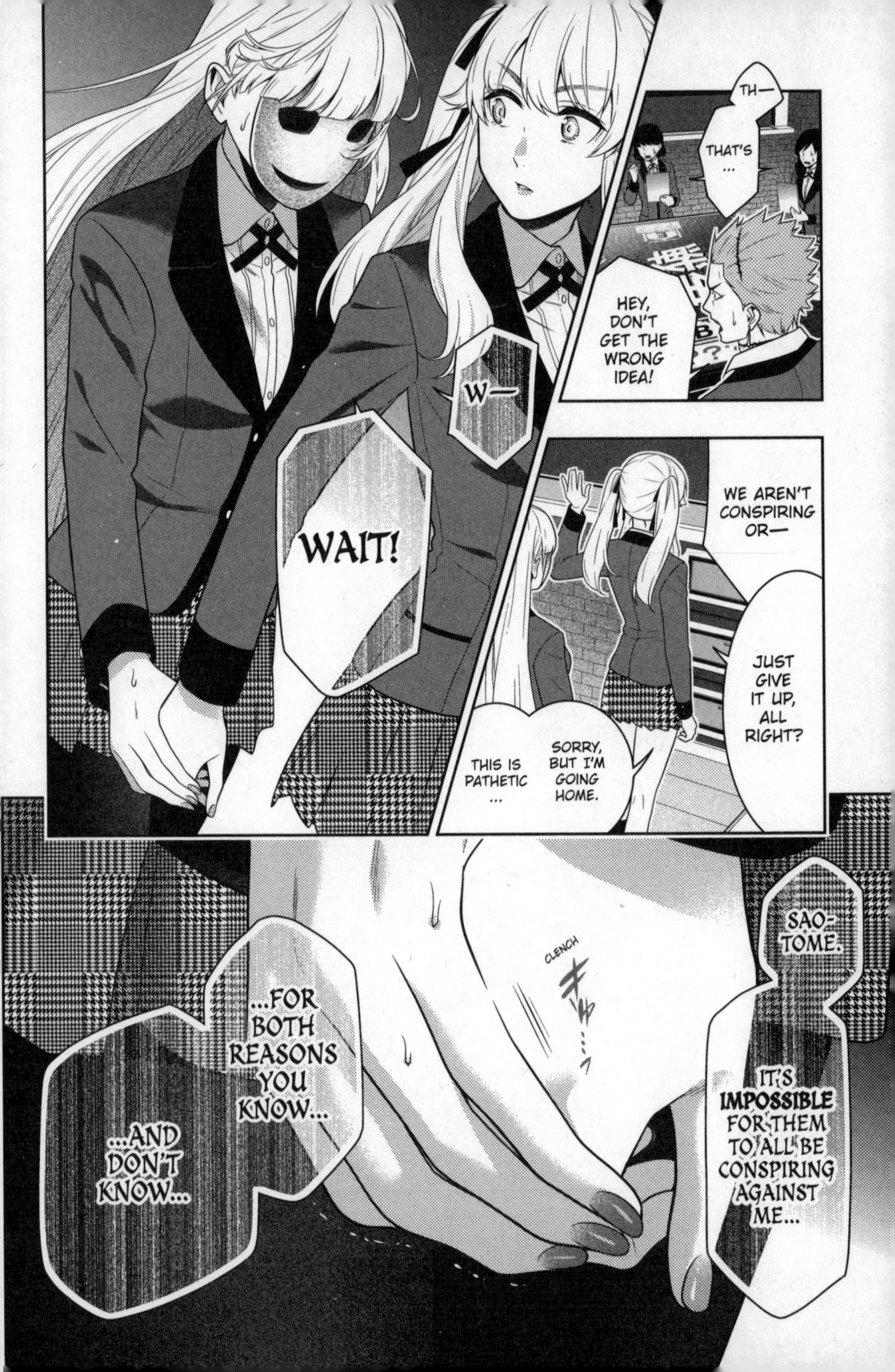
TH—
THAT'S ...
HEY, DON'T GET THE WRONG IDEA!
WE AREN'T CONSPIRING OR—
JUST GIVE IT UP, ALL RIGHT?
SORRY, BUT I'M GOING HOME.
THIS IS PATHETIC ...
W—
WAIT!
SAO-TOME.
IT'S IMPOSSIBLE FOR THEM TO ALL BE CONSPIRING AGAINST ME...
CLENCH
...FOR BOTH REASONS YOU KNOW...
...AND DON'T KNOW...

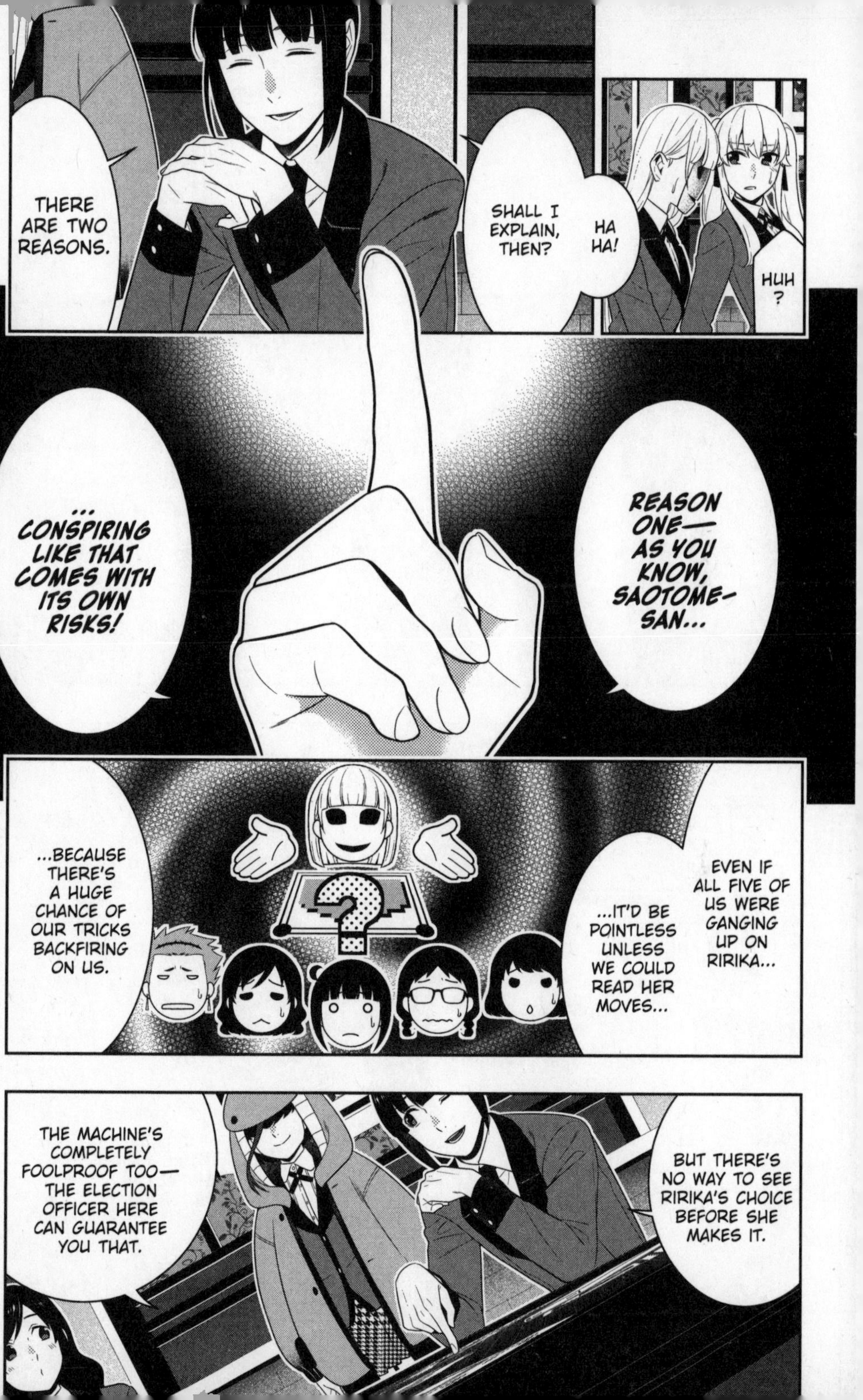
HA HA!
HUH?
SHALL I EXPLAIN, THEN?
THERE ARE TWO REASONS.
REASON ONE—AS YOU KNOW, SAOTOME-SAN...
...CONSPIRING LIKE THAT COMES WITH ITS OWN RISKS!
EVEN IF ALL FIVE OF US WERE GANGING UP ON RIRIKA...
...IT'D BE POINTLESS UNLESS WE COULD READ HER MOVES...
...BECAUSE THERE'S A HUGE CHANCE OF OUR TRICKS BACKFIRING ON US.
BUT THERE'S NO WAY TO SEE RIRIKA'S CHOICE BEFORE SHE MAKES IT.
THE MACHINE'S COMPLETELY FOOLPROOF TOO—THE ELECTION OFFICER HERE CAN GUARANTEE YOU THAT.

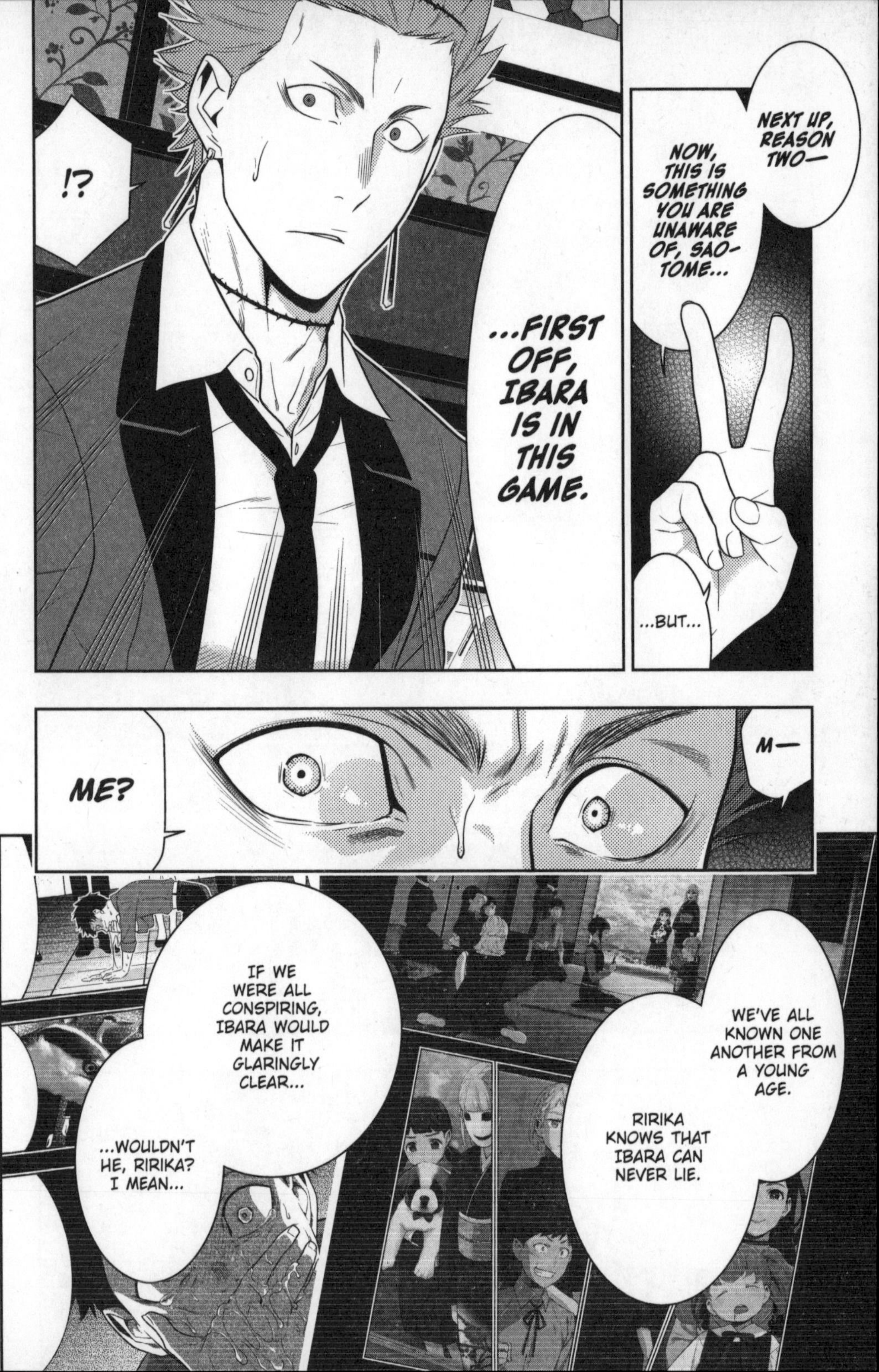
NEXT UP, REASON TWO—
NOW, THIS IS SOMETHING YOU ARE UNAWARE OF, SAO-TOME...
...BUT...
...FIRST OFF, IBARA IS IN THIS GAME.
!?
M—
ME?
WE'VE ALL KNOWN ONE ANOTHER FROM A YOUNG AGE.
RIRIKA KNOWS THAT IBARA CAN NEVER LIE.
IF WE WERE ALL CONSPIRING, IBARA WOULD MAKE IT GLARINGLY CLEAR...
...WOULDN'T HE, RIRIKA? I MEAN...

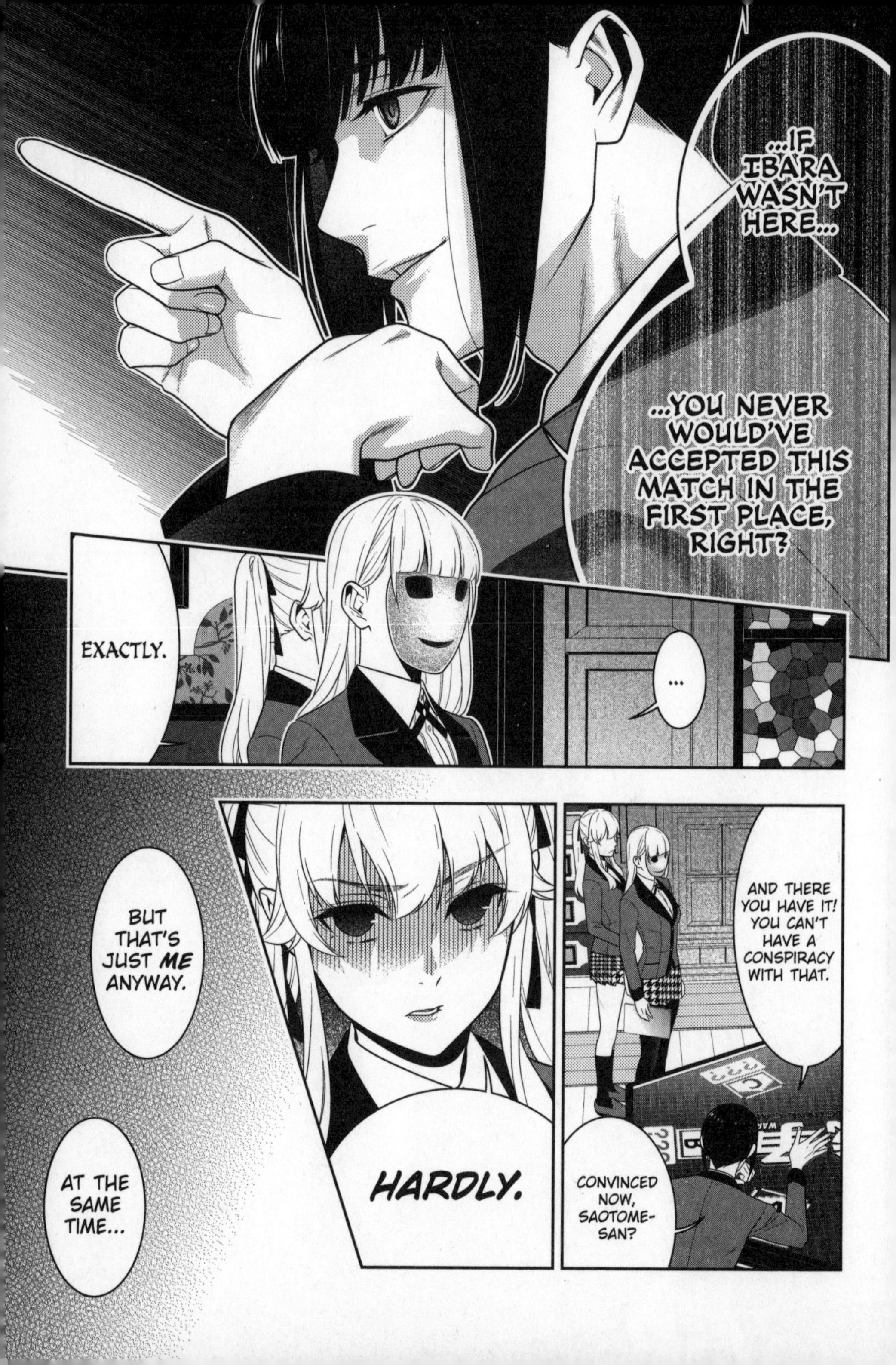
...IF IBARA WASN'T HERE...
...YOU NEVER WOULD'VE ACCEPTED THIS MATCH IN THE FIRST PLACE, RIGHT?
...
EXACTLY.
AND THERE YOU HAVE IT! YOU CAN'T HAVE A CONSPIRACY WITH THAT.
CONVINCED NOW, SAOTOME-SAN?
HARDLY.
BUT THAT'S JUST *ME* ANYWAY.
AT THE SAME TIME...

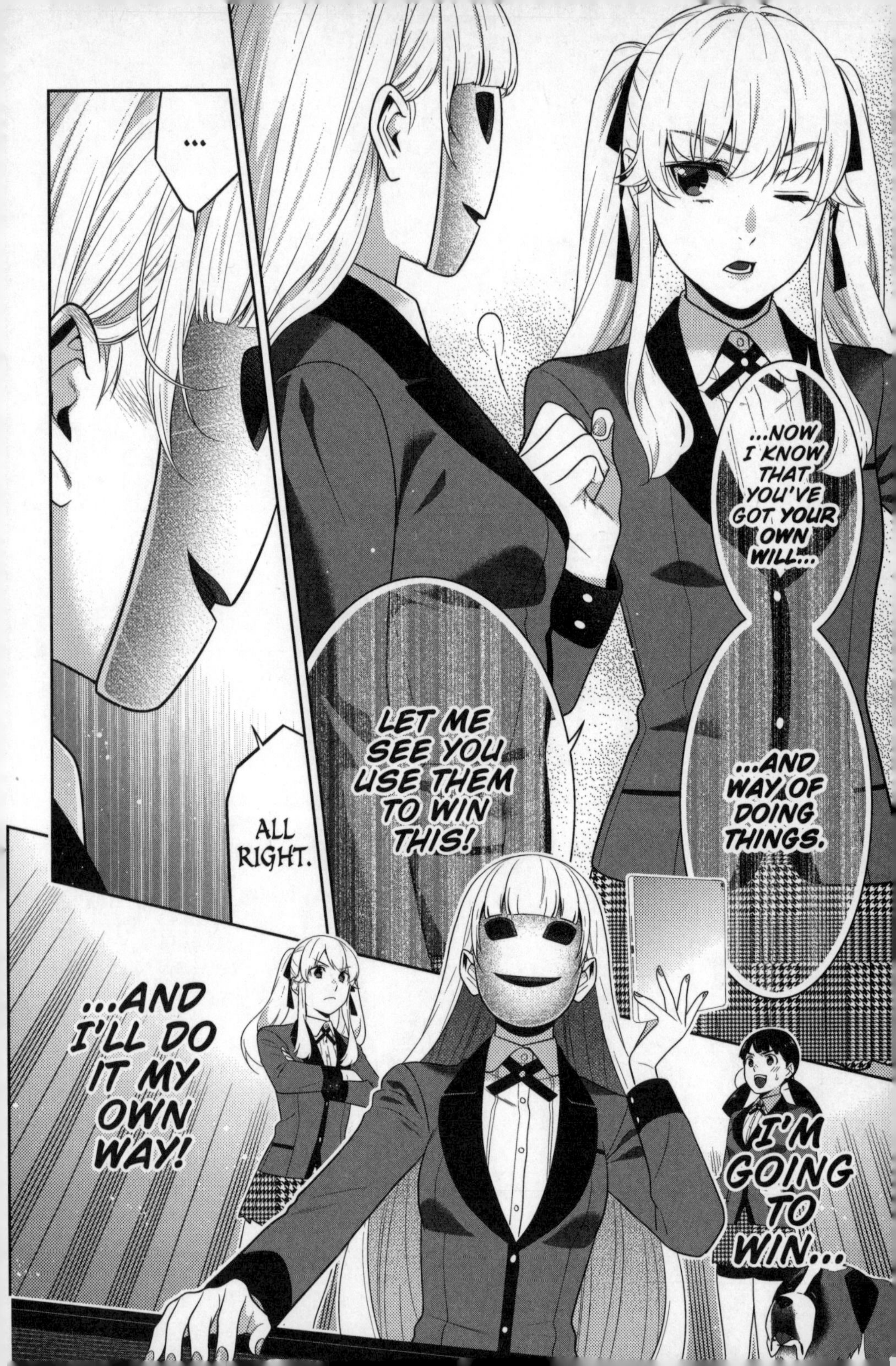
...NOW I KNOW THAT YOU'VE GOT YOUR OWN WILL...
...AND WAY OF DOING THINGS.
LET ME SEE YOU USE THEM TO WIN THIS!
...
ALL RIGHT.
I'M GOING TO WIN...
...AND I'LL DO IT MY OWN WAY!

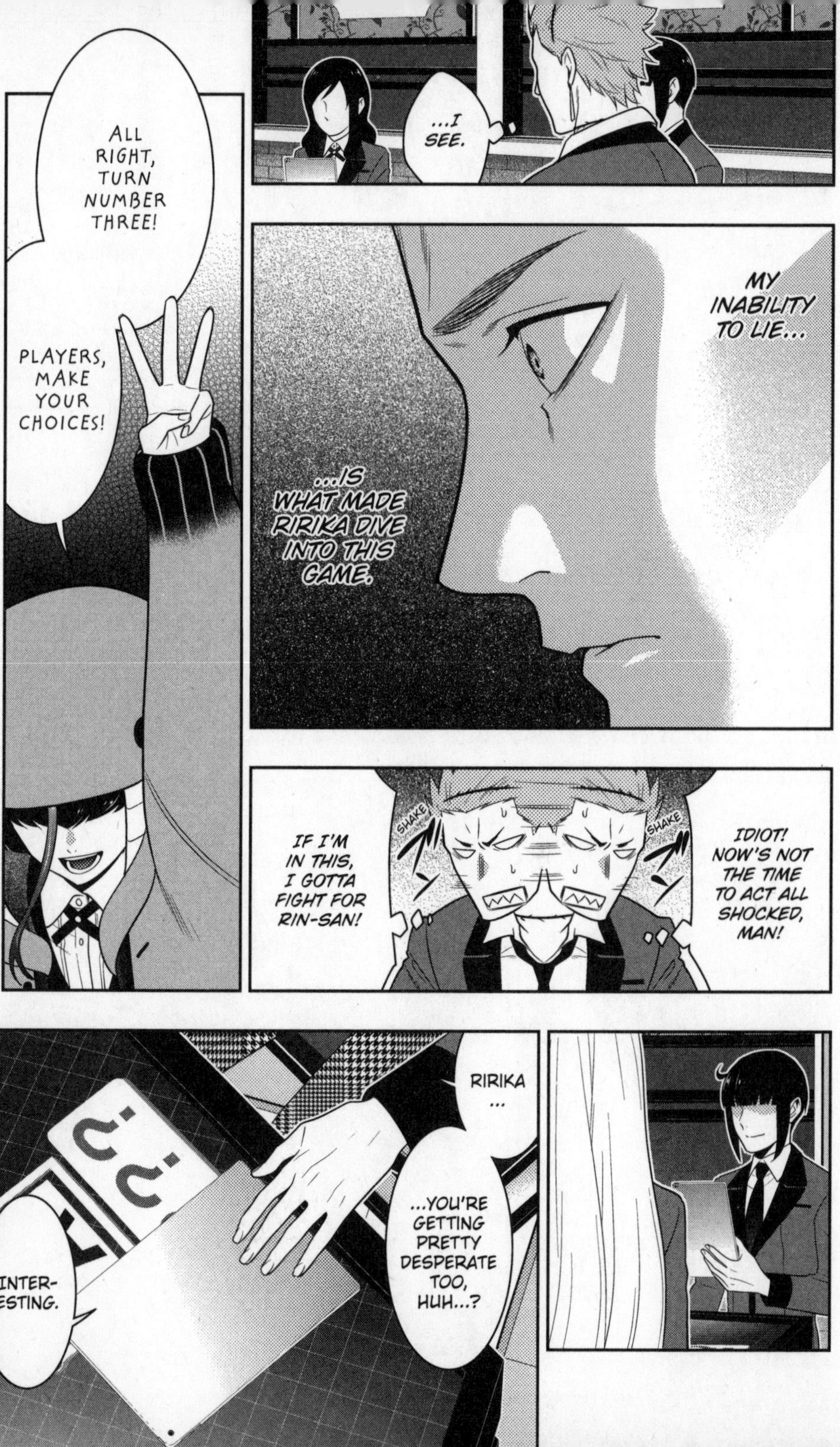
...I SEE.
MY INABILITY TO LIE...
...IS WHAT MADE RIRIKA DIVE INTO THIS GAME.
SHAKE
IDIOT! NOW'S NOT THE TIME TO ACT ALL SHOCKED, MAN!
SHAKE
IF I'M IN THIS, I GOTTA FIGHT FOR RIN-SAN!
ALL RIGHT, TURN NUMBER THREE!
PLAYERS, MAKE YOUR CHOICES!
RIRIKA...
...YOU'RE GETTING PRETTY DESPERATE TOO, HUH...?
INTER-ESTING.

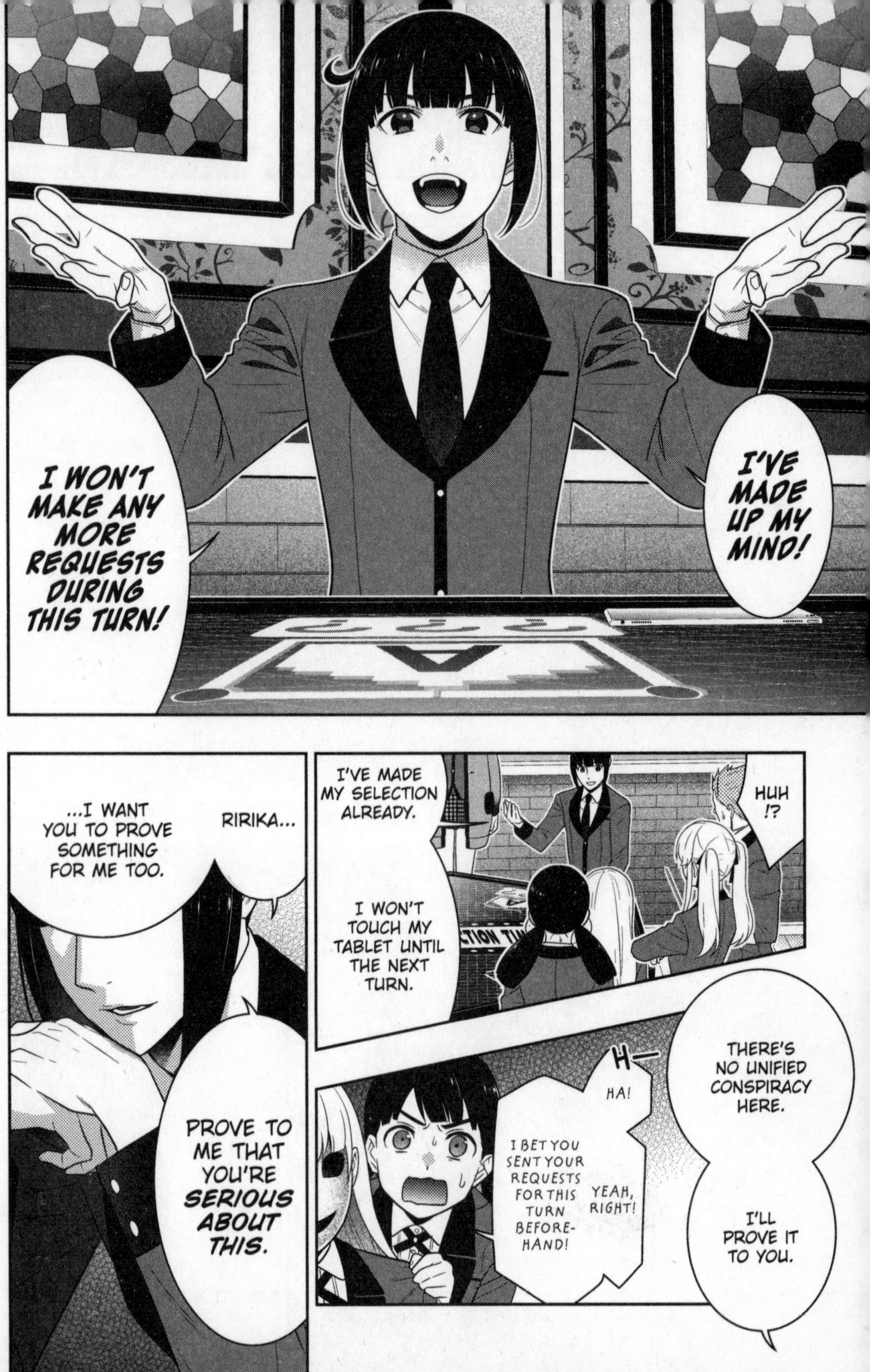
I'VE MADE UP MY MIND!
I WON'T MAKE ANY MORE REQUESTS DURING THIS TURN!
HUH!?
I'VE MADE MY SELECTION ALREADY.
I WON'T TOUCH MY TABLET UNTIL THE NEXT TURN.
H— HA!
YEAH, RIGHT!
I BET YOU SENT YOUR REQUESTS FOR THIS TURN BEFORE-HAND!
THERE'S NO UNIFIED CONSPIRACY HERE.
I'LL PROVE IT TO YOU.
RIRIKA...
...I WANT YOU TO PROVE SOMETHING FOR ME TOO.
PROVE TO ME THAT YOU'RE SERIOUS ABOUT THIS.

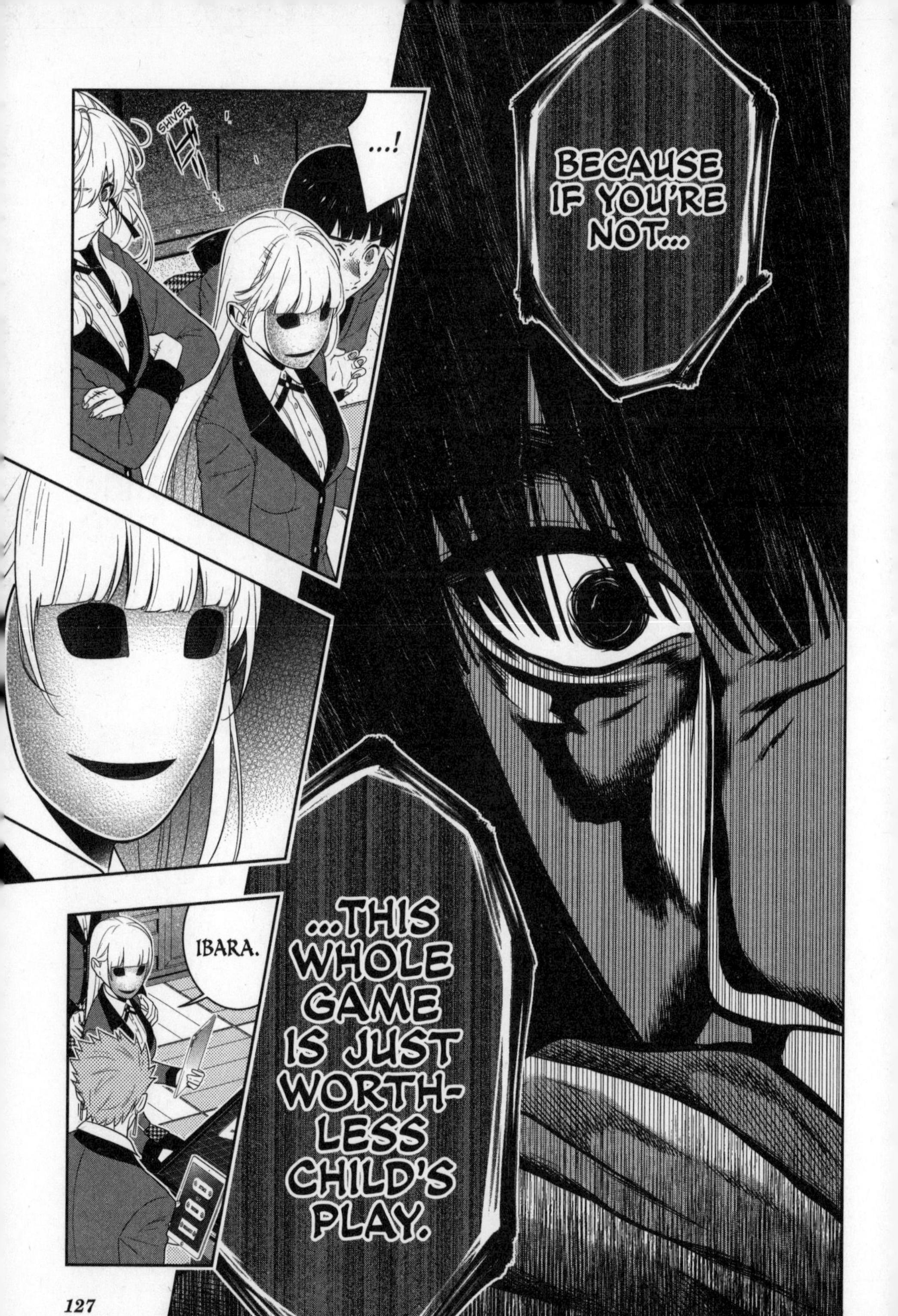
BECAUSE IF YOU'RE NOT...
...THIS WHOLE GAME IS JUST WORTH-LESS CHILD'S PLAY.
...!
SHIVER
IBARA.

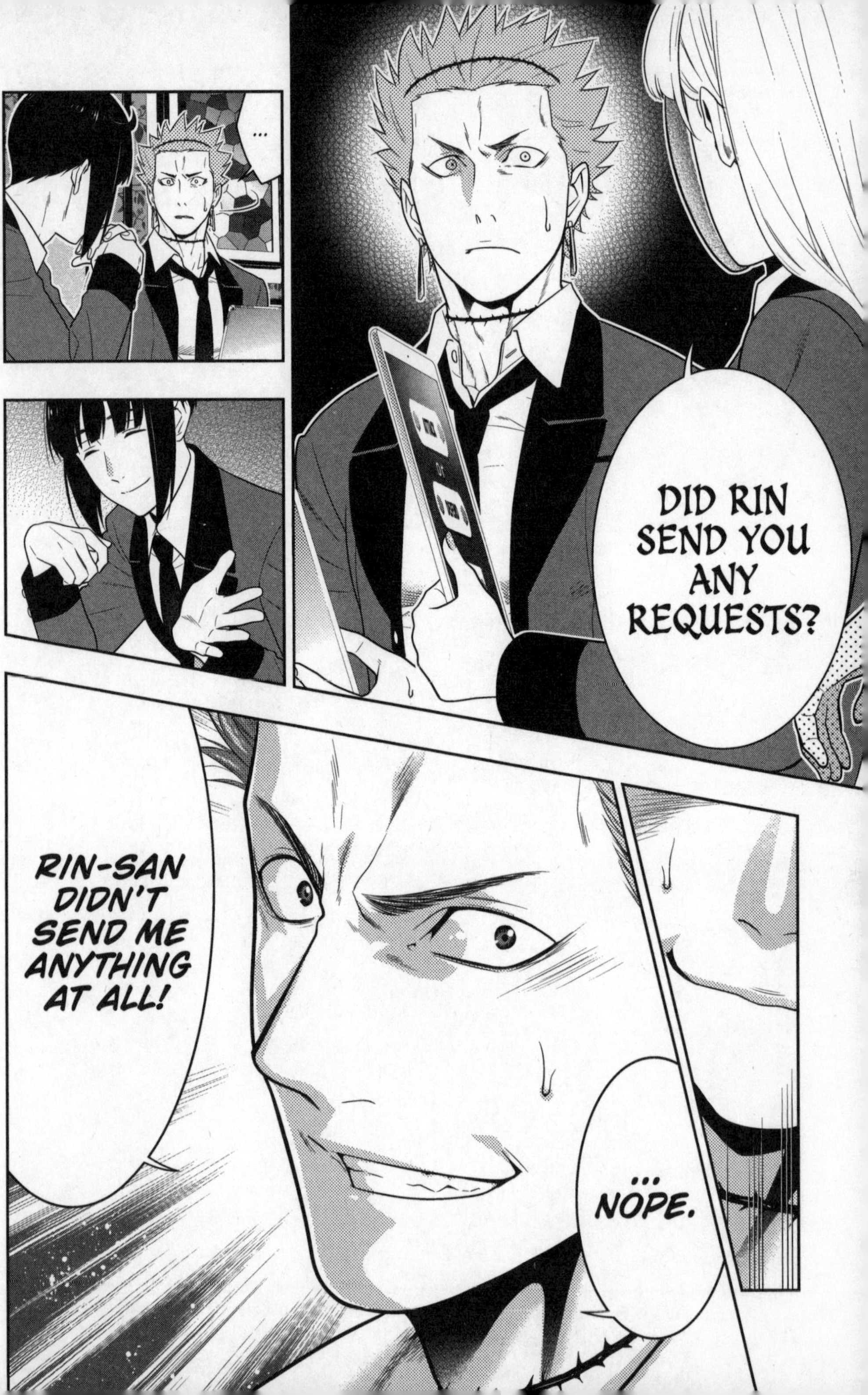
DID RIN SEND YOU ANY REQUESTS?
...
... NOPE.
RIN-SAN DIDN'T SEND ME ANYTHING AT ALL!

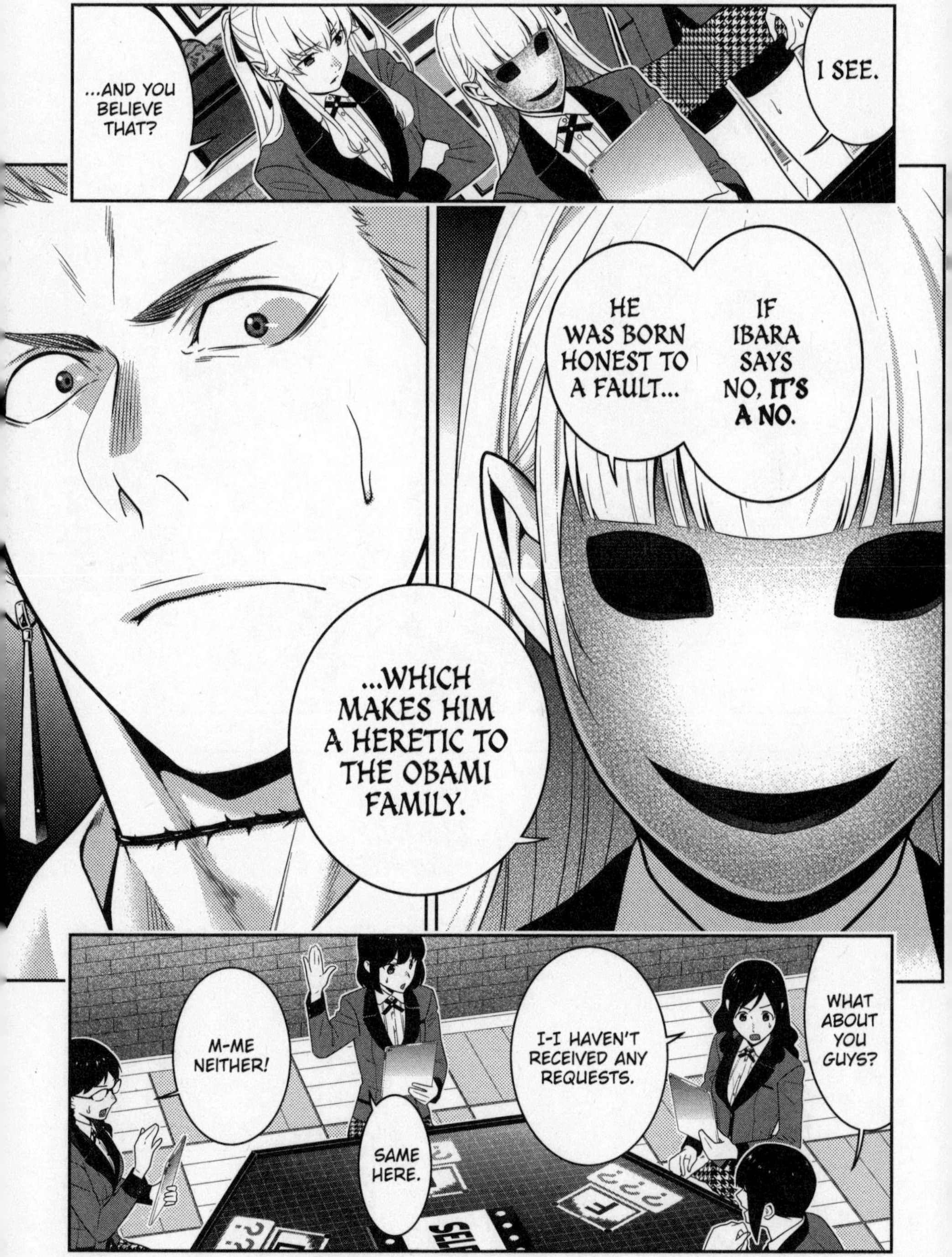
I SEE.
...AND YOU BELIEVE THAT?
IF IBARA SAYS NO, IT'S A NO.
HE WAS BORN HONEST TO A FAULT...
...WHICH MAKES HIM A HERETIC TO THE OBAMI FAMILY.
WHAT ABOUT YOU GUYS?
I-I HAVEN'T RECEIVED ANY REQUESTS.
SAME HERE.
M-ME NEITHER!

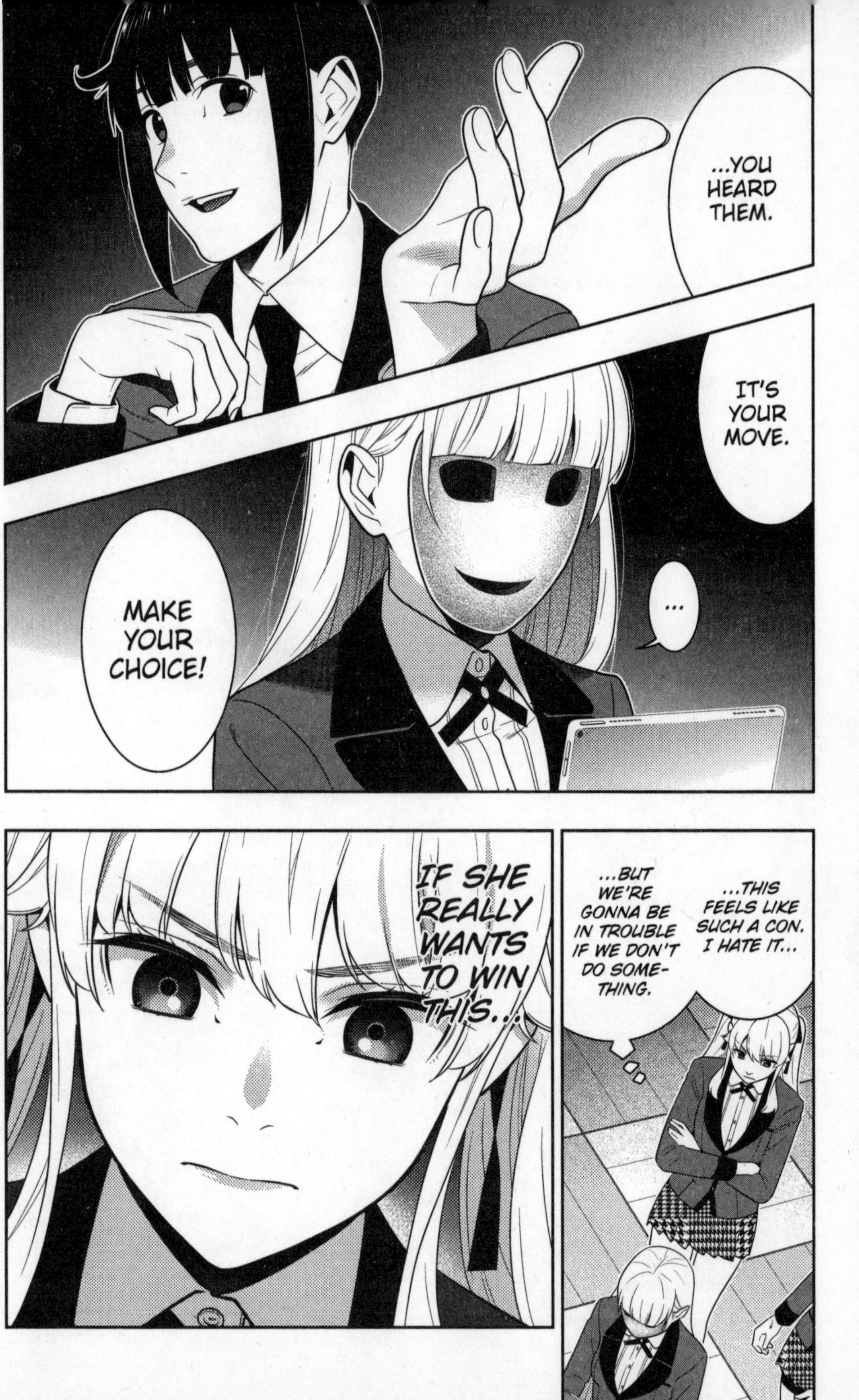
...YOU HEARD THEM.
IT'S YOUR MOVE.
...
MAKE YOUR CHOICE!
...THIS FEELS LIKE SUCH A CON. I HATE IT...
...BUT WE'RE GONNA BE IN TROUBLE IF WE DON'T DO SOME-THING.
IF SHE REALLY WANTS TO WIN THIS...

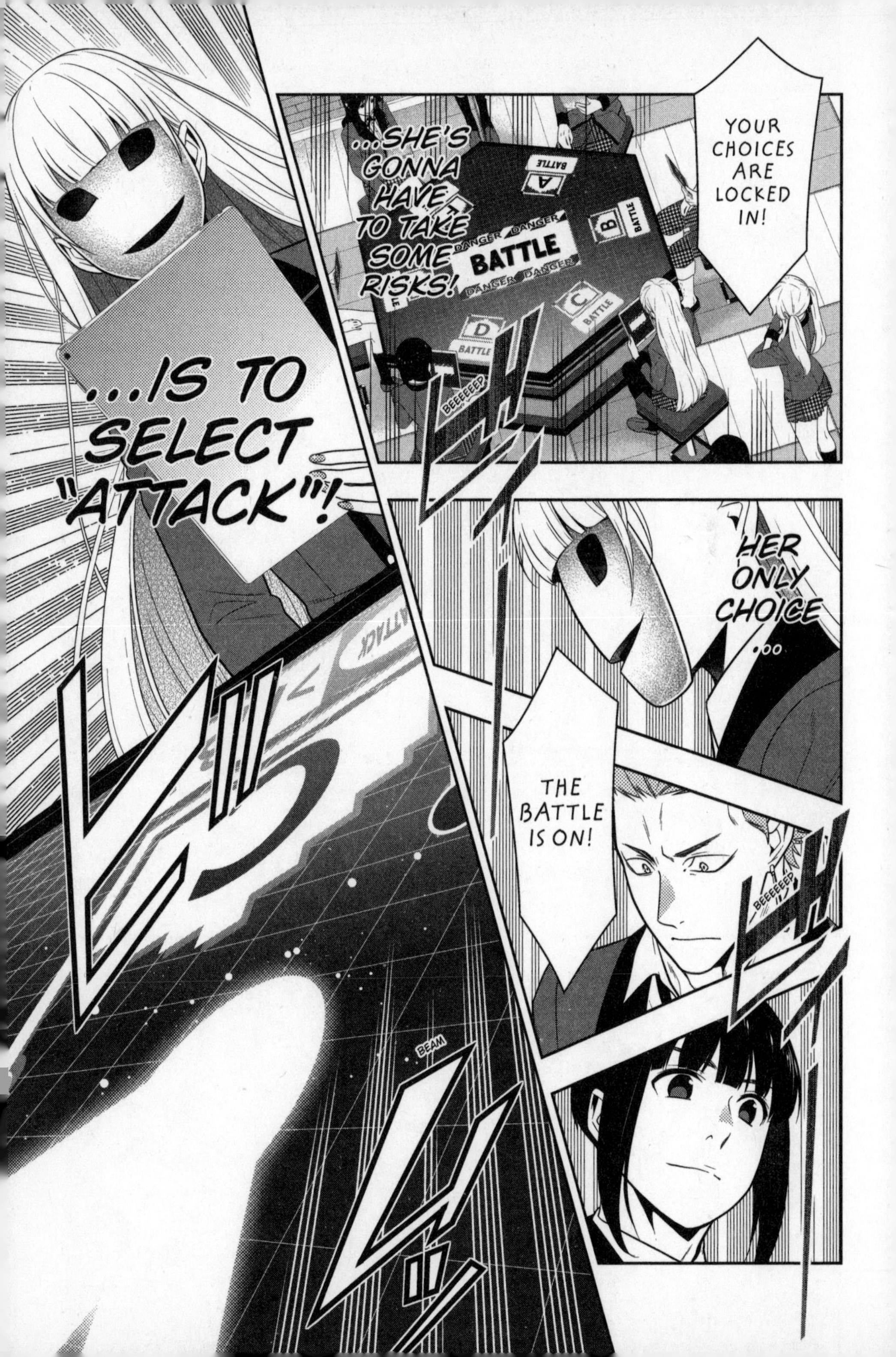
YOUR CHOICES ARE LOCKED IN!
...SHE'S GONNA HAVE TO TAKE SOME RISKS!
A BATTLE
B BATTLE
DANGER DANGER BATTLE DANGER DANGER
C BATTLE
D BATTLE
BEEEEEEP
HER ONLY CHOICE...
THE BATTLE IS ON!
BEEEEEEP
...IS TO SELECT "ATTACK"!
ATTACK
BEAM

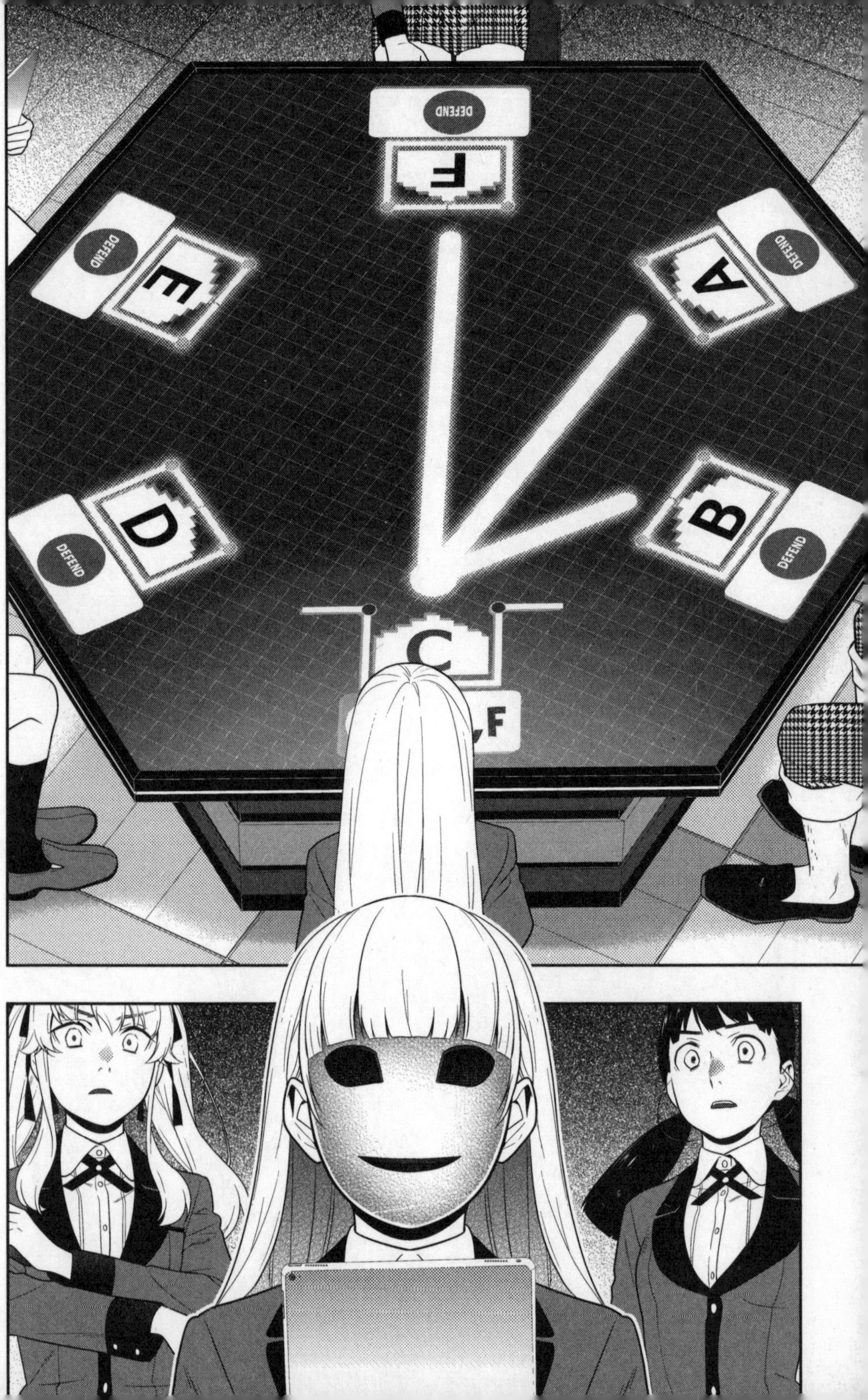
DEFEND
F
DEFEND
A
DEFEND
E
DEFEND
B
DEFEND
D
C
F

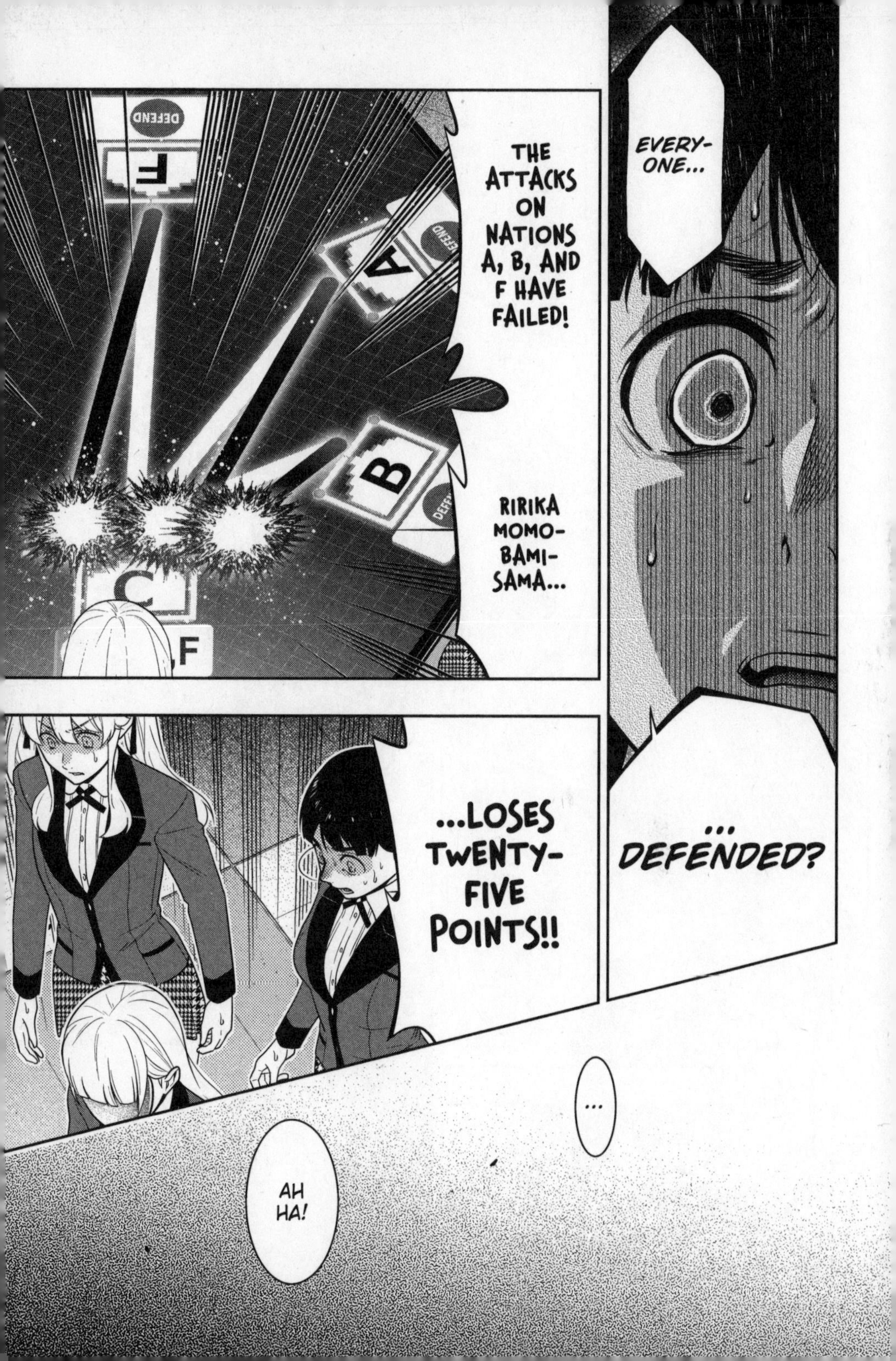
EVERY-ONE...
...DEFENDED?
THE ATTACKS ON NATIONS A, B, AND F HAVE FAILED!
RIRIKA MOMO-BAMI-SAMA...
...LOSES TWENTY-FIVE POINTS!!
...
AH HA!

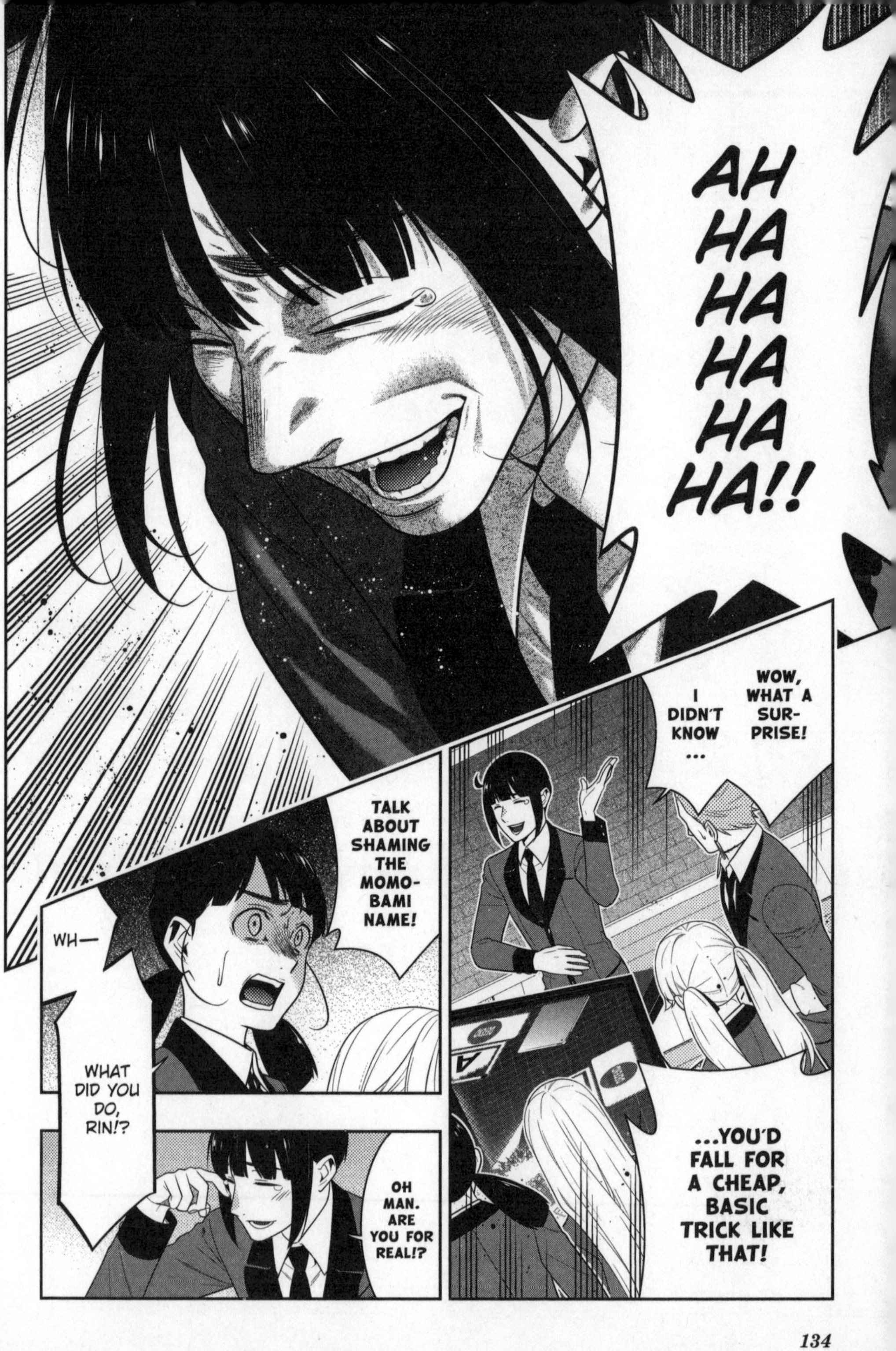
AH HA HA HA HA HA HA!!
WOW, WHAT A SUR-PRISE!
I DIDN'T KNOW ...
...YOU'D FALL FOR A CHEAP, BASIC TRICK LIKE THAT!
TALK ABOUT SHAMING THE MOMO-BAMI NAME!
WH—
WHAT DID YOU DO, RIN!?
OH MAN. ARE YOU FOR REAL!?

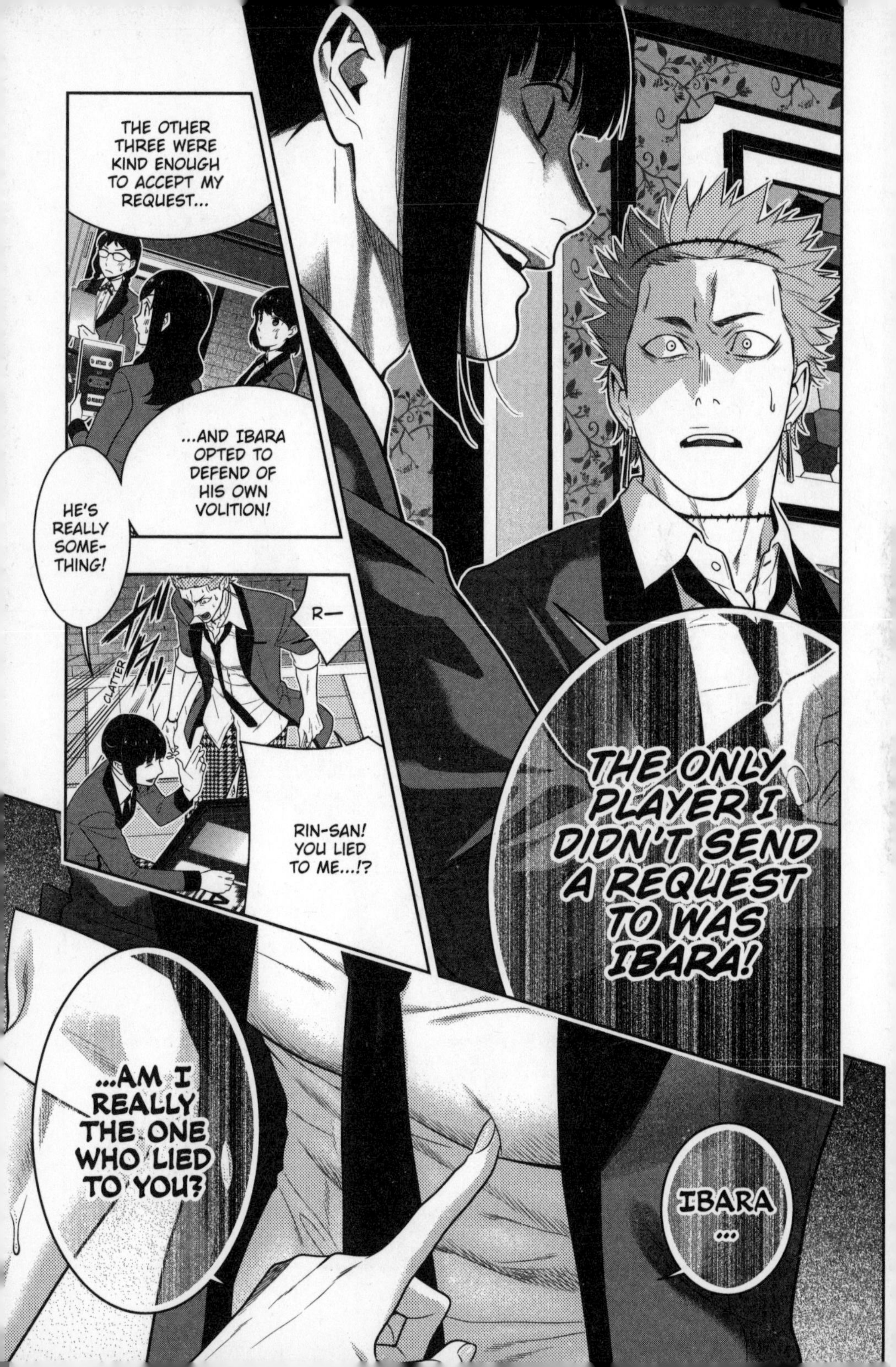
THE OTHER THREE WERE KIND ENOUGH TO ACCEPT MY REQUEST...
...AND IBARA OPTED TO DEFEND OF HIS OWN VOLITION!
HE'S REALLY SOME-THING!
R—
CLATTER
RIN-SAN! YOU LIED TO ME...!?
THE ONLY PLAYER I DIDN'T SEND A REQUEST TO WAS IBARA!
...AM I REALLY THE ONE WHO LIED TO YOU?
IBARA ...

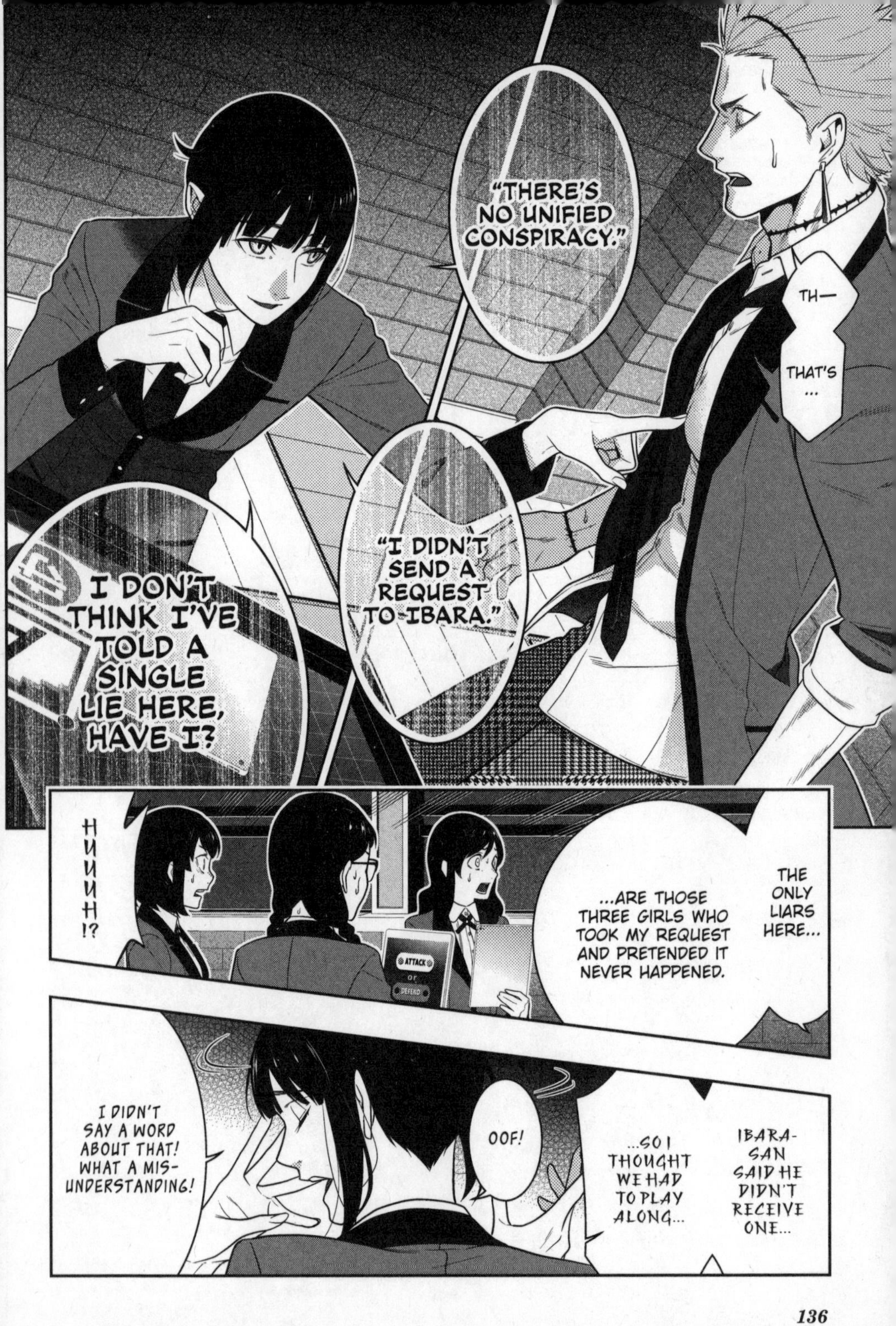
TH—
THAT'S ...
"THERE'S NO UNIFIED CONSPIRACY."
"I DIDN'T SEND A REQUEST TO IBARA."
I DON'T THINK I'VE TOLD A SINGLE LIE HERE, HAVE I?
THE ONLY LIARS HERE...
...ARE THOSE THREE GIRLS WHO TOOK MY REQUEST AND PRETENDED IT NEVER HAPPENED.
HUUUUH!?
ATTACK
or
DEFEND
IBARA-SAN SAID HE DIDN'T RECEIVE ONE...
...SO I THOUGHT WE HAD TO PLAY ALONG...
OOF!
I DIDN'T SAY A WORD ABOUT THAT! WHAT A MIS-UNDERSTANDING!

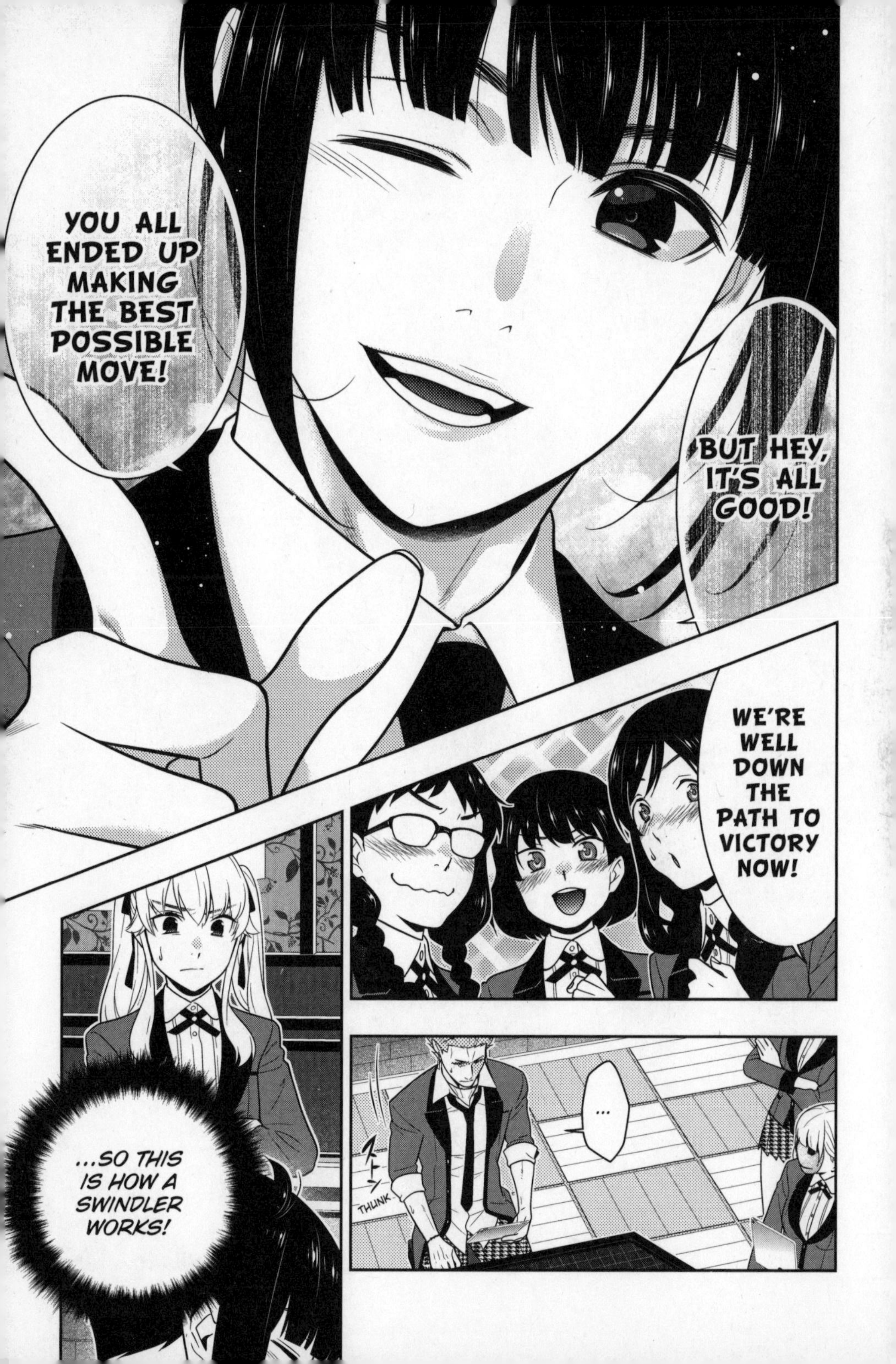
BUT HEY, IT'S ALL GOOD!
YOU ALL ENDED UP MAKING THE BEST POSSIBLE MOVE!
WE'RE WELL DOWN THE PATH TO VICTORY NOW!
...
ストン
THUNK
...SO THIS IS HOW A SWINDLER WORKS!

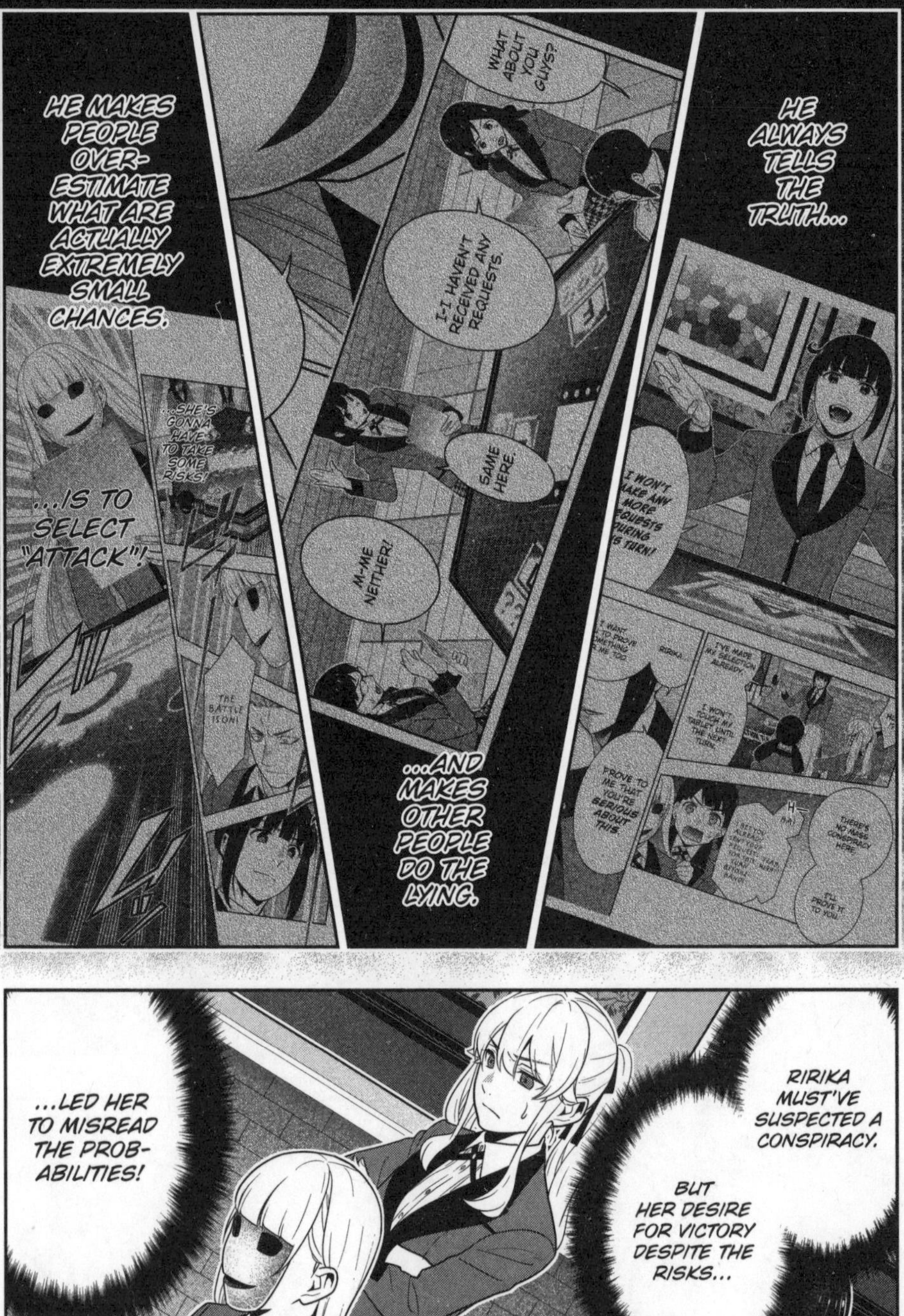
HE ALWAYS TELLS THE TRUTH...
I WON'T MAKE ANY MORE REQUESTS DURING THIS TURN!
RIRIKA...
I'VE MADE MY SELECTION ALREADY.
I WON'T TOUCH MY TABLET UNTIL THE NEXT TURN.
THERE'S NO MASS CONSPIRACY HERE.
I'LL PROVE IT TO YOU.
H— HA!
PROVE TO ME THAT YOU'RE SERIOUS ABOUT THIS.
WHAT ABOUT YOU GUYS?
I-I HAVEN'T RECEIVED ANY REQUESTS.
SAME HERE.
M-ME NEITHER!
...AND MAKES OTHER PEOPLE DO THE LYING.
HE MAKES PEOPLE OVER-ESTIMATE WHAT ARE ACTUALLY EXTREMELY SMALL CHANCES.
...SHE'S GONNA HAVE TO TAKE SOME RISKS!
...IS TO SELECT "ATTACK"!
THE BATTLE IS ON!
RIRIKA MUST'VE SUSPECTED A CONSPIRACY.
BUT HER DESIRE FOR VICTORY DESPITE THE RISKS...
...LED HER TO MISREAD THE PROB-ABILITIES!

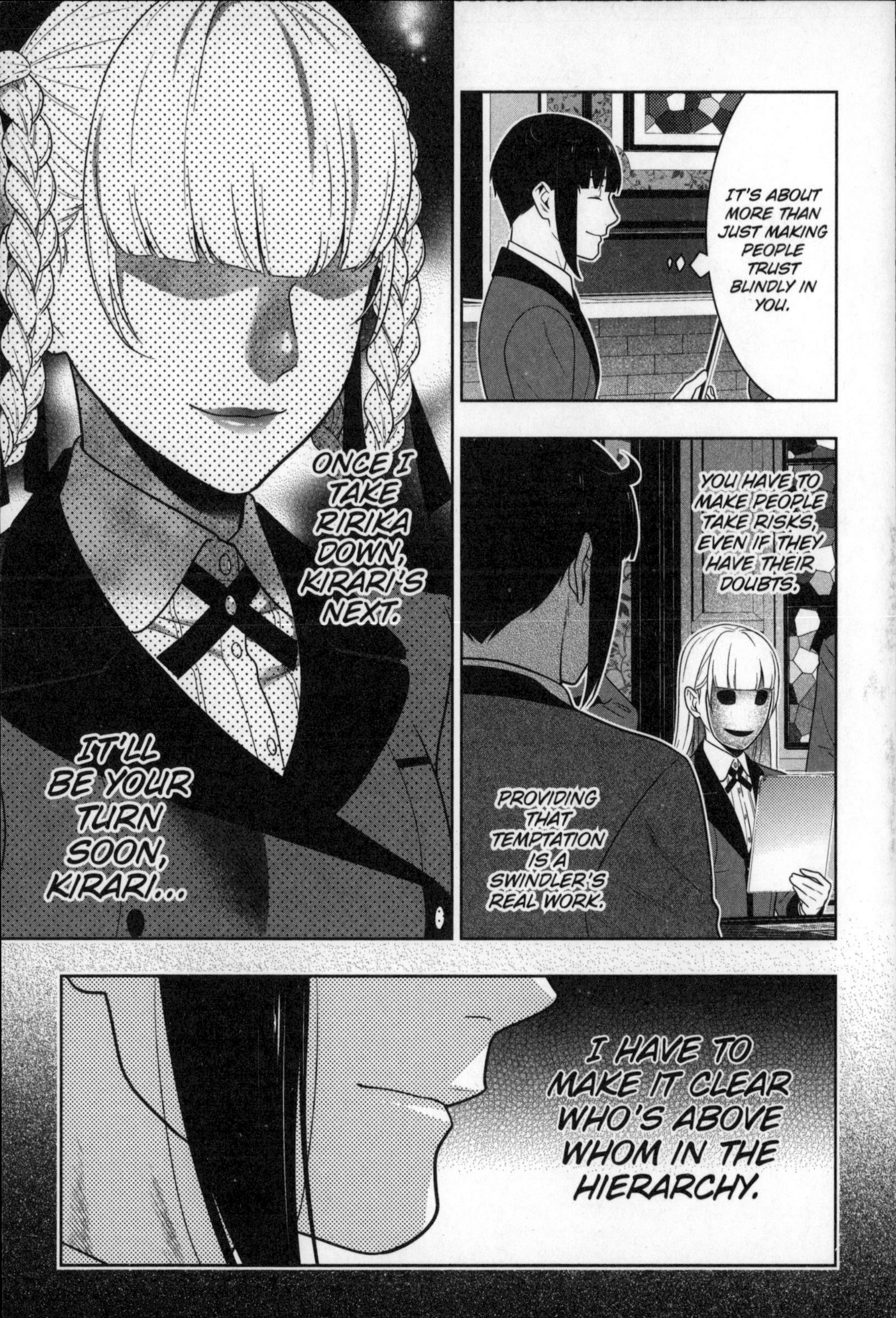
IT'S ABOUT MORE THAN JUST MAKING PEOPLE TRUST BLINDLY IN YOU.
YOU HAVE TO MAKE PEOPLE TAKE RISKS, EVEN IF THEY HAVE THEIR DOUBTS.
PROVIDING THAT TEMPTATION IS A SWINDLER'S REAL WORK.
ONCE I TAKE RIRIKA DOWN, KIRARI'S NEXT.
IT'LL BE YOUR TURN SOON, KIRARI...
I HAVE TO MAKE IT CLEAR WHO'S ABOVE WHOM IN THE HIERARCHY.

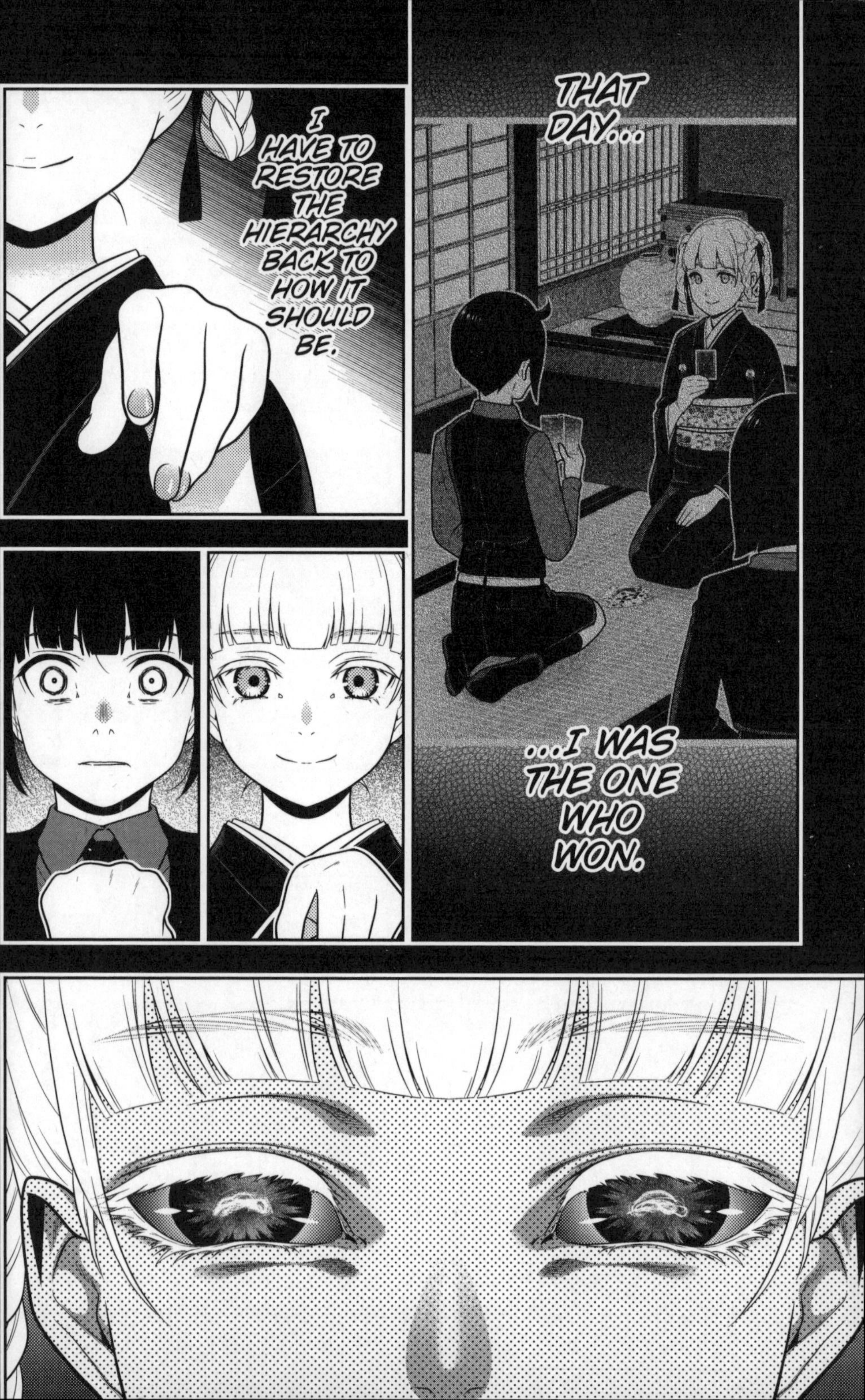
THAT DAY...
...I WAS THE ONE WHO WON.
I HAVE TO RESTORE THE HIERARCHY BACK TO HOW IT SHOULD BE.

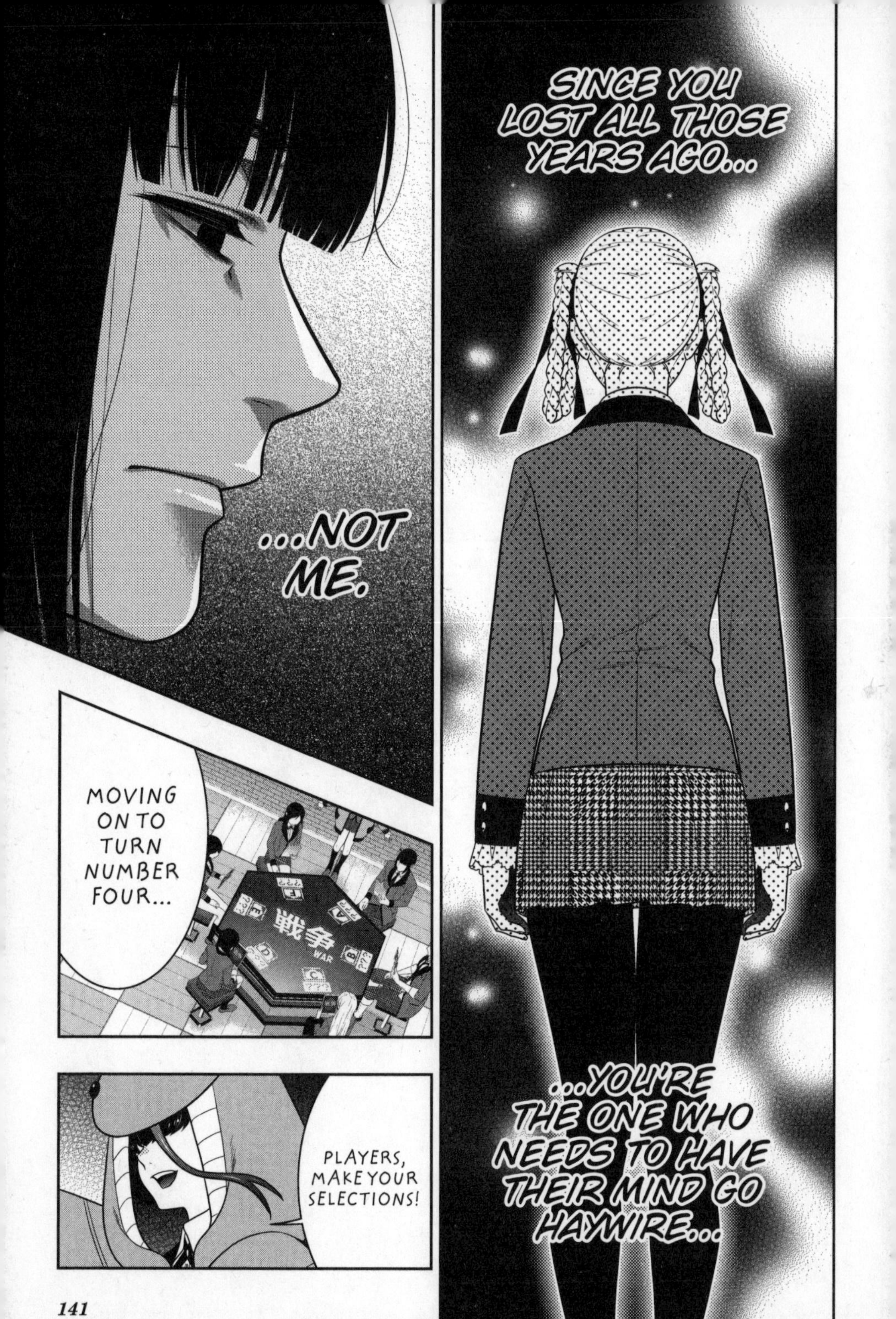
SINCE YOU LOST ALL THOSE YEARS AGO...
...YOU'RE THE ONE WHO NEEDS TO HAVE THEIR MIND GO HAYWIRE...
...NOT ME.
MOVING ON TO TURN NUMBER FOUR...
戦争
WAR
PLAYERS, MAKE YOUR SELECTIONS!

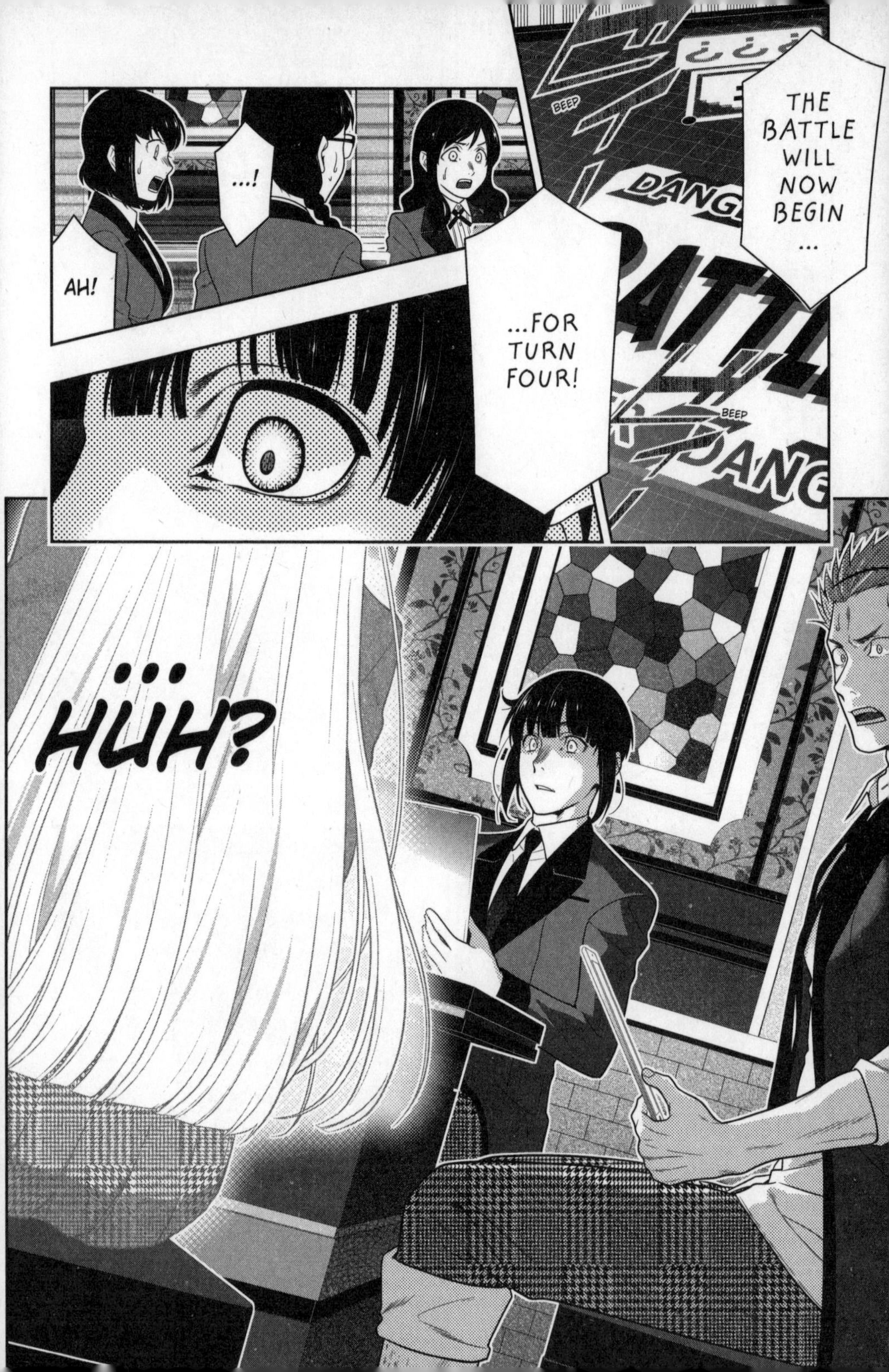
BEEP
THE BATTLE WILL NOW BEGIN ...
...FOR TURN FOUR!
BEEP
...!
AH!
...HUH?

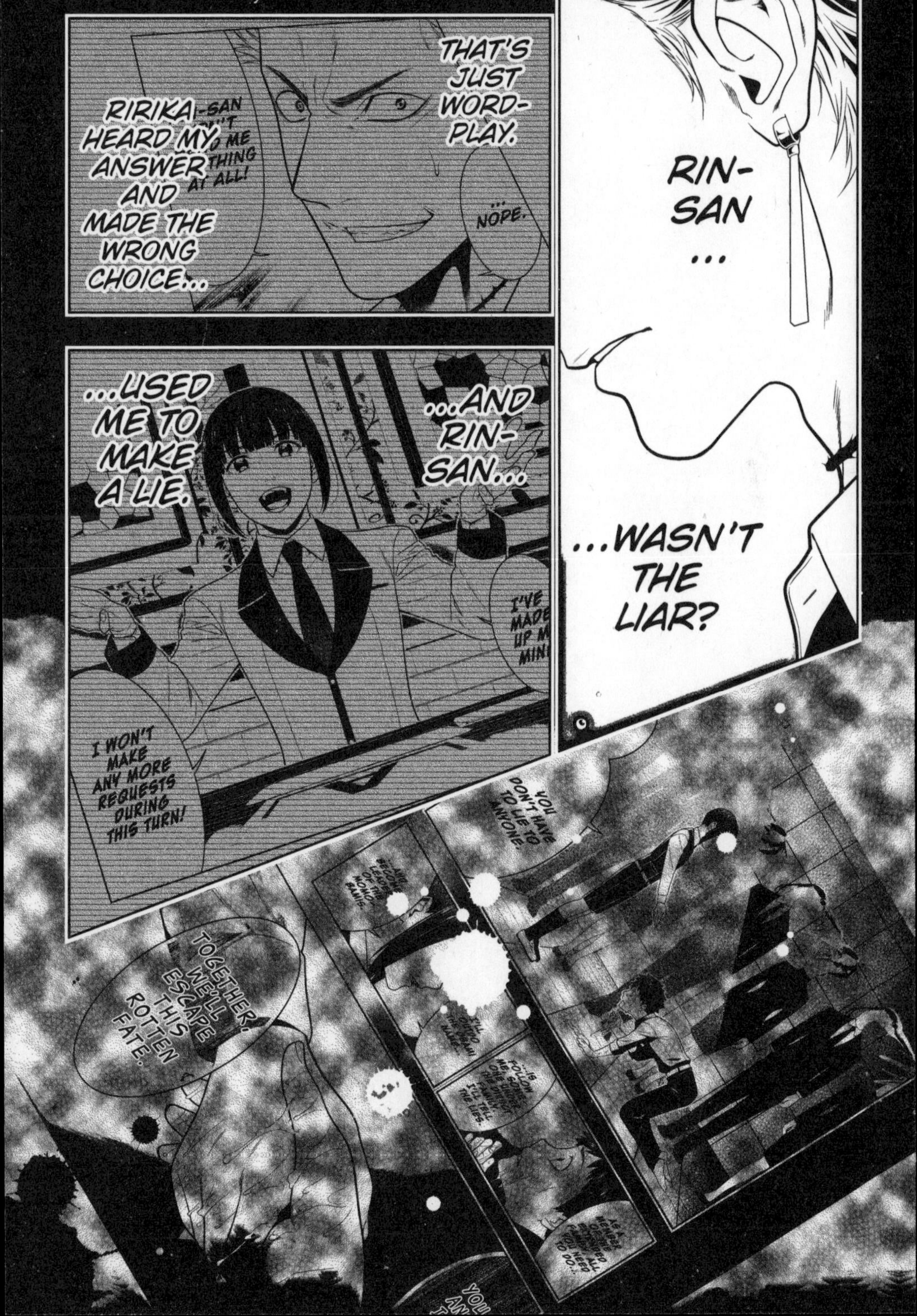
RIN-SAN ...
...WASN'T THE LIAR?
THAT'S JUST WORD-PLAY.
...NOPE.
RIRIKA HEARD MY ANSWER AND MADE THE WRONG CHOICE...
...AND RIN-SAN...
...USED ME TO MAKE A LIE.
I WON'T MAKE ANY MORE REQUESTS DURING THIS TURN!
YOU DON'T HAVE TO LIE TO ANYONE.
TOGETHER, WE'LL ESCAPE THIS ROTTEN FATE.

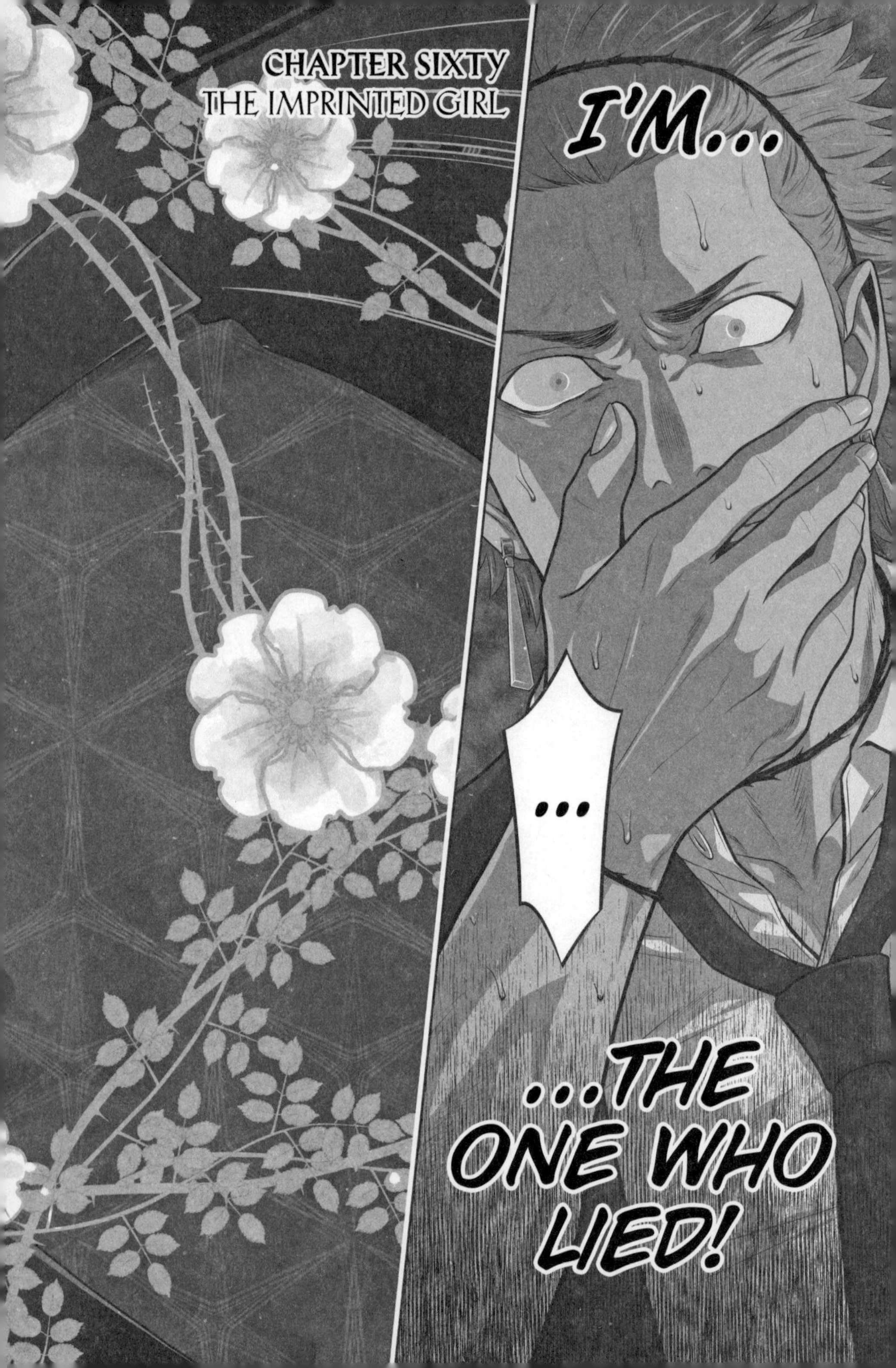
I'M...
...
...THE ONE WHO LIED!
CHAPTER SIXTY
THE IMPRINTED GIRL

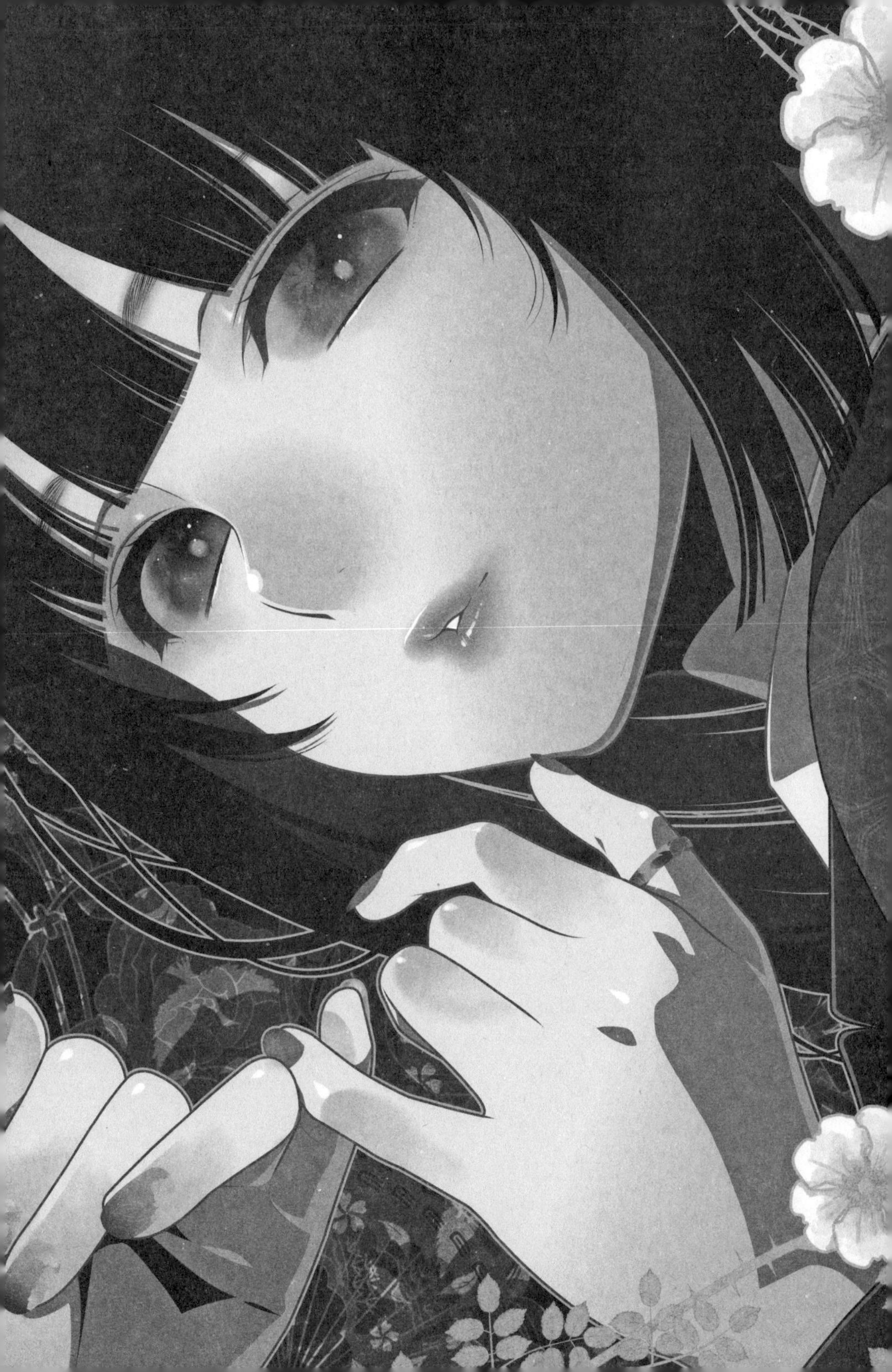

KAKEGURUI
— Compulsive Gambler —

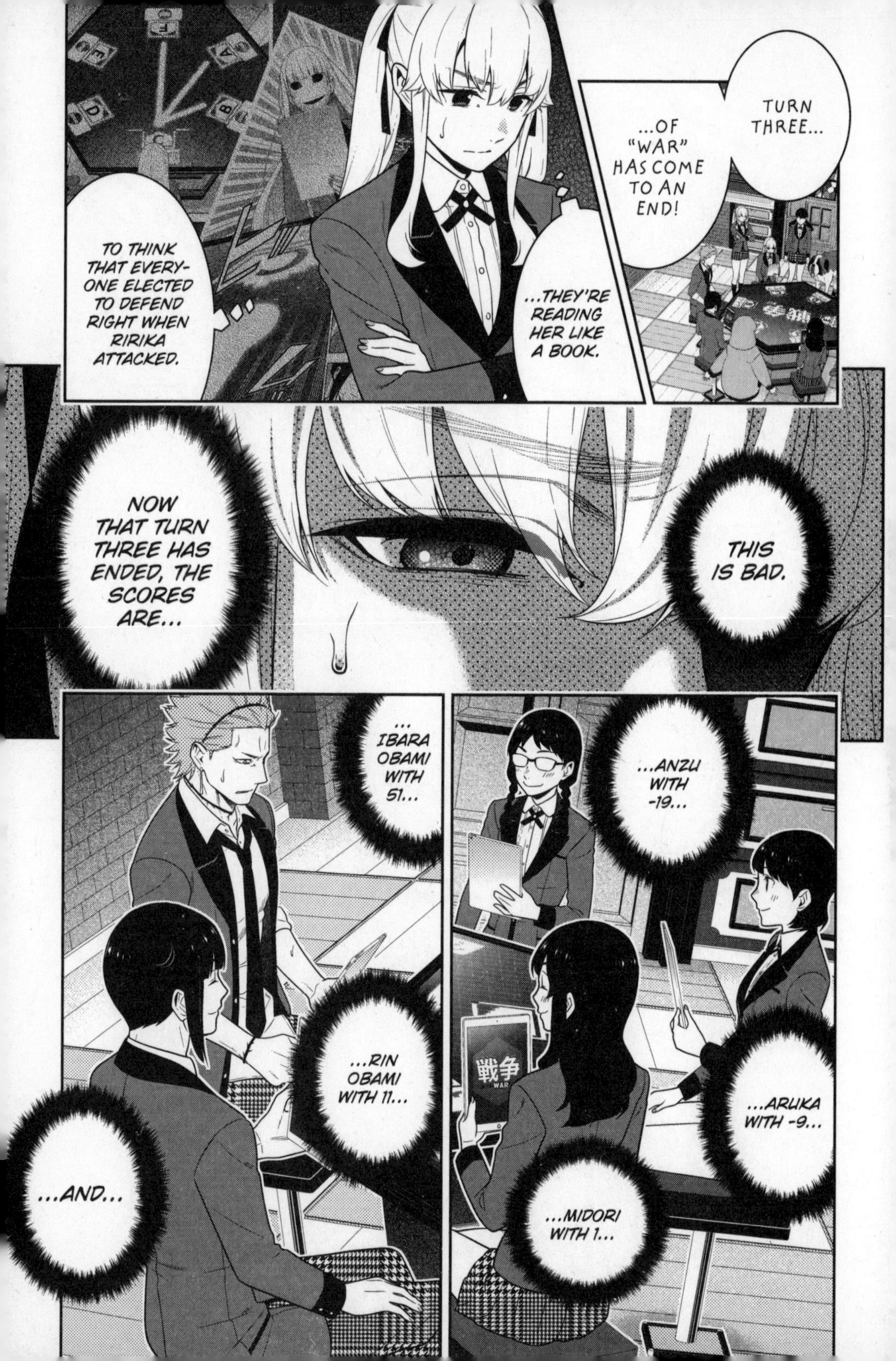
TURN THREE...
...OF "WAR" HAS COME TO AN END!
...THEY'RE READING HER LIKE A BOOK.
TO THINK THAT EVERYONE ELECTED TO DEFEND RIGHT WHEN RIRIKA ATTACKED.
THIS IS BAD.
NOW THAT TURN THREE HAS ENDED, THE SCORES ARE...
...ANZU WITH -19...
...ARUKA WITH -9...
戦争
WAR
...MIDORI WITH 1...
...IBARA OBAMI WITH 51...
...RIN OBAMI WITH 11...
...AND...

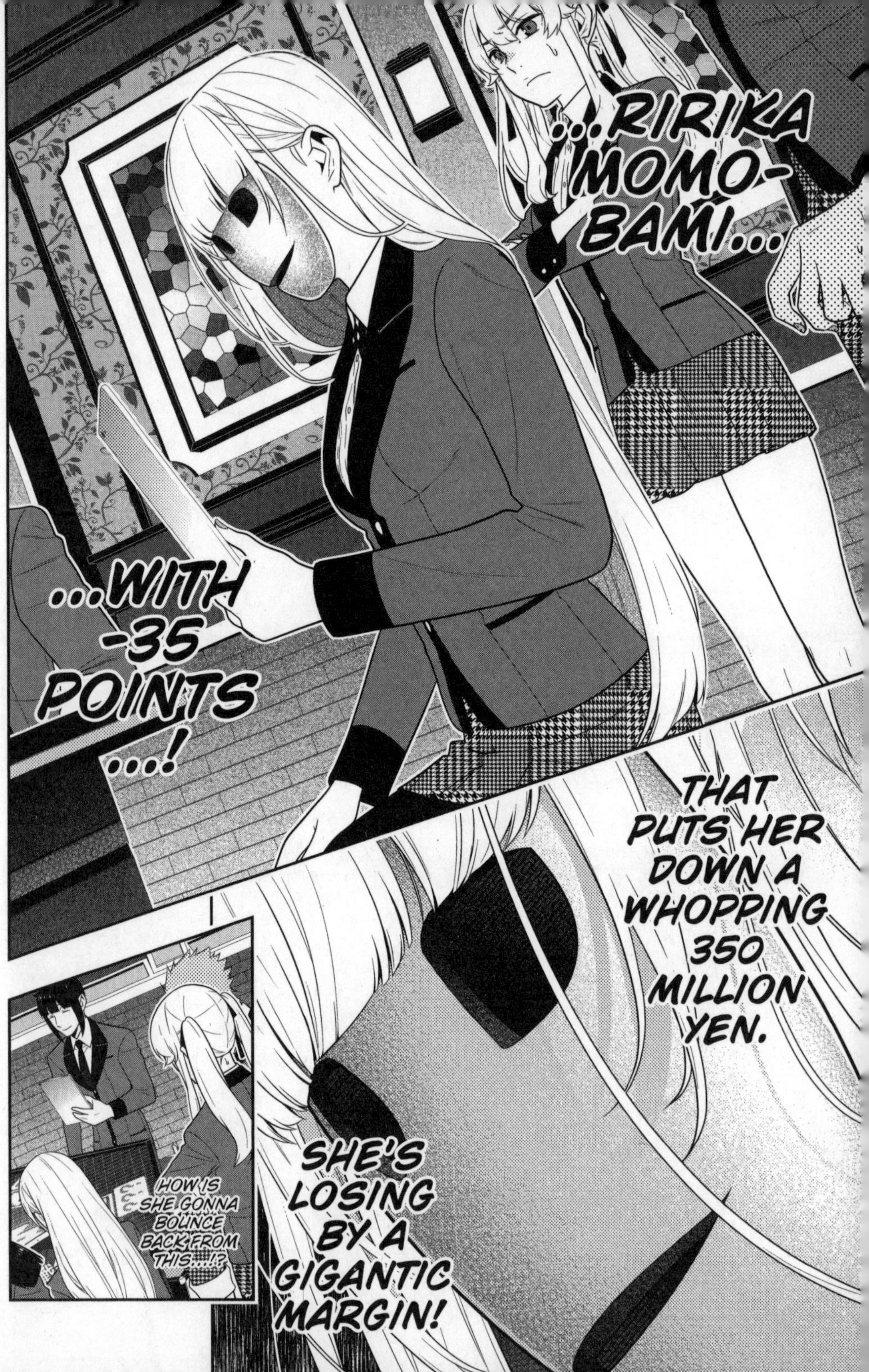
...RIRIKA MOMOBAMI...
...WITH -35 POINTS...!
THAT PUTS HER DOWN A WHOPPING 350 MILLION YEN.
SHE'S LOSING BY A GIGANTIC MARGIN!
HOW IS SHE GONNA BOUNCE BACK FROM THIS...!?

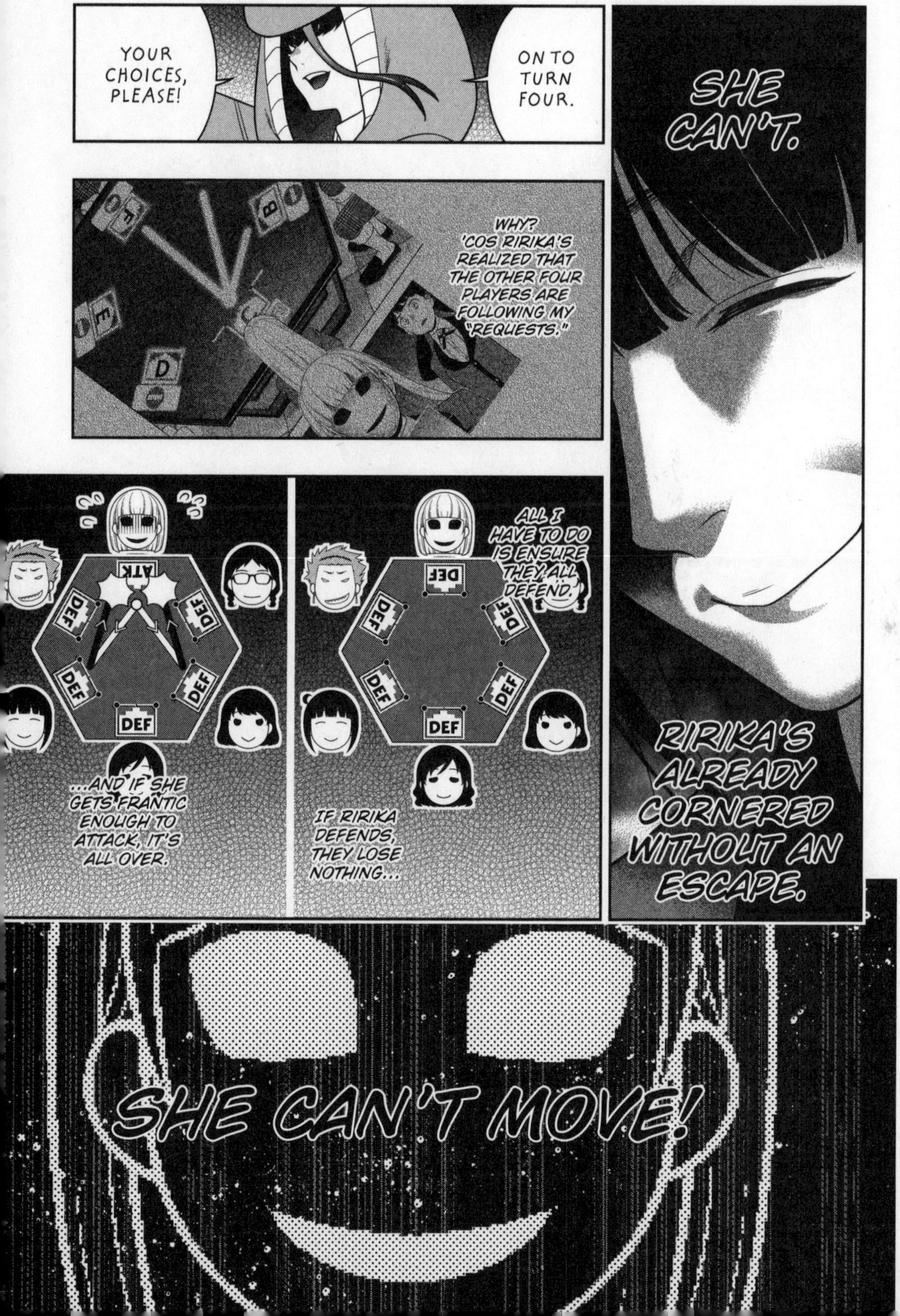
SHE CAN'T.
RIRIKA'S ALREADY CORNERED WITHOUT AN ESCAPE.
ON TO TURN FOUR.
YOUR CHOICES, PLEASE!
B
F
E
D
WHY? 'COS RIRIKA'S REALIZED THAT THE OTHER FOUR PLAYERS ARE FOLLOWING MY "REQUESTS."
ALL I HAVE TO DO IS ENSURE THEY ALL DEFEND.
DEF
DEF
DEF
DEF
DEF
DEF
IF RIRIKA DEFENDS, THEY LOSE NOTHING...
ATK
DEF
DEF
DEF
DEF
DEF
...AND IF SHE GETS FRANTIC ENOUGH TO ATTACK, IT'S ALL OVER.
SHE CAN'T MOVE!

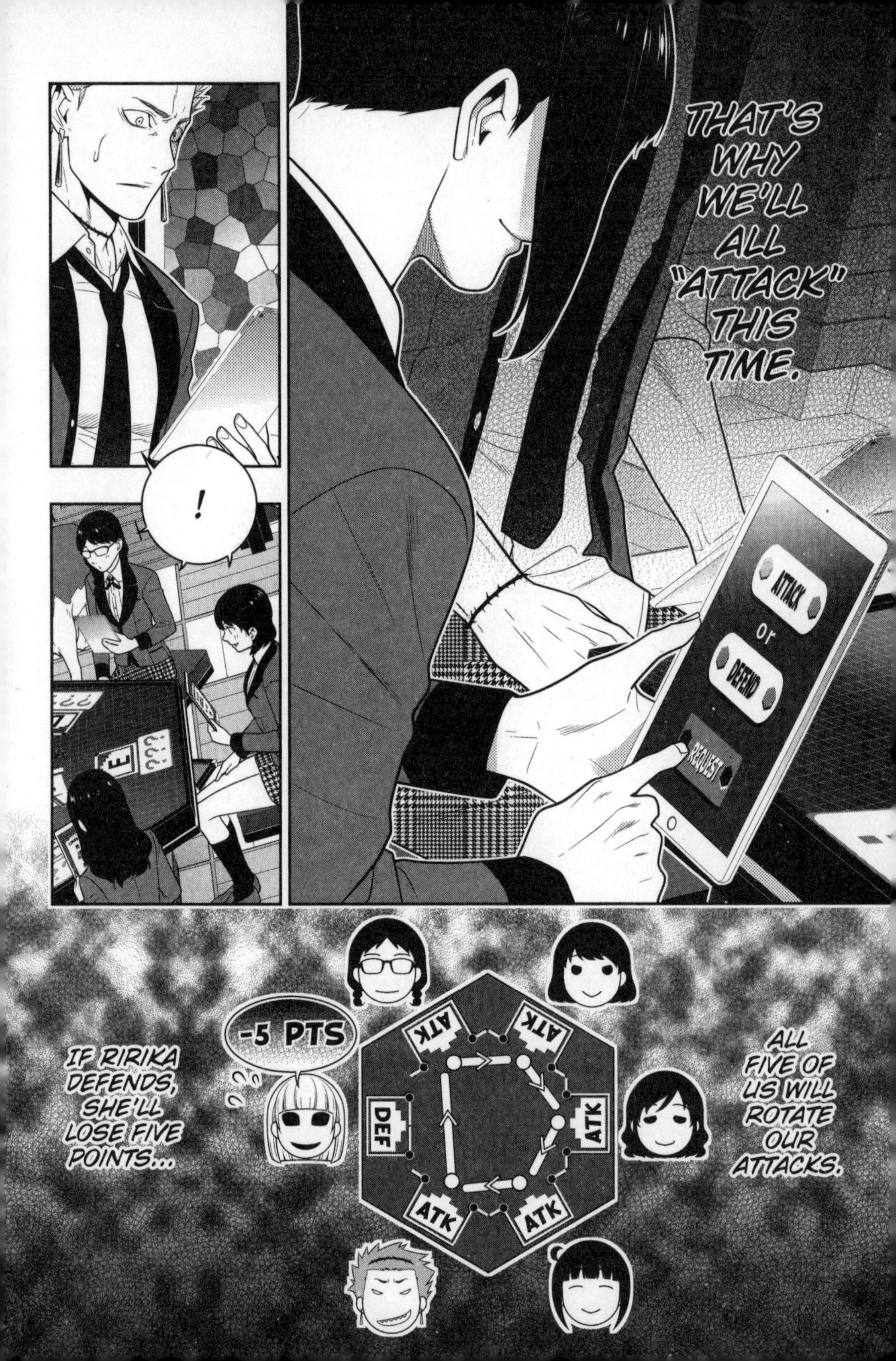
THAT'S WHY WE'LL ALL "ATTACK" THIS TIME.
ATTACK
or
DEFEND
REQUEST
!
ALL FIVE OF US WILL ROTATE OUR ATTACKS.
ATK
ATK
ATK
ATK
ATK
DEF
-5 PTS
IF RIRIKA DEFENDS, SHE'LL LOSE FIVE POINTS...

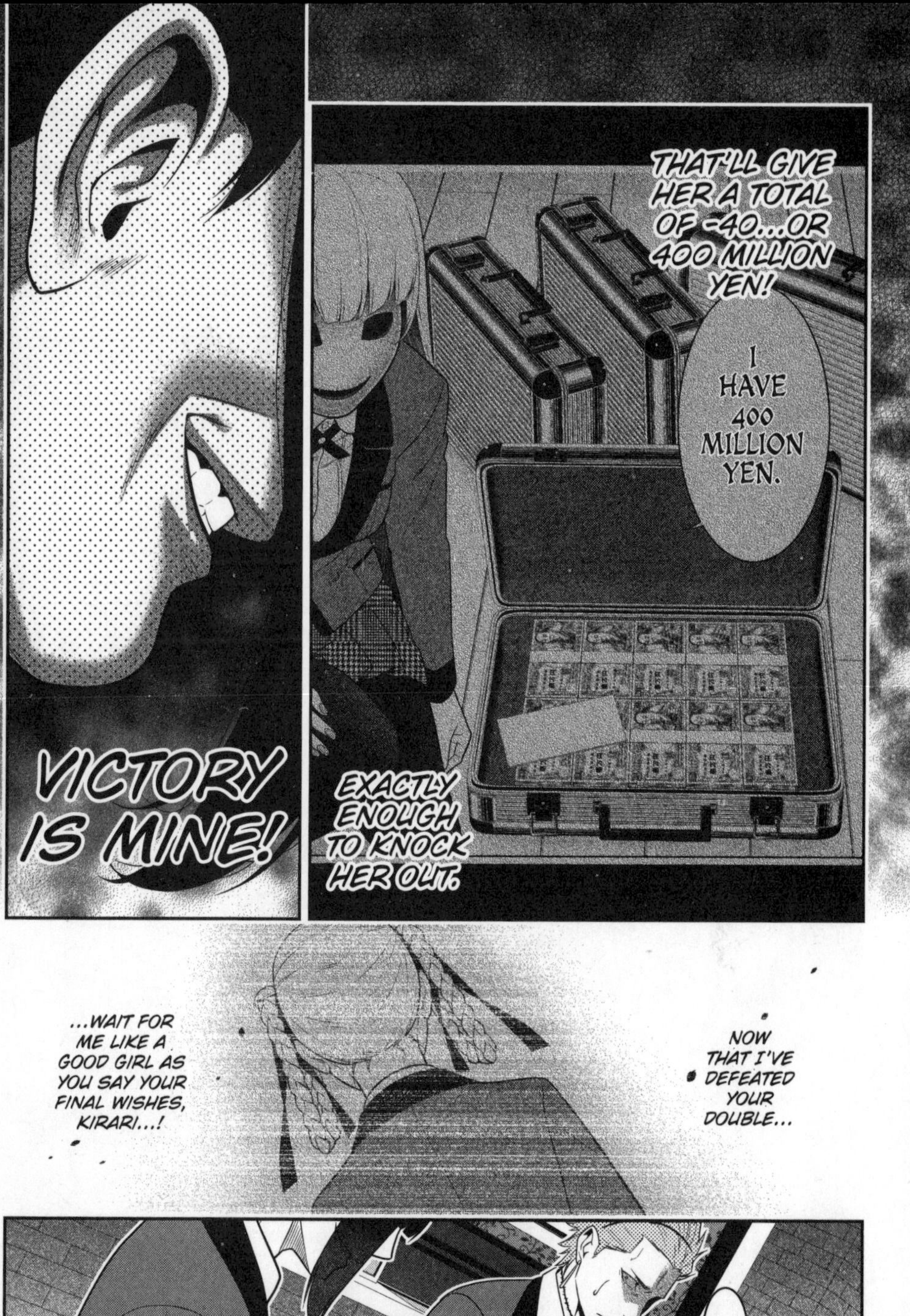
THAT'LL GIVE HER A TOTAL OF -40...OR 400 MILLION YEN!
I HAVE 400 MILLION YEN.
EXACTLY ENOUGH TO KNOCK HER OUT.
VICTORY IS MINE!
NOW THAT I'VE DEFEATED YOUR DOUBLE...
...WAIT FOR ME LIKE A GOOD GIRL AS YOU SAY YOUR FINAL WISHES, KIRARI...!
...

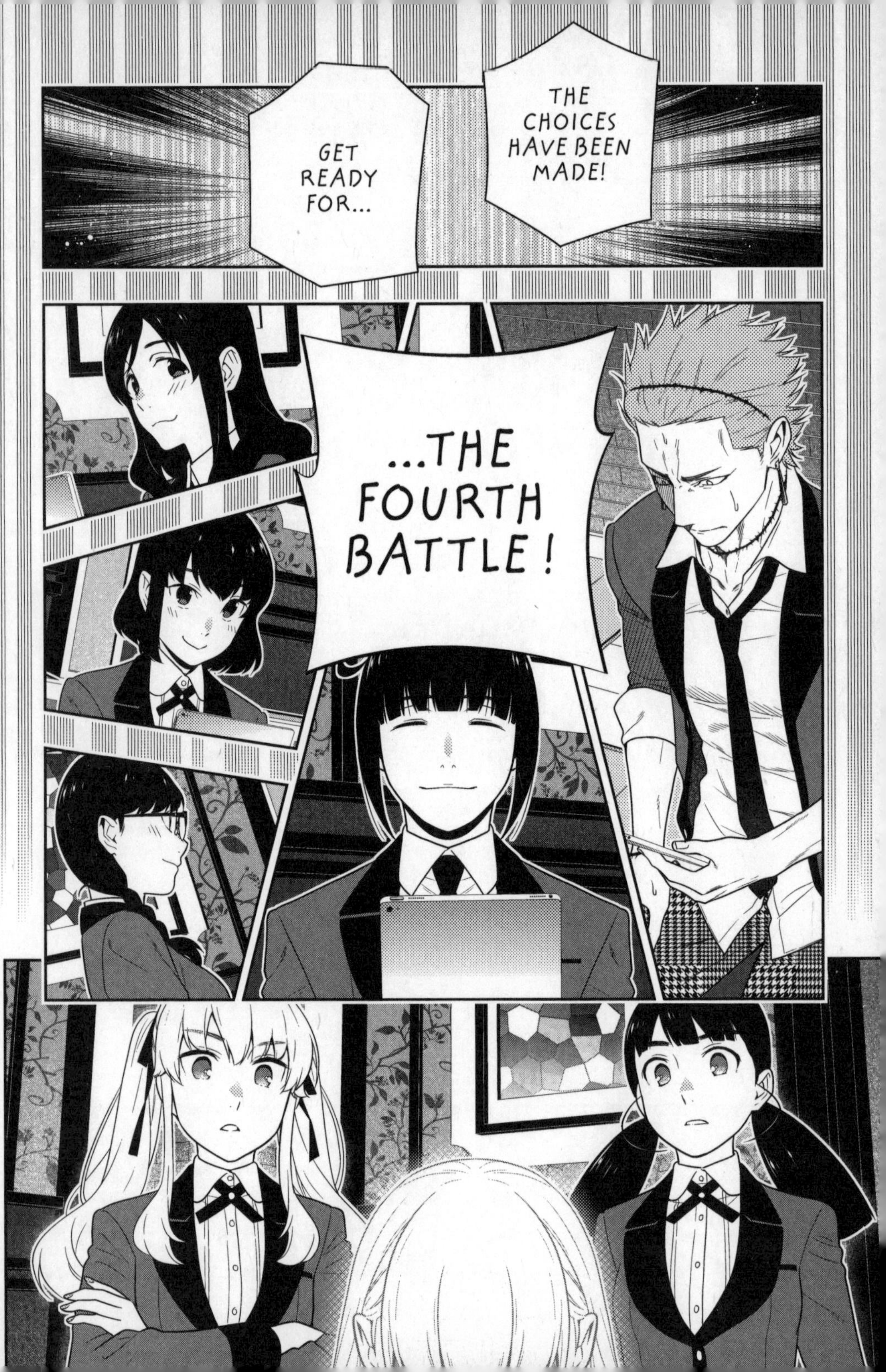
THE CHOICES HAVE BEEN MADE!
GET READY FOR...
...THE FOURTH BATTLE!

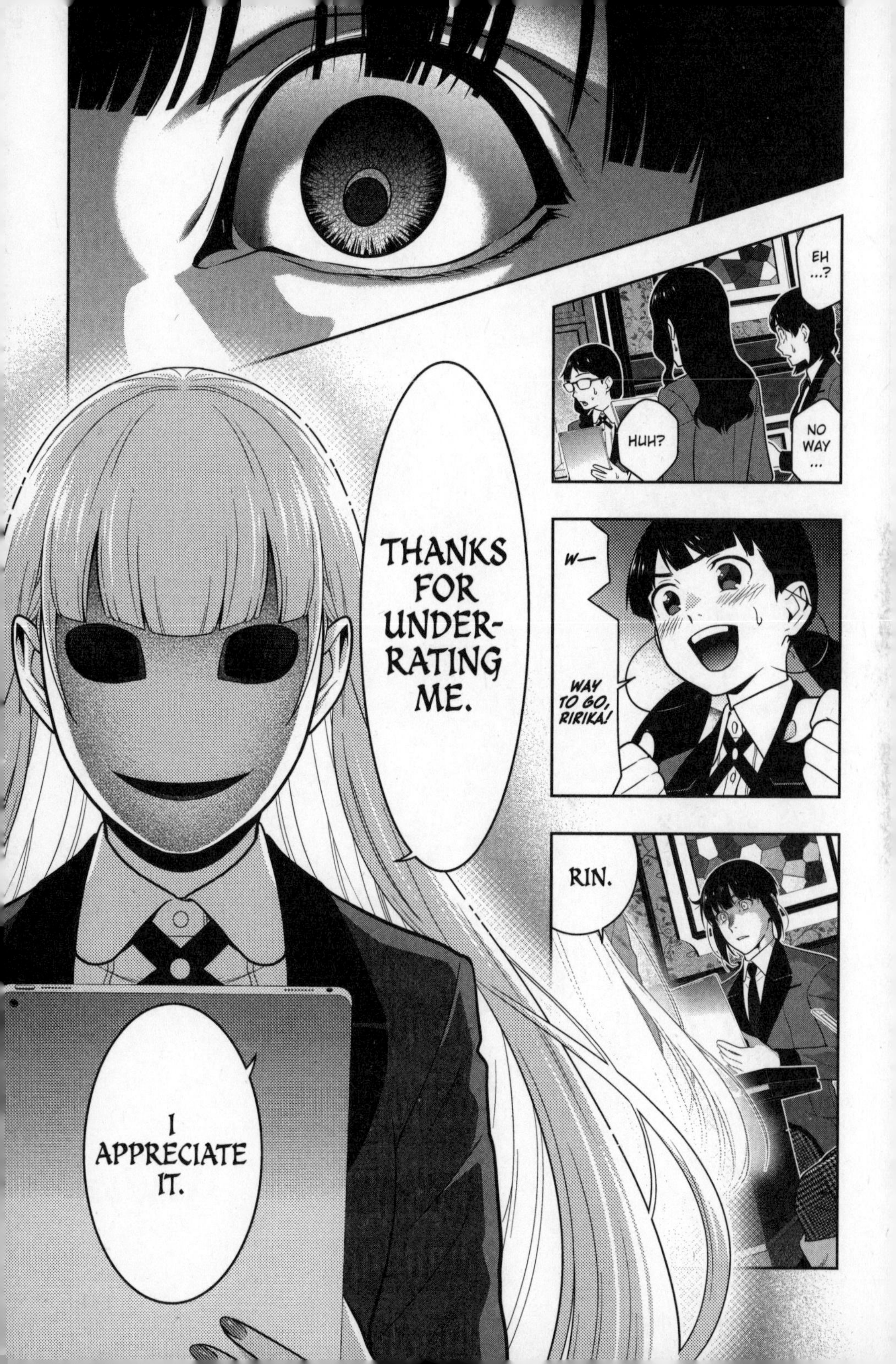
EH ...?
NO WAY ...
HUH?
W—
WAY TO GO, RIRIKA!
RIN.
THANKS FOR UNDER-RATING ME.
I APPRECIATE IT.

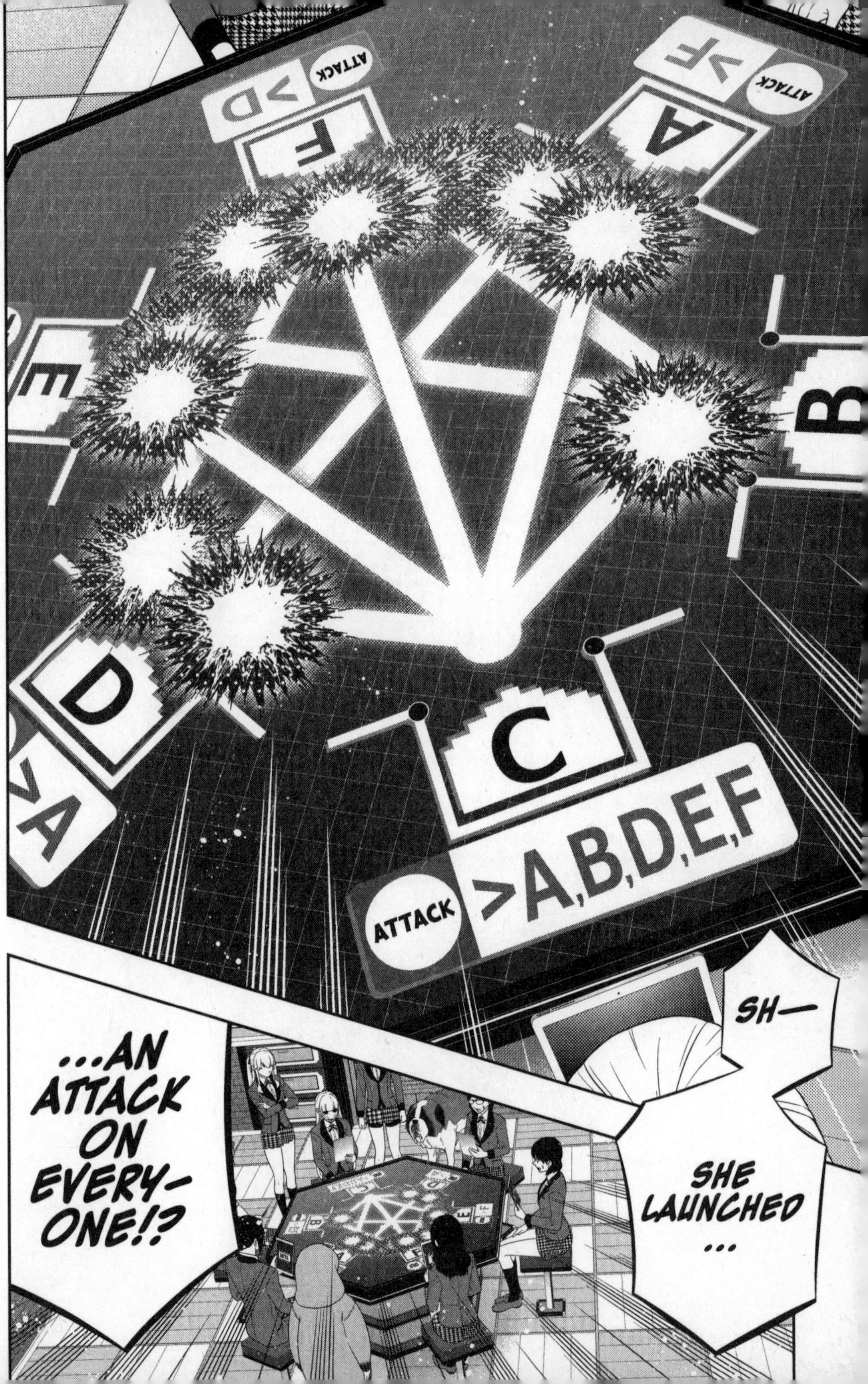
ATTACK >F
A
ATTACK >D
F
B
E
C
ATTACK >A,B,D,E,F
D
>A
SH—
SHE LAUNCHED ...
...AN ATTACK ON EVERY-ONE!?

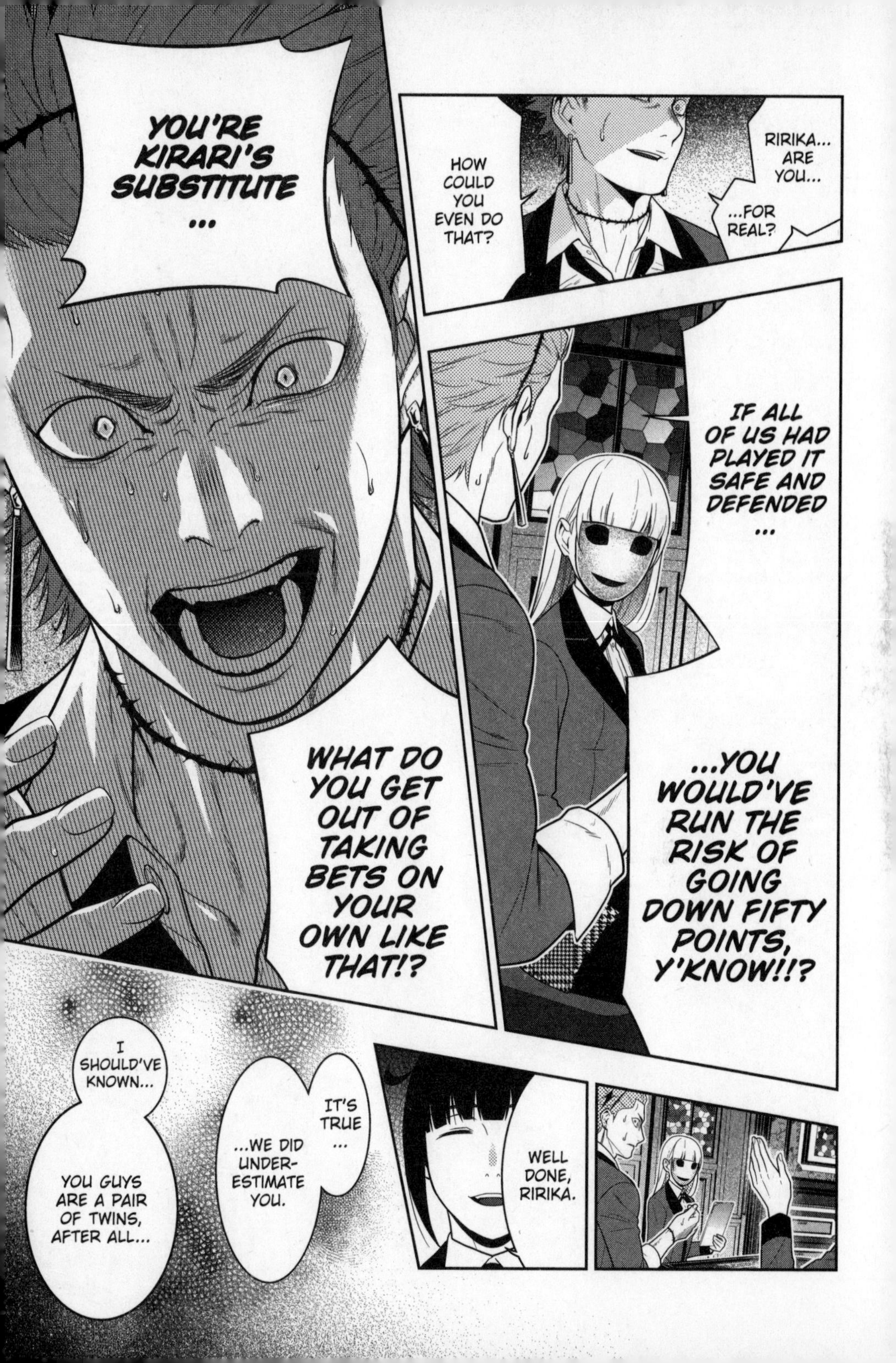
RIRIKA... ARE YOU...
...FOR REAL?
HOW COULD YOU EVEN DO THAT?
IF ALL OF US HAD PLAYED IT SAFE AND DEFENDED ...
...YOU WOULD'VE RUN THE RISK OF GOING DOWN FIFTY POINTS, Y'KNOW!!?
YOU'RE KIRARI'S SUBSTITUTE ...
WHAT DO YOU GET OUT OF TAKING BETS ON YOUR OWN LIKE THAT!?
WELL DONE, RIRIKA.
IT'S TRUE ...
...WE DID UNDER-ESTIMATE YOU.
I SHOULD'VE KNOWN...
YOU GUYS ARE A PAIR OF TWINS, AFTER ALL...

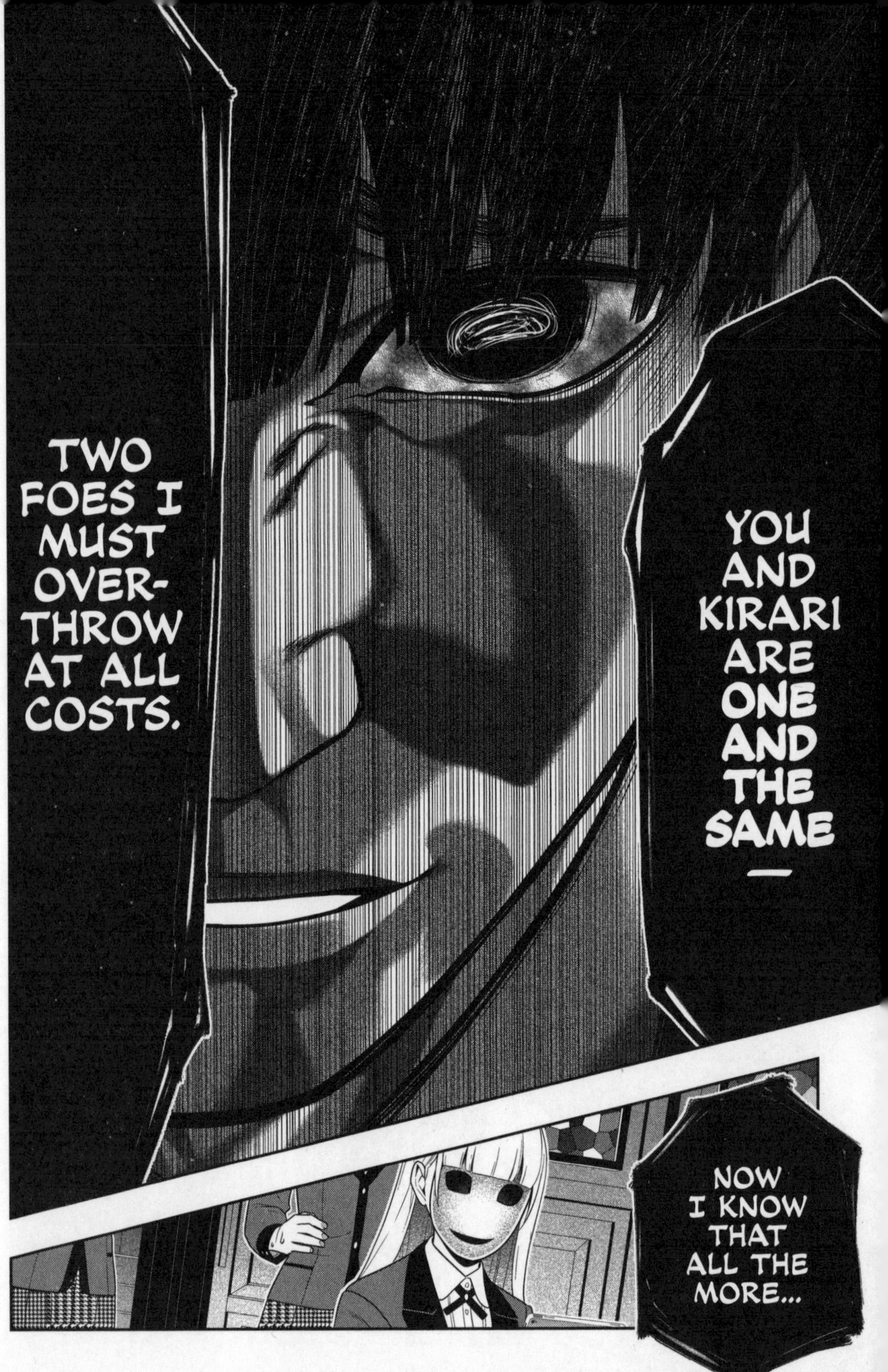
YOU AND KIRARI ARE ONE AND THE SAME —
TWO FOES I MUST OVER-THROW AT ALL COSTS.
NOW I KNOW THAT ALL THE MORE...

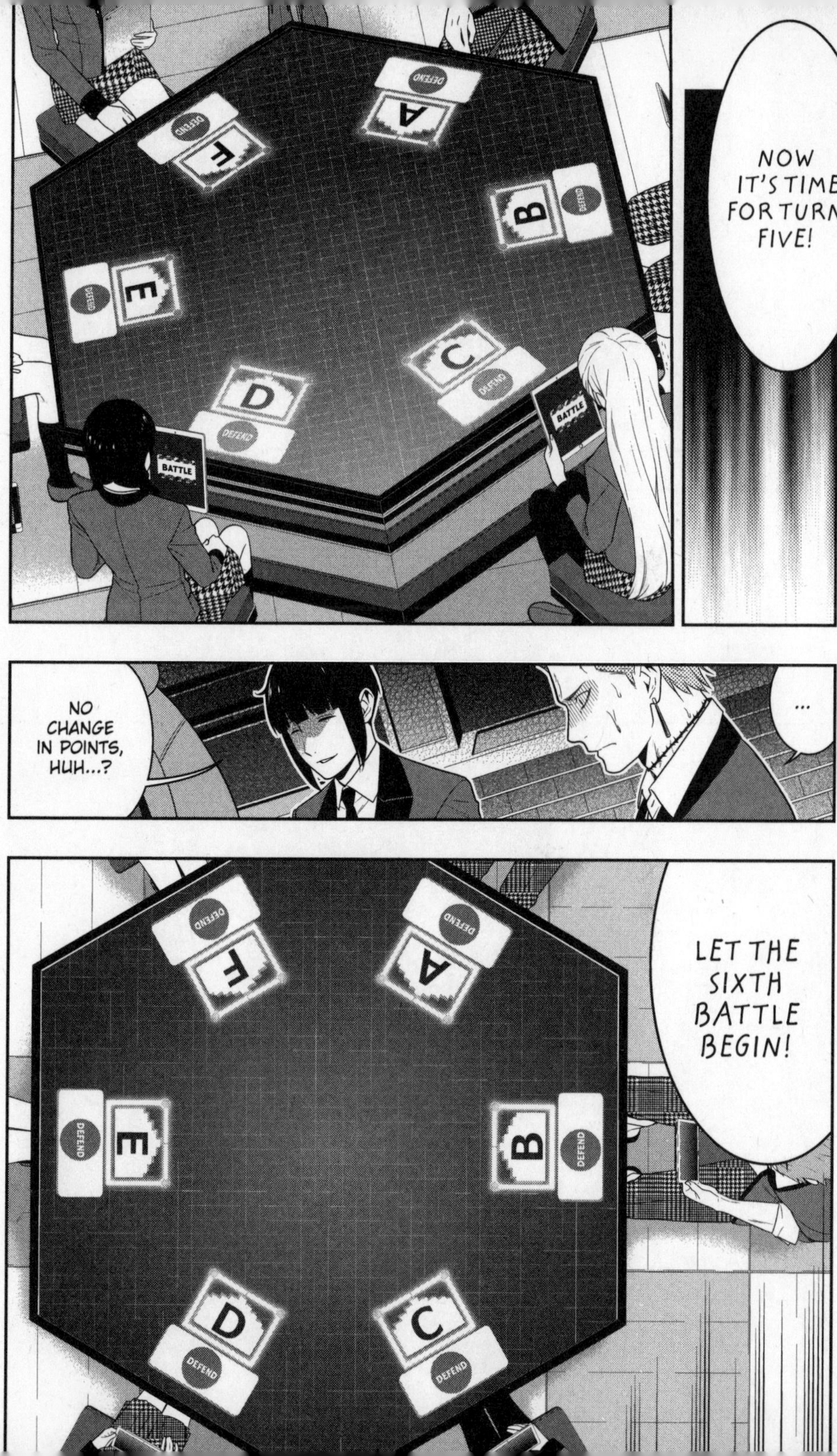
NOW IT'S TIME FOR TURN FIVE!
...
NO CHANGE IN POINTS, HUH...?
LET THE SIXTH BATTLE BEGIN!

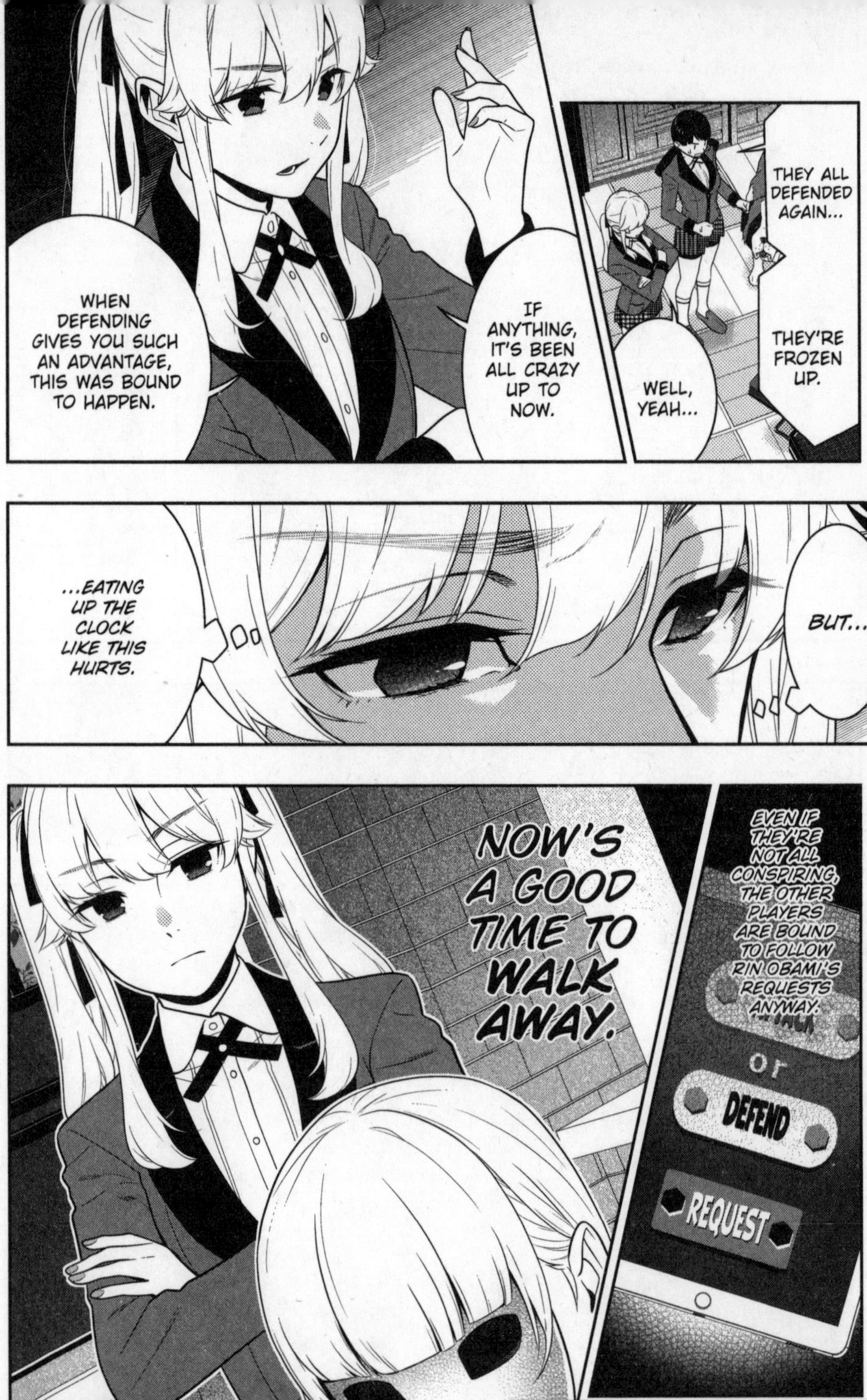
THEY ALL DEFENDED AGAIN...
THEY'RE FROZEN UP.
WELL, YEAH...
IF ANYTHING, IT'S BEEN ALL CRAZY UP TO NOW.
WHEN DEFENDING GIVES YOU SUCH AN ADVANTAGE, THIS WAS BOUND TO HAPPEN.
BUT...
...EATING UP THE CLOCK LIKE THIS HURTS.
EVEN IF THEY'RE NOT ALL CONSPIRING, THE OTHER PLAYERS ARE BOUND TO FOLLOW RIN OBAMI'S REQUESTS ANYWAY.
or
DEFEND
REQUEST
NOW'S A GOOD TIME TO WALK AWAY.

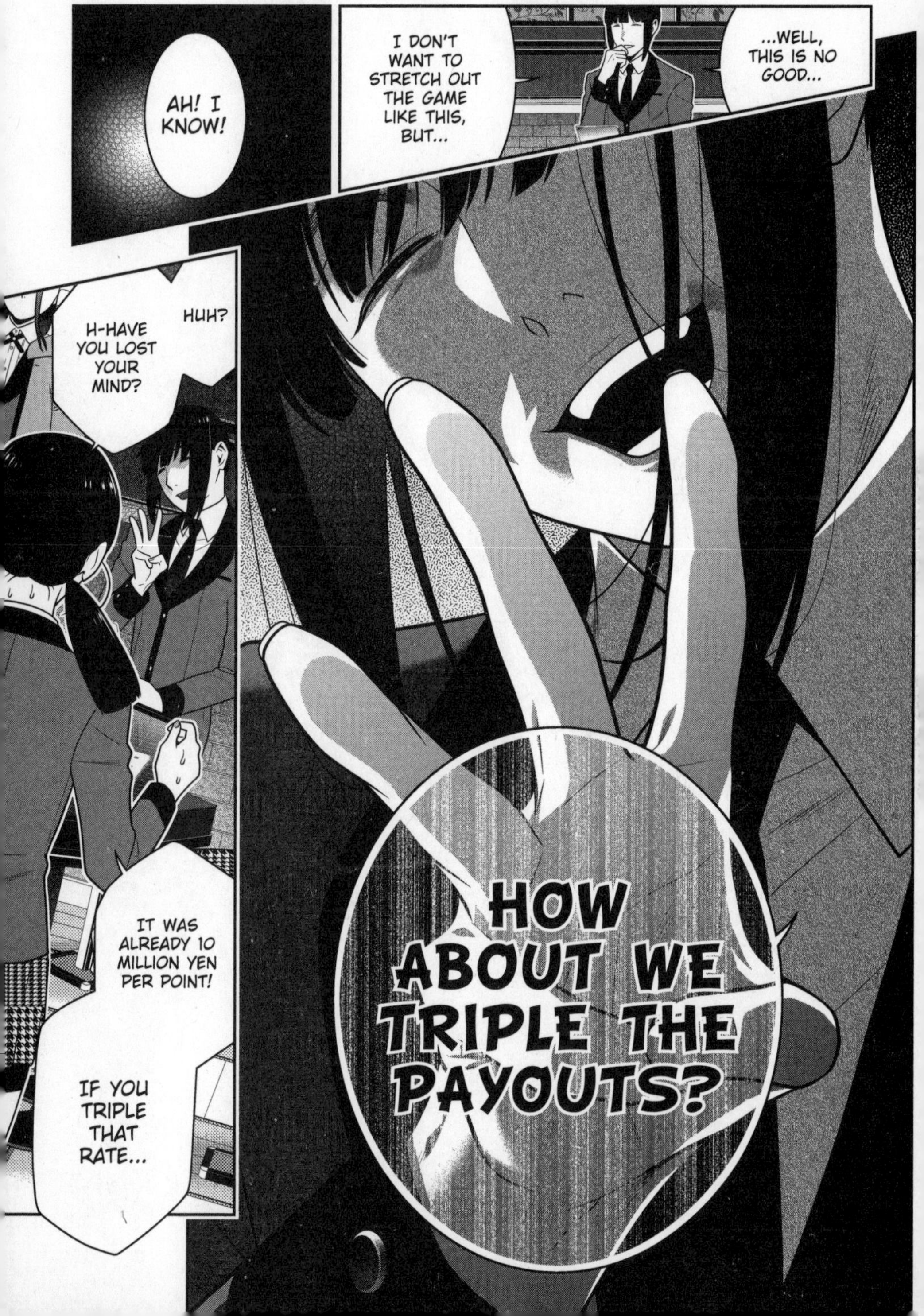
...WELL, THIS IS NO GOOD...
I DON'T WANT TO STRETCH OUT THE GAME LIKE THIS, BUT...
AH! I KNOW!
HOW ABOUT WE TRIPLE THE PAYOUTS?
HUH?
H-HAVE YOU LOST YOUR MIND?
IT WAS ALREADY 10 MILLION YEN PER POINT!
IF YOU TRIPLE THAT RATE...

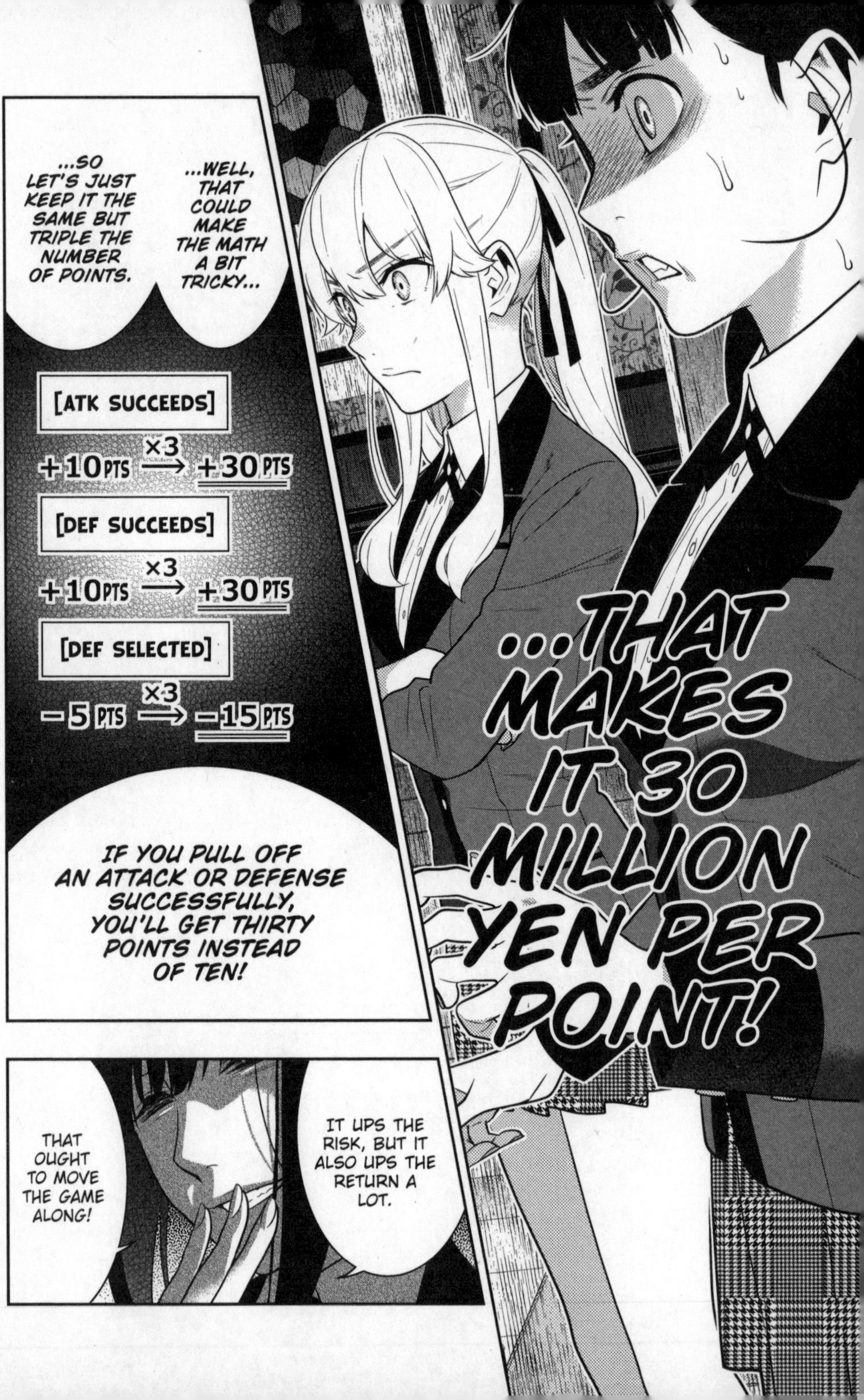
...THAT MAKES IT 30 MILLION YEN PER POINT!
...WELL, THAT COULD MAKE THE MATH A BIT TRICKY...
...SO LET'S JUST KEEP IT THE SAME BUT TRIPLE THE NUMBER OF POINTS.
[ATK SUCCEEDS]
+10PTS ×3 → +30PTS
[DEF SUCCEEDS]
+10PTS ×3 → +30PTS
[DEF SELECTED]
−5PTS ×3 → −15PTS
IF YOU PULL OFF AN ATTACK OR DEFENSE SUCCESSFULLY, YOU'LL GET THIRTY POINTS INSTEAD OF TEN!
IT UPS THE RISK, BUT IT ALSO UPS THE RETURN A LOT.
THAT OUGHT TO MOVE THE GAME ALONG!

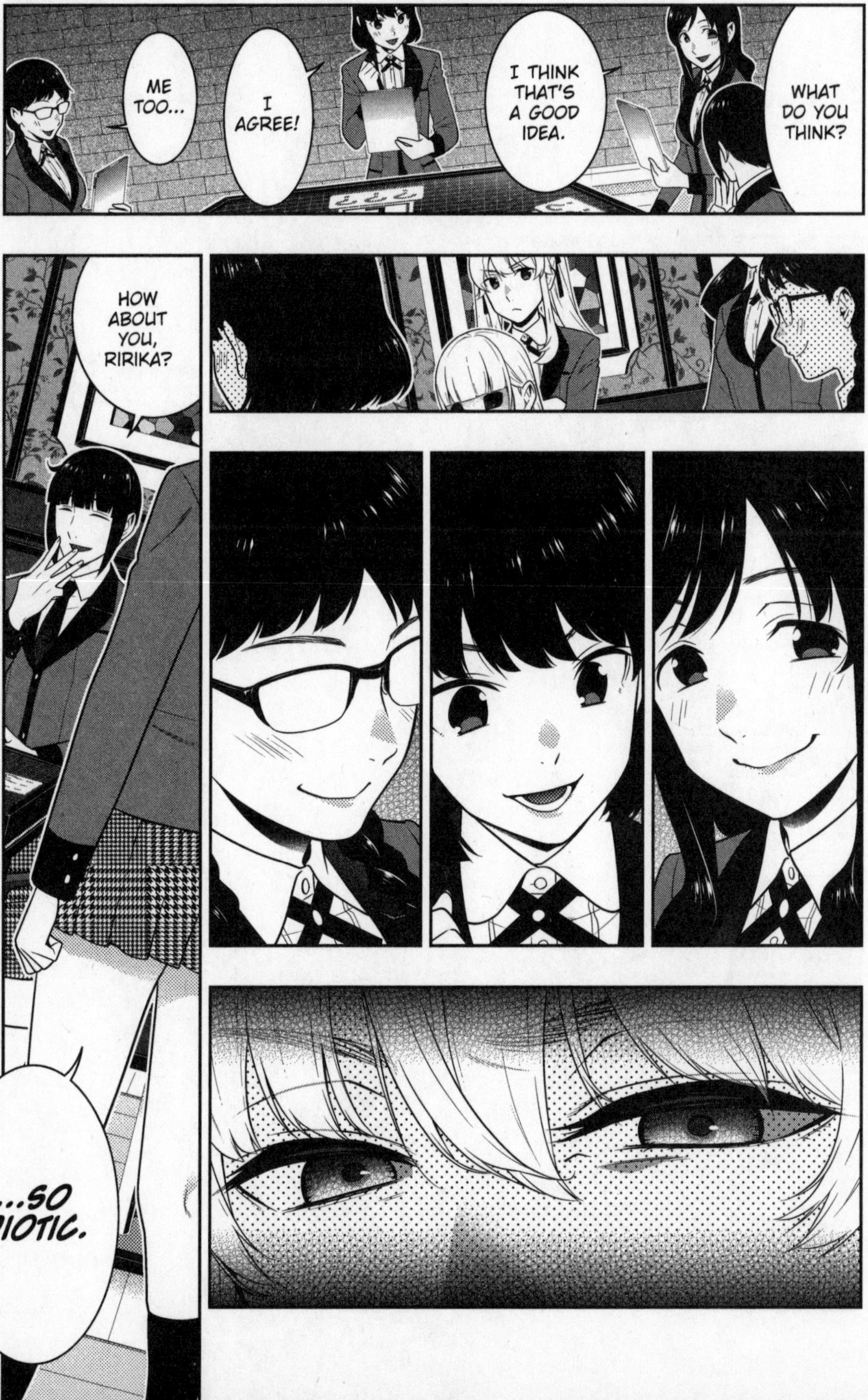
WHAT DO YOU THINK?
I THINK THAT'S A GOOD IDEA.
I AGREE!
ME TOO...
HOW ABOUT YOU, RIRIKA?
...SO IDIOTIC.

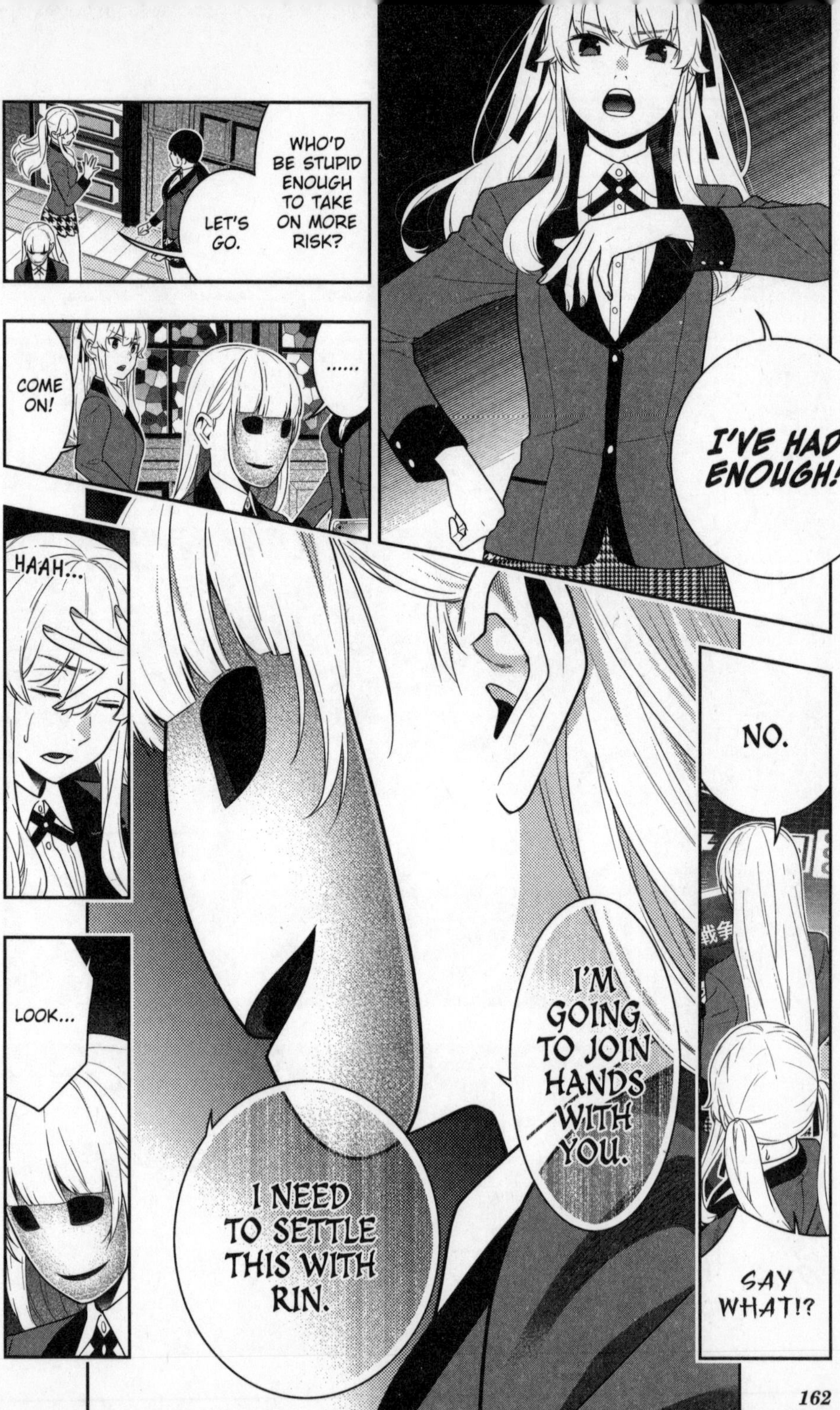
I'VE HAD ENOUGH!
WHO'D BE STUPID ENOUGH TO TAKE ON MORE RISK?
LET'S GO.
......
COME ON!
NO.
SAY WHAT!?
I'M GOING TO JOIN HANDS WITH YOU.
I NEED TO SETTLE THIS WITH RIN.
HAAH...
LOOK...

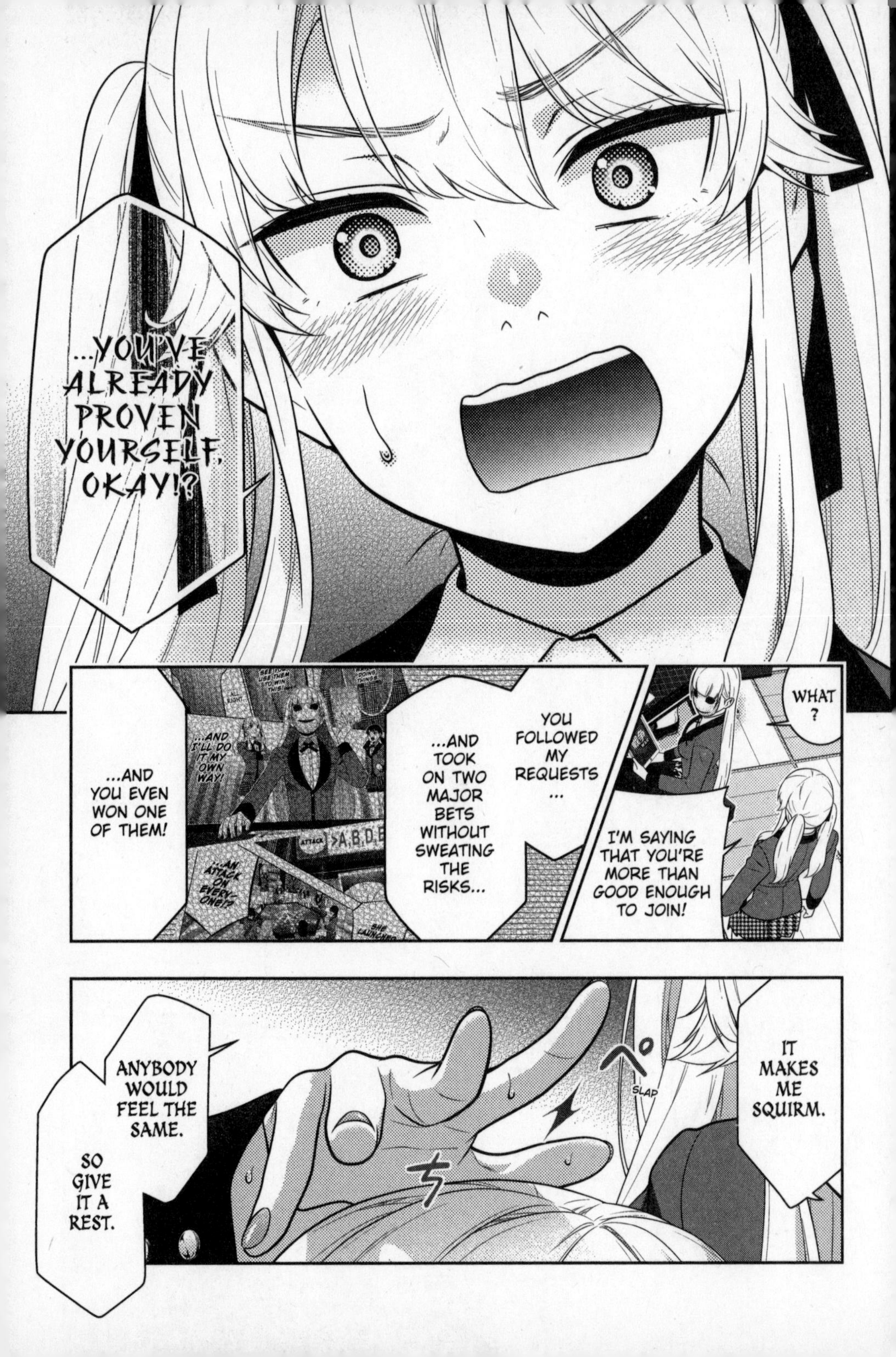
...YOU'VE ALREADY PROVEN YOURSELF, OKAY!?
WHAT?
I'M SAYING THAT YOU'RE MORE THAN GOOD ENOUGH TO JOIN!
YOU FOLLOWED MY REQUESTS...
...AND TOOK ON TWO MAJOR BETS WITHOUT SWEATING THE RISKS...
...AND I'LL DO IT MY OWN WAY!
...AN ATTACK ON EVERYONE!?
...AND YOU EVEN WON ONE OF THEM!
SLAP
IT MAKES ME SQUIRM.
ANYBODY WOULD FEEL THE SAME.
SO GIVE IT A REST.

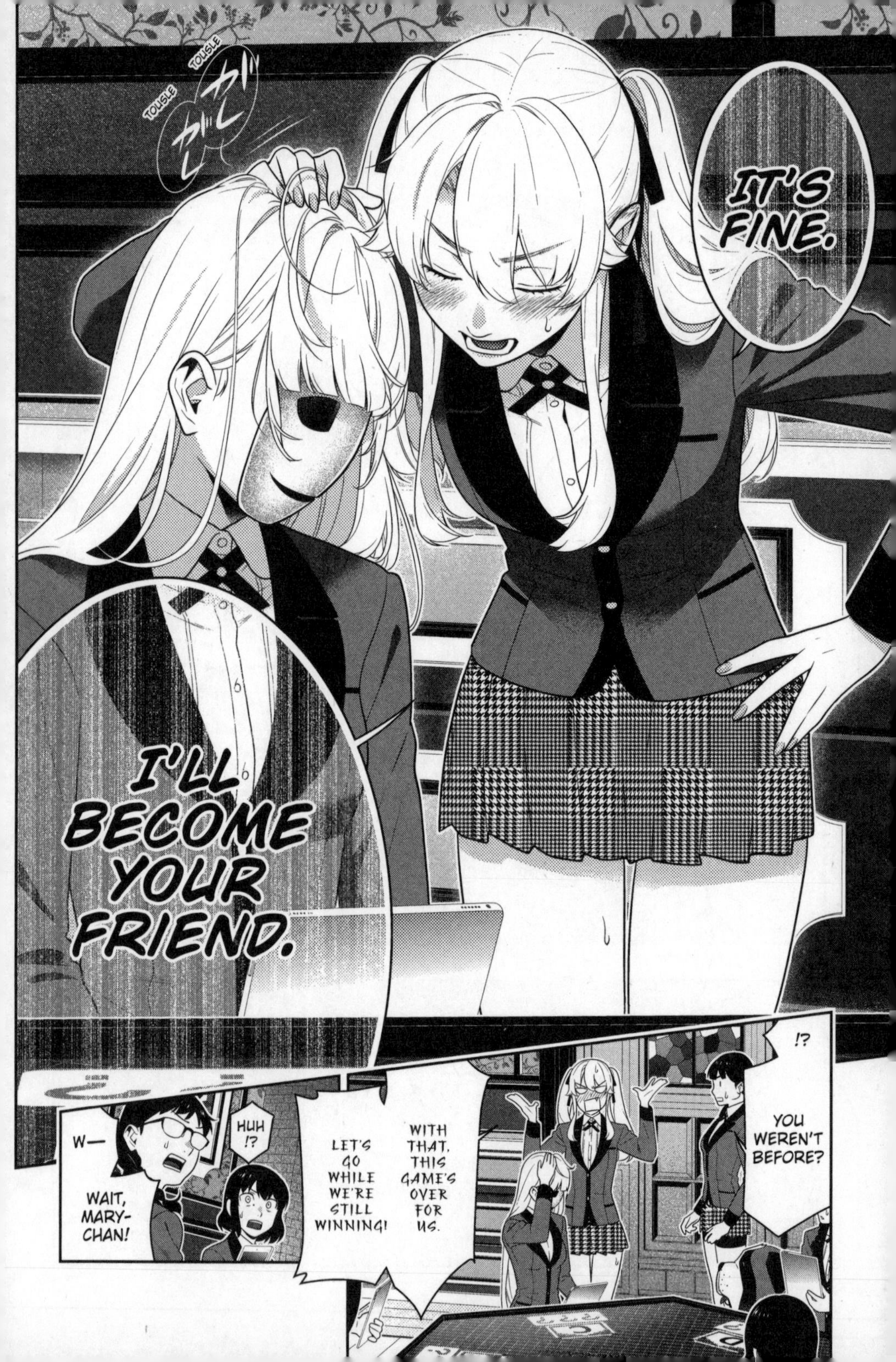

TOUSLE
TOUSLE
IT'S FINE.
I'LL BECOME YOUR FRIEND.
!?
YOU WEREN'T BEFORE?
WITH THAT, THIS GAME'S OVER FOR US.
LET'S GO WHILE WE'RE STILL WINNING!
HUH !?
W—
WAIT, MARY-CHAN!

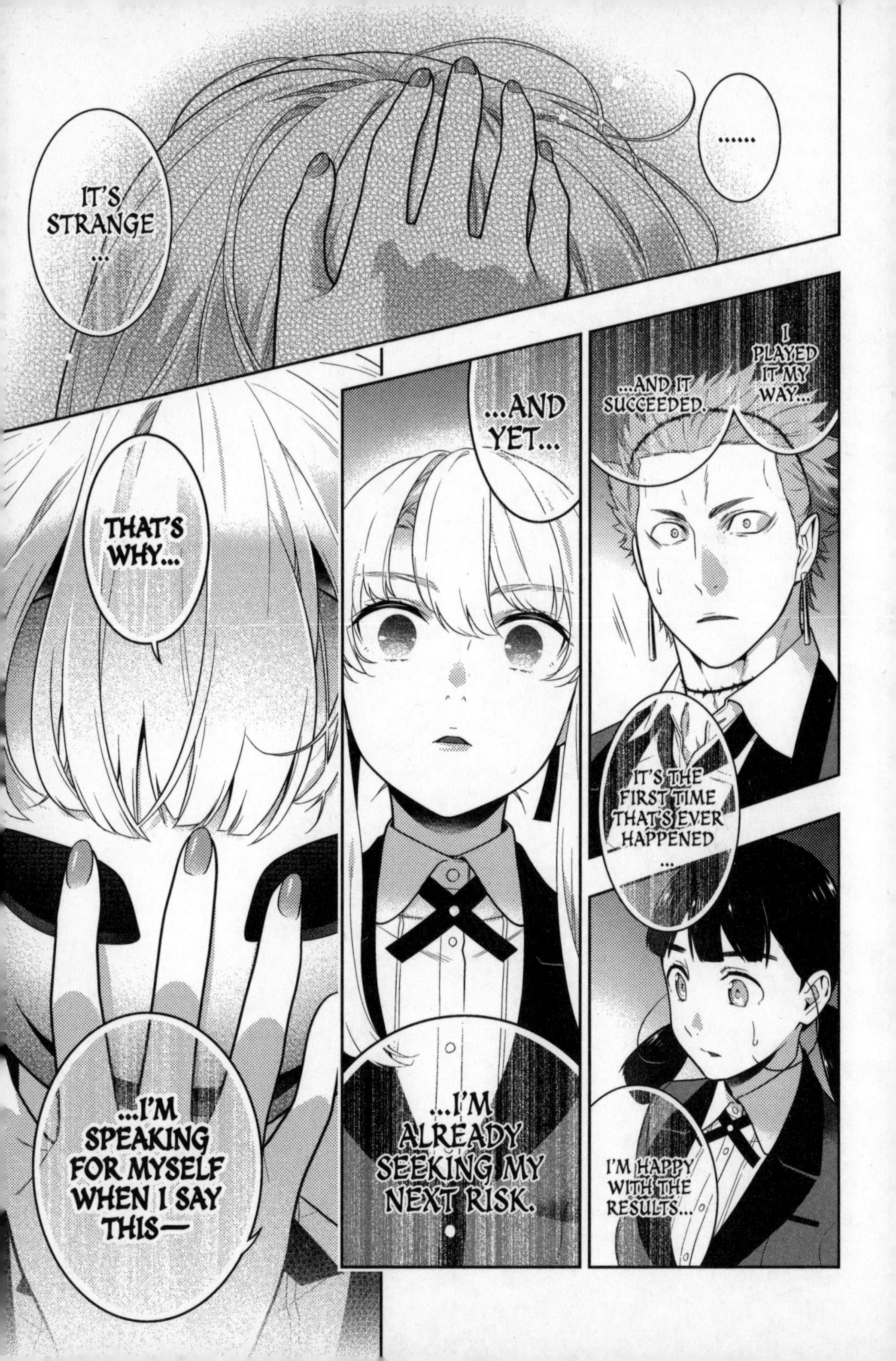
......
IT'S STRANGE ...
I PLAYED IT MY WAY...
...AND IT SUCCEEDED.
IT'S THE FIRST TIME THAT'S EVER HAPPENED ...
I'M HAPPY WITH THE RESULTS...
...AND YET...
...I'M ALREADY SEEKING MY NEXT RISK.
THAT'S WHY...
...I'M SPEAKING FOR MYSELF WHEN I SAY THIS—

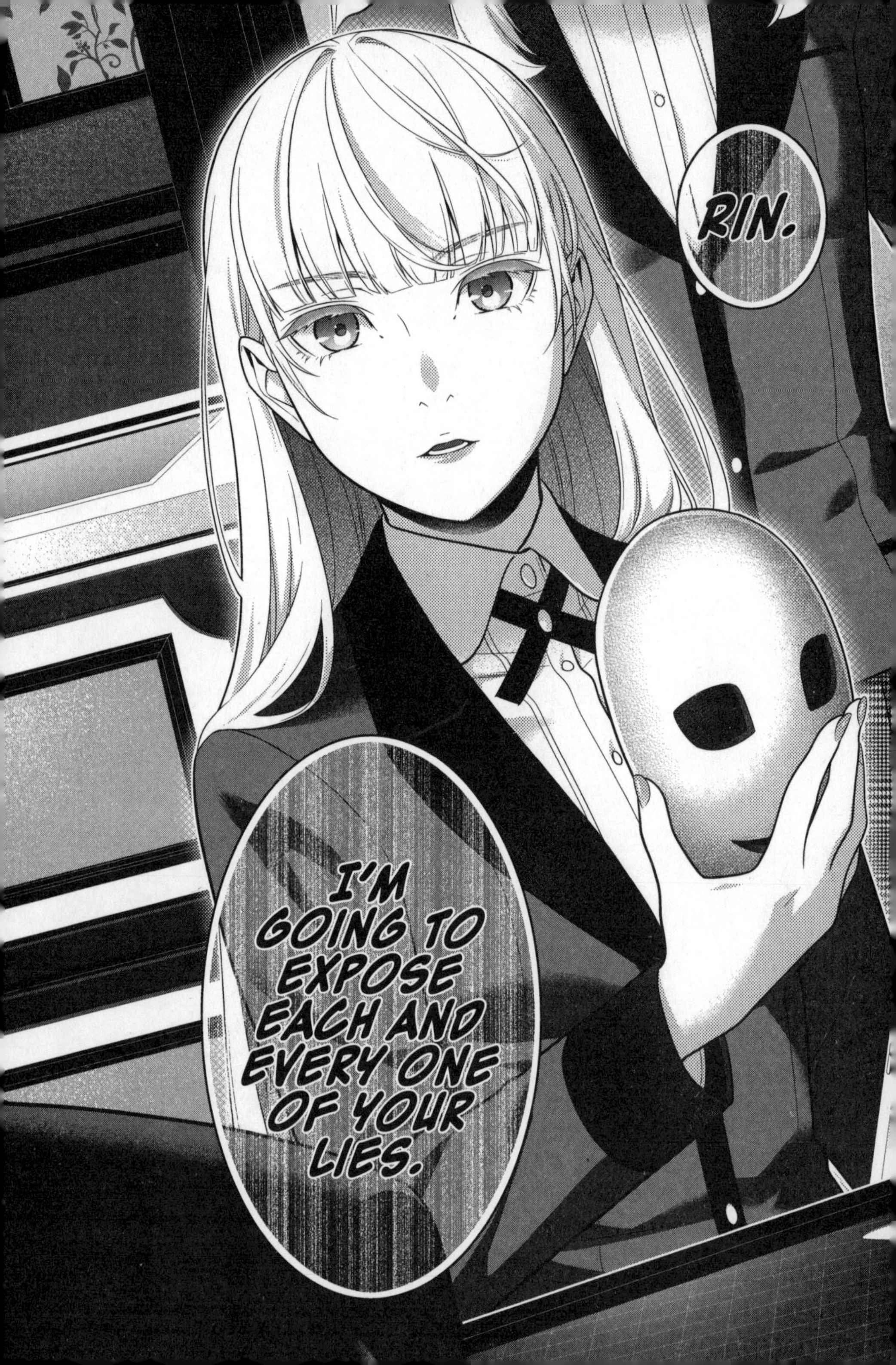
RIN.
I'M GOING TO EXPOSE EACH AND EVERY ONE OF YOUR LIES.

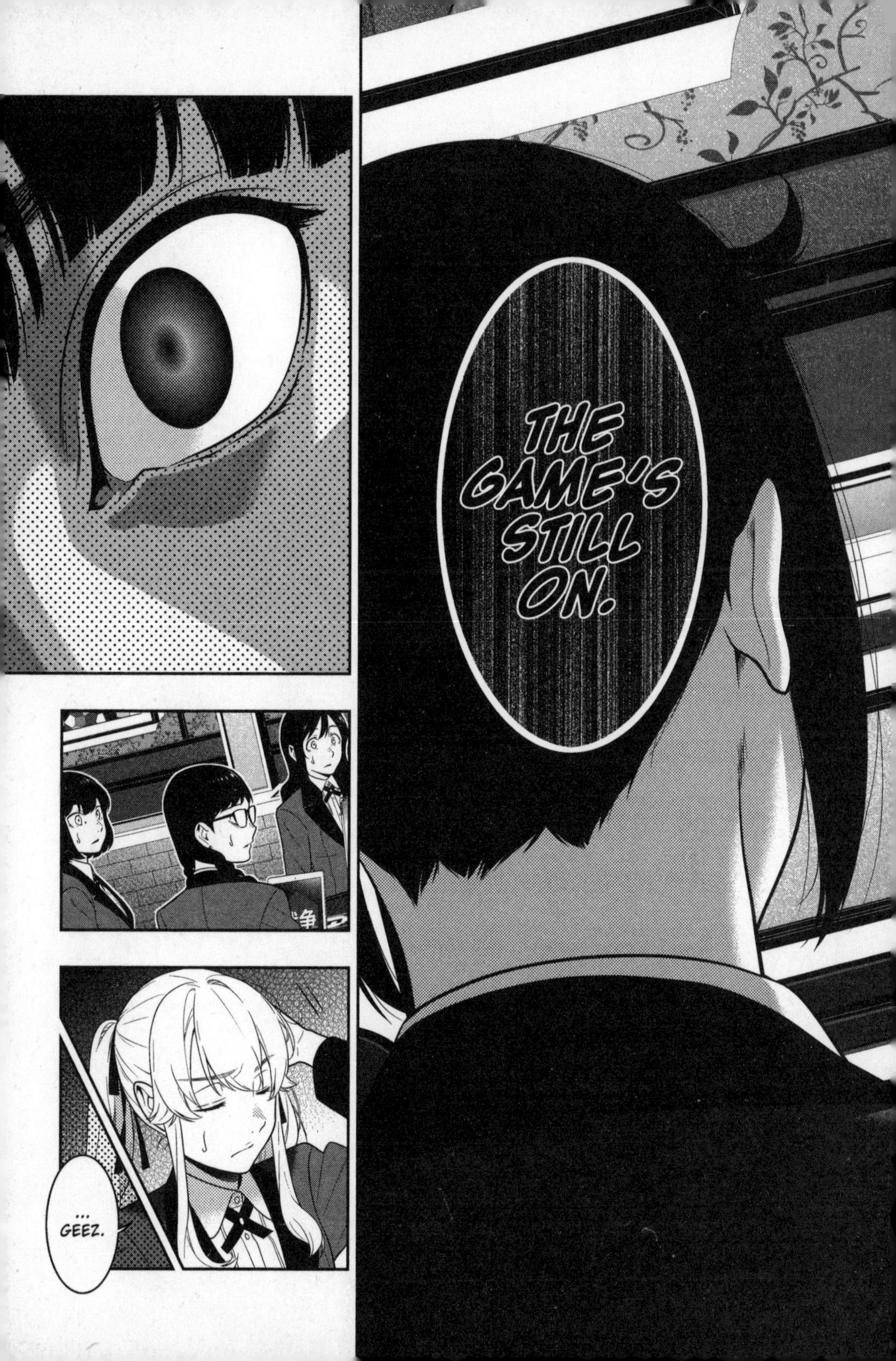
THE GAME'S STILL ON.
... GEEZ.

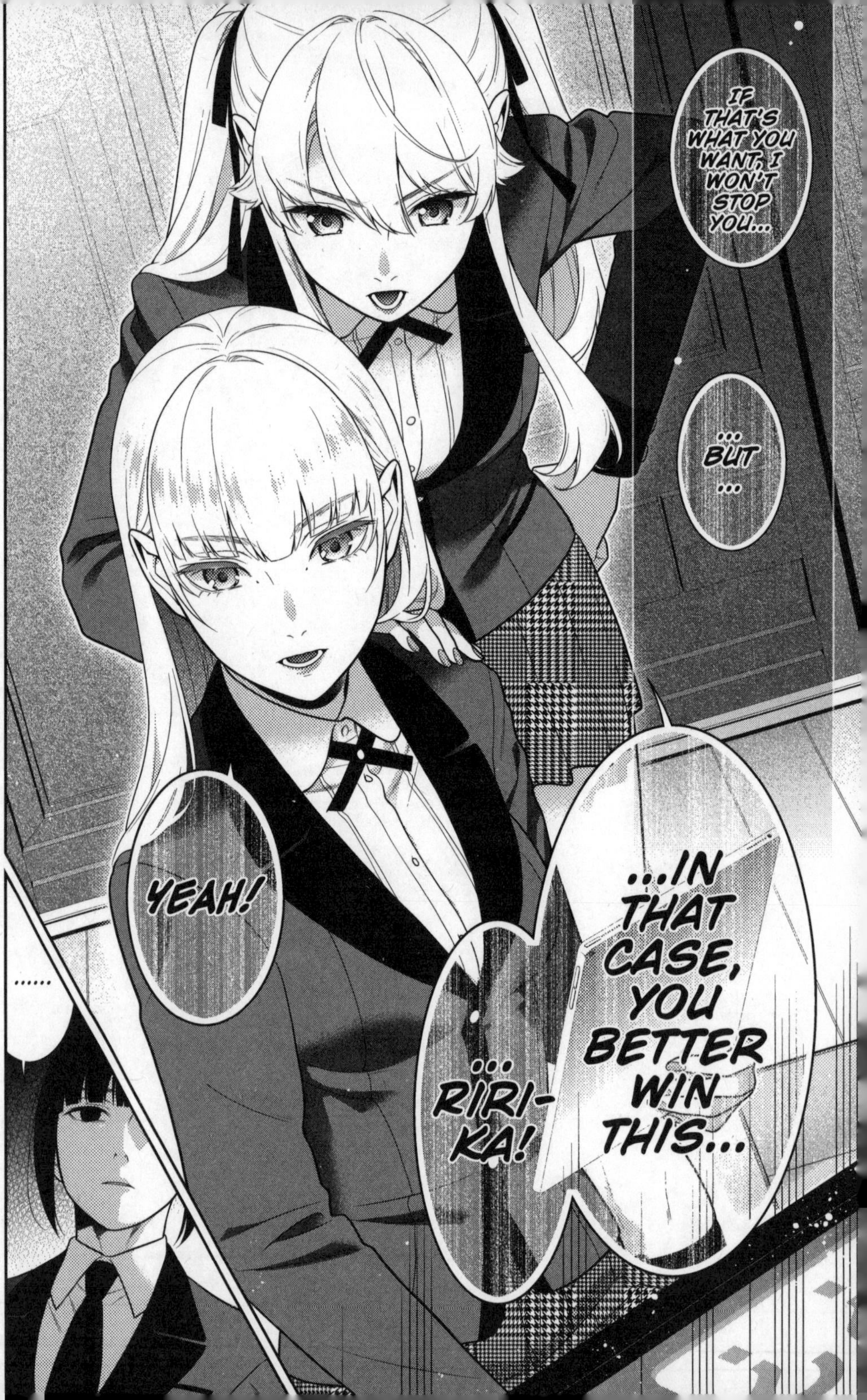
IF THAT'S WHAT YOU WANT, I WON'T STOP YOU...
...BUT...
...IN THAT CASE, YOU BETTER WIN THIS...
...RIRI-KA!
YEAH!
......

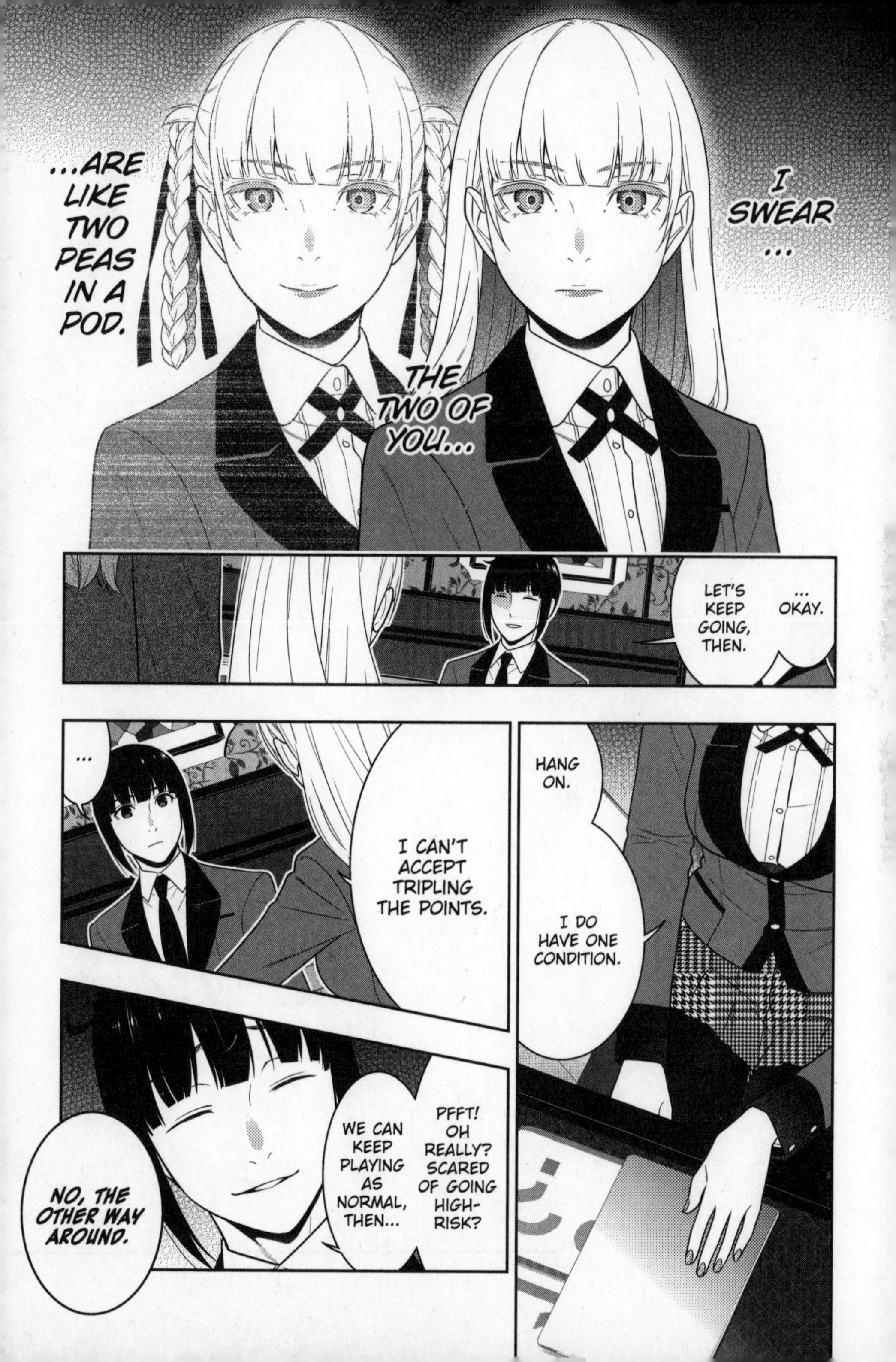
I SWEAR...
THE TWO OF YOU...
...ARE LIKE TWO PEAS IN A POD.
... OKAY.
LET'S KEEP GOING, THEN.
HANG ON.
I DO HAVE ONE CONDITION.
I CAN'T ACCEPT TRIPLING THE POINTS.
...
PFFT! OH REALLY? SCARED OF GOING HIGH-RISK?
WE CAN KEEP PLAYING AS NORMAL, THEN...
NO, THE OTHER WAY AROUND.

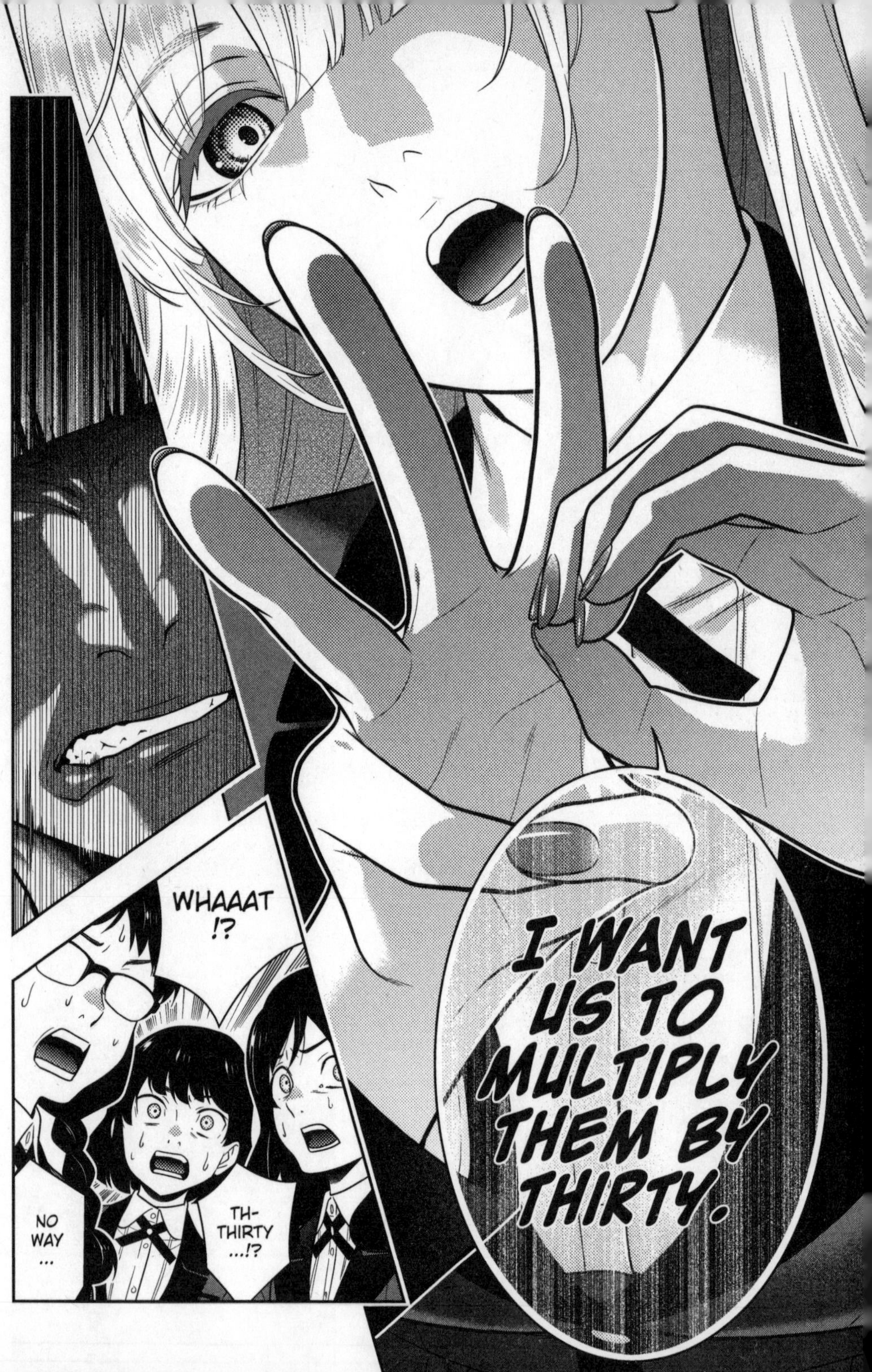
I WANT US TO MULTIPLY THEM BY THIRTY.
WHAAAT !?
TH-THIRTY ...!?
NO WAY ...

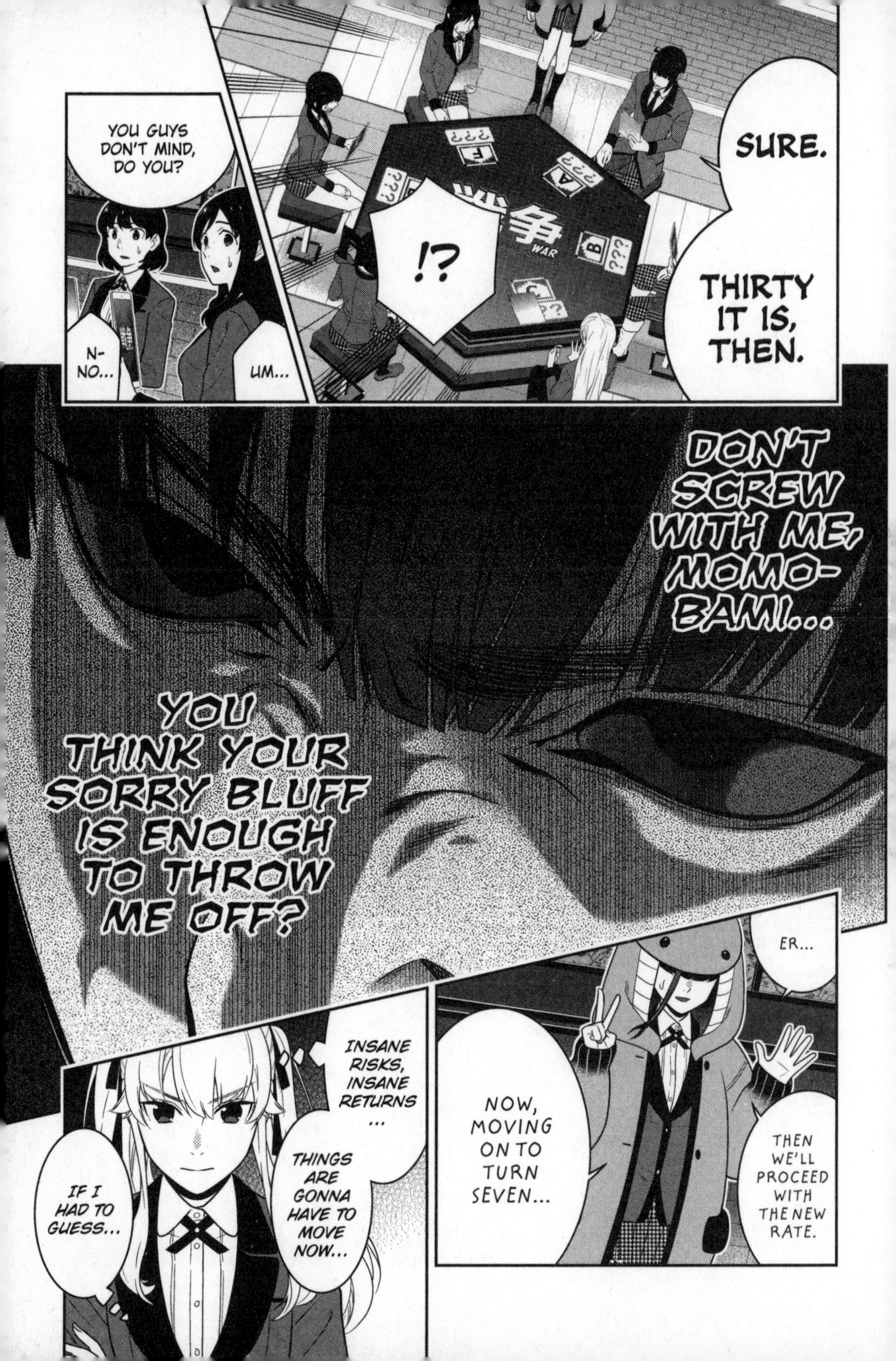
SURE.
THIRTY IT IS, THEN.
!?
争
WAR
YOU GUYS DON'T MIND, DO YOU?
N-NO...
UM...
DON'T SCREW WITH ME, MOMOBAMI...
YOU THINK YOUR SORRY BLUFF IS ENOUGH TO THROW ME OFF?
ER...
THEN WE'LL PROCEED WITH THE NEW RATE.
NOW, MOVING ON TO TURN SEVEN...
INSANE RISKS, INSANE RETURNS...
THINGS ARE GONNA HAVE TO MOVE NOW...
IF I HAD TO GUESS...

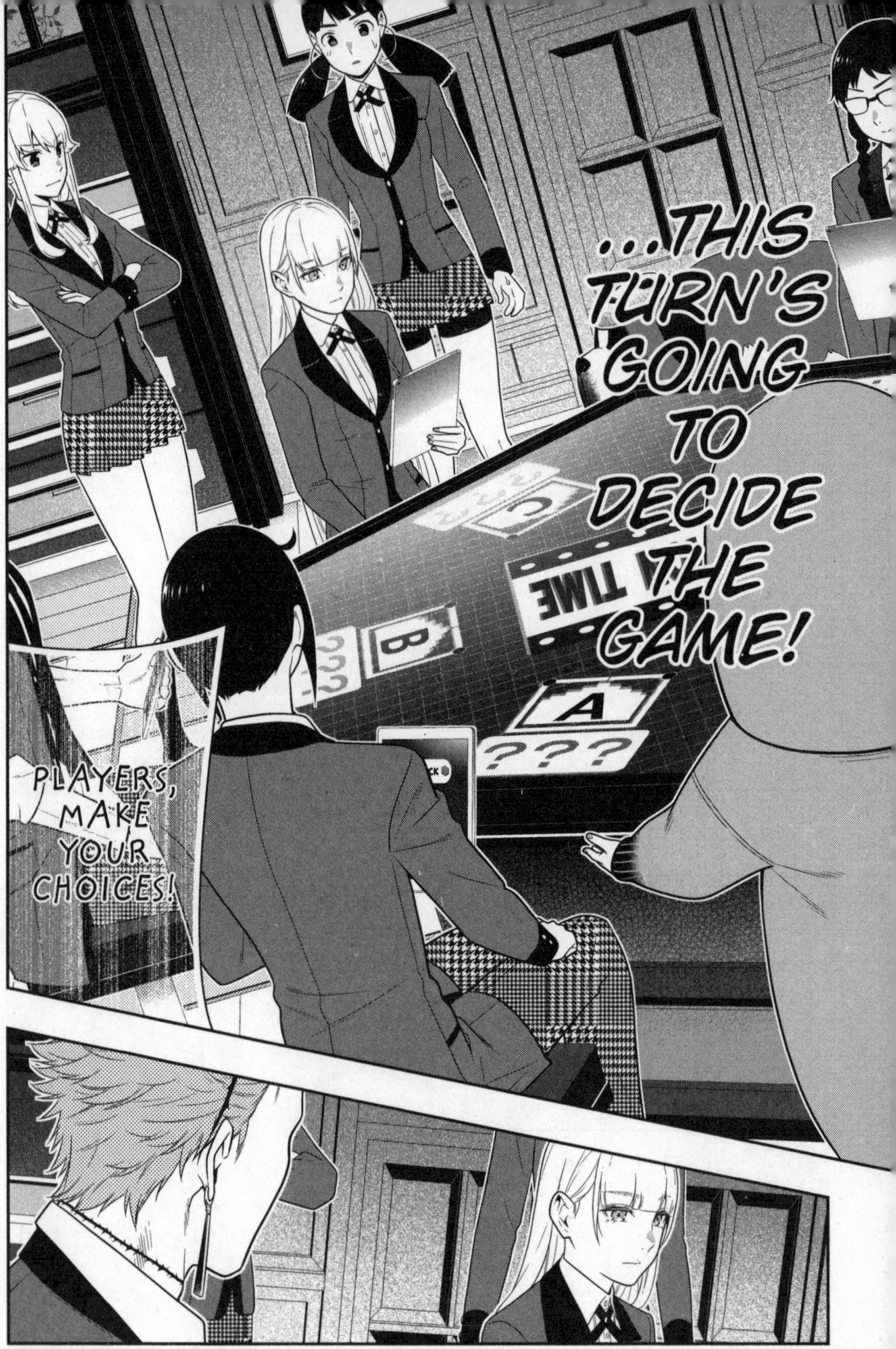
...THIS TURN'S GOING TO DECIDE THE GAME!
PLAYERS, MAKE YOUR CHOICES!

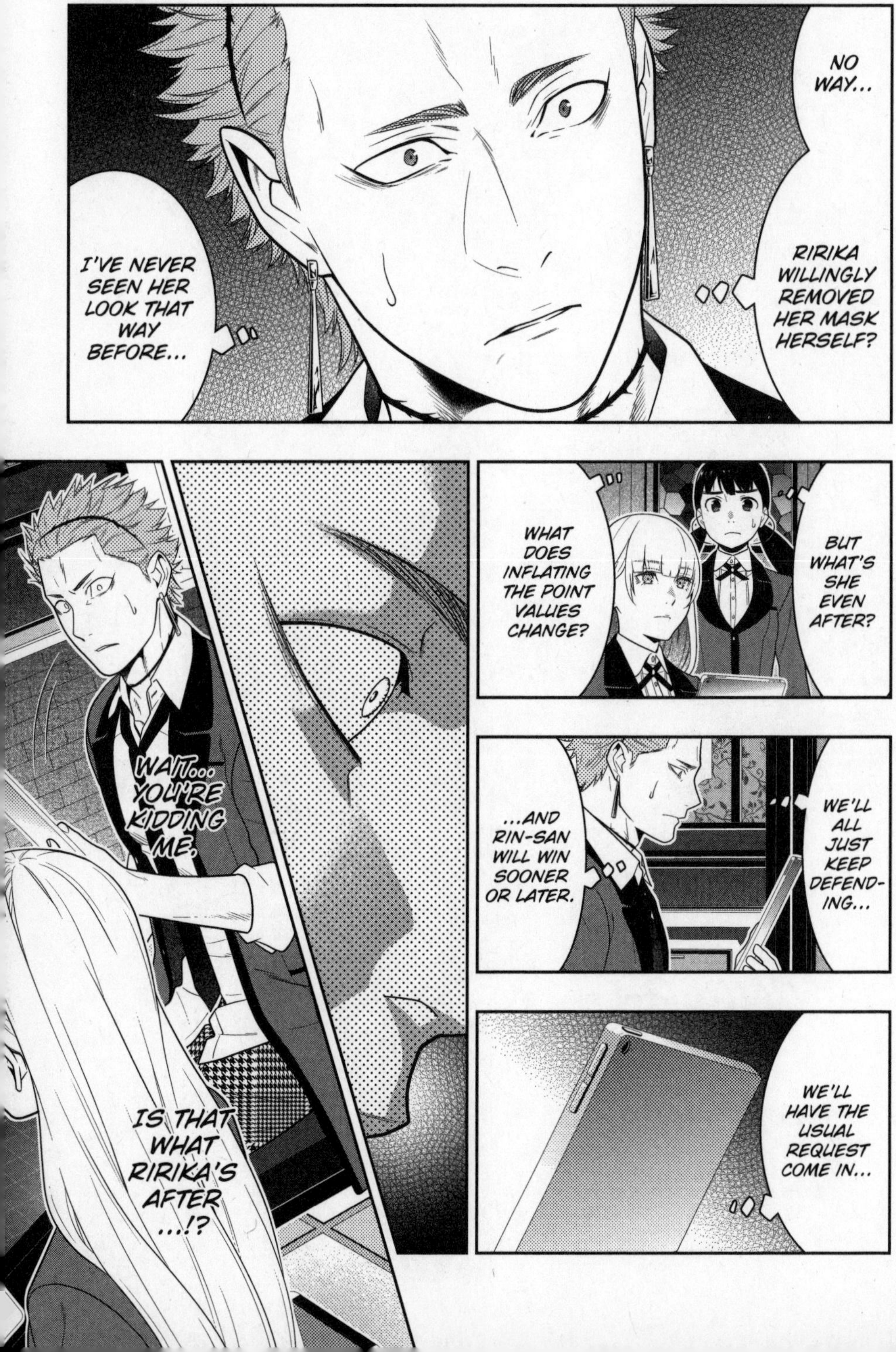
NO WAY...
RIRIKA WILLINGLY REMOVED HER MASK HERSELF?
I'VE NEVER SEEN HER LOOK THAT WAY BEFORE...
BUT WHAT'S SHE EVEN AFTER?
WHAT DOES INFLATING THE POINT VALUES CHANGE?
WE'LL ALL JUST KEEP DEFEND-ING...
...AND RIN-SAN WILL WIN SOONER OR LATER.
WE'LL HAVE THE USUAL REQUEST COME IN...
WAIT... YOU'RE KIDDING ME.
IS THAT WHAT RIRIKA'S AFTER ...!?

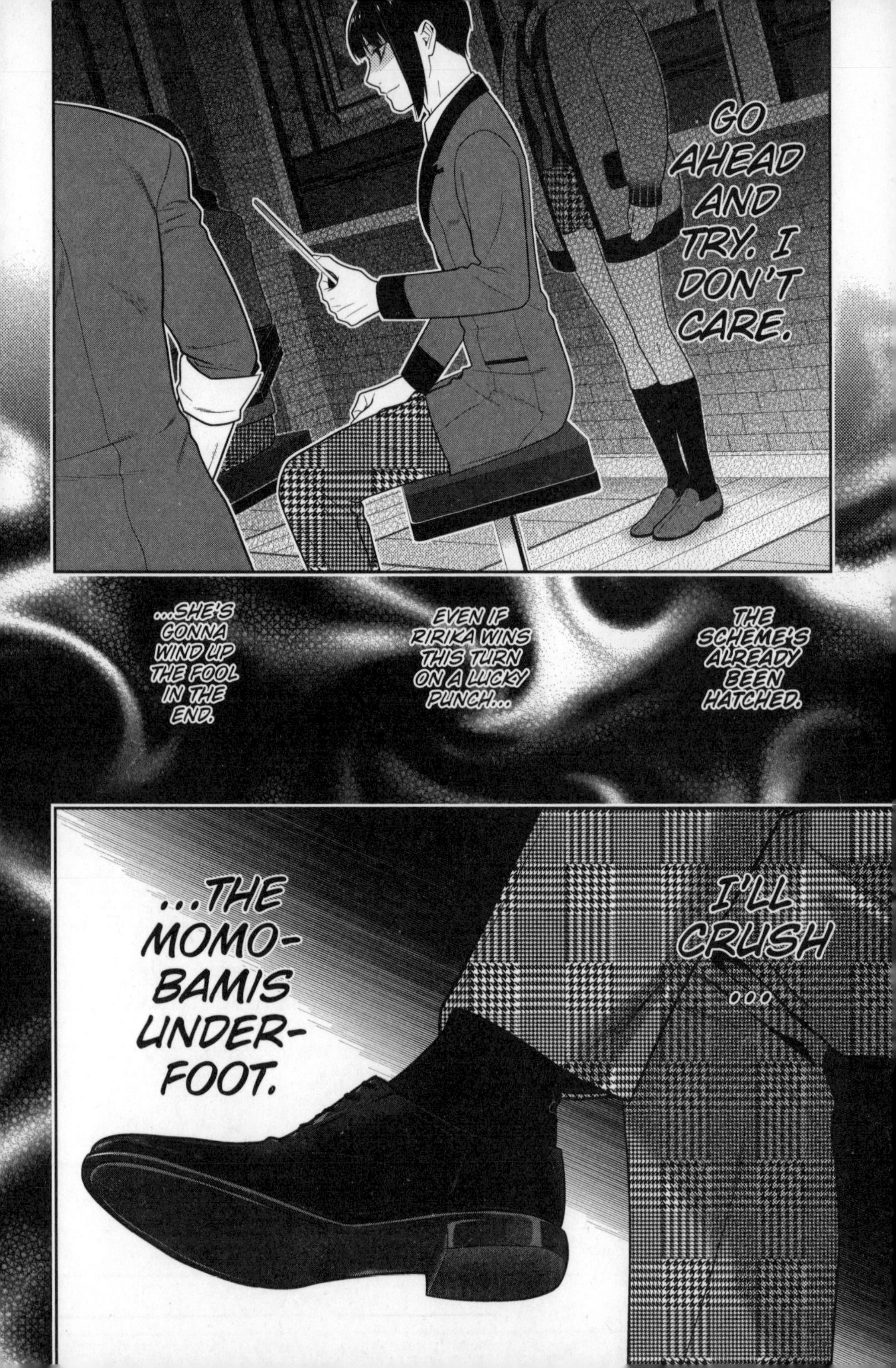
GO AHEAD AND TRY. I DON'T CARE.
THE SCHEME'S ALREADY BEEN HATCHED.
EVEN IF RIRIKA WINS THIS TURN ON A LUCKY PUNCH...
...SHE'S GONNA WIND UP THE FOOL IN THE END.
I'LL CRUSH...
...THE MOMO-BAMIS UNDER-FOOT.

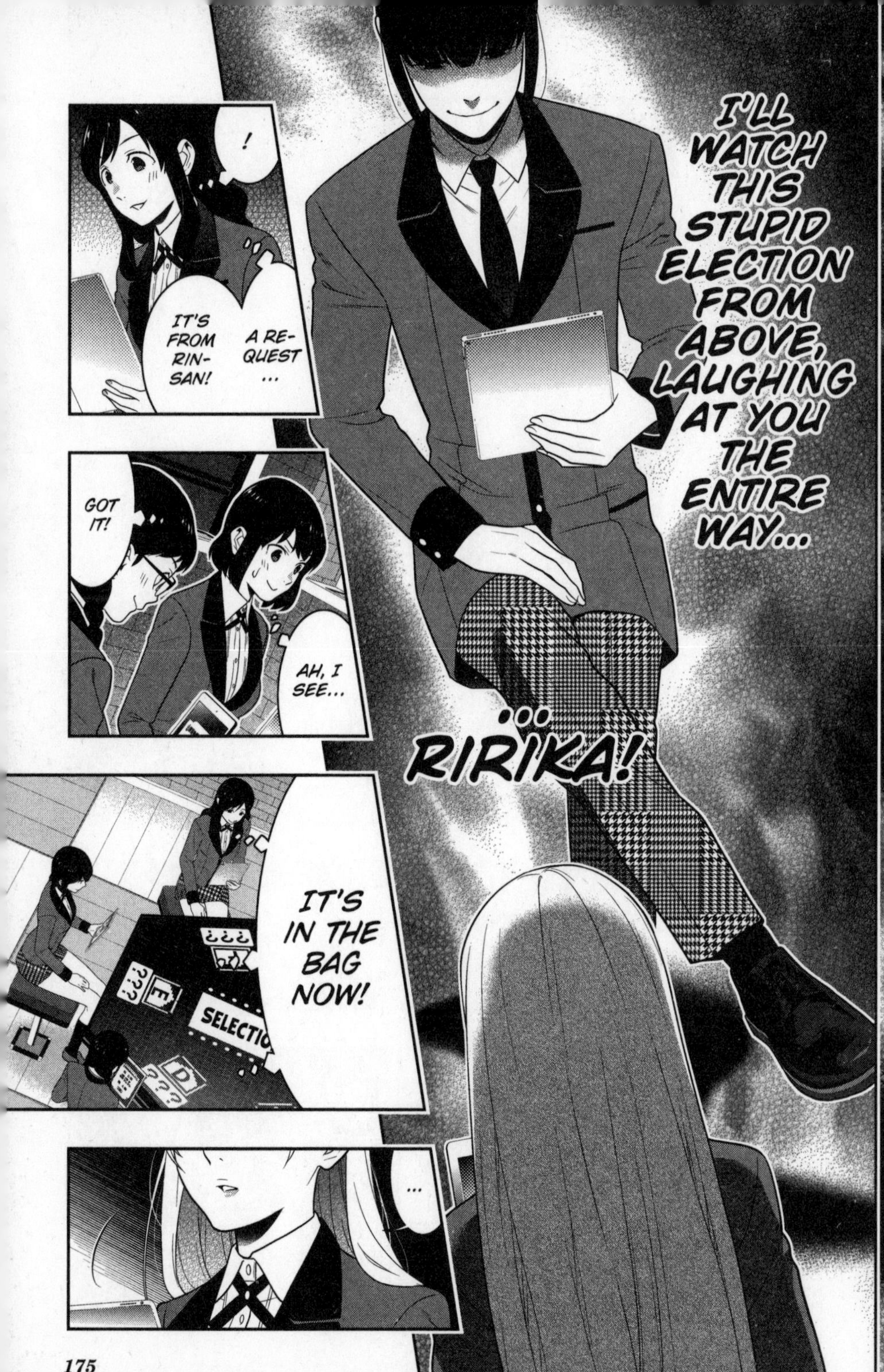
I'LL WATCH THIS STUPID ELECTION FROM ABOVE, LAUGHING AT YOU THE ENTIRE WAY...
...RIRIKA!
!
A REQUEST...
IT'S FROM RIN-SAN!
GOT IT!
AH, I SEE...
IT'S IN THE BAG NOW!
SELECTIO
...

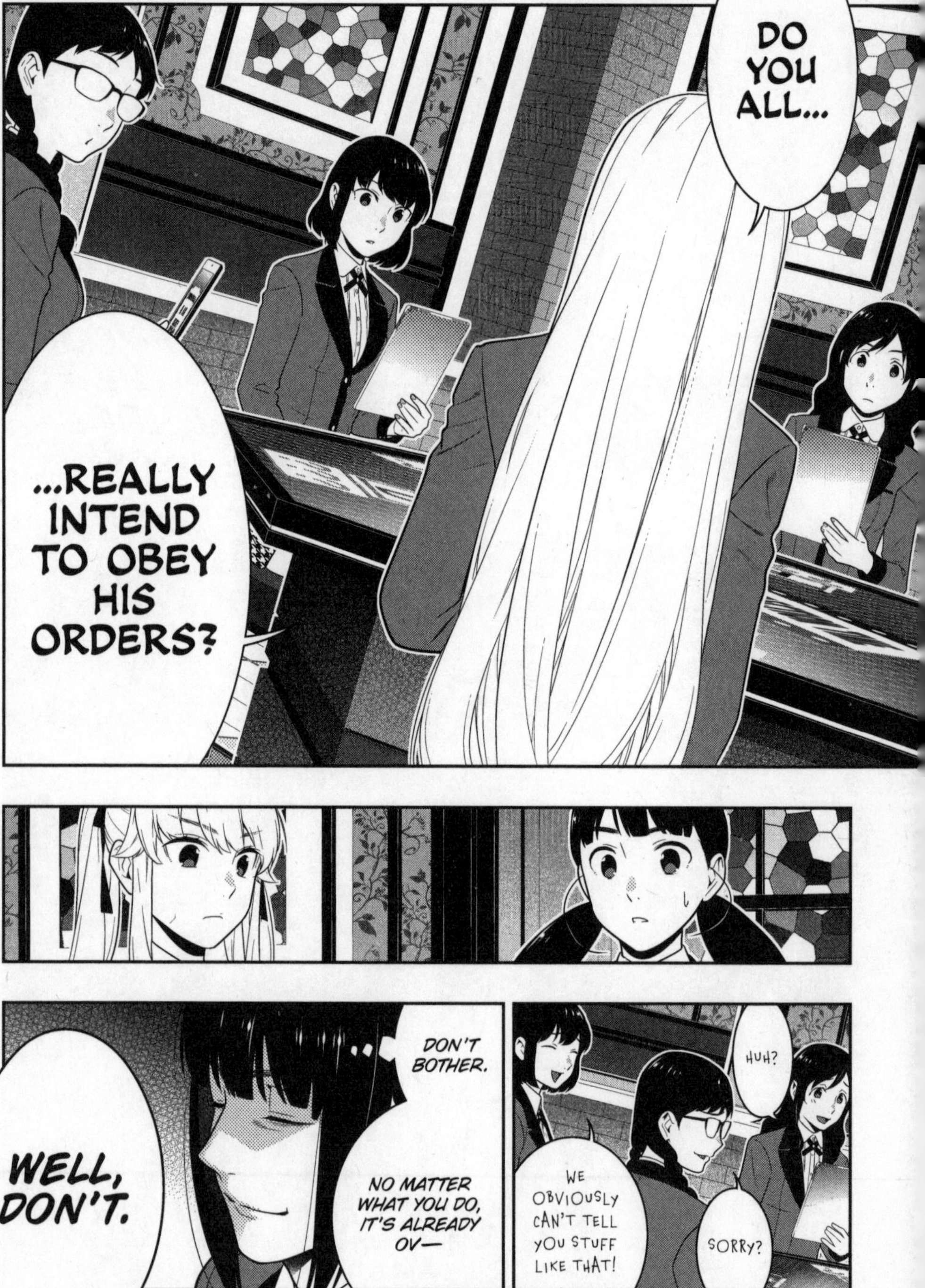
DO YOU ALL...
...REALLY INTEND TO OBEY HIS ORDERS?
HUH?
SORRY?
WE OBVIOUSLY CAN'T TELL YOU STUFF LIKE THAT!
DON'T BOTHER.
NO MATTER WHAT YOU DO, IT'S ALREADY OV—
WELL, DON'T.

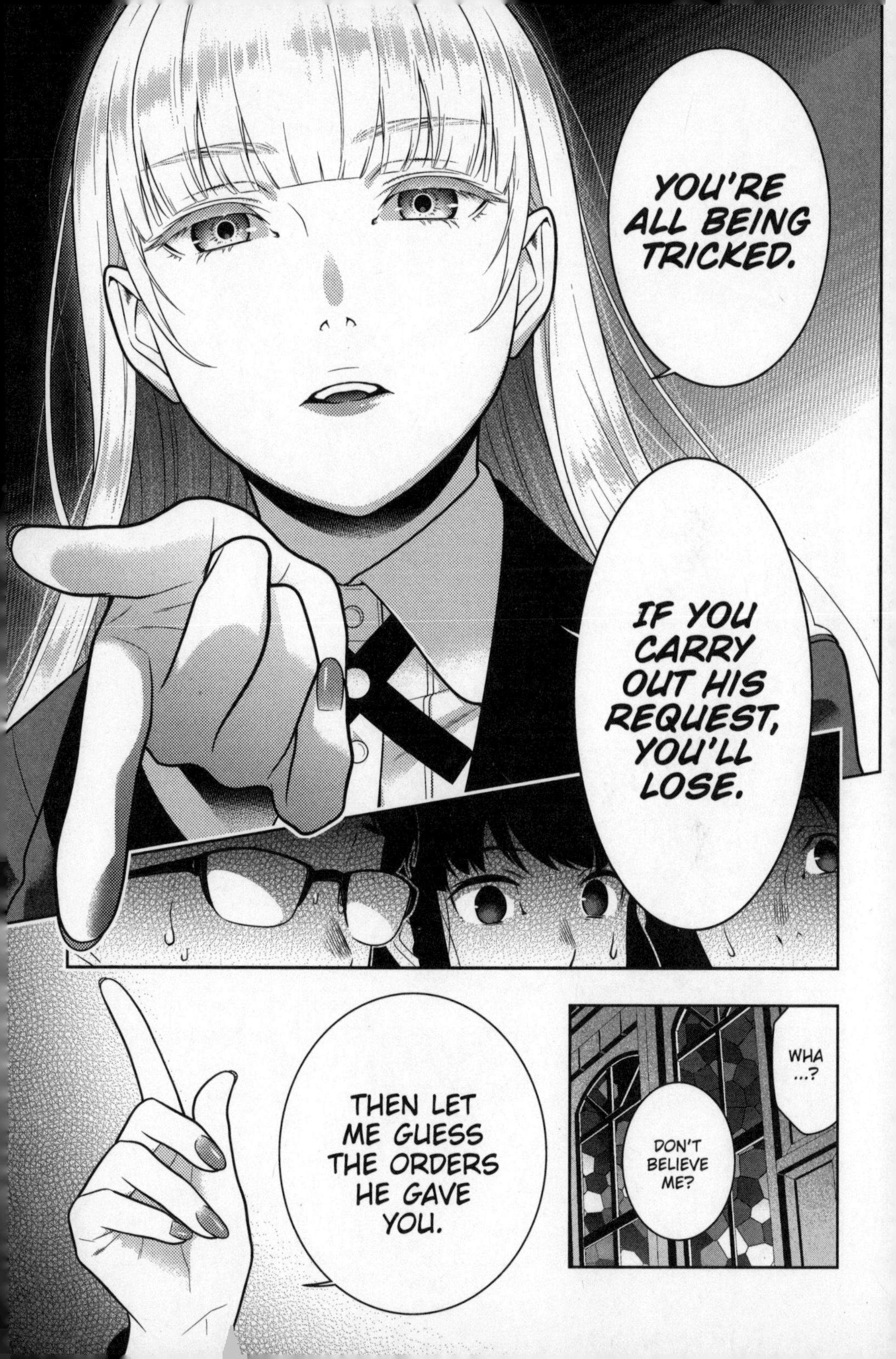
YOU'RE ALL BEING TRICKED.
IF YOU CARRY OUT HIS REQUEST, YOU'LL LOSE.
WHA ...?
DON'T BELIEVE ME?
THEN LET ME GUESS THE ORDERS HE GAVE YOU.

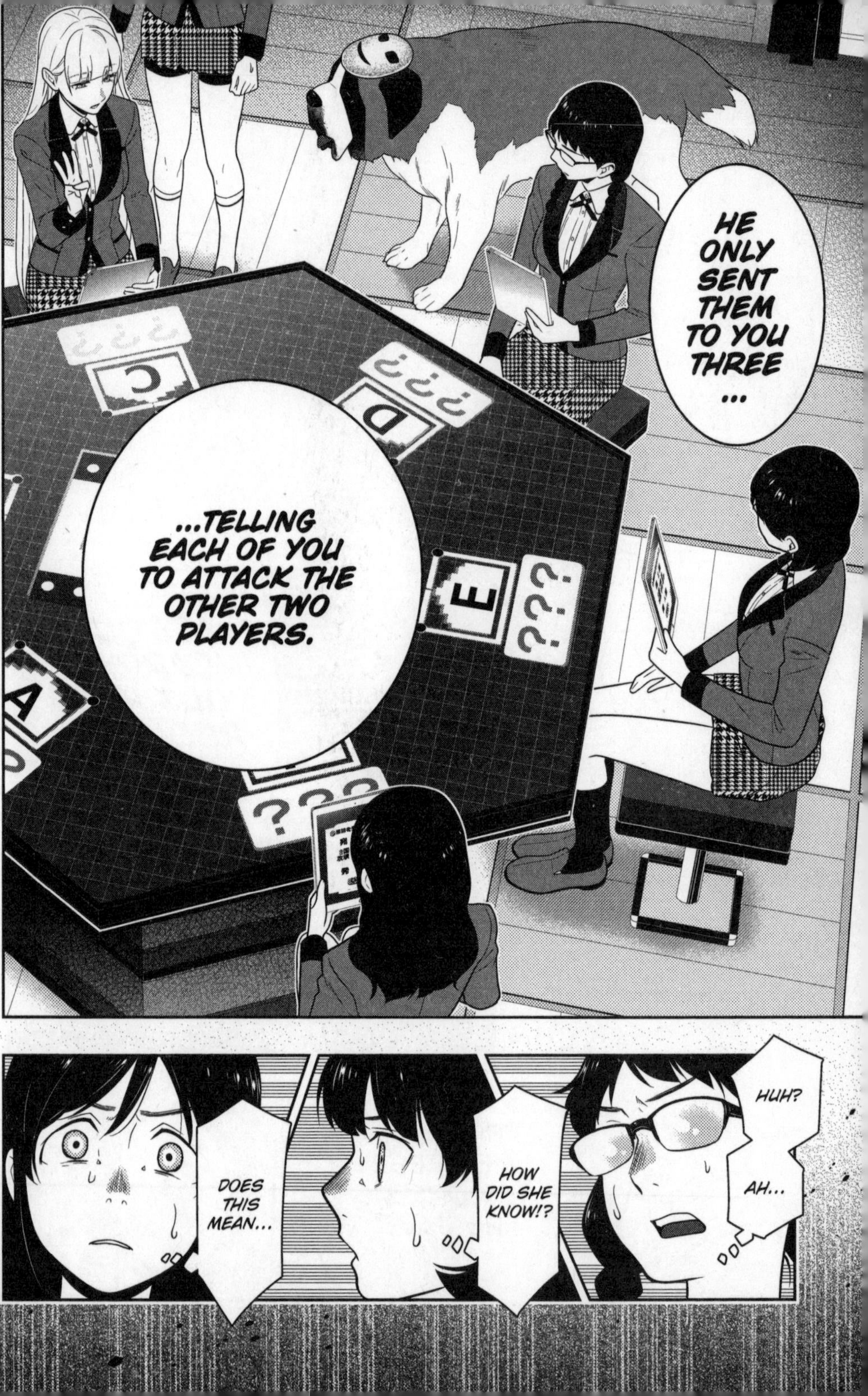
HE ONLY SENT THEM TO YOU THREE...
...TELLING EACH OF YOU TO ATTACK THE OTHER TWO PLAYERS.
HUH?
AH...
HOW DID SHE KNOW!?
DOES THIS MEAN...

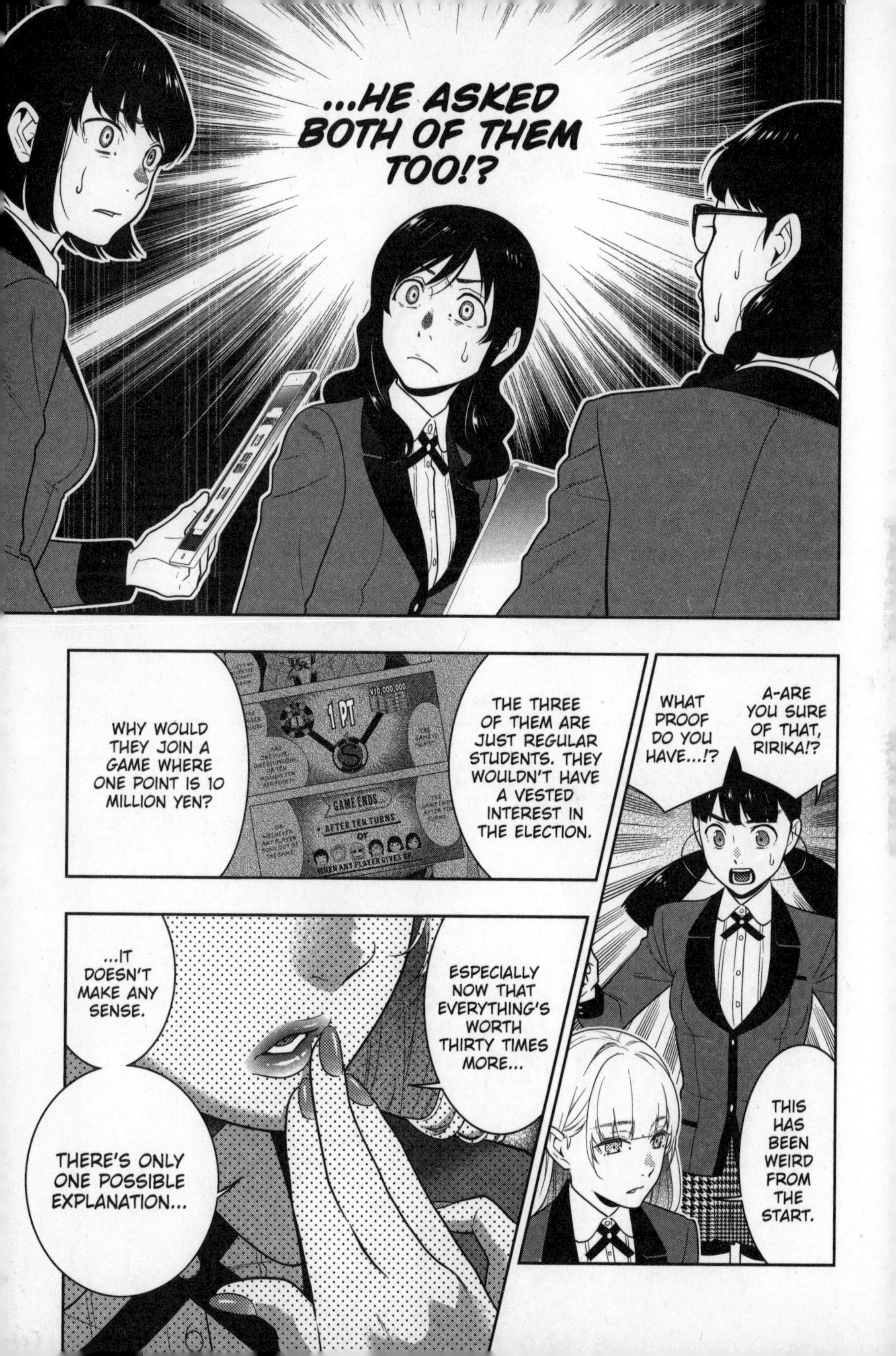
...HE ASKED BOTH OF THEM TOO!?
A-ARE YOU SURE OF THAT, RIRIKA!?
WHAT PROOF DO YOU HAVE...!?
THIS HAS BEEN WEIRD FROM THE START.
THE THREE OF THEM ARE JUST REGULAR STUDENTS. THEY WOULDN'T HAVE A VESTED INTEREST IN THE ELECTION.
¥10,000,000
1 PT
GAME ENDS...
AFTER TEN TURNS
OR
WHEN ANY PLAYER GIVES UP
WHY WOULD THEY JOIN A GAME WHERE ONE POINT IS 10 MILLION YEN?
ESPECIALLY NOW THAT EVERYTHING'S WORTH THIRTY TIMES MORE...
...IT DOESN'T MAKE ANY SENSE.
THERE'S ONLY ONE POSSIBLE EXPLANATION...

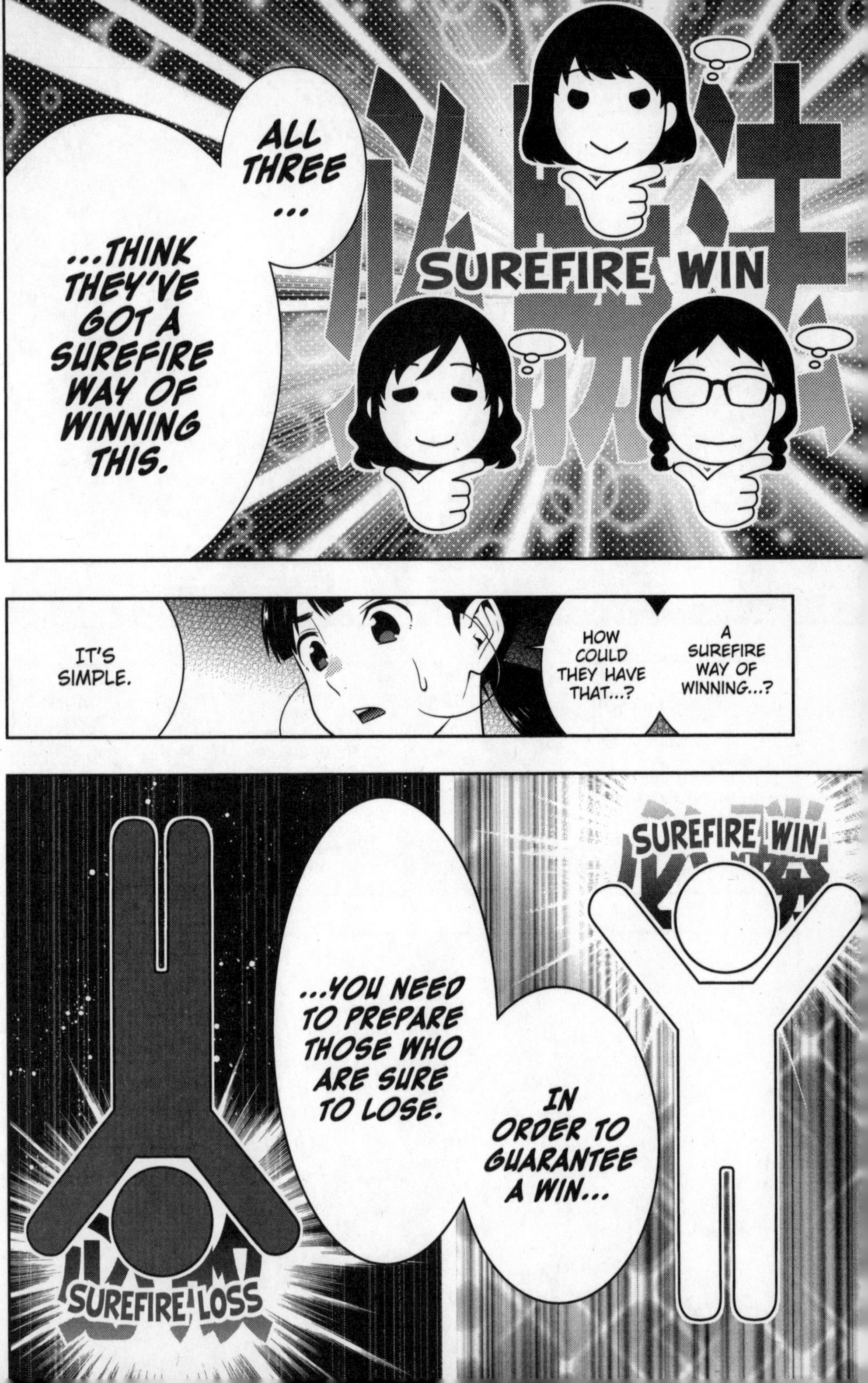
SUREFIRE WIN
ALL THREE ...
...THINK THEY'VE GOT A SUREFIRE WAY OF WINNING THIS.
A SUREFIRE WAY OF WINNING...?
HOW COULD THEY HAVE THAT...?
IT'S SIMPLE.
SUREFIRE WIN
IN ORDER TO GUARANTEE A WIN...
...YOU NEED TO PREPARE THOSE WHO ARE SURE TO LOSE.
SUREFIRE LOSS

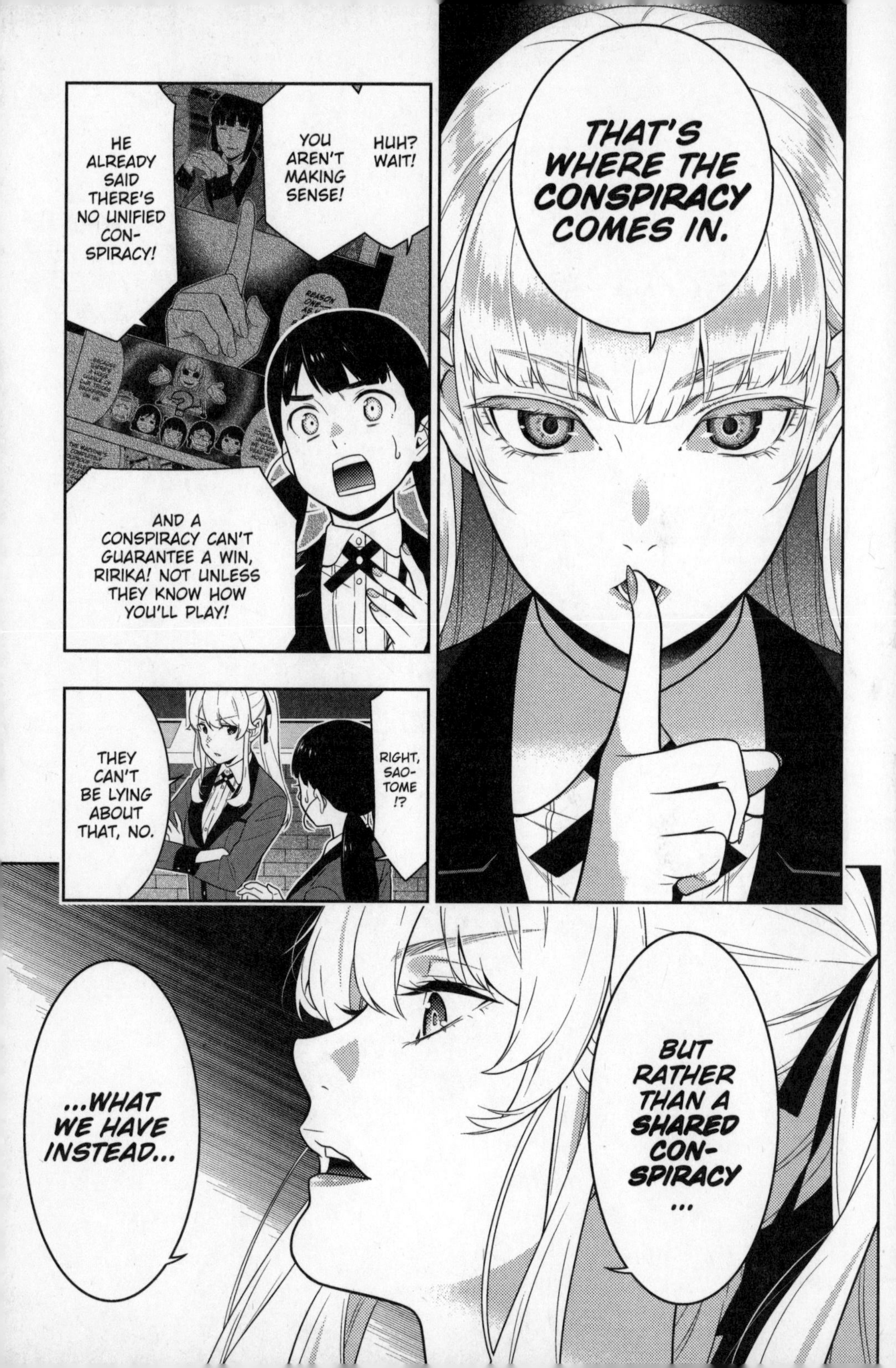
THAT'S WHERE THE CONSPIRACY COMES IN.
HUH? WAIT!
YOU AREN'T MAKING SENSE!
HE ALREADY SAID THERE'S NO UNIFIED CON-SPIRACY!
AND A CONSPIRACY CAN'T GUARANTEE A WIN, RIRIKA! NOT UNLESS THEY KNOW HOW YOU'LL PLAY!
RIGHT, SAO-TOME!?
THEY CAN'T BE LYING ABOUT THAT, NO.
BUT RATHER THAN A SHARED CON-SPIRACY...
...WHAT WE HAVE INSTEAD...

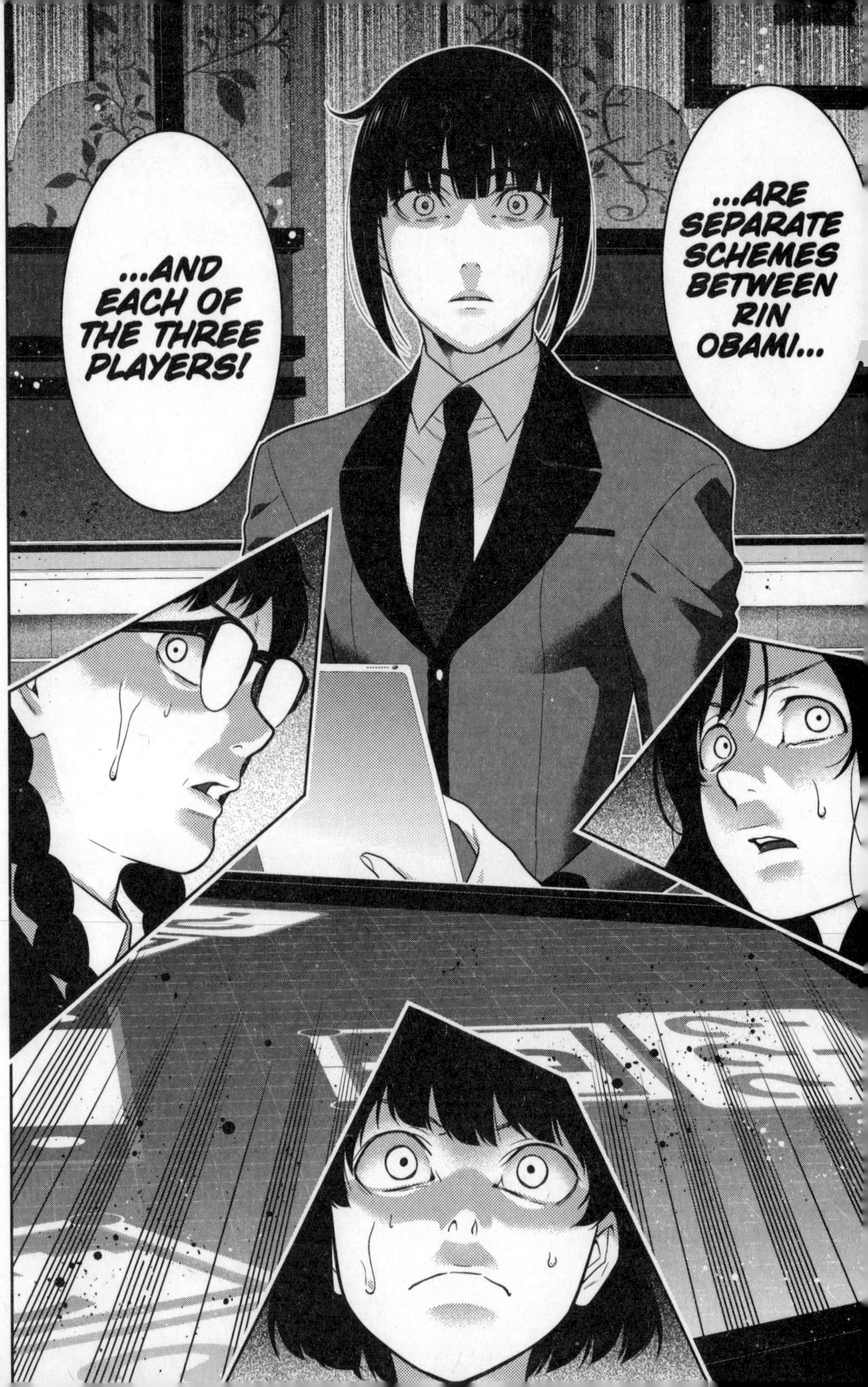
...ARE SEPARATE SCHEMES BETWEEN RIN OBAMI...
...AND EACH OF THE THREE PLAYERS!

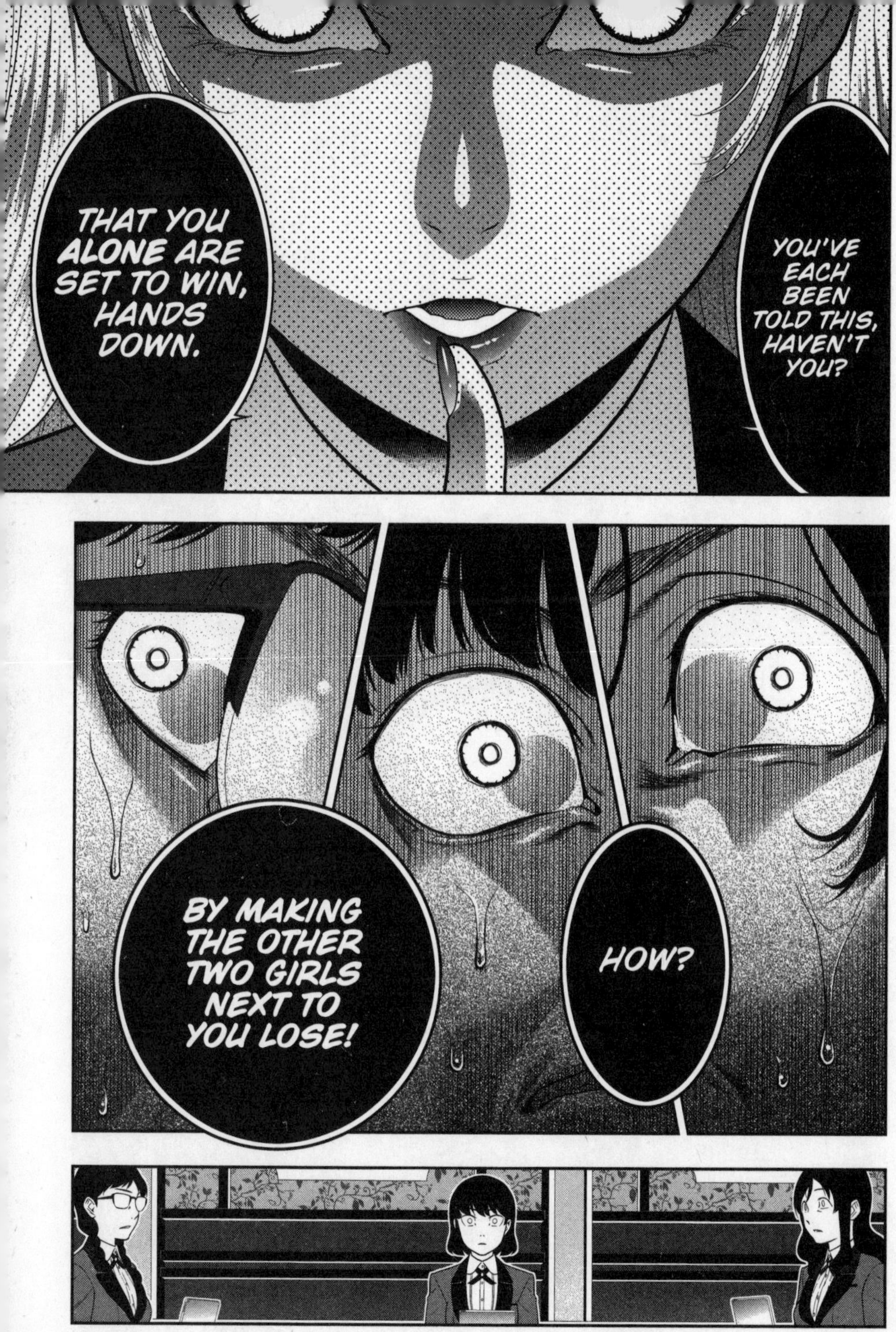
YOU'VE EACH BEEN TOLD THIS, HAVEN'T YOU?
THAT YOU ALONE ARE SET TO WIN, HANDS DOWN.
HOW?
BY MAKING THE OTHER TWO GIRLS NEXT TO YOU LOSE!

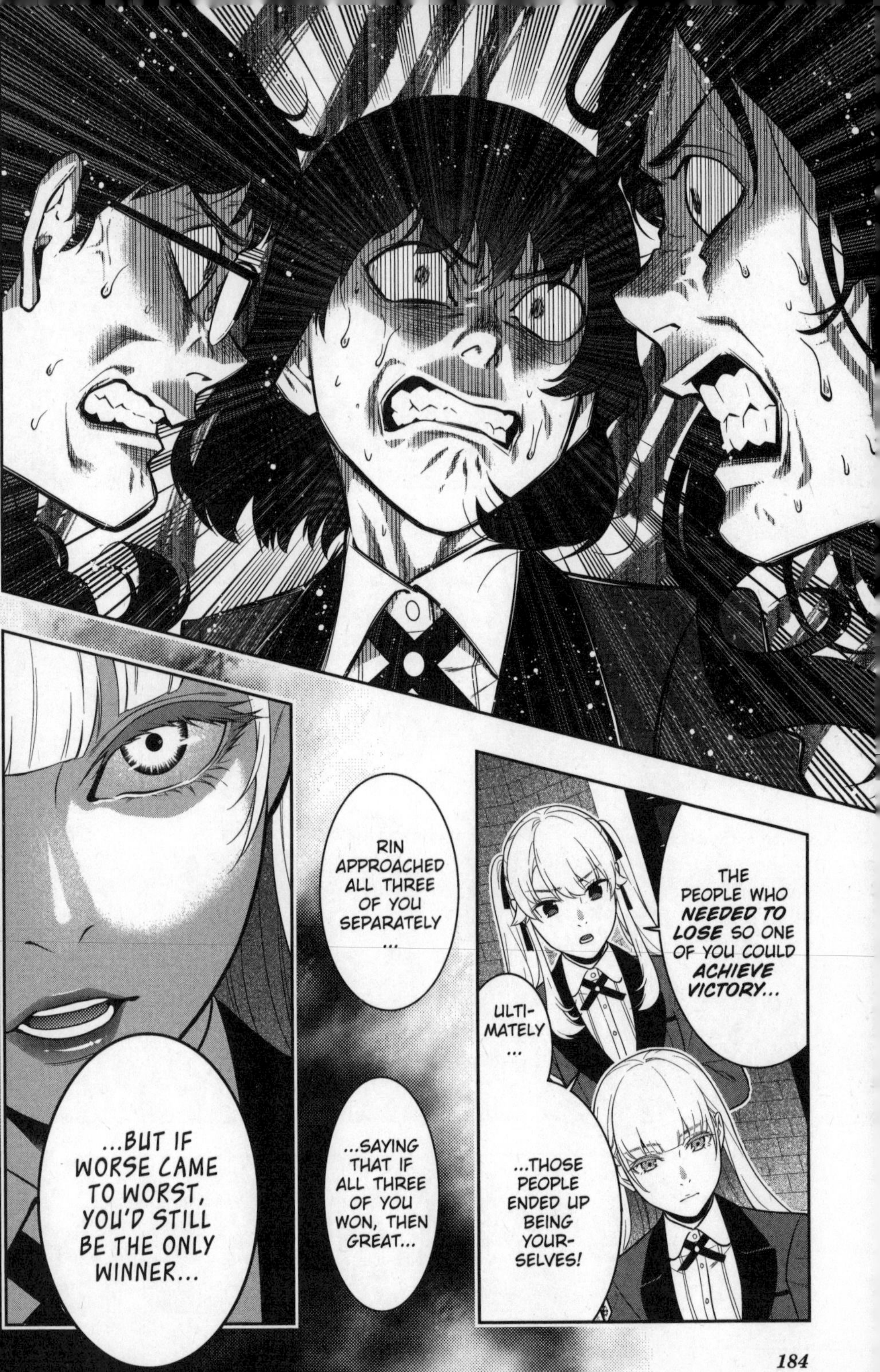
THE PEOPLE WHO NEEDED TO LOSE SO ONE OF YOU COULD ACHIEVE VICTORY...
ULTIMATELY...
...THOSE PEOPLE ENDED UP BEING YOURSELVES!
RIN APPROACHED ALL THREE OF YOU SEPARATELY...
...SAYING THAT IF ALL THREE OF YOU WON, THEN GREAT...
...BUT IF WORSE CAME TO WORST, YOU'D STILL BE THE ONLY WINNER...

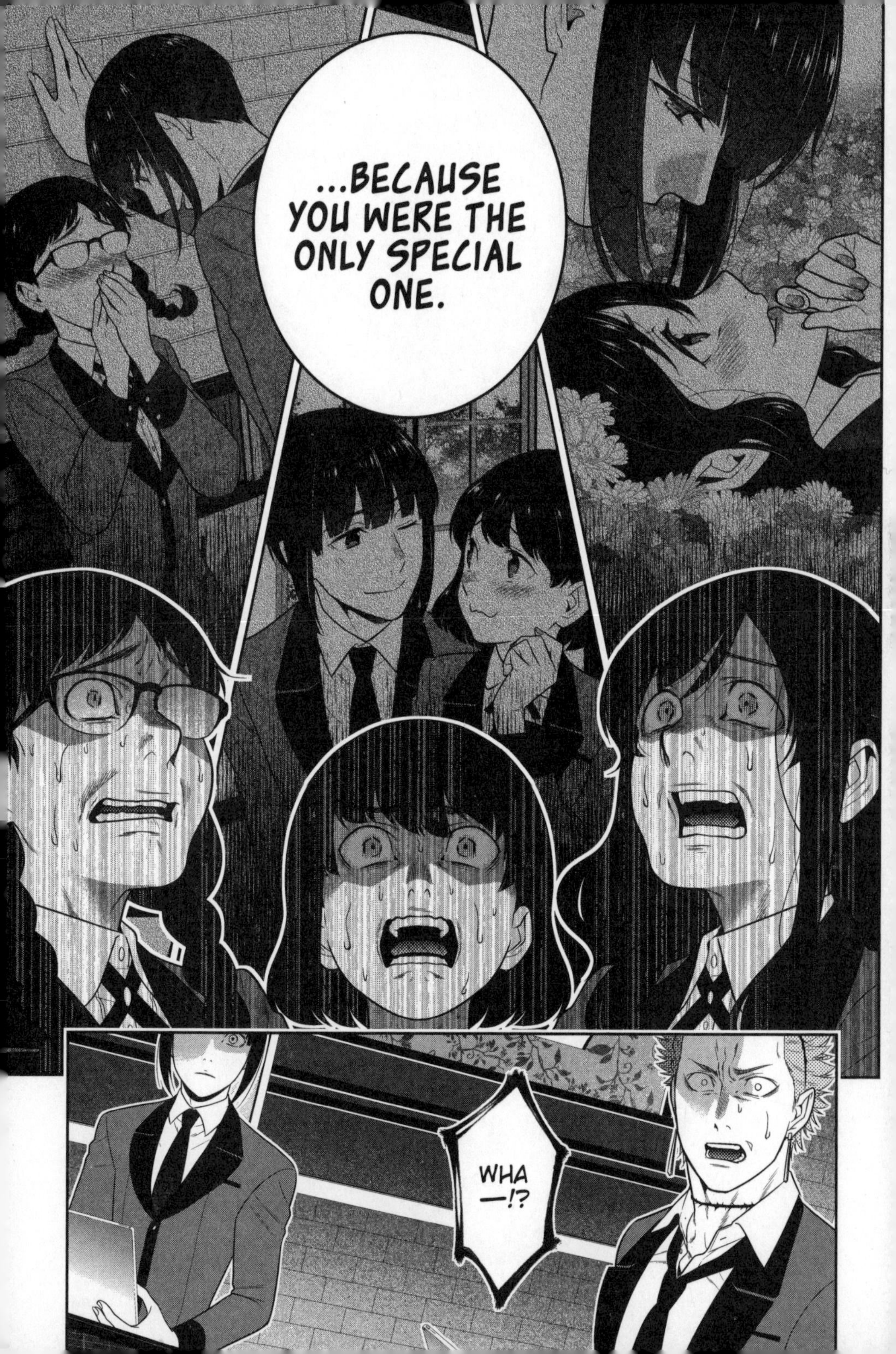
...BECAUSE YOU WERE THE ONLY SPECIAL ONE.
WHA—!?

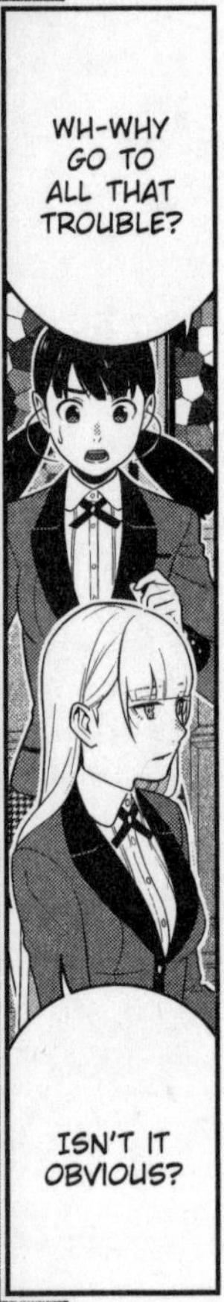
WH-WHY GO TO ALL THAT TROUBLE?
ISN'T IT OBVIOUS?
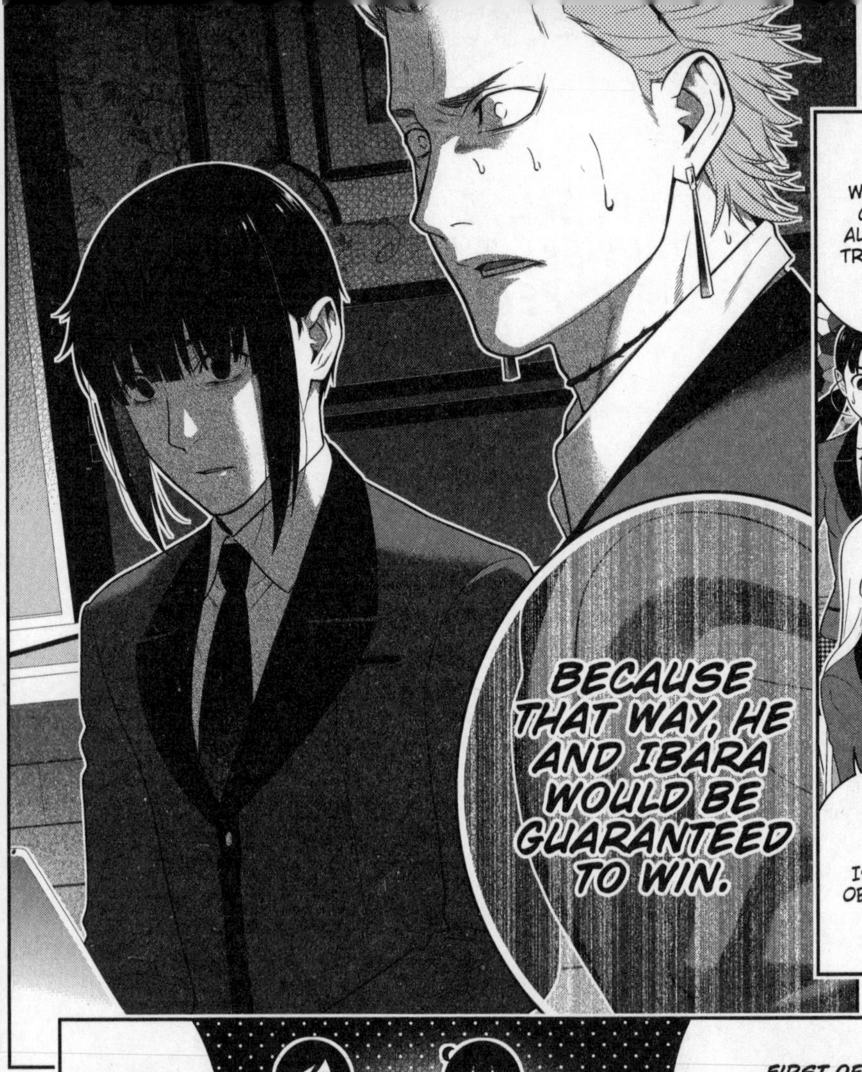
BECAUSE THAT WAY, HE AND IBARA WOULD BE GUARANTEED TO WIN.
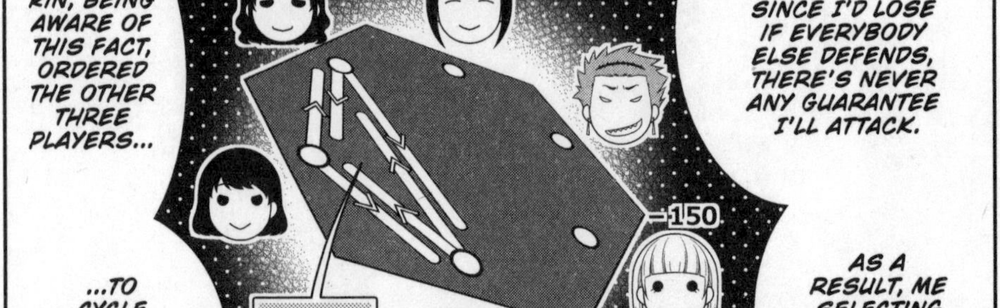
FIRST OFF, SINCE I'D LOSE IF EVERYBODY ELSE DEFENDS, THERE'S NEVER ANY GUARANTEE I'LL ATTACK.
RIN, BEING AWARE OF THIS FACT, ORDERED THE OTHER THREE PLAYERS...
−150
AS A RESULT, ME SELECTING "DEFEND" IS MORE LIKELY THAN NOT.
DEFEND
±0
...TO CYCLE THROUGH ATTACK ROUNDS.

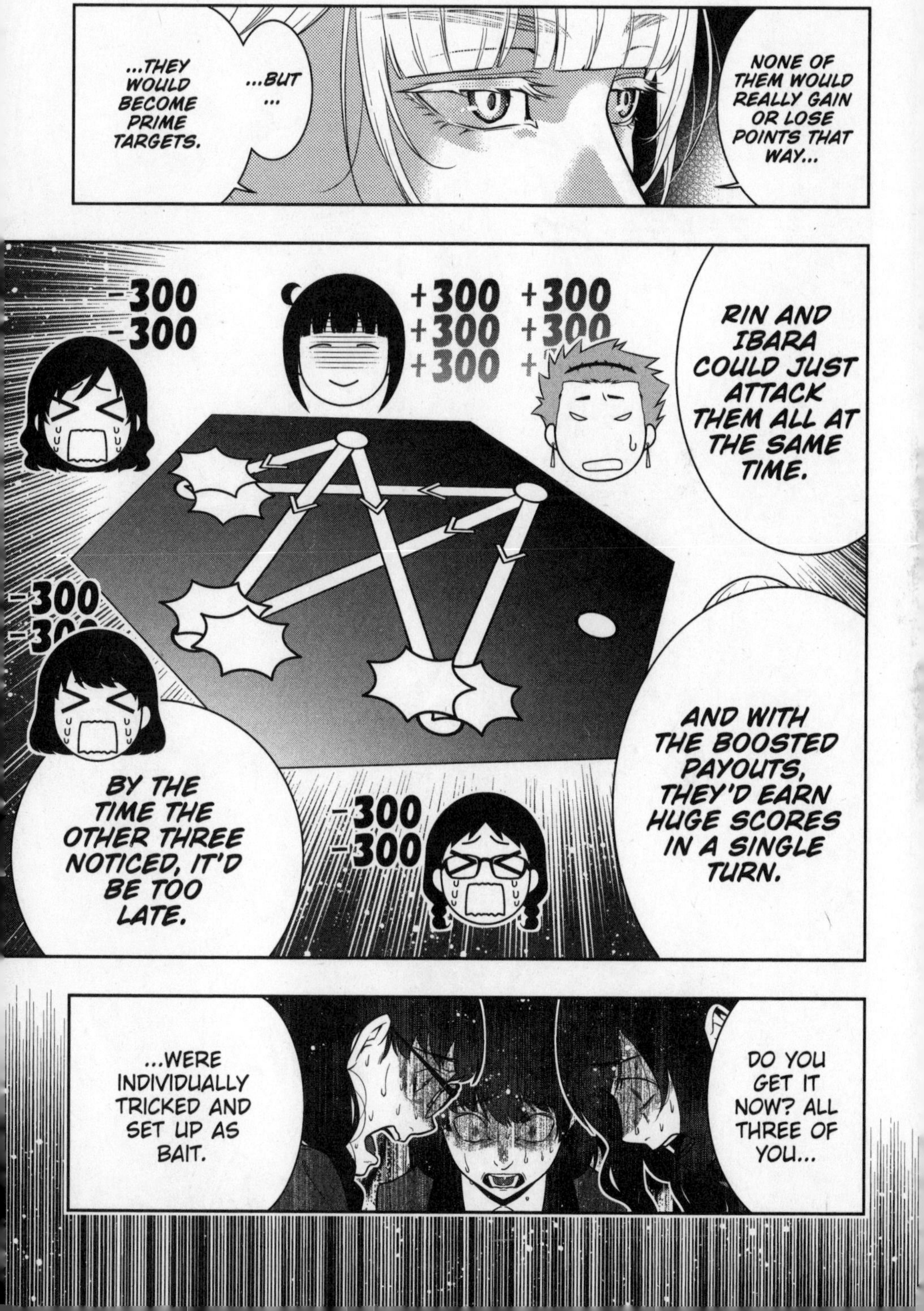
NONE OF THEM WOULD REALLY GAIN OR LOSE POINTS THAT WAY...
...BUT ...
...THEY WOULD BECOME PRIME TARGETS.
RIN AND IBARA COULD JUST ATTACK THEM ALL AT THE SAME TIME.
+300 +300
+300
+300
-300
-300
AND WITH THE BOOSTED PAYOUTS, THEY'D EARN HUGE SCORES IN A SINGLE TURN.
-300
-300
BY THE TIME THE OTHER THREE NOTICED, IT'D BE TOO LATE.
DO YOU GET IT NOW? ALL THREE OF YOU...
...WERE INDIVIDUALLY TRICKED AND SET UP AS BAIT.

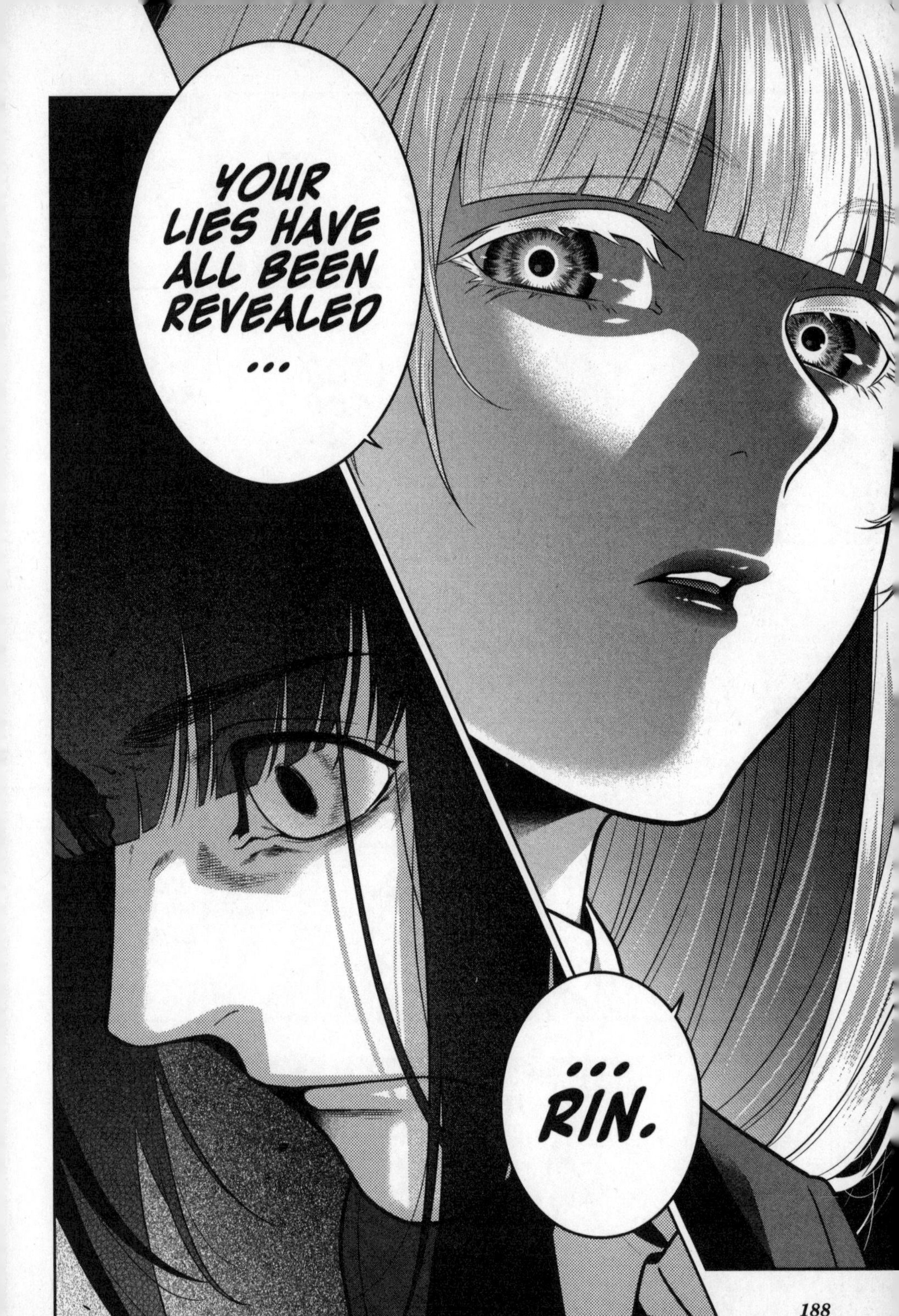
YOUR LIES HAVE ALL BEEN REVEALED ...
...RIN.

CHAPTER SIXTY-ONE
THE CONDESCENDING GIRL

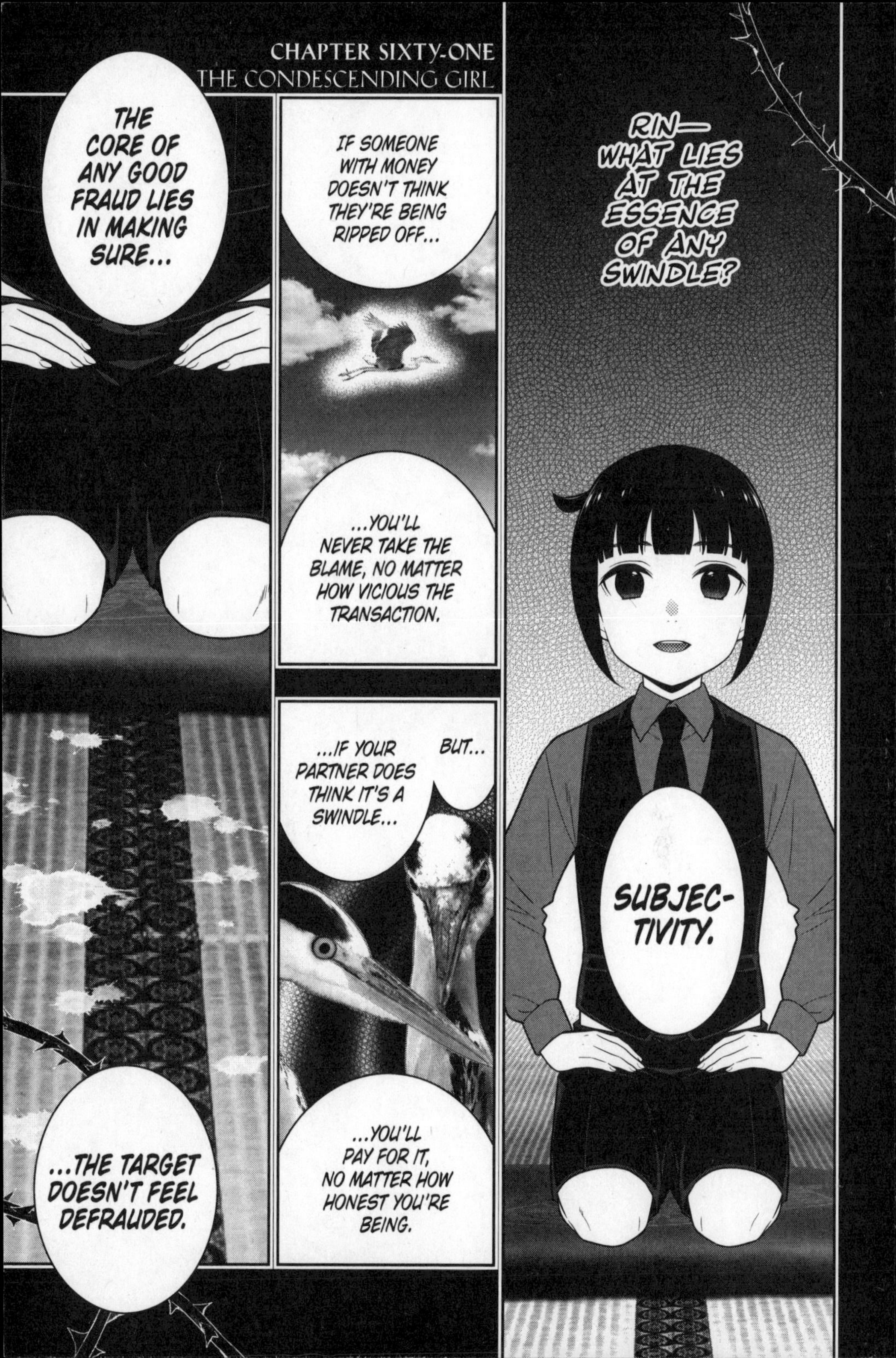
RIN—WHAT LIES AT THE ESSENCE OF ANY SWINDLE?
SUBJEC-TIVITY.
IF SOMEONE WITH MONEY DOESN'T THINK THEY'RE BEING RIPPED OFF...
...YOU'LL NEVER TAKE THE BLAME, NO MATTER HOW VICIOUS THE TRANSACTION.
THE CORE OF ANY GOOD FRAUD LIES IN MAKING SURE...
BUT...
...IF YOUR PARTNER DOES THINK IT'S A SWINDLE...
...YOU'LL PAY FOR IT, NO MATTER HOW HONEST YOU'RE BEING.
...THE TARGET DOESN'T FEEL DEFRAUDED.

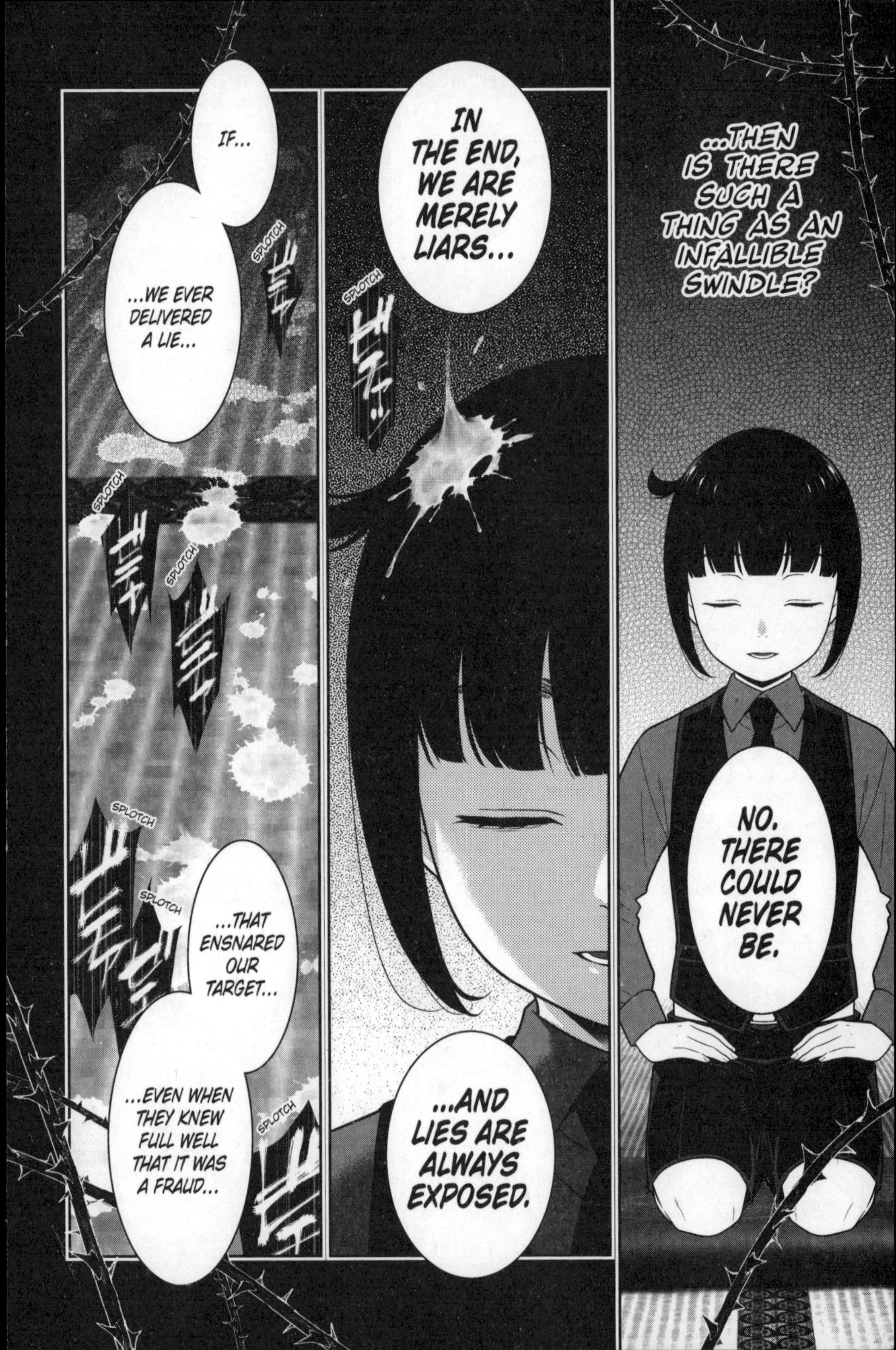
...THEN IS THERE SUCH A THING AS AN INFALLIBLE SWINDLE?
NO. THERE COULD NEVER BE.
IN THE END, WE ARE MERELY LIARS...
SPLOTCH
...AND LIES ARE ALWAYS EXPOSED.
IF...
...WE EVER DELIVERED A LIE...
SPLOTCH
SPLOTCH
SPLOTCH
SPLOTCH
SPLOTCH
...THAT ENSNARED OUR TARGET...
...EVEN WHEN THEY KNEW FULL WELL THAT IT WAS A FRAUD...
SPLOTCH

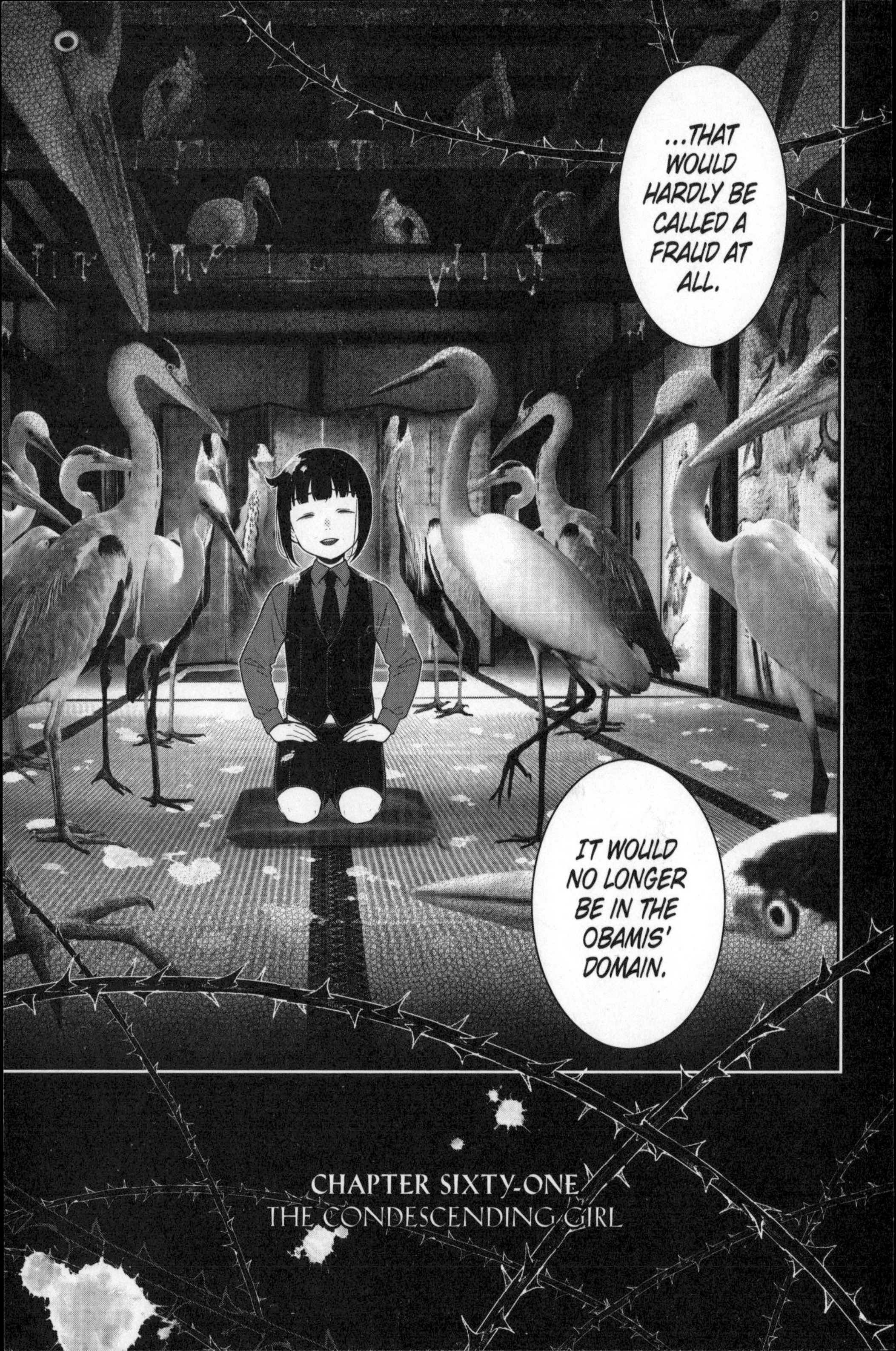
...THAT WOULD HARDLY BE CALLED A FRAUD AT ALL.
IT WOULD NO LONGER BE IN THE OBAMIS' DOMAIN.

CHAPTER SIXTY-ONE
THE CONDESCENDING GIRL

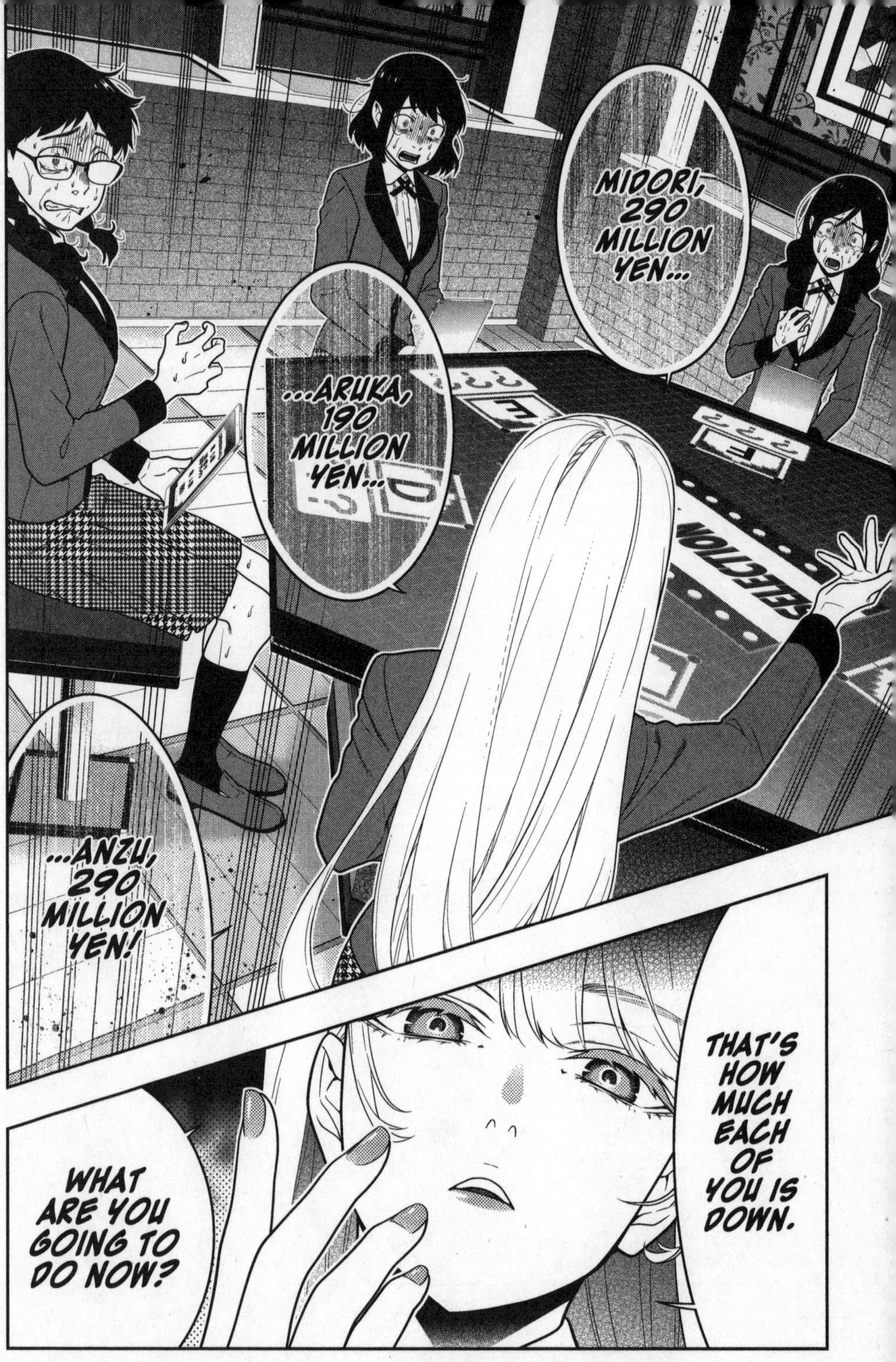
MIDORI, 290 MILLION YEN...
...ARUKA, 190 MILLION YEN...
SELECTION
...ANZU, 290 MILLION YEN!
THAT'S HOW MUCH EACH OF YOU IS DOWN.
WHAT ARE YOU GOING TO DO NOW?

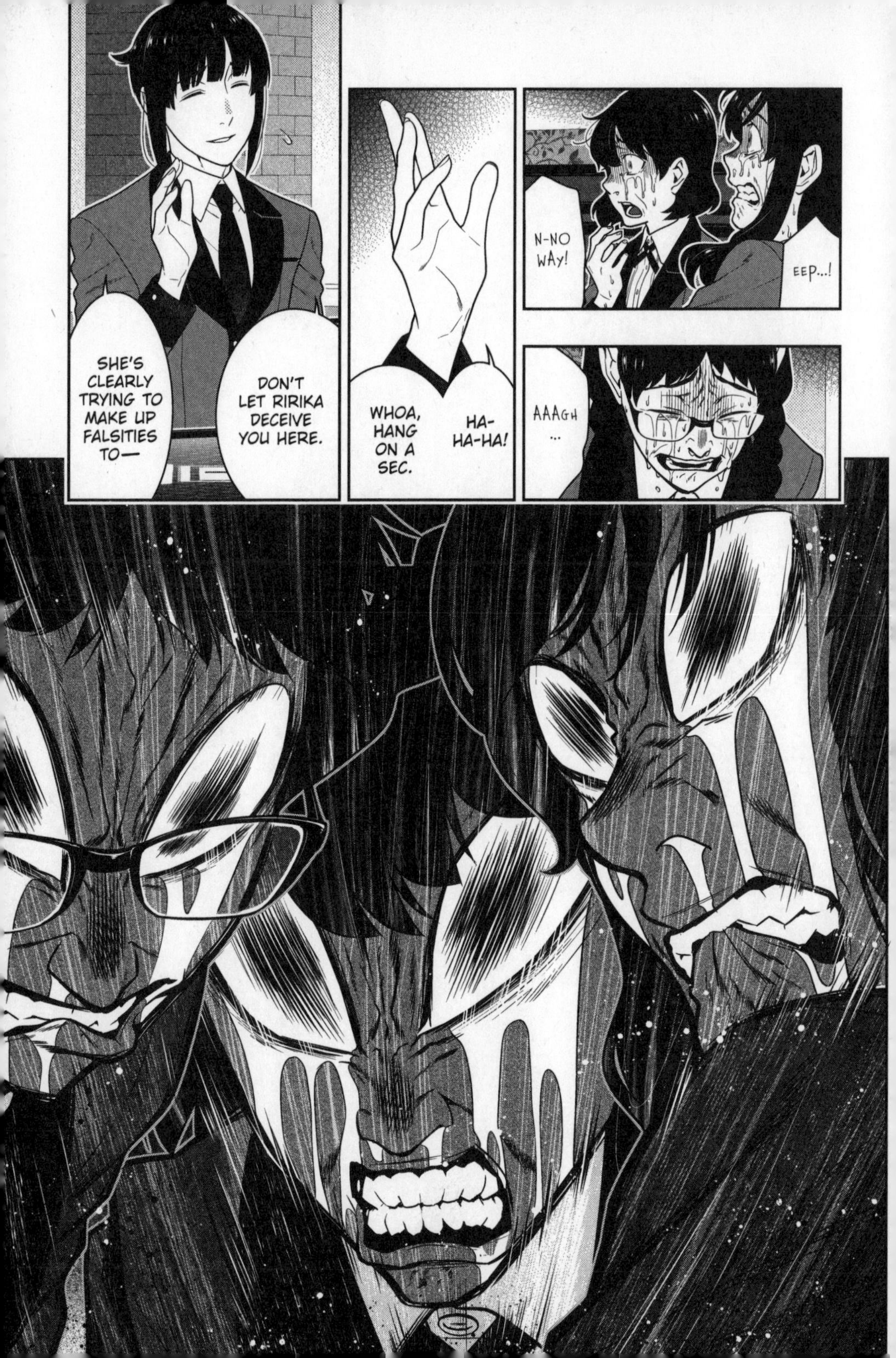
EEP...!
N-NO WAY!
AAAGH ...
HA-HA-HA!
WHOA, HANG ON A SEC.
DON'T LET RIRIKA DECEIVE YOU HERE.
SHE'S CLEARLY TRYING TO MAKE UP FALSITIES TO—

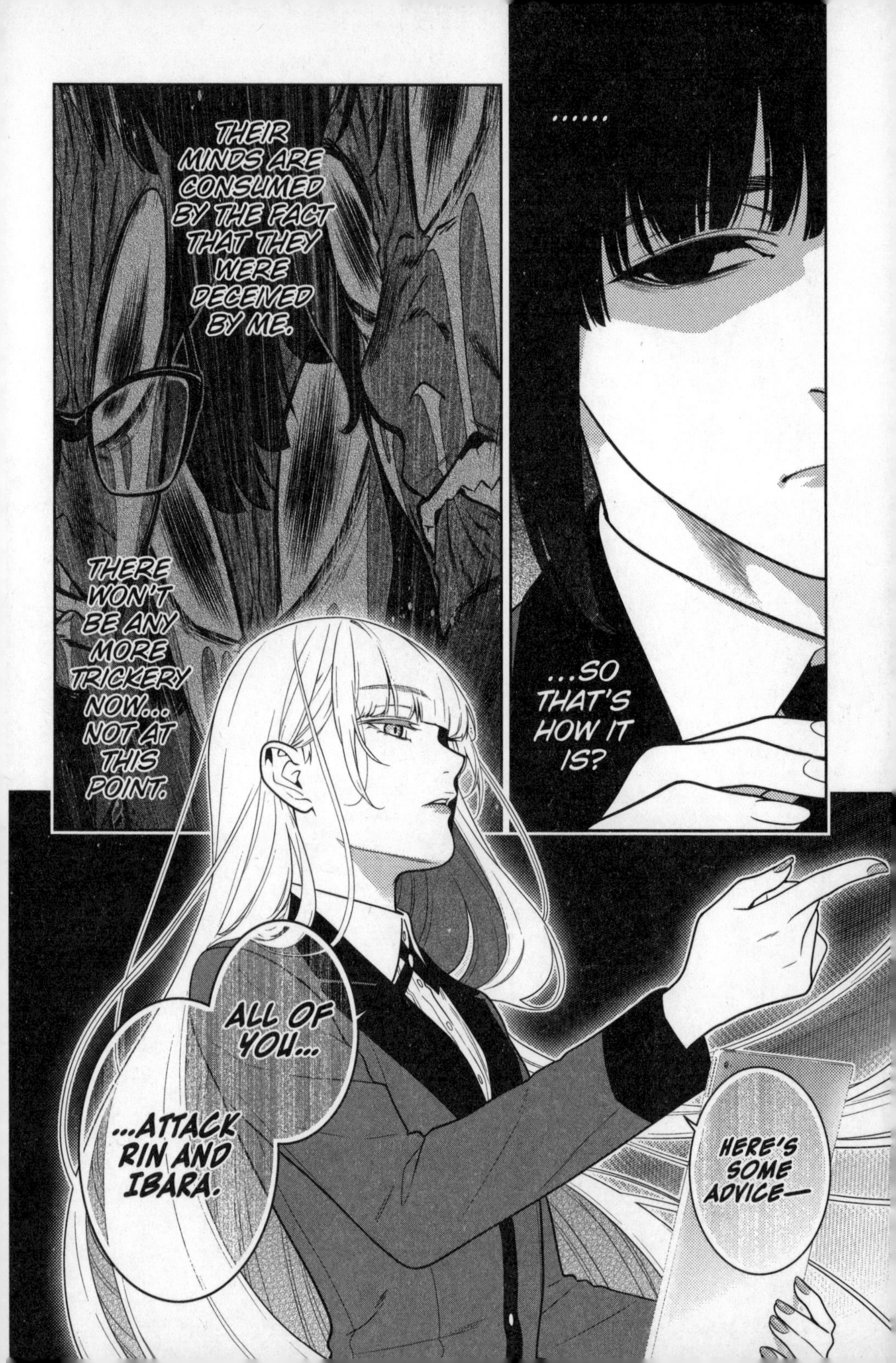
......
...SO THAT'S HOW IT IS?
THEIR MINDS ARE CONSUMED BY THE FACT THAT THEY WERE DECEIVED BY ME.
THERE WON'T BE ANY MORE TRICKERY NOW... NOT AT THIS POINT.
HERE'S SOME ADVICE—
ALL OF YOU...
...ATTACK RIN AND IBARA.

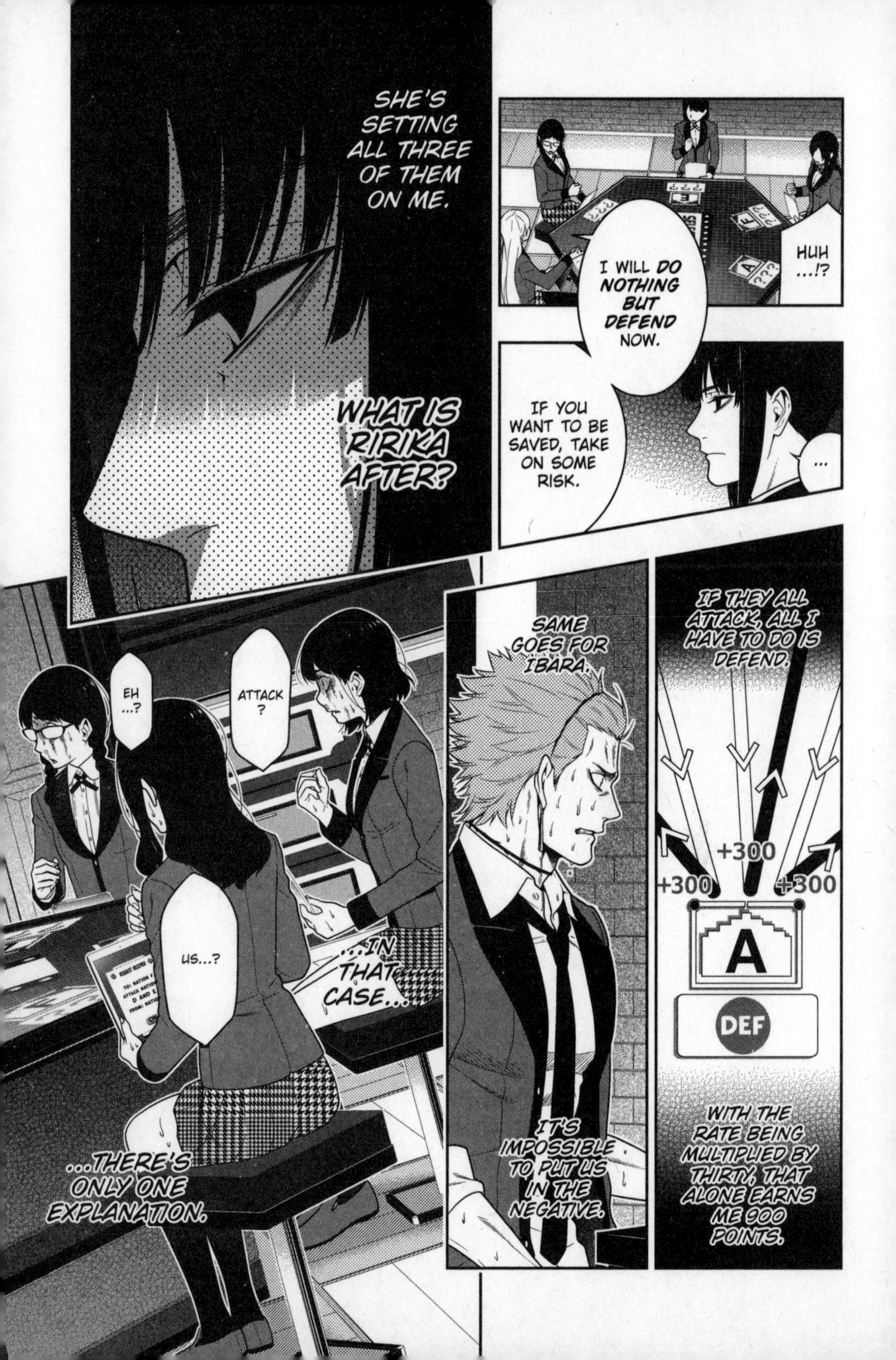
HUH ...!?
I WILL DO NOTHING BUT DEFEND NOW.
...
IF YOU WANT TO BE SAVED, TAKE ON SOME RISK.
SHE'S SETTING ALL THREE OF THEM ON ME.
WHAT IS RIRIKA AFTER?
IF THEY ALL ATTACK, ALL I HAVE TO DO IS DEFEND.
+300
+300
+300
A
DEF
WITH THE RATE BEING MULTIPLIED BY THIRTY, THAT ALONE EARNS ME 900 POINTS.
SAME GOES FOR IBARA.
IT'S IMPOSSIBLE TO PUT US IN THE NEGATIVE.
ATTACK ?
EH ...?
US...?
...IN THAT CASE...
...THERE'S ONLY ONE EXPLANATION.

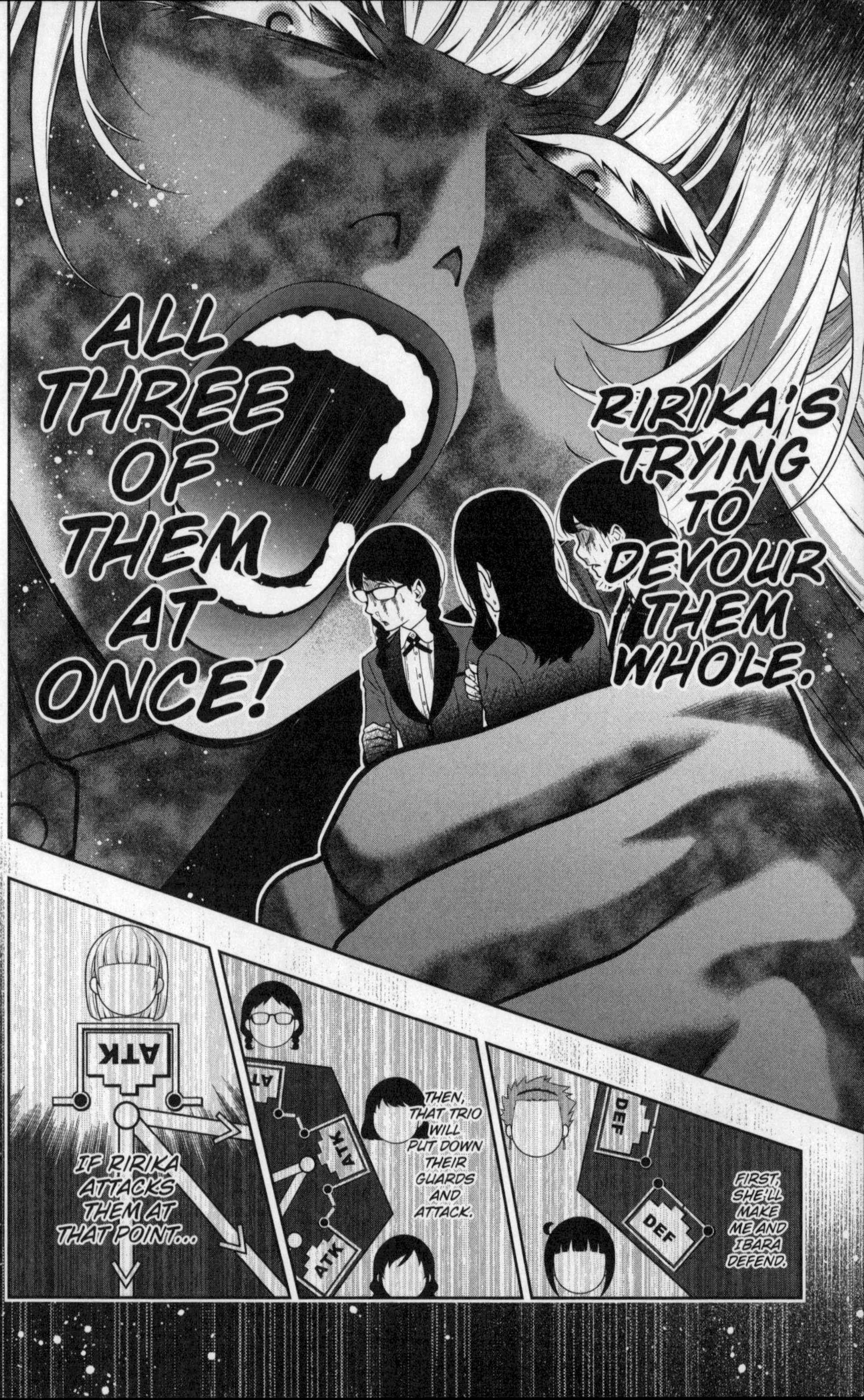
RIRIKA'S TRYING TO DEVOUR THEM WHOLE.
ALL THREE OF THEM AT ONCE!
DEF
DEF
FIRST, SHE'LL MAKE ME AND IBARA DEFEND.
ATK
ATK
THEN, THAT TRIO WILL PUT DOWN THEIR GUARDS AND ATTACK.
ATK
IF RIRIKA ATTACKS THEM AT THAT POINT...

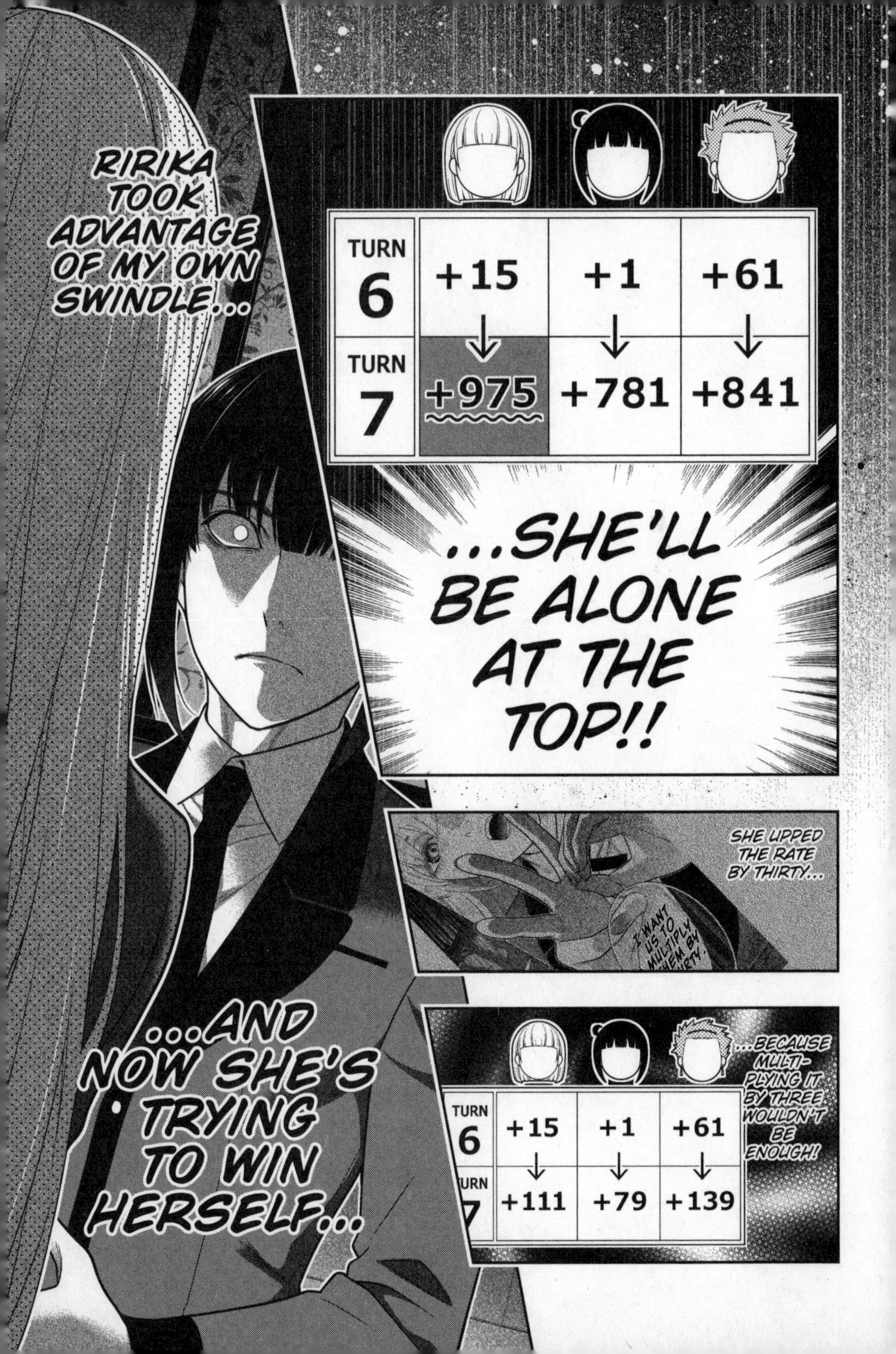
TURN 6: +15 / +1 / +61
TURN 7: +975 / +781 / +841
...SHE'LL BE ALONE AT THE TOP!!
SHE UPPED THE RATE BY THIRTY...
I WANT US TO MULTIPLY THEM BY THIRTY.
TURN 6: +15 / +1 / +61
TURN 7: +111 / +79 / +139
...BECAUSE MULTIPLYING IT BY THREE WOULDN'T BE ENOUGH!
RIRIKA TOOK ADVANTAGE OF MY OWN SWINDLE...
...AND NOW SHE'S TRYING TO WIN HERSELF...

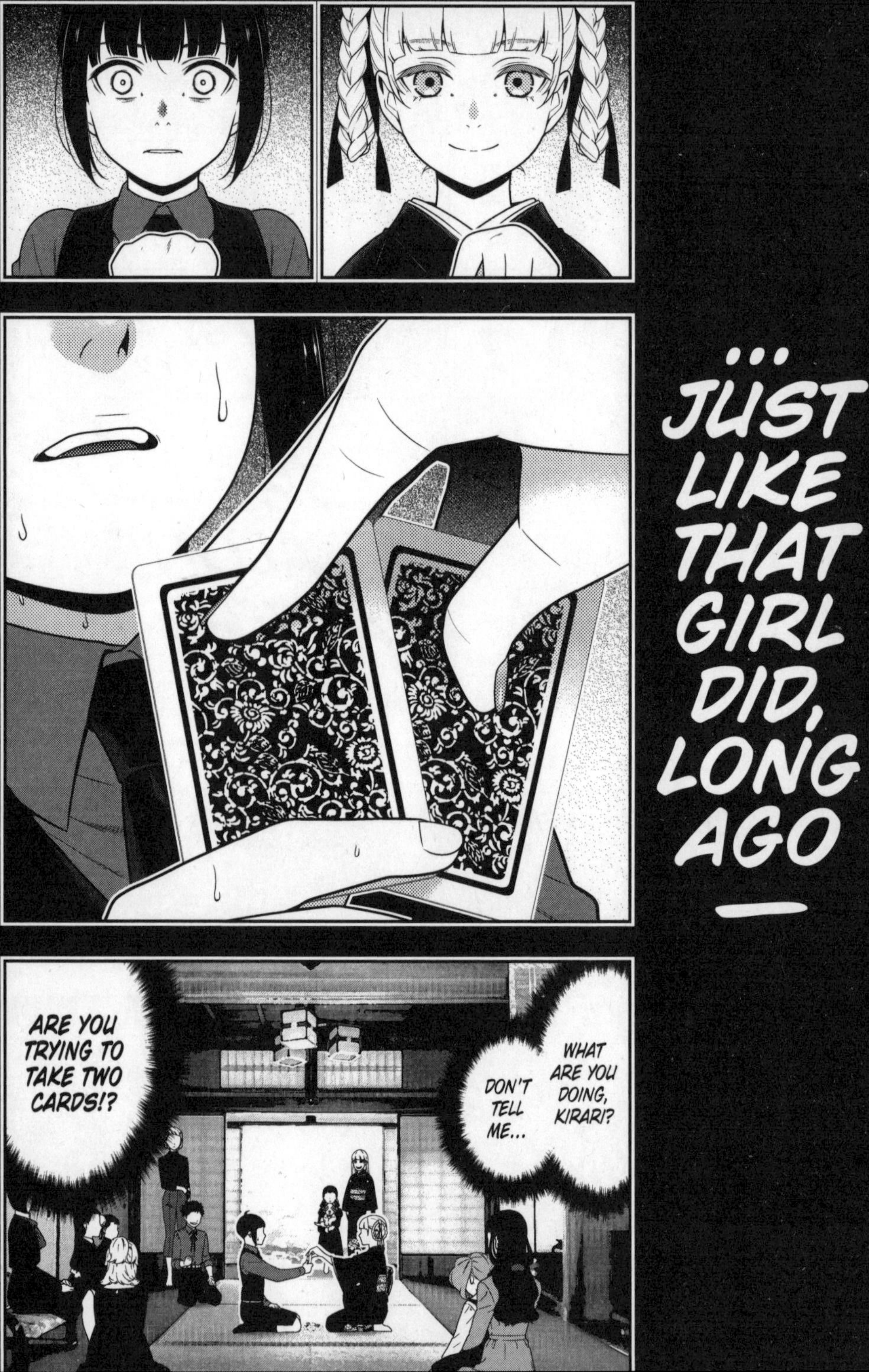
...JUST LIKE THAT GIRL DID, LONG AGO—
WHAT ARE YOU DOING, KIRARI?
DON'T TELL ME...
ARE YOU TRYING TO TAKE TWO CARDS!?

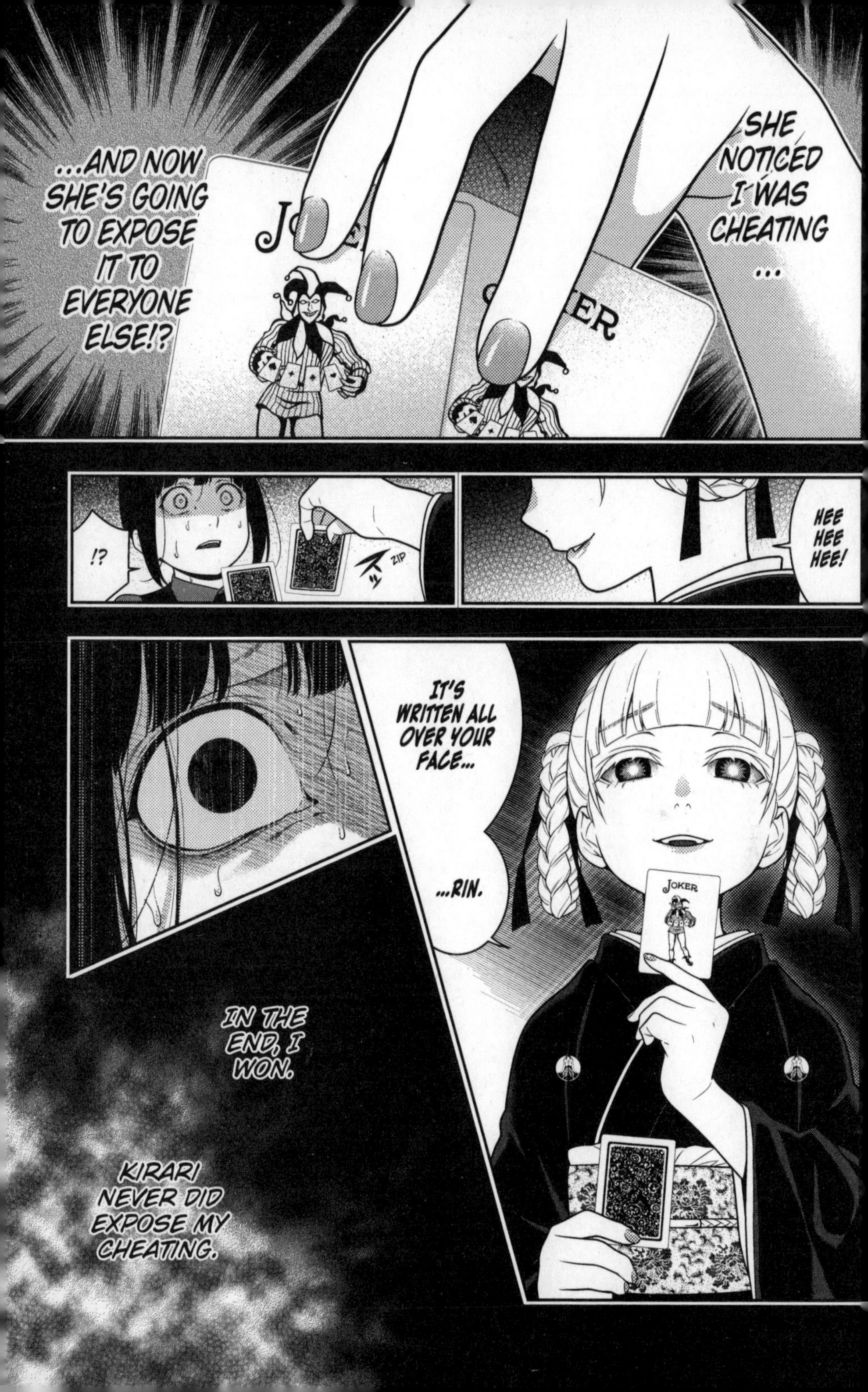
SHE NOTICED I WAS CHEATING ...
...AND NOW SHE'S GOING TO EXPOSE IT TO EVERYONE ELSE!?
HEE HEE HEE!
!?
ZIP
IT'S WRITTEN ALL OVER YOUR FACE...
...RIN.
JOKER
IN THE END, I WON.
KIRARI NEVER DID EXPOSE MY CHEATING.

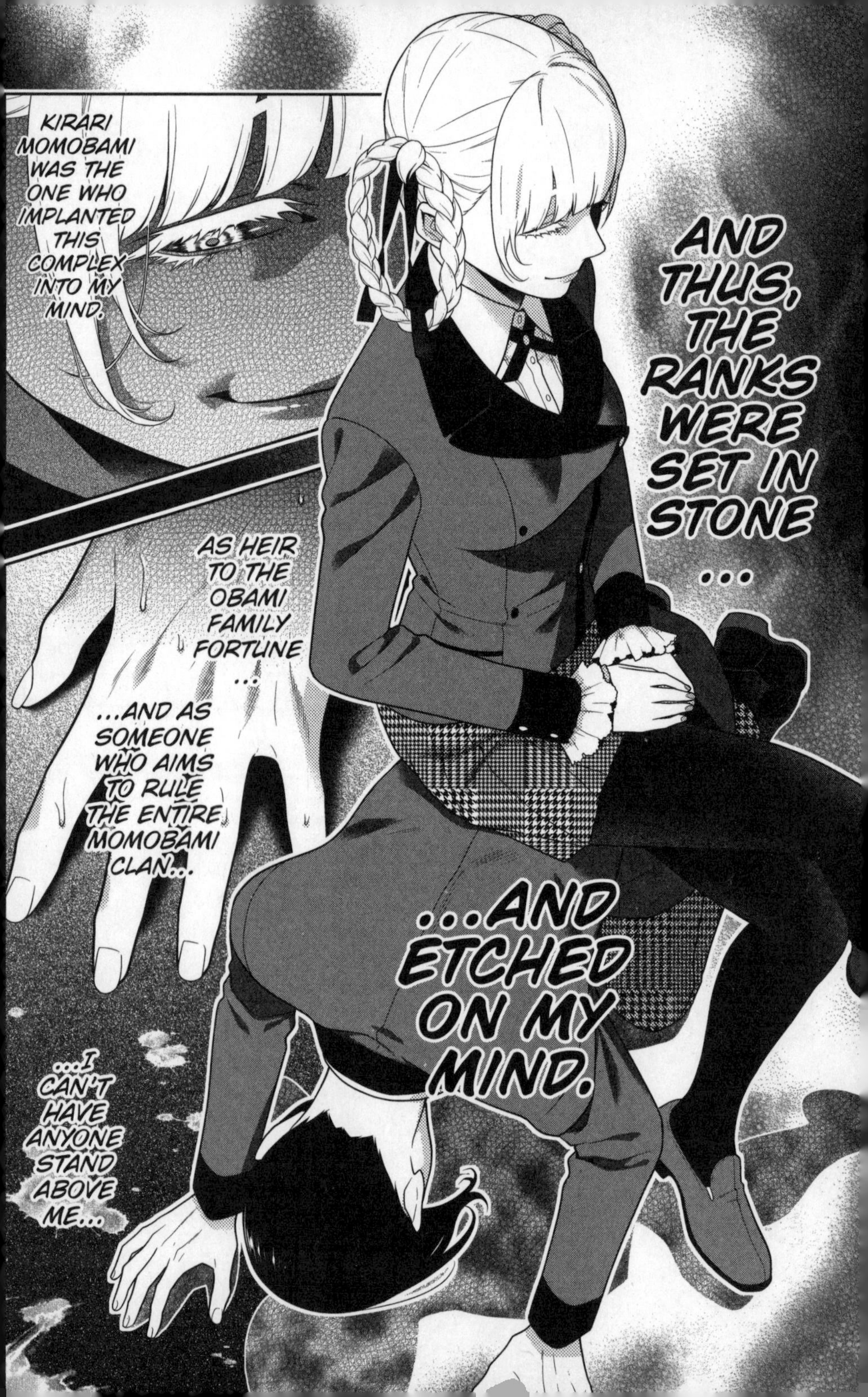
AND THUS, THE RANKS WERE SET IN STONE...
KIRARI MOMOBAMI WAS THE ONE WHO IMPLANTED THIS COMPLEX INTO MY MIND.
AS HEIR TO THE OBAMI FAMILY FORTUNE...
...AND AS SOMEONE WHO AIMS TO RULE THE ENTIRE MOMOBAMI CLAN...
...I CAN'T HAVE ANYONE STAND ABOVE ME...
...AND ETCHED ON MY MIND.

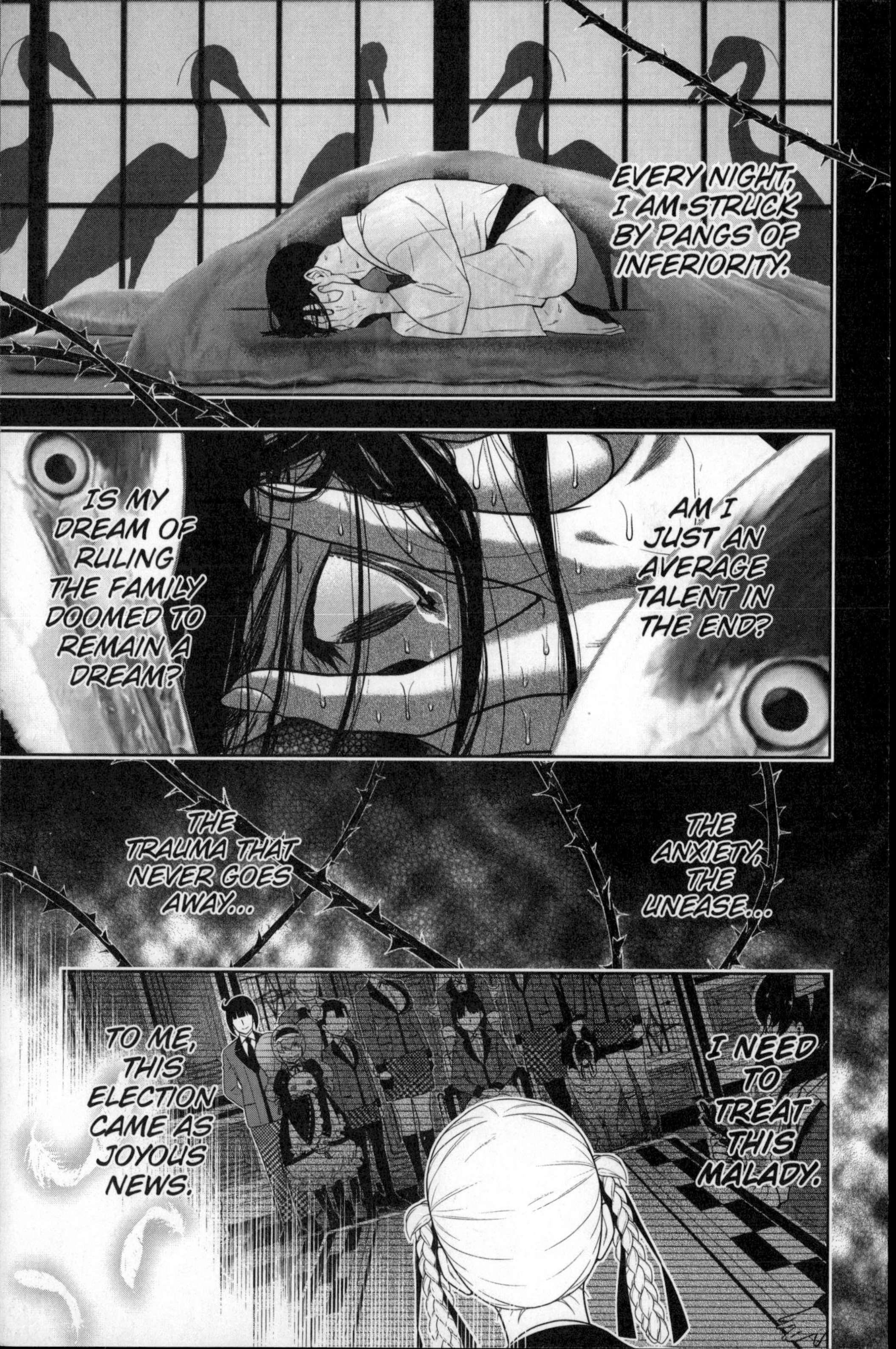
EVERY NIGHT, I AM STRUCK BY PANGS OF INFERIORITY.
AM I JUST AN AVERAGE TALENT IN THE END?
IS MY DREAM OF RULING THE FAMILY DOOMED TO REMAIN A DREAM?
THE ANXIETY, THE UNEASE...
THE TRAUMA THAT NEVER GOES AWAY...
I NEED TO TREAT THIS MALADY.
TO ME, THIS ELECTION CAME AS JOYOUS NEWS.

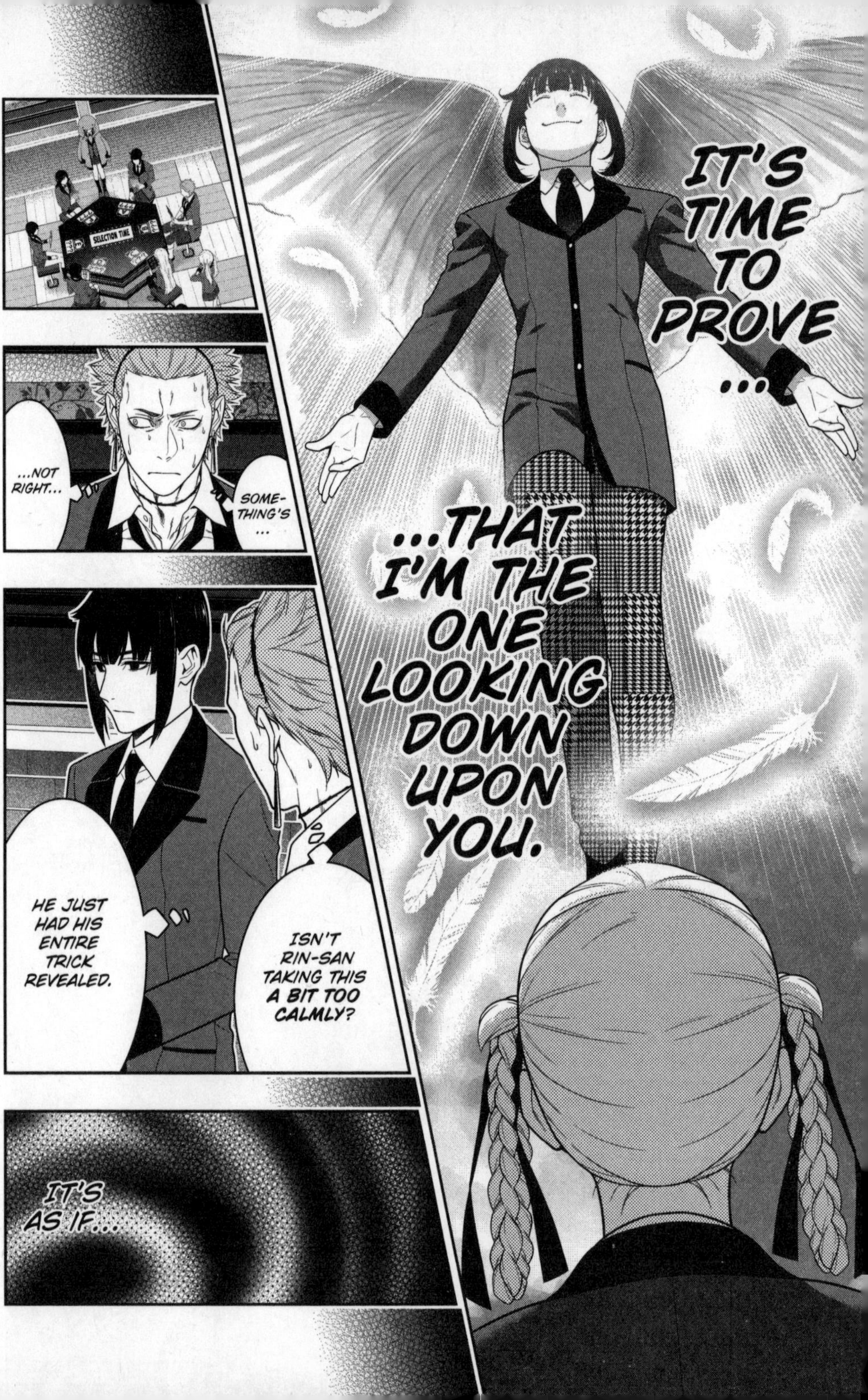
IT'S TIME TO PROVE...
...THAT I'M THE ONE LOOKING DOWN UPON YOU.
SELECTION TIME
SOME-THING'S...
...NOT RIGHT...
ISN'T RIN-SAN TAKING THIS A BIT TOO CALMLY?
HE JUST HAD HIS ENTIRE TRICK REVEALED.
IT'S AS IF...

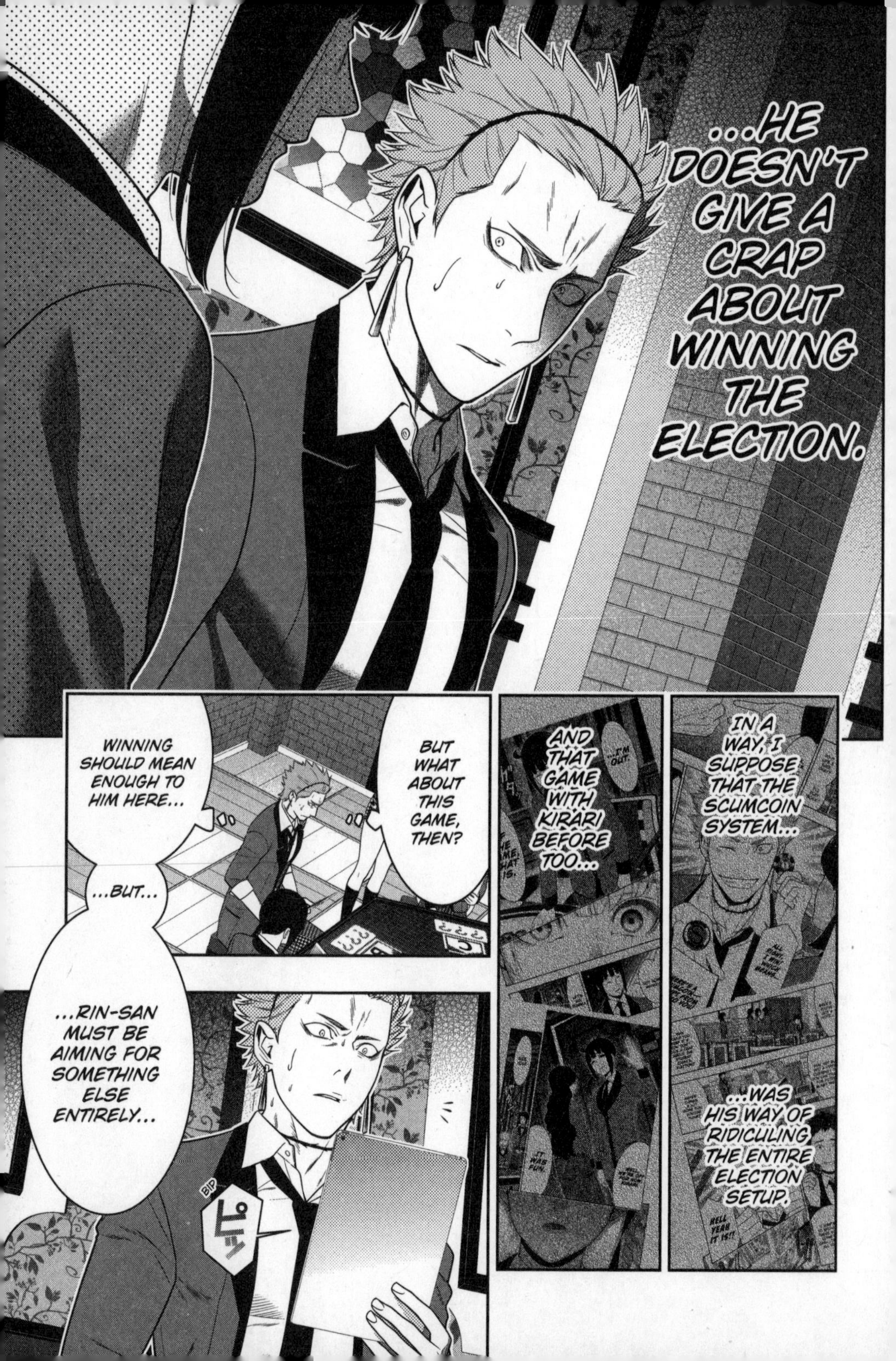
...HE DOESN'T GIVE A CRAP ABOUT WINNING THE ELECTION.
IN A WAY, I SUPPOSE THAT THE SCUMCOIN SYSTEM...
...WAS HIS WAY OF RIDICULING THE ENTIRE ELECTION SETUP.
HELL YEAH IT IS!!
AND THAT GAME WITH KIRARI BEFORE TOO...
...I'M OUT.
IT WAS FUN.
BUT WHAT ABOUT THIS GAME, THEN?
WINNING SHOULD MEAN ENOUGH TO HIM HERE...
...BUT...
...RIN-SAN MUST BE AIMING FOR SOMETHING ELSE ENTIRELY...
ピッ
BIP

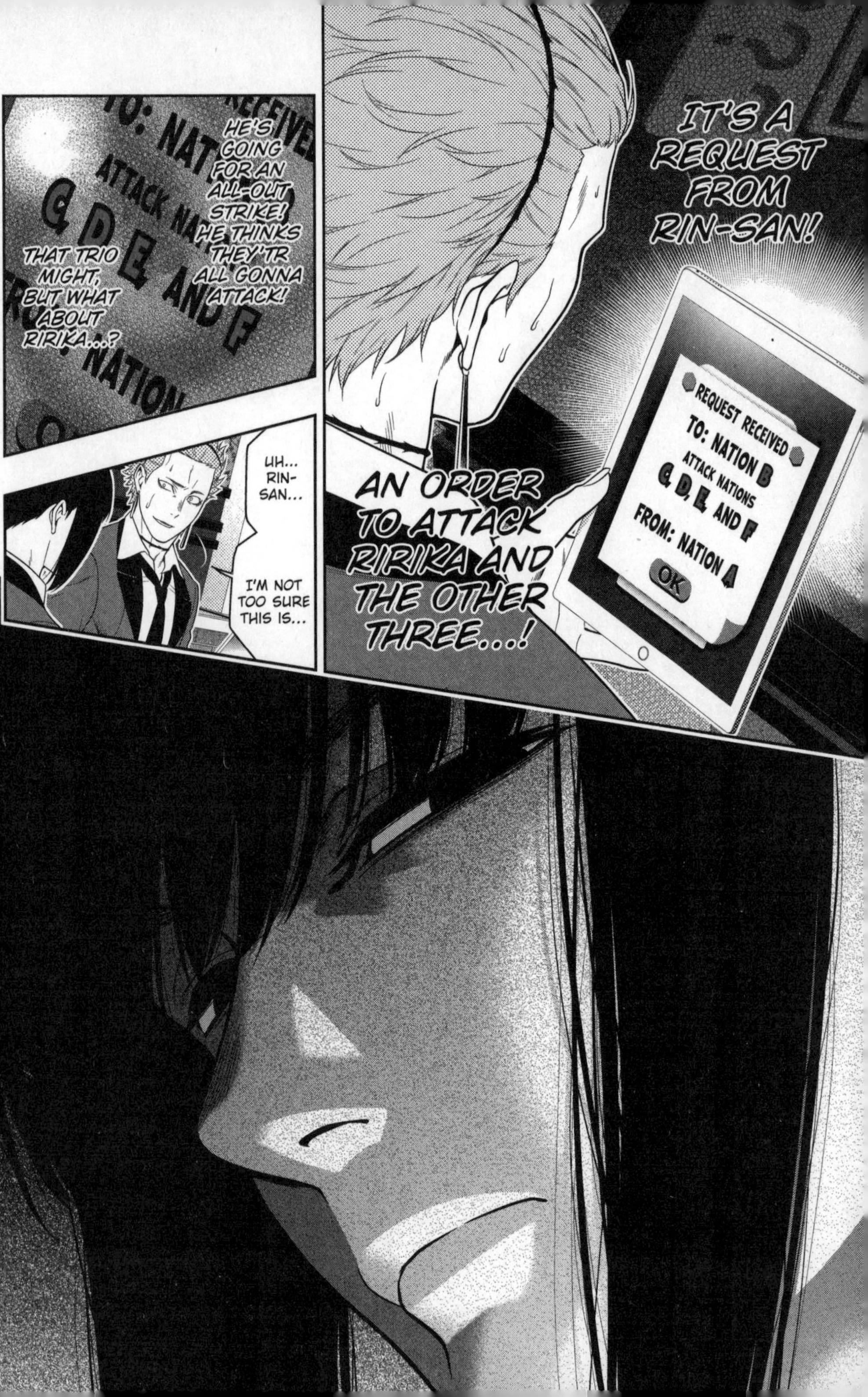
IT'S A REQUEST FROM RIN-SAN!
REQUEST RECEIVED
TO: NATION B
ATTACK NATIONS C, D, E, AND F
FROM: NATION A
OK
AN ORDER TO ATTACK RIRIKA AND THE OTHER THREE...!
HE'S GOING FOR AN ALL-OUT STRIKE! HE THINKS THEY'TR ALL GONNA ATTACK!
THAT TRIO MIGHT, BUT WHAT ABOUT RIRIKA...?
UH... RIN-SAN...
I'M NOT TOO SURE THIS IS...

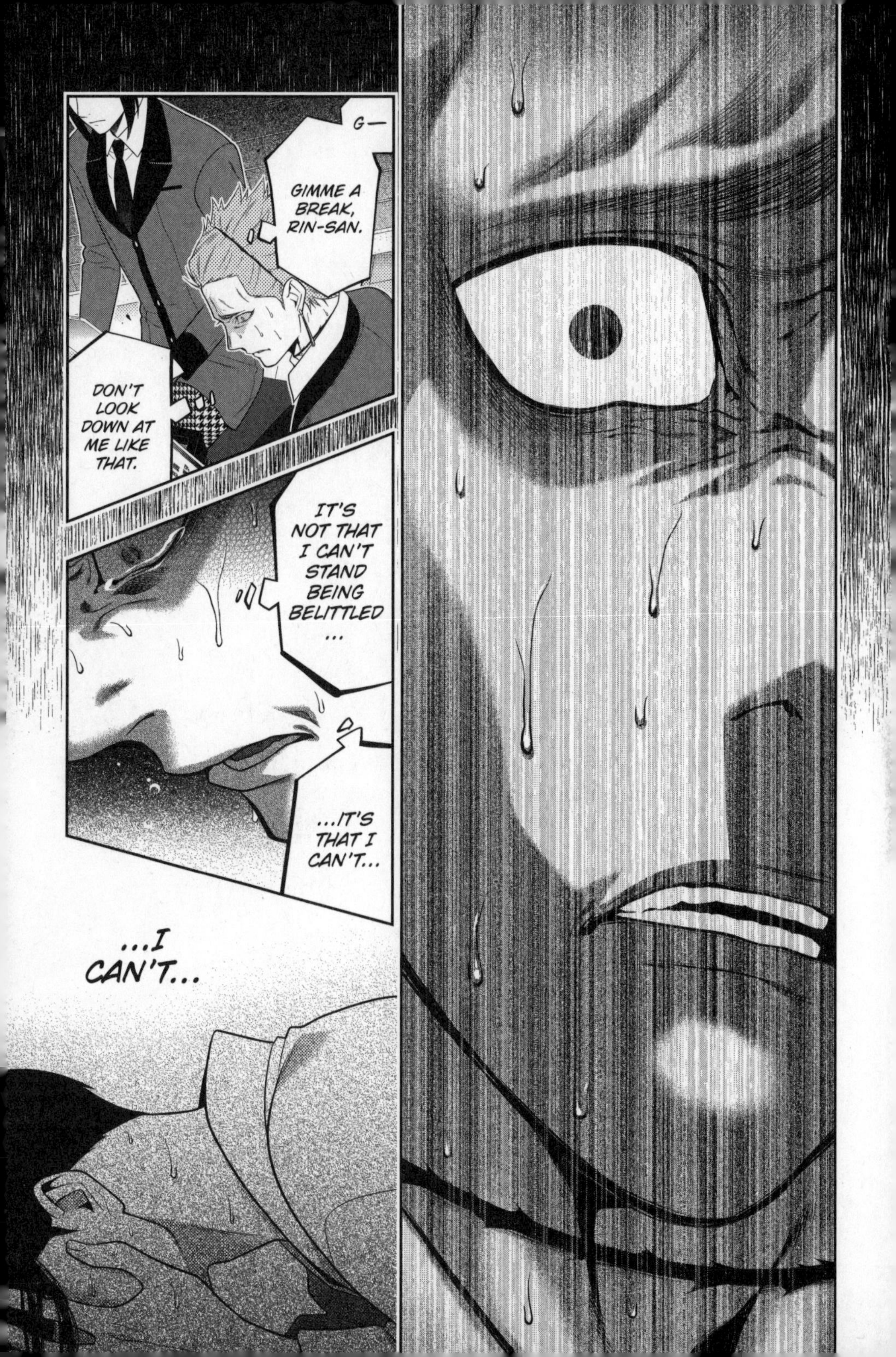
G—
GIMME A BREAK, RIN-SAN.
DON'T LOOK DOWN AT ME LIKE THAT.
IT'S NOT THAT I CAN'T STAND BEING BELITTLED...
...IT'S THAT I CAN'T...
...I CAN'T...

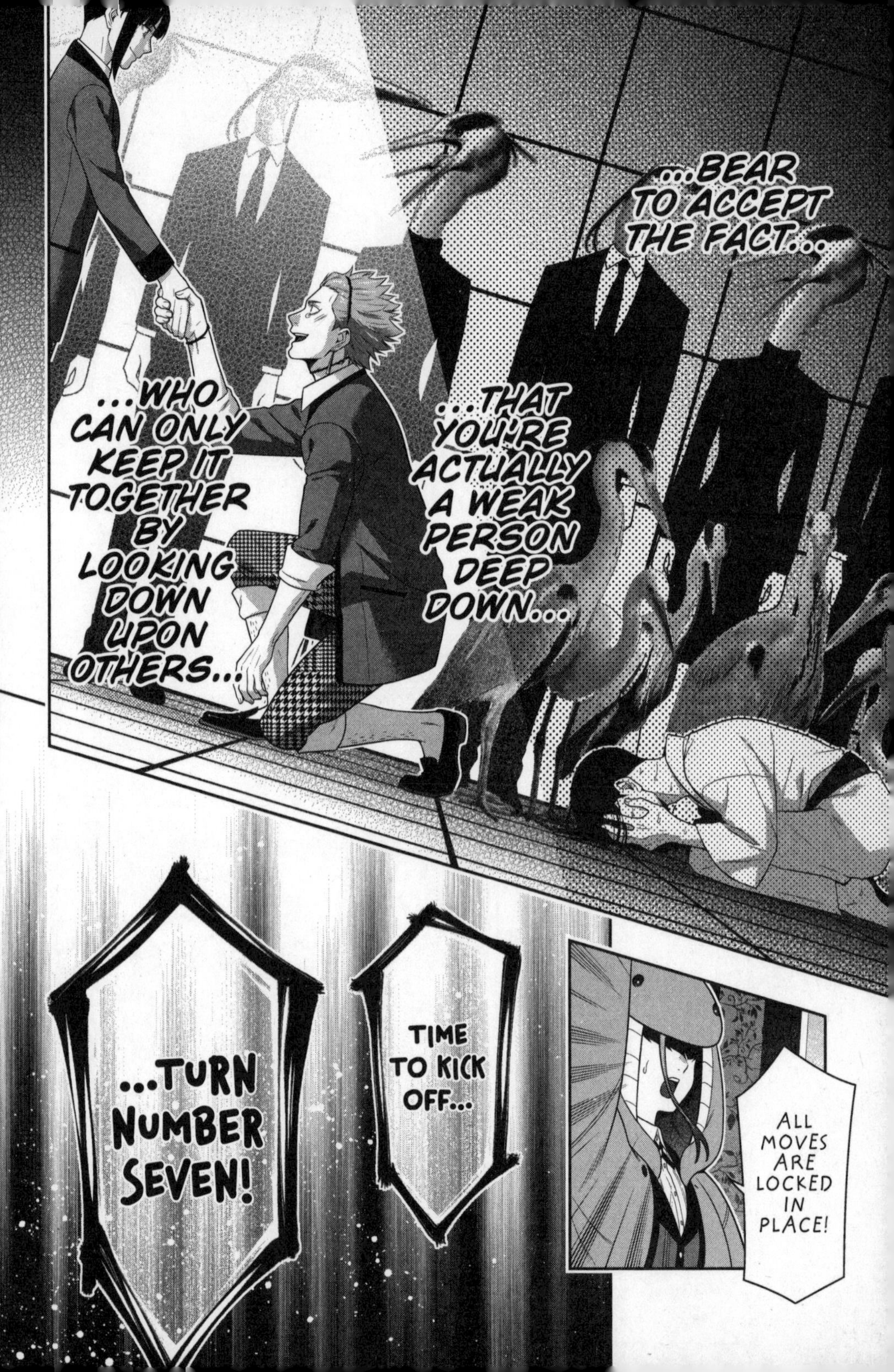
...BEAR TO ACCEPT THE FACT...
...THAT YOU'RE ACTUALLY A WEAK PERSON DEEP DOWN...
...WHO CAN ONLY KEEP IT TOGETHER BY LOOKING DOWN UPON OTHERS...
ALL MOVES ARE LOCKED IN PLACE!
TIME TO KICK OFF...
...TURN NUMBER SEVEN!

CHAPTER SIXTY-TWO
THE LIE-UNRAVELING GIRL

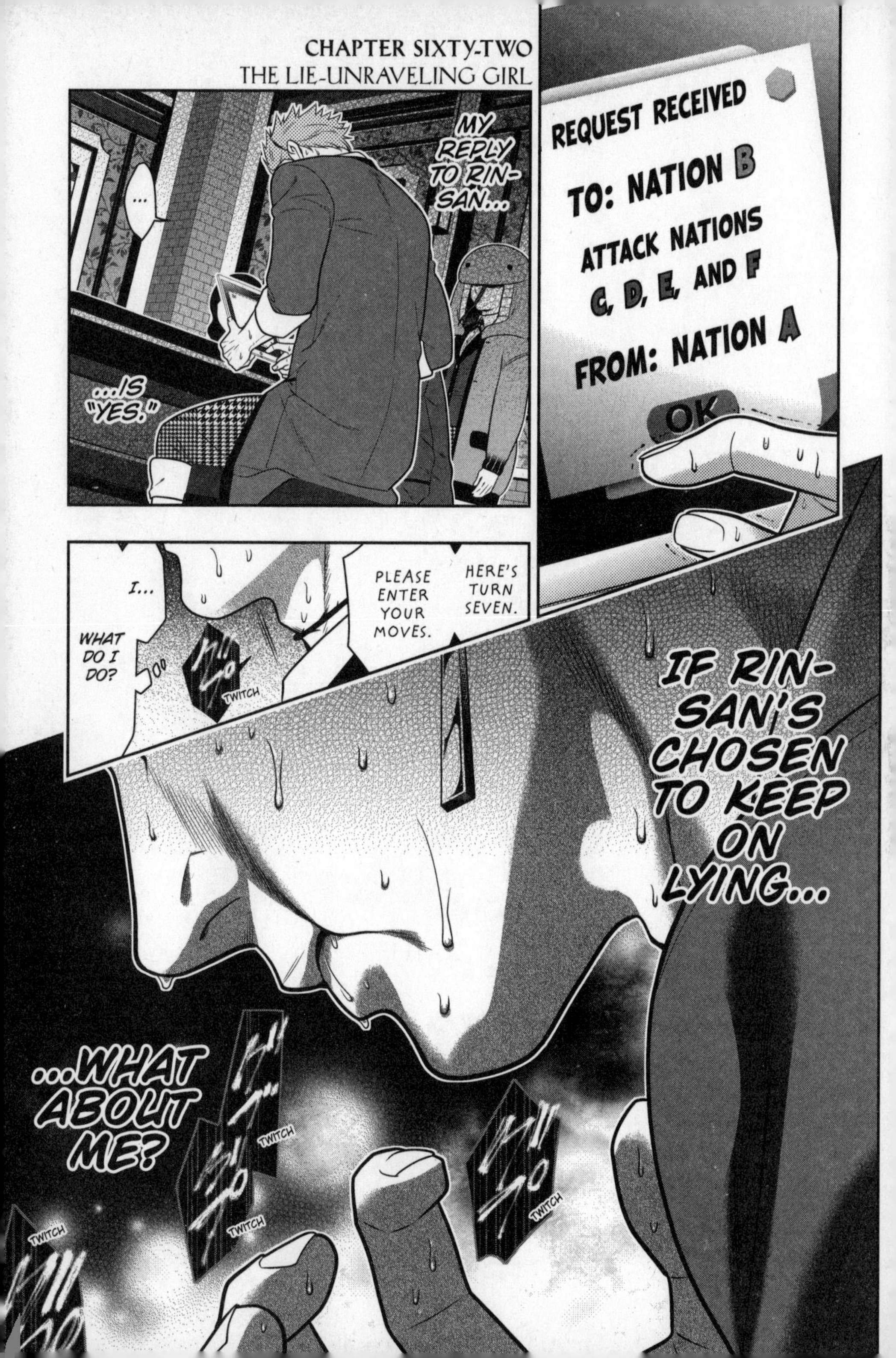
REQUEST RECEIVED
TO: NATION B
ATTACK NATIONS C, D, E, AND F
FROM: NATION A
OK
MY REPLY TO RIN-SAN...
...IS "YES."
...
HERE'S TURN SEVEN.
PLEASE ENTER YOUR MOVES.
I...
WHAT DO I DO?
TWITCH
IF RIN-SAN'S CHOSEN TO KEEP ON LYING...
...WHAT ABOUT ME?
TWITCH
TWITCH
TWITCH
TWITCH

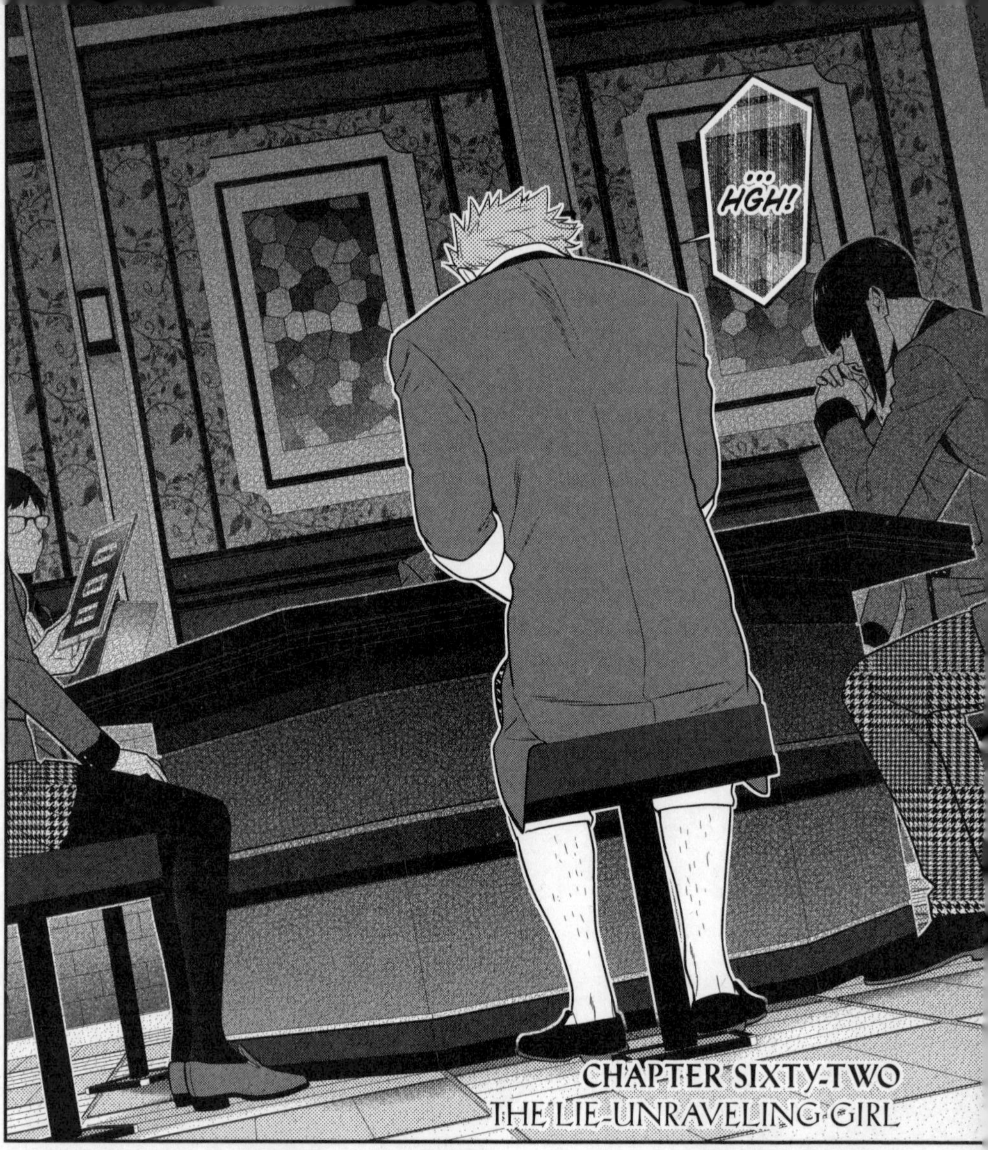
...HGH!
CHAPTER SIXTY-TWO
THE LIE-UNRAVELING GIRL

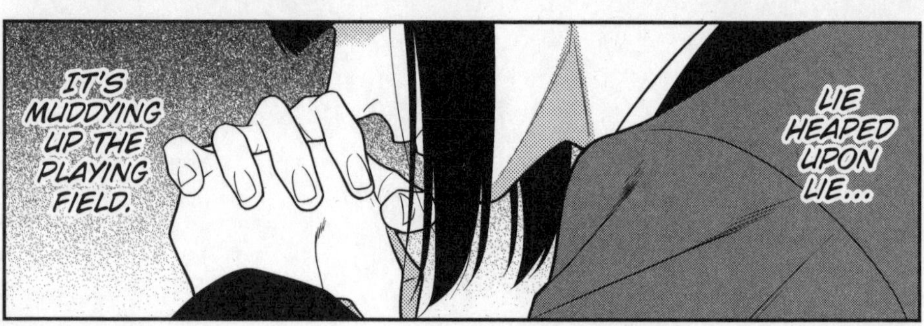
LIE HEAPED UPON LIE...
IT'S MUDDYING UP THE PLAYING FIELD.

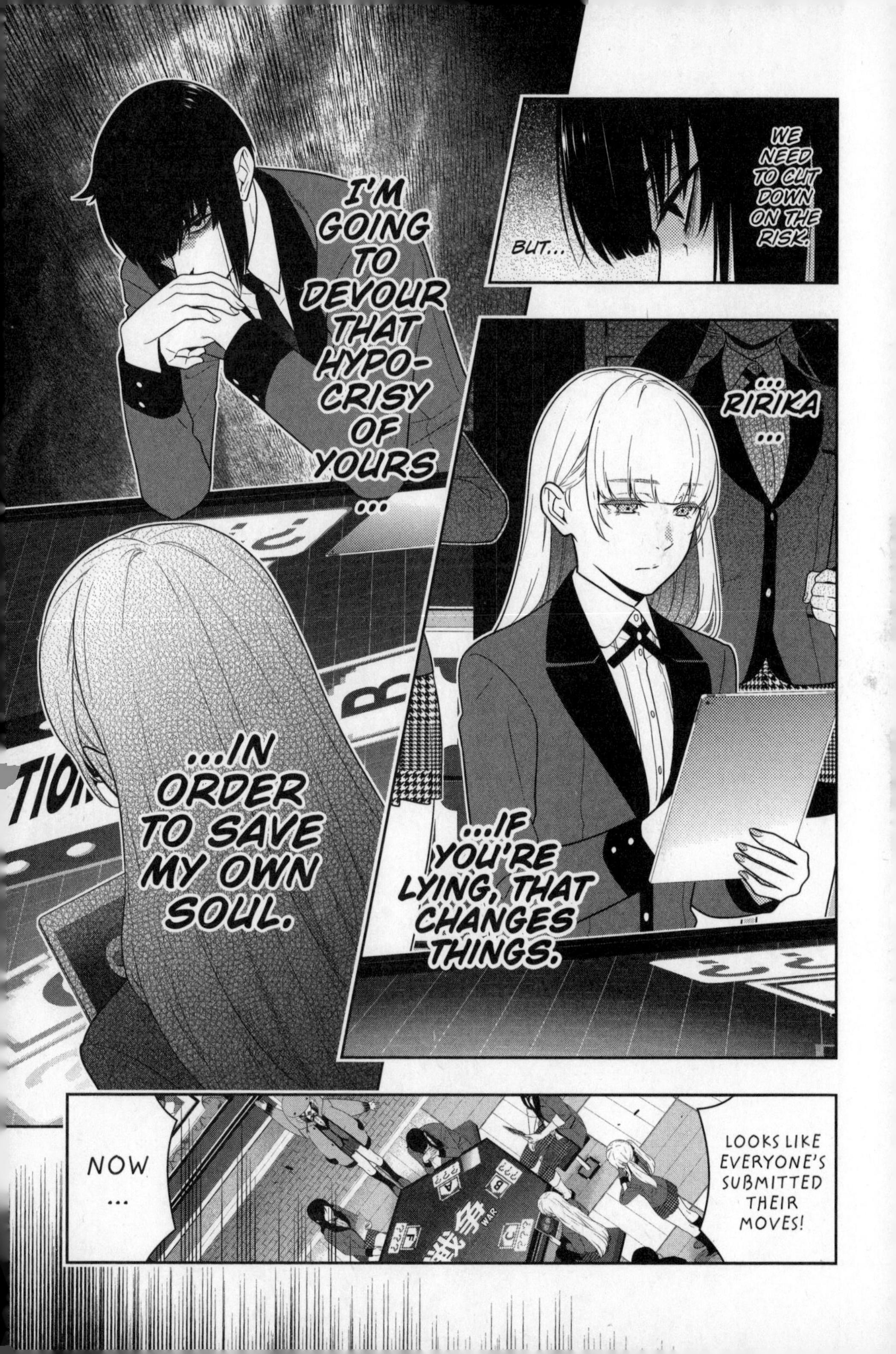
WE NEED TO CUT DOWN ON THE RISK.
BUT...
...RIRIKA...
...IF YOU'RE LYING, THAT CHANGES THINGS.
I'M GOING TO DEVOUR THAT HYPOCRISY OF YOURS...
...IN ORDER TO SAVE MY OWN SOUL.
LOOKS LIKE EVERYONE'S SUBMITTED THEIR MOVES!
NOW...

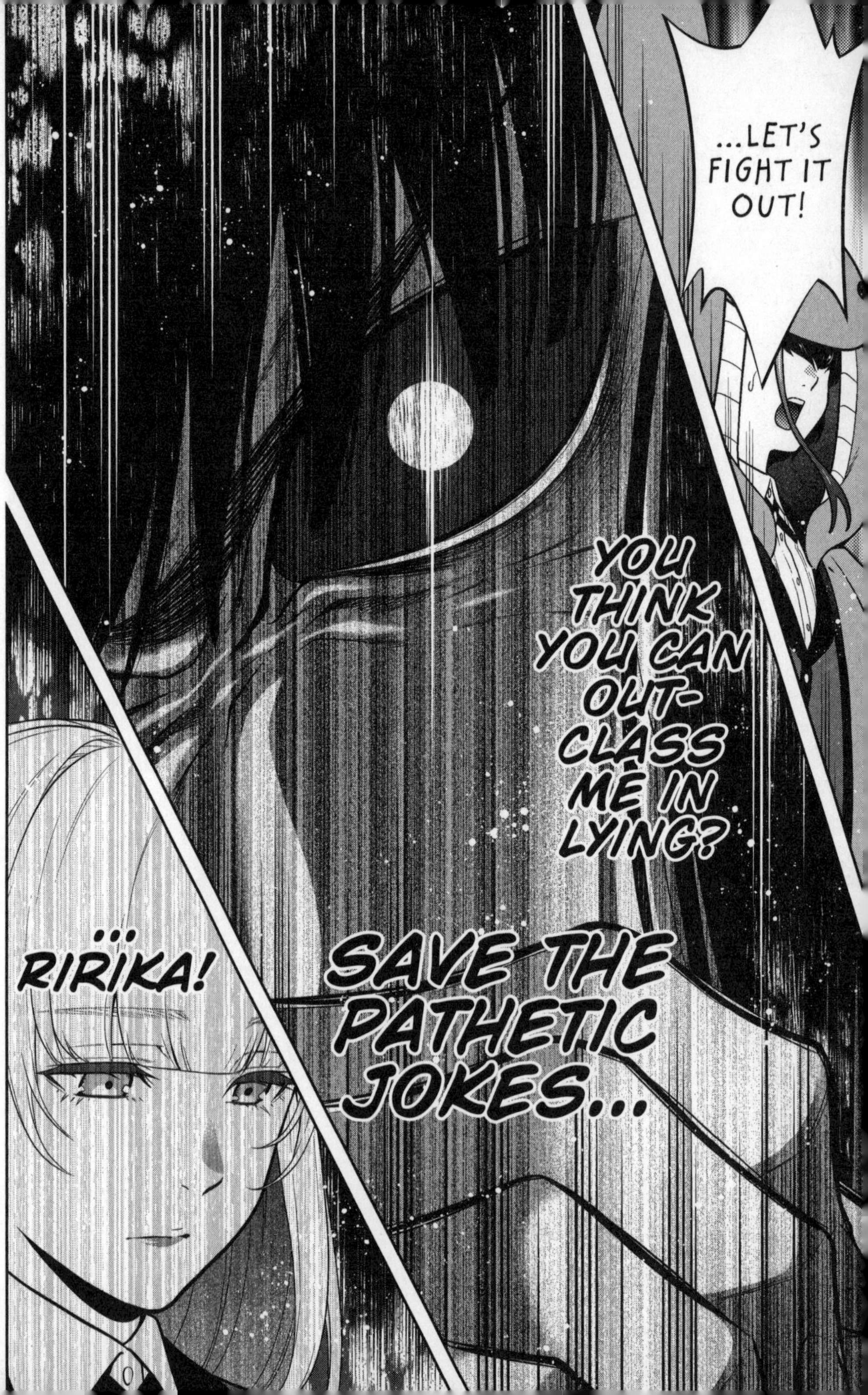
...LET'S FIGHT IT OUT!
YOU THINK YOU CAN OUT-CLASS ME IN LYING?
SAVE THE PATHETIC JOKES...
...RIRIKA!

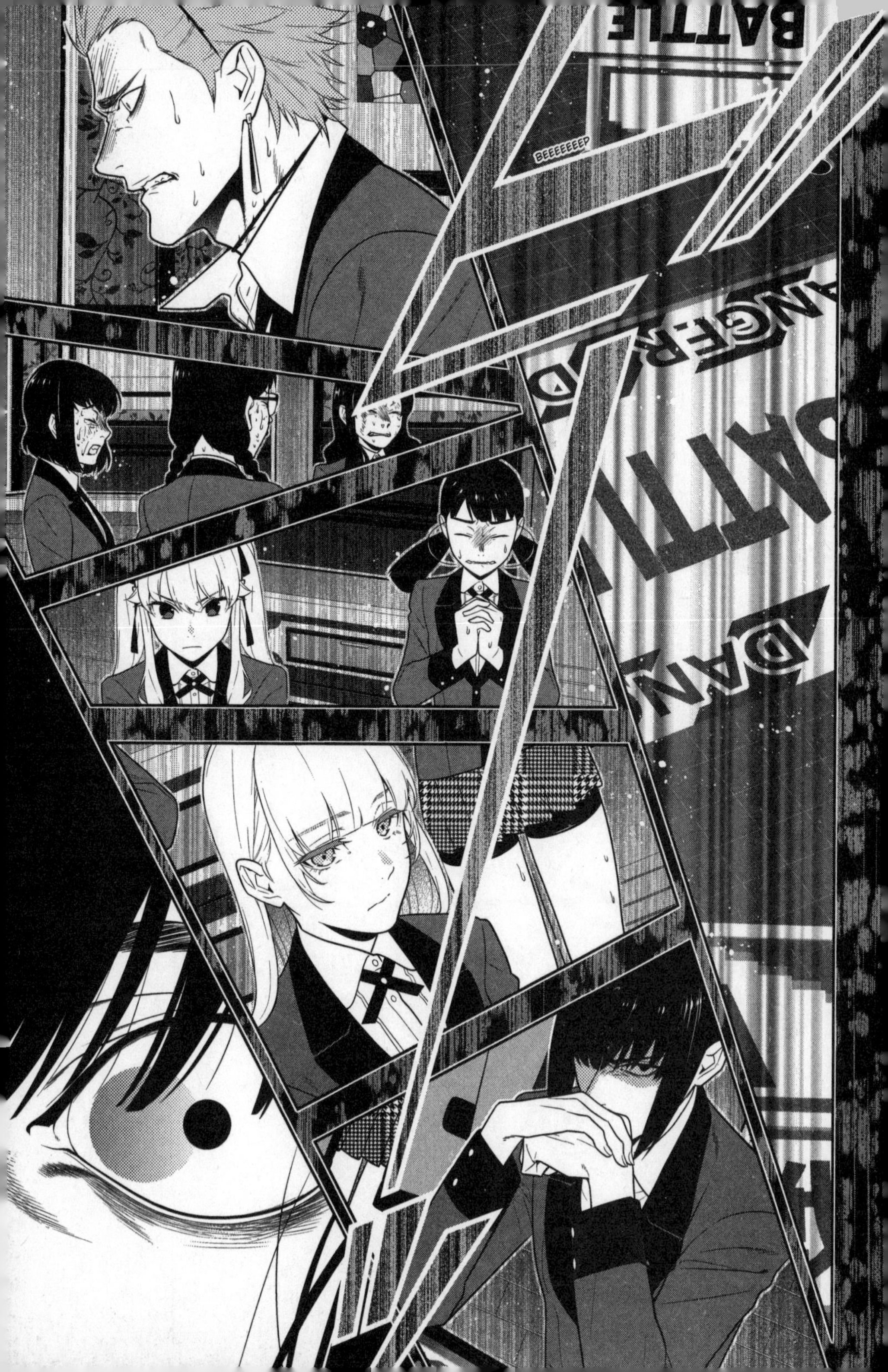
BEEEEEEEP

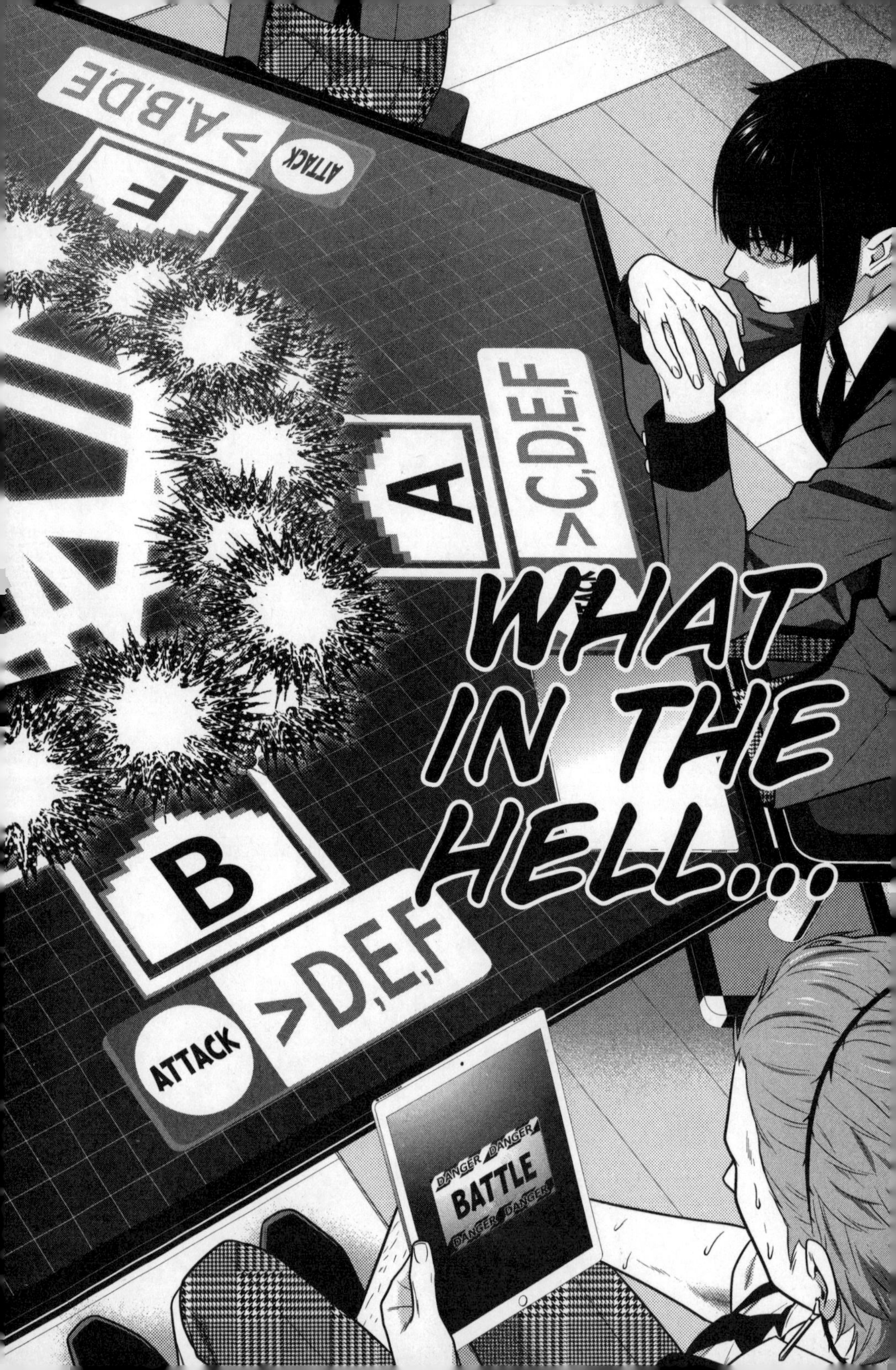
ATTACK
>A,B,D,E
F
A
>C,D,E,F
B
ATTACK
>D,E,F
WHAT IN THE HELL...
DANGER DANGER
BATTLE
DANGER DANGER

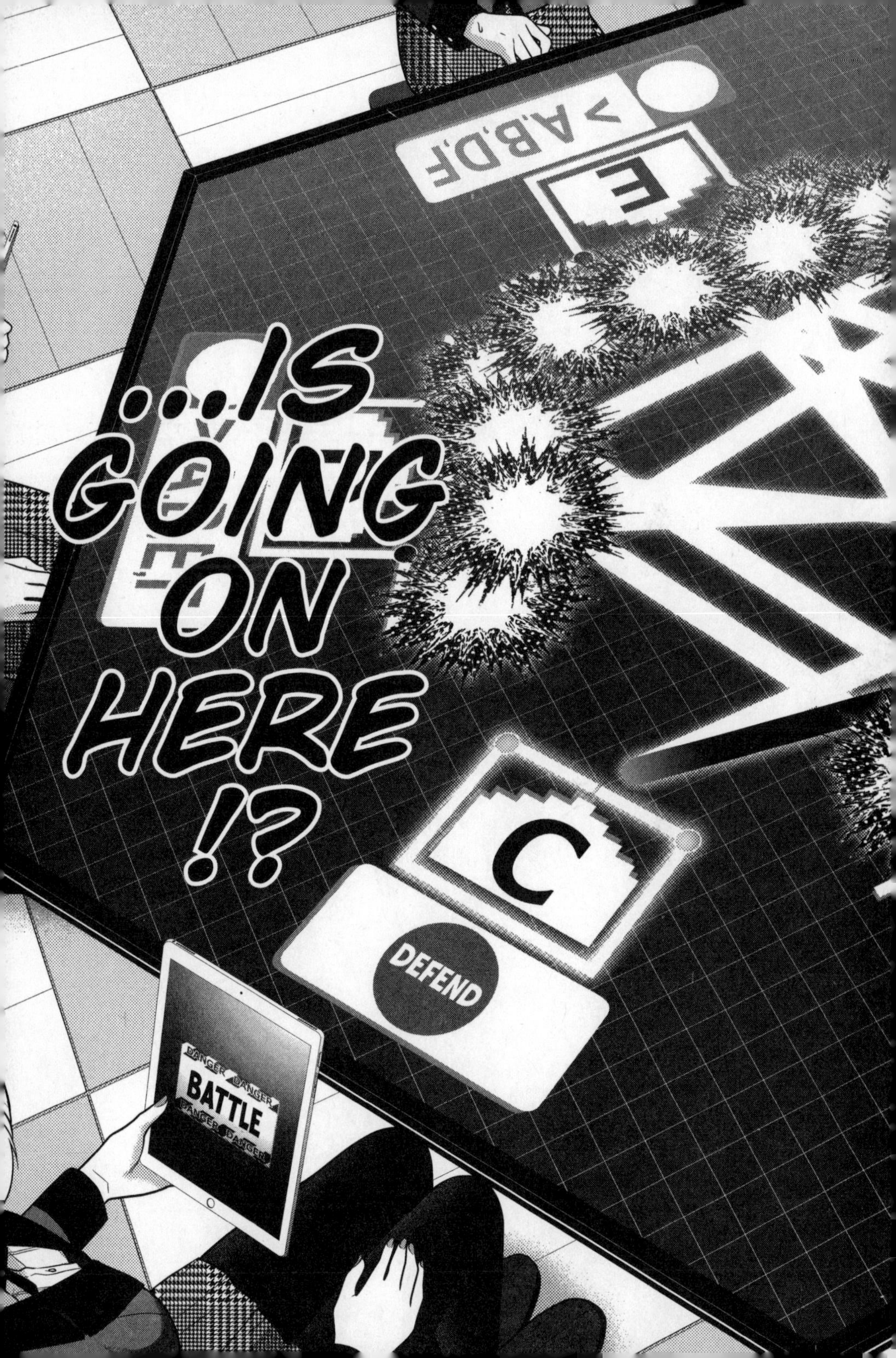
...IS GOING ON HERE!?
E
A,B,D,F
C
DEFEND
DANGER DANGER
BATTLE
DANGER DANGER

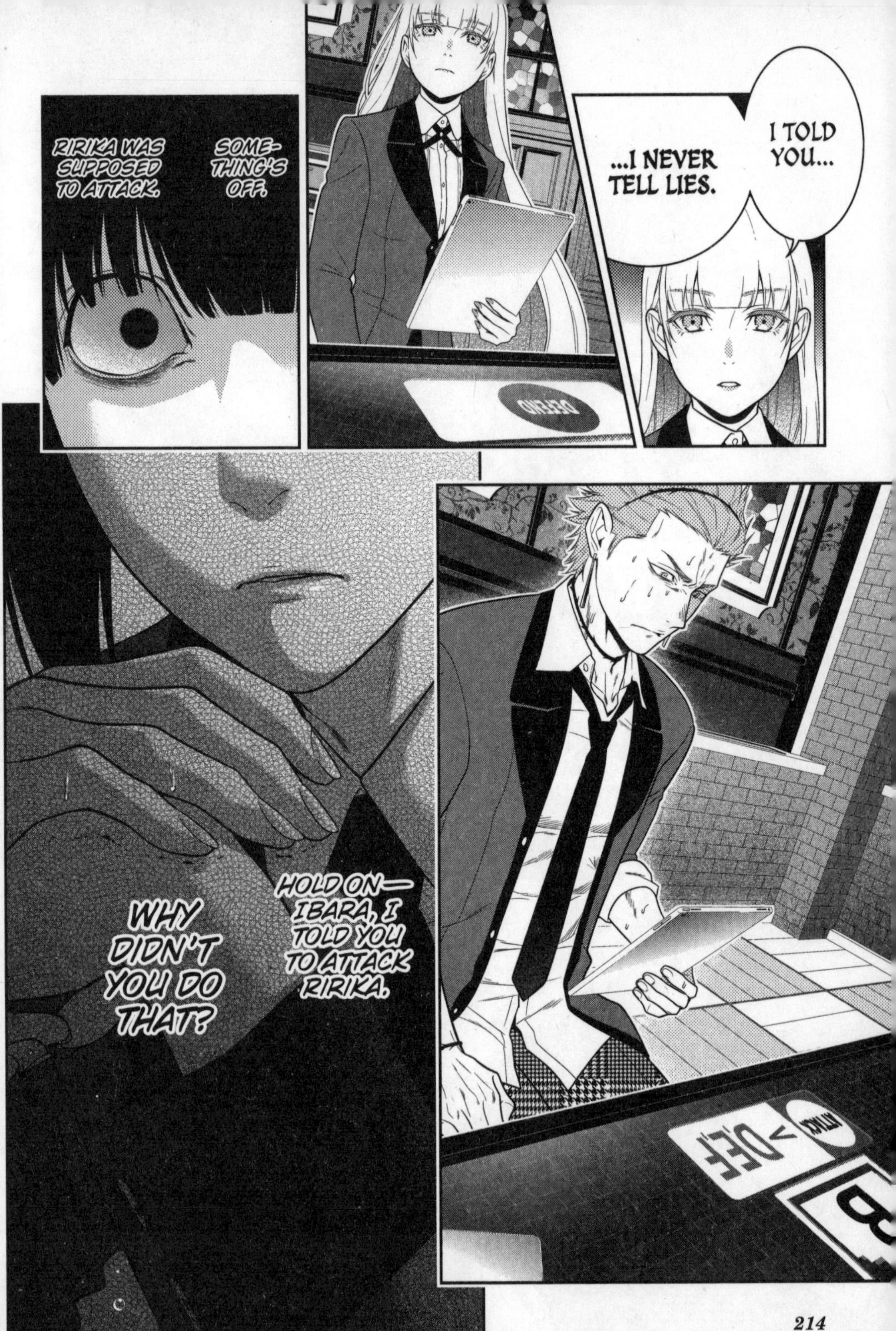
I TOLD YOU...
...I NEVER TELL LIES.
SOME-THING'S OFF.
RIRIKA WAS SUPPOSED TO ATTACK.
HOLD ON— IBARA, I TOLD YOU TO ATTACK RIRIKA.
WHY DIDN'T YOU DO THAT?

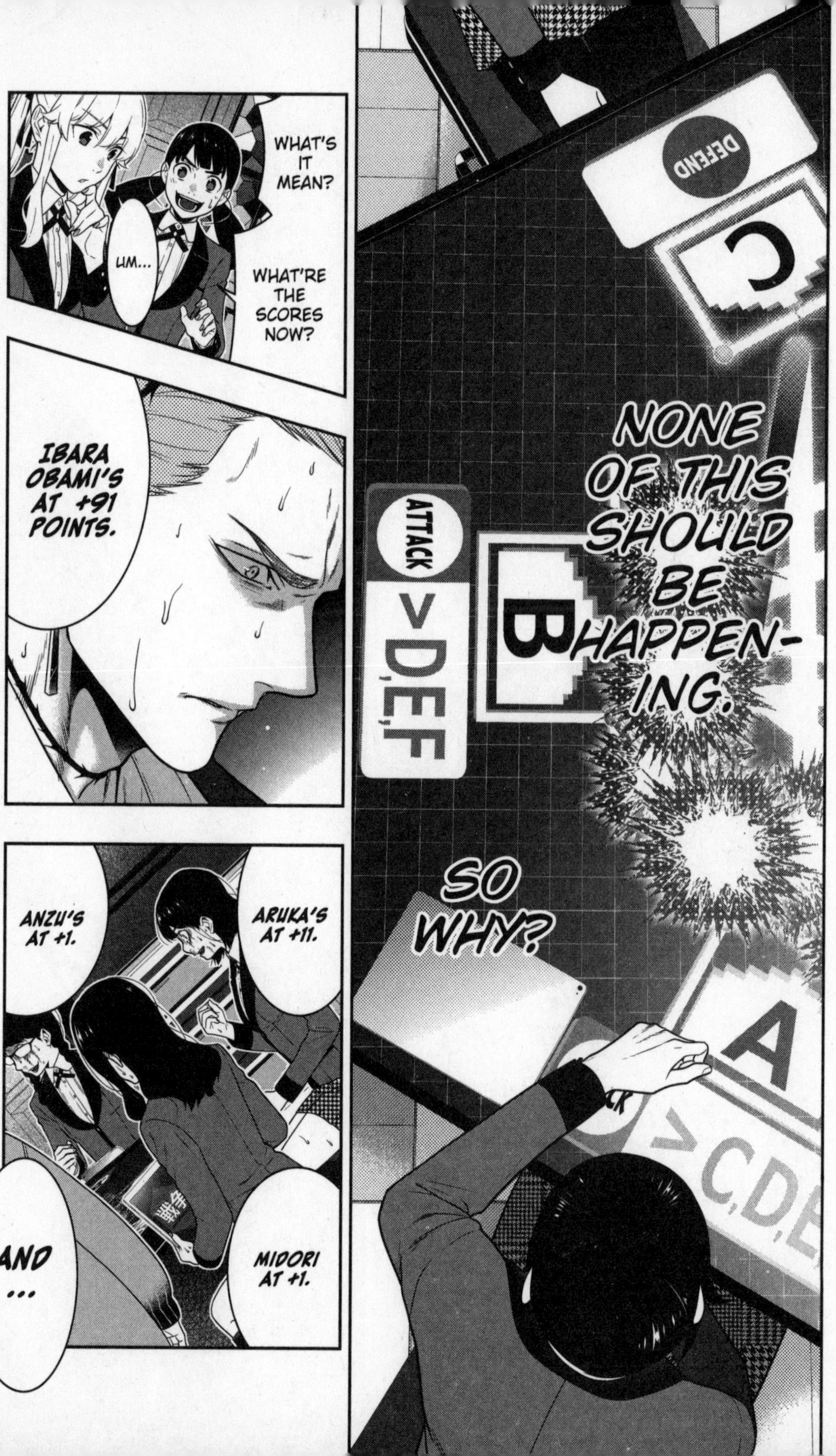
DEFEND
C
NONE OF THIS SHOULD BE HAPPEN-ING.
ATTACK
>D,E,F
B
SO WHY?
A
>C,D,E
WHAT'S IT MEAN?
UM...
WHAT'RE THE SCORES NOW?
IBARA OBAMI'S AT +91 POINTS.
ARUKA'S AT +11.
ANZU'S AT +1.
MIDORI AT +1.
AND ...

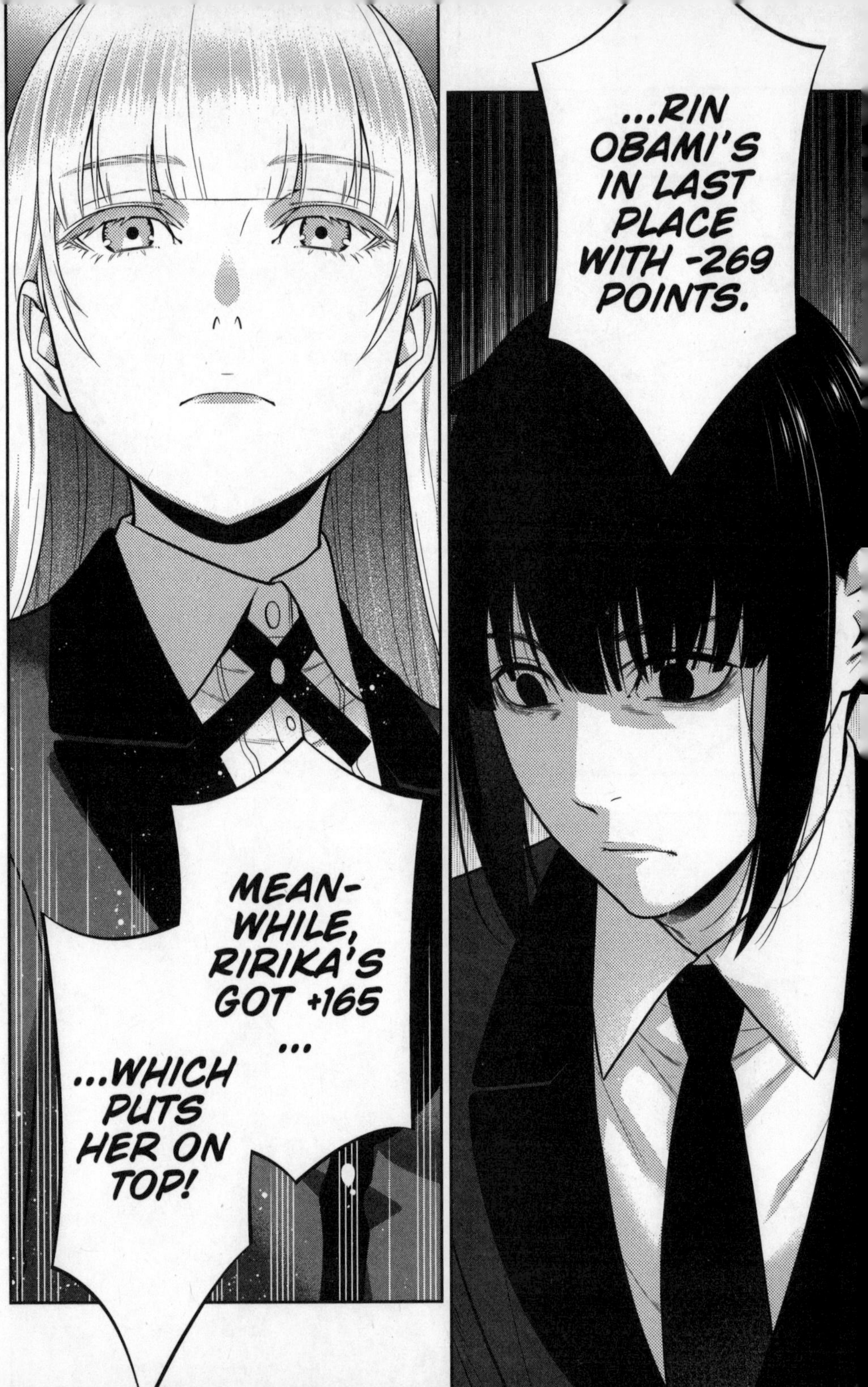
...RIN OBAMI'S IN LAST PLACE WITH -269 POINTS.
MEAN-WHILE, RIRIKA'S GOT +165...
...WHICH PUTS HER ON TOP!

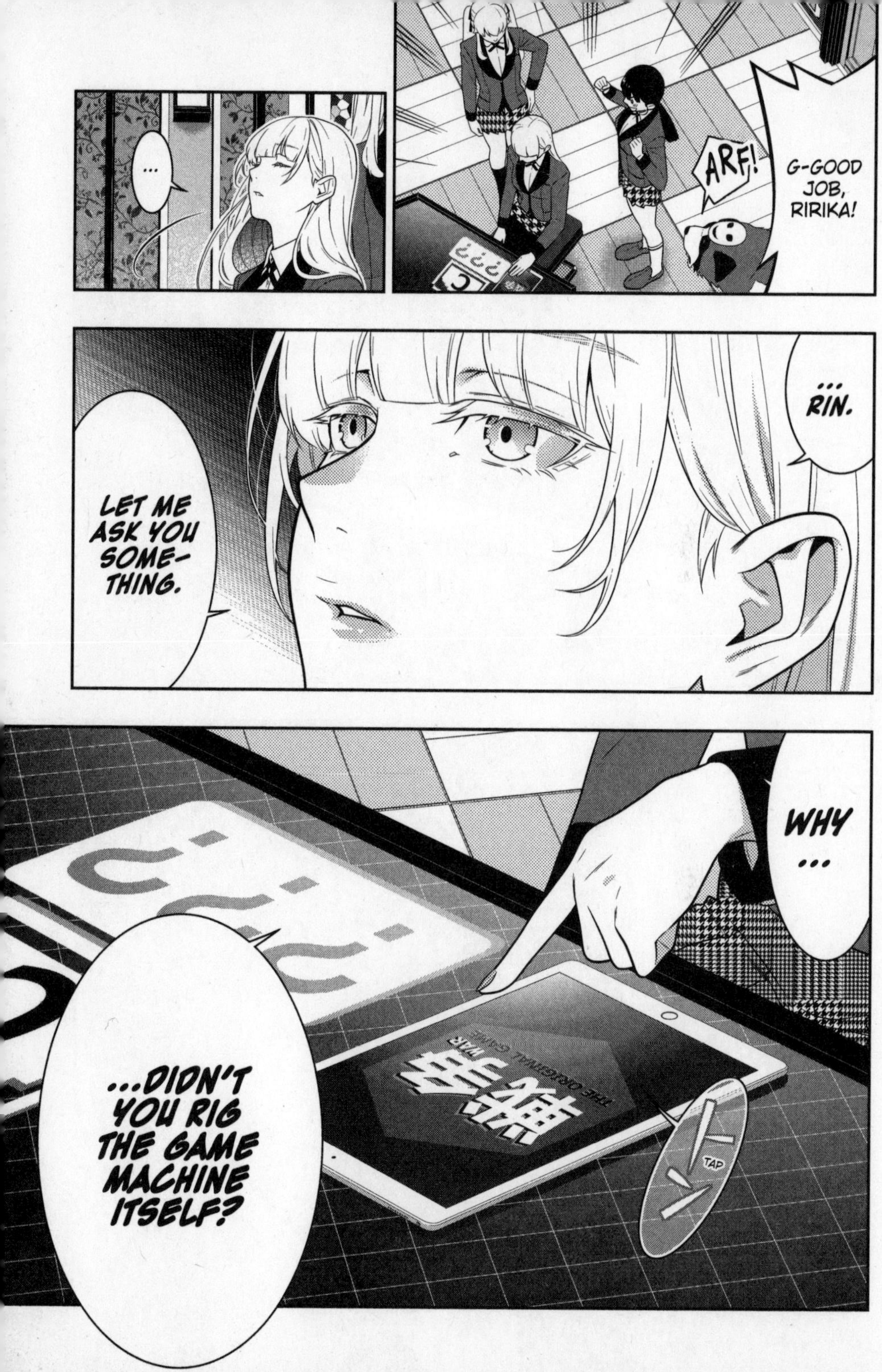
G-GOOD JOB, RIRIKA!
ARF!
...
... RIN.
LET ME ASK YOU SOME-THING.
WHY ...
...DIDN'T YOU RIG THE GAME MACHINE ITSELF?
TAP

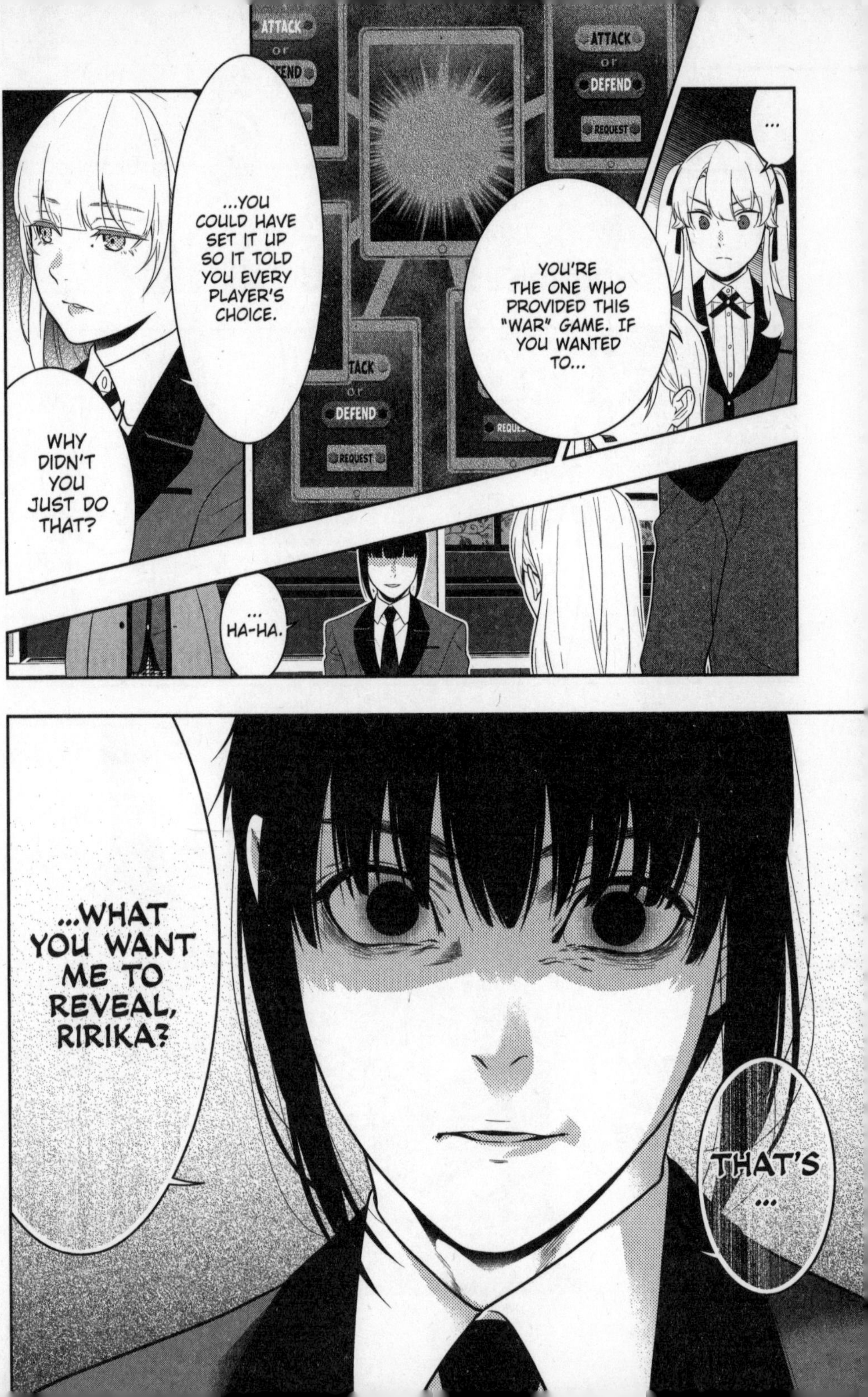
...
YOU'RE THE ONE WHO PROVIDED THIS "WAR" GAME. IF YOU WANTED TO...
...YOU COULD HAVE SET IT UP SO IT TOLD YOU EVERY PLAYER'S CHOICE.
WHY DIDN'T YOU JUST DO THAT?
ATTACK or DEFEND
REQUEST
... HA-HA.
THAT'S ...
...WHAT YOU WANT ME TO REVEAL, RIRIKA?

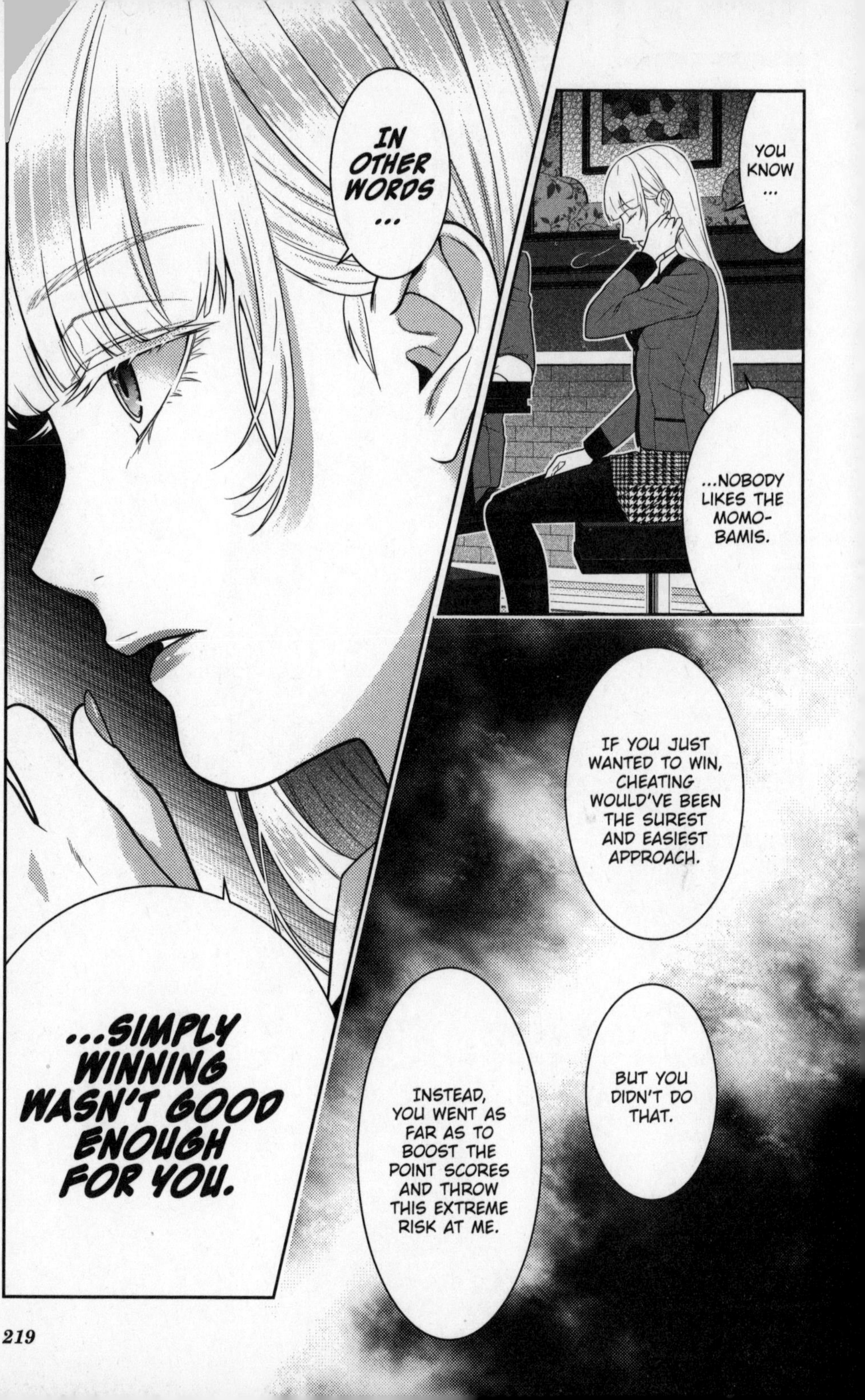
YOU KNOW ...
...NOBODY LIKES THE MOMO-BAMIS.
IF YOU JUST WANTED TO WIN, CHEATING WOULD'VE BEEN THE SUREST AND EASIEST APPROACH.
BUT YOU DIDN'T DO THAT.
INSTEAD, YOU WENT AS FAR AS TO BOOST THE POINT SCORES AND THROW THIS EXTREME RISK AT ME.
IN OTHER WORDS ...
...SIMPLY WINNING WASN'T GOOD ENOUGH FOR YOU.

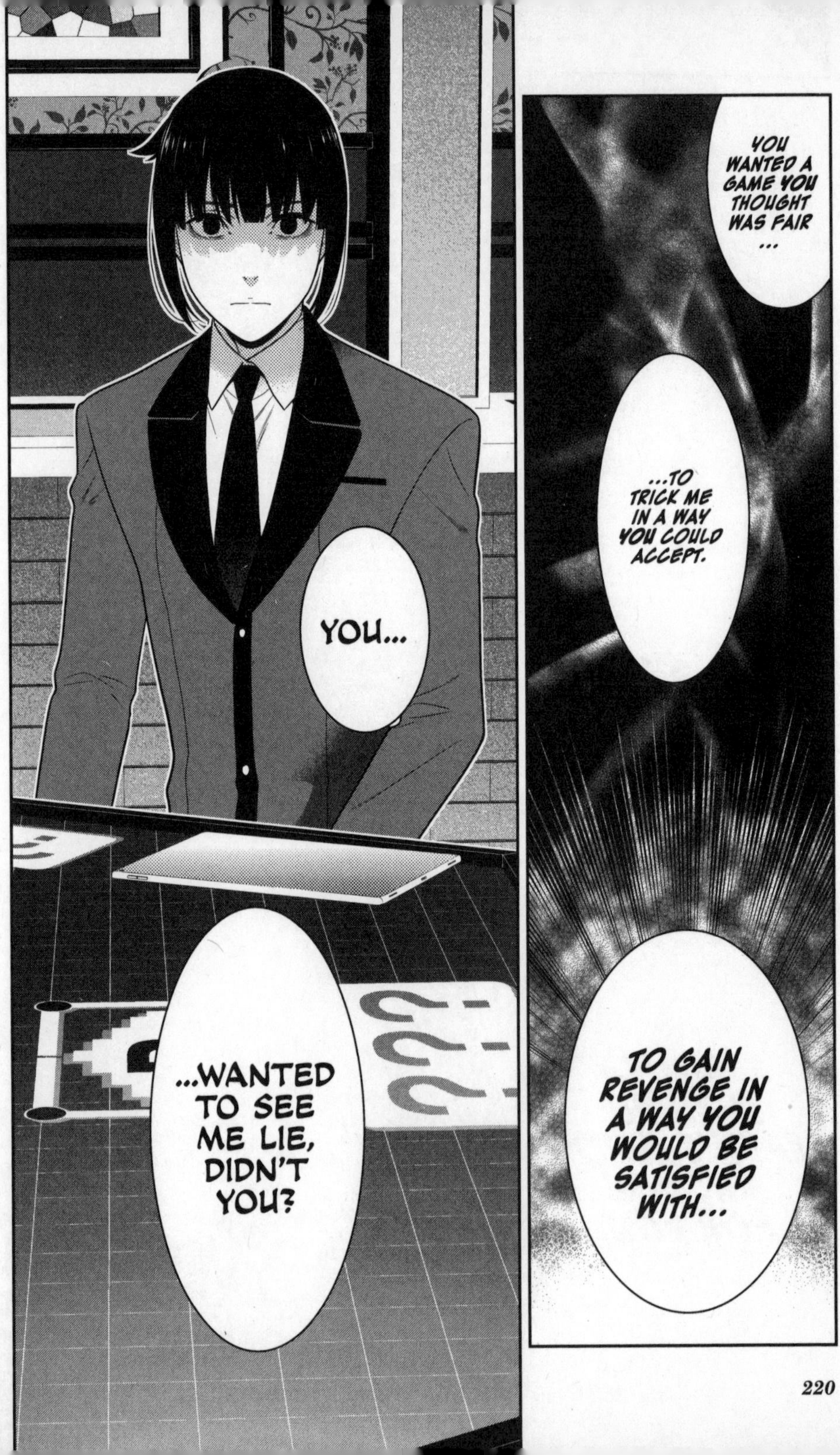
YOU WANTED A GAME YOU THOUGHT WAS FAIR ...
...TO TRICK ME IN A WAY YOU COULD ACCEPT.
TO GAIN REVENGE IN A WAY YOU WOULD BE SATISFIED WITH...
YOU...
...WANTED TO SEE ME LIE, DIDN'T YOU?

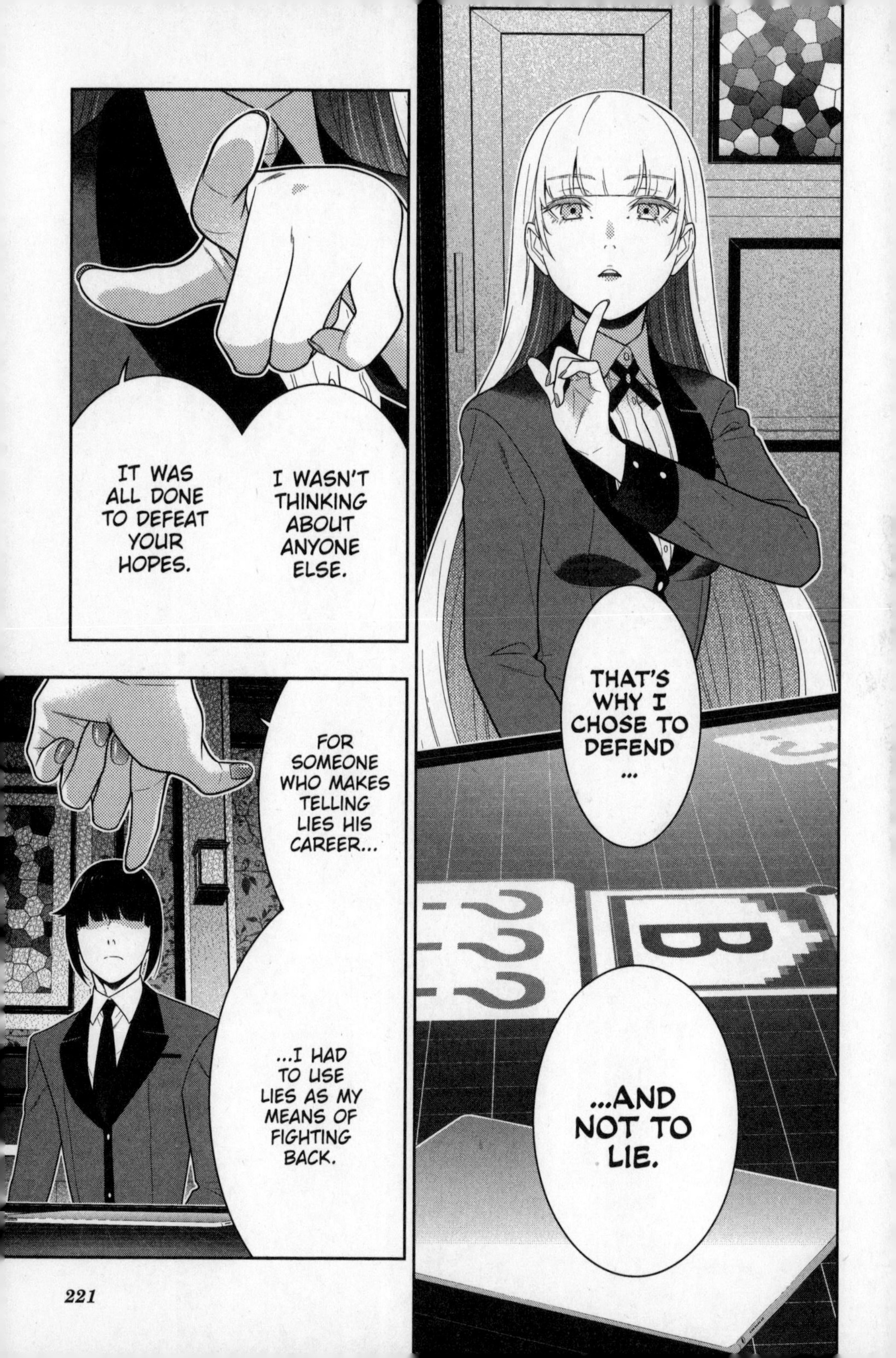
THAT'S WHY I CHOSE TO DEFEND ...
I WASN'T THINKING ABOUT ANYONE ELSE.
IT WAS ALL DONE TO DEFEAT YOUR HOPES.
...AND NOT TO LIE.
FOR SOMEONE WHO MAKES TELLING LIES HIS CAREER...
...I HAD TO USE LIES AS MY MEANS OF FIGHTING BACK.

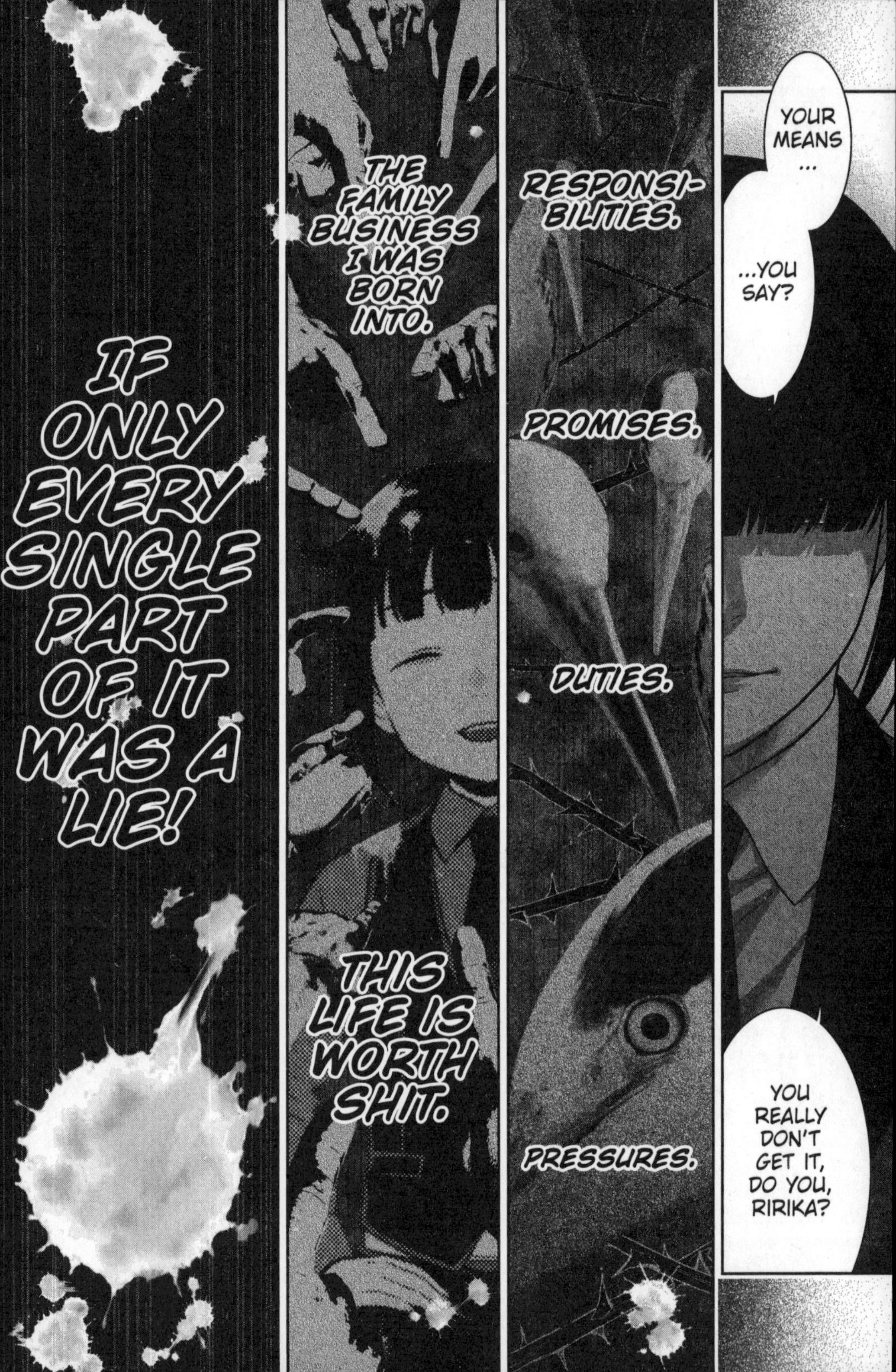
YOUR MEANS ...
...YOU SAY?
YOU REALLY DON'T GET IT, DO YOU, RIRIKA?
RESPONSI-BILITIES.
PROMISES.
DUTIES.
PRESSURES.
THE FAMILY BUSINESS I WAS BORN INTO.
THIS LIFE IS WORTH SHIT.
IF ONLY EVERY SINGLE PART OF IT WAS A LIE!

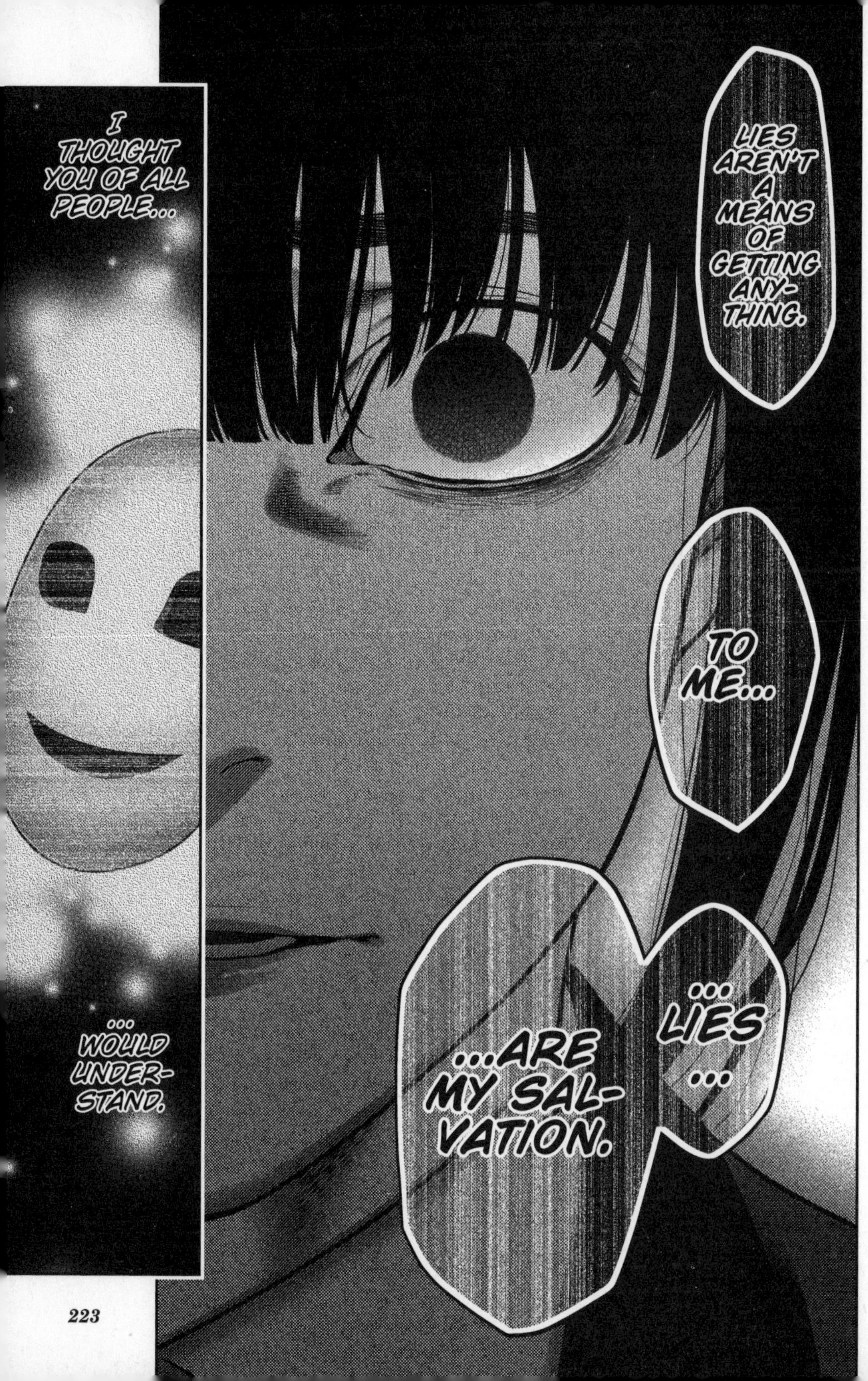
LIES AREN'T A MEANS OF GETTING ANY-THING.
TO ME...
...LIES...
...ARE MY SAL-VATION.
I THOUGHT YOU OF ALL PEOPLE...
...WOULD UNDER-STAND.

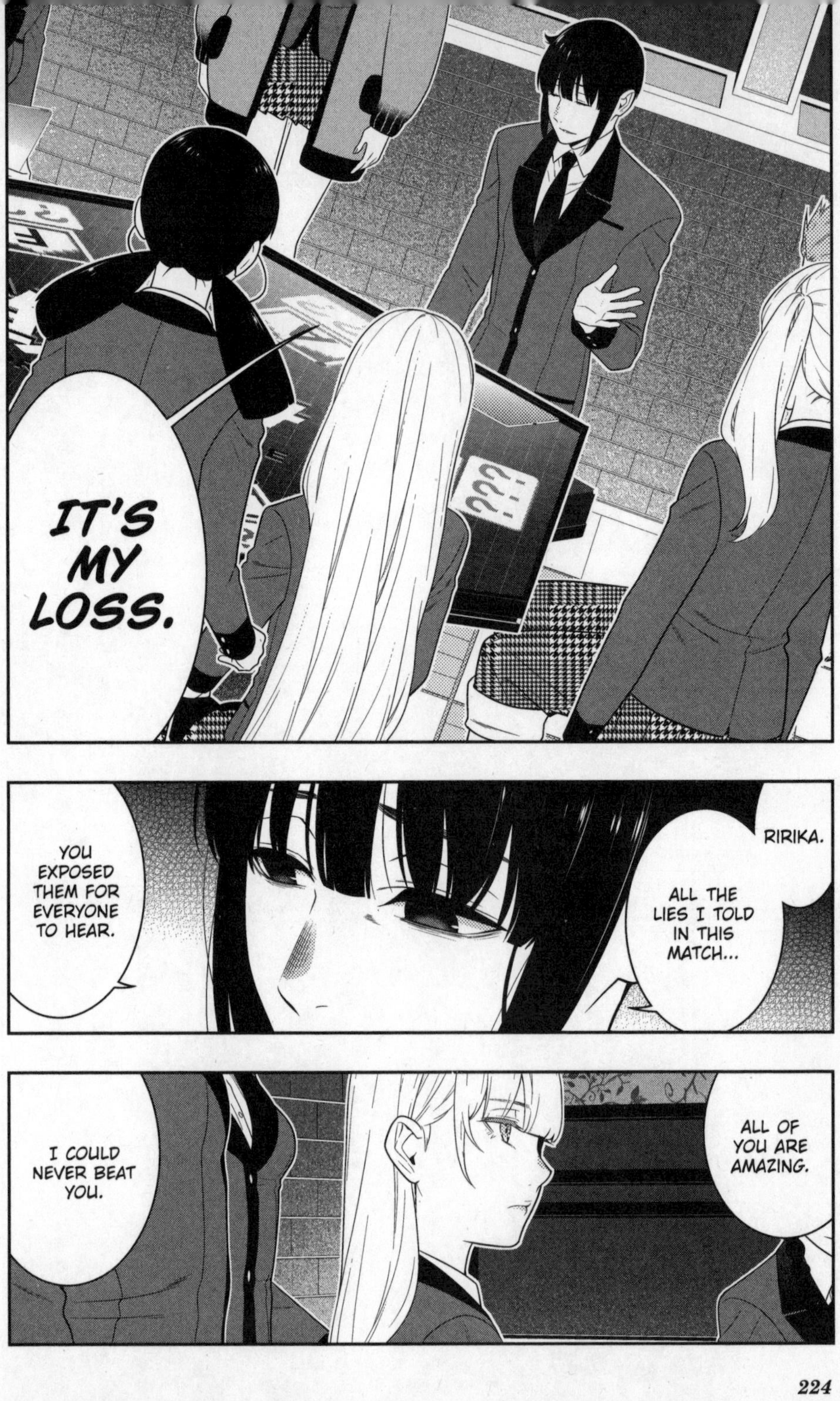
???
IT'S MY LOSS.
RIRIKA.
ALL THE LIES I TOLD IN THIS MATCH...
YOU EXPOSED THEM FOR EVERYONE TO HEAR.
ALL OF YOU ARE AMAZING.
I COULD NEVER BEAT YOU.

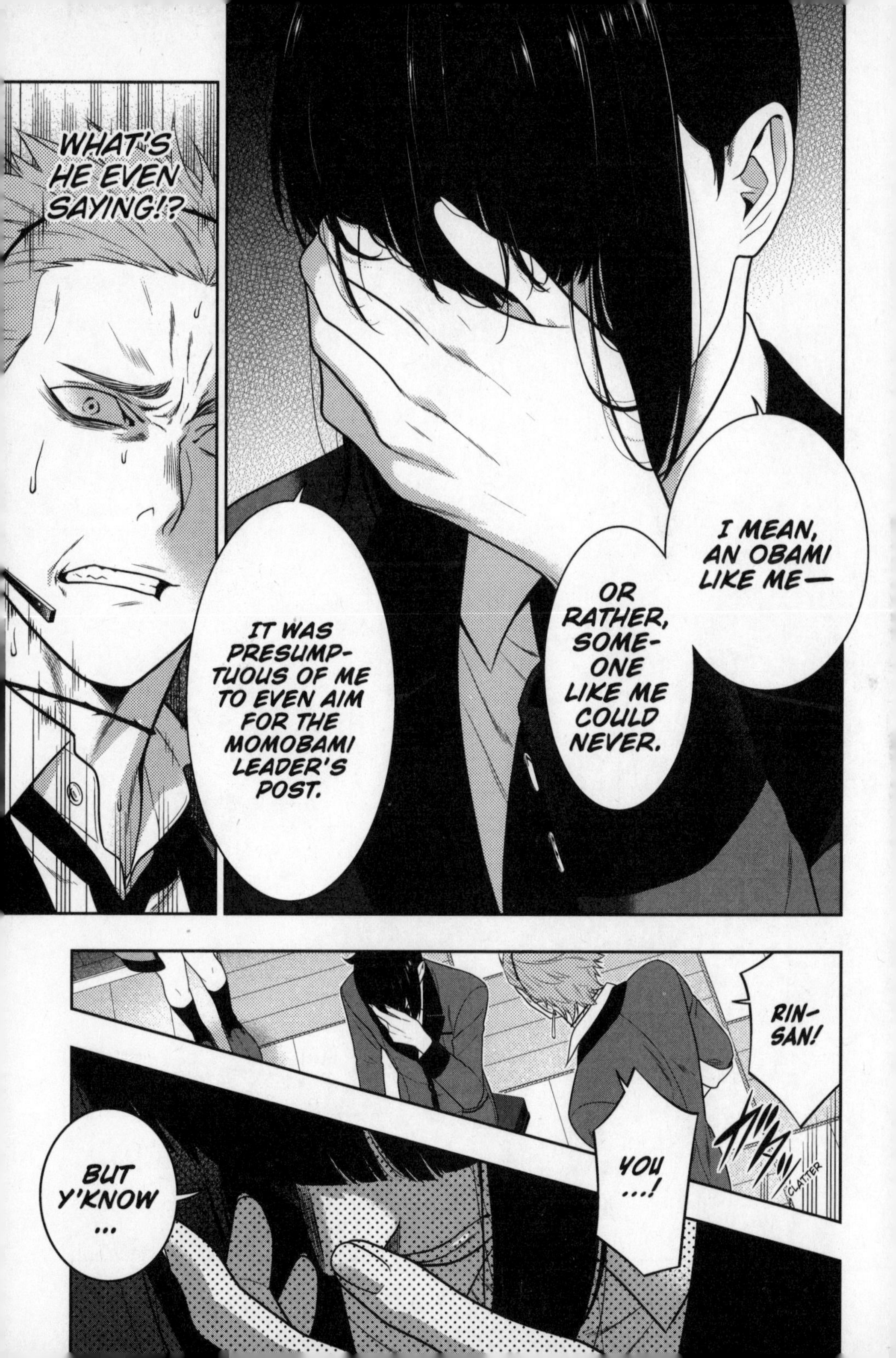
I MEAN, AN OBAMI LIKE ME—
OR RATHER, SOME-ONE LIKE ME COULD NEVER.
IT WAS PRESUMP-TUOUS OF ME TO EVEN AIM FOR THE MOMOBAMI LEADER'S POST.
WHAT'S HE EVEN SAYING!?
RIN-SAN!
CLATTER
YOU ...!
BUT Y'KNOW ...

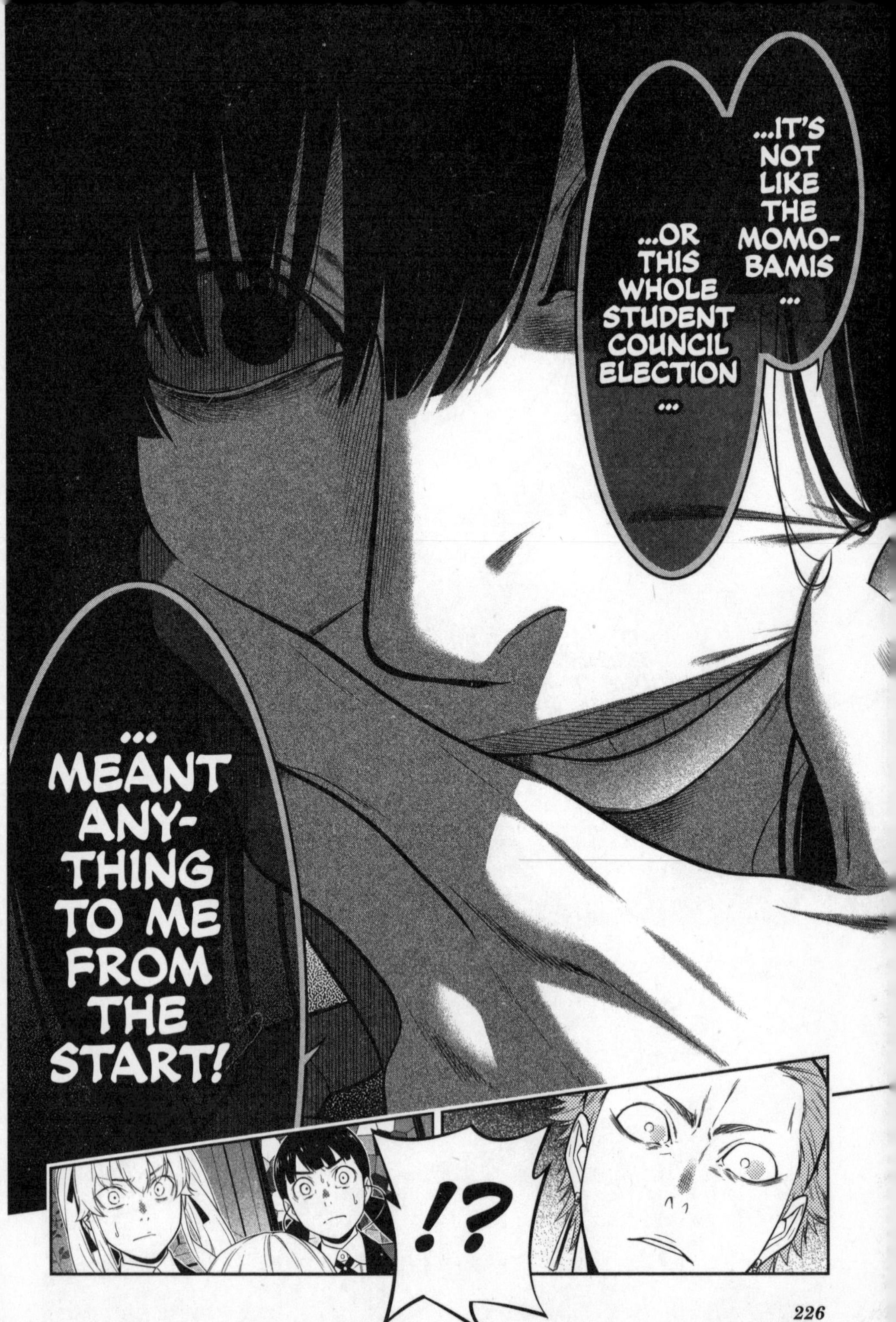
...IT'S NOT LIKE THE MOMO-BAMIS...
...OR THIS WHOLE STUDENT COUNCIL ELECTION...
...MEANT ANY-THING TO ME FROM THE START!
!?

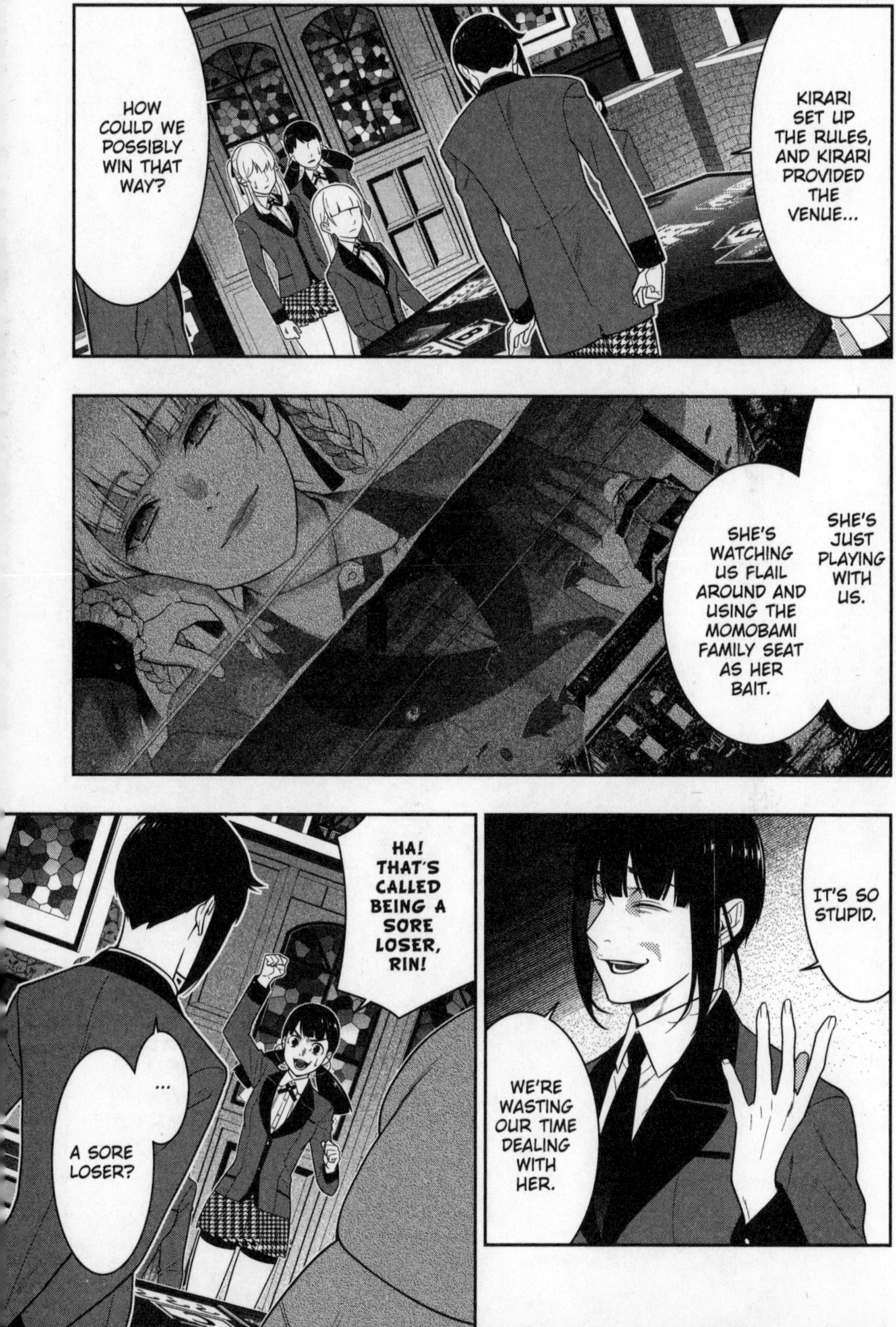
KIRARI SET UP THE RULES, AND KIRARI PROVIDED THE VENUE...
HOW COULD WE POSSIBLY WIN THAT WAY?
SHE'S JUST PLAYING WITH US.
SHE'S WATCHING US FLAIL AROUND AND USING THE MOMOBAMI FAMILY SEAT AS HER BAIT.
IT'S SO STUPID.
WE'RE WASTING OUR TIME DEALING WITH HER.
HA! THAT'S CALLED BEING A SORE LOSER, RIN!
...
A SORE LOSER?

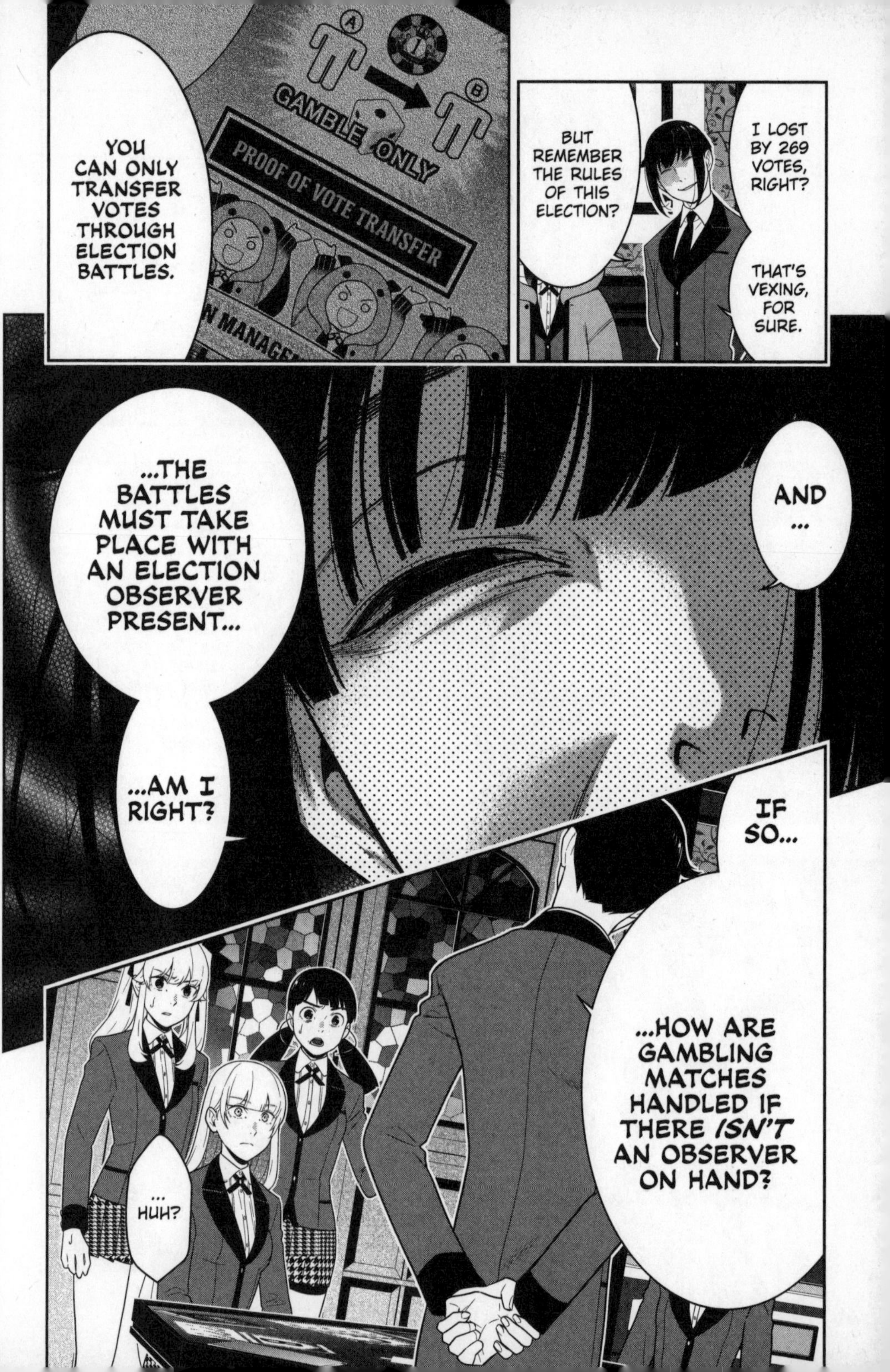
I LOST BY 269 VOTES, RIGHT?
THAT'S VEXING, FOR SURE.
BUT REMEMBER THE RULES OF THIS ELECTION?
YOU CAN ONLY TRANSFER VOTES THROUGH ELECTION BATTLES.
GAMBLE ONLY
PROOF OF VOTE TRANSFER
AND ...
...THE BATTLES MUST TAKE PLACE WITH AN ELECTION OBSERVER PRESENT...
...AM I RIGHT?
IF SO...
...HOW ARE GAMBLING MATCHES HANDLED IF THERE *ISN'T* AN OBSERVER ON HAND?
... HUH?

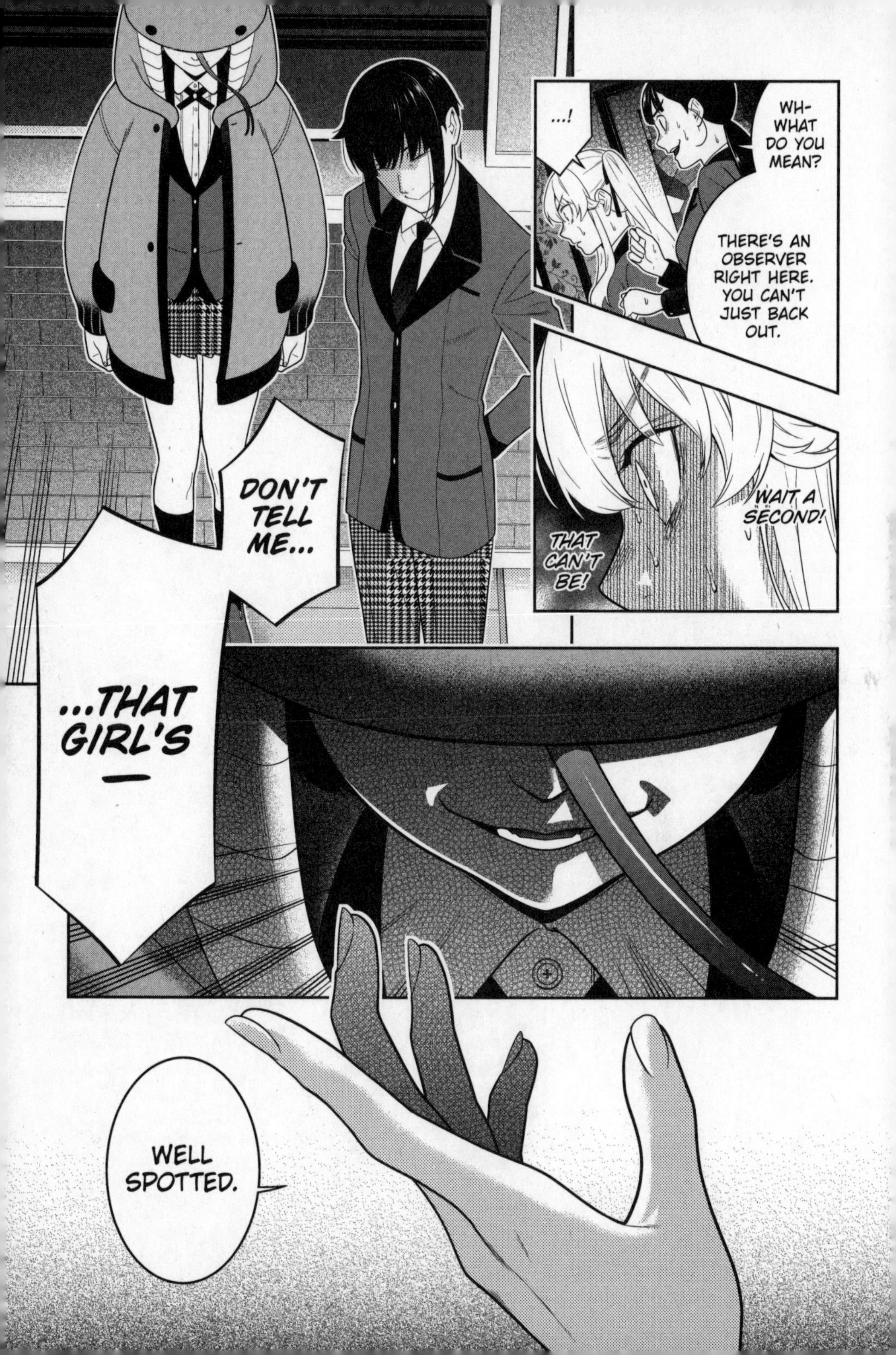

WH- WHAT DO YOU MEAN?
THERE'S AN OBSERVER RIGHT HERE. YOU CAN'T JUST BACK OUT.
...!
WAIT A SECOND!
THAT CAN'T BE!
DON'T TELL ME...
...THAT GIRL'S —
WELL SPOTTED.

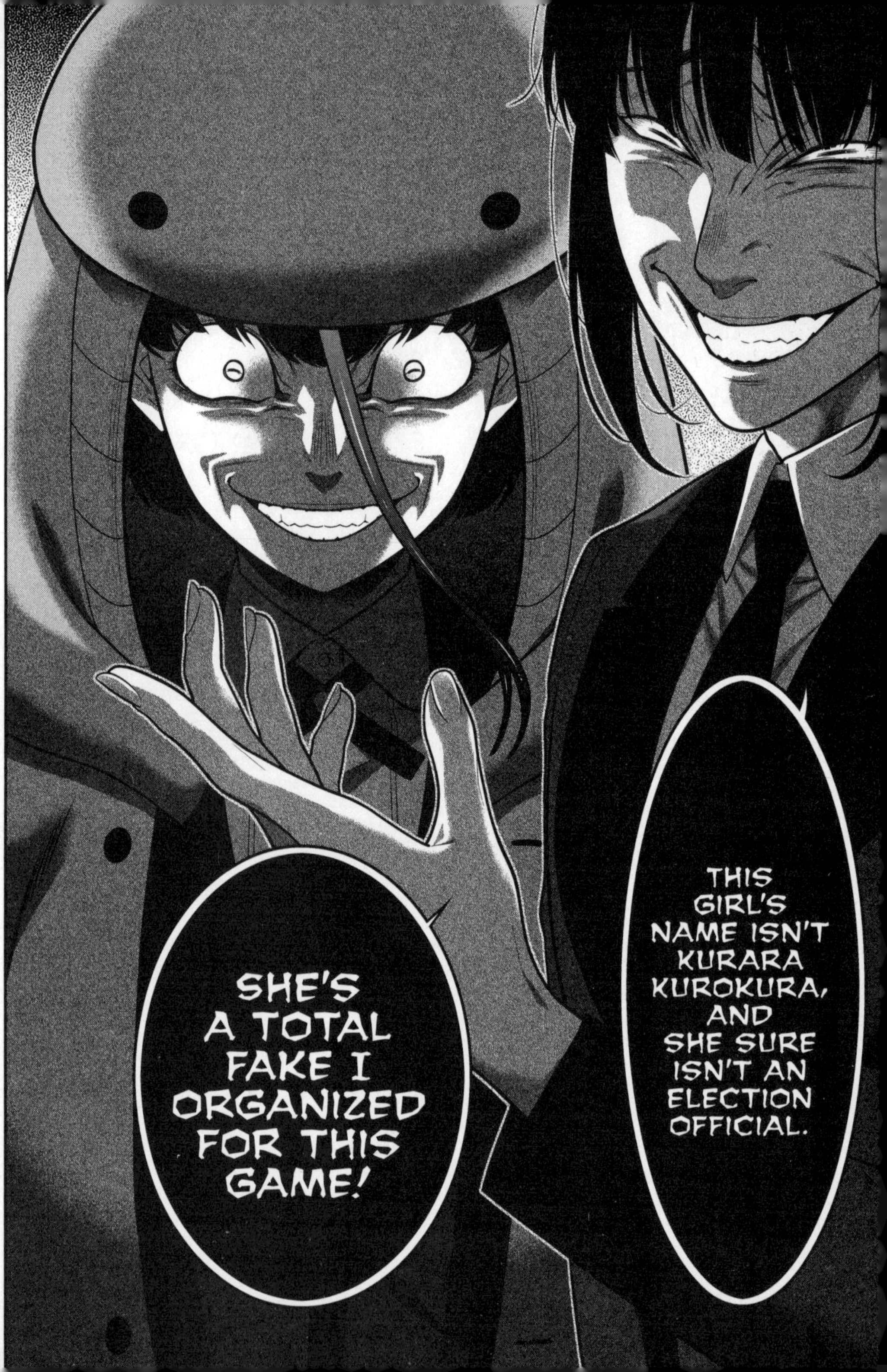
THIS GIRL'S NAME ISN'T KURARA KUROKURA, AND SHE SURE ISN'T AN ELECTION OFFICIAL.
SHE'S A TOTAL FAKE I ORGANIZED FOR THIS GAME!

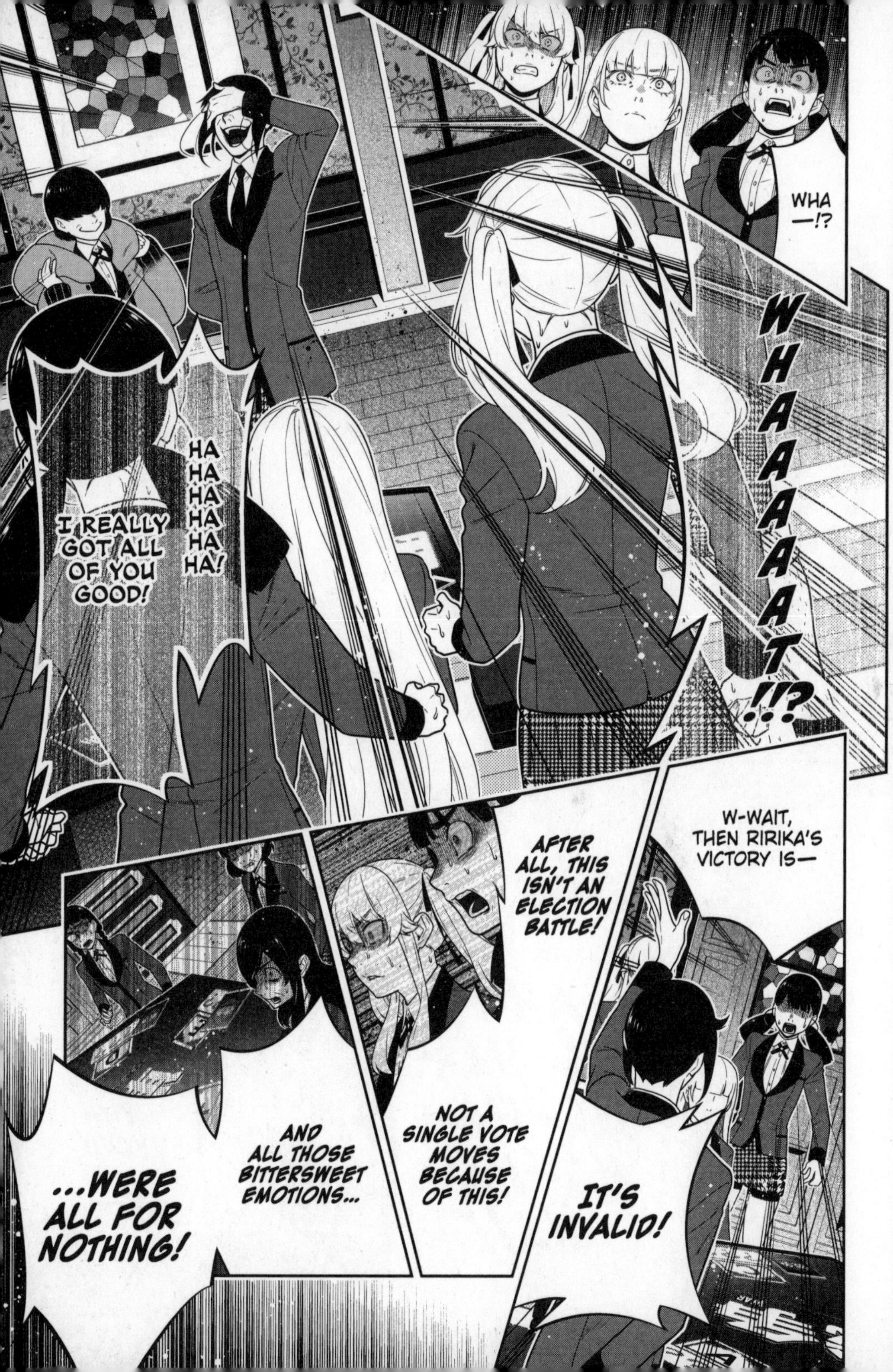
WHA—!?
WHAAAAAAT!!?
HA HA HA HA HA HA HA!
I REALLY GOT ALL OF YOU GOOD!
W-WAIT, THEN RIRIKA'S VICTORY IS—
IT'S INVALID!
AFTER ALL, THIS ISN'T AN ELECTION BATTLE!
NOT A SINGLE VOTE MOVES BECAUSE OF THIS!
AND ALL THOSE BITTERSWEET EMOTIONS...
...WERE ALL FOR NOTHING!

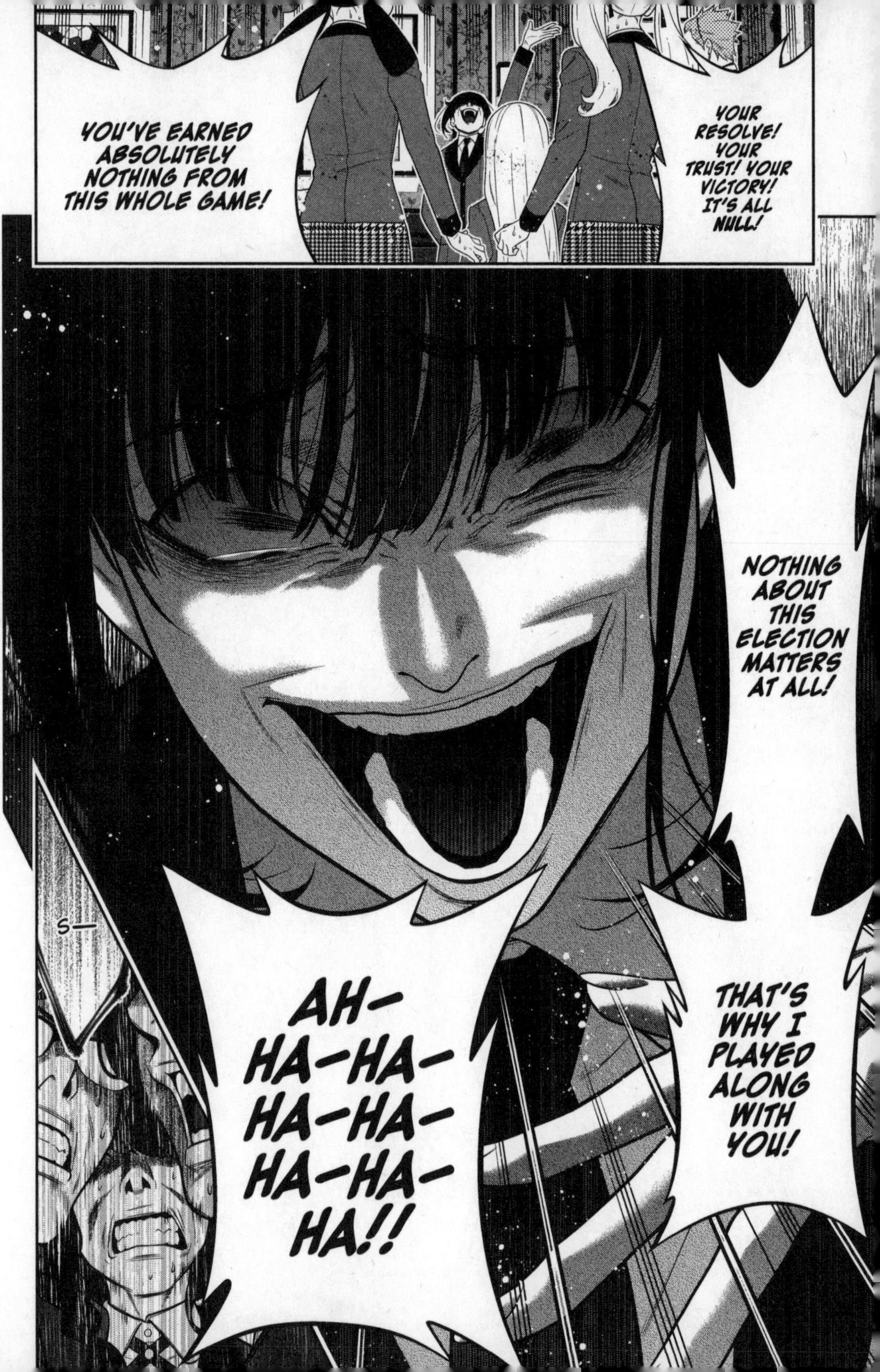
YOUR RESOLVE! YOUR TRUST! YOUR VICTORY! IT'S ALL NULL!
YOU'VE EARNED ABSOLUTELY NOTHING FROM THIS WHOLE GAME!
NOTHING ABOUT THIS ELECTION MATTERS AT ALL!
THAT'S WHY I PLAYED ALONG WITH YOU!
AH-HA-HA-HA-HA-HA-HA-HA-HA!!
S—

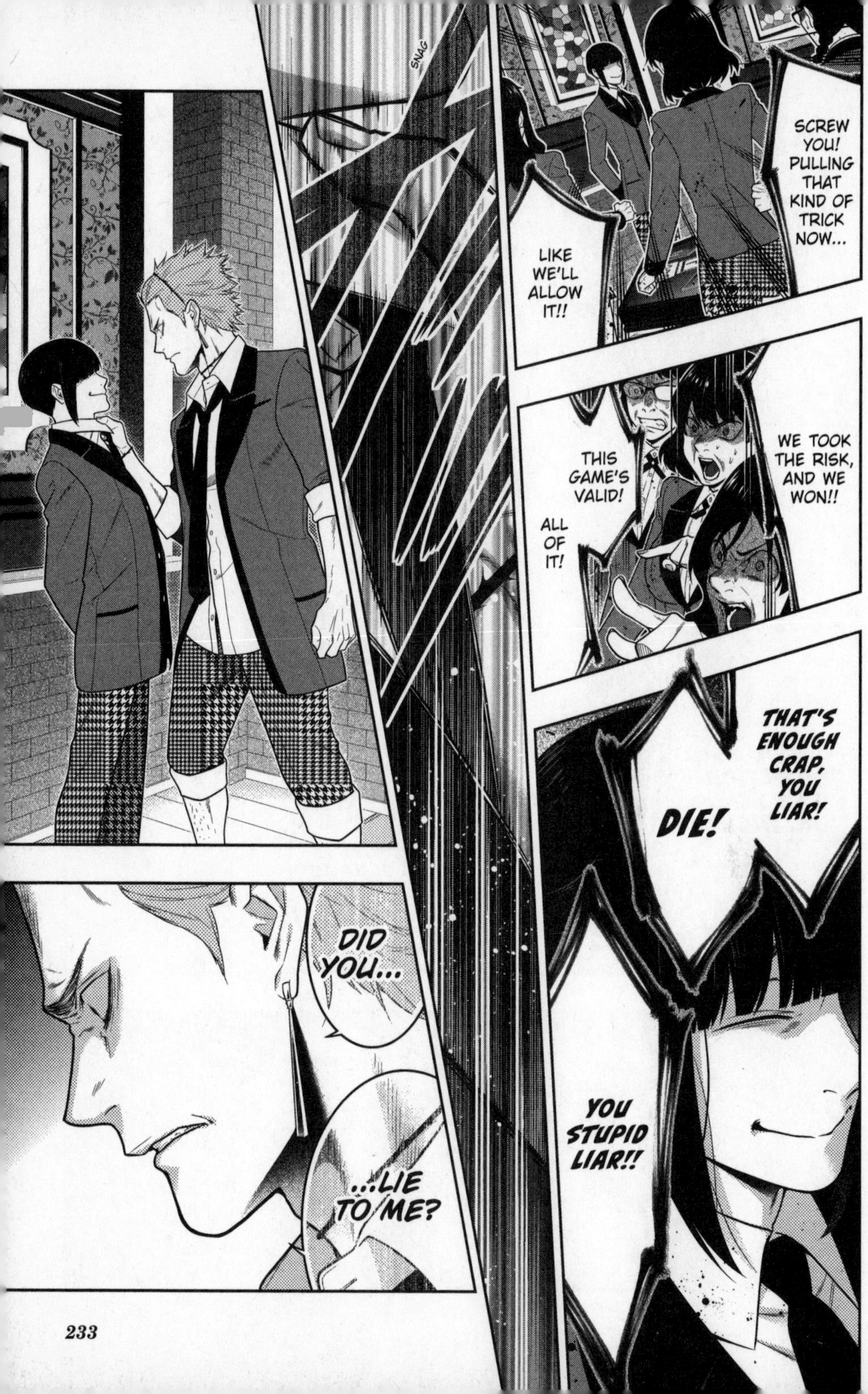
SCREW YOU! PULLING THAT KIND OF TRICK NOW...
LIKE WE'LL ALLOW IT!!
WE TOOK THE RISK, AND WE WON!!
THIS GAME'S VALID!
ALL OF IT!
THAT'S ENOUGH CRAP, YOU LIAR!
DIE!
YOU STUPID LIAR!!
SNAG
DID YOU...
...LIE TO ME?

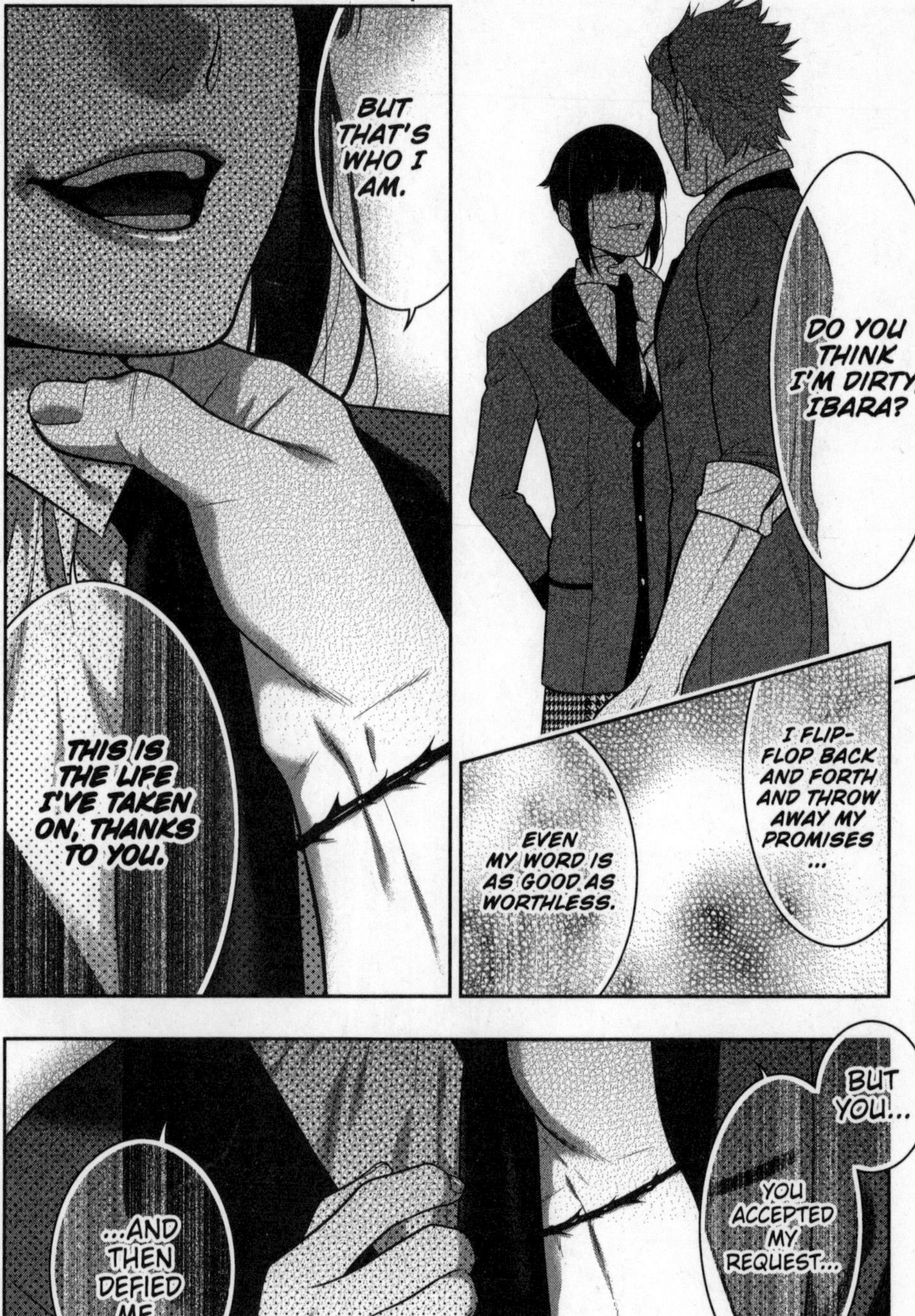
DO YOU THINK I'M DIRTY, IBARA?
I FLIP-FLOP BACK AND FORTH AND THROW AWAY MY PROMISES...
EVEN MY WORD IS AS GOOD AS WORTHLESS.
BUT THAT'S WHO I AM.
THIS IS THE LIFE I'VE TAKEN ON, THANKS TO YOU.
BUT YOU...
YOU ACCEPTED MY REQUEST...
...AND THEN DEFIED ME.

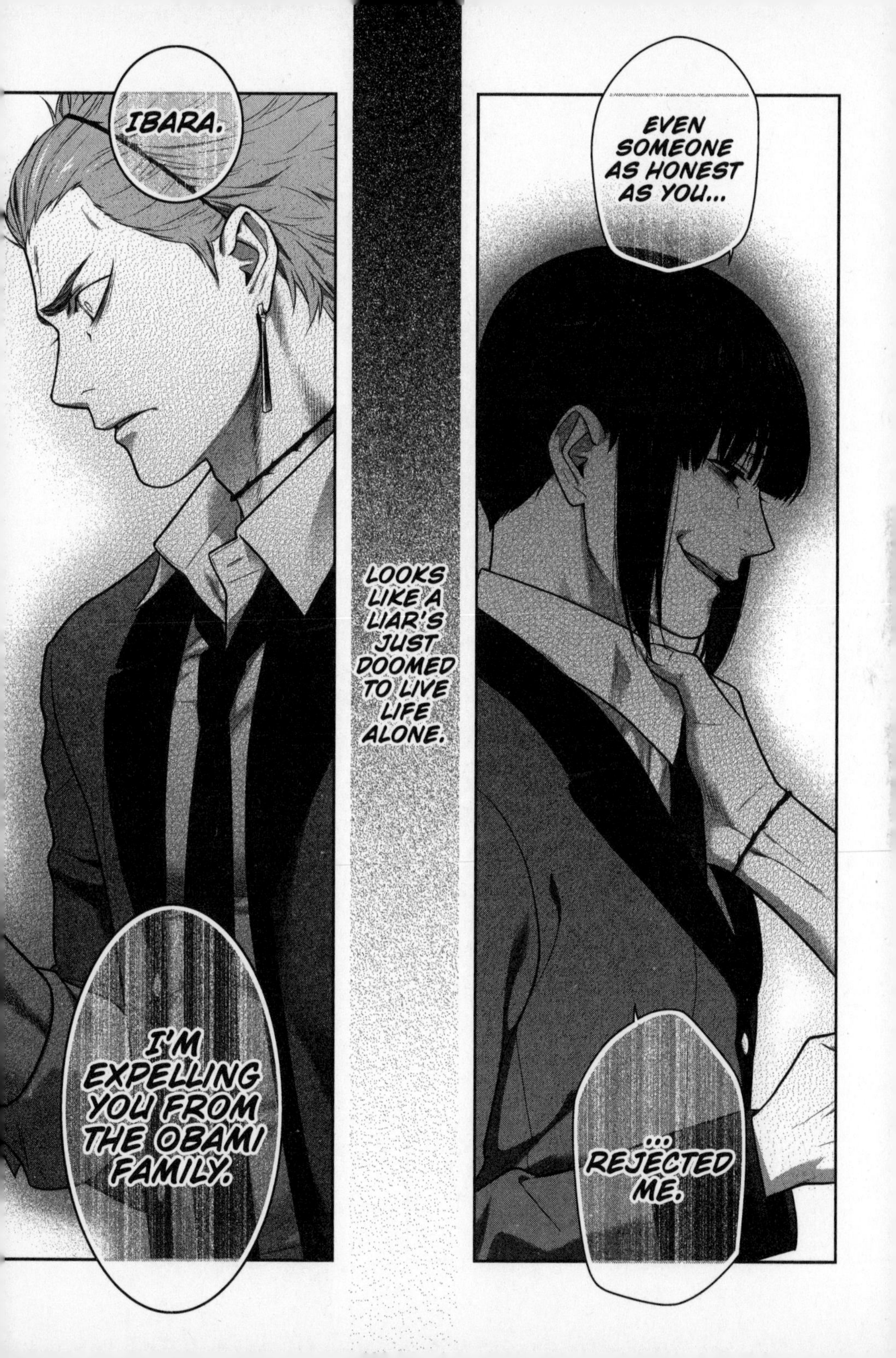
EVEN SOMEONE AS HONEST AS YOU...
...REJECTED ME.
LOOKS LIKE A LIAR'S JUST DOOMED TO LIVE LIFE ALONE.
IBARA.
I'M EXPELLING YOU FROM THE OBAMI FAMILY.

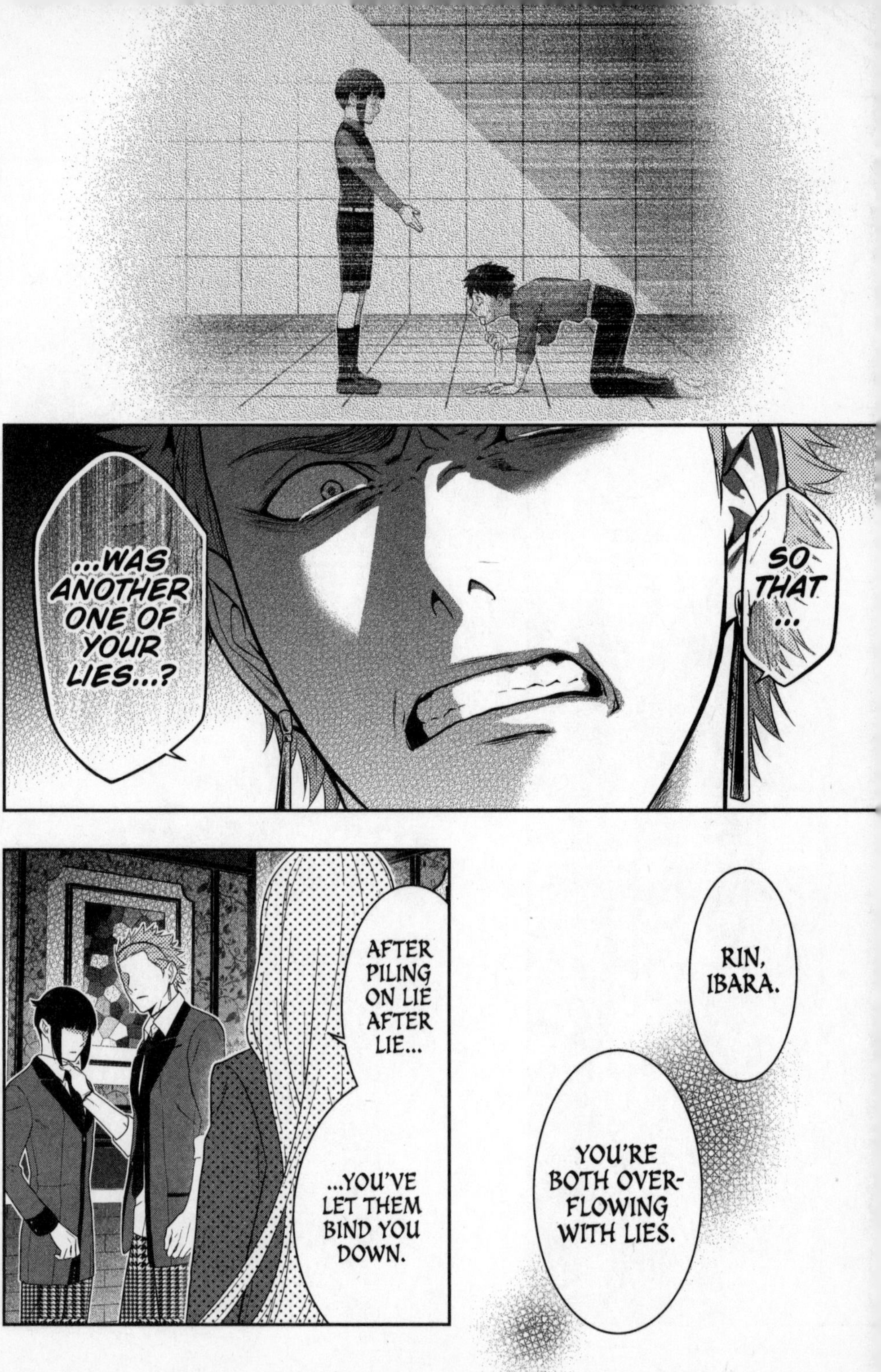
SO THAT...
...WAS ANOTHER ONE OF YOUR LIES...?
RIN, IBARA.
YOU'RE BOTH OVER-FLOWING WITH LIES.
AFTER PILING ON LIE AFTER LIE...
...YOU'VE LET THEM BIND YOU DOWN.

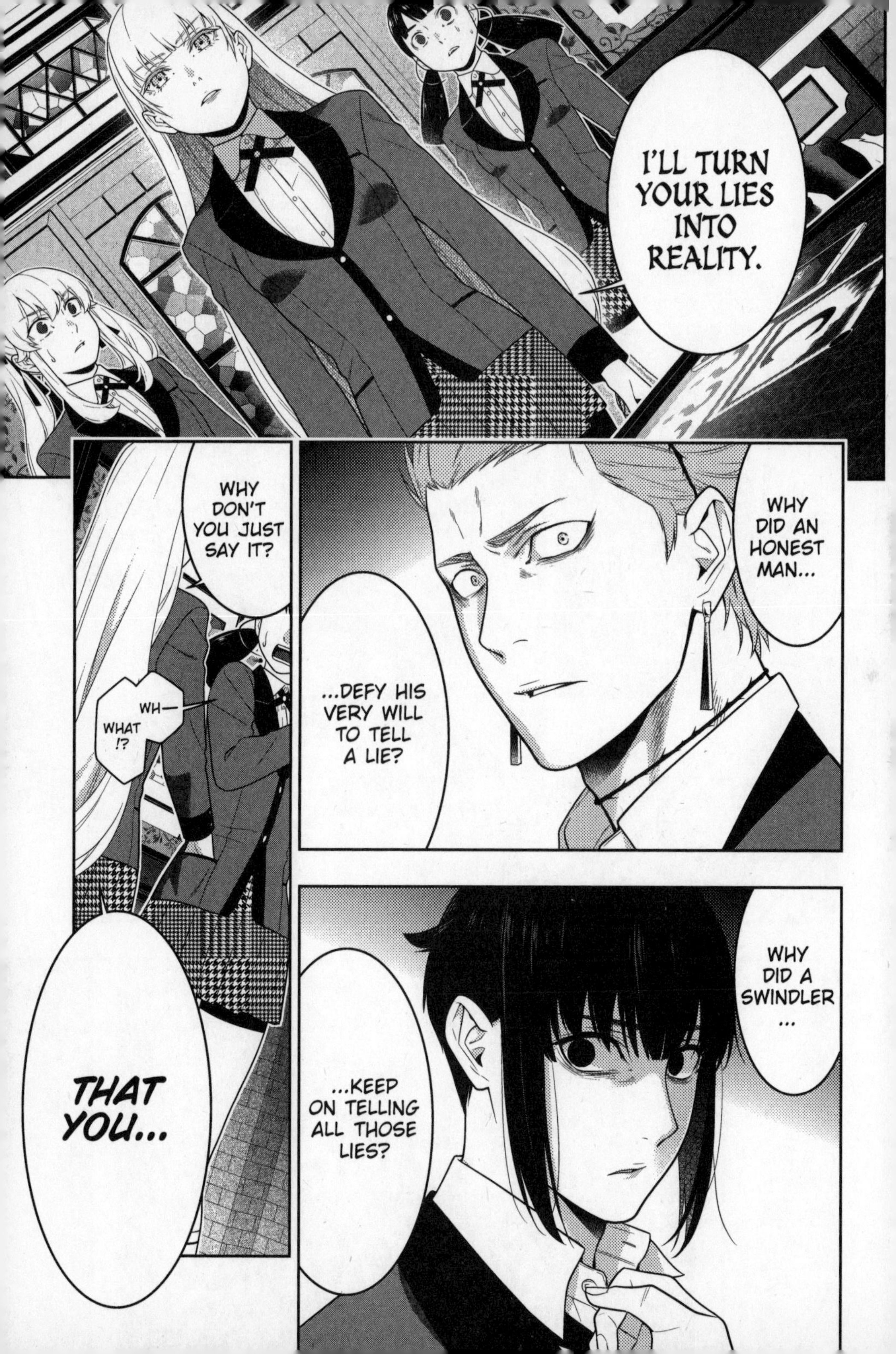
I'LL TURN YOUR LIES INTO REALITY.
WHY DID AN HONEST MAN...
...DEFY HIS VERY WILL TO TELL A LIE?
WHY DID A SWINDLER ...
...KEEP ON TELLING ALL THOSE LIES?
WHY DON'T YOU JUST SAY IT?
WH— WHAT !?
THAT YOU...

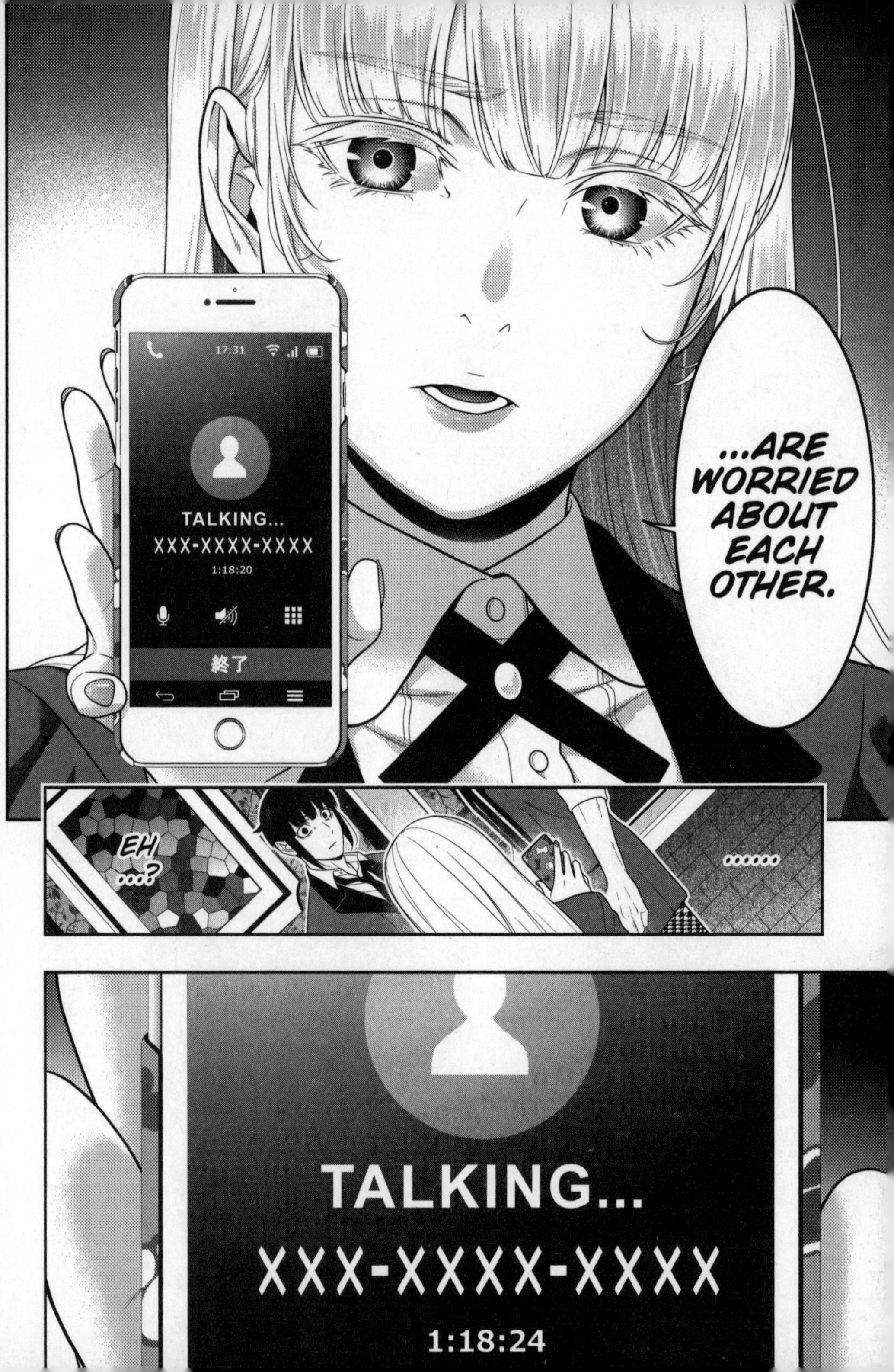
...ARE WORRIED ABOUT EACH OTHER.
17:31
TALKING...
XXX-XXXX-XXXX
1:18:20
終了
......
EH ...?
TALKING...
XXX-XXXX-XXXX
1:18:24

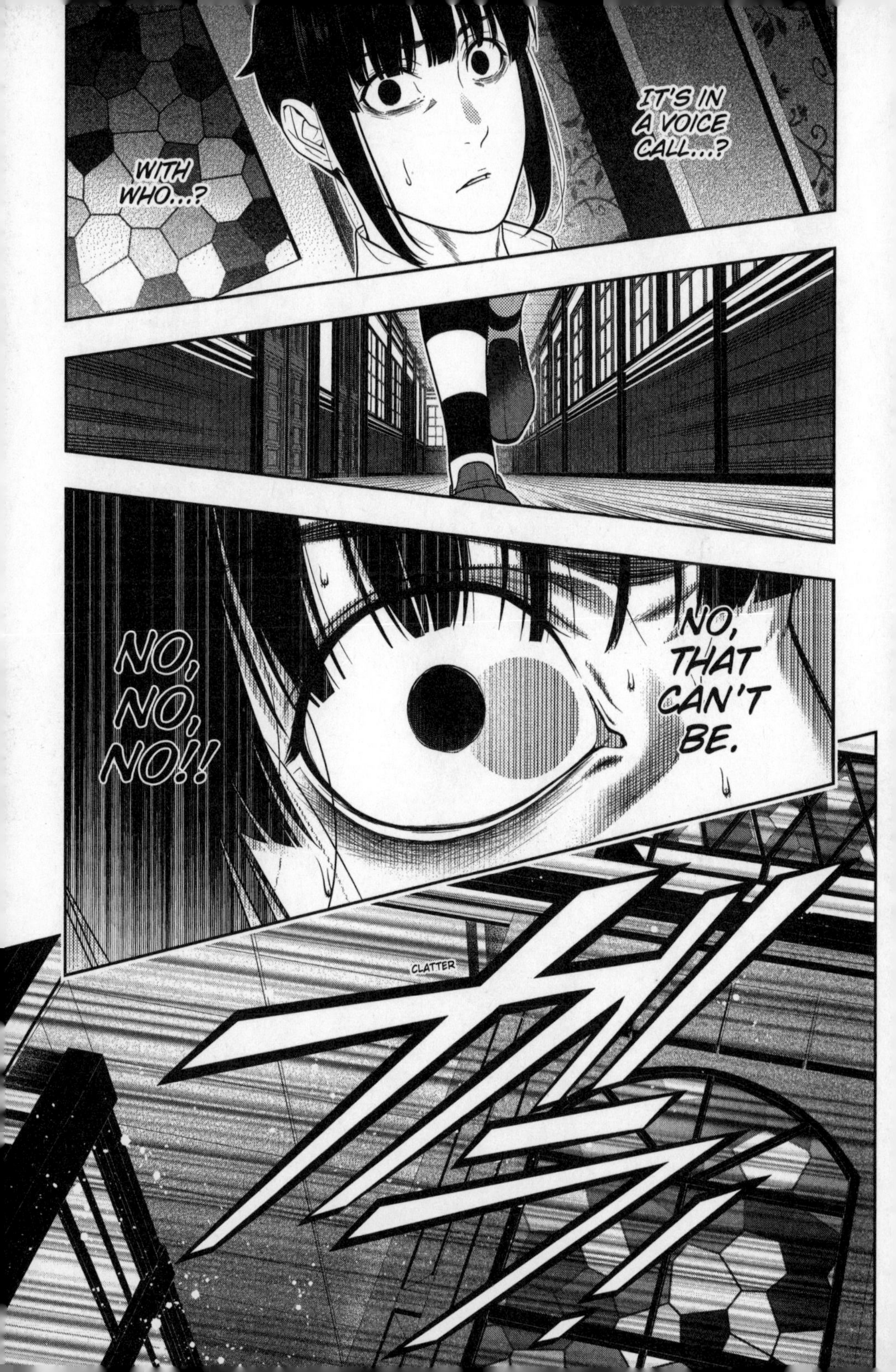
IT'S IN A VOICE CALL...?
WITH WHO...?
NO, THAT CAN'T BE.
NO, NO, NO!!
CLATTER

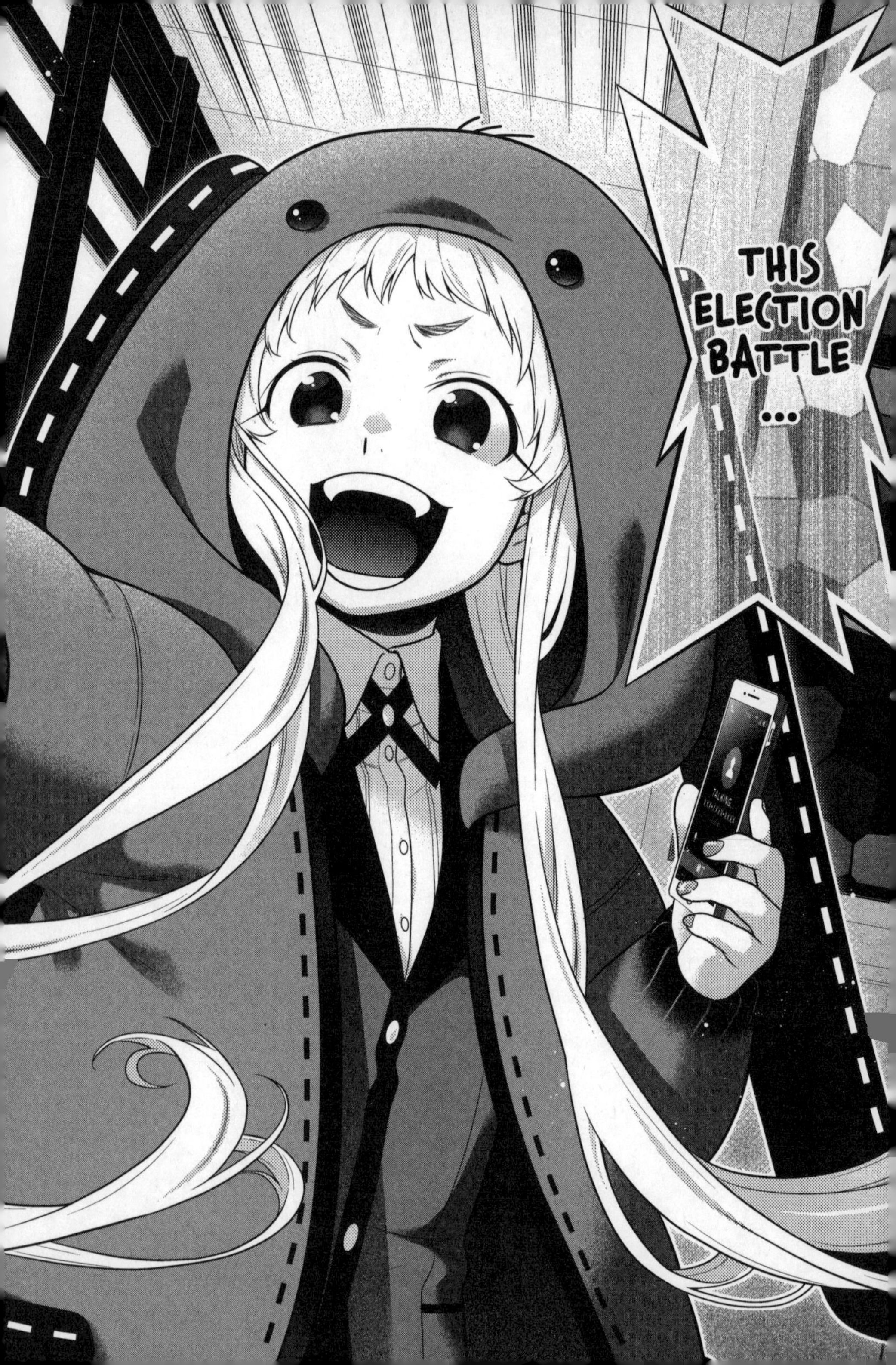
THIS ELECTION BATTLE ...

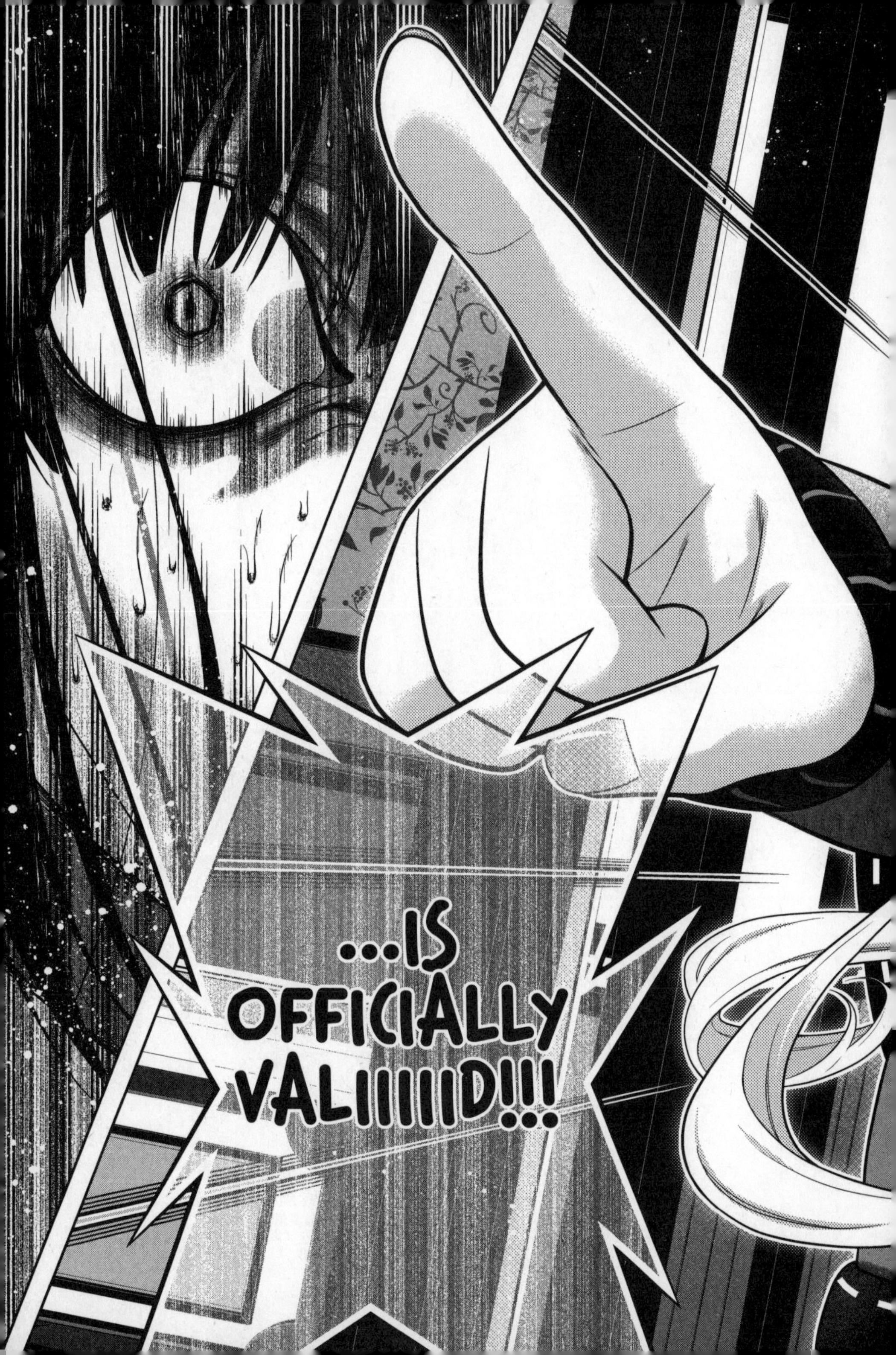
...IS OFFICIALLY VALIIIIID!!!

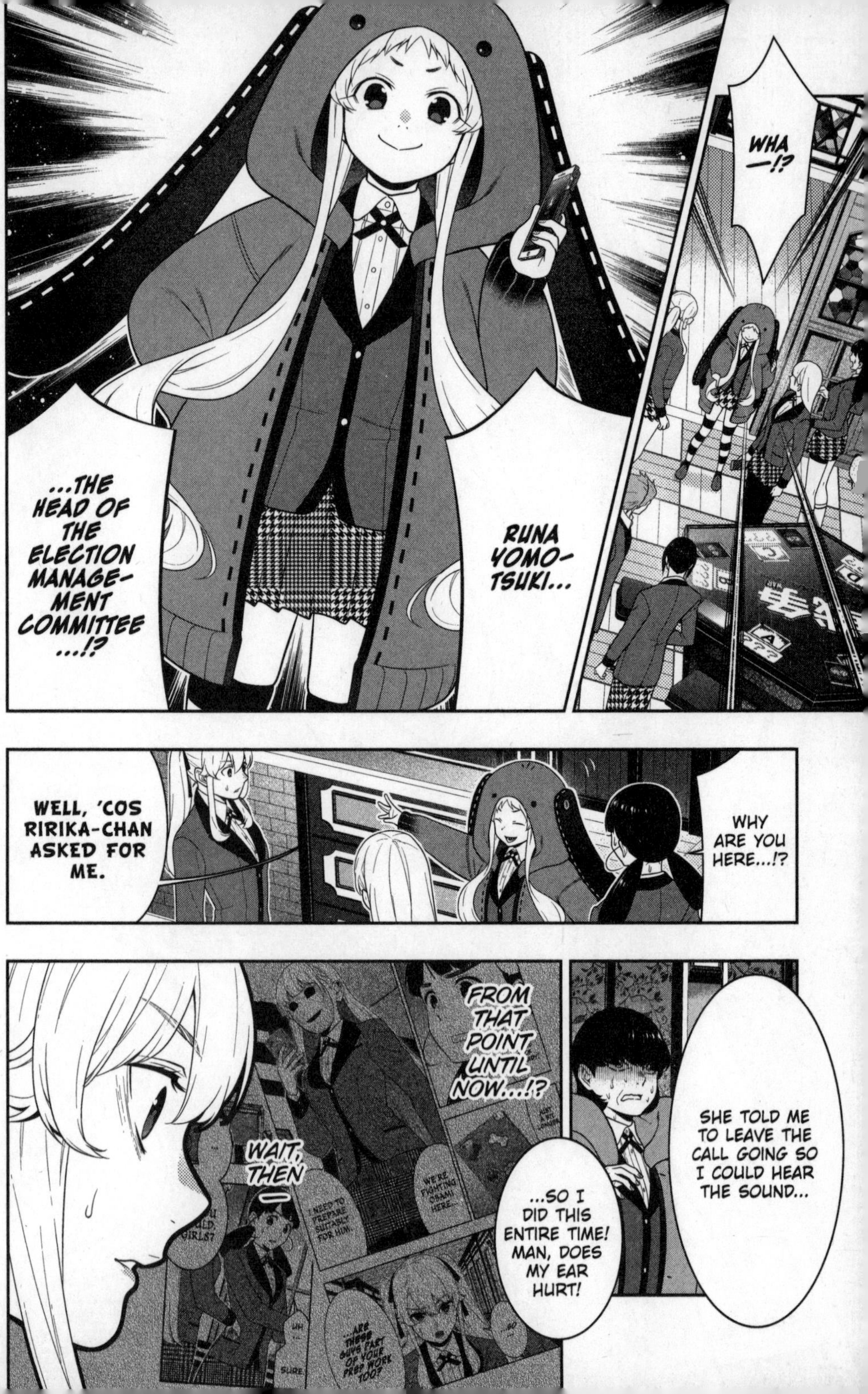
WHA—!?
RUNA YOMOTSUKI...
...THE HEAD OF THE ELECTION MANAGEMENT COMMITTEE ...!?
WHY ARE YOU HERE...!?
WELL, 'COS RIRIKA-CHAN ASKED FOR ME.
SHE TOLD ME TO LEAVE THE CALL GOING SO I COULD HEAR THE SOUND...
...SO I DID THIS ENTIRE TIME! MAN, DOES MY EAR HURT!
FROM THAT POINT UNTIL NOW...!?
WE'RE FIGHTING OBAMI HERE...
I NEED TO PREPARE SUITABLY FOR HIM.
WAIT, THEN —
...ARE THESE GUYS PART OF YOUR PREP WORK TOO?
SURE.

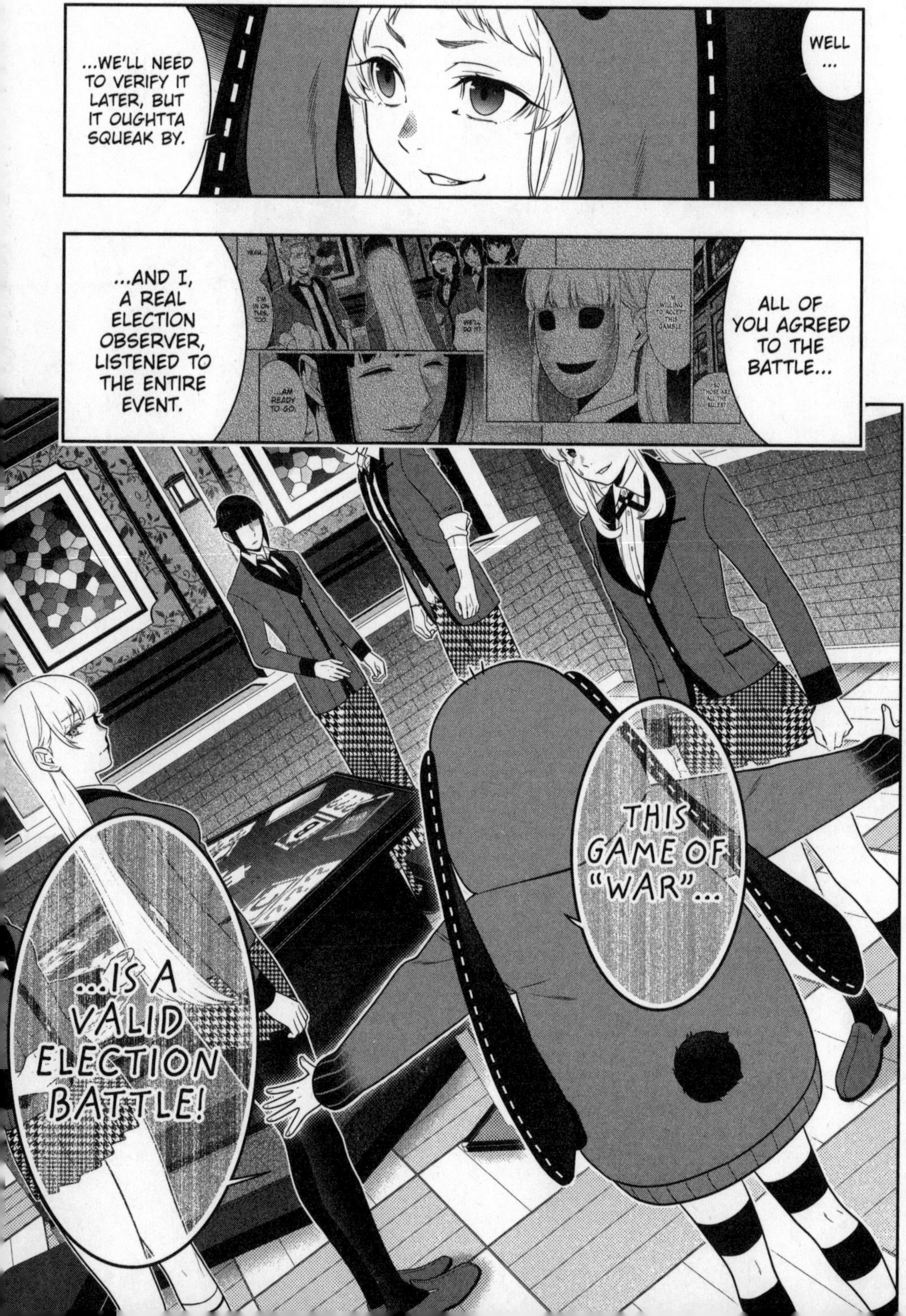
WELL ...
...WE'LL NEED TO VERIFY IT LATER, BUT IT OUGHTTA SQUEAK BY.
ALL OF YOU AGREED TO THE BATTLE...
I'M WILLING TO ACCEPT THIS GAMBLE.
...SO THOSE ARE ALL THE RULES?
WE'LL DO IT!
YEAH.
I'M IN ON THIS TOO.
...AM READY TO GO.
...AND I, A REAL ELECTION OBSERVER, LISTENED TO THE ENTIRE EVENT.
THIS GAME OF "WAR"...
...IS A VALID ELECTION BATTLE!

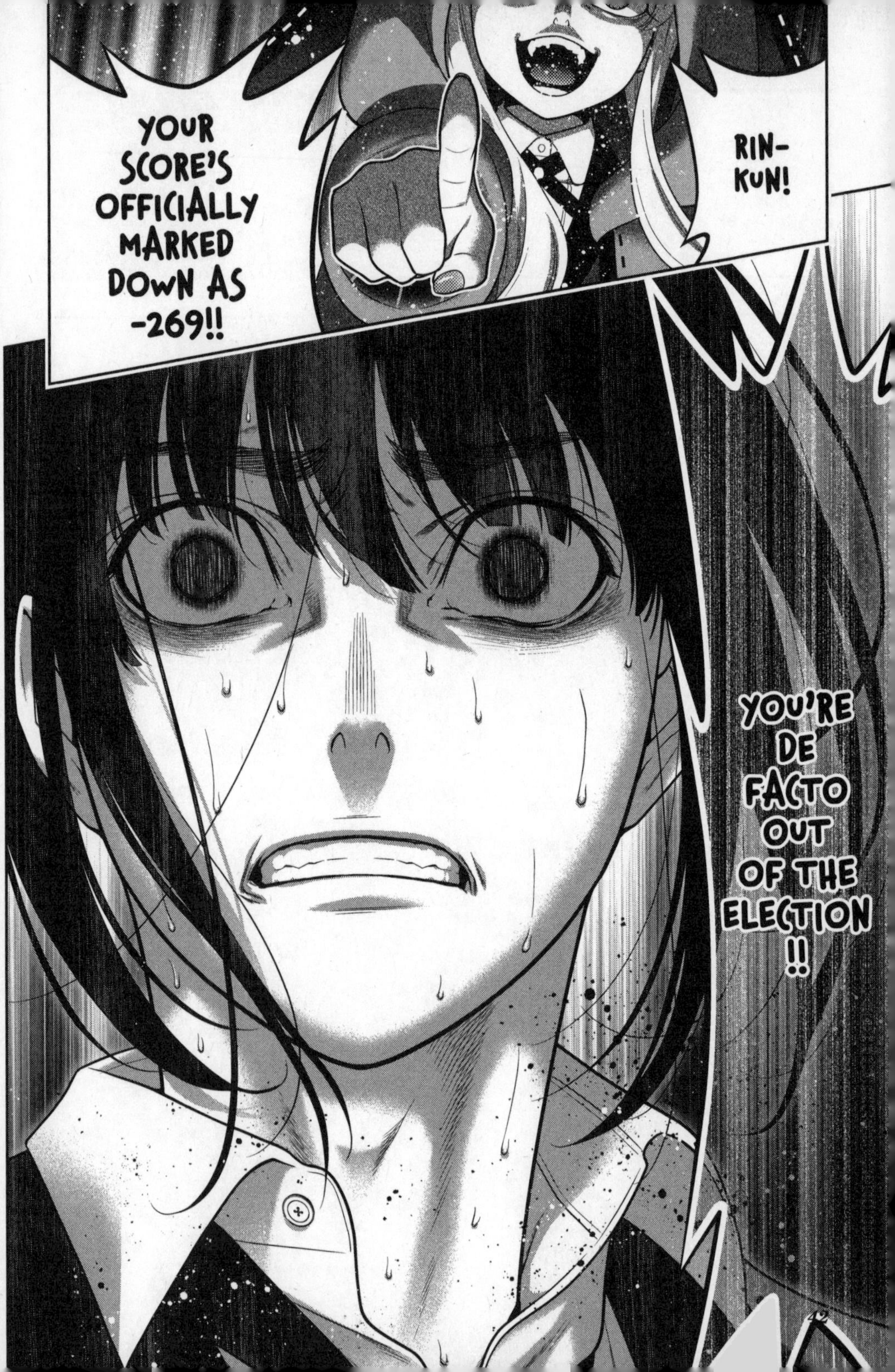
RIN-KUN!
YOUR SCORE'S OFFICIALLY MARKED DOWN AS -269!!
YOU'RE DE FACTO OUT OF THE ELECTION!!

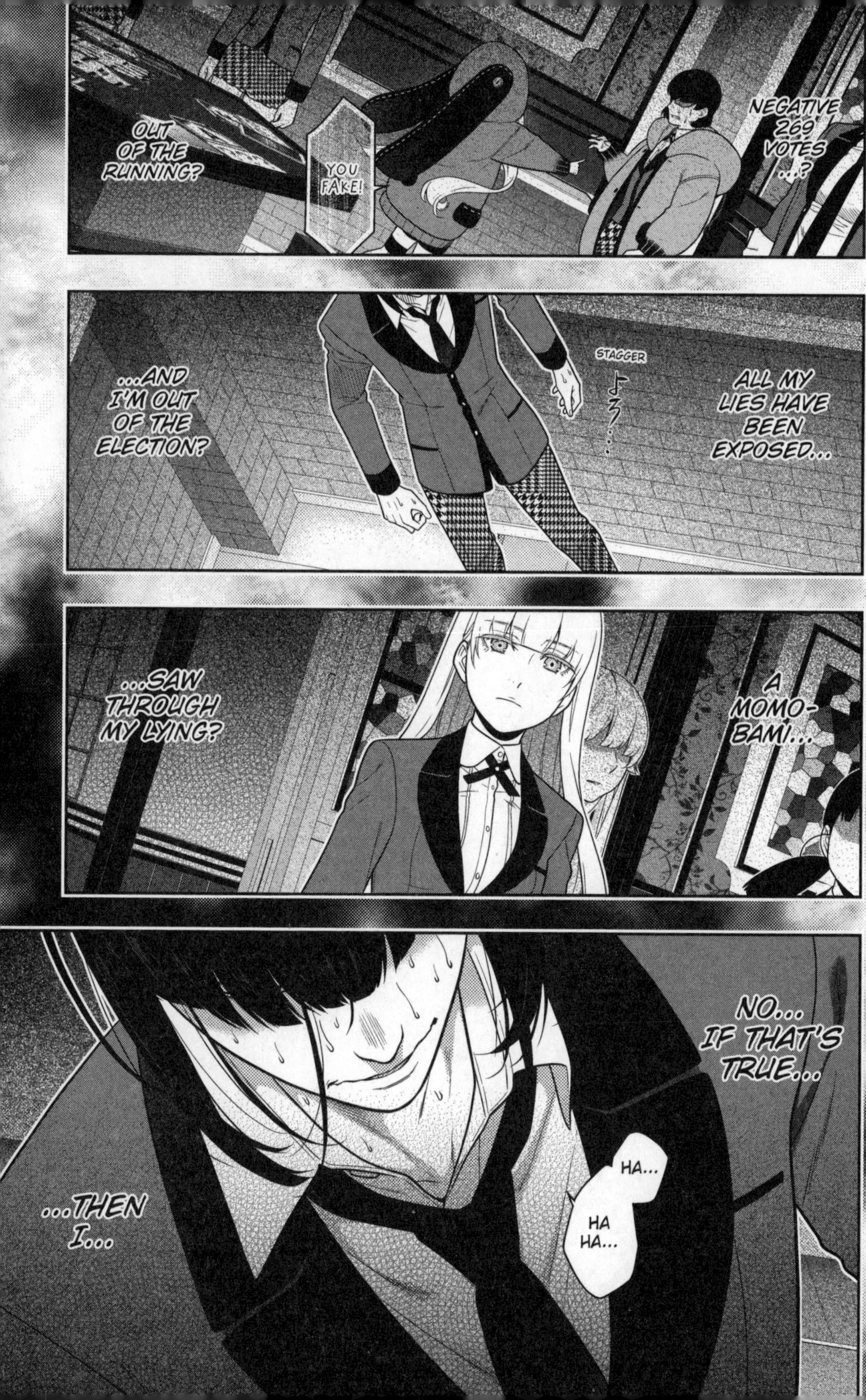
NEGATIVE 269 VOTES ...?
YOU FAKE!
OUT OF THE RUNNING?
ALL MY LIES HAVE BEEN EXPOSED...
STAGGER
...AND I'M OUT OF THE ELECTION?
A MOMOBAMI...
...SAW THROUGH MY LYING?
NO... IF THAT'S TRUE...
HA...
HA HA...
...THEN I...

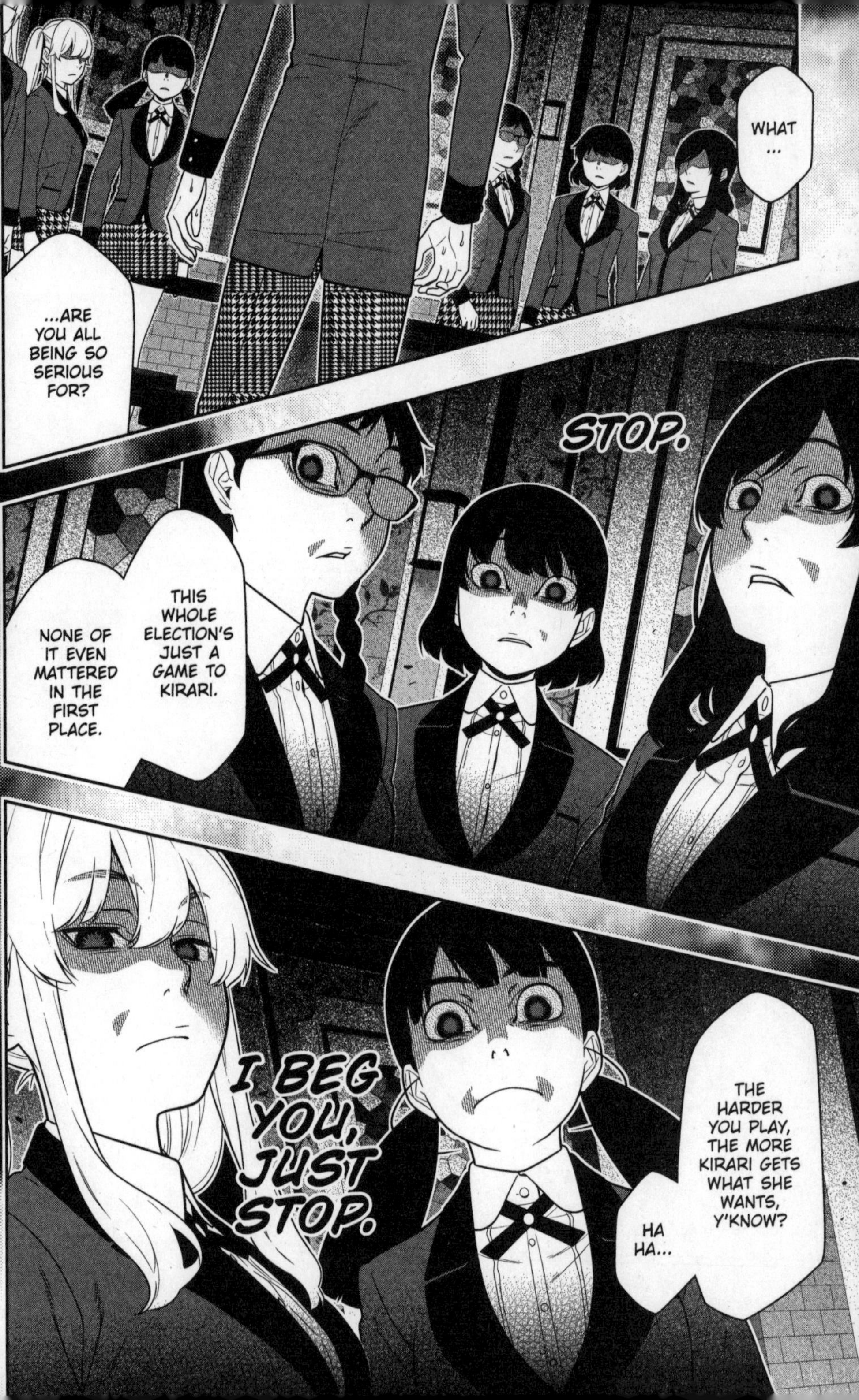
WHAT ...
...ARE YOU ALL BEING SO SERIOUS FOR?
STOP.
THIS WHOLE ELECTION'S JUST A GAME TO KIRARI.
NONE OF IT EVEN MATTERED IN THE FIRST PLACE.
THE HARDER YOU PLAY, THE MORE KIRARI GETS WHAT SHE WANTS, Y'KNOW?
HA HA...
I BEG YOU, JUST STOP.

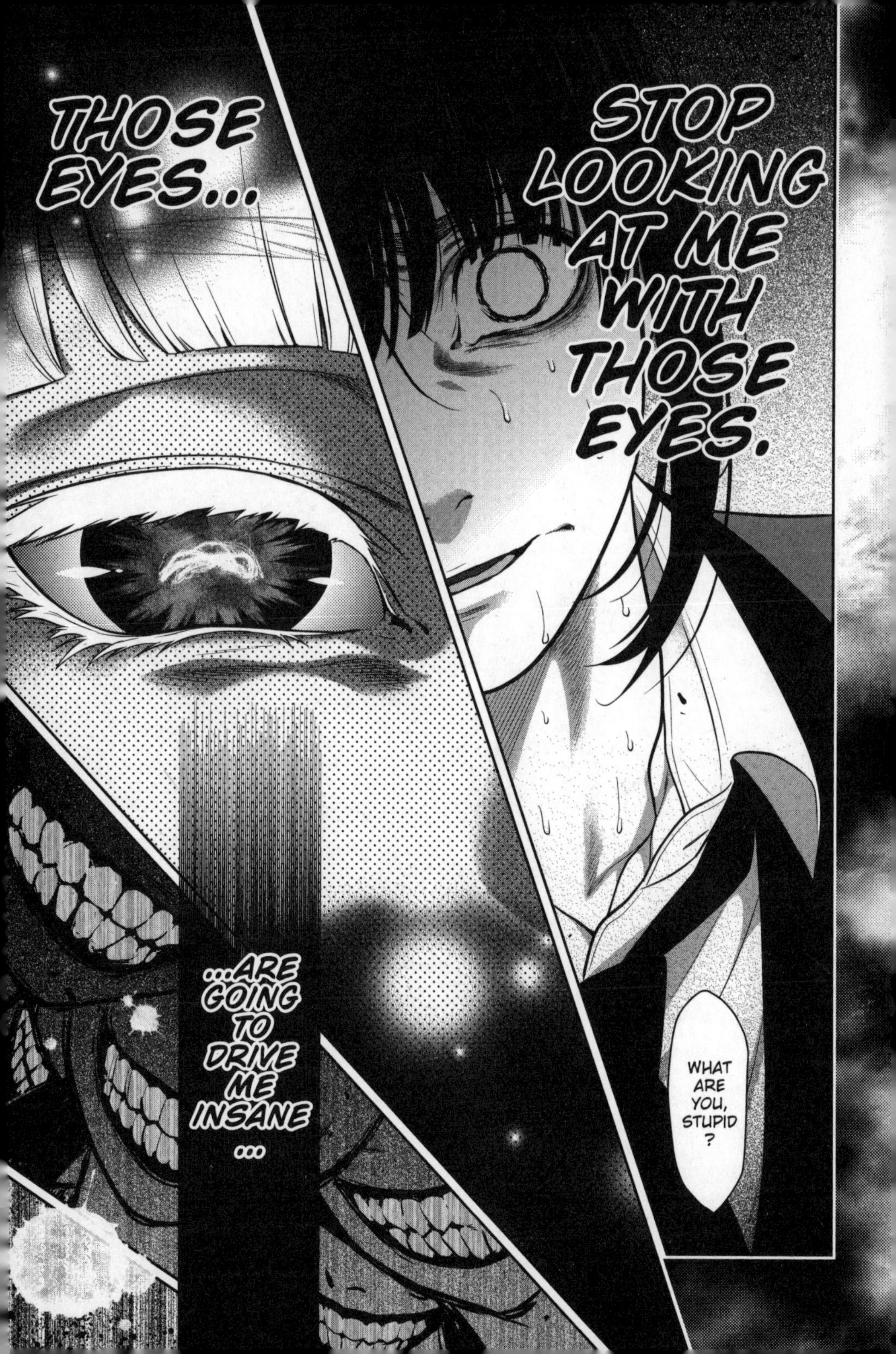
STOP LOOKING AT ME WITH THOSE EYES.
WHAT ARE YOU, STUPID?
THOSE EYES...
...ARE GOING TO DRIVE ME INSANE...

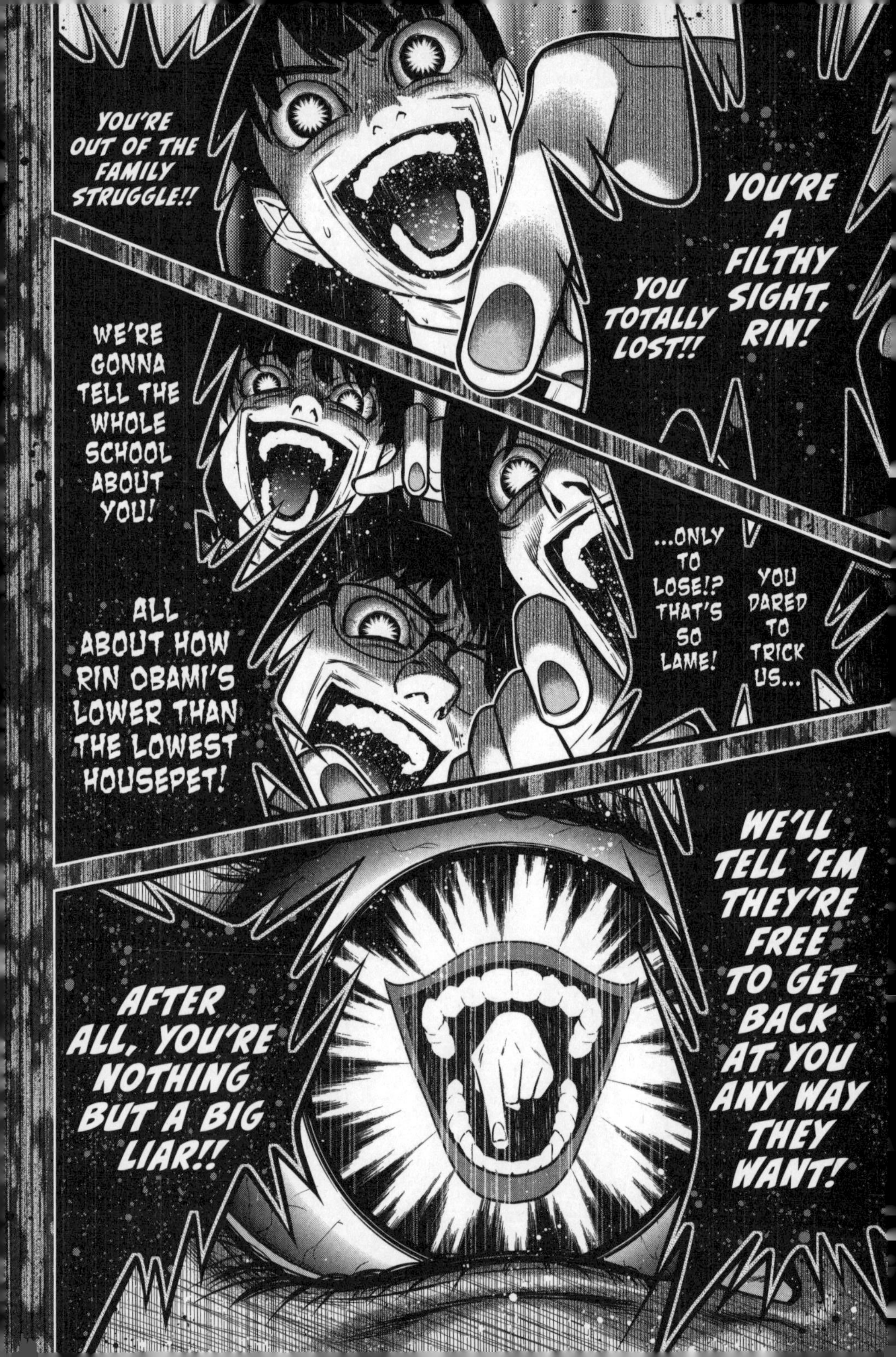
YOU'RE A FILTHY SIGHT, RIN!
YOU TOTALLY LOST!!
YOU'RE OUT OF THE FAMILY STRUGGLE!!
YOU DARED TO TRICK US...
...ONLY TO LOSE!? THAT'S SO LAME!
WE'RE GONNA TELL THE WHOLE SCHOOL ABOUT YOU!
ALL ABOUT HOW RIN OBAMI'S LOWER THAN THE LOWEST HOUSEPET!
WE'LL TELL 'EM THEY'RE FREE TO GET BACK AT YOU ANY WAY THEY WANT!
AFTER ALL, YOU'RE NOTHING BUT A BIG LIAR!!

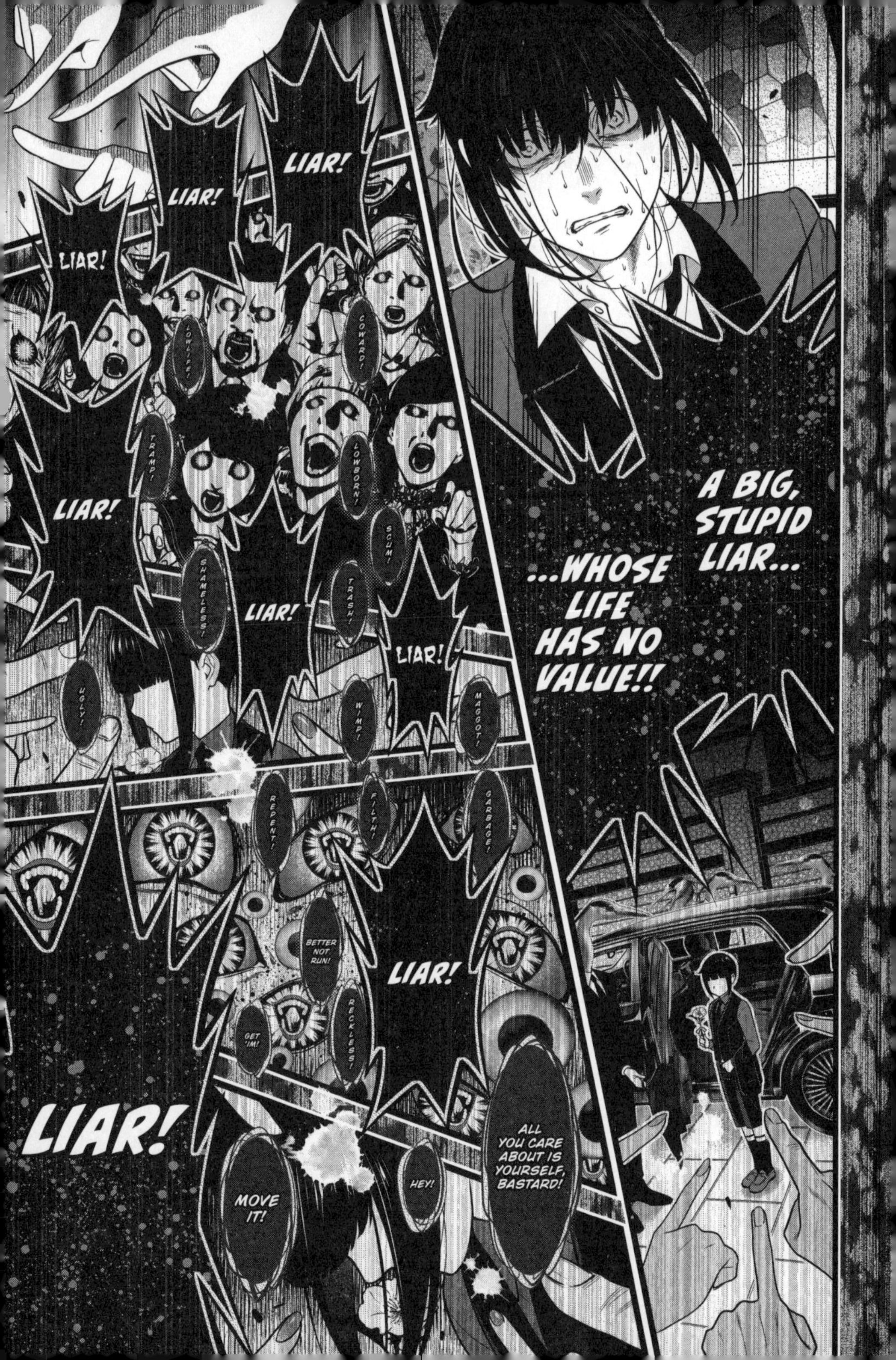
A BIG, STUPID LIAR...
...WHOSE LIFE HAS NO VALUE!!
LIAR!
LIAR!
LIAR!
COWARD!
LOWLIFE!
LOWBORN!
TRAMP!
LIAR!
SCUM!
SHAMELESS!
TRASH!
LIAR!
LIAR!
MAGGOT!
WIMP!
UGLY!
GARBAGE!
FILTH!
REPENT!
LIAR!
BETTER NOT RUN!
RECKLESS!
GET 'IM!
ALL YOU CARE ABOUT IS YOURSELF, BASTARD!
HEY!
MOVE IT!
LIAR!

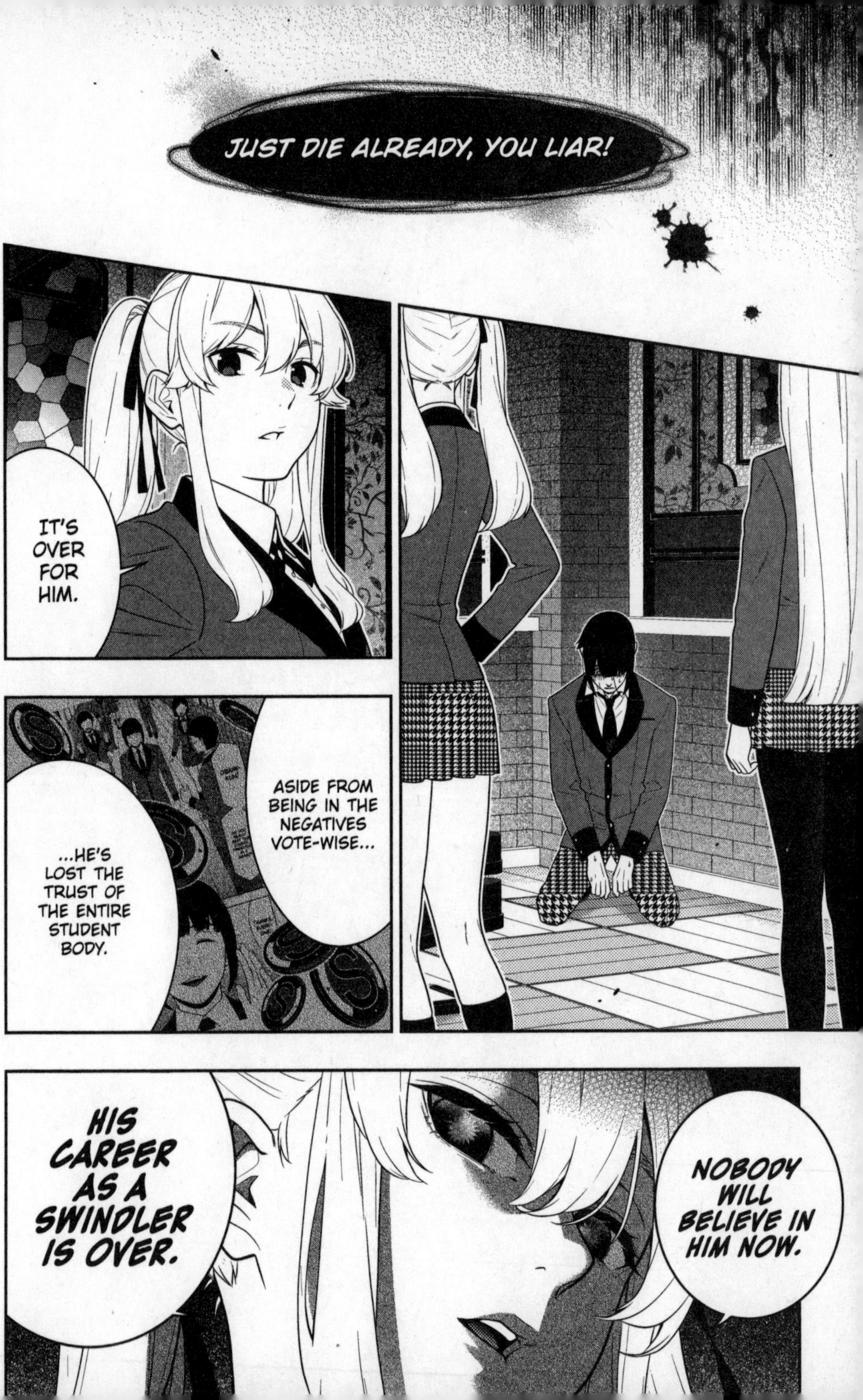
JUST DIE ALREADY, YOU LIAR!
IT'S OVER FOR HIM.
ASIDE FROM BEING IN THE NEGATIVES VOTE-WISE...
...HE'S LOST THE TRUST OF THE ENTIRE STUDENT BODY.
NOBODY WILL BELIEVE IN HIM NOW.
HIS CAREER AS A SWINDLER IS OVER.

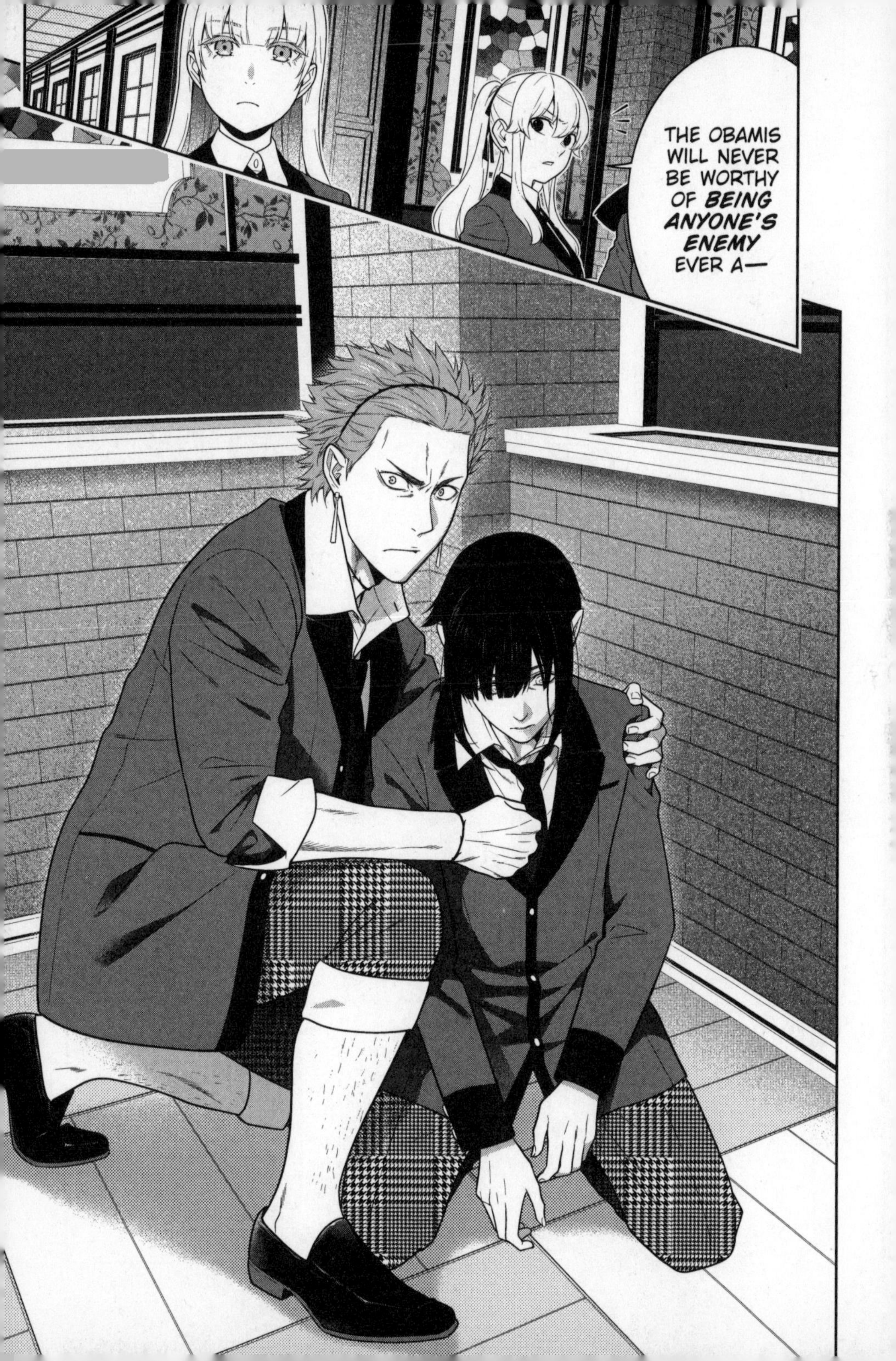
THE OBAMIS WILL NEVER BE WORTHY OF **BEING ANYONE'S ENEMY** EVER A—

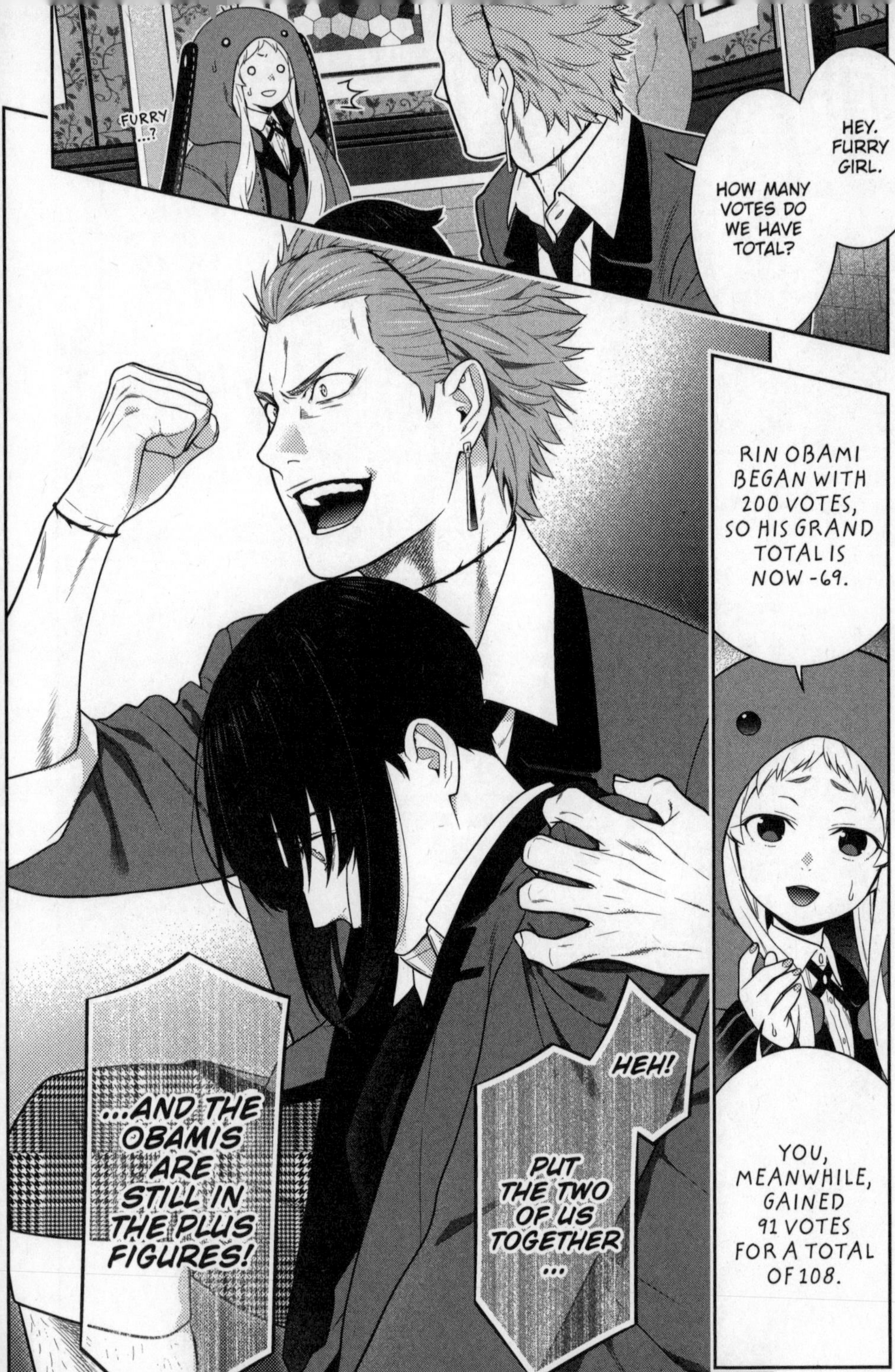
HEY. FURRY GIRL.
HOW MANY VOTES DO WE HAVE TOTAL?
FURRY ...?
RIN OBAMI BEGAN WITH 200 VOTES, SO HIS GRAND TOTAL IS NOW -69.
YOU, MEANWHILE, GAINED 91 VOTES FOR A TOTAL OF 108.
HEH!
PUT THE TWO OF US TOGETHER ...
...AND THE OBAMIS ARE STILL IN THE PLUS FIGURES!

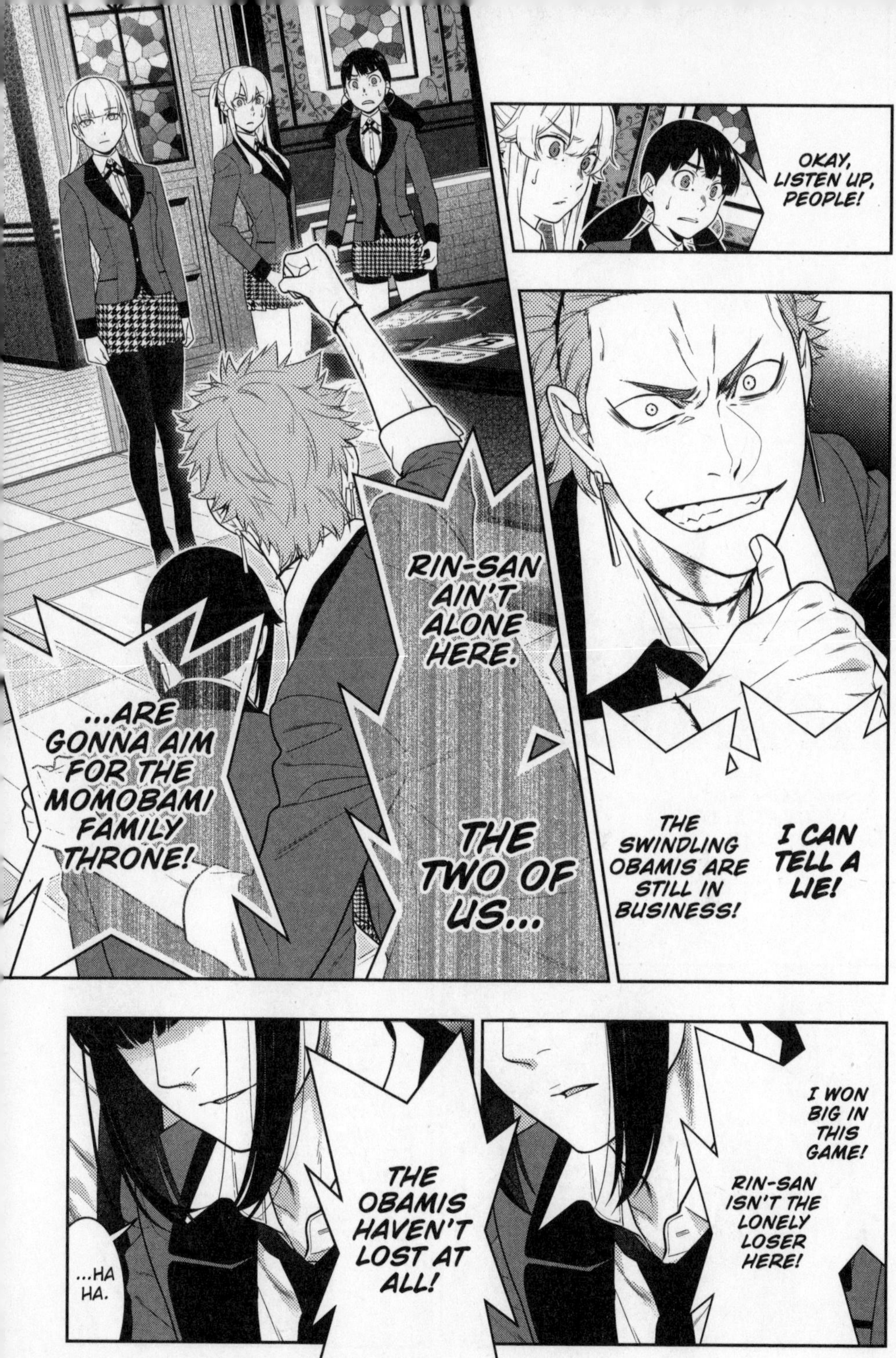
OKAY, LISTEN UP, PEOPLE!
I CAN TELL A LIE!
THE SWINDLING OBAMIS ARE STILL IN BUSINESS!
RIN-SAN AIN'T ALONE HERE.
THE TWO OF US...
...ARE GONNA AIM FOR THE MOMOBAMI FAMILY THRONE!
I WON BIG IN THIS GAME!
RIN-SAN ISN'T THE LONELY LOSER HERE!
THE OBAMIS HAVEN'T LOST AT ALL!
...HA HA.

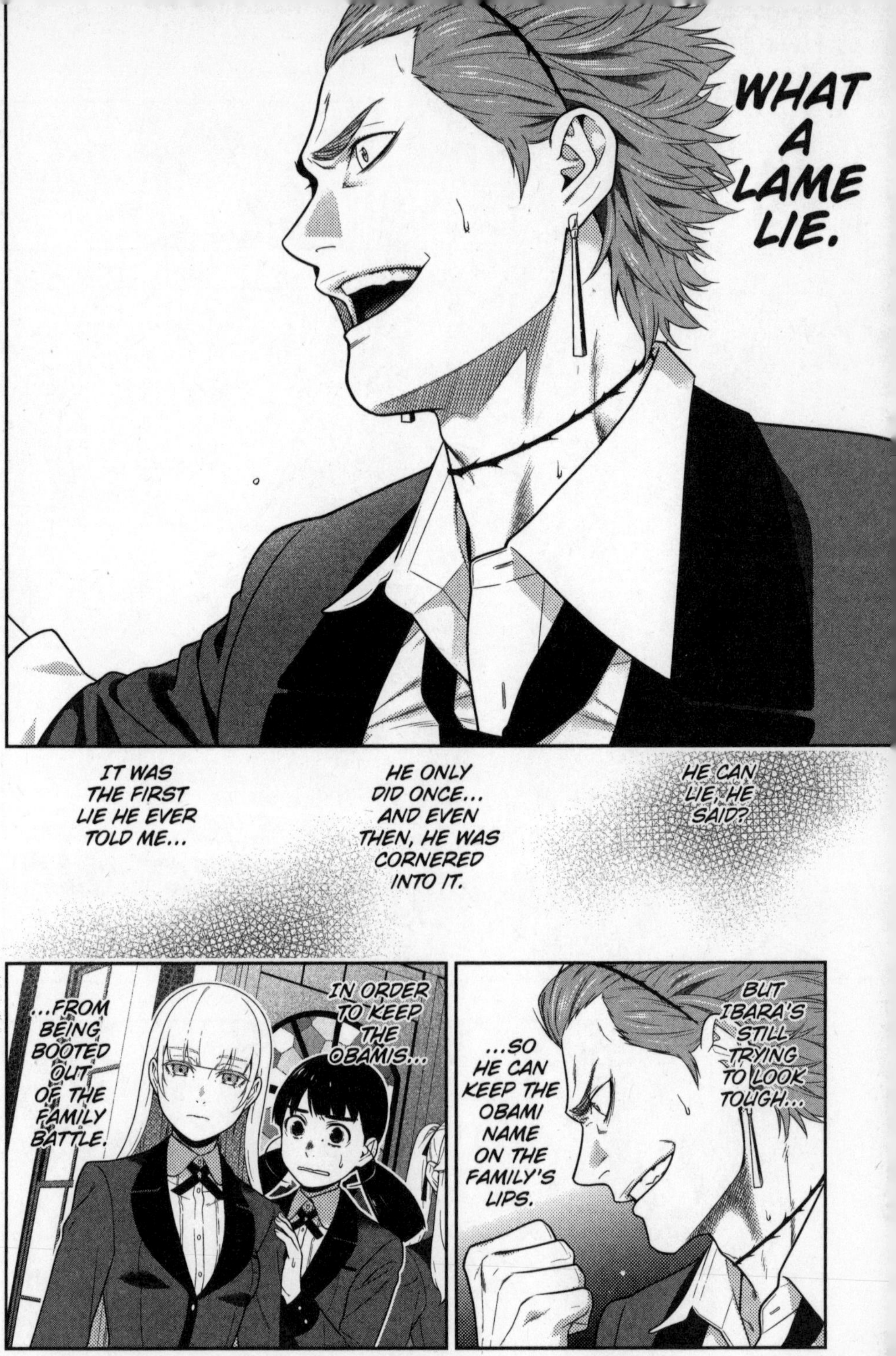
WHAT A LAME LIE.
HE CAN LIE, HE SAID?
HE ONLY DID ONCE... AND EVEN THEN, HE WAS CORNERED INTO IT.
IT WAS THE FIRST LIE HE EVER TOLD ME...
BUT IBARA'S STILL TRYING TO LOOK TOUGH...
...SO HE CAN KEEP THE OBAMI NAME ON THE FAMILY'S LIPS.
IN ORDER TO KEEP THE OBAMIS...
...FROM BEING BOOTED OUT OF THE FAMILY BATTLE.

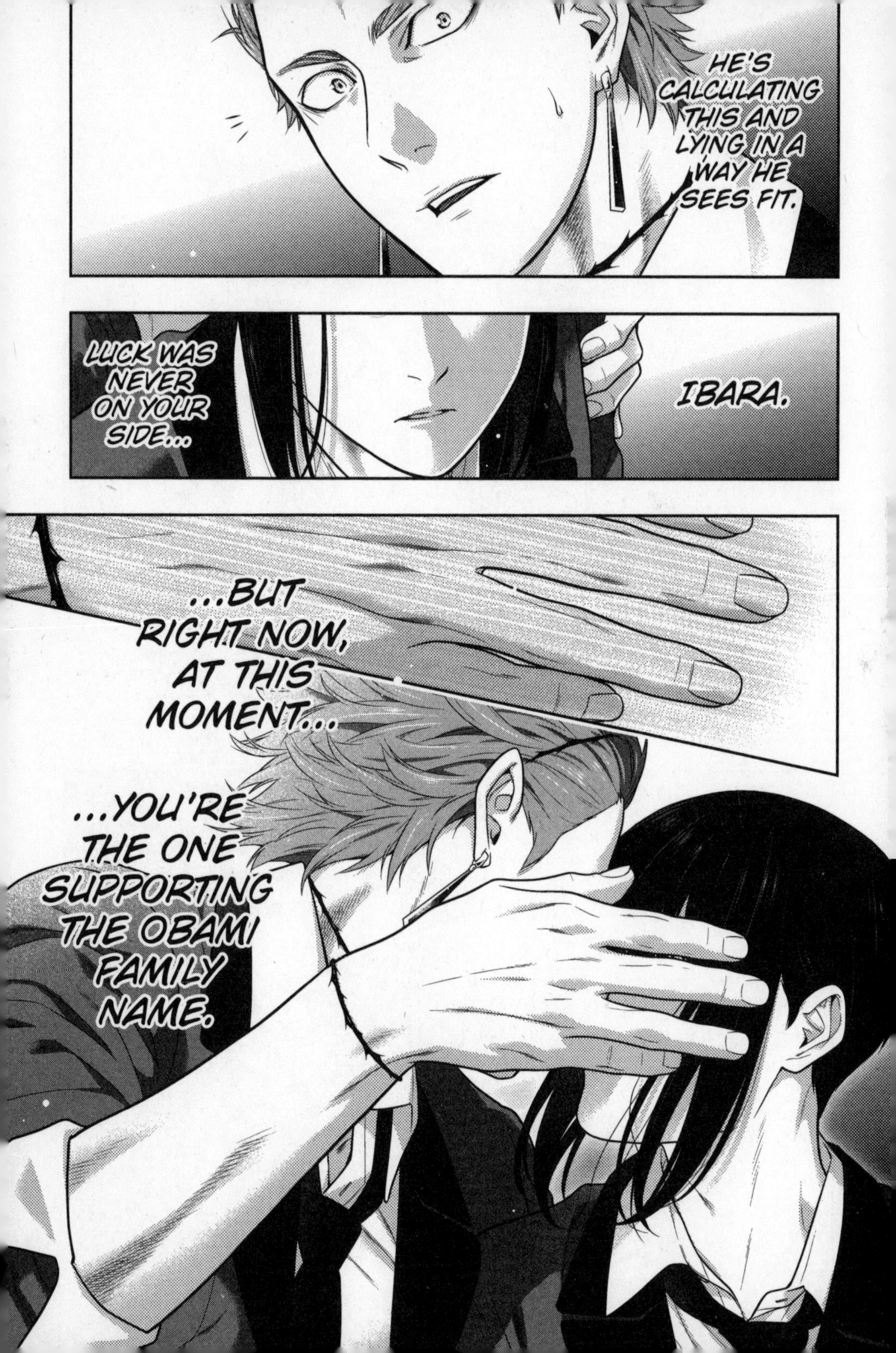
HE'S CALCULATING THIS AND LYING IN A WAY HE SEES FIT.
IBARA.
LUCK WAS NEVER ON YOUR SIDE...
...BUT RIGHT NOW, AT THIS MOMENT...
...YOU'RE THE ONE SUPPORTING THE OBAMI FAMILY NAME.

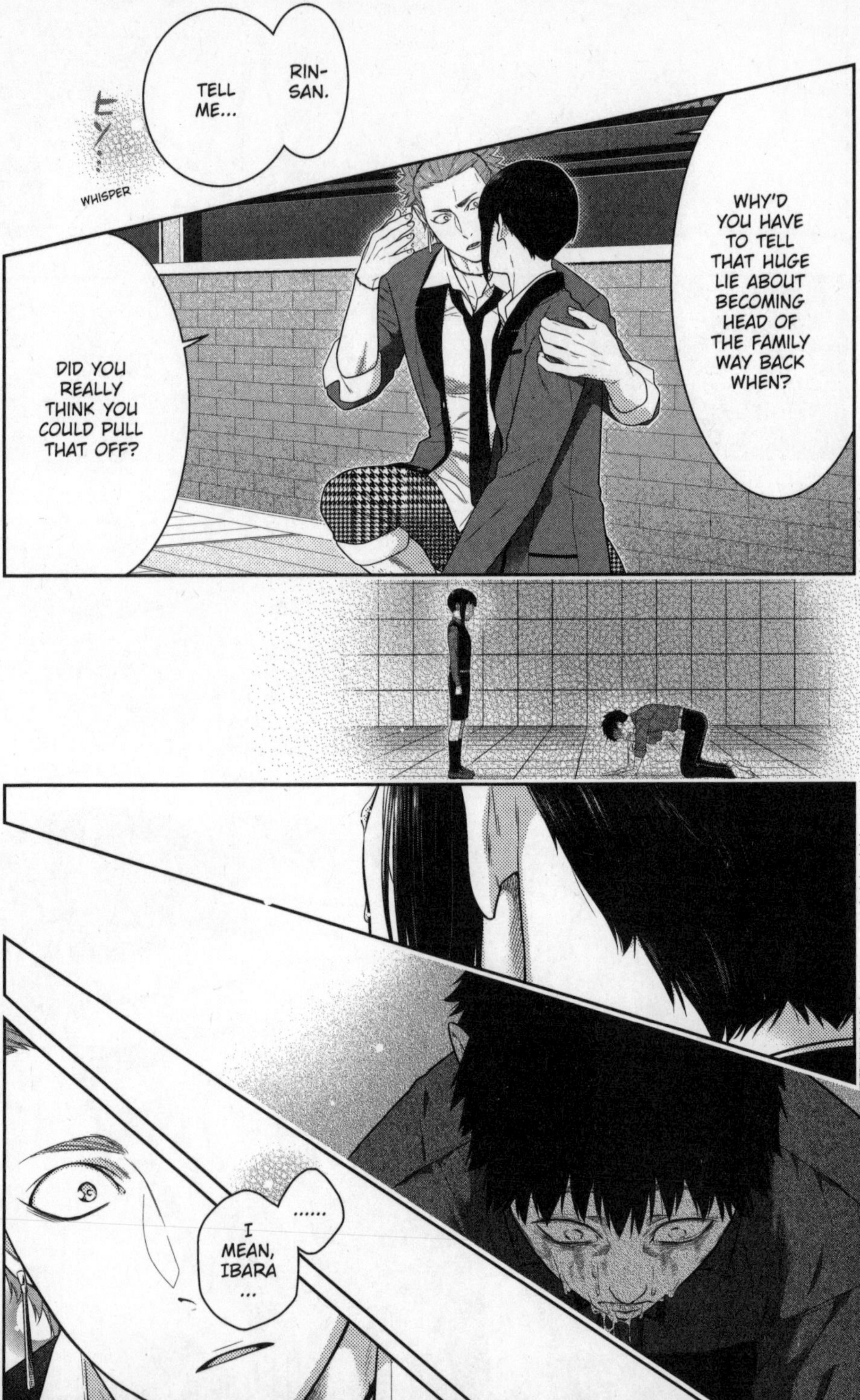
RIN-SAN. TELL ME...
ヒソ…
WHISPER
WHY'D YOU HAVE TO TELL THAT HUGE LIE ABOUT BECOMING HEAD OF THE FAMILY WAY BACK WHEN?
DID YOU REALLY THINK YOU COULD PULL THAT OFF?
......
I MEAN, IBARA ...

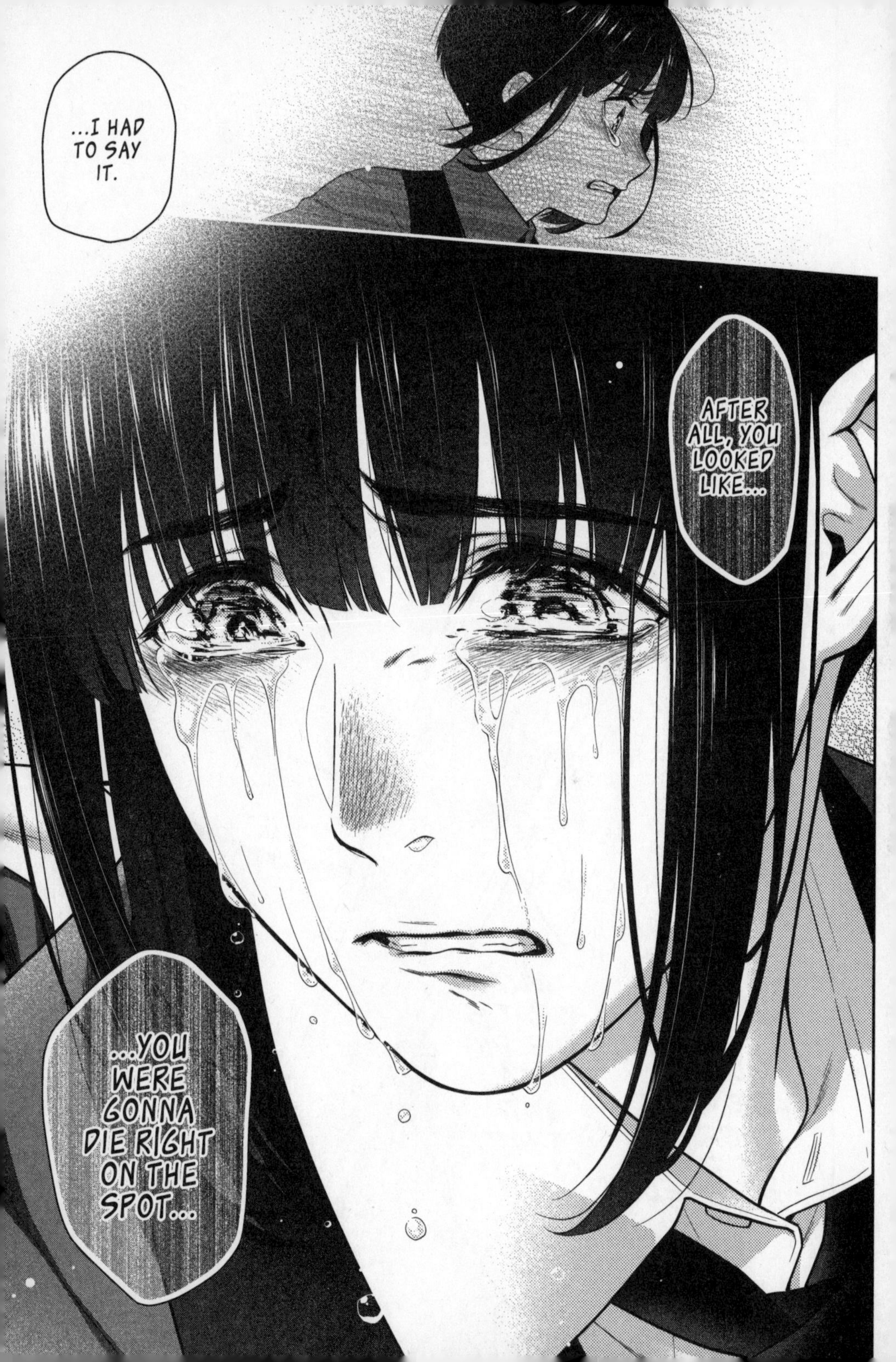
...I HAD TO SAY IT.
AFTER ALL, YOU LOOKED LIKE...
...YOU WERE GONNA DIE RIGHT ON THE SPOT...

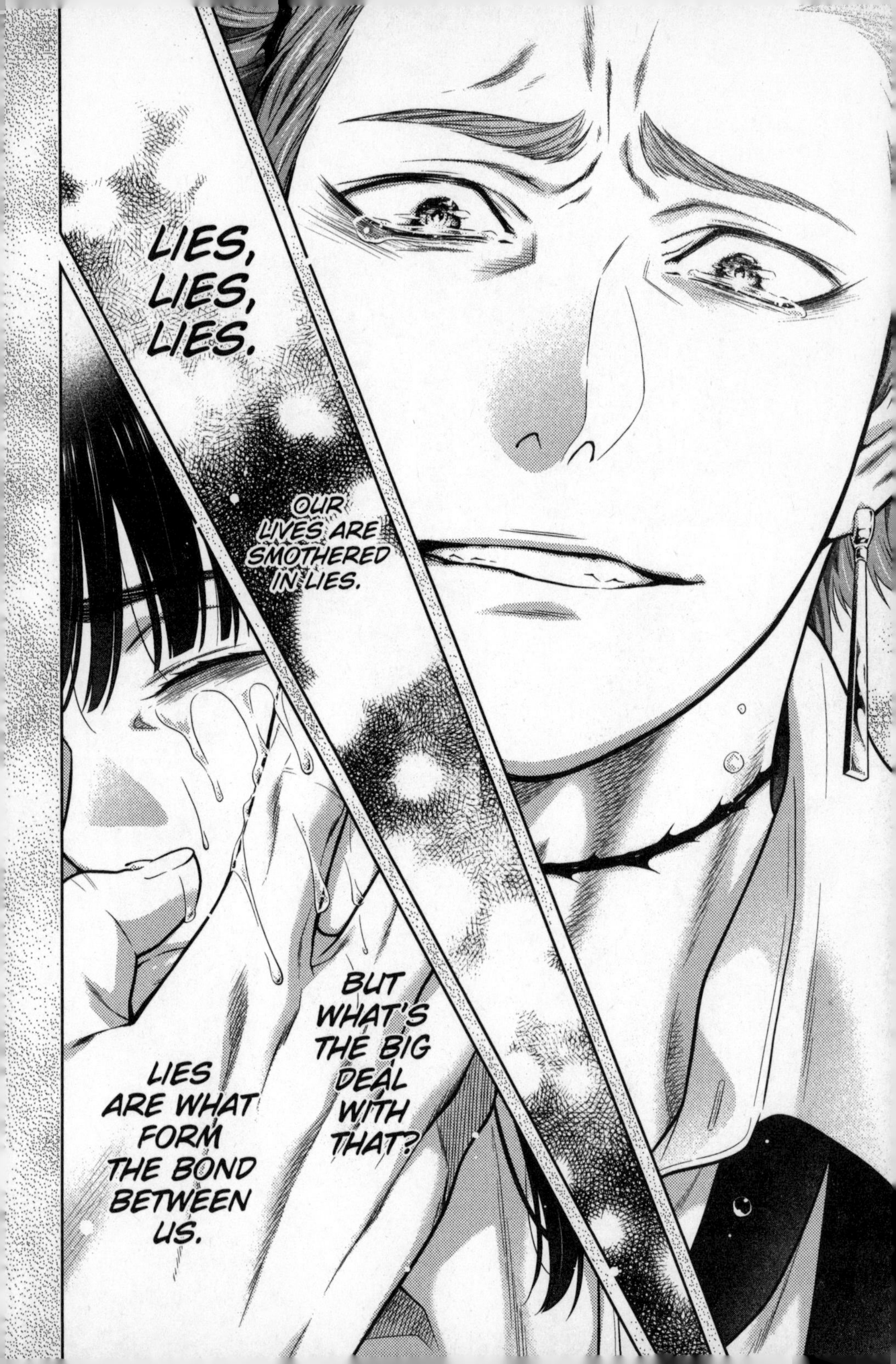
LIES, LIES, LIES.
OUR LIVES ARE SMOTHERED IN LIES.
BUT WHAT'S THE BIG DEAL WITH THAT?
LIES ARE WHAT FORM THE BOND BETWEEN US.

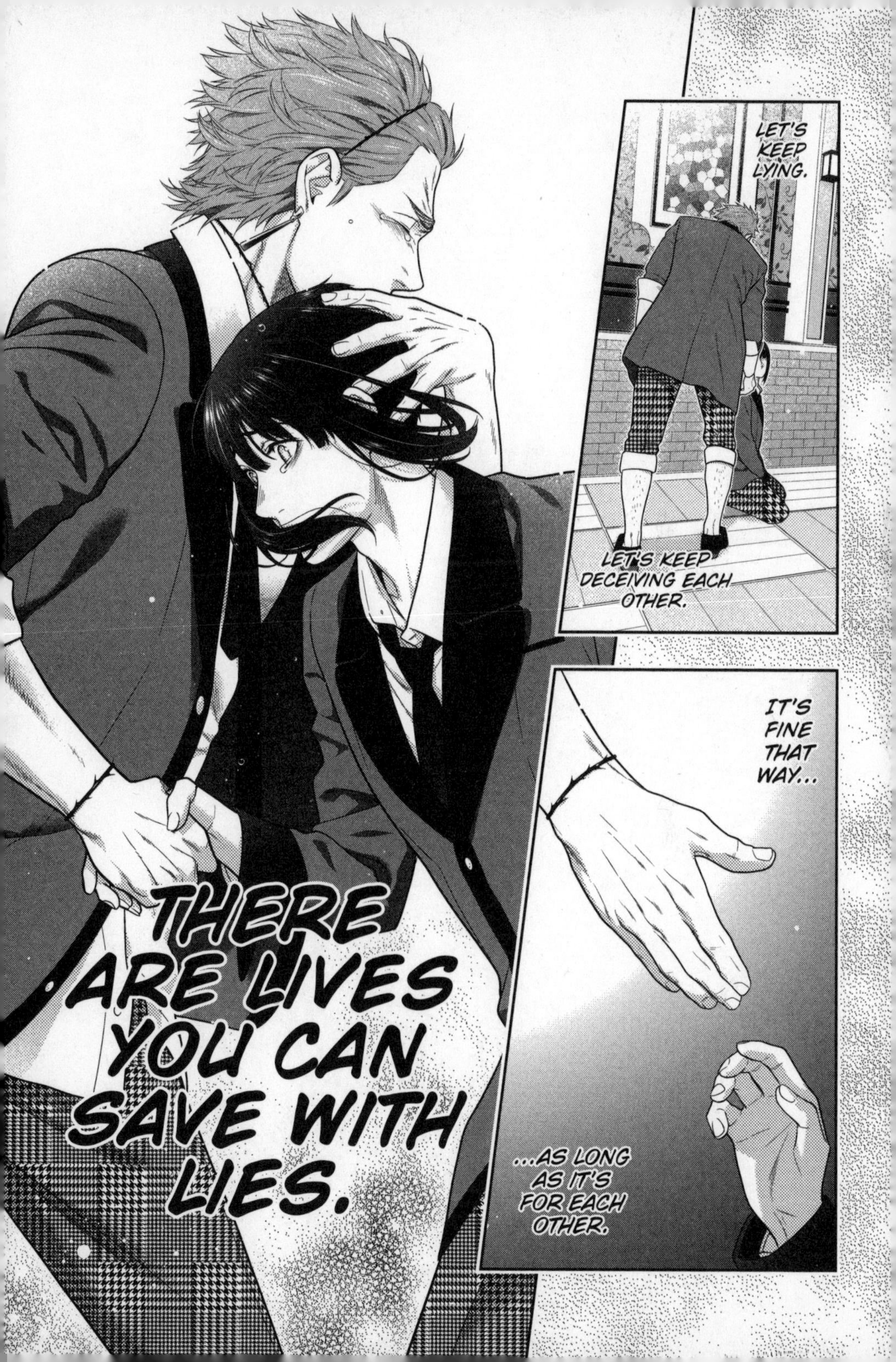
LET'S KEEP LYING.
LET'S KEEP DECEIVING EACH OTHER.
IT'S FINE THAT WAY...
...AS LONG AS IT'S FOR EACH OTHER.
THERE ARE LIVES YOU CAN SAVE WITH LIES.

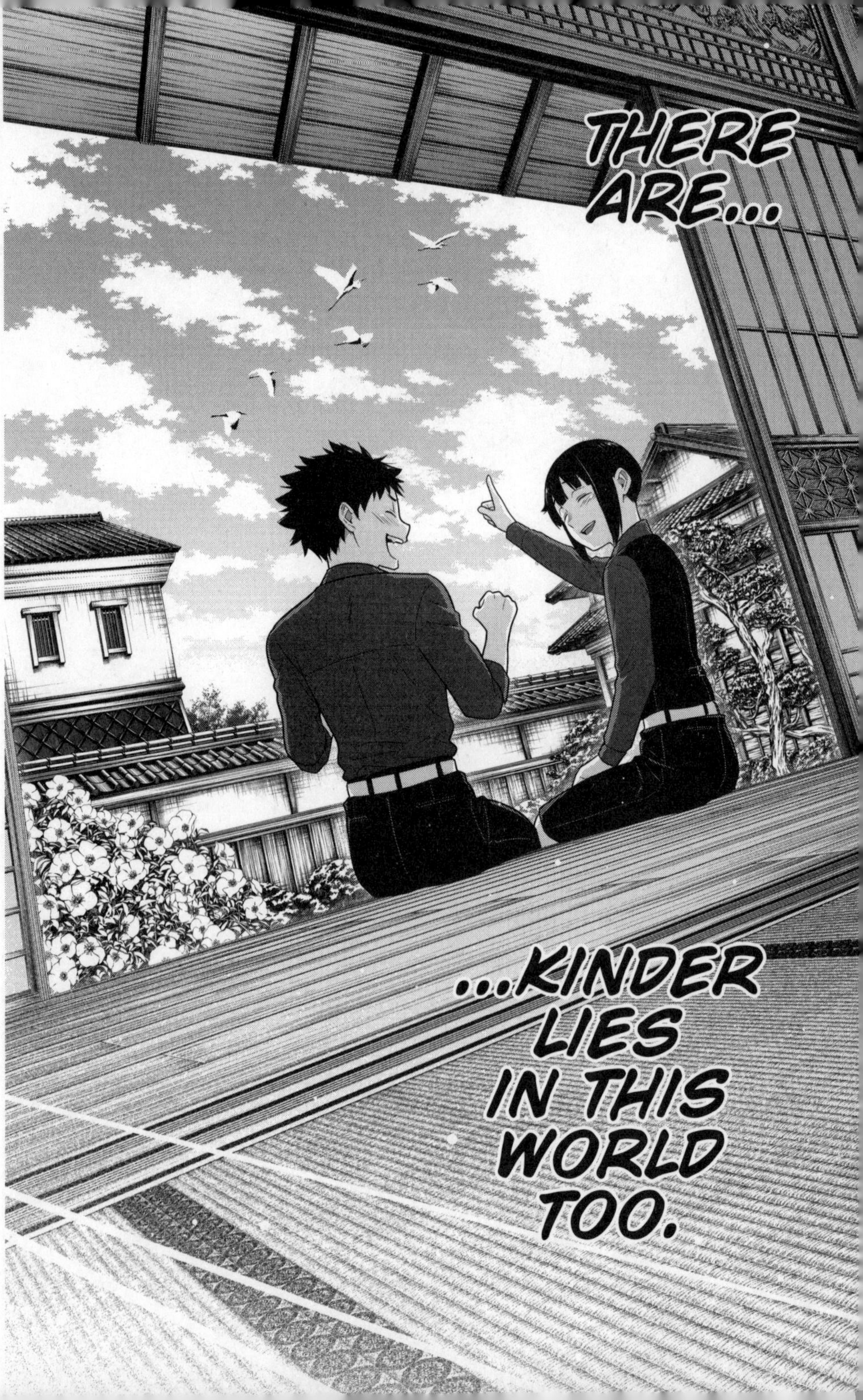
THERE ARE...
...KINDER LIES IN THIS WORLD TOO.

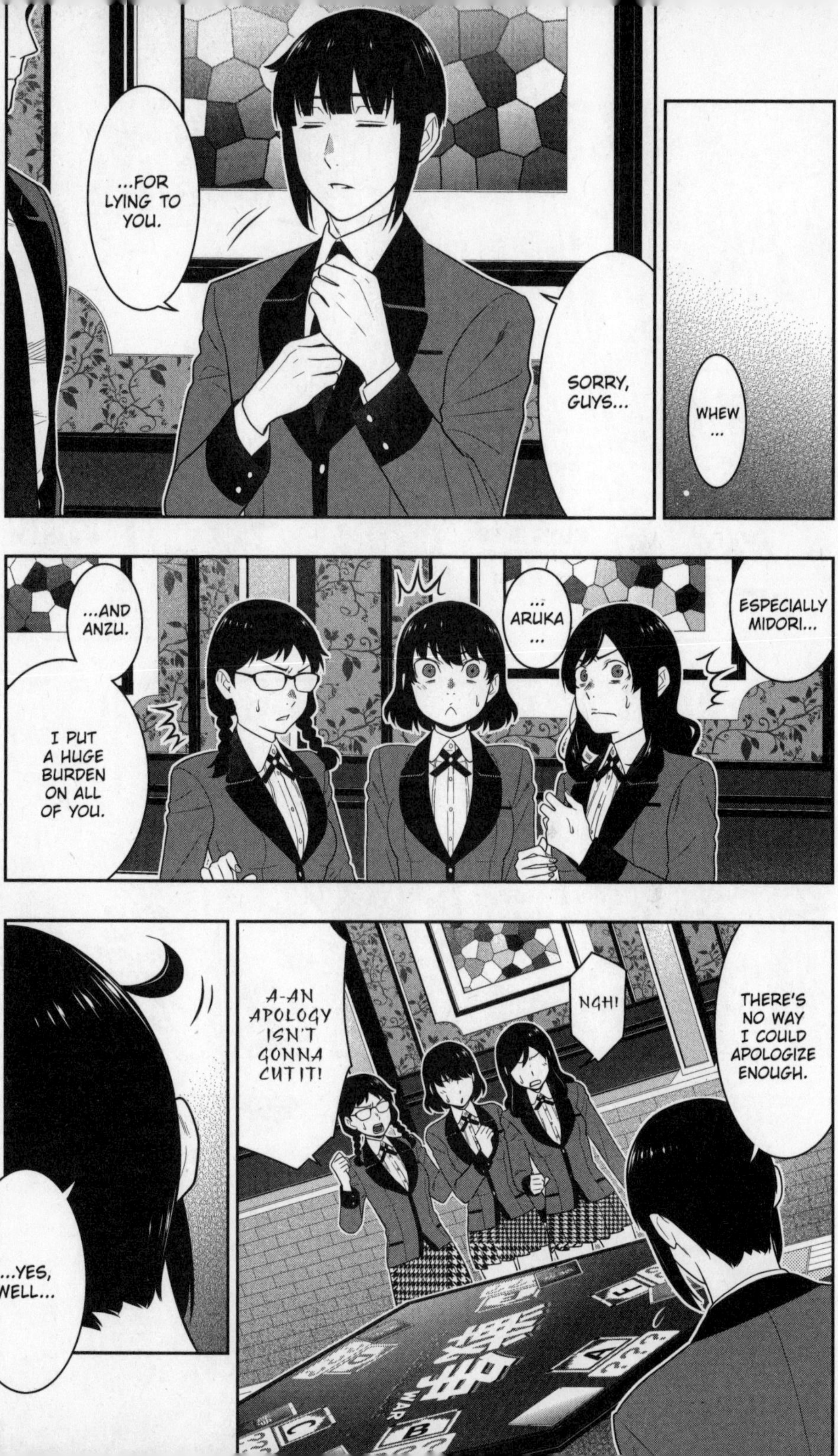
WHEW ...
SORRY, GUYS...
...FOR LYING TO YOU.
ESPECIALLY MIDORI...
... ARUKA ...
...AND ANZU.
I PUT A HUGE BURDEN ON ALL OF YOU.
THERE'S NO WAY I COULD APOLOGIZE ENOUGH.
NGH!
A-AN APOLOGY ISN'T GONNA CUT IT!
...YES, WELL...

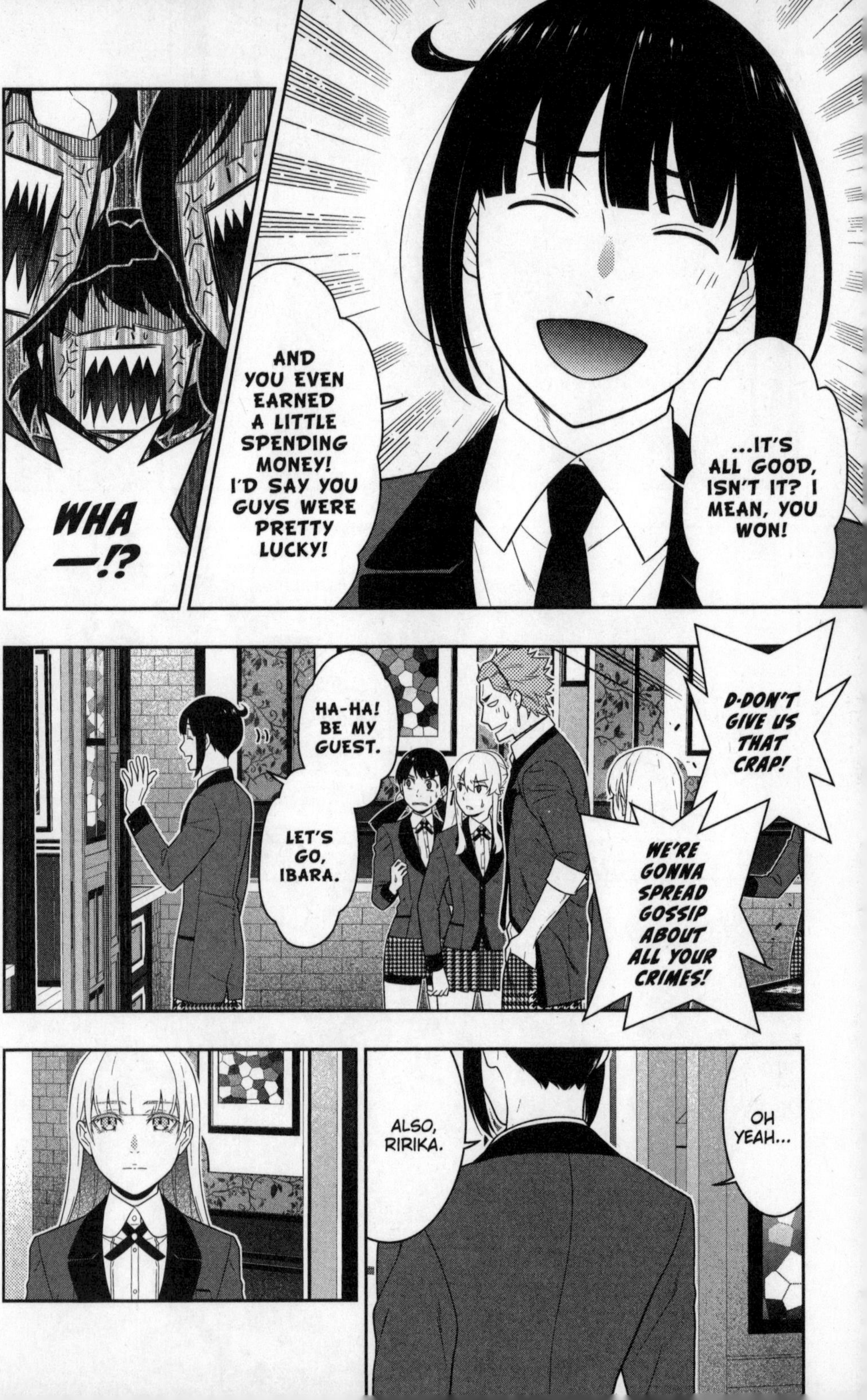
...IT'S ALL GOOD, ISN'T IT? I MEAN, YOU WON!
AND YOU EVEN EARNED A LITTLE SPENDING MONEY! I'D SAY YOU GUYS WERE PRETTY LUCKY!
WHA—!?
D-DON'T GIVE US THAT CRAP!
WE'RE GONNA SPREAD GOSSIP ABOUT ALL YOUR CRIMES!
HA-HA! BE MY GUEST.
LET'S GO, IBARA.
OH YEAH...
ALSO, RIRIKA.

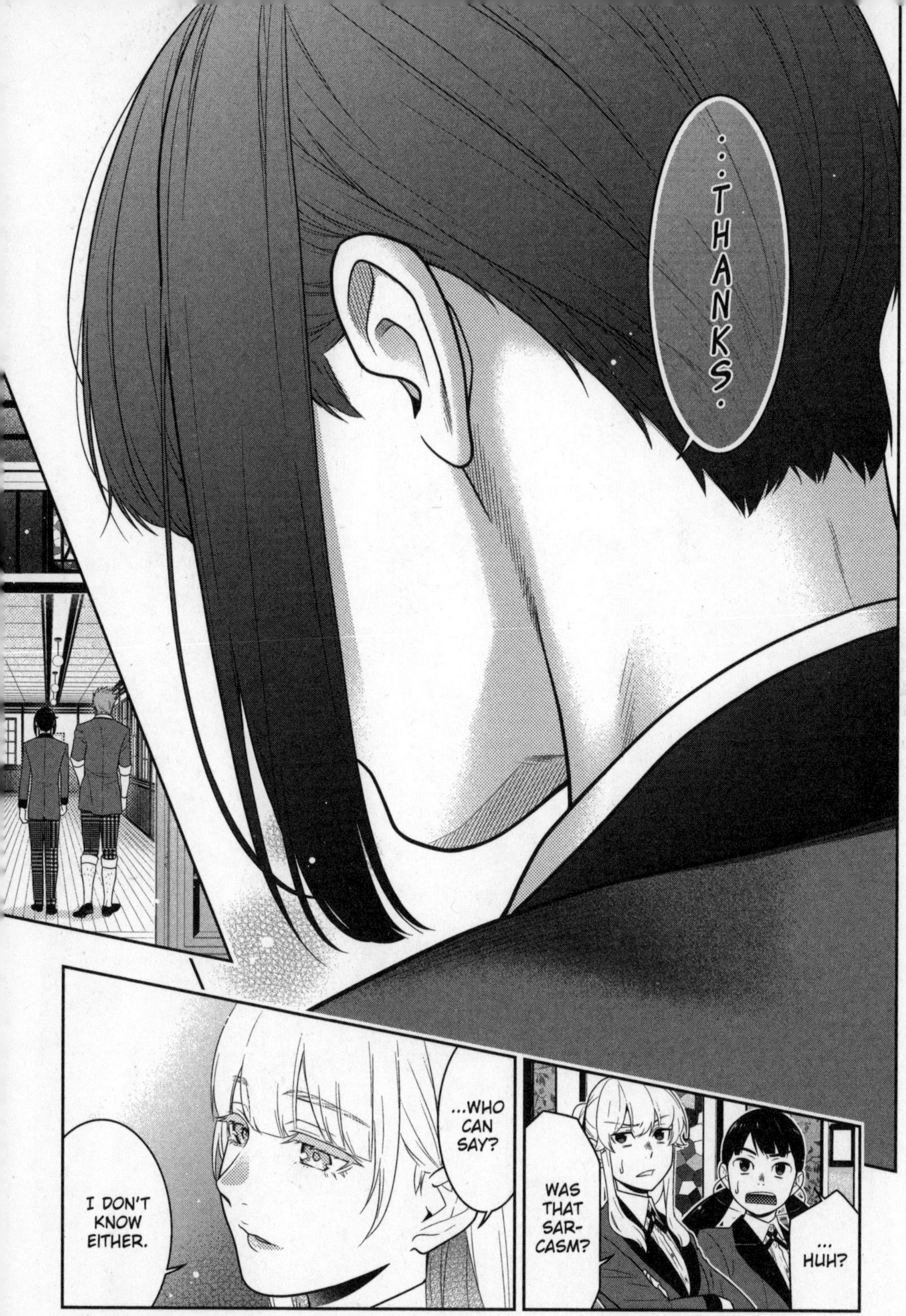
...THANKS.
...HUH?
WAS THAT SAR-CASM?
...WHO CAN SAY?
I DON'T KNOW EITHER.

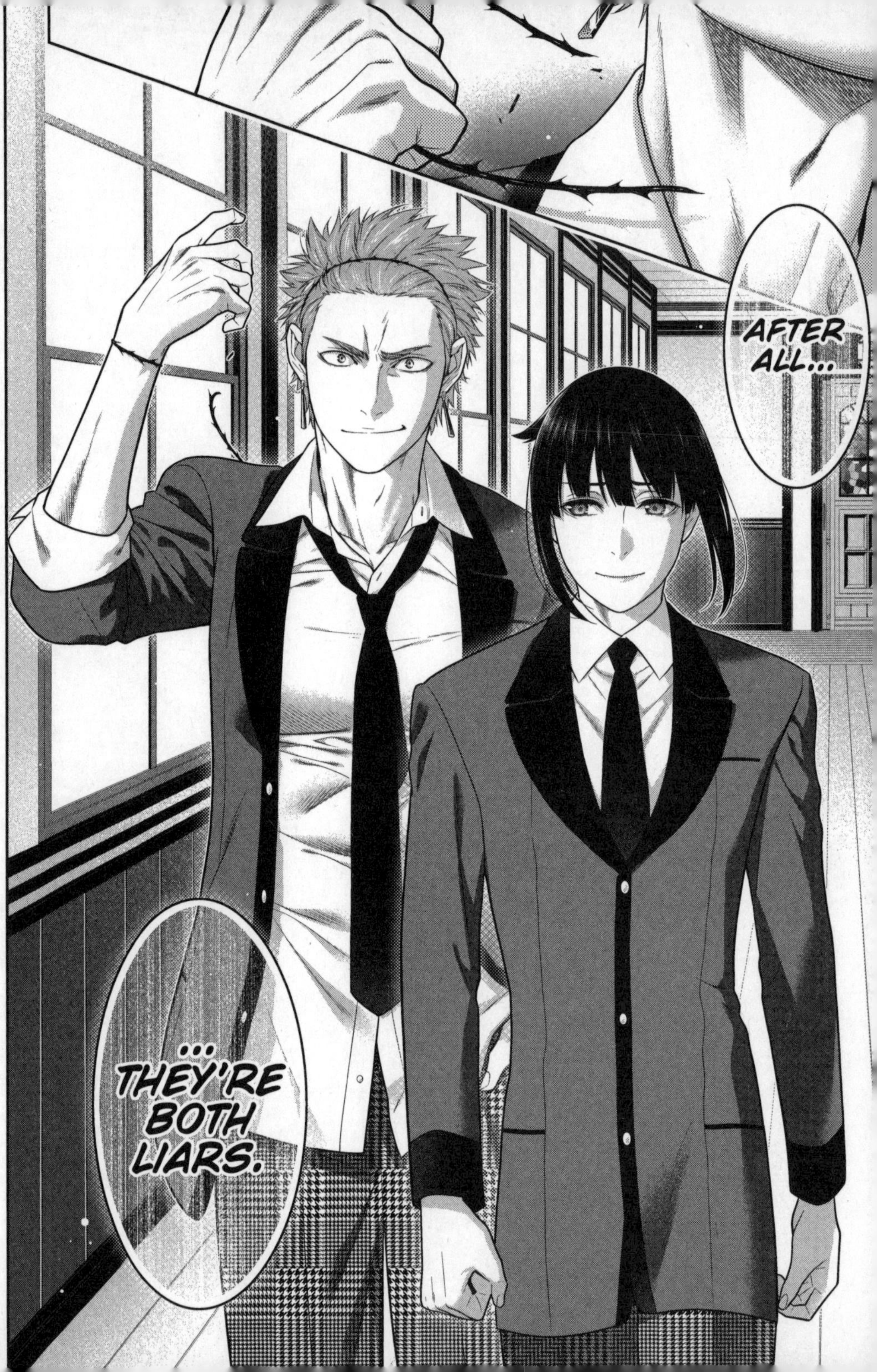
AFTER ALL...
...THEY'RE BOTH LIARS.

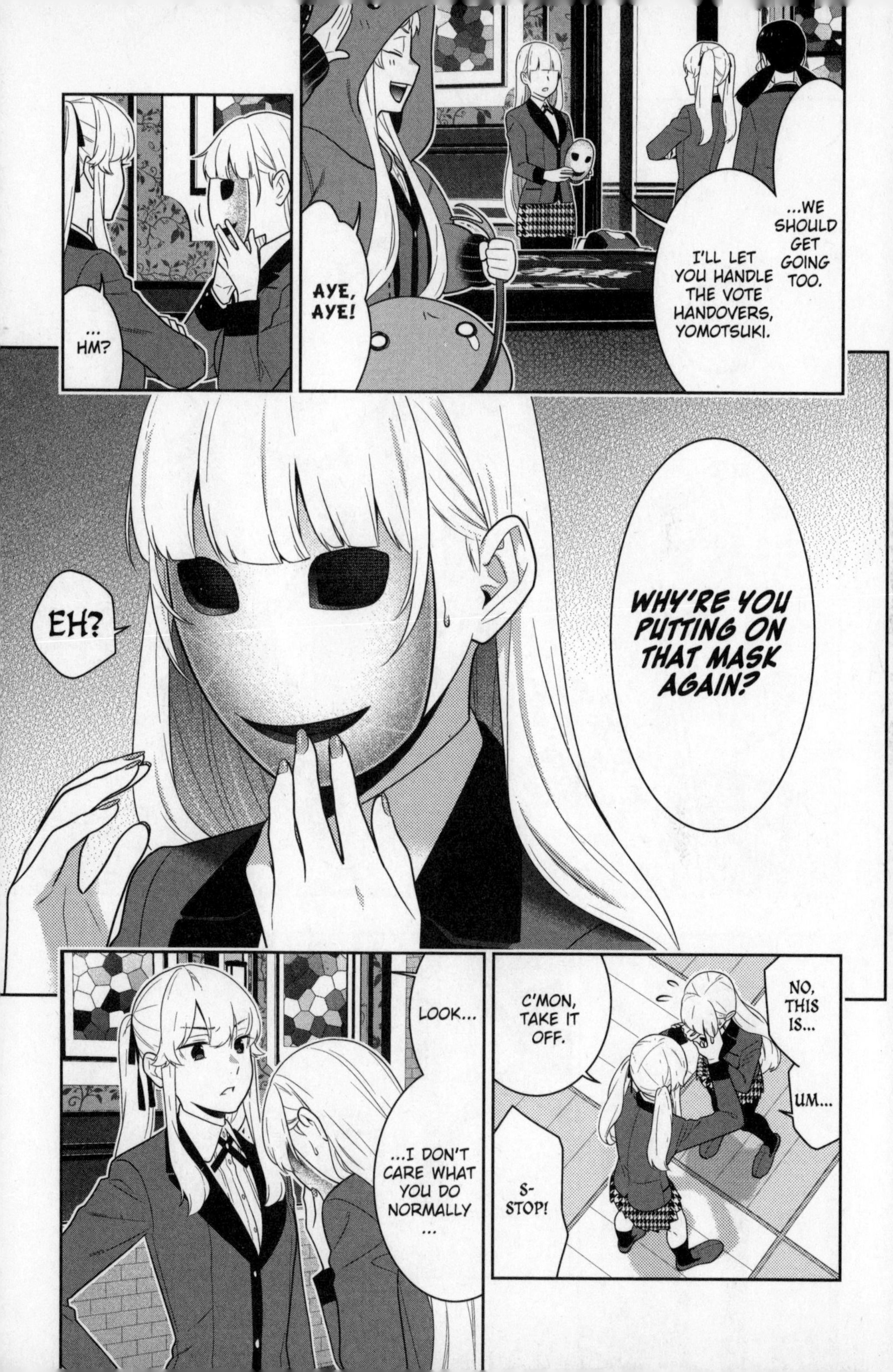
...WE SHOULD GET GOING TOO.
I'LL LET YOU HANDLE THE VOTE HANDOVERS, YOMOTSUKI.
AYE, AYE!
...HM?
WHY'RE YOU PUTTING ON THAT MASK AGAIN?
EH?
NO, THIS IS...
C'MON, TAKE IT OFF.
UM...
S-STOP!
LOOK...
...I DON'T CARE WHAT YOU DO NORMALLY...

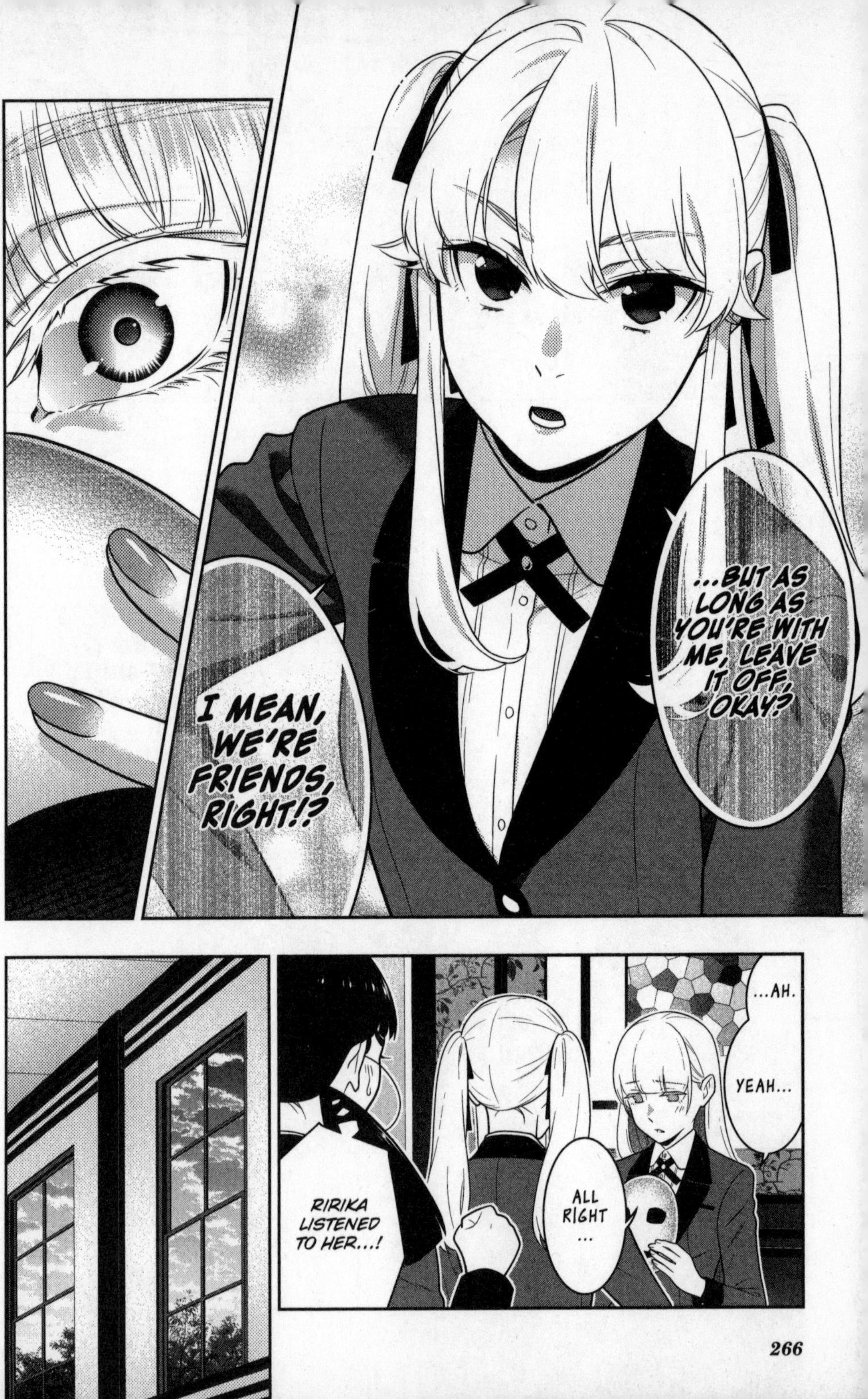
...BUT AS LONG AS YOU'RE WITH ME, LEAVE IT OFF, OKAY?
I MEAN, WE'RE FRIENDS, RIGHT!?
...AH.
YEAH...
ALL RIGHT...
RIRIKA LISTENED TO HER...!

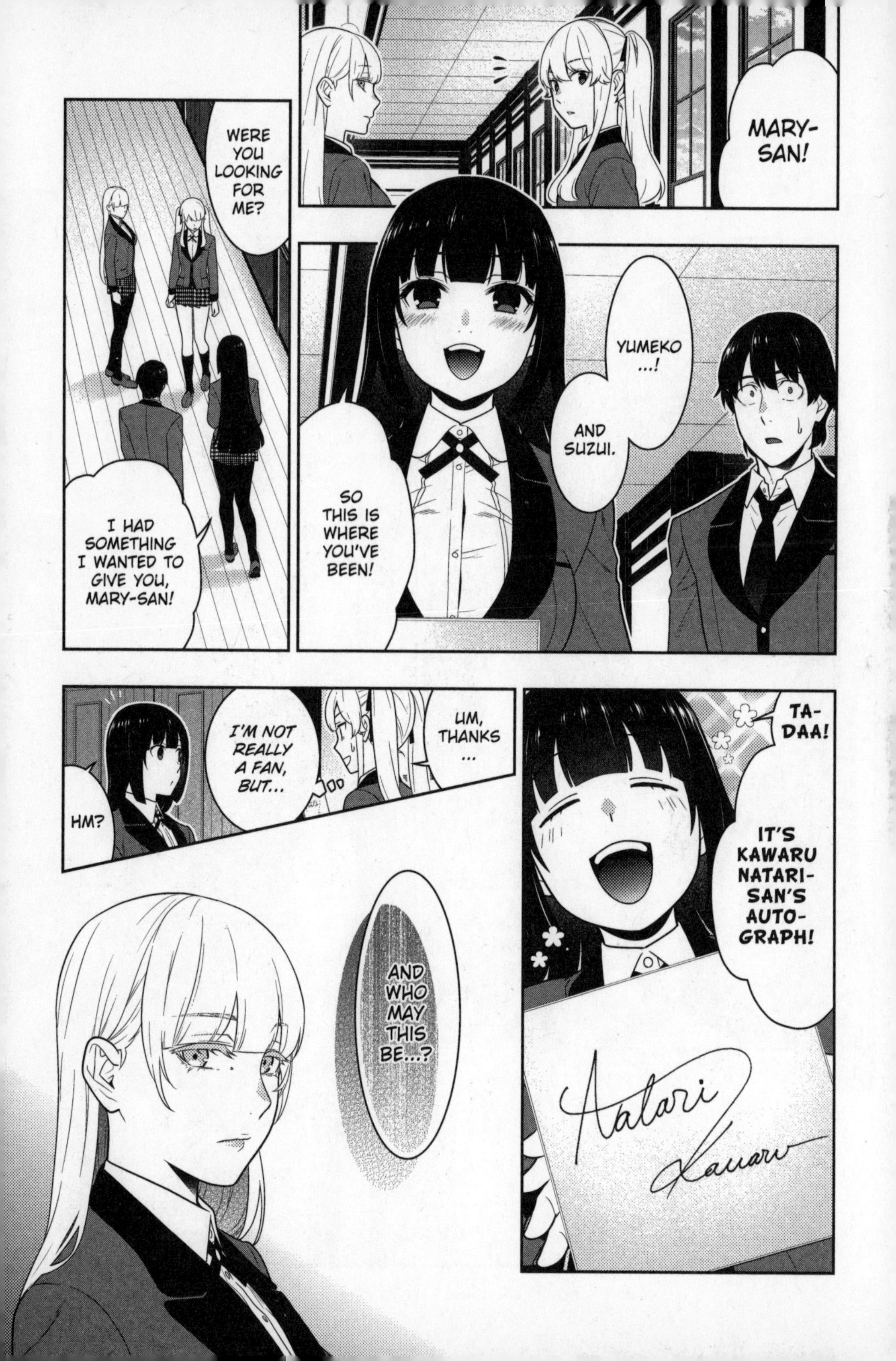
MARY-SAN!
YUMEKO ...!
AND SUZUI.
SO THIS IS WHERE YOU'VE BEEN!
WERE YOU LOOKING FOR ME?
I HAD SOMETHING I WANTED TO GIVE YOU, MARY-SAN!
TA-DAA!
IT'S KAWARU NATARI-SAN'S AUTO-GRAPH!
Natari Kawaru
UM, THANKS ...
I'M NOT REALLY A FAN, BUT...
HM?
AND WHO MAY THIS BE...?

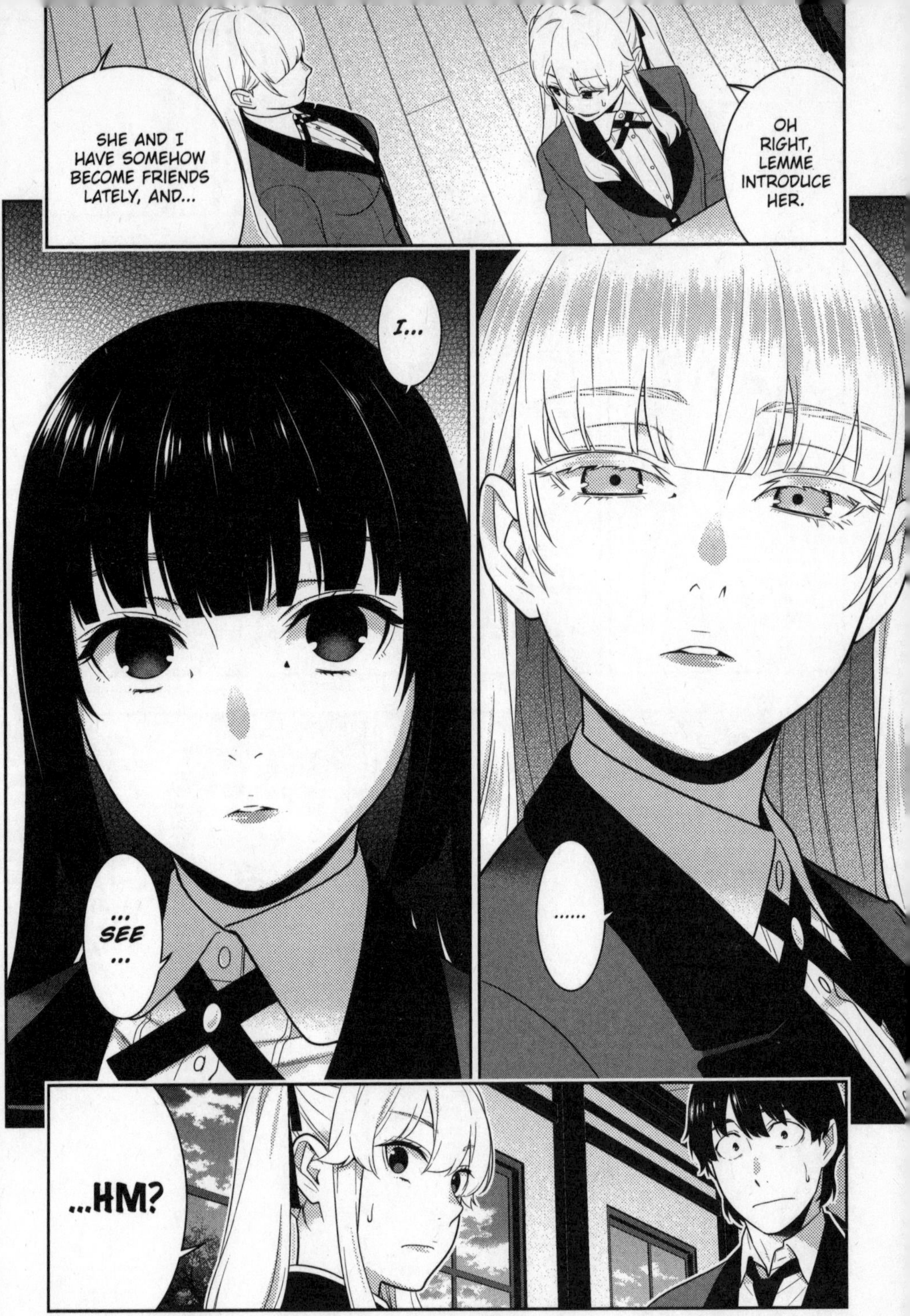
OH RIGHT, LEMME INTRODUCE HER.
SHE AND I HAVE SOMEHOW BECOME FRIENDS LATELY, AND...
......
I...
... SEE ...
...HM?

KAKEGURUI 11 END

TIME FOR SOME END-OF-THE-VOLUME BONUS COMICS!

RUNA-CHAN—TURNING LIES INTO REALITY

※THIS HAS NO RELATION TO THE ACTUAL STORY.

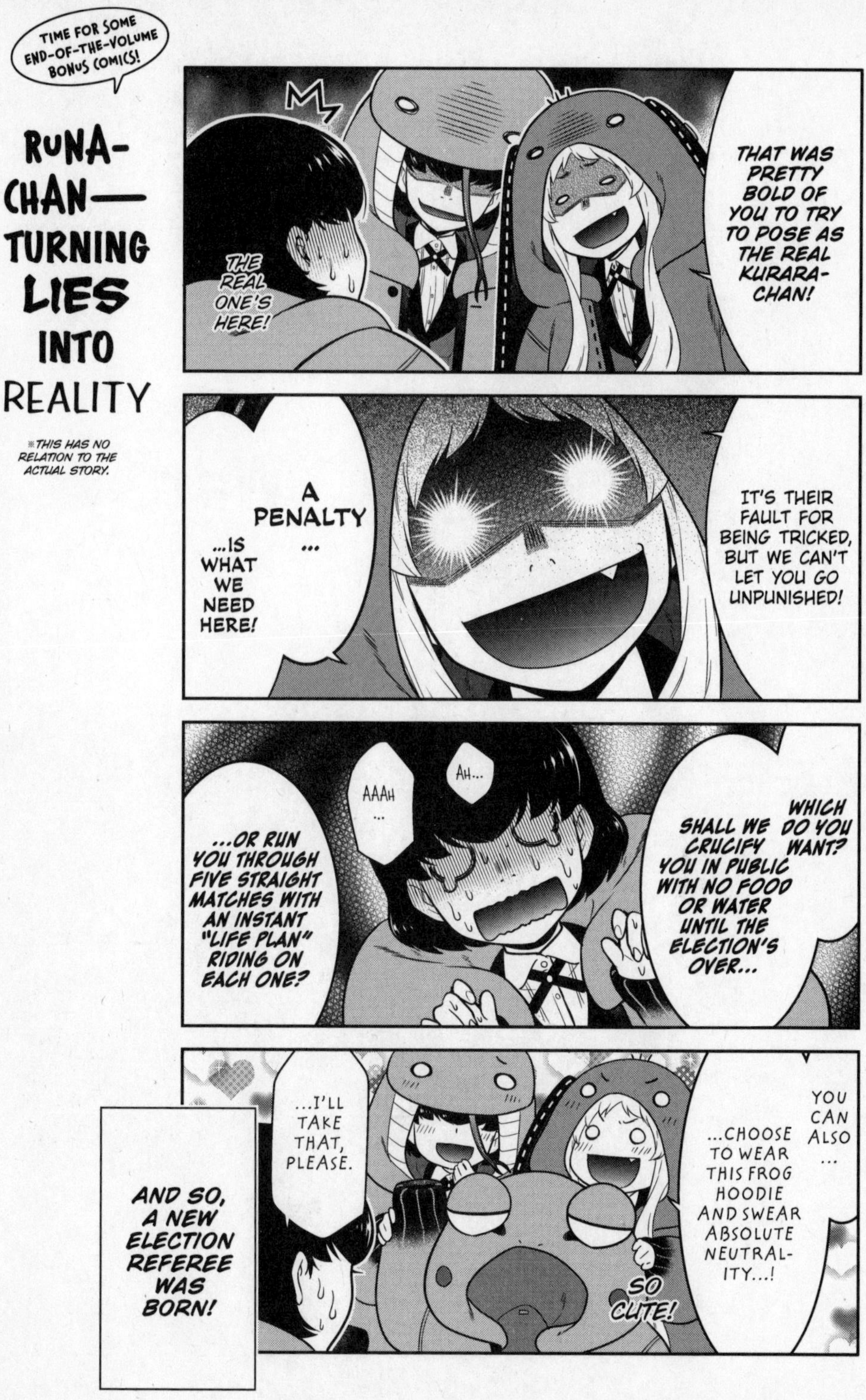
THAT WAS PRETTY BOLD OF YOU TO TRY TO POSE AS THE REAL KURARA-CHAN!
THE REAL ONE'S HERE!
IT'S THEIR FAULT FOR BEING TRICKED, BUT WE CAN'T LET YOU GO UNPUNISHED!
A PENALTY ...
...IS WHAT WE NEED HERE!
WHICH DO YOU WANT?
SHALL WE CRUCIFY YOU IN PUBLIC WITH NO FOOD OR WATER UNTIL THE ELECTION'S OVER...
AH...
AAAH ...
...OR RUN YOU THROUGH FIVE STRAIGHT MATCHES WITH AN INSTANT "LIFE PLAN" RIDING ON EACH ONE?
YOU CAN ALSO ...
...CHOOSE TO WEAR THIS FROG HOODIE AND SWEAR ABSOLUTE NEUTRAL-ITY...!
SO CUTE!
...I'LL TAKE THAT, PLEASE.
AND SO, A NEW ELECTION REFEREE WAS BORN!

GAMBLING, THAT IS MY RAISON D'ÊTRE.

This game is run entirely by computer, a rarity in the *Kakegurui* world.
I think defending generally gives you the advantage, but you can't win by just doing that.
If all participants are competing equally, I think there's a lot of potential for strategy—you could form alliances via requests, or even betray your so-called friends. But what if everyone isn't equal? That's the question I explored in this volume.

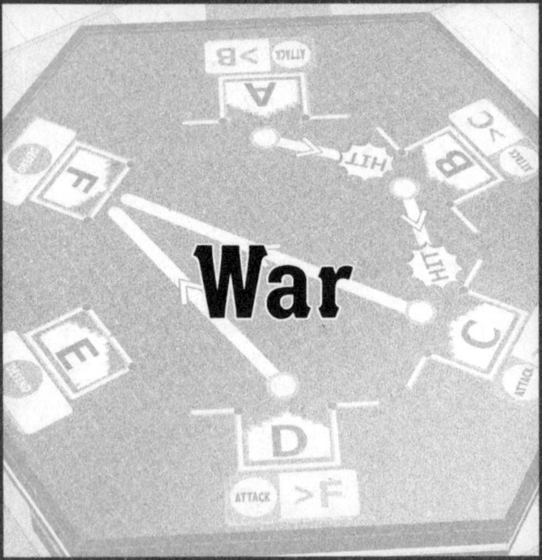

ATTACK
>B
A
B
>C
ATTACK
HIT
HIT
War
F
E
C
ATTACK
D
ATTACK
>F

Thank you for picking up Volume 11 of *Kakegurui*. This volume puts Obami, one of the strongest in the Momobami family, front and center. The Momobamis work in assorted fields, but Obami's line of work pairs rather well with being a gambler. Seeing him compete was super exciting for me as I wrote this story. The election is starting to reach its climax, and hopefully you're all waiting with bated breath to see how it turns out.

My thanks go out to Naomura-sensei and his assistants, as always, for depicting the subtle psychology behind each competition in such wonderful fashion on paper. I also thank my editors Sasaki-san and Yumoto-san for being so kind as to answer my calls to talk things over in the middle of the night. Tanaka too. And of course, all my readers. Please continue to support us!

Between *Kakegurui XX* (the second season of the anime), the TV drama, and the movie, this tale's spreading out across all kinds of media. I think they're all beautifully done, so here's to hoping you check them out! See you guys later in Volume 12!

Homura Kawamoto

Afterword

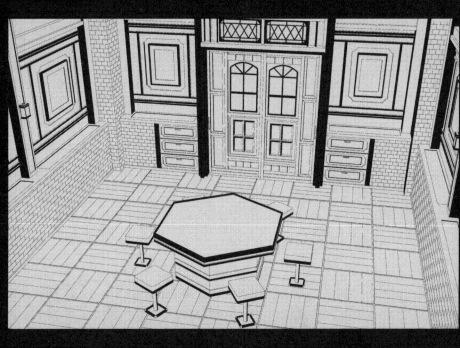

Thank you for picking up Volume 11 of *Kakegurui*.
The *Kakegurui XX* anime, the second season of the live-action drama, the movie, the smartphone app, etc.
Everything feels like a happy dream to me.
I could go on to ridiculous levels about how moved and thankful I am, but I'm deliberately going to hold back on this page for now. (LOL)

Oh, one more thing! The autograph Yumeko breaks out in the final scene was provided (well, scanned, that is) by Ayahi Takagaki, who voices Kaware Natari and provided that wonderful rendition of "Amazing Grace" in the anime. In other words, it's totally authentic. Pretty awesome, huh!? A huge thanks to her for that!

See you guys in the next volume.

SPECIAL THANKS:

My editors • Kawamoto-sama •
Imeko • Hz-sama • AO-sama

Toru Naomura (artist), March 2019

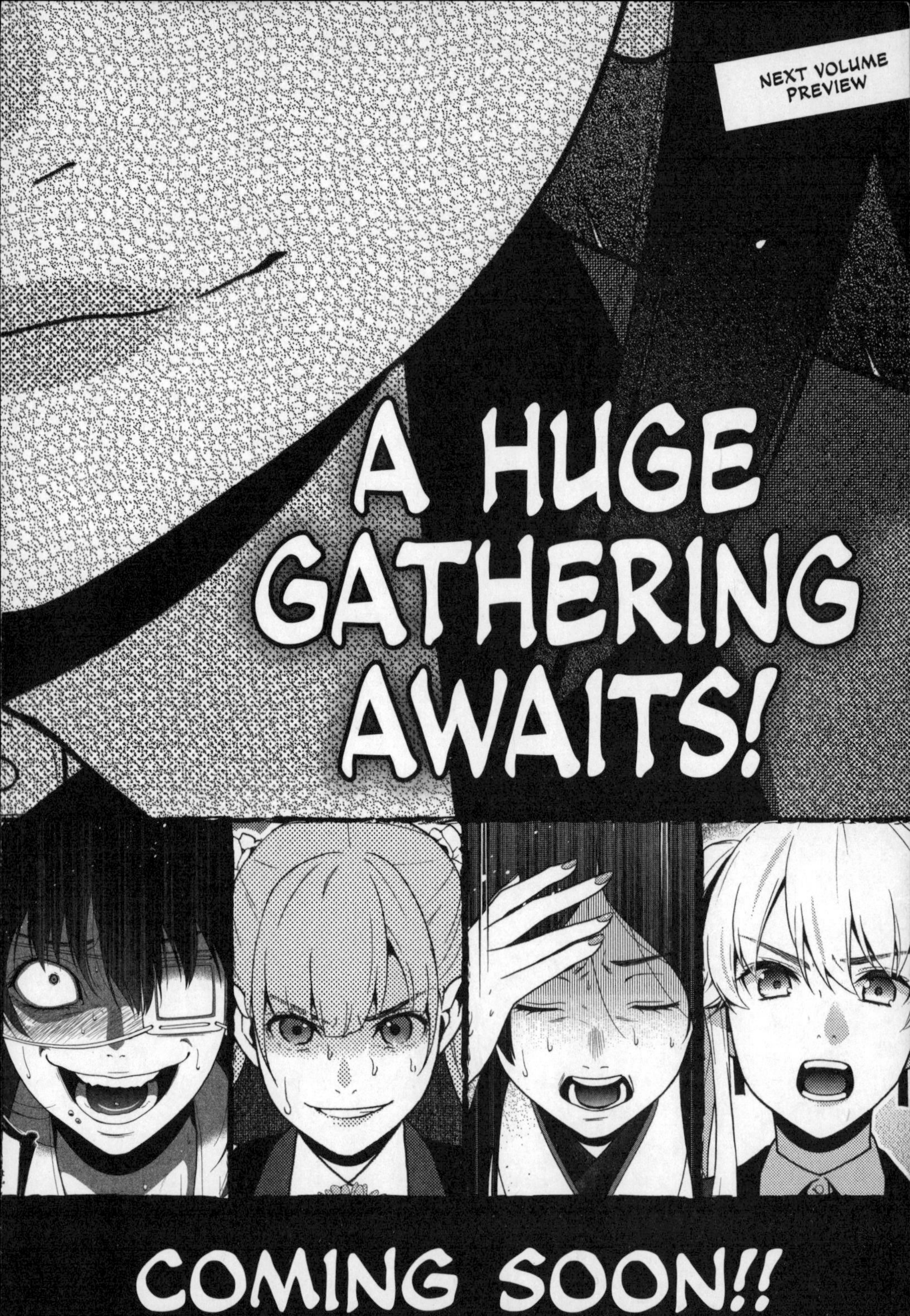
NEXT VOLUME PREVIEW
A HUGE GATHERING AWAITS!
COMING SOON!!

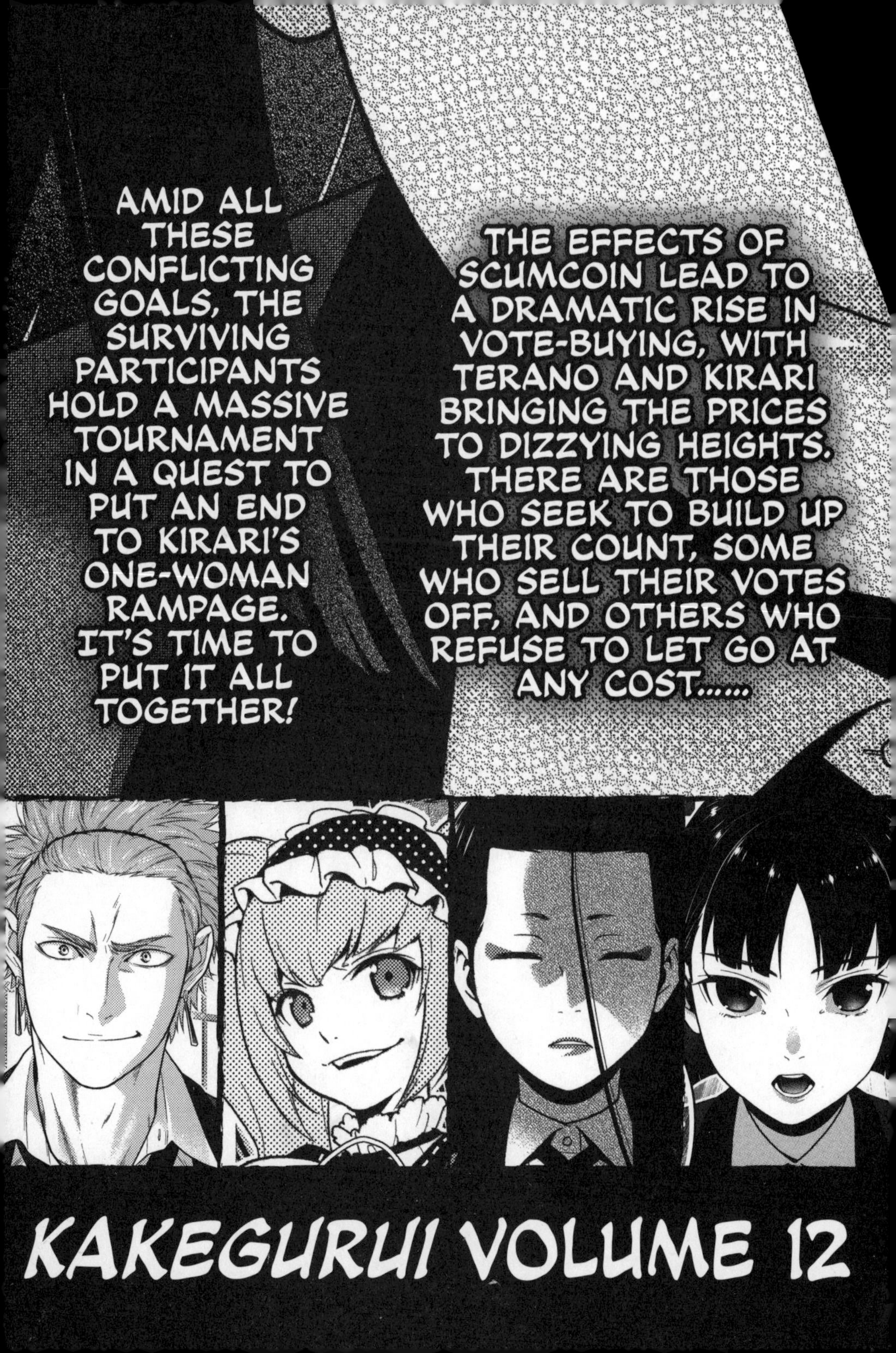
THE EFFECTS OF SCUMCOIN LEAD TO A DRAMATIC RISE IN VOTE-BUYING, WITH TERANO AND KIRARI BRINGING THE PRICES TO DIZZYING HEIGHTS. THERE ARE THOSE WHO SEEK TO BUILD UP THEIR COUNT, SOME WHO SELL THEIR VOTES OFF, AND OTHERS WHO REFUSE TO LET GO AT ANY COST......
AMID ALL THESE CONFLICTING GOALS, THE SURVIVING PARTICIPANTS HOLD A MASSIVE TOURNAMENT IN A QUEST TO PUT AN END TO KIRARI'S ONE-WOMAN RAMPAGE. IT'S TIME TO PUT IT ALL TOGETHER!
KAKEGURUI VOLUME 12

(11)

STORY: **Homura Kawamoto**
ART: **Toru Naomura**

Translation: Kevin Gifford
Lettering: Anthony Quintessenza

KAKEGURUI Vol. 11 ©2019 Homura Kawamoto, Toru Naomura/SQUARE ENIX CO., LTD. First published in Japan in 2019 by SQUARE ENIX CO., LTD. English translation rights arranged with SQUARE ENIX CO., LTD. and Yen Press, LLC through Tuttle-Mori Agency, Inc.

English translation ©2019 by SQUARE ENIX CO., LTD.

Yen Press
150 West 30th Street, 19th Floor
New York, NY 10005

Visit us at yenpress.com
facebook.com/yenpress
twitter.com/yenpress
yenpress.tumblr.com
instagram.com/yenpress

First Yen Press Edition: December 2019
The chapters in this volume were originally published as ebooks by Yen Press.

Yen Press is an imprint of Yen Press, LLC.
The Yen Press name and logo are trademarks of Yen Press, LLC.

The publisher is not responsible for websites (or their content) that are not owned by the publisher.

Library of Congress Control Number: 2017939211

ISBNs: 978-1-9753-8754-9 (paperback)
        978-1-9753-8755-6 (ebook)

10 9 8 7 6 5 4 3 2 1

WOR

Printed in the United States of America